COLLIN COUNTY COMMUNITY

W9-BLM-547

99

Learning Resource Center
Collin County Community College District
SPRING CREEK CAMPUS
Plano, Texas 75074

Strange Bedfellows

Bedfellows

THE FIRST

AMERICAN

AVANT-GARDE

STEVEN WATSON

ABBEVILLE PRESS PUBLISHERS

NEW YORK LONDON PARIS

C O N T

BEFORE 1913
Cradles of Modernism

*"1912 was really
an extraordinary year. . . .
the evidence of a New Spirit
come suddenly to birth."*
FLOYD DELL

1913-1914

*"In that year of 1913,
barriers went down and people
reached each other."*
MABEL DODGE

Floyd Dell

7 a.m. Sunday, July 27,
1911.

F. Dell.

INTRODUCTION

There rest under the same blanket (or rather, toss feverishly)
anarchists, terrorists, degenerates, rowdies, scavengers,
dreamers, poets, liberators and patriots.

Charles Vezin, President of the Art Students League,
commenting on the Armory Show in February 1913

*S*trange Bedfellows: The First American Avant-Garde presents a group
portrait of a small band of cultural renegades who flourished from
1913 to 1917. At the center of this loose network were the poets and
artists who created the forms and syntax of modernism—in free verse
and Imagist poetry, in Cubism and abstract art—and catalyzed similar
developments in music, drama, and fiction. But the avant-garde also
depended on those who organized its events, articulated its theories,
and made its work known to the public. Thus, *Strange Bedfellows* is
populated by critics and collectors as well as artists, editors and journalists as well as poets, salon hosts and hostesses as well as distinguished guests. As the critic Paul Rosenfeld observed, "Complex works
of art speak not through individuals but ensembles." [1]

The alienation of this avant-garde from bourgeois taste and morality demanded an alternative society. New York's Greenwich Village
became its center (and its most sympathetic audience), although out-
posts were established uptown, in Europe, and in Chicago. Both a geographical entity and a state of mind, the Village was where individuals
could go to reinvent themselves through psychoanalysis, feminism,
fashion, revolutionary politics, and unorthodox sexual relationships.
This process of self-discovery was often distinct from aesthetic innovation, but some figures—notably Marcel Duchamp and the Baroness
Elsa von Freytag-Loringhoven—fused modern art and modern life.

The avant-garde's aspiration to live in perpetual revolution inevitably created the conditions for its rapid overthrow, both by popularizers
and by succeeding avant-gardes. During the brief period chronicled
in *Strange Bedfellows,* the avant-garde progressed through three dis-

Floyd Dell (1887–1969).
*Floyd Dell—7 a.m. Sunday,
July 27, 1911.* Pencil on
paper, 6¼ × 7¾ in.
(15.8 × 19.6 cm). Floyd Dell
Papers, The Newberry Library,
Chicago

7

tinct stages—foundation, revolution, and colonization. These roughly correspond to the major sections of the book.

Mainstream culture in turn-of-the-century America was moribund. In the years before the formation of the American avant-garde, the National Academy of Design seemed incapable of responding to change, American poetry had lain fallow for a generation, and theater consisted of little more than crude melodrama and frothy comedy. It was almost a cliché to remark that all art had already been painted and all poetry had been written. The cultural establishment was ripe for takeover.

Although the avant-garde considered itself the antithesis of the old order, its foundations were built on the accomplishments and accumulated wealth of the nineteenth century. Future radicals met one another through institutions as old as Harvard and through clubs that were both fusty and nonconformist. The credo of one such club suggests their common denominator: "A place where hearts beat high and hands grasp firm, where poverty is not disgrace and where charity does not chill. A place where kindred virtues have fled for refuge, and where Mrs. Grundy has no sway." [2] Many artists, writers, and saloneuses also traveled to Europe in search of the most up-to-date ideas and personalities. Through brief sojourns or permanent expatriation, they experienced the modern revolution firsthand in Paris and London. These nineteenth-century establishments, maverick clubs, and Continental milieus provided the cradles of American modernism.

In the fall of 1912 the poet Ezra Pound wrote, "If it lie within your desire to promote the arts you must not only subsidize the man with work still in him, but you must gather such dynamic particles together, you must set them where they will interact, and stimulate each other." [3] Shortly after he wrote this, the American avant-garde reached the critical mass necessary for its revolutionary stage. No longer isolated, the avant-gardists were inspired by a shared impulse, in the journalist Hutchins Hapgood's words, "to loosen up the old forms and traditions, to dynamite the baked and hardened earth so that fresh flowers can grow." [4] Its members joined forces to subvert the Academy, capitalist commerce, and Victorian morality. Painters aspired to abstraction rather than likeness, and poets stripped their work of rhetorical excess. Long hair replaced short, sandals supplanted shoes, and women smoked cigarettes instead of sipping tea. Concepts like the New Woman, Free Love, and Human Sex became more than fashionable slogans that popped up in little magazines and Village conversations; the avant-garde tried to live them.

In the early days—before that oxymoronic entity the avant-garde institution had a chance to develop—the avant-garde was just a loose skein of tangled social circles. The most defined unit of organization was the salon—held at various times by the Steins, Mabel Dodge, the Stettheimers, and the Arensbergs. At once large and intimate, attended by the enlightened rich and the bohemian poor, these gatherings became an instrumental feature of avant-garde life. Describing the importance of the salon hostess, Hutchins Hapgood observed, "Her personality may be made the means by which all intellectual and political movements may come together charmingly, socially, and learn to see the humanity in each."[5] In these convivial settings and in slightly more formal clubs, the avant-garde first discovered itself.

The desire to demolish an outmoded culture made unlikely allies of bohemians experimenting with liberated life-styles, anarchists demanding political revolution, and modernists inventing new aesthetics. It was commonly remarked that "all revolution is synonymous," and Margaret Anderson went so far as to declare "Revolution *is* Art."[6] Years later Mabel Dodge recalled the exuberance of that momentary partnership: "Looking back upon it now, it seems as though everywhere, in that year of 1913, barriers went down and people reached each other who had never been in touch before. . . . The new spirit was abroad and swept us all together."[7]

During this stage the agenda for the modern revolution was set. The fact that it was disconcertingly open-ended mattered little at first, for the overriding hope for a fusion of art, politics, and life-style led to a high tolerance for diversity. John Quinn described the era as "an age of experiment rather than accomplishment," Alfred Stieglitz referred to his gallery as an artistic laboratory, and Floyd Dell characterized the new bohemia as an intellectual nursery.[8]

When the avant-garde came together in common cause—to present an exhibition, to publish a magazine, to stage a play—it avoided the structures of conventional organizations. Rarely did a group follow a written agenda or subdivide into committees. Authority was dispersed among its members, and George Cram Cook's dictum held sway: "Work done in the spirit of play has the only true seriousness."[9] Decisions were made democratically and the participatory process became as important as the results.

One poet wrote during this period, "Only after the common cause is won will we have time to fight among ourselves."[10] And as the frontiers of modernism began to be colonized, that time arrived. Where once the outpost had been a single little magazine or a lone gallery, several now appeared on the cultural scene. As soon as chic galleries began to sell modern art and mainstream publishers started to print contemporary poetry, the idealism of the avant-garde was undermined by the possibility of commercial success. Criticism and competition soon displaced the earlier sense of unity and support.

Membership in the revolutionary avant-garde was usually determined by self-election. All comers had been welcomed to Mabel Dodge's Evenings and to the meetings where the *Masses* was edited. The little magazines accommodated both radical formal experiments from Europe and homespun American verse. Painters became Cubists and Futurists by applying these new terms to themselves. But the intrusion of scavengers—fake free-versers, bohemian entrepreneurs, ersatz Cubists—encouraged avant-garde circles to define their membership more warily and to assert the need for stringent aesthetic standards. Hierarchical organizations, replete with officers and paid staff, began to replace ad-hoc gatherings.

The avant-garde trained its eye on posterity. Stieglitz published a special issue of *Camera Work* to eulogize the spirit of 291; the Provincetown Players turned Village values and characters into plays; Amy Lowell, Harriet Monroe, and Ezra Pound published anthologies of the best new poetry; Marius de Zayas and Lowell wrote books that placed modernism in historical perspective. Many, though certainly not all, of the major characters began to appear more retrospective than radical.

Strange Bedfellows closes as the first American avant-garde began to transform itself into official high culture. As the avant-garde's artifacts entered the world of the museum, and its poets were elected to the literary canon, the avant-garde's pioneering spirit became the source of nostalgic veneration. "It is a great thing to be living when an age passes," observed the *Little Review* editor Jane Heap. This book attempts to capture the irreverent, messianic spirit of that crucial moment.[11]

BEFORE 1913

Cradles of Modernism

"1912 was really an
extraordinary year. . . .
the evidence of a
New Spirit come
suddenly to birth."

FLOYD DELL

CHICAGO

On October 12, 1892, exactly four hundred years after Christopher Columbus discovered America, the World's Columbian Exposition was dedicated. On that warm, windless afternoon in Chicago the Beaux-Arts buildings of the White City seemed to rise out of Lake Michigan, on mud flats that had previously housed only shanties. An official delegation arrived at the great Hall of Manufacture and Liberal Arts: the vice president of the United States, twenty carriages of commissioners and as many Supreme Court justices and foreign counsels, as well as a five thousand–member chorus and a five hundred–piece orchestra. In all, a hundred fifty thousand people were spread over twenty-five acres.

After a fanfare and the swelling song of the white-gowned chorus, a tall, full-throated actress recited Harriet Monroe's "Columbian Ode." Few among the acres of people caught the exact words, but all could

Hail to thee, fair Chicago! On thy brow
America, thy mother, lays a crown.
Bravest among her daughters brave art thou,
Most strong of all her heirs of high renown.

Harriet Monroe, "Cantata," 1889

recognize the uplifting tone and inspirational cadences. Unlike the creators of the Beaux-Arts decoration that dominated the Exposition architecture, Monroe had eschewed all classical references—her Columbian laurels were distinctly American, woven of "dewy flowers / Plucked from wide prairies."

Monroe climbed the stairs of the officials' platform, her frail beauty nearly overpowered by an imposing bun of dark hair and the grand puffed shoulders of her black-and-white gown. The recitation of her "Columbian Ode" had resulted from her iron-willed tenacity on behalf of poetry. The committee that had planned the fair had recognized all the arts—except poetry. That all-too-familiar neglect had been overcome by Monroe's triumph this afternoon. It would be her sole victory for twenty years.

The ceremonial reverence accorded the arts that day reflected their function as civilizing ornaments to Chicago's industry. Members of the city's newly prosperous business class were determined to create a city that offered more than the stench of stockyards and the soot of factories. The barons of meat-packing, railroads, and grain established what came to be called the Upward Movement, through the efforts of their wives. Their drive for gentility financed the city's most prominent institutions, including the University of Chicago, the Art Institute, the Newberry Library, and an enlarged Historical Society. "Centers of social activity are thus forming," exulted the editor of the *Dial* in 1892, "in which artists and scholars and educators will gather, at which ideas and ideals will prevail, and which, as an informal 'Academy,' will set standards that shall mitigate and transform the grossness of our hitherto material life." [1]

The informal Academy invoked by Chicago's leading literary magazine was embodied in a gathering called the Little Room. [2] Begun in the early 1890s for a communal taking of tea after the Chicago Symphony Orchestra's matinees, the Little Room flourished until about 1910. Chicago's literary and artistic elite met Friday afternoons in Ralph Clarkson's Tintype Studio on the top floor of the Fine Arts Building. Among the regulars were the prominent authors Henry Fuller, Hamlin Garland, and Robert Herrick; the sculptor Lorado Taft; the journalist Clara Laughlin; the theater director Anna Morgan; and the poets Harriet Monroe and

OPPOSITE, TOP
Harriet Monroe, c. 1890

OPPOSITE, BOTTOM
Dedication of World's Columbian Exposition, interior of Manufacturer's Building, 1893

Members of the Little Room
in an evening of High Jinks

THE LITTLE ROOM

I want to be a writer,
And with the writers stand,
A thought within my cranium,
A pen within my hand;
And if I write a novel
Or something that will boom—
Perhaps I'll be invited
To join "The Little Room."
The members of this "Little Room"
Have very clannish been;
Perhaps they will not "rush" me
If I too eager seem.
But time, alas! is going,
Ambition doth consume,
And soon I'll be too aged
To join "The Little Room."
To this mysterious chamber
The "hoi polloi" ne'er come;
No one can cross the portal
Unless some work he's done—
Some stunt in art or poesy,
Or maybe writ a tune.
Ah! then he may find entrance
Into "The Little Room."

M. Stranger, n.d.
(to be sung to
the tune of "I Want
to Be an Angel")

William Vaughn Moody.[3] In the candlelit studio they nibbled small plates of peppermints and carefully trimmed sandwiches, ceremoniously filled their cups from a samovar, and retired to settees where they listened to music played on a grand piano. From time to time the high-minded atmosphere was enlivened by guests such as young Isadora Duncan, who waltzed one afternoon in sandaled feet. One newspaper noted, "The members of the Little Room occasionally descend from their pedestal of high art and the perfection of pink tea" to indulge in the high jinks of vaudeville evenings.[4]

The refined air that usually pervaded the Little Room proved as significant to it as any of the ideas that were informally discussed there. This cultivated haven provided a bridge between the city's monied society and its arts community. One historian called it "Chicago's best available substitute for a fully developed, leisured and cultivated class."[5] It also supplied an official cultural establishment against which Chicago's avant-garde would rebel.

In the early twentieth century Chicago offered a beacon to those dissatisfied with midwestern towns where cultural life was limited to Booster Clubs and potluck suppers in the church basement. In the picture drawn by Sherwood Anderson, Hamlin Garland, Sinclair Lewis, and H. L. Mencken, village life offered the proto-avant-gardist nothing but the impetus to revolt. Yet from these small towns came the American bohemians who settled along Chicago's Fifty-seventh Street and in New York's Greenwich Village. One of these village (and Village) residents, Floyd Dell, later observed: "As immigrants to America are often devout Americans in heart before they arrive, so these immigrants to Greenwich Village were addicted to the ideas and practices of the Village back in their home towns."[6]

Dell in his hometown—Davenport, Iowa—exemplified the eager young bohemians starting to sprout in the soil of small-town America. The youngest son of a long-unemployed butcher, Dell watched his family clinging to respectability but "losing its hold upon the golden ladder."[7] He would climb his own golden ladder, whose first rungs consisted of books from the public library. After he dropped out of school to support his family, Dell got his education from Edward Bellamy's *Looking Backward* and Karl Marx's *Communist Manifesto*, which laid the foundation for his early conversion to socialism; from Robert Ingersoll's tirades against religion, which inspired his early atheism; and from Richard Hovey's "Songs from Vagabondia," which transformed him, in imagination at least, into a bohemian. At sixteen Dell joined Davenport's socialist local, attending meetings in which discontented workers like himself (he worked in a candy factory) debated the value of the Industrial Workers of the World (I.W.W.). He also wrote muckraking articles for the *Tri-City Workers' Magazine*, a local socialist publication.

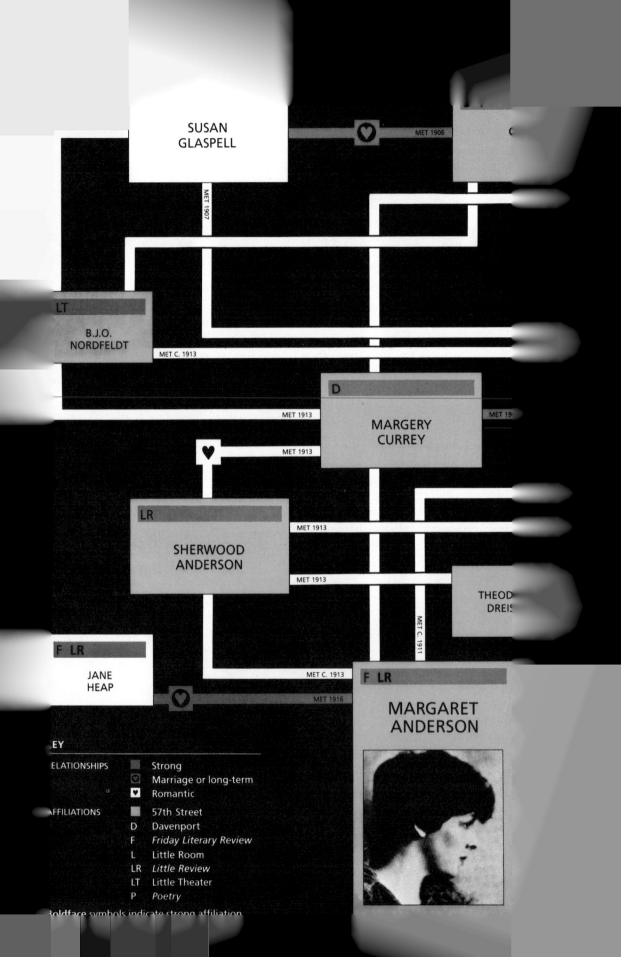

SUSAN
GLASPELL

MET 1906

MET 1907

LT
B.J.O.
NORDFELDT

MET C. 1913

MET 1913

D

MARGERY
CURREY

MET 19

MET 1913

MET 1913

LR

SHERWOOD
ANDERSON

MET 1913

MET 1913

THEOD
DREIS

MET C. 1911

F LR
JANE
HEAP

MET C. 1913

MET 1916

F LR

MARGARET
ANDERSON

KEY

RELATIONSHIPS
- ♡ Strong
- ♡ Marriage or long-term
- ♥ Romantic

AFFILIATIONS
- 57th Street
- D Davenport
- F *Friday Literary Review*
- L Little Room
- LR *Little Review*
- LT Little Theater
- P *Poetry*

Boldface symbols indicate strong affiliation

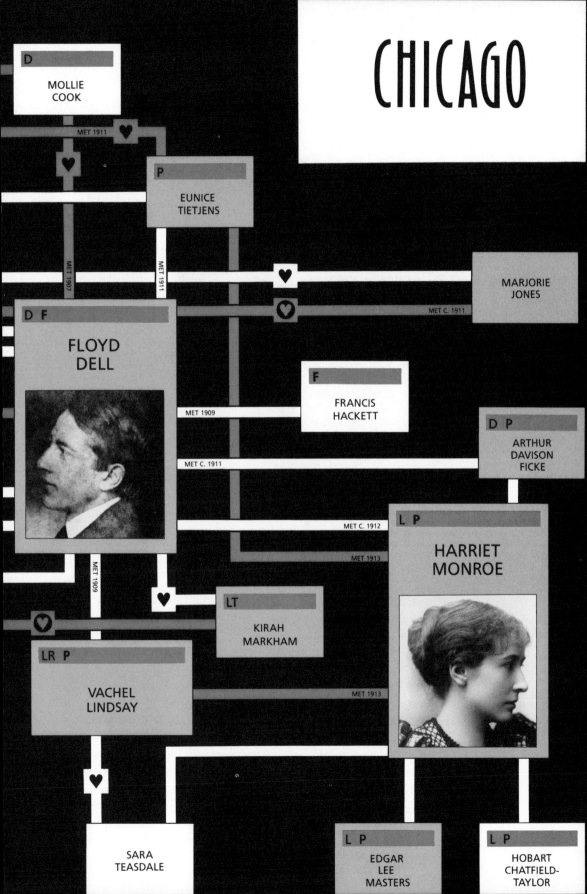

CHICAGO

D MOLLIE COOK

MET 1911 ♥

♥

P EUNICE TIETJENS

MET 1907

MET 1911

♥ MARJORIE JONES

♥ MET C. 1911

D F FLOYD DELL

MET 1909 **F** FRANCIS HACKETT

MET C. 1911 **D P** ARTHUR DAVISON FICKE

MET C. 1912 **L P** HARRIET MONROE

MET 1913

MET 1909

♥ **LT** KIRAH MARKHAM

♥

LR P VACHEL LINDSAY

MET 1913

♥

SARA TEASDALE

L P EDGAR LEE MASTERS

L P HOBART CHATFIELD-TAYLOR

Floyd Dell in Davenport,
c. 1908

Dell inspired both maternal tenderness and libidinal impulses. Many
women were drawn to this boy-poet, whose slender face, sensitive
blue eyes, and thatch of long brown hair prompted comparisons with
Shelley and Keats. Appropriately, his first infatuation was with the public librarian, "the goddess of the shrine of books."[8] Their chaste romance was a mixture of earnest discussion of new ideas and unspoken
sexual yearning. Astonished by the verse that Dell gave her one afternoon, she showed it to her friend George Cram Cook, who announced
that she should fly a flag over the library to honor this local prodigy.

Cook was in his early thirties, a tall, robust figure who had already
experienced many civilizations far more advanced than Davenport's—
including Florence, Heidelberg, Harvard, and bohemian San Francisco.
Introduced by the librarian, he and Dell became friends and soon organized the Monist Society in the fall of 1906. Its aim, in Cook's words,
was to disseminate an independent "philosophy in the guise of religion, or religion in the guise of philosophy."[9] The society attracted a
motley congregation—as one member put it, "all of us who were out
of sorts with what we were supposed to believe."[10] Davenport's intelligentsia—emancipated clubwomen, free-thinking Germans, politicians
seeking a new constituency, and public library habitués—met on Sunday afternoons in a barren hall over a saloon to talk about such ad-

vanced topics as evolution and socialism. Susan Glaspell, one of the Monist Society's more devoted members, observed, "We were the queer fish of the town; get the queer fish into one pond and it's a queer pond—but it moves the water around." [11]

At the meetings of the Monist Society, Cook, Glaspell, and Dell began friendships that would endure long after they left Davenport.[12] Glaspell, a tall thirty-year-old woman with sad eyes and a sweet, intelligent smile, appeared to one friend as "fragile as old lace." [13] A Davenport native, she wrote romantic stories filled with local color, in which the heroine invariably resembled the author. The protagonist of "The Return of Rhoda," for example, was a small-town girl who had tasted the sophistication of Chicago only to return to Iowa, concluding, "There's no place like home."

As for Cook, his stentorian orations at the Monist Society could not obscure a sense of personal failure. He had written two indifferent novels, his first marriage had dissolved miserably, and his ideal Hellenic community consisted of an unprofitable farm he shared with a barefoot anarchist wife named Mollie. Cook's self-evaluation from this period presages his career: "Enthusiastic; able to suffer martyrdom for an idea. Indolent, uninspired, nine-tenths of the time." [14] Years later Dell observed of Cook, "It is a miserable fate to be a non-producing 'man of genius' anywhere, but it is perhaps worst of all in one's home town." [15] To the adolescent Dell, however, Cook was an ideal mentor, and life on his farm nine miles out of Davenport offered a romantic alternative to small-town provincialism. Dell and Cook argued about Marx while they sprayed apple trees, and they antiphonally chanted Sappho while carrying vegetables to town. In the evenings they smoked corncob pipes in front of the fireplace and planned novels about each other.[16] "In the whole history of Iowa there has probably not been so stimulating a hired man," Glaspell later observed about Dell, "and perhaps since the beginnings of growth seeds have not matured in so lively a stream of intellectual life." [17]

This Edenic existence was complicated by the transformation of friendships into sexual liaisons. Fifty years later Dell remembered the moment when his librarian became his lover: "To lie in the woods with a goddess, to unbutton her shirtwaist and fondle and kiss her beautiful breasts, to lift her skirt and see and caress her beautiful thighs—there was a touch of heroic impiety about it." [18] Cook's young wife, Mollie, was also attracted to Dell, which drove her husband to jealousy, though he was meanwhile falling in love with Susan Glaspell, who idealized Cook as a larger-than-life poet. The clandestine nature of Glaspell's previous affairs prompted Cook to jibe that she "lacked the convictions of her courage"; but their own romantic relationship was shadowed by the fact that Cook and Mollie had a young child and Mollie was pregnant with a second.[19] In the summer of 1908 Dell met Margery Currey.

George Cram Cook as a young man

Learning Resources Center
Collin County Community College District
SPRING CREEK CAMPUS
Plano, Texas 75074

A cigarette-smoking Vassar graduate who taught English at Davenport High School, she read extensively and extolled the suffragette movement and sexual freedom, expressing her radical sentiments with inveterate cheeriness. She was twelve years older than Dell, but he observed, "She was a girl of twenty-one in looks, and I was a man of thirty-one in mental powers, tastes and habits."[20] He initiated their courtship by recommending that she read Friedrich Engels's *Socialism, Utopian and Scientific.*

Finding this tangle of romances exhausting, Dell wrote a poem entitled "Now That Our Youth Has Begun to Fade." Although such a romantic sentiment is hard to take seriously from a boy still in his teens, a chapter in Dell's life was indeed closing. In his autobiographical novel, *Moon-Calf* (1920), his desire to escape small-town life and to flee the complications of romance took shape in a single word: "'Chicago!' he said to himself. The rhythm of a word that said itself over and over in his mind: 'Chicago! Chicago!'"[21]

Dell arrived there in the fall of 1908 with twenty dollars in his pocket, and he soon began working for the influential *Chicago Evening Post.* This newspaper, widely read by Chicago's intelligentsia and financial elite, initiated a section called the *Friday Literary Review* on March 5, 1909. The *Review* proved so important that this date is often cited as the beginning of what has come to be known as the Chicago Literary Renaissance. The *Review* provided a primary link between a mainstream audience and advanced writing, publishing European writers such as Henri Bergson, Joseph Conrad, Anatole France, Henrik Ibsen, George Bernard Shaw, and H. G. Wells.

Joining the *Friday Literary Review* soon after it started, Dell served as assistant to the editor Francis Hackett, who instructed him, "You will wash up the dishes in the kitchen, while I sit in the parlor and discourse enlightenment to the suburbs."[22] After two years of writing hundreds of unsigned reviews, Dell was elevated to the *Review*'s editor on July 28, 1911.[23] At age twenty-four he became Chicago's most powerful literary arbiter. He used his new position to hire George Cram Cook as the *Review*'s associate editor, to encourage local writers, and to praise expatriates such as Ezra Pound.[24]

One poet Dell supported was Vachel Lindsay, who introduced himself to Dell in 1909 with the words, "I serve no woman but the Virgin Mary, reverence no knight but Galahad, pray to no God but the Christ-Apollo (despite much contrary advice in your publication)."[25] Thirty-six-year-old Lindsay had recently returned from five years in New York, where his study with the artist Robert Henri had yielded the valuable suggestion that Lindsay's poetry should take precedence over his painting. After returning from the metropolis he became an agrarian troubadour who tramped through villages preaching the Gospel of Beauty. A hobo in a derby, he would present himself at farmhouse doors and

This book is to be used in exchange for the necessities of life on a tramp-journey from the author's home town, through the west and back, during which he will observe the following rules: (1) Keep away from cities. (2) Keep away from the rail-roads. (3) Have nothing to do with money. (4) Ask for dinner about quarter after eleven. (5) Ask for supper, lodging and breakfast about quarter of five. (6) Travel alone. (7) Be neat, truthful, civil and on the square. (8) Preach the Gospel of Beauty.

In order to carry out the last rule there will be three exceptions to the rule about baggage. (1) The author will carry a brief printed statement, called "The Gospel of Beauty." (2) He will carry this book of rhymes for distribution. (3) Also he will carry a small portfolio with pictures, etc., chosen to give an outline of his view of the history of art, especially as it applies to America.

Vachel Lindsay, c. 1911

remove several documents from a bundle tied to the end of his stick. Among them were booklets with the explanatory title *Rhymes to Be Traded for Bread.*

Dell pronounced Lindsay "indubitably a poet!" and in 1911 he in-troduced the shy and ungainly man to Chicago gatherings. Dell vividly recalled one evening, for instance, when Lindsay joined a group of poets around a driftwood fire. After Dell and Cook loudly sang the po-etry of William Butler Yeats, Lindsay stepped forward to recite one of his own poems. But his voice was so soft—Dell called it "a monoto-nous mauve whisper"—that it barely registered above the lapping waves of Lake Michigan.[26]

Margaret Anderson had decided early on that beauty was a necessity—to revolt against her neurotic mother, to escape from small-town In-diana, to save herself from mediocrity. Since Anderson's family moved every year to satisfy her mother's compulsion for redecorating, the love of beauty provided Margaret's only roots. She later wrote, "I had been ecstasied from the age of six instead of learning anything."[27] Piano took precedence over Greek, literature consisted of lyric poetry, and her chief memories from three years of formal education at Western College for Women were of afternoon violet hunts and evenings loung-ing on moonlit balconies.

In the fall of 1908, the same season Dell moved to Chicago, twenty-one-year-old Anderson decided she could no longer tolerate her family life in Columbus, Indiana. She consulted *Good Housekeeping*'s per-

Margaret Anderson

sonal advisor, Clara Laughlin, who was also the literary editor of a religious weekly called the *Continent* and a member of the Little Room. Anderson wrote a letter describing her alienation and closed by asking if she was crazy. Laughlin responded by return post, and her answer delighted Anderson: No, she wasn't crazy, her letter was the most interesting Miss Laughlin had received, and perhaps she should come to Chicago to discuss it further. Anderson impulsively boarded a train, and as soon as Lake Michigan came into view she knew Chicago would be her home. She ordered white lilacs for her hotel room, arranged them with the lake in the background, and stared out at the lighthouse that trained its beams on her window. Illuminated by the hypnotic searchlight, Anderson began to repeat a vow: "I will become something beautiful. I swear it."[28]

Anderson next took a room in the YWCA. Although it was a cell that smelled of laundry and her weekly allowance was only eight dollars, she remained undaunted. She purchased one extravagantly expensive (seventeen dollars) light-blue georgette shirtwaist with ruffles at the wrist, washed and ironed it nightly and wore it daily, always adorned with a fresh yellow rose that cost a nickel. When money ran low Anderson sold two silk negligées and her calfskin-bound volume of Ibsen, and when she could no longer abide her YWCA cell—"that narrow room so tragically turned away from the lake"—she charged four Oriental rugs at Fleming H. Revell's to mask its dreariness.[29]

Anderson's real home was the cluster of buildings that housed Chicago's high culture: Orchestra Hall, the Art Institute, the Annex, the Auditorium Building, and the Fine Arts Building. Collectively these

BELOW, LEFT
Fine Arts Building, 1903

BELOW, RIGHT
A studio in the Fine Arts Building, 1918

buildings represented the proud legacy of the Upward Movement. Its social center, the Fine Arts Building, had inscribed over its doors a motto to which Margaret Anderson passionately subscribed: "All passes, art alone endures." Within this single building were the Little Room, the Chicago Literary Club, the Fortnightly Club, the Caxton Club, Mrs. Chatfield-Taylor's bindery, Ralph Fletcher Seymour's etching studio, artists' studios, and the Dial Bookstore.

The Little Theater—of all the occupants of the Fine Arts Building the most important to the American avant-garde—inhabited a converted storage room at the back of the fourth floor. It opened in December 1912, with a production of *The Trojan Women,* and is often cited as America's first little theater. Directed by the elegant Englishman Maurice Browne and his wife, Ellen van Volkenberg, its amateur casts were made up of artists and bohemians who appreciated the chance for public self-expression. Among them was a twenty-one-year-old actress named Kirah Markham, whose dark beauty attracted two men in the audience—Floyd Dell and Theodore Dreiser. One of the set designers was the Post-Impressionist painter B.J.O. Nordfeldt, and the other was a former Art Institute student named Jane Heap, who talked like a brilliant truck driver and insisted on dressing with the men rather than the women.

Heap would later become the center of Anderson's life, but in these earlier days the Dial Bookstore (designed by Frank Lloyd Wright) proved most important to her. She spent her days working there in the company of Chicago's best society, who drank tea while browsing. Every day when the bookshop closed at 5:30, Anderson would take the same route—through the Fine Arts Building, into the Auditorium Hotel, past the white-gloved black attendant and the nude statues and the onyx columns of the block-long Peacock Alley to the elegant Elizabethan Room. Here she lounged on davenports beneath rich tapestries, wrote letters, and read, attended by hotel maids as if she were royalty. The imperious Anderson stood five feet ten inches tall, and her regal carriage made her seem even taller. With red-gold hair, full lips, and blue eyes, Anderson was, as she put it, "extravagantly pretty in those days—extravagantly and disgustingly pretty. I looked like a composite of all the most offensive magazine covers." [30]

Literature was Anderson's passion. She not only sold books at the Dial Bookstore but also reviewed them for the *Friday Literary Review.* As Floyd Dell recalled, she did so "more enthusiastically than anybody had ever written before in the whole history of book-reviewing." [31] In addition, she soon inherited Clara Laughlin's job as literary editor of the *Continent.* Anderson's relations with Francis Fisher Browne (editor of the *Dial* and her employer at the bookstore) changed one day when the elderly man was walking through the shop muttering Matthew Arnold's "eyes too expressive to be grey, too something to be brown,"

I was always pretending that I was a poor working-girl, always forgetting that I really was poor—also a working-girl.

Margaret Anderson

and Anderson chimed in with the missing word, "lovely." From that moment they developed a relationship based on their shared love of lyric poetry. It ended abruptly when Browne kissed Anderson one afternoon, but before that the editor took her behind the scenes at the *Dial*. Here she learned the basics of composition, monotype, linotype, page makeup, and proofreading—an early education in magazine production that would prove indispensable to Anderson's editorship of her own magazine.

Unlike Margaret Anderson and Floyd Dell, Sherwood Anderson was no longer young when he escaped to Chicago. The thirty-six-year-old's achievements included a family, his paint store in Elyria, Ohio, and reams of inspirational copy he had written for *Agricultural Advertising*. He was bored with it all—the smell of paint, the burdens of domestic life, the hypocrisy of his all-American optimism. On the morning of November 28, 1912, he walked into his office, stood near the heater, and said to his secretary, "I feel as though my feet were wet, and they keep getting wetter." [32] He then walked out the door in his dark business suit, scurried across fields, filled his pockets with corn, and nibbled at the ears. An inner voice whispered to him, "You must leave all that and everything that has been a part of that life behind you." [33] Three days later he turned up in a Cleveland drugstore, his suit spattered with mud. He had no idea who he was.

Anderson would later describe his breakdown as a conversion experience, a revolt against provincialism in which he played the role of a midwestern Gauguin. Chicago was Anderson's Tahiti, and he arrived there in February 1913, feeling newborn but ill equipped to write. He needed the nurturing of a community of writers and artists to complete his mid-life transformation. He found that fellowship one summer evening in the bohemian enclave known as Fifty-seventh Street. Close-set rows of artists' houses fronted both sides of Fifty-seventh Street and Stony Island Avenue for one and a half blocks on Chicago's South Side (now the site of the University of Chicago). The colony rose from the ashes of the Columbian Exposition: the fairgrounds had burned a few months after the fair closed but many of the hastily constructed outbuildings had survived.

The artists' colony was born in 1900 when the Swedish painter B.J.O. Nordfeldt appropriated one of the outbuildings as his studio. Over the next decade many of the single-story shops and storerooms with gingerbread-ornamented façades were converted into studios and makeshift dwellings for Nordfeldt's friend Thorstein Veblen, painters, photographers, etchers, writers, metal craftsmen, and performers. [34] Each residence featured a single room that was inadequately warmed by a potbelly stove, minimal kitchen facilities, and an outhouse; to bathe, one stood in a large iron sink and squeezed a sponge over one's head. The buildings did, however, offer certain amenities: storefront windows that admitted abundant light, expansive high-ceilinged rooms that provided space, and leafy backyards that supplied the setting for communal picnics. On hot summer nights one could escape to the shores of Lake Michigan, just a few blocks away. Most important, the rent was just twelve dollars a month.

One evening a few months after his arrival in Chicago, Sherwood Anderson crept past the gloomy trestles of a railroad embankment and shyly approached Fifty-seventh Street, where he heard laughter and voices. Through the half-drawn green curtains of Margery Currey's broad studio window, he saw silhouettes and flickering shadows in a candlelit room. The conversation was drowned out by the rattle of passing streetcars, but when he could pick out words, he told himself: "'Here is the kind of talk for which I have been hungry.' . . . Here was a world of men and women, of my own age, absorbed in the things in which I wanted to absorb myself. Could I ever enter that world?"[35] Anderson was too timid to go in that first evening, but when he attended the next week's party he found the dialogue he had been seeking.

Evenings at Fifty-seventh Street were informal affairs—sandwiches, hot dogs, and chop suey with gin or wine served in sherbet glasses, guests seated on couches or the floor. Gatherings lasted until the early morning, when spirited intellectual discussion and songs on Margery Currey's grand piano gave way to a quieter tone of reverie and poetry reading. Although writers were a minority of the residents along Fifty-seventh Street, they were in the majority at these evenings. The graying lawyer-poet Edgar Lee Masters often tucked a poem in his pocket to be recited late in the evening. Vachel Lindsay traveled from Springfield and quietly read "My sweetheart is the girl beyond the Moon / For Never have I been in love with woman. . . ."[36] Theodore Dreiser would visit when he was in Chicago, compulsively folding his white handkerchief into precise squares and muttering, "A mad world, my masters."[37] Carl Sandburg, who rarely spoke, could occasionally be coaxed to read from the writings that later composed *Chicago Poems.* The poet Eunice Tietjens sometimes wore a Japanese robe and struck the postures of No theater, while Margaret Anderson appeared in her ruffled georgette shirtwaist. Harriet Monroe would offer her Victorian verse. Maurice Browne and Ellen van Volkenberg represented Chicago's new Little Theater, which rehearsed in a nearby studio. There were also writers for the *Chicago Evening Post* (Llewelyn Carey, Charles Hallinan) and neighborhood residents such as Ernestine Evans, known as a "worshipper of genius," and Lou Wall Moore, a middle-aged, harelipped sculptor who played Cassandra in one of the Little Theater's first productions. Sherwood Anderson read the manuscript of his first novel, *Windy McPherson's Son,* and eventually became so loquacious that he would talk to chairs if he had no other audience.

What linked these disparate people was Floyd Dell and Margery Currey, who married in 1909 and became Chicago's exemplary modern couple. As the Davenport poet Arthur Davison Ficke wrote of them in his "Ode to a Futurist": "Why does all of sharp and new / That our modern age can brew / Culminate in you?"[38] Their party-giving skills were complementary. Currey provided the framework for the evening (she later became, appropriately, a frame designer), furnishing both the organization and the warmth essential to such events. Dell had become a dandy, wearing a broad black scarf, Windsor tie, spats, gloves, and cane. As Margaret Anderson recalled, Currey "presented him as an impersonal being whose only function in life was to talk."[39]

But I could discern little advance out of the routine of small day-by-day occupations and earning toward the larger exercise and recognition of powers within me which seemed to be going to waste. I did not utterly despair—there was consolation in mere living. But how could I reach out toward higher fulfillment, more courageous adventure?—This was my spirit's query during a long period of compromise and self-critical discouragement.

Harriet Monroe

Harriet Monroe declared on the front page of the *Chicago Tribune* in 1911, "The modern English-speaking world says 'Shut up!' to its poets, a condition so unnatural, so destructive to new inspiration, that I believe it can only be temporary and absurd."[40] In the nearly two decades that had passed since the recitation of her "Columbian Ode," Monroe had written ornate poetry that rarely saw print and plays that went unproduced. To heat her study she occasionally burned some of the thousands of unsold copies of her "Ode." She had rejected her few opportunities for romance because they were not "flawless like a diamond" while witnessing the marriage of her siblings and the decline of her family's once-respectable fortune. At fifty-one she was a spinster whose passion focused on poetry and whose bitterness was directed at its neglect. She asked herself, "How could I reach out toward higher fulfillment, more courageous adventure?"

In 1911 she returned from a trip around the world that had allowed her to view Chicago and poetry's marginal position from an international perspective. With new urgency she concluded that America needed a poetry magazine and that she must publish it. Although her magazine would introduce America to modern poetry, it was firmly rooted in the nineteenth-century gentility of the Upward Movement and the social networks of the Little Room. No one better exemplified the magazine's conservative base than the Little Room member Hobart

Chatfield-Taylor. He had founded a xenophobic magazine, *America*, which was dedicated to fighting immigration, encroaching realism in literature, and anarchist bombs. He envisioned a poetry magazine that would showcase Chicago's cultural credentials, and in November 1911 he formulated the plan that would transform Monroe's mission into a functioning poetry magazine. He suggested that one hundred prominent Chicago citizens contribute fifty dollars per year for five years. The commitment of these guarantors would cover office and production costs, and the money from subscriptions would pay the writers. This system of guarantors relied more on civic pride than on enlightened patronage: support came not from an intellectual or literary community but from the builders of power plants and farm machinery, the autocrats of utilities and railroads, the leaders of Sears Roebuck and meat-packing plants.

For the next year Monroe personally solicited Chicago's leading citizens. Her task was difficult, for the city's elite was more willing to import literary lions from Europe than to nurture local cubs. She used her friendships at the Little Room, tapped the same individuals who had supported the Upward Movement, and approached old family friends. By the summer of 1912 Monroe had elicited commitments from 108 guarantors. She began spending her days in the Chicago Public Library's reading room, surveying all verse published in English from 1907 to the present. In August she sent a "poet's circular" to those writers she most respected and appended personal letters to fifty of the poets she most wanted to publish.[41] "We promise to refuse nothing because it is too good," Monroe wrote. "We shall read with special interest poems of modern significance. . . ."[42]

Monroe could not have known how perfectly timed was her invitation. In 1912 a thirty-year fallow season in American poetry came to an end as young poets throughout the country began to publish. In Springfield, Illinois, Vachel Lindsay published *Rhymes to Be Traded for Bread,* and in Brookline, Massachusetts, Amy Lowell published her first poetry volume, *A Dome of Many-Coloured Glass.* There were also books by Donald Evans, Robinson Jeffers, and Edgar Lee Masters, and in London, Ezra Pound published two books (*Ripostes* and *Cavalcanti*). Each of these publications was accomplished without the knowledge of the other poets. But that August of 1912 they all received Monroe's announcement of *Poetry,* which promised to end the poets' isolation. The title of Edna St. Vincent Millay's 1912 debut, "Renascence," seemed to forecast a new era in poetry.

HARVARD

Walter Arensberg at Harvard, from the *Harvard Alum,* 1900

Wallace Stevens, c. 1900

Harvard's Class of 1900 began their undergraduate careers at a time when Boston was suffering from "grandfather on the brain." The city had reigned throughout the nineteenth century as America's cultural capital, while across the river Harvard served as both a Brahmin finishing school and an intellectual center. The new students included several future architects of modernism: Pitts Sanborn, who would edit a little magazine (*Trend*) and write music criticism; Arthur Davison Ficke and Witter Bynner, poets who would stage America's first avant-garde hoax; Paul Sachs, who would train a generation of museum directors; and, most prominently, Walter Arensberg, who would support avant-garde artists and poets, and Wallace Stevens, who would pioneer modern poetry. These young men hardly constituted a circle, for their connections with each other were sometimes only a matter of recognizing a face in Harvard Yard or reading one another's work in the *Harvard Advocate,* but even such casual relationships linked them to the most influential old-boy network in America.

Between Walter Arensberg and Wallace Stevens the mutual sympathies ran much deeper. Both were Pennsylvanians; had four siblings; were influenced by George Santayana, Charles Eliot Norton, and Benjamin Jowett; had an interest in poetry—and harbored the sensibility of a dandy.

Walter Conrad Arensberg was the privileged eldest son of a steel magnate whose Pittsburgh-based McCollough-Dalzell Company thrived in the post–Civil War industrial boom. Young Walter knew the luxury of growing up in a fashionable home, receiving violin lessons, and polishing his manners in a drawing room whose walls were hung with engravings in heavy frames. His thin frame, wispy hair, and infectious enthusiasm projected a boyish charm. As his classmate Wallace Stevens observed, "His interest amounted to excitement." [1]

Upon arriving at Harvard, Arensberg installed a large photograph of the Mona Lisa on his mantelpiece, steeped himself in the aesthetic philosophy of Walter Pater, and decided to study literature and philosophy. His choice was made with a minimum of struggle. A friend recalled that "Walter was nothing if not highbrow."[2] He explored the subtle twists of his own mind, pondered questions of appearance and reality, constructed intricate acrostics. His penchant for cerebral games was reflected in his method of chess playing: while walking in the country, he would call out moves on an imaginary board. He wrote Symbolist-inflected poetry that appeared in the *Harvard Advocate* and served two terms as president of Delta Upsilon, Harvard's literary society. The pinnacle of his Harvard career was his election as editor of the *Harvard Monthly*. Among the poems he published in that prestigious periodical were Keatsian sonnets by John Morris II and Hilary Harness. The author hiding behind both pseudonyms was Wallace Stevens, and his withdrawal into anonymity suggests that his literary vocation was as troubled as Arensberg's was effortless.

Stevens went to Harvard in 1897 as a "special student"—a status that acknowledged both his academic ability and the economic hardship his education was causing the Stevens family back in Reading, Pennsylvania. With diligence Stevens managed to graduate with the Class of 1900, having earned respectable grades while carrying on a richer and more conflicted life outside the classroom. "Harvard feeds subjectivity," he wrote in his journal, "encourages an all consuming flame + that, in my mind, is an evil in so impersonal a world. Personality must be kept secret before the world."[3] One of his Harvard stories, "Part of His Education," dramatizes the tension between two contrasting personalities: a dandy who is ridiculed for ordering a crème de menthe by his friend, a conventional fellow who drinks beer. To his classmates Stevens seemed the epitome of a regular fellow—robust, modest, amiable—but in his imagination he sipped crème de menthe.[4]

By graduation Stevens had published stories and poems in the Harvard magazines, had served as president of both the Signet Club and the *Harvard Advocate,* and had confided to a professor that he aspired to be a poet—to which the professor uncharitably responded, "Jesus Christ!"[5] In June 1900 Stevens's last Harvard poem appeared. He would not publish another for fourteen years. Shortly before graduation Stevens had written in his journal: "I should be content to dream along to the end of my life—and opposing moralists be hanged. At the same time I should be quite content to work and be practical. . . . I must try not to be a dilettante—half dream, half deed. I must be all dream or all deed."[6] Instead, he compromised: he worked during the day as an insurance lawyer and devoted evenings to his journal. ("This is my own diary," he wrote, "of which I am the house, the inhabitant, the lock, and the key."[7]) In 1909 he married Elsie Kachel, a strikingly beautiful Reading girl seven years younger than he, who served as the model for the figure on the Liberty dime. She became Stevens's muse, and his only poems were written for her, often on the occasion of her birthday. Elsie, who had completed only one year of high school and subscribed

HARVARD STUDENTS

Walter Arensberg,
    Class of 1900
Bernard Berenson,
    Class of 1887
Van Wyck Brooks,
    Class of 1908
Witter Bynner,
    Class of 1902
George Cram Cook,
    Class of 1893
T. S. Eliot,
    Class of 1910
Arthur Davison Ficke,
    Class of 1904
John Gould Fletcher,
    Class of 1907
    (attended 1903–7
    but did not graduate)
Hutchins Hapgood,
    Class of 1892
Paul Haviland,
    Class of 1901
Robert Edmond Jones,
    Class of 1910
Walter Lippmann,
    Class of 1910
Eugene O'Neill,
    Class of 1916
John Quinn,
    earned L.L.B. in 1895
John Reed,
    Class of 1910
Paul Sachs,
    Class of 1900
Leo Stein, special student,
    1892–94
Wallace Stevens,
    Class of 1900

Between lovers and the like personality is well-enough; so with poets + old men etc. + conquerors + lambs etc.; but for young men etc. it is most decidedly well-enough to be left alone.

Wallace Stevens,
journal entry,
July 28, 1900

to the canons of conventional taste, felt threatened by the elegance and abstraction of his poems. When Stevens wanted to recite them, he would retreat into the closet of their small apartment.

Walter Arensberg graduated cum laude in June 1900 and was named class poet. Many of his classmates expected Arensberg, whose family money emancipated him from practical concerns, to pursue an exceptionally creative career. He settled in Florence for a year and translated Dante's *Divine Comedy* into English terza rima. Perhaps he was trying to assume the mantle of his professor Charles Eliot Norton, who had done a prose translation of Dante's masterpiece. In 1912 Arensberg bought Norton's home, Shady Hill, a white Federal-style mansion that lay one thousand yards northeast of Harvard Yard and carried a distinguished pedigree; the first mayor of Boston had built it in 1815 and Norton had reigned there during the late nineteenth century as Harvard's first professor of art history and America's arbiter of high culture. Arensberg settled into Norton's study and wrote poetry in the company of two Welsh terriers.

By this time he had worked as an art critic on the *New York Post* from 1904 to 1906 and had written elegant translations of poems by Jules Laforgue, Stéphane Mallarmé, and Paul Verlaine. In June 1907 Arensberg married Louise Stevens (the sister of a Harvard classmate), who had inherited the family's medium-sized fortune derived from a textile factory in Ludlow, Massachusetts. Louise had studied music seriously, but her shyness prevented her from singing professionally. With two independent incomes, one of the most eminent addresses in America, and a knowledgeable interest in the arts, the Arensbergs were well equipped to become patrons of the modern age. As Wallace Stevens observed about his Harvard classmate, "He was just the man to become absorbed in cubism and in everything that followed."[8]

Across the Charles River in Brookline during that June of 1900, Amy Lowell was preparing the parlor of the family estate for her father's funeral. The Oriental rugs were cleaned, the sterling doorknobs polished, and flowers from her father's beloved gardens were arranged in memorial festoons. Twenty-six-year-old Amy Lowell was now officially on her own. Unofficially, this had always been her relationship to her parents.

Lowell's mother, an invalid suffering from Bright's disease, was chronically short-tempered and incapable of raising her last child, who was sometimes known as "the post-script." Lowell's father was a stern and canny businessman who expended his energy on family charities and his passion on his exotic greenhouse gardens. Amy commanded their attention with her precocious bravado—at the age of two she drove the two-horse coach to church and back, and she later entertained her parents' after-dinner guests with puns—but the relationship was never close. According to a popular Boston rumor, Amy was raised by the coachman.

Amy Lowell

Key figures in the Brahmin aristocracy, the Lowell family had arrived in America in 1639 and quickly prospered—first as merchants and shippers, later as prominent lawyers, diplomats, historians, and ministers. During the nineteenth century, when Boston was known as "the Athens of the New World," Lowells were the driving forces behind its leading institutions—Harvard, the Boston Athenaeum, the Massachusetts Institute of Technology, and of course the Lowell Institute. Amy's great-uncle was the poet James Russell Lowell.

Amy's awareness of her forebears was acute, especially since she was such an odd late-blooming flower on the Lowell family tree. A tomboyish, roly-poly child, she grew to barely five feet tall but weighed 250 pounds. Her feet were small, her ankles dainty, and her head normally proportioned, but she called her body "a great, rough, strong, masculine thing," and once declared, "I'm a disease!" [9] Her doctors, baffled by the glandular disorder that plagued Lowell from the age of ten, simply counseled her to eat less. Her dieting reached its extreme in 1898, when she accompanied four women on a stylish dahabeah up the Nile, eating only tomatoes and asparagus and sweating profusely as they drifted past ancient temples. This method, known as banting, was popular among fashionable ladies, but for Lowell it resulted in the loss of only a few pounds, gastritis, and a seven-year headache.

After her father died, Amy faced an uncertain future. As a Lowell, she enjoyed limitless privilege; as a woman beyond marriageable age, her options were considerably narrower. [10] Her first act was to buy Sevenels—named for the seven Lowells (*L*'s)—from her brothers and sisters, and to remodel it to reflect her priorities. She created a baronial library, moved her bed back into the nursery she called the Sky Parlor,

She was always the child, a Gargantual child with the reach of a khan or a brigand. . . .

Van Wyck Brooks on Amy Lowell

and installed a huge tiled bathtub for her painstaking toilette. In honor of the seven Lowells, she bought seven large sheepdogs, and in memory of her father, she assumed his place on Boston committees. Her true vocation would not become clear to her until she attended a 1902 performance of Gabriele D'Annunzio's *La Gioconda* and became so infatuated with Eleonora Duse that she returned for all nine Boston performances and trailed her to Philadelphia. While watching the elegiac tragedienne, Lowell had a vision "that revealed me to myself," and when she finally met the actress, lying on her bed in a filmy dressing gown, Duse "talked as if soul to soul." [11] This experience inspired Lowell to write seventy-one lines of blank verse. It contained "every cliché and every technical error which a poem can have," Lowell recalled, "but it loosed a bolt in my brain and I found out where my true function lay." [12]

Lowell began to spend her nights in Sevenels's library—seated in her father's huge leather chair with her feet on his round hassock and a lit Manila cigar between her fingers—writing verses in large gestural script. She wrote prodigiously but not well. In 1912, at the age of thirty-eight, she presented her poems to the respected Boston publisher Houghton Mifflin and magisterially convinced the firm to publish them. *A Dome of Many-Coloured Glass*—a Keatsian rehashing of such time-worn subjects as the seasons, eternity, nature—caused barely a ripple even in Boston. Eighty copies were sold and the few reviews were tepid. Amy Lowell had become an author, but she hadn't yet found her voice.

Shortly after he graduated in 1910, John Reed looked back on his undergraduate years as "the Harvard Renaissance"—and his appellation was not merely the inflated sentiment of a recent graduate. Evidence of a renaissance could be seen in the embryonic accomplishments of his classmates, who would figure prominently in shaping the American avant-garde: Conrad Aiken, Charles and Albert Boni, T. S. Eliot, Robert Edmond Jones, and Walter Lippmann. The new spirit could be seen in student articles that urged greater connection between the university and the outside world and declared that the traditional Harvard education must expand to embrace "revolutions, rejuvenations and catastrophes." [13] The renaissance was also embodied in the variety of new clubs that had recently sprung up on campus. Most prominent was the Socialist Club, founded in 1908. In its wake smaller political organizations formed: the Social Politics Club, the Harvard Men's League for Women's Suffrage, the Anarchist Club, the Single Tax Club. In contrast to clubs like Porcellian, Fly, and others along Mount Auburn Street—which existed mainly to initiate young men into the Brahmin aristocracy—the new clubs were issue oriented. The Harvard trustees felt sufficiently threatened by these new groups to curtail on-campus "systematic propaganda on contentious questions of contemporaneous social, economic, political or religious interests."[14] But the clubs' collective presence gave students a way to force the ivory tower to open up to the twentieth century. The clubs' common aim, as Reed wrote, was "to realize right here and now what had been vague dreams," and they spawned a new breed of activist-intellectuals who aspired not only to understand the world but to change it.[15] Walter Lippmann wrote, "The shaping of the future lies in our hands; for the first time in history an enlightened nation may consciously prepare for the future to suit its own purposes."[16]

Some students, like the young Missourian T. S. Eliot (known as Tom), scarcely participated in these progressive activities. Bloodless, intellectual, nattily dressed, he outwardly conformed to Harvard's social caste, aspiring to the clubs on Mount Auburn Street and the traditional literary clubs. But mostly he buried himself in his studies, which provided a well-polished shield for his intense shyness. Eliot's significant undergraduate experiences included his discovery of Symbolist poetry and his introspective wanderings around Boston, which he described as "quite civilized but refined beyond the point of civilization."[17] They inspired such early poems as "The Love Song of J. Alfred Prufrock."

T. S. Eliot, age 19, at Harvard, 1907

At the other extreme was Walter Lippmann, who spearheaded Harvard's progressive movement. Stocky, self-assured, and intellectually dazzling, the Manhattan Jew had no place in Harvard's time-honored clubs. Instead, he organized the Socialist Club and became active in the Social Politics Club, the Debating Club, and Harvard's magazines. He used his podiums to articulate his newly adopted socialist creed, going beyond theoretical debate to proposing concrete reforms. He urged the university to raise its wages for workers, to allow women speakers on campus, to offer a course in socialism, and he even proposed a socialist platform that extended beyond Harvard Yard. In his senior year he mounted a challenge to the elite clubs whose members had traditionally dominated class offices, and he organized the heads of progressive clubs into a super club that became a powerful radical faction on campus.[18] Lippmann was so ambitious and his political sense so rational that John Reed introduced him, only half-jokingly, as "the future President of the United States."[19]

Reed fluctuated wildly between the old and the new at Harvard. Arriving in 1906 as an outsider—a native of Portland, Oregon, and a graduate from a non–Ivy League prep school—he felt compelled to be recognized as a big man on campus. After two days he was ready to write a book on the university, brashly declaring, "Hell, we'll find out doing the thing!"[20] This quickly jettisoned idea was merely the first of Reed's attempts to storm Harvard's ivy-covered walls. He tried out for the football team and the freshman crew; he trooped through Cambridge, rattling windows and shouting "The British are coming!"; he left calling cards on the gravestones of Boston's most distinguished

John Reed, age 18, 1905

families. His classmates initially dismissed him as a grandstanding arriviste who didn't know "cricket from non-cricket,"[21] but Reed's drive to be recognized was gradually rewarded. He began writing for the *Harvard Lampoon,* the *Harvard Advocate,* and the *Harvard Monthly;* he joined the water-polo team and the varsity swimming team; and he was accepted by many campus clubs.

Reed's activities at Harvard, however self-contradictory and juvenile, presaged his role in America's new bohemia. He wrote a play for the Cosmopolitan Club about the ancient Tower of Babel, portraying its workers organizing a union and striking; in the same season he wrote the lyrics for a frothy Hasty Pudding production called *Diana's Debut.* He scorned the "Harvard spirit" as adolescent but was happiest as a football cheerleader, enjoying "the supreme blissful sensation of swaying two thousand voices in great crashing choruses."[22] His conflict was dramatized in his senior year, during one of the most important of Harvard rituals—the election of officers for graduation week. The Harvard Renaissance had bred a spirit of rebellion against the domination of these offices by the Mount Auburn Street elite, and the poorer dorm residents, led by Walter Lippmann, launched their own candidates. Reed was torn when the Mount Auburn aristocrats, in an effort to broaden their appeal, invited him to join their ticket and defeat the "democratic revolution." He chose social status over democracy, but the underdogs won the election. Reed arrived at his graduation as one who had not only sold out but lost.

The quadrangle's greensward was filled the afternoon of June 24, and an east wind tempered the heat as the Class of 1910 marched to the graduation ceremony. Harvard President Abbott Lowell (Amy's brother) walked with former United States President Theodore Roosevelt in the procession to Memorial Hall, which was filled with the largest audience in Harvard's history. The class orator, William Ohler, stressed Harvard's need to be engaged in society. T. S. Eliot recited his farewell ode: "For the hour that is left us Fair Harvard, with thee, / Ere we face the importunate years. . . ."[23] The entire class sang Eliot's words to the tune of "Fair Harvard" and then marched up the aisle and out into the world.

Shortly after graduation John Reed set out on his own gritty version of the Grand Tour—he sailed on a decrepit British cattle boat and planned to travel across Europe and Asia on foot. He never got as far as he had hoped; after brief stays in London and Spain he settled in Paris's Latin Quarter for several months. He alternated between hobnobbing with Harvard's expatriate set—dressing fastidiously for cocktails and smoking Philip Morrises—and exploring lower-class bohemian life. Reed danced all night at the Bal Bullier, drank in Le Rat Mort, the Moulin Rouge, and L'Abbaye, and welcomed "freedom from every boundary, moral, religious, social."[24] Declaring that Paris embodied the dream he had unconsciously held all his life, he struggled to capture it in his writing. But his euphoria was mixed with homesickness and self-doubt, and by the spring after his graduation Reed had returned to America.

On the south side of Greenwich Village's Washington Square he shared a thirty-dollar-a-month third-floor flat with three Harvard classmates and soon began writing his own homegrown version of *La Bohème*. His fifteen hundred lines of pastiche verse were old-fashioned in style but modern in subject; "The Day in Bohemia" was the first epic of Greenwich Village. In lively doggerel Reed painted a picture of aesthetic teas, cold-water flats, elegant hangouts like the Hotel Brevoort, and Village characters like Harry Kemp and Lincoln Steffens.

At the beginning of 1913 Reed hawked his poem on the streets for a dollar and found that the Village fell in love with its own reflection, hailing him as the Village Bard. Although Reed wrote before the Village had established its key avant-garde institutions, his poem described the playful spirit of the bohemia-to-be:

Yet we are free who live in Washington Square,
We dare to think as Uptown wouldn't dare,
Blazing our nights with arguments uproarious;
What care we for a dull world censorious
When each is sure he'll fashion something glorious?[25]

PARIS

n the fall of 1903 Gertrude Stein and her older brother Leo set up housekeeping in Paris's sixth arrondissement at 27, rue de Fleurus. They were an odd couple. Tall and angular, with a scraggly red beard, thirty-one-year-old Leo resembled a rabbinical Ichabod Crane. Whatever he saw through his gold-rimmed spectacles prompted theoretical discourse—one friend observed that all he wanted in life was an Ear. Twenty-nine-year-old Gertrude was both fleshy and earthy, and her broad, handsome features had the authoritative solidity of a monument. In connoisseur Bernard Berenson's words, she was "the proto-Semite, a statue from the Ur of the Chaldees."[1] In contrast to her brother, Gertrude did not expound; she was more likely to emit a hearty laugh that came out, as her friend Mabel Dodge observed, "like a beefsteak."[2] Leo spent his life pondering their differences, and a few days before his death in 1947 he provided the final summary. "The differences between Gertrude's character and mine were profound," he wrote. "Her critical interest was entirely in character, in people's personalities. She was practically inaccessible to ideas and I was accessible to nothing else."[3]

Nonetheless, Gertrude and Leo were tightly bonded; to one observer they appeared to be "the happiest couple on the Left Bank."[4] In addition to the interdependence that had resulted from being orphaned during adolescence, at that point in 1903 they shared a sense of personal and professional crisis. Each had arrived at a dead end.

Leo had long borne the burden of being a genius unable to focus his erratic brilliance. He had studied philosophy at Harvard (1892–96) and biology at Johns Hopkins University in Baltimore (1897–1900); in 1900 he decided that his calling was aesthetics. He settled in Florence to immerse himself in quattrocento art (which he discussed with his informal mentor, Bernard Berenson) and to write a biography of Andrea Mantegna, the Renaissance painter. But he soon abandoned this project, too, upon discovering that two other books on Mantegna were already in preparation. Leo wandered on to London and Paris, vaguely planning to return to America. In Paris an epiphany struck: he felt that he was "growing into an artist" and, standing nude before the fireplace in his hotel room, he began to draw.[5] Although his career as an artist was as short-lived as his preceding preoccupations, it inspired him to rent the atelier on the rue de Fleurus that became his home. At this point Leo's achievements were as eclectic as the collection of objects he had brought from Florence: terra-cotta saints, Venetian glass, ivory daggers, Japanese prints, and a marble head of Dionysus.

Gertrude seemed equally directionless. She had begun promisingly at Radcliffe, where she was considered "the ideal student" by her mentor, William James.[6] "Don't reject anything," he counseled her. "If you reject anything, that is the beginning of the end as an intellectual."[7] On his advice she studied medicine at Johns Hopkins, sharing a flat with her brother. After her third year Gertrude's interest and her grades plummeted. "Gertrude, Gertrude," implored a feminist friend, "remember the cause of women." To which she replied, "You don't know what it is to be bored."[8] She had her first lesbian affair in Baltimore, spending long hours with an emancipated Johns Hopkins student

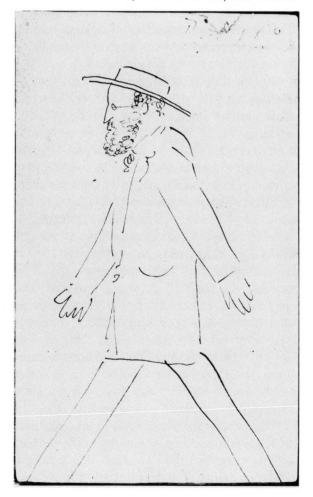

Pablo Picasso (1881–1973). *Leo Stein*, 1905. Pen and ink on paper, 6¾ × 4½ in. (17.1 × 11.4 cm). Mr. and Mrs. Jerome B. Rocherolle

named May Bookstaver. The relationship ended after a year, when Bookstaver left her for another woman. The experience threatened Stein's previously unshakable self-confidence, but it inspired her first sustained writing and her first attempt to explore her own psychology. This novel, *Q.E.D.*, completed shortly after Gertrude moved to the rue de Fleurus, lay unseen in the studio cupboard for nearly three decades. It marked the beginning of her vocation as a writer and gave her hope. "One plunges here and there with energy and misdirection during the storm and stress of the making of a personality," she wrote, "until at last we reach the twenty-ninth year the straight and narrow gateway of maturity and life which was all uproar and confusion narrows down to form and purpose and we exchange a great dim possibility for a small hard reality."[9]

Twenty-seven, rue de Fleurus was located on a street that jogged the few blocks between Luxembourg Gardens and rue Notre Dame. The boulevard Montparnasse met the boulevard Raspail less than half a mile from the Steins' door. By 1900 this intersection had become the heart of the artists' neighborhood, Montparnasse, overtaking Montmartre as the densest concentration of artists in the western world.[10] The model market was held on the broad boulevards each Monday morning, and in 1903 the Café de la Rotonde joined the Café du Dôme (started in 1898) as a center of bohemian life. An international assortment of artists lingered over café crèmes on the terrace, or drank with the German artists at the Dôme's zinc bar, or retired to its back rooms to play billiards or join the continuous all-American poker game. The artists who moved to Montparnasse over the next decade formed a community that would stimulate the growth of modernism in America: Patrick Henry Bruce, Jo Davidson, Mina Loy, John Marin, Elie Nadelman, Walter Pach, Edward Steichen, Maurice Sterne, and others. And in 1905 Gertrude and Leo's older brother, Michael, and his wife, Sarah, moved a few blocks away, on rue Madame.

Gertrude and Leo found their new home on the rue de Fleurus to be ideal—the two-story courtyard apartment provided comfortable living quarters, and an attached atelier featured good northern light. Although they were close to the artists' community, they kept enough distance to lead quiet, sensible lives. They were the first on the Left Bank to install a Yale lock; they immediately hired a staunch house-keeper named Hélène, who cooked them plain food and attended to their bourgeois comfort; and they preferred a stroll in Luxembourg Gardens to an evening in a Montparnasse café.

The origin of the Steins' modern art collection dates to the fall of 1904. It was triggered partly by an unexpected surplus of eight thou-sand francs in their bank account and partly by Bernard Berenson's suggestion that Leo see the paintings of Paul Cézanne—but the chief catalyst was the 1904 Salon d'Automne. There the Steins first encountered the diversity of modern painting: Pierre Bonnard, Edgar Degas, Paul Gauguin, Edouard Manet, Pierre-Auguste Renoir, Henri de Toulouse-Lautrec, Vincent van Gogh, Edouard Vuillard. Leo, who was more intrigued than Gertrude, recalled that he "looked again and again at every single picture, just as a botanist might at the flora of an unknown land."[11] His obsessive study inspired his first broad treatise on "L'Art Moderne." Within a few pages he summarized the theoretical underpinnings of modernism; identified its four most influential artists as Manet, Renoir, Degas, and Cézanne; and described their individual contributions to the history of painting. It was a performance of dazzling prescience and connoisseurship. (That this modern credo was buried in a letter was characteristic, for Leo's discourses were tossed off in ephemeral forms like conversations or correspondence.) Leo had found his vocation. As Gertrude later wrote, "My brother needed to be talking and he was painting but he needed to talk about painting."[12]

At the next year's Salon d'Automne, Leo had a fateful confrontation with Henri Matisse's *Woman with a Hat.* "The nastiest smear of paint that I had ever seen," Leo later wrote. "It was what I was unknowingly waiting for."[13] It took him several days to decide to pay Matisse's price of 500 francs (roughly one hundred dollars), but that decision marked his new commitment to the most radical direction in painting. Over the next two years he became, in the measured judgment of art historian Alfred Barr, "possibly the most discerning connoisseur and collector of twentieth-century painting in the world."[14] The tasteful Japanese prints that had filled the Steins' walls were banished to Leo's study (which was dubbed the "salon des refusés") and replaced with a row of canvases by Cézanne, Gauguin, Matisse, and Picasso. Soon a second tier of paintings was added and then a third, and by 1908 the collection crowded the three available walls of the atelier. Their ornate gold frames hung only a few inches apart, in true Salon style, and the paintings were skied right up to the ceiling. Not all of them could be seen, for at the upper reaches the gaslights cast only flickering illumination. But nowhere else in Paris—or in the world— could modern painting be found in such quantity and quality as on those three walls. As Leo later described his pursuit of the modern, he felt "like a Columbus setting sail for a world beyond the world."[15]

Within a few weeks of Leo's introduction to Matisse, Gertrude experienced something similarly inspiring when the writer Henri-Pierre Roché introduced her to Pablo Picasso. She was immediately convinced of Picasso's genius—although she took an equally immediate dislike to his painting—and was delighted by his derogatory comments about her brother. Drawn to her striking physical presence, Picasso soon asked her to sit for a portrait.[16] The sitting assumed marathon proportions and proved seminal for both Picasso and Stein. Gertrude re-

called spending nearly ninety afternoons posing in a broken armchair in Picasso's studio in the Bateau Lavoir. Dressed in the blue overalls usually worn by Parisian plumbers, Picasso painted and repainted the figure before him, while his mistress Fernande Olivier read aloud from *The Fables* of La Fontaine. As the sittings stretched on, silence replaced Olivier's reading, and during these mute spells Gertrude formulated the stories that would become *Three Lives* (1909), her first published work. Declaring that he could no longer see Stein when he looked at her, Picasso took a long summer vacation from the painting. On his return he wiped out Stein's portrait and painted primitive features in flat planes; they resembled an Iberian mask as much as his sitter. Friends remarked that Stein looked nothing like the painting, to which Picasso nonchalantly replied, "She will." Stein was enchanted and later called it "the only reproduction of me which is always I, for me." [17] For Picasso the *Portrait of Gertrude Stein* was an essential step in his transition to Cubism.

The events of the fall of 1905—Leo's purchases from the Salon d'Automne and new friendships with Matisse and Picasso—began the most important period in the Steins' joint career as collectors of art and of artists. As their holdings grew, Matisse began to treat 27, rue de Fleurus as a museum dedicated to him. He brought friends and often stayed for dinner, if he approved of what Hélène had prepared. Soon Henri-Pierre Roché was escorting foreign visitors to the apartment, and Picasso was arriving with the bohemian crew from the Bateau Lavoir. People visited at all times of day, and Gertrude found that the many knocks at the door interrupted the internal rhythm of her words, so she began to write at night. She sat at the heavy Florentine table and filled schoolchildren's notebooks with her generous scrawl, forging her new identity as a writer.

By 1907 the visitors were arriving in such great numbers that Gertrude and Leo instituted what was then a common social formula. Their closest artist friends received standing invitations to early supper on Saturday evenings. Then, from nine until the early morning, the Steins were At Home for the writers, artists, mistresses, and patrons who constituted Paris's modern community. For them 27, rue de Fleurus became as notable a feature of the Parisian landscape as the Cirque Medrano or the Bateau Lavoir.

Guests passed through an archway into a dim passage that opened onto a small courtyard, where they faced a pair of large wooden doors and a small knocker. Gertrude answered the door herself, and if she did not recognize a visitor, she would ask, "De la part de qui venez-vous?" ("Who sent you?"). The question was merely a formality: everyone was admitted. The disquieting modernity of the paintings inside contrasted with the amiable clutter of Leo's miscellany. Renaissance chairs clustered around a long Tuscan refectory table next to a cast-iron stove.

Gertrude Stein in the studio, 27, rue de Fleurus, c. 1905

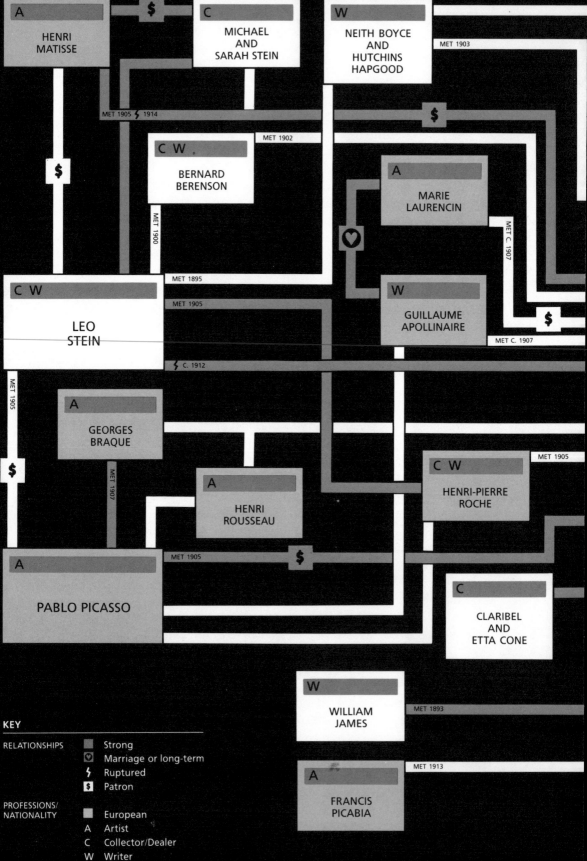

A
HENRI
MATISSE

$

C
MICHAEL
AND
SARAH STEIN

W
NEITH BOYCE
AND
HUTCHINS
HAPGOOD

MET 1903

MET 1905 ⚡ 1914

$

C W
BERNARD
BERENSON

MET 1902

A
MARIE
LAURENCIN

MET C. 1907

♡

MET 1900

MET 1895

C W
LEO
STEIN

MET 1905

W
GUILLAUME
APOLLINAIRE

$

MET C. 1907

⚡ C. 1912

A
GEORGES
BRAQUE

MET 1907

A
HENRI
ROUSSEAU

C W
HENRI-PIERRE
ROCHE

MET 1905

MET 1905

$

A
PABLO PICASSO

MET 1905

$

C
CLARIBEL
AND
ETTA CONE

W
WILLIAM
JAMES

MET 1893

KEY

RELATIONSHIPS   ▢ Strong
     🖤 Marriage or long-term
     ⚡ Ruptured
     $ Patron

PROFESSIONS/
NATIONALITY   ▢ European
     A   Artist
     C   Collector/Dealer
     W   Writer

A
FRANCIS
PICABIA

MET 1913

PARIS

ALICE B. TOKLAS

MABEL DODGE
W
MET 1911

MINA LOY
A W
MET C. 1907

GERTRUDE STEIN
C W
MET 1907
MET 1911

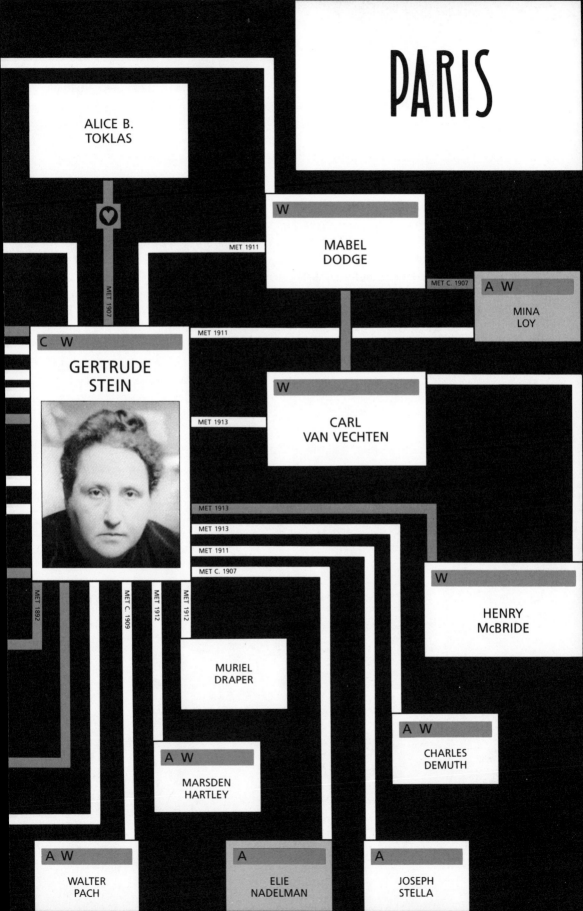

CARL VAN VECHTEN
W
MET 1913

HENRY McBRIDE
W

MET 1913
MET 1913
MET 1911
MET C. 1907

MET 1892
MET C. 1909
MET 1912
MET 1912

MURIEL DRAPER

CHARLES DEMUTH
A W

MARSDEN HARTLEY
A W

WALTER PACH
A W

ELIE NADELMAN
A

JOSEPH STELLA
A

A Henry IV buffet and sideboards, chests, and little tables all carried a full complement of objects—ranging from Elie Nadelman's *Venus* and a bronze Buddha to curio-shop figurines, tiny alabaster urns, carved eagles, horeshoe nails, and pipe holders. The guests' clothing ranged just as widely, from Gertrude's loose corduroy garb and Matisse's business suit to the flashy tweed suits, bowler hats, and loud ties of artists who liked dressing "à l'américaine."[18] Some guests never strayed far from the platters of ham and cheese, the slender baguettes, and the wine set out on the refectory table.

The Steins' burgeoning art collection inspired heated discussion. The fleshy Renoirs were easy to like, as were the vibrantly colored Gauguins, but Matisse's Fauve paintings and Picasso's early Cubist works offered more of a challenge. "I have never in my life seen so many dreadful paintings in one place," exclaimed Mary Cassatt on her only visit, "and I want to be taken home at once."[19] For Marsden Hartley, the paintings offered "a new kind of words for an old theme" and made him feel "like a severed head living of itself by mystical excitation."[20] When Gertrude's former mentor, William James, looked at the collection shortly before his death, he took a step back and exclaimed, "I always told you that you should keep your mind open."[21]

By ten o'clock the studio buzzed with conversation and Latin Quarter gossip, and the crowd of several dozen spilled into the Steins'

Collection of Leo and Gertrude Stein in the studio, 27, rue de Fleurus

living quarters. A few figures stood out in the tumult. Leo was always at the middle of it and always delivering "trenchant affirmations," gesturing with concise jabs that seemed to nail down Truth.[22] Gertrude reigned from one of the high-back Renaissance chairs, her legs tucked under her. In those early days her authority owed less to what she said than to her engaging demeanor and her composed certitude. The art-laden walls were Leo's province, the guests Gertrude's. Quietly observing from her chair, occasionally letting loose an infectious laugh, she quickly sized up her guests and decided who would be invited back. "What differentiated her from all other collectors was the fact that she collected geniuses rather than masterpieces," observed critic Henry McBride. "She recognized them a long way off."[23]

Geniuses filled the studio. Poet and critic Guillaume Apollinaire turned up with his lover, the nearsighted painter Marie Laurencin, who gazed at the paintings through her lorgnette. Apollinaire declaimed about new trends in art with an authority developed on the spot. Max Jacob was the most theatrical of the Montmartre contingent. He rolled up his trousers to imitate a barefoot dancer or donned a translucent veil to sing arias in a tuneful but ridiculous soprano.[24] Gertrude thought that Picasso encircled by his friends looked "like Napoleon surrounded by his marshals," while her friend Alice B. Toklas observed that the group surrounded him "like the cuadrilla does a bullfighter."[25] Picasso reigned over his corner of the room with reluctant authority, for he was self-conscious about his halting French and bored by people who sought explanations for his art.

Commanding another part of the studio was Matisse, who once declared that he and Picasso were "as different as the North Pole is from the South Pole."[26] It was here that the two men met in 1906, perhaps the only territory in all of Paris sufficiently neutral to accommodate them both. With his neatly trimmed beard and his devoted wife, Matisse looked just like a bourgeois businessman. He enjoyed convincing listeners about the superiority of modern art and repeatedly offered the same dictum that he presented to his students: "You must be able to walk firmly on the ground before you can start walking a tightrope."[27] He stood with such fellow Fauves as André Derain, and he was usually attended by a knot of his students.[28]

Although the French dominated the gatherings, the company was truly international, including the Russian pàtron Sergei Shchukin, the Polish émigré–sculptor Elie Nadelman (whom Gertrude early regarded as a genius and also the coldest man she'd ever met), and numerous Hungarians; the royal Infanta Eulalia of Spain even paid a visit. Henri-Pierre Roché circulated through the crowd, dubbed by Gertrude "the general introducer" and by Leo "the liaison officer."[29] Although Roché wrote about art and casually dealt in it, his métier was social. Gertrude recalled his perennial response to artists and writers hungry for encouragement: "Good, good, excellent."[30]

Saturdays brought a mixture of nationalities to Miss Stein's but while there was much confusion and the light was not good, one could see an extraordinary jumble of paintings, a few of them worth examining.

Manierre Dawson,
journal entry,
November 2, 1910

A visit to the Steins held special significance for Americans. By 1910 the At Homes had come to symbolize the new age to the artist-expatriates who traveled to France to study. They came in sufficient numbers to prompt Edward Steichen to organize a group called the New Society of American Artists in Paris. As one of them put it, "Paris had become the Mecca for any ambitious artists in search of the new verb in art."[31] The Paris residents who became Saturday night regulars included Patrick Henry Bruce, Charles Demuth, Marsden Hartley, Alfred Maurer, Walter Pach, Morgan Russell, Edward Steichen, Maurice Sterne, and Max Weber. As they brought along other Americans, the network grew increasingly transatlantic, exposing an entire generation of American artists and collectors to modern art. Pach brought Joseph Stella; Maurer brought Arthur Dove and later William Glackens, who in turn escorted his patron, the irascible Dr. Barnes. Steichen brought the painter Katherine Dreier, Alfred Stieglitz, and the young collector Agnes Ernst. The young modernist Manierre Dawson arrived one Saturday evening in 1910 with a small painting under his arm and made the first sale of his career. Max Weber's introduction of the photographer Alvin Langdon Coburn in about 1909 resulted in a masterly portrait of Gertrude.

Gertrude Stein's biographer has described 27, rue de Fleurus as "a cultural halfway house between the European vanguard and the merest beginnings of the avant-garde in the United States."[32] And there, at the vortex of modernity, were two Americans.

Beginning in the fall of 1910 another circle of modernists began to meet each Sunday afternoon. In the middle-class Parisian suburb of Puteaux, behind the studios of František Kupka, Raymond Duchamp-Villon, and Jacques Villon, congregated a group of artists and aestheticians. More exclusively French than the Steins' circle, equally radical in their aesthetic experiments, the all-male Puteaux group met among the gladiolas and spreading shade trees of a scruffy garden. There they shot arrows, played chess, and invented games with toy horses. One of the participants recalled that the purpose of their afternoon play was "to gain elasticity and to moisten our deep thoughts with the sweat of our armpits and for the health of our bodies!"[33] This compound of frivolous play and abstract discussion prompted Walter Pach to remark, "No other place I have ever known can tell so much of the contrast between the outer tranquility of a life and its intensity within."[34]

The Puteaux afternoons offered an informal laboratory where new aesthetics, new philosophies, and new mathematics were combined. "Our interest in forming a group, so as to meet frequently and exchange ideas, suddenly began to seem an urgent necessity," recalled Albert Gleizes.[35] Familiar with earlier avant-garde movements from Impressionism through Fauvism, the Puteaux group admiringly invoked

Jacques Villon, Marcel Duchamp, and Raymond Duchamp-Villon at Puteaux, 1912

Cézanne, Cubism, and Futurism, salting their discussion with allusions to non-Euclidean geometry and the fourth dimension. They wanted to fix modern art within a historical context, and their discussions gave rise to Jean Metzinger and Albert Gleizes's 1912 book, *Du Cubisme* (Of Cubism), and Apollinaire's publication in 1913 of *Les Peintres cubistes* (The Cubist Painters).

The youngest member of the group, twenty-three-year-old Marcel Duchamp, balked at these attempts to define modern art. His laconic style of subversion was already developing: while enrolled in art classes at the Académie Julian he spent most of his time across the street shooting billiards in a café, and after observing the luscious colors of Impressionist painting he created a canvas that was mostly black and white. The most constant feature of his painting was his refusal to commit to a single style—he painted in, and then rejected, the manner of Pierre Bonnard, the Fauves, Cézanne—and he practiced what one Puteaux colleague called "a continuous challenge to common sense. . . ."[36] Gertrude Stein saw in Duchamp's cool blue eyes and striking profile the image of "a young Norman conqueror," while a fellow artist perceived him as "a public danger. . . ."[37] In Francis Picabia he found ideally subversive company.

"Anybody called Francis is elegant, unbalanced and intelligent"; Gertrude Stein's observation succinctly sketched Picabia's character.[38] Pampered, plump, and darkly handsome, Picabia was nine years older than Duchamp and already reputed to be a high liver. A smoker of opium, a driver of fast and expensive cars, an habitué of Left Bank cafés like the Dôme and the Rotonde, Picabia compulsively sampled the newest trends in art and life and was given to leaping up to contradict any dogma he heard. "Picabia and I already opposed the very idea of a valid theory," Duchamp recalled, "well aware of how far one's gray matter is from one's lips."[39]

Drawn together by their distrust of doctrines, Duchamp and Picabia digested avant-garde styles, trying out everything from Cézanne to Cubism, then moved on. "They emulated each other in their extraordinary adherence to paradoxical, destructive principles," Picabia's wife, Gabrielle Buffet-Picabia, recalled.[40] Their bond was both immediate and enduring, and it would persist throughout their lives. Years later, when asked who was his best friend, Duchamp unhesitatingly replied, "Picabia, of course. As a co-pilot you might say."[41]

By January 1912 Duchamp had completed a canvas for the following month's Salon des Indépendants. He called it *Nude Descending a Staircase,* a title that distressed some of his Puteaux confreres. A nude, they said, should recline. "Even their little revolutionary temple couldn't understand that a nude could be *descending* the stairs," Duchamp recalled.[42] At Gleizes's request he withdrew the painting; it would arouse much greater controversy the following year at the Armory Show in

New York. The frustrating episode prompted Duchamp to consider giving up painting, but it also proved instructive to the young artist. "It helped liberate me completely from the past, in the personal sense of the word," Duchamp observed. "I said, 'All right, since it's like that, there's no question of joining a group—I'm going to count on no one but myself, alone.'"[43] Duchamp pursued a solitary course that skirted the popular aesthetic paths, both old and modern. In his epochal book, *Les Peintres cubistes,* Apollinaire predicted, "Perhaps it will be the task of an artist as detached from aesthetic preoccupations, and as intent on the energetic as Marcel Duchamp, to reconcile art and the people."[44]

By 1913 life at 27, rue de Fleurus had undergone a metamorphosis; its outlines were familiar, its essence completely transformed. No longer the lion of his own Saturday Evenings, Leo had retreated to his study. "He was tired of the mob," said Walter Pach. "He wanted to talk stomach ache and politics and esthetics—but mostly stomach ache."[45] Modern art's premier connoisseur had grown bored with it, the most revolutionary stage of his collecting having lasted only about three years (1904–7). He dismissed Matisse as lacking in "rhythm" about the same time his prices started to climb in 1909, outstripping the buying power of the modest Stein fortune. The painter now frequented the Saturday Evenings of Michael and Sarah Stein, whose patronage of Matisse continued unabated.[46] Picasso came in for Leo's sourest condemnation. Cubism was the ostensible culprit, but his comments are entangled with Leo's changing perception of Gertrude and her Picasso-influenced writing. "Both [Picasso] and Gertrude are using their intellects, which they ain't got, to do what would need the finest critical tact, which they ain't got, neither, and they are . . . turning out the most Godalmighty rubbish that is to be found."[47] Having refused to accept Cubism as the next step in the evolution of modern art, Leo declared that he was regarded as "no longer a prophet in Israel . . . at best only a Jeremiah."[48]

As Leo was decamping from the modern movement, Gertrude was entering a richly experimental period in her development as a writer. She moved from the naturalistic narrative of *Q.E.D.* and *Three Lives* to the abstraction of "Portrait of Mabel Dodge at the Villa Curonia" (1912) and *Tender Buttons* (1914). Her nocturnal sessions had become a ritual, and her loosely looped words, which looked as if they had simply floated onto the page, filled notebooks that were rapidly piling up. She received no support from her brother, and on at least one occasion his ridicule sent her to bed in tears.

Gertrude's persistence owed a great deal to a small encouraging audience. The journalist Hutchins Hapgood, for example, was an advocate of *Three Lives* as early as 1906 and tried to interest a publisher in it. Mabel Dodge responded to Stein's epic *The Making of Americans*

When Jesus said, "Verily, verily," the second verily added much to the expression. But if he said, "Verily, verily, verily, verily, verily, verily, verily, verily," it wouldn't have been so good.

Leo Stein to
Hutchins Hapgood

with the grand exclamation, "I am perfectly convinced, it is the fore-runner of a whole epoch of new form and expression. . . . I feel it will alter reality as we know it."[49]

Stein was sustained by painters, too. She worked sitting beneath a large painting by Cézanne and saw an affinity between the structure of his brush strokes and the accumulation of her simple repetitive sentences. She increasingly allied herself with Picasso, convinced that they were attempting the same thing in their respective media. Buoyed by her coterie, she finally achieved independence from her dominant brother—as she put it at the time, "she was knowing that sound was coming out of her and she was thinking about being a very different one in being one than he was in being one."[50] She felt vindicated when Alfred Stieglitz published her abstract "word portraits" of Matisse and Picasso in his journal, *Camera Work,* in 1912; this was her first publication in an American magazine.

Having found a small audience, Gertrude was now ready for a larger one, both in Paris and in her native America. "I always wanted to be historical, from almost a baby on, I felt that way about it," Gertrude wrote at the end of her life.[51] In the summer of 1913 she met the two men who would campaign for her recognition in America: Henry McBride and Carl Van Vechten. Despite the efforts of these devoted lieutenants, however, *gloire* would be a long time coming to her.

Henry McBride had visited Paris several times and already knew such notables as Roger Fry and Henri Matisse. That summer of 1913 he was there for the first time as an art critic. He now had his own audience—the readers of the *New York Sun*—to whom he introduced the modern art he loved. When he met Gertrude, he was immediately attracted by her sense of humor, and later that year he wrote her a letter describing one bond between them: "In this country of rural peda-

Think of the Bible and Homer think of Shake-speare and think of me.

Gertrude Stein

Alvin Langdon Coburn (1882–1966). *Gertrude Stein,* 1913. Gelatin silver print, 5⅞ × 4¼ in. (15.1 × 10.8 cm). International Museum of Photography at George Eastman House, Rochester, New York

gogues and long faced parsons, to laugh at all is to be thought frivolous. I laugh a great deal (so do you)."[52] Stein trusted him sufficiently to let him read her abstract plays, and McBride tried to negotiate their production at the 1915 Panama-Pacific International Exposition in San Francisco. His unsuccessful attempt was only one of many efforts he would make to introduce Stein to the American public in the coming years. When McBride attended his first Saturday Evening, he sensed that the salon's pioneering period was over. Not for any lack of guests—as he wrote, "the crowd of pilgrims became too dense for even Gertrude's energy to cope with." But modern art could no longer incite heated disagreements and the Evenings were no longer the scene of altercations. "How could they be?" McBride asked. "Everybody had been vindicated."[53]

Carl van Vechten, 1917

Gertrude wrote that she first saw Carl Van Vechten at the second performance of *Le Sacre du printemps* and was impressed by the tiny pleats puckering his orange evening shirt. So taken was she that when she returned home to write that evening, she bypassed the revolutionary impact of Diaghilev, Nijinsky, and Stravinsky in favor of that shirt: "A touching white shining sash and a touching white green undercoat and a touching white colored orange and a touching piece of elastic suddenly."[54]

A stylish entrance against a modern backdrop suited Carl Van Vechten well.[55] When a magazine columnist in 1915 looked back on the advent of male fashion, she simply wrote, "Then Carlo came."[56] The thirty-two-year-old was devoted to fashion—not only in dress but in dance, in music, and in people. As his summary of Paris suggested, Van Vechten sought the cutting edge of advancing culture: "To be truly Parisian, one must be of the minute," he wrote in 1908. "The Boulevardiers demand a new catch word, a new idea, every day."[57] Van Vechten was a modern propagandist, but in place of the theorizing favored by Leo Stein, he assumed the hybrid role of critic, gossip columnist, and press agent. His enthusiasms reveal his evolved taste: opera diva Mary Garden; dancers Ruth St. Denis, Isadora Duncan, Vaslav Nijinsky, and Anna Pavlova; composer Richard Strauss. Since the luminaries he praised on the pages of the *New York Times* (where he worked from 1906 to 1913) often became his friends, he traveled in many circles; like Henri-Pierre Roché, he was a "general introducer." The dynamics between Van Vechten and Gertrude Stein could not have been more complementary: her voracious appetite for appreciation and her determined will to power were matched by his keen sense of publicity and his penchant for star making. Stein became his next passionate enthusiasm, one that uncharacteristically endured the whims of fashion and continued long after her death as he shepherded her scrawled notebook to publication. Near the end of her life Gertrude recalled, "Carl was one of the earliest ones that made me certain."[58]

Elie Nadelman (1882–1946).
Female Figure (Gertrude Stein), c. 1907. Bronze, height: 29½ in. (74.9 cm). Private collection.

By 1913 Gertrude had established a routine that reflected her philosophy, "If you are way ahead with your head you naturally are old fashioned and regular in your daily life."[59] The mainstay of her domestic life was her devoted companion and lover, Alice Babette Toklas, who moved into 27, rue de Fleurus in August 1910. Toklas's darkly exotic appearance led many to take her for a gypsy, and her self-effacing demeanor prompted some to dismiss her as a secretary-companion; both perceptions were incorrect. Although Toklas did indeed gather Stein's notebooks each morning, dutifully transcribing the scrawl on her new Smith-Premier typewriter, and did act as housekeeper and cook, the relationship provided more than the calm domestic foundation necessary for Gertrude's writing. Stein and Toklas were a devoted and highly erotic couple, and Toklas's support for Stein's writing was unswerving. She told Stein that *The Making of Americans* was "more exciting than anything else had ever been. Even more exciting than Picasso's pictures promise to be."[60]

After Toklas moved into the rue de Fleurus, the uneasy equilibrium between brother and sister became permanently unbalanced. Leo's contempt for Gertrude's writing yielded adolescent parodies such as his rendition of the "Portrait of Mabel Dodge":

Mabel Dodge
Hodge Podge
What is up,
What is down,
What's a smile,
What's a frown,
What is passion,
What is pose.[61]

Brother and sister finally communicated only by irritated notes, the sort that remind the recipient to turn off the light in the front hall. By February 1913 Leo sulkily decided to leave the rue de Fleurus for Florence. The rupture was final. Gertrude would see Leo only once in the remaining three decades of his life—a brief and accidental encounter on a Paris street in 1931, which Gertrude tersely acknowledged in a short piece, "She Bowed to Her Brother." After Leo's departure all that remained of their relationship was the collection of paintings that climbed the atelier walls. The epistolary determination of custody was coolly amicable; their tastes had veered so sharply that there remained no bone left to pick. "I'm going to Florence a simple-minded person of the 'Old School' without a single Picasso, hardly any Matisses, only 2 Cézanne paintings and some acquarelles, and 16 Renoirs," Leo reported to a friend. "Rather an amusing baggage for a leader in the great modern fight. But *que voulez vous.* The fight is already won and lost."[62]

LONDON

zra Pound arrived at London's Victoria Station on August 14, 1908, with no letters of introduction and only three pounds in his pocket. Prominent among the twenty-two-year-old's sparse belongings were copies of his slim, self-published volume of poems, *A Lume Spento* (With Tapers Quenched). The poems were undistinguished juvenilia, but the book's existence suggests that Pound had already developed his own acute sense of priorities: a volume of his poems was more essential than cash for making an entrance into the literary capital of the world. He reported to his father: "I've got a fool idea that I'm going to make good in this bloomin' village," and soon expressed his youthful optimism in verse: "'Tis the white stag, Fame, we're a-hunting / Bid the world's hounds come to horn!" [1]

Although the report that Pound was "born in a blizzard [and] his first meal consisted of kerosene" [2] was Ford Madox Ford's fabrication, Pound's actual circumstances were only slightly less primitive. He was born in Hailey, Idaho, a town that boasted only one street, and he was reared in the rural outskirts of Philadelphia. Pound's earliest verse was published in his elementary-school magazine, and during early adolescence he decided that poetry was his calling. More recently he had taught Romantic languages in the cultural backwater of Crawfordsville, Indiana. His position at Wabash College was short-lived—Pound was fired for alleged sexual impropriety—but the dismissal and severance pay freed him to travel. [3] After briefly returning to Philadelphia to bid his friend William Carlos Williams farewell and to urge his paramour, Hilda Doolittle, to follow him abroad, Pound set out on the RMS *Slavonia* for the alluring world on the other side of the Atlantic Ocean.

Just as young American painters traveled to Paris, so many writers of Pound's generation—Conrad Aiken, Van Wyck Brooks, Hilda Doolittle, T. S. Eliot, John Gould Fletcher, Robert Frost, Elinor Wylie—made the pilgrimage to London. They hoped to be befriended by other young writers, published by small presses, and discussed by intellectuals—experiences that added up to, in Van Wyck Brooks's words, "an intensity of literary living." [4] London in 1908, however, offered less vitality

Ezra Pound, 1908

The common verse of Britain from 1890 was a horrible agglomerate compost, not minted, most of it not even baked, all legato, a doughty mess of third-hand Keats, Wordsworth, heaven knows what, fourth-hand Elizabethan sonority blunted, half-melted, lumpy.

Ezra Pound

than Paris offered its painters, for it was adrift between two literary generations. The reigning figures (Arnold Bennett, Joseph Conrad, Thomas Hardy, Henry James, William Butler Yeats) represented an earlier period, while the modern generation (Pound, H. G. Wells, D. H. Lawrence, Wyndham Lewis) had not yet begun to publish. Recalling the literary landscape, Pound called it an "arthritic milieu," filled with "gargoyles" and fading éminences grises.[5]

Nonetheless, Pound was also accurate in reporting back to William Carlos Williams that "London, deah old Lundon [*sic*], is the place for poesy."[6] Despite the dearth of avant-garde experimentation, London had a stimulating continuity of literary tradition and established resources for poets that New York lacked. "There was *more* going on and what went on went on *sooner* than in New York," Pound recalled.[7] In the borough of Kensington, poets had their own community, which Ford Madox Ford called "a high class Greenwich Village."[8] In Elkin Mathews's bookshop on Vigo Street, near Piccadilly Circus, poets congregated for readings and to browse through new volumes of verse. In the British aristocratic tradition, London also offered select gatherings for poets that resembled gentlemen's clubs (the Poets' Club, the Square Club) or drawing-room salons and literary soirées (William Butler Yeats's Monday Evenings, Dorothy Shakespear's teas). In the more democratic tradition of pubs and coffee houses, poets also gathered in Kensington bun shops and at gatherings hosted by T. E. Hulme at the Tour Eiffel restaurant. London boasted, as well, several organs for disseminating advanced writing, including Ford Madox Ford's *English Review* and the ailing *New Age,* which A. R. Orage took over in 1907 and transformed into a vehicle for Fabianism and literature.

Pound's obsession with London was entirely understandable, for it was only within the crucible of this literary metropolis that the young American could remake himself as a modern poet and an impresario of poetry. In August 1909 he moved to Kensington, where he lived in a tiny second-floor flat at 10 Church Walk. Before venturing into London's literary society, he devised an elaborate persona. During his lengthy morning toilet he would sculpt his auburn hair into a high pompadour and meticulously trim his beard. He would don green baize pants, shirts with loose velvet collars and lapis lazuli buttons, and spats. Having fastened a lone turquoise earring to his earlobe and balanced a rimless pince-nez on his nose, he would fetch his ebony cane and descend to the streets of Kensington with, as Iris Barry recalled, a "perpetual air of majestic flowing and billowing."[9] His conversation was studded with foreign phrases and snippets of medieval Provençal uttered in an accent that was unmistakably Philadelphian. At the dinner table Pound sometimes chewed on the floral decorations and launched into recitations that, in Yeats's words, sounded "like something on a very bad phonograph." [10] Pound had scrupulously modeled himself on his hero, James McNeill Whistler, but the London literary community dismissed him as a gaudy imitation of a bit player in *La Bohème*. This dandyish aspect did attract attention at least, and nine months after his arrival *Punch* crowned Pound "the new Montana (U.S.A.) poet, Ezekiel Ton, who is the most remarkable thing in poetry since Robert Browning." [11] Pound later described the formula that resulted in his precipitate rise: "I made my life in London by going to see Ford in the afternoons and Yeats in the evenings." [12]

William Butler Yeats entered Pound's life in stages. At first he was simply "a dim sort of figure with associations set in the past," whom Pound regarded as the preeminent poet of the English language. Yeats also provided the chief link to a literary avant-garde, embodied in the Rhymers Club, established in 1891. Lured to London because he wanted "to sit at Yeats's feet and learn what he knew," [13] the young poet mailed Yeats a copy of *A Lume Spento* as a letter of introduction. Yeats, however, was away in Ireland. In his absence Pound moved a step closer to him by taking tea at the home of Yeats's former mistress, Olivia Shakespear, in January 1909.[14] He excitedly reported to a friend that he had sat on the same hearth rug from which Yeats had reigned and recited one of Yeats's poems in a voice quavering with emotion. Both Olivia Shakespear and her twenty-two-year-old daughter, Dorothy, were enchanted by the performance. Pound subsequently paid court to Mrs. Shakespear (who was twenty-one years older than he), calling her "undoubtedly the most charming woman in London," while her daughter developed a schoolgirlish crush on Pound.[15]

Listen to it—Ezra! Ezra! And a third time Ezra! He has a wonderful, beautiful face, a high forehead, prominent over the eyes; a long delicate nose, with little red nostrils; a strange mouth, never still, & quite elusive; a square chin, slightly cleft in the middle—the whole face pale; the eyes gray-blue; the hair golden-brown, and curling in soft wavy crinkles. Large hands, with long, well-shaped fingers, and beautiful nails.

Dorothy Shakespear, journal entry, February 1909

After Yeats returned to London in May 1909, Mrs. Shakespear escorted Pound to one of his Monday Evenings. They mounted the creaking stairs at the Woburn Buildings and entered a large room lit by candles in tall green candlesticks. Pound was surrounded by Blake engravings, Aubrey Beardsley drawings, and Pre-Raphaelite paintings, bookcases filled with fine editions by William Morris, and a chest containing Yeats's manuscripts and tarot cards. The guests, seated in high-backed chairs, included a mixture of young poets and members of the Abbey Theatre. Pound had finally reached the hub of the literary community and, looking across the dim room, he beheld the tall cloaked figure of the Master.

At the age of forty-four Yeats was experiencing the pains and disappointments of middle age. His literary powers were apparently waning, and he was plagued by diminishing sight, indigestion, and headaches. His grand affair with Maud Gonne was over, and his close friend John Synge had died just a few months earlier. Yeats wrote that his days were "full of all sorts of nothings."[16] A colleague compared him to an "old umbrella forgotten at a picnic-party," but Pound's nickname, "the Eagle," suggests a more heroic figure.[17]

At first merely one of Yeats's peripheral acolytes, Pound gradually advanced into the inner circle. His most obvious value to Yeats was practical; he ran errands, wrote letters, taught him fencing, and read to him in the failing evening light. In such close proximity Pound found his idol was "a bit wooly at the edges," and their approaches to poetry often diverged.[18] (Pound's pencil was always sharp, and by 1913 he went so far as to "correct" Yeats's poetry.) Gradually the disciple became the self-designated master at Yeats's Monday Evenings. As one regular guest recalled, "He dominated the room, distributed Yeats's cigarettes and Chianti, and laid down the law about poetry."[19] That law owed less to Yeats, however, than it did to two of London's other prominent literary figures: Ford Madox Ford and T. E. Hulme.

In the spring of 1909 the popular novelist May Sinclair introduced "the greatest poet to the greatest editor in the world," by which she meant Pound and Ford Madox Ford.[20] The meeting took place in Ford's maisonette flat, which also served as the offices of the *English Review*. Thirty-five-year-old Ford had begun the magazine shortly after Pound's arrival in London, and during his eighteen months as editor Ford published not only the most distinguished writers of an older generation (Arnold Bennett, Joseph Conrad, Henry James, Yeats), but he also introduced the writers he dubbed "les jeunes" (Pound, D. H. Lawrence, Wyndham Lewis).[21] Ford's new mistress, Violet Hunt, described the magazine as "a Forlorn Hope led for the supremacy of the Kingdom of Literature gone derelict."[22] The *English Review* became a hinge between the generations, and in the process it strengthened Ford's tenuous position within London's literary community.

Ford's output was prodigious: by the time he began the *English Review* he had published over twenty books in genres ranging from historical novels and fairy tales to criticism and poetry; he was also credited as a master of the comic bon mot. Ford's personal fictions included claims to an aristocratic family tree and exaggerations of his own accomplishments. Whatever his faults, Ford was essential to the literary community. He had a brilliant understanding of the craft of

Alvin Langdon Coburn (1882–1966). *W. B. Yeats,* Dublin, January 24, 1908. Photogravure, 8 × 6¼ in. (20.3 × 15.8 cm). International Museum of Photography at George Eastman House, Rochester, New York

writing, he listened warmly, judged with Olympian assurance, and valued writers over all other beings. He became the mentor to an emerging generation of writers. Ford's literary goals were relatively simple: to purge literature of verbal excess and archaic rhetoric and to use colloquial language to "present modern English life as it is lived." [23] Over dinners and on endless walks with Pound through the streets of Kensington, Ford hammered away at the necessity of writing that was impressionistic and granite hard; Pound's willing acceptance of this advice laid the groundwork not only for his own poetry but also for the movement he later named Imagisme. Pound's debut in the *English Review* in June 1909 was merely one instance of Ford's embracing new writers excluded from established literary journals. [24] He maintained an open-door policy based on personal contact between writers and the editor. (For example, when Wyndham Lewis got no answer on ringing Ford's bell, he marched in, found the editor soaking in a bathtub, announced that he was a man of genius, and read a complete essay, which promptly appeared in the *English Review*.) Ford's own description of his position as an editor cannot be bettered: "A sort of half-way house between nonpublishable youth and real money—a sort of green baize swing door that everyone kicks both on entering and leaving." [25]

Pound entered Ford's life at the crucial point when Ford had not only started the *English Review* but had also begun a serious affair with the novelist Violet Hunt. [26] Ford was already married, and many of their old friends would not countenance the illicit relationship. Since Ford enjoyed entertaining and Hunt was a vivacious, "smart" hostess, the duo assembled a new and younger circle. The old-guard literary crowd was replaced by a motley group that included Pound, Wyndham Lewis, Walter de la Mare, Rebecca West (still in her teens), the sculptor Jacob Epstein, the artist C.R.W. Nevinson—and later Richard Aldington, Hilda Doolittle, and the artist Henri Gaudier-Brzeska. They congregated at South Lodge, Hunt's villa in South Camden—a modest semidetached residence with a patch of garden and a large drawing room. At first, late Victorian etiquette was observed; guests arrived in "London clothes"—top hats, gloves, and canes—and sat down to tea. Ford initiated verse games, at which he was a master—contests in the spontaneous composition of bouts-rimés and sonnets beginning "Ah God." Quail and champagne were served against a background of Pre-Raphaelite memorabilia.

When Ezra Pound appeared, the tenor of South Lodge changed "from a rather stuffy and conventional Campden [*sic*] Hill villa into a stamping ground for *les jeunes*." [27] Wyndham Lewis modernized the villa by painting an explosive red abstraction in its study, and Pound modernized the guest list. He was indispensable to these gatherings—even the parrot at South Lodge greeted his entrance by screaming "Ezra! Ezra!"—and he functioned as a social director whose peculiarly

He ran the English Review *like an infant in charge of a motor car.*

Ezra Pound on
Ford Madox Ford

American exuberance electrified these once genteel afternoons. Instead of "London clothes," he sported a bright bohemian uniform, and he moved the action from the drawing room to the tennis courts across the road. The most vivid image of Pound during this era is on these courts, exchanging violent volleys with Ford. He would leap excitedly, with "the flaps of his polychrome shirt flying out like the petals of some flower." [28] A game with Pound, Ford recalled, was "like playing against an inebriated kangaroo that has been rendered unduly vigorous by injection of some gland or other." [29] This vignette captures two aspects of Pound's character. On the surface he seemed a court jester, "playing like a mischievous urchin," as one friend recalled, "letting off his gaminesque little jokes." [30] But this gamin also commandeered the courts, and he was loath to give them up to other players. As Ford later recalled with only slight exaggeration, Pound had soon "taken charge of me, the review, and finally of London." [31]

Just as Yeats symbolized the previous generation and Ford was the door that swung open to both the past and the future, T. E. Hulme represented the coming generation. An odd figure in London's poetry circles, he was a philosopher who did not consider himself a poet. He boasted about his stint as a lumberjack in Canada, his dismissal from Cambridge for misbehavior, and his latest heterosexual exploit in the Piccadilly tube station. His close friend Jacob Epstein summed him up as "capable of kicking a theory as well as a man downstairs when the occasion demanded." [32] Hulme had nevertheless been invited to join Sir Edmund Gosse's conservative Poets' Club, the reigning circle of established English poets. He accepted and attended their stuffy gatherings until—inspired by an article by F. S. Flint that concluded "The Poets' Club is Death"—Hulme seceded and formed a splinter group that would pursue the more scabrous tradition of Paul Verlaine.[33]

Beginning March 25, 1909, the group met on Thursday nights at the Tour Eiffel restaurant in Soho. Those present have been mostly forgotten—Hulme, Joseph Campbell, Florence Farr, F. S. Flint, Edward Storer, F. W. Tancred—but the stylistic foundations for modern poetry were laid during those evenings among the Tour Eiffel's small tables and pink-shaded lamps. Predicting "a period of dry, hard, classical verse," Hulme wrote, "The great aim is accurate, precise, and definite description." [34] Hulme's group proposed to replace existing forms of poetry with pure vers libre and Japanese tanka and haiku.

At their third meeting Ezra Pound joined the group and declaimed his poem "Sestina: Altaforte" with such force that the management promptly erected a folding screen around him to shield the restaurant's other customers. Pound contributed little to the poetry discussions, which were dominated by the coruscating analytical intelligence of Hulme, and two years later he described the Thursday evenings as "dull enough at the time, but rather pleasant to look back upon." This recollection is disingenuous.[35] From these gatherings Pound "took very much," observed F. S. Flint. "He took away the whole doctrine of what he later called Imagisme."[36]

Pound took pleasure in guiding American visitors through London. His oldest friend, twenty-six-year-old William Carlos Williams, arrived in March 1910. "Ez" and "Bill" had met at the University of Pennsylvania in the fall of 1902 while Williams was studying medicine and Pound was pursuing literature. Their bond was originally formed from mutual loneliness—Williams immediately recognized Pound as a fellow outsider—but they soon shared an interest in poetry as well. Williams provided Pound's first sympathetic audience, and Pound became Williams's first mentor, encouraging his decision to embrace both medicine and poetry. "Before meeting Pound is like B.C. and A.D.," Williams later reflected. "He was the livest, most intelligent and unexplainable thing I'd ever seen."[37] The roles defined during those undergraduate days would endure long after they entered adulthood and Williams had grown impatient with Pound's pronouncements.

William Carlos Williams

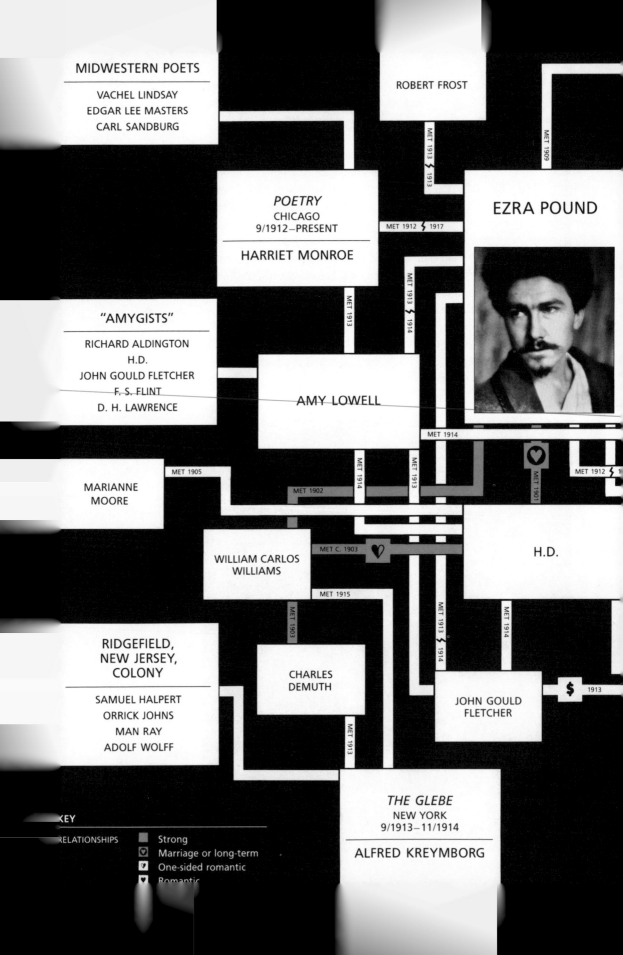

MIDWESTERN POETS

VACHEL LINDSAY
EDGAR LEE MASTERS
CARL SANDBURG

ROBERT FROST

MET 1913 ∮ 1913

MET 1909

POETRY
CHICAGO
9/1912–PRESENT

HARRIET MONROE

MET 1912 ∮ 1917

EZRA POUND

MET 1913 ∮ 1914

MET 1913

"AMYGISTS"

RICHARD ALDINGTON
H.D.
JOHN GOULD FLETCHER
F. S. FLINT
D. H. LAWRENCE

AMY LOWELL

MET 1914

MARIANNE
MOORE

MET 1905

MET 1914

MET 1913

MET 1901

MET 1912 ∮

MET 1902

WILLIAM CARLOS
WILLIAMS

MET C. 1903 ♥

H.D.

MET 1915

RIDGEFIELD,
NEW JERSEY,
COLONY

SAMUEL HALPERT
ORRICK JOHNS
MAN RAY
ADOLF WOLFF

MET 1903

CHARLES
DEMUTH

MET 1913 ∮ 1914

MET 1914

JOHN GOULD
FLETCHER

$ 1913

MET 1913

THE GLEBE
NEW YORK
9/1913–11/1914

ALFRED KREYMBORG

KEY

RELATIONSHIPS
■ Strong
♡ Marriage or long-term
♥ One-sided romantic
♥ Romantic

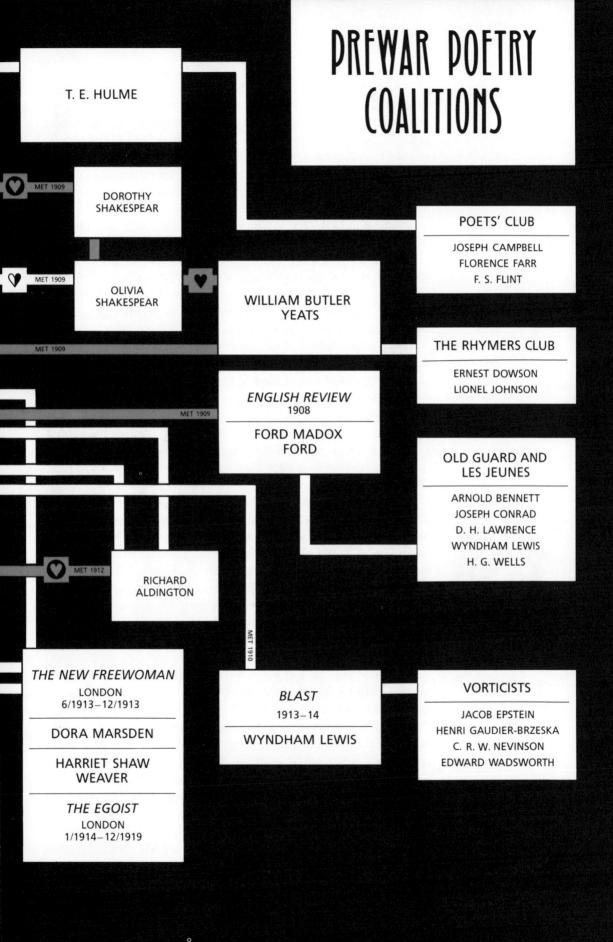

PREWAR POETRY COALITIONS

T. E. HULME

MET 1909

DOROTHY SHAKESPEAR

MET 1909

OLIVIA SHAKESPEAR

WILLIAM BUTLER YEATS

MET 1909

POETS' CLUB
JOSEPH CAMPBELL
FLORENCE FARR
F. S. FLINT

THE RHYMERS CLUB
ERNEST DOWSON
LIONEL JOHNSON

ENGLISH REVIEW
1908

FORD MADOX FORD

MET 1909

OLD GUARD AND LES JEUNES
ARNOLD BENNETT
JOSEPH CONRAD
D. H. LAWRENCE
WYNDHAM LEWIS
H. G. WELLS

MET 1912

RICHARD ALDINGTON

MET 1910

THE NEW FREEWOMAN
LONDON
6/1913–12/1913

DORA MARSDEN

HARRIET SHAW WEAVER

THE EGOIST
LONDON
1/1914–12/1919

BLAST
1913–14

WYNDHAM LEWIS

VORTICISTS
JACOB EPSTEIN
HENRI GAUDIER-BRZESKA
C. R. W. NEVINSON
EDWARD WADSWORTH

While Williams practiced pediatric medicine in Rutherford, New Jersey, Pound kept him in touch with the cosmopolitan tastes of London. He prescribed doses of Yeats, Algernon Swinburne, and Robert Browning and offered such inspirational advice as "Remember a man's real work is *what he is going to do,* not what is behind him. *Avanti e coraggio!*" [38] When Williams arrived in London, Pound proudly escorted him through its literary landscape and in the process consolidated his role as "little Bill's" mentor.[39]

"Bill has arrived," Pound wrote to his mother, "and I am attempting to broaden his mind." [40] Williams stayed in Pound's tiny flat at 10 Church Walk for one intense week so packed with literary introductions and cultural excursions that Williams had scarcely a moment to himself. His schedule included trips to the National Gallery and the British Museum, a reading of Ibsen's *Ghosts,* and dinner with the Shakespears. The most memorable event was one of Yeats's Monday Evenings, which presented a scene unlike anything the New Jersey pediatrician had ever witnessed. In the candlelit room Yeats recited Ernest Dowson's "Cynara" to a hushed audience of Abbey Theatre members. Although Williams appreciated Yeats's voice, he quickly recognized "it was not my dish." [41] In fact, Pound's cultural tour convinced Williams that he had no place in this metropolis of exiles. The "intense literary atmosphere," he wrote, "though it was thrilling every minute of it, was fatiguing in the extreme. I don't know how Ezra stood it, it would have killed me in a month." [42]

One warm Saturday morning a year or so later, in July 1911, Williams stood at New York's Twenty-third Street ferry terminal to see his friend Hilda Doolittle off to London. Williams and Doolittle were two points of an old romantic triangle; the third was Pound, who had met Doolittle at a Halloween party ten years earlier. Tall and lithe, fifteen-year-old Hilda was then just a tomboyish schoolgirl, but a few years later, in 1905, Pound became attracted to her unvarnished beauty. His courtship had elements of both pedagogy and unabashed romanticism. He called her "Dryad" and bestowed kisses in a treehouse. He wrote romantic poems that rhapsodized her bond to nature, then typed them on vellum and sewed the leaves together to create his first volume, *Hilda's Book.* [43] At other times he dictated a rigorous syllabus of Greek and Latin poets, Ibsen, Maurice Maeterlinck, William Morris, and the Rossettis. (Even on their picnics Pound continued his tutoring by introducing Doolittle to an exotic comestible called brie cheese.) Pound's pedagogical attention came at an especially welcome moment, for Doolittle had recently failed her freshman English class at Bryn Mawr and doubted her academic competence. Though Pound was drawn to her "tree-born spirit of the wood," he was determined to fashion Doolittle into a cosmopolitan. She considered him "immensely sophisticated, immensely superior," and quickly fell under the spell of his rabid

Hilda Doolittle, high school graduation picture, 1904

self-confidence.[44] "He drags me out of the shadows," she wrote, and vowed that both her mind and her emotions belonged to Pound.[45] A half-century later she still romanticized their evenings in the tree-house: "We sway with the wind. There is no wind. We sway with the stars. They are not far away."[46]

Pound introduced Doolittle to Williams in 1905. Although Williams thought Pound's paeans to her physical beauty exaggerated and ceded to Pound the role of lover, he was attracted by her fresh spirit, her "bizarre beauty," and fascinated by a quality "which is found in wild animals at times, a breathless impatience."[47] Jealousy intensified when Hilda invited them both to visit her father's observatory and coyly wrote to Williams (whom she called "William Squared") that she would "so like to know *two* of the rising young poets of the age."[48]

This competitive relationship climaxed in a spontaneous mock duel fought with walking sticks in the vestibule of Pound's family home. Both men had belonged to the University of Pennsylvania fencing team, and Pound would practice this elegant combative sport for years to come. Williams, the superior swordsman, effectively parried Pound's lunging thrusts until Pound, losing control, swung the wooden stick with full force and struck Williams just below the eye. Williams promptly lay down his cane and declared the duel over. But he never forgot it: three decades later he was still fulminating that he "could have shoved the stick through [Pound's] mouth and out his ass hole if it had been important enough to do so."[49]

Just before embarking for Europe in 1908, Pound proposed to Doolittle. His mother offered a sapphire ring on her son's behalf, and Hilda confided to Williams that she was prepared to spend the rest of her life with Pound. When he announced the proposal to her father, Professor Doolittle stared at him and gasped, "Why, you're nothing but a nomad!"[50] The engagement quickly ended when Hilda discovered that Pound had also proposed to another woman, Mary Moore of Trenton, New Jersey. His largess with engagement rings was characteristic, for he found it as hard to commit himself to a single woman as to a single style of poetry. "The engagement, such as it was," Doolittle wrote, "was shattered like a Venetian glass goblet, flung on the floor."[51] She suffered a physical and emotional breakdown, withdrew from Bryn Mawr, and found solace in a romance with a beautiful female poet named Frances Gregg.

When Doolittle departed for London in the summer of 1911 she considered herself a resounding failure—a liability to her family, an academic dropout with no prospects for marriage. As she later wrote, "She had burned her candle of rebellion at both ends, and she was left unequipped for the simplest dealing with the world."[52] She told her family that she would travel for four months to complete her education, but Williams knew that she hoped to renew her engagement to Pound. To

Hilda Doolittle, age 19, 1905

further complicate her relationships, she traveled with Frances Gregg, who was infatuated with both Doolittle and Pound.

When Doolittle arrived in London, Pound went through elaborate paces to introduce her to London and its "celebrities and lesser oddities."[53] Calling himself her "nearest male relative," he escorted her to afternoons at Hunt's South Lodge and Monday Evenings at Yeats's, introduced her to Elkin Mathews's bookshop and the drawing rooms of literary hostesses. It was not her writing that Pound was presenting to London—she had just begun to write poetry at the end of 1911 and had yet to find her own voice—but Doolittle herself. "You are a poem," Pound said, "though your poem's naught."[54] He sponsored her in London society as a figure of the new Hellenism, for everything Greek was fashionable in the London of 1911. One could see it in the sandals that replaced high-button boots, in the loose cut of the new dresses by Mariano Fortuny and Paul Poiret, in the preference for lean, willowy bodies and loosely knotted hair adorned with a band across the forehead. For the first time in her life Hilda Doolittle was in vogue. Her height (nearly five foot eleven) was considered dramatic rather than gawky, and her features were admired as exemplifying the chiseled angularity of classical statuary. "You're odd here, you're a great success," Pound told her.[55]

Aided by novelist May Sinclair's loan of her apartment, the romance between Pound and Doolittle resumed, and again Pound's kisses were followed by a ring, this time a pearl. But this was merely one alliance among many; the romantic relationships within Pound's crowd were extremely complicated. Pound was at its center, yet he seems to have been minimally motivated by sex itself. His friends described him as a sexual naïf, and Williams observed, "If he ever got under a gal's skirt it must have been mainly with his imagination."[56] His love affairs instead amplified his drive for social power.

Within this crowd Pound chiefly pursued Dorothy Shakespear—spurred in part by her connection to Yeats. Partly out of jealousy, her mother, Olivia, made repeated attempts to end the romance—banning the poet from the Shakespears' home, derogating her daughter as a self-absorbed woman unworthy of Pound's attention, and finally imploring Pound, "You *ought* to go away—Englishmen don't understand yr [sic] American ways. . . ."[57] But by 1912 Dorothy Shakespear was wearing Pound's ring on a thin chain around her neck.

During the first months of that year the web of romances was further tangled by the arrival from Portsmouth of the nineteen-year-old poet Richard Aldington. Dashingly handsome, dressed with theatrical panache, he shared an interest in classicism with both Pound and Doolittle. After Pound introduced him to Doolittle, the two began to spend days together in the British Museum, reading and looking at the classical Greek friezes. Doolittle's attraction to Aldington (six years her

Alvin Langdon Coburn
(1882–1966). *Ezra Pound*,
1913. Gelatin silver print,
8⅜ × 6⅜ in. (21.3 ×
16.2 cm). International
Museum of Photography at
George Eastman House,
Rochester, New York

junior) increased in direct proportion to her independence from Pound, and she enjoyed the opportunity to be worshiped rather than sculpted. Soon Aldington became the Other Man to Dorothy Shakespear's Other Woman. Pound condescendingly dubbed him "the Faun" but didn't display his characteristic territoriality—not even when Aldington moved into 6 Church Walk, two stories above Doolittle's flat and across a paved courtyard from Pound's. Soon after that, Church Walk became the scene of many poetry discussions.

In the early fall days of 1912 Imagisme was born with the nearly simultaneous occurrence of three events that marked the end of Pound's first stage in London. No longer a disciple, gofer, or jester, he became the founder and chief impresario of a movement.

America, my country, is almost a continent and hardly yet a nation, for no nation can be considered historically as such until it has achieved within itself a city to which all roads lead, and from which there goes out an authority.

Ezra Pound, "Patria Mia," September 1912

In October 1912 Pound's *Ripostes* was published by Elkin Mathews; although this collection of poems reflected the modernizing of Pound, the book has historical interest chiefly because of its curious appendix. Entitled "The Complete Works of T. E. Hulme" (which consisted of five poems totaling thirty-three lines), the piece was an awkward bow to Hulme as Pound prepared to appropriate Hulme's ideas. Pound's facetious preface, written in January 1912, contains the first reference to Imagisme. "As for the future, *Les Imagistes,* the descendants of the forgotten school of 1909, have that in their keeping." [58] Aldington later doubted that Pound had had any idea about what an Imagiste might be but simply liked the sound of the name and "kept it *in petto* for the right occasion. If there were no Imagists, obviously they would have to be invented." [59]

The scene of that invention was the tea-and-bun shop at the British Museum. Doolittle and Aldington met Pound there one September day in 1912, and she cautiously showed him a poem. Her typed manuscript, entitled "Hermes of the Ways," offered proof that she had learned from her mentor and was entering her literary maturity. Pound slashed at the manuscript with his pencil—"Cut this out, shorten this line"—removed his pince-nez in astonishment, and exclaimed, "But Dryad, this is poetry!" He then inscribed the bottom of the page: "H.D. Imagiste." [60] This bun-shop transaction was the consummation of their long and equivocal engagement; like the Pygmalion of George Bernard Shaw's eponymous play, written the next year, Pound had fashioned his identically named Miss Doolittle into a Galatea of modern poetry.

The preceding month Pound had received a letter bearing a Chicago postmark and an unfamiliar signature. Pleased to read that his poems had given Harriet Monroe "a very special pleasure" and plainly intrigued by her plan for a monthly magazine called *Poetry,* he promptly wrote to Monroe, "I *am* interested." He then delivered his first set of challenges and pronouncements:

> Are you for American poetry or for poetry? The latter is more important, but it is important that America should boost the former, provided it don't mean a blindness to the art. The glory of any nation is to produce art that can be exported without disgrace to its origin. . . .

> P.S. Any agonizing that tends to hurry what I believe in the end to be inevitable, our American Risorgimento, is dear to me. That awakening will make the Italian Renaissance look like a tempest in a teapot! The force we have, and the impulse, but the guiding sense, the discrimination in applying the force, we must wait and strive for.[61]

NEW YORK

In the early years of the twentieth century, America's tiny avant-garde congregated in three garret rooms at a no longer fashionable address. The man who presided there eschewed publicity, contending that "those who love and understand and have the art-nose will find their way."[1] Those who did arrive at 291 Fifth Avenue, between Thirtieth and Thirty-first streets, discovered in the building's foyer a small sign with the words PHOTO and SECESSION separated by a golden orb. They stepped into a rickety elevator that one regular remembered as being "about as large as a nickel-plated toast rack on end," a lanky West Indian hoisted them by rope and pulley to the top floor of the once-elegant brownstone, and they turned left into the little rooms beyond.[2] Something about the natural light that filtered into the Little Galleries of the Photo-Secession—commonly known as 291—seemed hallowed. Many visitors regarded this place as a modern chapel.

At the center of the largest room (fifteen feet square) stood an altarlike platform topped by a hammered-brass bowl filled with seasonal foliage. The painter Marsden Hartley recalled that a spirit seemed "to come up out of this bowl like a singular wraith."[3] Photographs and abstract paintings were carefully positioned on the grayed olive burlap

Alfred Stieglitz (1864–1946). *291 Interior*, 1914. Photogravure, 7 × 9⅜ in. (18 × 23.9 cm). International Museum of Photography at George Eastman House, Rochester, New York

walls, and though they often seemed inscrutable, they carried the weight of icons.

The nasal voice of Alfred Stieglitz broke the hushed silence of these little rooms every weekday from ten in the morning until seven in the evening. The middle-aged Stieglitz wrapped himself in a black cloak that protected him from the cold of the unheated rooms and made his slight frame—topped by an aureole of iron gray hair that sprouted even from his ears—seem more majestic.[4] He declaimed about the art on the wall, posed Socratic questions, offered parables and riddles. Visitors to the gallery could not see the works on exhibition without interacting with Stieglitz. His never-ending sermon was as essential to experiencing the art as the holy words of communion that precede the sip of wine.

The small congregation was united by a collective faith. "All that one group was able to do was done by the spirit of 291," recalled Hartley, "for that group was never but a single spirit and a single voice."[5] Though never defined by a manifesto, their shared convictions can be summarized: the creative process was emotional rather than rational, intuition was more important than technical mastery, profound subjectivity was akin to spirituality, art provided the means to regenerate society. During one difficult period, one of Stieglitz's colleagues reminded him that 291 was pursuing "a path full of thorns indeed but of thorns that wouldn't cover you with blood, but with glory" and that the group was "not working for today, nor for tomorrow, nor for ourselves, but for all times and for everybody."[6] Stieglitz called the goal "purity," and by that he could mean either the artist's liberation from representation or the gallery's autonomy from commerce.

The crusade was rooted in a turn-of-the-century circle of photographers—most prominently Alfred Stieglitz, Gertrude Käsebier, Edward Steichen, and Clarence H. White—who aspired to accord photography the same importance as a means for self-expression as painting. Their work, in a style known as Pictorialism, transcended photography's documentary function, incorporating such painterly conventions of the day as otherworldly subjects, impressionistic atmosphere, and diaphanous lighting. Since their profession was not recognized by the art establishment, these photographers were auspicious recruits for the avant-garde battle.[7] Stieglitz capitalized on these aspirations in 1902 when he formed the Photo-Secession, a term that called to mind recent "Secessions" by artists in Munich and Vienna.[8] The Photo-Secession was a loose professional organization that initially had no club rooms, no president, no secretary, no dues, no regular meetings. But within the year the group issued a statement of principles and created a hierarchy of membership ruled by a council that consisted of Stieglitz and eleven allies.[9] They circulated members' work to international exhibitions and ensured that Pictorialist photography was discussed.

More important to the formation of an American avant-garde was

Alvin Langdon Coburn (1882–1966). *Alfred Stieglitz,* 1912. Platinum print, diameter: 8¾ in. (22.2 cm). International Museum of Photography at George Eastman House, Rochester, New York

Cover of *Camera Work*, 1905.
Photograph by Edward
Steichen

the premiere in January 1903 of the magazine *Camera Work,* with
Stieglitz as its editor. He treated the magazine as a precious object, meticulously presenting the Photo-Secessionists' photographs as art rather
than as illustration. With its extraordinary quality of reproduction—
achieved by using such complex techniques as photogravure, four-
color halftone, collotype, and two-color letterpress—*Camera Work*
looked like no other magazine, and the ideals it espoused appeared in
no other photography or art magazines of the day.

The foundation of the Little Galleries of the Photo-Secession on
November 24, 1905, marked the next step in the group's development.
The gallery was funded mostly by Stieglitz, although Photo-Secession
photographers also contributed dues amounting to four hundred dollars a year for the gallery's upkeep. Until the Armory Show in 1913, the
primary American campaign for modernism was centered at 291, where
such Parisian masters as Paul Cézanne, Henri Matisse, Pablo Picasso,
Auguste Rodin, and Henri de Toulouse-Lautrec were introduced to New
York. It also presented the first American modernists—Arthur Dove,
Marsden Hartley, John Marin, Max Weber—and offered the pleasures
of "minor" arts such as the caricatures of Marius de Zayas, the visionary
theater designs of Edward Gordon Craig, and the photographs of
Baron Adolf de Meyer and Alvin Langdon Coburn.

The formation of this influential enterprise can be traced to the
spring of 1900, when Stieglitz met Edward Steichen.[10] The twenty-one-
year-old Steichen had just renounced the life of a commercial artist in
Milwaukee to travel to Paris as a photographer and painter. Stieglitz
admired the vigor he saw in Steichen's work and promptly bought three
photographs for the then-generous sum of five dollars apiece. It was
exactly the gesture of encouragement that Steichen most needed at a
crucial juncture in his life.

Expansive in his ambitions and practical in his skills, Steichen was
the perfect foil for the messianic Stieglitz. Steichen embodied the self-
confident energy of youth; Stieglitz expressed the doubts of middle
age. As a frequent resident in Paris from 1900 to 1914, Steichen was in
a better position than Stieglitz to view the emergence of modernism.
He met the people who gathered at the Steins', saw modern art in studios and galleries, and shared his knowledge on regular trips to New
York. Since he regarded himself as both a painter and a photographer,
Steichen was the Photo-Secessionist most committed to broadening
the battle to include painting and sculpture.

Trying to sort out their respective contributions to 291 makes clear
how interdependent the two were. Stieglitz was responsible for publishing and editing *Camera Work;* Steichen designed the cover and interior layout. Steichen initiated the idea of the Little Galleries of the
Photo-Secession, suggested its location in his former studio at 291 Fifth
Avenue, and designed the galleries in Vienna Secession style; Stieglitz

supplied the money to lease the rooms and became the full-time director. Stieglitz determined the exhibition schedule, but many of the exhibitions for which the gallery is best known (Marin, Matisse, Rodin, Henri Rousseau) were conceived and curated by Steichen.

Ever since meeting Rodin in 1901 Steichen had corresponded with Stieglitz about the possibility of showing drawings, paintings, and sculpture at 291—specifically, work by Rodin. Steichen was unpleasantly surprised when Stieglitz peremptorily announced that the gallery's first nonphotographic exhibition, in January 1907, would consist of symbolic landscapes painted by the now-forgotten Pamela Colman Smith. This event signaled 291's transition from a professional organization of photographers to a more comprehensive avant-garde enterprise. The art in photography and the antiphotographic in art now came together on the gallery walls: painting, sculpture, photography, caricatures, even children's drawings were shown. "The Secession Idea is neither the servant nor the product of a medium," Stieglitz explained to his congregation. "It is a spirit. Let us say it is the Spirit of the Lamp. . . ."[11] No longer devoted solely to the intramural skirmishes of the photography community, *Camera Work* published articles on Henri Bergson and the Unconscious, works by Oscar Wilde, Maurice Maeterlinck, Wassily Kandinsky, and Gertrude Stein. "The Photo-Secession can now be said to stand for those artists who seceded from the photographic attitude toward representation of form," Stieglitz wrote in *Camera Work*.[12]

But the photographers would have none of his convoluted argument. Furious at what they regarded as betrayal, many of the Photo-Secessionists boycotted the nonphotographic exhibitions.[13] *Camera Work*'s circulation plummeted: its 1,000 subscribers in 1903 had fallen to 304 by 1912.

The expanded crusade of 291 inspired other changes in the Stieglitz circle, notably the modernization of Stieglitz himself. His academic taste in painting had previously been embodied in the dark, heavily framed nineteenth-century canvases that hung Salon style in his home. He laughed loudly on first viewing a work by Cézanne, and when informed that a single watercolor cost a thousand francs, he crowed: "You mean a dozen. Why there's nothing there but empty paper with a few splashes of color here and there."[14] A turning point came in the summer of 1909 when Stieglitz was squired through the Paris art world by Steichen. What did he see during his three-week visit? On a visit to 27, rue de Fleurus, Stieglitz looked at the Steins' collection tiered up to the ceiling. He listened to Leo's pronouncements—that Matisse was a better sculptor than Rodin, that Whistler was a second-rate artist— and offered to publish this heresy in *Camera Work*. (During this visit Gertrude Stein remained a silent figure in the background, but it was her writing rather than her brother's that would appear in *Camera*

Work.) Stieglitz visited Michael and Sarah Stein's burgeoning collection of Matisse's paintings and saw African sculpture in ethnographic museums plus modern paintings at such galleries as Vollard, Durand-Ruel, and Bernheim-Jeune. In Paris he also met the dapper photographer Baron Adolf de Meyer and first saw the paintings of John Marin. The artists whose work he encountered formed the core of subsequent exhibitions at 291.

Stieglitz would later claim that 167,000 people visited 291 during the years 1905–12. There is no way to confirm those figures, but a larger public did start attending the shows there, enticed by broader coverage in mainstream newspapers. Although the critics usually disparaged the exhibitions, their attention conferred a certain credibility on modern art, and even the most philistine lampoons lured curious visitors. At the much-reviled Matisse exhibition in 1908, for example, Stieglitz claimed that four thousand people crowded into the little rooms.

This public was complemented by the more intimate group of visitors who gathered in Stieglitz's back room around a wood stove, the only source of heat on the floor. These regulars could be classified as follows: gallery artists (Arthur Dove, Marsden Hartley, John Marin, Abraham Walkowitz, Max Weber); writers and critics (Charles Caffin, Benjamin De Casseres, Sadakichi Hartmann, Alfred Kreymborg, J. Nilsen Laurvik); and organizers (Paul Haviland, Agnes Ernst Meyer, Marius de Zayas). Up to a dozen of the back-room regulars would meet at 291 about noon each weekday for a ritual called the Round Table. Before the short walk to the Holland House (Fifth Avenue and Thirtieth Street) or the Prince George Hotel (14 East Twenty-eighth Street) for lunch, the needier artists would briefly huddle around the desk of Stieglitz's secretary, Marie Rapp, to camouflage their frayed coats by rubbing black ink and cigarette ashes into the offending spots.

The reshuffling of forces at 291 after the photographers withdrew led to the emergence of two trios: John Marin, Marsden Hartley, and Arthur Dove; and Agnes Ernst Meyer, Paul Haviland, and Marius de Zayas. The former represented Stieglitz's best hope for American modern art, and the latter worked behind the scenes to support 291 and *Camera Work*.

Steichen first showed Marin's vibrant watercolors to Stieglitz in 1908, and before he had even met the painter, Stieglitz hung twenty-four of them at 291 in March 1909. When the two men met in June that year, Stieglitz dared Marin to pursue his most personal creative instincts rather than satisfy his financial needs, and Stieglitz backed up this challenge with a practice known as grubstaking—guaranteeing a regular income so the painter could work without worrying about how to survive. Although Marin had received much of his artistic education in Paris (where he lived from 1905 to 1910), on his return to the United

States he began to paint exclusively American subjects, a practice he would continue throughout his life. Increasingly, his jubilant paintings incorporated jagged forms and forceful diagonals that reflect the urban dynamism of New York. "While these powers are at work pushing, pulling sideways, downwards, upwards," he wrote, "I can hear the strife and there is great music being played." [15]

When thirty-one-year-old Marsden Hartley first visited 291 in the spring of 1909, he felt rootless. This chronic feeling stretched back to his childhood; as he later recalled, "From the moment of my mother's

death [when Hartley was eight years old] I became psychologically an orphan, in consciousness a lone thing left to make its way. . . ." [16] Stieglitz was impressed by Hartley's paintings, whose thick daubs of vivid color the artist described as Neo-Impressionist, and he was also moved by his poverty (he survived on four dollars a week) and his desperate commitment to art. He promptly decided to keep the gallery open into the summer months in order to give Hartley his first exhibition.

With his avian profile and melancholy ice blue eyes, Hartley was a striking character, who masked his poverty by pinning a fresh gardenia to his lapel and swinging a silver-headed cane. His psychological and financial neediness would never be satisfied—his contradictory demands for both privacy and constant expressions of approval were impossible to meet—but 291 provided him momentary respite. In Stieglitz he encountered his first mentor, in the back room he met a

ABOVE, LEFT
Marius de Zayas (1880– 1961). *Caricature of John Marin and Alfred Stieglitz*, 1913. Charcoal on paper, 24¼ × 18⅝ in. (61.6 × 47.5 cm). The Metropolitan Museum of Art, New York; The Alfred Stieglitz Collection, 1949

ABOVE, RIGHT
Marius de Zayas (1880– 1961). *Marsden Hartley*, 1911. Ink and watercolor on paper, 28½ × 22⅝ in. (72.4 × 57.7 cm). The Metropolitan Museum of Art, New York: The Alfred Stieglitz Collection, 1949

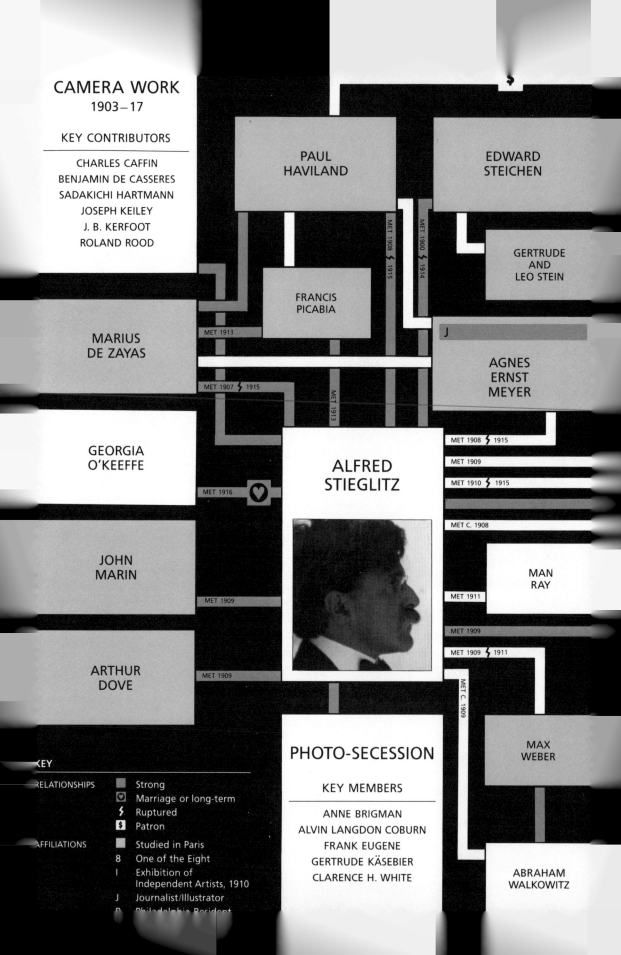

CAMERA WORK
1903–17

KEY CONTRIBUTORS

CHARLES CAFFIN
BENJAMIN DE CASSERES
SADAKICHI HARTMANN
JOSEPH KEILEY
J. B. KERFOOT
ROLAND ROOD

PAUL HAVILAND

EDWARD STEICHEN

MET 1908 ⚡ 1915

MET 1900 ⚡ 1914

GERTRUDE AND LEO STEIN

FRANCIS PICABIA

MARIUS DE ZAYAS

MET 1913

J

MET 1907 ⚡ 1915

MET 1913

AGNES ERNST MEYER

GEORGIA O'KEEFFE

MET 1908 ⚡ 1915

MET 1909

MET 1910 ⚡ 1915

ALFRED STIEGLITZ

MET 1916 ♥

MET C. 1908

JOHN MARIN

MAN RAY

MET 1911

MET 1909

MET 1909

MET 1909 ⚡ 1911

ARTHUR DOVE

MET 1909

MET C. 1909

PHOTO-SECESSION

KEY MEMBERS

ANNE BRIGMAN
ALVIN LANGDON COBURN
FRANK EUGENE
GERTRUDE KÄSEBIER
CLARENCE H. WHITE

MAX WEBER

ABRAHAM WALKOWITZ

KEY

RELATIONSHIPS
- ⬛ Strong
- ♥ Marriage or long-term
- ⚡ Ruptured
- $ Patron

AFFILIATIONS
- ⬛ Studied in Paris
- 8 One of the Eight
- I Exhibition of Independent Artists, 1910
- J Journalist/Illustrator

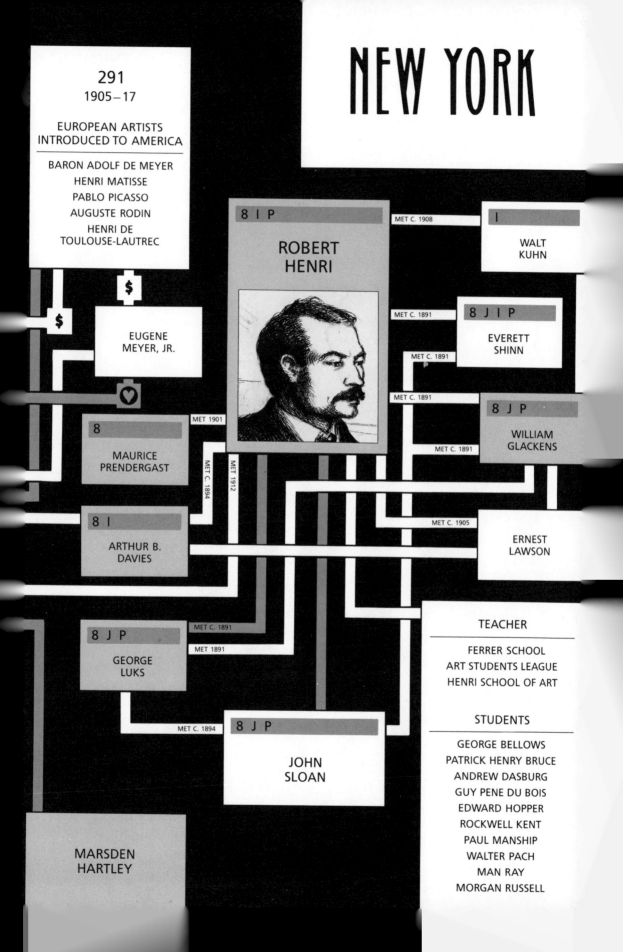

NEW YORK

291
1905–17

EUROPEAN ARTISTS
INTRODUCED TO AMERICA

BARON ADOLF DE MEYER
HENRI MATISSE
PABLO PICASSO
AUGUSTE RODIN
HENRI DE
TOULOUSE-LAUTREC

8 I P
ROBERT
HENRI

MET C. 1908

I
WALT
KUHN

$

$

EUGENE
MEYER, JR.

MET C. 1891

8 J I P
EVERETT
SHINN

MET C. 1891

8
MAURICE
PRENDERGAST

MET 1901

MET C. 1891

8 J P
WILLIAM
GLACKENS

MET C. 1891

MET C. 1894

MET 1912

8 I
ARTHUR B.
DAVIES

MET C. 1905

ERNEST
LAWSON

8 J P
GEORGE
LUKS

MET C. 1891

MET 1891

TEACHER

FERRER SCHOOL
ART STUDENTS LEAGUE
HENRI SCHOOL OF ART

STUDENTS

GEORGE BELLOWS
PATRICK HENRY BRUCE
ANDREW DASBURG
GUY PENE DU BOIS
EDWARD HOPPER
ROCKWELL KENT
PAUL MANSHIP
WALTER PACH
MAN RAY
MORGAN RUSSELL

MET C. 1894

8 J P
JOHN
SLOAN

MARSDEN
HARTLEY

community of like-minded artists, and from the exhibitions he gained inspiration. Immersing himself in European modernism, looking for hours at the work of Matisse, Picasso, and Weber, he painted brilliant abstract canvases for his next exhibition, in 1912. His new work so excited Agnes Ernst Meyer that she bought a painting, which financed a trip to Paris and began the next chapter in Hartley's peripatetic life. Throughout his adult years he would never occupy the same rooms for more than ten months, but he did try to establish a space for himself within avant-garde circles; in the next few years he would become a member of the Stein salon, Mabel Dodge's Evenings, the Arensberg gatherings, and the Stettheimers' parties. Repeatedly he returned to the Stieglitz circle, his most enduring home.

Arthur Dove first went to 291 at the end of 1909, a genial twenty-nine-year-old free-lance magazine illustrator from Geneva, New York. After he spent a year in Paris (1908–9), where his close friend Alfred Maurer introduced him to the art community, the colors in Dove's Impressionist-inflected paintings brightened considerably. But when he met Stieglitz shortly after his return, his work was still a pastiche of other styles. Unpretentious, level headed, affectionately known as "the whispering kid," Dove had a personality that complemented Stieglitz's, and their relationship would endure until the latter's death. Stieglitz invited the painter to exhibit in a group show in March 1910 that marked the beginning of his public career. Dove later called Stieglitz "one who has always known" and wrote, "I could not have existed as a painter without that superencouragement." [17]

Arthur Dove in Paris, 1908–9

Ten of Dove's pastels hung at 291 in February 1912. These voluptuous organic forms constituted the most advanced abstractions yet exhibited by an American. They reflected the modern experiments of Parisian artists even though Dove was thousands of miles from the art center; seeing exhibitions at 291 had provided his link to French avant-garde art. After this revolutionary debut Dove devoted his time to surviving as a chicken farmer in Westport, Connecticut, but even during this underground period his spirit was buoyed by 291.

These artists have become well known through their now-classic paintings, but the work of 291's second trio is not so visible. Nonetheless, their work was just as essential to 291's operation.

At the beginning of 1907 Stieglitz walked into the studio of the caricaturist Marius de Zayas and, without introducing himself, offered him an exhibition.[18] Although de Zayas initially declined, this offer marked the beginning of a relationship vital to 291. With his waxed mustache and graceful bearing, the twenty-six-year-old exuded a cosmopolitan aristocracy embodied in his urbane wit; in his fluent command of French, Spanish, and English; in his impeccable manners; and in the elegantly spare line of his caricatures. He was raised in Veracruz, Mexico—his father was Mexico's poet laureate and the publisher of

Alfred Stieglitz (1864–1946). *Marius de Zayas,* 1912. Platinum print, 8¾ × 7¼ in. (22.5 × 18.3 cm). National Gallery of Art, Washington, D.C.; Alfred Stieglitz Collection

two liberal newspapers—but the family's money had recently been confiscated by the conservative Mexican regime, and de Zayas had emigrated. He now made his living drawing for the *New York Evening World.* Through his contact with 291 de Zayas moved into the art world and replaced Steichen as Stieglitz's key lieutenant. First associated with 291 as a gallery artist, he exhibited in 1909, 1910, and 1913. In 1911 he began writing regular articles on art for *Camera Work.*

By the time de Zayas traveled to Paris in 1910, he wrote to Stieglitz, "I was prepared to see with open eyes."[19] In contrast to the purity of 291, the Parisian art circles were dominated by jealous feuds, "humbug," and commercialism, and he found nothing equal to the little rooms. "To me they appear bigger than many of the colossal rooms of the Louvre," he wrote to Stieglitz.[20] Establishing friendships in Paris with Arthur B. Carles, Marin, Steichen, and Picasso, de Zayas laid the foundation for his role as a modernist missionary.

Looking closely at the work in the Salon d'Automne, he was also inspired to articulate a philosophical rationale for modern art. In an age in which science had replaced religion, he argued, art provided spiritual expression, and modern art represented the highest evolution of the human intellect. His ideas appeared in *Camera Work,* and in 1913 he collaborated with Paul Haviland on *A Study of the Modern Evolution of Plastic Expression,* which articulated the gospel of early modernism.[21]

Paul Haviland arrived at 291 in January 1908, attracted by an exhibition of Rodin's drawings, and he later wrote that "the spirit of the place immediately took a strong hold on me."[22] A descendant of the Limoges porcelain dynasty in France, Haviland had a thorough education in art and degrees from the University of Paris and Harvard (A.B., 1901). His photographer brother, Frank Burty, kept him informed about the modern art revolution in Paris. He wore finely tailored suits, with his hands slung casually in his pockets, and the cultivated tones of his lightly accented English marked him as a gentleman.

Haviland combined heartfelt support of avant-garde art with the thoroughly practical outlook of a businessman, and his relationship to Stieglitz was loyal but not servile. This even-handed combination later earned Haviland the designation as "the balance wheel" of the group.[23] At a crucial moment in 1908 Haviland proved a godsend to the Stieglitz enterprise. The gallery rent was doubled at the same time that the Photo-Secessionists were withdrawing their financial support, and Stieglitz had resigned himself to closing 291. Haviland assured 291's future by offering to guarantee the rent for a three-year lease. A regular contributor to *Camera Work,* he documented the critical response to 291's exhibitions in his "Photo-Secession Notes," and in 1910 he became the magazine's associate editor.

Twenty-year-old Agnes Ernst arrived at 291 one April morning in 1908, on assignment from the *New York Morning Sun* to interview

OPPOSITE
Marius de Zayas (1880–1961). *Stieglitz (L'Accoucheur d'Idées),* c. 1909. Charcoal on paper, 24½ × 18¾ in. (62.3 × 47.8 cm). The Metropolitan Museum of Art, New York; The Alfred Stieglitz Collection, 1949

LEFT
Marius de Zayas (1880–1961). *Paul Haviland,* c. 1910. Charcoal on paper, 22 × 16 in. (55.9 × 40.6 cm). Harry H. Lunn, Jr.

Edward Steichen (1879–1973). *Mrs. Eugene Meyer,* c. 1910. Photograph, 11⅞ × 10¹/₁₆ in. (30.2 × 25.6 cm). The Metropolitan Museum of Art, New York; The Alfred Stieglitz Collection, 1949

Stieglitz. A recent Barnard graduate, she had just begun working as the paper's first female reporter. Riding up in the tiny elevator, she didn't know what to expect; six hours later, she recalled, "I felt at 291 that my sails were filled by the free air I craved."[24] From then on, she became a supporter of modern art and a regular at 291, where she was known as "The Sun Girl"—a nickname that related to her personal radiance as well as to her employer.

Beginning in the summer of 1908 Ernst spent a year in Europe. With Steichen's help she negotiated the networks of Parisian modernism—visiting museums on the arm of Rodin, interviewing Matisse at the Salon d'Automne, and viewing the Stein collection. "Over here I feel almost like an apostle," she wrote to Stieglitz, "and every time a *Camera Work* comes, I wave it like a red flag in the face of my friends."[25] Upon returning to New York she married the investment banker Eugene Meyer in 1910 and became the conduit between her husband's money and modern artists. Chief among the American recipients of her largess were Hartley, Marin, Steichen, Walkowitz, and Weber, and the Meyers also supported 291 by collecting the work of such European modernists as Constantin Brancusi, Cézanne, Picasso, Rodin, and Toulouse-Lautrec. Stieglitz concluded, "They are the only 'rich people' who have done anything at all for 291."[26]

Although all these figures were essential to the functioning of 291, they depended on Stieglitz as their catalyst.[27] In turn, Stieglitz depended upon the circle surrounding him. As one regular observed, "291 is a man who lives through a company, a crowd busy expressing a man."[28] The personnel shifted—from the Photo-Secessionists to the trio of de Zayas, Ernst, and Haviland to later acolytes such as Waldo Frank and Paul Rosenfeld—but an adulatory circle remained a constant in Stieglitz's life.

The consistency with which Stieglitz gathered a brilliant company around himself seems especially remarkable in light of the strains he put on relationships. He was controlling, quarrelsome, contentious, hypochondriacal, and garrulous.[29] His unrelenting devotion to 291 was mixed with self-pitying demands for appreciation, and when he suffered his periodic depressions, he attributed them to the disloyalty of colleagues. "In every innovator there is something of a redeemer, and every redeemer is crucified by those he wants to redeem," wrote Marius de Zayas, and Stieglitz often perceived himself as just such a martyr.[30] He could not abdicate personal control even for the good of 291—any more than he could relinquish control over the fine tones in his photographs or the scrupulous printing of each issue of *Camera Work.* His need to control was part of a despotic side that led to severed relations. One colleague declared himself "tired of your dictatorship"; another called him "incapable of a relationship of equality"; and Steichen observed, "Stieglitz only tolerated people close to him when they completely agreed with him and were of service."[31] Nevertheless, Stieglitz was able to attract the most advanced artists of the day, and he gave them the kind of support that came from no other quarter. At times, the entire avant-garde crusade seemed to depend solely on his leadership. As he wrote to one colleague: "No one can help. It's all too personal—like a work of art."[32]

Although Stieglitz's humorless fulminations against America's soul-less materialism could seem endless, they were precisely what was needed at this first stage of the avant-garde. Stieglitz created the in-spirational oral gospel of early modernism, and he delivered it tirelessly. His commitment was unsullied by commerce: he didn't advertise ex-hibitions, never locked the gallery's doors, kept no records, accepted no commission from his artists, and sold work only to those he judged ca-pable of appreciating it. 291 was a laboratory rather than a gallery, Stieglitz insisted, and he was "merely a trustee" for beauty.[33]

Stieglitz and his circle were not the only ones crusading against the art-world status quo. Their chief co-combatant was Robert Henri, an artist and teacher who shared Stieglitz's belief in freedom, progress, and ex-perimentation. In most other respects Henri was dramatically unlike Stieglitz, and the two men took potshots at one another. Whereas Stieglitz was a bourgeois urban Jew, Henri was a westerner who wore a ten-gallon hat and whose father had shot and killed a card-game op-ponent. While Stieglitz considered Picasso the one to watch, Henri thought his art execrable, and of all the modern artists he appreciated only Georges Rouault. Henri focused on portraying life in the streets; Stieglitz aspired to the spiritual realm. Only in their opposition to the turn-of-the-century art establishment were Stieglitz and Henri allied.

Henri's protégés, known as "the stock company," fell into roughly two groups.[34] One—George Bellows, George Luks, Jerome Myers, John Sloan—hewed closely to the realist line, which dictated "truth" over "beauty" and "life" over "art."[35] The other—Arthur B. Davies, William Glackens, Walt Kuhn, Ernest Lawson, Maurice Prendergast—was attracted less to contemporary urban subjects than to the for-malism of European Impressionism and Symbolism. Although their styles diverged dramatically, these two groups were tied together by bonds that included shared geography (Glackens, Henri, Lawson, Luks, and Everett Shinn had all emigrated from Philadelphia to New York around the turn of the century); shared training (many studied with Henri at the New York School of Art); shared occupation (several had switched from newspaper illustration to painting); shared exhibitions (*The Eight, The Exhibition of Independent Artists*); shared antipathy to-ward the Academy; and shared belief in the future of American art. Henri's combination of charisma and despotism welded them into a group and spearheaded their efforts to overthrow the Academy.

It is sometimes a ques-tion in our minds whether it is Mr. Stieglitz or the pictures on the wall at the Photo-Secession that constitute the exhibition.

Henry McBride,
New York Sun,
November 30, 1916

John Sloan (1871–1951). *Robert Henri,* 1905. Etching, 18⅞ × 15¹⁄₁₆ in. (48 × 38.4 cm). The Metropolitan Museum of Art, New York; Gift of Mrs. Harry Payne Whitney, 1926

Henri instructed his students to throw away their tiny brushes, forget about art, and paint life.[36] The brushy realism they specialized in lacks the formal innovation now associated with modernism, but their subjects were undeniably modern: Lower East Side slums, the Sixth Avenue El, shopgirls washing their hair on tenement rooftops. Looking to the skyscraper, they proclaimed "its every line indicative of our virile young lustiness."[37] Trained in popular journalism, Henri's protégés made paintings that were accessible to a broad public and that could be used for political reform, espousing the radical social values of the modern era without speaking the sometimes hermetic modern tongue. Their political commitment extended beyond their canvases—Henri was a philosophical anarchist, Sloan ran for office as a socialist, and most of the others were leftists. In the course of addressing their social concerns they would integrate strikers and suffragettes, immigrants and anarchists into the avant-garde alliance.

One urgent mission was to force open the door so tightly sealed by the rigid Academy. "The Academy" was shorthand for the well-oiled art machine that celebrated the aesthetics of such institutions as the Ecole des Beaux-Arts in Paris, the Royal Academy of Arts in London, and the National Academy of Design in New York. It propounded rules for correctly limning the human figure, mandated edifying classical subject matter, and abjured innovation. By its own lights, the Academy functioned successfully, and the artists who followed the rules were often commercially successful.

Henri's crew fit neither the "long-hair, flowing ties" style of bohemian artists nor the "frock-coat, high-hat" manner of academic artists. Dubbed the "the outlaw salon" by the yellow press, they gathered every Thursday night in such restaurants as Mouquin's or Petitpa's to drink beer and discuss not only art but also baseball, bull-fighting, and the merits of different shaving creams, ending finally with a poker game.[38] Here one could find the pugnacious George Luks, who was funny until he'd drunk so much beer that he challenged his colleagues to a boxing match. Everett Shinn, the dandy among them, described his recent trips to the theater. The amiable John Sloan talked socialism and art, while the more conservative William Glackens championed the bright Impressionist palette he had developed in Paris. The increasingly deaf Maurice Prendergast loudly asserted that his colleagues should learn more from Cézanne. Most reserved of the group was Arthur B. Davies, gazing fastidiously through his pince-nez.

To the emerging American avant-garde this group contributed a series of exhibitions that restructured the machinery of art exhibition in America. Reacting to the Academy's rejection of Bellows, Glackens, Luks, and Shinn, they defied its jurisdiction by taking charge of their own exhibitions and ensuring their own economic survival. The first of these exhibitions was staged in February 1908, by a group the newspapers called the Eight: Davies, Glackens, Henri, Lawson, Luks, Prendergast, Shinn, and Sloan. Renouncing juries and formal organization, the Eight rented William Macbeth's gallery at 450 Fifth Avenue and mounted their own exhibition. It proved an unexpected success, attracting critical attention (a substantial article appeared in the newspapers each day of its run, and a majority of critics praised the show), numerous visitors (attendance was high, and the exhibition traveled to six other cities), and sales (seven paintings were sold, totaling $4,000).[39]

Heartened by this achievement, this core group expanded to mount a larger show in April 1910, modeled on the Société des Indépendants in Paris. They adopted the Société's slogan, "no juries, no prizes," and presented the *Exhibition of Independent Artists* in an improvised gallery on West Thirty-fifth Street. Crowded into the third floor, backed by floor-to-ceiling stretches of cheesecloth, and lit by electric bulbs were 260 paintings, 20 sculptures, and 219 drawings and etchings. Sales were low (five paintings sold, totaling only seventy-five dollars), and the critical response was mixed, but the show's most important feature was

The National Academy is no more national than the National Biscuit Company.

John Sloan

its democratic, artist-run organization. Henri emphasized a major goal of the enterprise, that "the people of America learn the means of expressing themselves in their own time and in their own land." [40] The communal effort raised the morale among the artists, and after celebrating in Mouquin's red plush dining room, Sloan exulted that they had mounted "the best exhibition ever held on this continent (that is, composed of American art exclusively)." [41]

No one could have anticipated that the Independents Show would offer both training and rehearsal for the Armory Show. That epochal event in February 1913 signaled the beginning of a new era of modernism. It spelled the equivocal success of Stieglitz's and Henri's separate campaigns: one had introduced modernist aesthetics to America, and the other had developed exhibition strategies independent of the Academy. But the Armory Show also marked the end of their greatest influence: its modernism rendered Henri's aesthetics passé, and its circus hoopla made Stieglitz's elevated approach obsolete. Two quotations foreshadow the changes to come:

> "But the poor Independents must look to their laurels. Already they are back numbers and we shall look soon to see them amalgamate with the much abused old National Academy of Design."
>
> The art critic Arthur Hoeber in the *New York Globe*, 1911, after seeing Picasso's exhibition at 291 [42]

> "Isn't my work for the cause about finished?"
>
> Alfred Stieglitz, May 22, 1912 [43]

FLORENCE

I n the fall of 1905 Mabel Dodge crossed the Apennines and beheld the city of Florence. She gazed on the stately Duomo, the towers and palaces of Renaissance civilization, and the blue-green hills, broken by spiky verticals of dark cypresses and olive trees. It looked to her as if the old master paintings she had seen in reproduction had come to life. Inhaling the city's fragrance of old stone and laurel trees, dust and roses, she vowed, "I will make you mine."[1]

Dodge's declaration reflected her desperate desire to establish a home after twenty-six years of emotional rootlessness. She had grown up in luxury but starved of parental love, and her native Buffalo, with its ersatz Tuscan villas, had offered only a Gilded Age imitation of civilization. Her first marriage had ended abruptly when her husband was killed in a hunting accident, leaving her a son, and her subsequent affair with a married doctor had ended in scandal. Her second marriage followed soon after, in 1904, to a Boston Beaux-Arts architect named Edwin Dodge, who provided material comfort but not passion. In the absence of love or beauty, Mabel would descend into a state of neurasthenia that not even her compulsive shopping sprees could alleviate. Florence inspired her to transform her misery into a life of art. She proceeded in a sequence that would be repeated many times over the years—from the streets of Greenwich Village to the sands of New Mexico. She created her setting; she animated it with guests; she installed a man at its center.

With Edwin she set about designing a highly personalized backdrop in a quattrocento estate called the Villa Curonia; this joint enterprise proved to be the most intimate episode in their marriage. Describing their collaboration, Mabel wrote, "He was to make the shell, I to line it."[2] Edwin restored the villa and unearthed an exemplary cinquecento courtyard. Using fifty thousand dollars from her mother, Mabel decorated the villa's endless rooms with precious and not so precious *objets* to match her changing tempers. Appreciative Florentine merchants dubbed her "questo angelo vestito in bianco" ("this angel dressed in white"). Her friend Mina Loy recalled, "Her palace was tremendous

We Americans, for whom the world is in its infancy, lay claim to the past of your continent— it is ours.

Mabel Dodge, c. 1912

BELOW AND RIGHT
The Villa Curonia

OPPOSITE
Mabel Dodge at the Villa
Curonia. Photograph by
Jacques-Emile Blanche

and stuffed with things bought in the flurry of a woman with taste."[3] The intimate Yellow Salon was gay and French, the medieval bedroom hushed, the huge dining room voluptuous. On the polished wood floor stood a legion of Meissen and Staffordshire dogs; gardenias and jasmine bloomed in terra-cotta tubs. What Mabel called "the million billion organized glints and sparkles" reflected her need for animation, but it was the Renaissance civilization embodied in the villa itself that enclosed her with a solid frame. "I knew quite well the kind of queen I wanted to be and the type of royal residence in which I would immolate myself," she later wrote. "It would allow one to be both majestic and careless, spontaneous and picturesque, and yet always framed and supported by a secure and beautiful authenticity of background."[4] Strewing her old clothes on her bedroom floor—because "they have no emotion"—she dressed for her new role in Renaissance coats, rich brocades, and chiffon turbans.[5] One friend observed that she looked "for all the world as if she had always been a part of the *mise-en-scène*."[6]

From five to seven one afternoon the refurbished Villa Curonia was first opened to international society. Roses were arranged in front of velvet tapestries, and a long table was laden with fruit and flowers. At the first appearance of a star in the Tuscan sky, a soloist burst into "Song to the Evening Star" from *Tannhäuser*. Sipping champagne, titled guests strolled on the garlanded loggia, gazed out at the twilit hills, and admired the pair of white peacocks in the villa's garden. "Tintorettoish," Mabel declared happily.[7] The fête had been an unequivocal success, but when she surveyed the resulting disarray and inhaled the lingering scents of cigarette smoke and chocolate, she felt nauseated.

She was overcome by "a fatigue from straining myself to fill an empty form that could be blown into a fullness for a while, but that would always collapse when one ceased to blow it up."[8]

While artists and writers in Paris and London looked ahead to the modern age, the residents of Florence looked resolutely backward. For Ezra Pound, sitting in his cramped Kensington quarters, the Renaissance was an inspiring metaphor; for the Florentines, the cinquecento seemed more real than the twentieth century. As Dodge observed, "life was built up around the productions of the dead," and that included the ancient villas, the churches filled with frescoes, and the old family names—the Rucellai, the Serristori, the Antinori—that dominated Florentine society.[9]

In Paris when a man's mind has so diliquessed [sic] that even the semi-dilletanti of that tolerant capital can't stand him, it is said "Jones ought to go to FLORENCE."

Ezra Pound to
Harriet Monroe,
January 31, 1915

Since the international community that visited Florence was not welcomed by the local aristocrats, American and English hostesses stepped into the breach. In a city with little industry, gossip became the main enterprise; intrigues and romances fueled the endless social rounds. "One was always 'visiting,'" Mabel Dodge recalled, "people, paintings, architecture, scenery, palaces, villas, museums, gardens, and galleries."[10] In this hothouse atmosphere were trained the *salonneuses* of the modern age. Dodge described the role as "a *femme du monde* whose wheel of life is society," and who judged her guests by title, hereditary honors, beauty, and wit (in descending order of importance).[11] As Virgil Thomson later observed: "You will find that the great American hostesses all spent time in Florence. In Paris you learn wit, in London you learn to crush your social rivals, in Florence you learn poise."[12]

Mabel Dodge assumed the style of an old world hostess. Sumptuously dressed and reclining on a chaise longue, she gazed raptly at all that surrounded her. The actor Robert de La Condamine acknowledged her specialized skill when he inscribed a book "To Mabel, who has the courage to sit still and the wisdom to keep silent."[13] Dodge's uncanny ability to mirror the speaker may have been rooted in emotional deprivation, but it neatly dovetailed with the hostess's role in nineteenth-century society, and she added to it her own erotic note. Mina Loy observed, "She had the divine female quality of lending to every latest science or philosophy—no matter how mathematical or how austere—a ribald flavor of lubriciousness."[14]

Dodge's At Homes differed from those of other Florentine hostesses. Some of her gatherings were elegantly contrived costume balls, but most were informal events where the hostess smoked cigarettes and some guests even removed their shirts. Dodge's guests came from the city's international underbelly as well as from the margins of local society. She welcomed artists, homosexuals, Jews, bohemians, scandalous lovers, and political exiles. "She was the only woman who had conquered Palms [Florence]," Mina Loy observed, "and blown herself up for a voluntary ostracism in which she could pick out some more bizarre ingredients from which to compound her inquisitive career."[15]

Dodge could choose from a large crowd of people who appreciated Florence for its tolerance of deviation from various norms.[16] Here lived the Queen of Saxony, who had fled to Florence in romantic pursuit of her children's tutor, and the actress Eleonora Duse, who recuperated at the Villa Curonia after her heartless treatment at the hands of Gabriele D'Annunzio. Bernard Berenson and Charles Loeser, former Harvard classmates and now rival connoisseurs who hadn't exchanged words in fifteen years, made their visits to the villa separately. Dealers in antiquities (known as the "bone-and-rag trade") like waxen Arthur Acton mixed with such incarnations of the fin-de-siècle aesthete as the club-footed and silver-tongued actor Robert de La Condamine. In one conversation at the Villa Curonia the theater visionary Edward Gordon Craig grew so excited when Dodge proposed mounting a Renaissance pageant that he offered to forgo his contract with the Moscow Art Theatre.[17] The epicene sculptor Pen Browning (son of Robert Browning and Elizabeth Barrett Browning) appeared regularly, along with the sculptors Jo Davidson and Janet Scudder, the successful and eccentric playwright Constance Fletcher, the music teacher Isidor Braggiotti, and Americans considered too arriviste for other society. This congregation was a step lower than proper society, and Mary Berenson, among others, had her doubts about them. "Tastes differ!" she wrote. "Mabel Dodge made friends with all the people in Florence whom we consider peculiarly undesirable."[18] Harold Acton, the last survivor of the Villa Curonia gatherings, viewed this crowd through the eyes of a young boy, recalling it as "a paradise of exiles, a sunny place for shady people," whose "eccentricity flourished in the clear Tuscan light."[19]

From this mixture of guests at the Villa Curonia, two of Mabel Dodge's close friends stand out. Mina Loy arrived in Florence in 1906 with her husband, Stephen Haweis.[20] Born in London to a middle-class family, she had spent the last four years in Paris studying painting at the Académie Colarossi in Montparnasse; she exhibited her Post-Impressionist watercolors in the Salon d'Automne from 1904 to 1906. Dodge thought Loy was as "lovely as a Byzantine Madonna," and others remarked on her chiseled patrician features, her luxuriant dark hair parted in the middle, and pale skin at the nape of her neck. Her intellect was razor-sharp and her wit so cerebral that she intimidated many men. Despite her looks, intelligence, artistic talent, and a modest house on the Costa San Giorgio, Loy was profoundly depressed. "How beautiful she is and how dried out, no sap!" exclaimed Mabel Dodge.[21]

Loy's depression stretched back to her childhood, but it was exacerbated by her sour marriage (in 1903) to a philanderer, the death of their first child in infancy, and her dissatisfaction with living in what she considered a cultural backwater. Her initial social connections in

Mina Loy

Florence came through her husband, a painter of limited talent and a descendant of one of England's oldest families. She made the required rounds of social calls on the English colony, but she felt ill at ease in this precious and wholly uncurious world of "Anglo-Saxon closed up-ness."[22] She wrote to Carl Van Vechten, "Most of my time I spend in utter aloneness—among moving crowds—that gives me the real fillip of Being."[23]

Loy mixed her own egg tempera and painted Symbolist images of morbid figures. She designed her own clothes and hats. Or she simply closed the shutters and lay down. When she emerged on the streets— smoking cigarettes and even whistling—she refused to wear the black dresses that were the traditional public uniform of women in Italy; black made her look like a death's head, she maintained. Loy instead presented a provocative picture to the Florentine populace in her lemon-and-magenta hobble skirts, her beige poncho and amber candelabra earrings—one pair of which featured flies with extended wings trapped in the resin.

Loy came alive at the Villa Curonia—she called herself "a hermit crab occasionally lured to expansiveness under Mabel Dodge's flower-ing trees."[24] Loy called Dodge "Moose," made her the godmother of her second child, and pronounced her "the most ample woman personality alive."[25] In a story inspired by Dodge, Loy later described her own first step from being a passive beauty to being a creator: "Amazingly responsive, Ova's [Loy's] consciousness expanded with this first impetus towards liberation—here was an adoptable standard— easy and the mind free of the middle-class god of monstrosities. . . ."[26] Alice B. Toklas witnessed Loy's new freedom when she visited the Villa Curonia in the autumn of 1912: while André Gide conversed with a reclining Mabel Dodge, Mina Loy danced gaily around the room with an unseen partner to unheard music.

Muriel Draper and her new husband, Paul, arrived in Florence in 1909 on their honeymoon; Muriel was four months pregnant. Both de-scended from old New England stock—the Danas, the Howes, the Saltonstalls among them—so Muriel's prenuptial pregnancy was a major family embarrassment. To blur the date of the birth, a trip to Flor-ence was prescribed, with the plausible guise of Paul's musical educa-tion. He studied voice with Isidor Braggiotti and Muriel accompanied him on the piano. Her musicianship was merely competent, however; her métier was talk.

Years later Mabel Dodge recalled her first vision of Muriel Draper, who was coming down the stone steps of the Villa Curonia: "Bending slightly backwards, she was like a hard, slender, polished ivory figure carved from an elephant's tusk; she seemed to have been produced complete from that curving, unyielding form and ever afterwards to have retained, like a special destiny, the arbitrary character of the mate-

Roy Sheldon. *Portrait of Muriel Draper,* 1929. Onyx. Yale Collection of American Literature, The Beinecke Rare Book and Manuscript Library, Yale University, New Haven, Connecticut

rial from whence she had emerged."[27] Against her pale, silky complexion her extravagantly painted thick lips stood out, and her electric blue eyes were piercing. Her features were so irregular that she verged on ugliness, but her disquieting looks provided a theatrical complement to her talk.

Dodge considered Draper the most gifted monologist since Oscar Wilde. Although Draper's formal education had ended at thirteen, when the local school sent her home for asking too many questions, she could deliver a mot juste with acerbic authority.[28] Her odd wit helped her to manage the considerable adversity in her life; as Dodge observed, she was "forever overcoming with a pointed phrase the stupidities of life."[29] These included a husband who loved women and alcohol; he sometimes disappeared for days and squandered their limited income. But even during the Drapers' straitened years in Florence—when they occupied a small villino on the Via San Leandro and Muriel's wardrobe consisted of one broadcloth dress with a cascade of lace—she acted like an aristocrat. "But Muriel was not only a lady in the quaint, old-fashioned sense of that word," Dodge cautioned. "She always had, in addition, an infinitely elegant and royal air that permitted her any license of speech or gesture that she cared to indulge. . . ."[30]

Mabel Dodge had created her setting and enlivened it with illustrious company. Her next step—installing a man at the center of her milieu—personally touched Loy and Draper and was noted by visitors to the Villa Curonia. Even nine-year-old Harold Acton pegged her as "a Turkish delight type, her languid eyes gazing with prurient expression."[31] Her eroticized responses were not directed solely toward men but occasionally to women and the world at large. Loy later wrote, "Gloria's [Mabel's] instinct had come to desire to stuff everything into her vulva to see what marvelous creative modification it had undergone in the process before chucking it away."[32] Dapper, reticent Edwin could never satisfy her needs—nor was it likely that any man could.

At first she pursued Italians—including a penniless homosexual descendant of the Medicis, and her chauffeur, whom she aestheticized into "a knight, a page, a courtier." But her affairs ended disastrously. Bindo Peruzzi de Medici committed suicide, and when she found herself unable to respond sexually to her chauffeur, she swallowed shards of glass and a bottle of laudanum.

By the time Mina Loy and Muriel Draper arrived in Florence, Dodge had reined in her passions; though still erotically obsessed, she had directed her feelings into more acceptable channels. To Loy and Haweis she became a marital arbiter and urged them to separate.[33] She inserted herself into the Drapers' marriage as a romantic muse. Exclaiming "God! Mabel! You are life!"[34] Paul Draper embarked on an affair with her in 1910 while Muriel was struggling through the final stages of pregnancy. Oblivious to Muriel's feelings, Dodge considered herself a necessary element in the artistic process—every musician must conceive a passion for his muse, and thus their affair belonged not to the personal realm but to the grander arena of art. (She was suitably pleased by her effect on the musician, for his repertoire thereafter expanded beyond classics to embrace more up-to-date compositions by César Franck.) But this affair tore a hole in the Drapers' marriage that would never mend. After a costume party at the Villa Curonia, Muriel secretly threw herself over an embankment and lay there limp as a rag doll, until she was found and revived by stiff doses of brandy. After that her increasingly brittle wit shielded her feelings, and she became less vulnerable to the pains of romantic relationships.

Although Florence seemed resolutely unmodern, it was there that three New Women—Muriel Draper, Mina Loy, and Mabel Dodge—found their way out of the fin-de-siècle dead end. "No scratching on the surface of the rubbish heap of tradition will bring about Reform," wrote Mina Loy, "the only method is Absolute Demolition."[35]

The Drapers left Florence for London in the summer of 1911 so that Paul could further his musical studies.[36] While Paul trained his light, precise tenor for the stringent demands of lieder singing, Muriel created London's chief music salon in the years before the Great War. By this time both the Drapers had come into their family inheritances, so Muriel leased an out-of-the-way studio at 19 Edith Grove; stripped it to its brick walls; added a fireplace, a skylight, and a Bechstein piano; and illuminated it with tall candles.

Her gatherings began around midnight, after the music crowd returned from the evening's concerts and arrived at Edith Grove carrying their instruments. The nucleus comprised young musicians, including Harold Bauer, Pablo Casals, and Artur Rubinstein. In the room's flickering light they performed impromptu chamber music for a rapt audience that often included Lady Emerald Cunard, Norman Douglas, Ruth Draper, and Henry James. The guests drank champagne, sometimes dozed on scattered pillows, and when dawn came they retired to the dining room for scrambled eggs and raspberries.

It was during these years that Muriel molded her distinctive persona as a hostess, and her style and appearance inspired others to call her the White Negress. "Good taste is the worst vice," she often said, and wore hats appointed with white love birds, ravens' wings, and ospreys springing up above her forehead. The middle-of-the-night hours of her salon were unheard of in London society, and the setting she created suggested bohemia rather than old money. Her torrent of salty language alarmed some of her guests; Henry James declared himself both "tickled" and "affrighted." Nevertheless, Muriel Draper conquered London, and even John Singer Sargent painted her. As one friend has observed, "She made being American chic."[37]

Curie
of the laboratory
of vocabulary
  she crushed
the tonnage
of consciousness
congealed to phrases
  to extract
a radium of the word

          Mina Loy

Mina Loy's transition from the fin de siècle to the modern was catalyzed by Gertrude Stein, whom she met in Florence in 1911. When Loy read *The Making of Americans,* she instantly grasped Stein's radical experiments with language; as Stein observed of Loy in *The Autobiography of Alice B. Toklas,* "She has always been able to understand."[38] Both women had traveled in overlapping Parisian art circles, both were influenced as much by the revolution in painting as by contemporary writing, and both were intrigued by the psychology of sexuality and the mind's cognitive structure. Loy was inspired by Stein's prose to explore a new poetic syntax, and in 1913 she began writing pithy aphorisms that reflected not only Stein's influence but also Loy's own uncompromising rejection of the past. Entitled "Aphorisms on Futurism," they were published in *Camera Work* after Dodge sent them to Stieglitz.[39]

In 1913 Loy met the Futurists. By this time Stephen Haweis had taken Dodge's advice and left for Australia, and Frances Stevens, a beautiful young American painter influenced by Futurism, became a boarder at 54 Costa San Giorgio.[40] While visiting Stevens, several of the

Futurists met Loy. As a result of her romantic liaisons with two of Futurism's leaders, Giovanni Papini and Filippo Tommaso Marinetti, she would play a significant role in the movement, and they would play a role in her transformation into a New Woman and New Poet.[41]

Papini was a small, unattractive, respected writer-philosopher who published *Lacerba* (1913–15), a Florence-based little magazine that was the chief organ of Futurist writing and images. Loy found him deeply sympathetic and entertained fantasies of marrying him, but Papini was already married, and Catholic to boot; however iconoclastic his Futurist beliefs, he was unwilling to abandon his wife and commit himself to Loy.

By the end of 1913 Loy knew Marinetti, the founder of Futurism and its chief leader. Their romance was primarily cerebral, and it lasted only a few intense months. But it proved profoundly important to Loy's artistic development, and she credited him for "twenty years added to my life from mere contact with his exuberant personality."[42] In the thirty-seven-year-old Marinetti, Loy found an intellectual comrade even more eager than she to dynamite the old era, as demonstrated by his radical experiments with syntax, *parole in libertà* (words freed). Loy wrote to Dodge, "My roots are being tugged out—for experiment—in exquisite and terrific anguish."[43]

Eventually Loy's relationships with Papini and Marinetti led to rivalry. In a New York gossip column George Cram Cook described her as "the woman who split the Futurist movement."[44] While this may have been an exaggeration, Papini and Marinetti did begin a feud simultaneous with their romances with Loy. The painful conclusions of these romances intensified Loy's sense of isolation and her conviction that women must create their own identities. She wrote a "Feminist Manifesto" (1914), which called for women to "leave off looking for men to find out what you are *not*—seek within yourselves to find out what you are."[45] Her romantic relationships had impelled her to feminist politics; nevertheless, she longed for a man. "The only thing that frightens me," she wrote, "is the fear of not finding someone who appeals to me as much."[46]

Mabel Dodge's transformation was also inspired by Gertrude Stein, whom she first encountered in Paris during the spring of 1911. Her immediate infatuation with Stein and her literary experiments reflected Dodge's readiness for change; she had grown weary of the golden Tuscan views, the tortured romances, and the Berensons' increasingly refined games of connoisseurship. When Stein and Alice B. Toklas arrived at the Villa Curonia in October 1912, they found the Dodge household entangled in romance: Dodge was conducting a thoroughly modern flirtation with her son's football-playing tutor. Stein spent her nights writing in Edwin's study, adjacent to Mabel's white boudoir. One evening as Stein sat down at Edwin's large table, the twenty-two-year-

ANARCHISTS in art are art's instantaneous aristocracy.

Mina Loy

old tutor crept down the red-tiled corridor and presented himself at Mabel's door. She surreptitiously provided entry, and the two made a slow procession to the bed where they lay for several hours silently entwined in the moonlight. No one knows what Stein could hear through the adjoining wall, but the loosely scrawled pages that Toklas gathered up the next morning began, "The days are wonderful and the nights are wonderful and the life is pleasant."

So opened Stein's "Portrait of Mabel Dodge at the Villa Curonia," the portrait that would prove pivotal to the career of both its author and its subject.[47] Most of Dodge's friends were puzzled by the portrait—even Mina Loy and Muriel Draper claimed to understand nothing beyond the cover. Dodge, however, discerned a coherent likeness of her personality among the shifting phrases and fluid repetition.[48] She quickly had three hundred copies printed, bound, and wrapped in vivid Florentine wallpaper and distributed them among her friends, as if it were a calling card introducing the new Mabel Dodge.

The month after Stein's visit, Dodge left Florence, ostensibly to attend to the education of her son, John. Steeling herself for the return to America, she selected a few favorite objects from the Villa Curonia to carry to her unknown future. The three Dodges and their manservant, Domenico, embarked on the long voyage home in November 1912. Mabel installed herself at the ship's stern, training her eyes on the horizon even long after Europe had disappeared. She wept. "I felt nowhere," she later wrote, "suspended 'between two worlds.'"[49] Then the Statue of Liberty came into view and the skyline of New York, its heights shrouded in mist. Mabel dragged her son to the stern, the only people still looking back to the Old World. Through her sobs, Mabel instructed her son, "Remember, it is *ugly* in America."[50]

PORTRAIT
GALLERY

Man Ray (1890–1976).
Portrait of Alfred Stieglitz,
1913. Oil on canvas, 10½ ×
8½ in. (26.7 × 21.6 cm).
Alfred Stieglitz Collection,
Yale Collection of American
Literature, The Beinecke Rare
Book and Manuscript Library,
Yale University, New Haven,
Connecticut

Arthur Dove (1880–1946).
Portrait of Alfred Stieglitz,
1925. Camera lens, photo-
graphic plate, clock and
watch springs, and steel
wool on cardboard, 15⅞ ×
12⅛ in. (40.4 × 30.7 cm).
Collection, The Museum of
Modern Art, New York;
Purchase

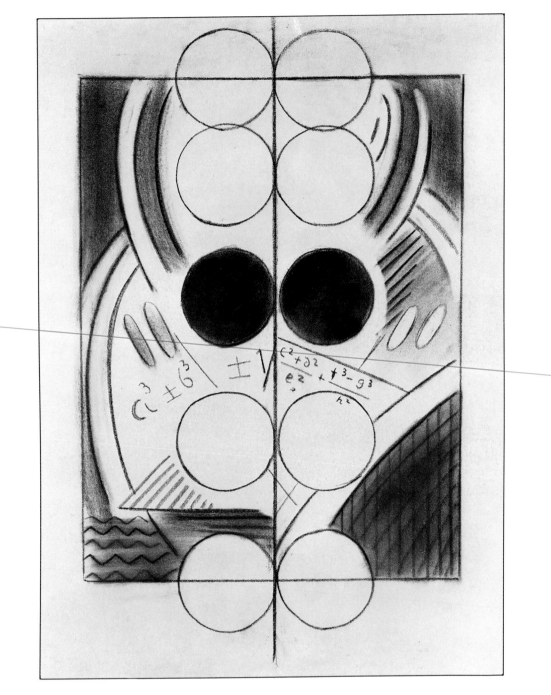

Marius de Zayas (1880–
1961). *Alfred Stieglitz,*
c. 1912–13. Charcoal on
paper, 24¼ × 18⅜ in.
(61.6 × 46.5 cm). The
Metropolitan Museum of
Art, New York; The Alfred
Stieglitz Collection, 1949

Pablo Picasso (1881–1973).
Leo Stein, 1906. Gouache on
cardboard, 9¾ × 6¾ in.
(24.8 × 17.2 cm). The
Baltimore Museum of Art;
The Cone Collection, formed
by Dr. Claribel Cone and
Miss Etta Cone of Baltimore,
Maryland

OPPOSITE
Charles Demuth (1883–1935). *Poster-Portrait of Georgia O'Keeffe,* 1924. Oil on panel, 20½ × 16½ in. (52.1 × 41.9 cm). Yale Collection of American Literature, The Beinecke Rare Book and Manuscript Library, Yale University, New Haven, Connecticut; Gift of Georgia O'Keeffe

ABOVE
Charles Demuth (1883–1935). *Poster-Portrait of Arthur Dove,* 1924. Oil on panel, 20 × 23½ in. (50.8 × 59.7 cm). Yale Collection of American Literature, The Beinecke Rare Book and Manuscript Library, Yale University, New Haven, Connecticut; Gift of Georgia O'Keeffe

Charles Demuth (1883–1935). *Poster-Portrait of John Marin,* 1925. Oil on panel, 26¼ × 33 in. (66.6 × 83.8 cm). Yale Collection of American Literature, The Beinecke Rare Book and Manuscript Library, Yale University, New Haven, Connecticut

Marius de Zayas (1880–1961).
Francis Picabia, 1914. From
Camera Work.

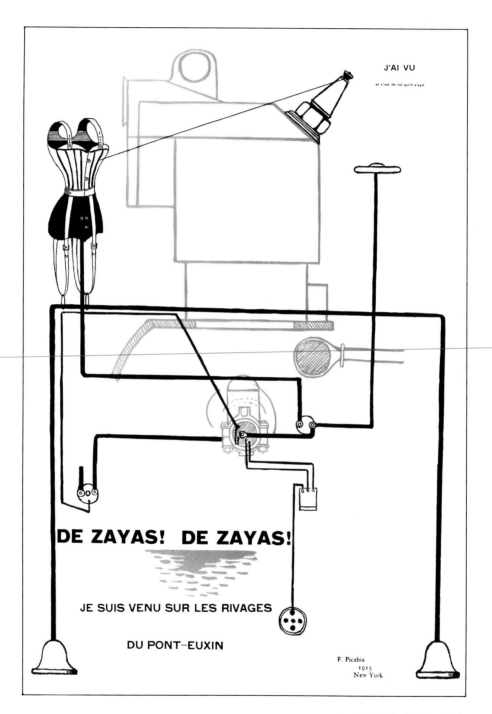

Francis Picabia (1878–1953).
De Zayas! De Zayas!, 1915.
From *291*.

Pablo Picasso (1881–1973).
Gertrude Stein, 1906. Oil on
canvas, 39¼ × 32 in.
(99.7 × 81.3 cm). The
Metropolitan Museum of
Art, New York; Bequest of
Gertrude Stein, 1946

ABOVE
Charles Demuth (1883–1935). *Love, Love, Love (Homage to Gertrude Stein),* 1928. Oil on wood, 20 × 23¾ in. (51 × 53 cm). Thyssen-Bornemisza Collection, Lugano, Switzerland

OPPOSITE
Marsden Hartley (1877–1943). *One Portrait of One Woman,* c. 1913. Oil on composition board, 32 × 21⅜ in. (81.3 × 54.3 cm). University Art Museum, University of Minnesota, Minneapolis; Bequest of Hudson Walker from Ione and Hudson Walker Collection

RIGHT
Wyndham Lewis (1884–
1957). *Ezra Pound,* 1920.
Black crayon on paper,
12¾ × 14⁹⁄₁₆ in. (32.4 ×
37.1 cm). Estate of Mrs. G. A.
Wyndham Lewis

BELOW
Henri Gaudier-Brzeska
(1891–1915). *Hieratic Head
of Ezra Pound,* 1914. Marble,
36 × 19 × 16½ in. (91.4 ×
48.3 × 41.9 cm). Patsy R. and
Raymond D. Nasher
Collection

OPPOSITE
Charles Demuth (1883–
1935). *I Saw the Figure Five
in Gold,* 1928. Oil on
composition board, 36 ×
29¾ in. (91.4 × 75.6 cm).
The Metropolitan Museum of
Art, New York; The Alfred
Stieglitz Collection, 1949

RIGHT

B.J.O. Nordfeldt (1878–1955). *Floyd Dell.* Oil painting on fabric, 48½ × 37½ in. (123.2 × 95.3 cm). Floyd Dell Papers, The Newberry Library, Chicago

BELOW

Florine Stettheimer (1871–1944). *Henry McBride, Art Critic,* 1922. Oil on canvas, 30 × 26 in. (76.2 × 66 cm). Smith College Museum of Art, Northampton, Massachusetts; Gift of Ettie Stettheimer, 1951

OPPOSITE

Florine Stettheimer (1871–1944). *Portrait of My Sister, Carrie W. Stettheimer, with Doll's House,* 1923. Oil on canvas, 37⅞ × 26⅛ in. (96.3 × 66.3 cm). Columbia University in the City of New York; Gift of the Estate of Ettie Stettheimer, 1967

OPPOSITE
Florine Stettheimer (1871–1944). *Portrait of Marcel Duchamp,* 1923. Oil on board with frame designed by artist, 30 × 26 in. (76.2 × 66 cm). Estate of Virgil Thomson

LEFT
Florine Stettheimer (1871–1944). *Soirée,* c. 1915. Oil on canvas, 27¾ × 29⅜ in. (70.5 × 74.5 cm). Yale Collection of American Literature, The Beinecke Rare Book and Manuscript Library, Yale University, New Haven, Connecticut

Top left: Ettie Stettheimer, Maurice Sterne, Isabelle Lachaise. Bottom left: Gaston Lachaise and Albert Gleizes. Seated center: Avery Hopwood and Leo Stein; above them, an unidentified Hindu poet. Far right, reading down, Juliet Roche (Mme Gleizes), Florine Stettheimer, part of an unidentified figure.

BELOW
Florine Stettheimer (1871–1944). *Picnic at Bedford Hills,* 1918. Oil on canvas, 40 × 50 in. (101.6 × 127 cm). The Pennsylvania Academy of the Fine Arts; Gift of Miss Ettie Stettheimer

Florine Stettheimer seated with parasol, Ettie Stettheimer lying on carpet talking with Elie Nadelman, Carrie Stettheimer and Marcel Duchamp setting out food.

Florine Stettheimer (1871–1944). *La Fête à Duchamp,* 1917. Oil on canvas, 35 × 45½ in. (88.9 × 115.6 cm). Private collection

The guests are shown at different stages of the party. Upper left: Marcel Duchamp waves from a car driven by Francis Picabia, and in the left foreground they enter the garden through an arch of flowers. Facing them are Florine Stettheimer and Albert Gleizes, with Fania Marinoff seated in the swing. Center, by the refreshment table: Carrie Stettheimer pours tea for the Marquis de Buenavista; beside the table, Avery Hopwood speaks to Juliet Roche (Mme Gleizes). Seated by the tree on right: Ettie Stettheimer listens to two likenesses of Leo Stein. Lying on the grass, front right: Picabia and Henri-Pierre Roché. Seated on chairs at center: Elizabeth Duncan and Carl Van Vechten. At top: the entire party is seated at the table on the terrace, with Ettie proposing a toast and Duchamp responding.

Florine Stettheimer (1871–1944). *Sunday Afternoon in the Country,* 1917. Oil on canvas, 50½ × 36½ in. (128.3 × 92.7 cm). The Cleveland Museum of Art; Gift of Ettie Stettheimer

Foreground: Edward Steichen photographing Marcel Duchamp, attended by Ettie Stettheimer; Baron de Meyer seated with back turned; Baroness de Meyer under a parasol with Paul Reimers; and Rosetta Walter Stettheimer playing Patience. Center: Ratan Devi and Adolph Bolm with a parasol, Arnold Genthe with Mme Bolm, Alfred Seligsberg with arms crossed, Carrie Stettheimer and Albert Sterner with Jo Davidson. Background: left, Marie Sterner watching Paul Thévenaz; right, Paul Calfin, the Marquis de Buenavista, against a tree, Florine Stettheimer painting at her easel.

Beatrice Wood (b. 1893). *Lit de Marcel* [Marcel's Bed], 1917. Watercolor and pencil on paper, 8¾ × 5¾ in. (22.2 × 14.6 cm). Francis M. Naumann, New York

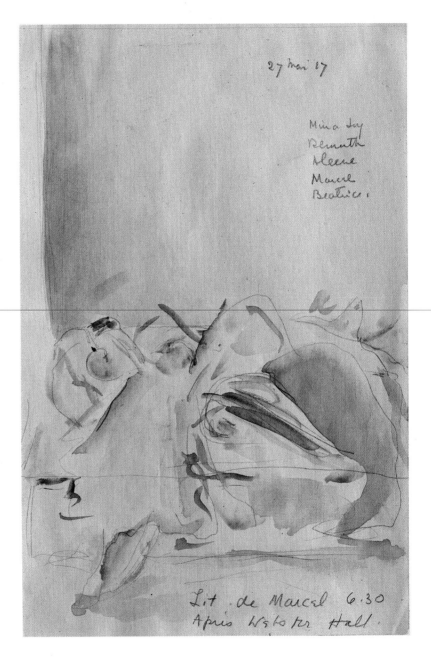

1913-1914

"In that year of 1913, barriers went down and people reached each other."

MABEL DODGE

VILLAGE I:
NEW BOHEMIA ON
WASHINGTON SQUARE

The boundaries of Greenwich Village are not easily drawn. In fact, the anarchist Hippolyte Havel once declared that since it was a state of mind, "it has no boundaries."[1] Politically known as the Ninth Ward and commonly called the American Ward, the Village officially runs from Fourteenth Street south to Vandam, from Fifth Avenue west to the Hudson River. Washington Square is generally considered the geographical and spiritual heart of the Village. Surveying the nine acres of the square's "established repose" in the midst of the "shrill city," Henry James saw in it "the look of having something of a social history."[2] Some Villagers preferred to view their community as a brave new world beyond the reach of history, social or otherwise, but it inevitably responded to outside forces.

The process began before the revolutionary war, when Indians were displaced by Dutch farmers, who were in turn displaced by English aristocrats, who named their hamlet Green Wich. Its population surged between 1818 and 1823, when a yellow-fever epidemic drove New York City residents northward to escape the contagion of the congested city streets at the foot of Manhattan. In the period that followed, Georgian mansions were built around the potter's field and hanging ground that became Washington Square. The Village escaped the post–Civil War industrial boom largely because the erratic zigzag of its streets—based on Indian trails and cowpaths—proved less conducive to industrial enterprise than the efficient grid imposed on the rest of Manhattan. As the wealthy followed industry farther north, the Village remained a residential enclave within the bustling city. Except for the still-posh north side of Washington Square, it became a neighborhood in decline, with plenty of spaces large enough for studios and with rent and food costs low enough to attract plebeian artists and writers. Italian immigrants colonized the region south of Washington

Bohemia, bordered on the North by hope, work and gaiety, on the South by necessity and courage, on the West and East by slander and the hospital.

Henry Murger, 1849

A new Bohemia . . . is a spiritual geography. It is bounded on the North by the Feminist Movement, on the East by the Old World Bohemia . . . on the South by the Artistic Temperament and on the West by the I.W.W. [Industrial Workers of the World].

Hutchins Hapgood, c. 1913

Square, moving up the dozen blocks from Mulberry Street to Bleecker Street. Irish immigrants settled in the West Village, and a small black community formed on Gay Street. Although the area was still called the American Ward, eighty percent of its residents were immigrants or first-generation citizens. The stage was set for the New Bohemia.

Now over fifty years old and left in disrepair, the once-fashionable homes of the Knickerbocker aristocracy were divided into small, cheaply rented rooms. The upper class's stables and liveries—which lost their original function as automobiles replaced horses—were transformed into artists' studios. As a popular slogan put it: "Stables into studios, liveries into libraries."[3] Established artists renovated stables on Washington Mews and MacDougal Alley; younger artists found cheaper studios on side streets such as Waverly Place, Minetta Lane, Gay Street, Christopher Street, Carmine Street, Patchin Place, and Milligan Place. Cooperative clubs where painters and writers rented studios—the Tile Club, Club A, and the Benedick—also emerged in the early years of the twentieth century, offering America's closest counterpart to the genteel version of bohemia called "European style."[4] The artistic cliques that developed within each club were independent and mutually indifferent, reinforcing the fragmented state of the Village bohemia.

The disparate community that made up the New Bohemia—the Real Villagers, as one historian has called them—constituted less than a tenth of the Village population.[5] They included social workers, settlement-house workers, teachers, artists, and writers. Around 1910 new residents followed the first influx of these bohemians into the area, stemming the Village's economic decline. Composed mostly of young businessmen and childless couples who favored a more bourgeois

---

The Archaeology of Greenwich Village

1. Sapponcanican. *A Native American village.*
2. Bossen Bouwerie. *A seventeenth-century Dutch farm settlement.*
3. Green Wich. *A pre-Revolutionary English hamlet.*
4. Greenwich. *A post-Revolutionary rural suburb.*
5. The Washington Square period (1825–50). *Georgian mansions are built around the potter's field and site for public hangings that became Washington Square.*
6. The American Ward period (1850–90). *Industry passes the Village by, and it remains a residential enclave.*
7. The "Real" Village (1890–1910). *Working-class Italians inhabit the Village.*
8. The Bohemian period (1910–20). *Artists, writers, social workers, and single women dominate the Village.*

BUSINESSES

1. The Benedick, 80 Washington Square East (1879–c. 1925). An aristocratic residence with suites for bachelor gentlemen.

2. Claire Marie Press, 3 East 14th Street (1913–14). Run by poet Donald Evans and best known for publishing Gertrude Stein's *Tender Buttons.*

3. Club A, 3 5th Avenue (founded early 1900s). A genteel bohemian cooperative lodging for writers, including William Dean Howells, Jack London, Upton Sinclair, Mark Twain, and Mary Heaton Vorse.

4. Golden Swan (popularly known as the Hell Hole), West 4th Street and 6th Avenue (through 1910s). This seedy Irish bar was the hangout of Dorothy Day, Charles Demuth, Hippolyte Havel, and Eugene O'Neill, and later provided the raw material for O'Neill's *Iceman Cometh.*

5. Gonfarones, 179 MacDougal Street. Beginning in the early 1900s, it was "a resort of scribes, artists, cranks and lovers." (Albert Parry, *Garrets and Pretenders*, p. 258.)

6. Hotel Brevoort, 5th Avenue and 8th Street (through 1910s). Its restaurant provided the meeting ground for the moneyed and the bohemian.

7. Hotel Lafayette, University Place and 9th Street (through 1910s). Another hotel with French atmosphere, often compared to the Brevoort.

8. "House of Genius," 61 Washington Square South (through 1910s). Mme Catherine Branchard transformed this 1840s home into a boardinghouse favored by creative types, including Stephen Crane, Floyd Dell, Theodore Dreiser, O. Henry, Harry Kemp, Frank Norris, Eugene O'Neill, Adelina Patti, and John Sloan.

9. Liberal Club, 137 MacDougal Street (1913–18). "A Meeting Place for Those Interested in New Ideas." Polly's, run by the doyenne of Village restaurateurs, Polly Holladay, was in the basement (1913–15).

10. *Masses*, 91 Greenwich Avenue (June 1913–December 1917). Editorial offices for the magazine that, according to Floyd Dell, stood for "fun, truth, beauty, realism, freedom, peace, feminism, revolution."

11. Mother Bertolotti's, 85 West 3d Street (c. 1910–c. 1917). A family restaurant offering fifteen-cent meals of spaghetti and red wine.

12. O'Connor's Saloon (aka the Working Girls Home), 1 Christopher Street (through 1910s). A rough saloon "favored by the lesser lights."

13. Pen and Brush Club, 16 East 10th Street (c. 1890–c. 1945). An arts organization headed by Ida Tarbell.

14. Washington Square Bookshop, 135 MacDougal Street (1913–14). Run by Albert and Charles Boni, it became an informal lending library and site of Liberal Club plays. Also was the residence of B.J.O. and Margaret Nordfeldt (from 1914).

15. Washington Square Gallery, 47 Washington Square South (1914–16). Run by Robert Coady, editor of *Soil*, it showed "primitive" sculpture and art by European modernists.

16. Webster Hall, 119 East 11th Street (through 1910s). Site of many Village balls, such as the Pagan Routs, Anarchist Ball, Blindman's Ball.

RESIDENCES

17. Willa Cather, 82 Washington Place (1909–13).

18. Willa Cather, 5 Bank Street (1913–27).

19. George Cram Cook, 42 Bank Street (1913); Henrietta Rodman (from c. 1912).

20. Floyd Dell, 45 Washington Square South (1913).

21. Mabel Dodge, 23 5th Avenue (1912–17).

22. Theodore Dreiser, 165 West 10th Street, #7 (1914–19); Kirah Markham lived with him part of the time.

23. Max Eastman and Ida Rauh, 27 West 11th Street (1912).

24. Max Eastman and Ida Rauh, 118 Waverly Place (1914–c. 1915).

25. Bobby Edwards (the Village troubadour), 46 Washington Square South (through 1910s).

26. William Glackens, 29 Washington Square West (1913–19).

27. William Glackens (studio), 3 Washington Square North (through 1910s); John Sloan's studio (through 1910s).

28. Harry Kemp, 10 Van Nest Place (from 1912); Sinclair Lewis (from 1912).

29. Ernest Lawson, 64 Washington Square South (through 1910s).

30. Ernest Lawson (studio), 23 Mac-Dougal Alley (c. 1912–c. 1915).

31. Everett Shinn, 112 Waverly Place (c. 1910–c. 1915).

32. John Sloan, 35 6th Avenue (from 1913).

33. John Reed, 42 Washington Square South (1912–15); Lincoln Steffens (1912–13).

34. Gertrude Vanderbilt Whitney (studio), 19 MacDougal Alley (from 1907).

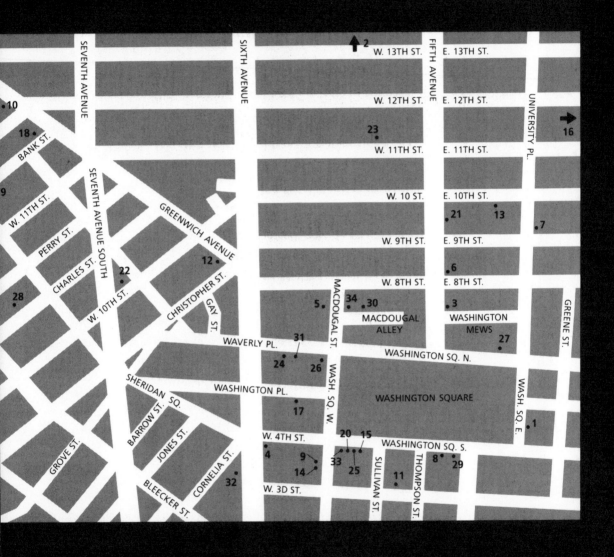

Washington Square, c. 1900. Etching. Museum of the City of New York

style, this group was drawn to the Village's redbrick houses and quaint mews. "And so today," observed one Village spokesman in 1916, "we find the aristocracy of money living in close quarters with the aristocracy of mind."[6] Many of the latter lived on the south side of Washington Square, which was known as Genius Row. For thirty dollars a month the more prosperous could rent an entire floor in an old house, consisting of two high-ceilinged public rooms with deep windows and fireplaces, a hall bedroom, a kitchen with a gas range, and a bathroom. For as little as eight dollars a month the more penurious could rent a bedroom in a similar house that had been divided into tiny warrens. The residents of the most illustrious of these artsy boardinghouses— Madame Catherine Branchard's "House of Genius" at 61 Washington Square South—included the writers Willa Cather, Stephen Crane, Theodore Dreiser, O. Henry, Lincoln Steffens, and Frank Norris; the opera diva Adelina Patti; and later Floyd Dell and Eugene O'Neill. One roomer, the poet Orrick Johns, described his quarters as containing no more than a cot, a kitchen table and chair, a coal grate, and a chipped plaster cast of the Venus de Milo. John Reed established his bohemian version of the Harvard Club several doors away, at 42 Washington Square South, and then immortalized his life there in "The Day in Bohemia." Between the House of Genius and 42 Washington Square South stood a row of brightly painted Italian restaurants, where a fifteen-cent lunch included minestrone, bread, wine, and tip.

Visitors to the south side of the square encountered a new dress code. Village men wore flannel shirts with soft rolled collars (newly known as "sport shirts") or tweedy coats complemented by a black bow tie or a black stock. Artistic types such as John Sloan might wear an orange tie with a green shirt, or what Floyd Dell called "the Windsor tie of artistic freedom," or even use a necktie as a belt.[7] Hair was worn long and kept meticulously clean. Women rejected corseted wasp waists and constricting hobble skirts in favor of smocks or loose-fitting suits in vivid colors that ran the spectrum from bilious yellow-green to bright magenta. Batik was especially popular, and sandals were ubiquitous. Women styled their hair to simulate a wild bird's nest or Irene Castle's bob, often topped by a felt hat or a "pancake style" in Hindoo blue. Women said "damn" in public, smoked cigarettes in amber holders, ordered alcoholic drinks in Village cafés.

The blurring of sartorial and behavioral boundaries was best expressed in a little magazine of the period: "But how charming, after all, when men grow dainty and women daring! . . . It is no longer a question of, are you a *Man* or, are you a *Woman?*—the answer is, I am an *Individual.*"[8] Such individuality was expressed in apartments as well. The artists William and Marguerite Zorach, for example, lived in an apartment dominated by lushly colored murals and furniture painted intense hues—lemon yellow, purple, cobalt, vermilion. The disquieting effect, one visitor noted, "was appropriate to the sensational mood of the times."[9]

Behind a border of trees on the north side of Washington Square stood a succession of redbrick Georgian mansions known as the "Old Row." The polished silver nameplates on their mahogany doors identified New York's patrician families: Rhinelander, Lydig, Van Rensselaer (as Villager Djuna Barnes described them, "all those whose names rustle like silk petticoats . . ."[10]) The northeast corner of the square had recently housed such cultural aristocrats as William Dean Howells, William James, and Edith Wharton. Moving up Fifth Avenue, one came to the Hotel Brevoort —situated, as its stationery announced, at the "Coin de la 5me Avenue et de la 8me Rue." It was a stately black brick building dating to 1835, with winding staircases and elegant rooms. Housed in its cellar was a tavern that boasted such authentically Gallic

---

Way down South in Greenwich Village
There they wear no fancy frillage,
For the ladies of the square
All wear smocks and bob their hair.
There they do not think it shocking
To wear stencils for a stocking,
That saves the laundry bills
In Washington Square.

Bobby Edwards and others,
The Village Epic (sung,
accompanied by ukulele), 1910s

Susan Glaspell in a Village apartment

We were supposed to be a sort of "special" group—radical, wild. Bohemians, we have even been called. But it seems to me we were a particularly simple people, who sought to arrange life for the thing we wanted to do, needing each other as a protection against complexities, yet living as we did because of an instinct for the old, old things, to have a garden, and neighbors, to keep up the fire and let the cat in at night.

Susan Glaspell

accoutrements—bootblacks in black-and-red-striped waistcoats and absinthe behind the bar—that a visitor might imagine having stepped from Fifth Avenue right into the Latin Quarter. In these convivial rooms the north side of the square met the south side, usually gathering after ten o'clock. One Village novel of the period divided the world into "two sorts of people . . . those that at one time or another one might expect to meet in the cellar of the Brevoort and those one would not." [11] The upper classes went to the Brevoort cellar when they were feeling bohemian; artists and writers went there to celebrate the sale of an article or a painting.

Next to the Brevoort lived Mabel Dodge, in a five-story brick house at the corner of Fifth Avenue and Ninth Street. Looking north along Fifth Avenue, she saw the townhouses and Beaux-Arts mansions of the Four Hundred; looking south, she saw Stanford White's arch looming over Washington Square. Beginning in 1913 her four generously proportioned rooms at 23 Fifth Avenue became the discussion center that linked Village bohemia and fashionable New York society.

When Dodge moved to New York at the end of 1912, she described herself as "Ariadne with the tide low." [12] Whenever her tide was out, Dodge would begin her familiar three-stage campaign. First she created a theatrical environment, then she filled it with people, and finally, she found a man to serve as its center. Her inexorable drive prompted the editor Max Eastman to observe, "Many famous salons have been established by women of wit or beauty; Mabel's was the only one ever established by pure will power." [13]

"I have always known how to make rooms that had power in them," Dodge said. "Whatever the need at any time I have been able to make for myself a refuge from the world, so I know that even if I had nothing I could somehow create an *ambiente* to creep into." [14] Her New York rooms were a far cry from the formality of the Villa Curonia. Since this was the New World, Dodge decreed that whiteness would reign—as if she could obliterate the past by creating a tabula rasa. The woodwork was painted white, white paper covered the walls, white linen curtains hung from the cornices, and a white bearskin rug lay before the white marble fireplace. As Dodge put it, "It seemed to me I couldn't get enough white into that apartment." [15] Only a few reminders of the Villa Curonia could be seen, most notably the chandelier that hung in the main parlor, bedecked with life-size canaries and bluebirds perched among garlands of porcelain roses.

Momentarily satisfied, Dodge lounged in her pristine cocoon, garbed as a Renaissance courtesan. But soon the gnawing sense of emptiness returned, and she proceeded to the next phase: filling her rooms. "*People!*" Dodge later exclaimed. "Never, for fifty years, have I left off pursuing, fusing, speculating, identifying, grouping, devouring

Interior of 23 Fifth Avenue

You attract, stimulate, and soothe people, and men like to sit with you and talk to themselves. You make them think more fluently, and they feel enhanced.

Lincoln Steffens to
Mabel Dodge, 1913

and rejecting!" [16] The writer Lincoln Steffens suggested, "Why not organize all this accidental, unplanned activity around you. . . . Have Evenings! . . . You might even revive General Conversation!" [17] In another place and time Steffens's suggestion might have inspired parties dimly remembered only by their participants. In the Greenwich Village of 1913 his proposal resulted in a cultural phenomenon: the scattered fragments of the New Bohemia coalesced at Mabel Dodge's Evenings. Steffens considered it "the only successful salon I have ever seen in America." [18]

In a circle of violet ink at the top of Dodge's thick white stationery appeared Walt Whitman's dictum: "Do I contradict myself? Very well, then, I contradict myself." Those words encapsulate Dodge's style as hostess. Dressed in Renaissance costume or a shell pink décolleté gown, she reigned from a great armchair near the hearth. Rarely moving and rarely speaking, she managed the Evenings without appearing to manage them. The only sign of agitation was her finely arched foot as it nervously beat the air through every discussion. As Hutchins Hapgood described her, "There was no mental form to her surging and changing

Mabel Dodge, c. 1915. Photograph by Gertrude Käsebier

I am the mirror wherein man sees man,
Whenever he looks deep into my eyes
And looks for me alone, he there descries
The human plan.

Mabel Dodge, July 1914

inner existence." [19] Dodge lacked emotional stability, intellectual brilliance, incisive wit, and beauty, but her silent smile and intelligent eyes—what Carl Van Vechten called her "perfect mask"—encouraged whoever was talking at the moment. Her sibylline expression inspired the speaker to feel, as one of them put it, as if he had suddenly been made fluent in a foreign language. Some attributed her effect to her "high vibration," and others felt "a magnetic field in which people become polarized and pulled in and made to behave very queerly." [20] Marsden Hartley wrote to Alfred Stieglitz, "Like yourself, [Mabel Dodge is] a real creator of creators." [21]

Two key men introduced Dodge to *tout le monde:* Carl Van Vechten and Hutchins Hapgood. Since both were journalists, they easily gained entrance into diverse New York circles—both high and low, political and cultural.

Carl Van Vechten first appeared at 23 Fifth Avenue in early 1913, suffering from a bad cold but eager to interview Dodge about Gertrude Stein's "Portrait of Mabel Dodge at the Villa Curonia." Scrutinizing Van Vechten, Dodge judged him a "young soul" in need of molding, and after a whiskey and soda, they began the stylish conversation that would continue daily for the next several months. [22] She called him the first to "animate" her "lifeless rooms"; he concluded at the end of his life that she "had more effect on my life than anybody I ever met. . . ." [23] Though just one year older than Van Vechten, Dodge played the role of worldly Auntie Mame to his Iowa native, and he rewarded her by eagerly absorbing her instruction. Van Vechten observed: "She had some bad qualities and the worst one was what made her great. She adored to change people. I loved what she did for me and accepted her guidance with pleasure." [24] Sexuality posed no threat to this friendship; though he married twice, Van Vechten was sexually attracted primarily to men, and his dandified behavior aroused amusement rather than passion in Dodge. In the absence of erotic tension, these two could be pals; she quickly became Mike to his Carlo. [25]

Each morning before dressing they would telephone one another to plan their day. Van Vechten would arrive at 11 A.M., "ruddy and washed-clean like a well-groomed hog," to escort Dodge around Manhattan in her long, flowing dresses, a hat with drooping feathers and

She is a dynamo [with] a face that could express anything and nothing more easily than any I have ever seen before. It is a perfect mask.

Carl Van Vechten
on Mabel Dodge

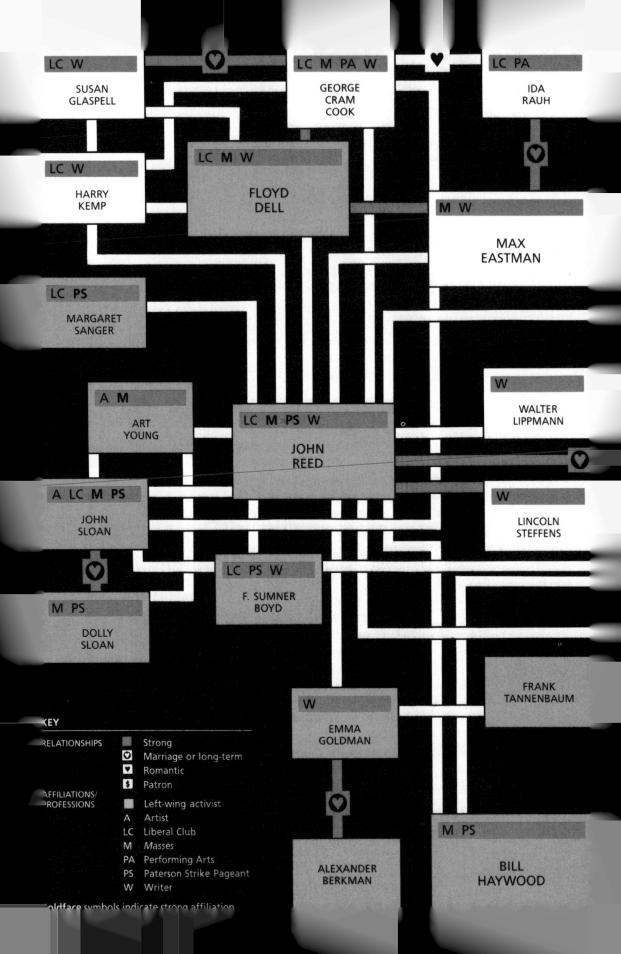

SUSAN GLASPELL — LC W

GEORGE CRAM COOK — LC M PA W

IDA RAUH — LC PA

HARRY KEMP — LC W

FLOYD DELL — LC M W

MAX EASTMAN — M W

MARGARET SANGER — LC PS

ART YOUNG — A M

JOHN REED — LC M PS W

WALTER LIPPMANN — W

JOHN SLOAN — A LC M PS

LINCOLN STEFFENS — W

F. SUMNER BOYD — LC PS W

DOLLY SLOAN — M PS

FRANK TANNENBAUM

EMMA GOLDMAN — W

ALEXANDER BERKMAN

BILL HAYWOOD — M PS

KEY

RELATIONSHIPS
- ■ Strong
- ♥ Marriage or long-term
- ♥ Romantic
- $ Patron

AFFILIATIONS/
PROFESSIONS
- ■ Left-wing activist
- A Artist
- LC Liberal Club
- M *Masses*
- PA Performing Arts
- PS Paterson Strike Pageant
- W Writer

Boldface symbols indicate strong affiliation

THE NEW BOHEMIA

LC
POLLY HOLLADAY

LC M
HIPPOLYTE HAVEL

LOUIS HOLLADAY

W
LOUISE NORTON

W
ALLEN NORTON

LC PA PS
ROBERT EDMOND JONES

W
CARL VAN VECHTEN

W
DONALD EVANS

LC PS W
MABEL DODGE

A
MAURICE STERNE

W
A. A. BRILL

LC W
HUTCHINS HAPGOOD

LC W
NEITH BOYCE

A
FRANCIS PICABIA

A
ALFRED STIEGLITZ

PA
ISADORA DUNCAN

A W
MARSDEN HARTLEY

A
ANDREW DASBURG

Florine Stettheimer (1871–1944). *Portrait of Carl Van Vechten,* 1922. Oil on canvas, 30⅜ × 26⅛ in. (77.1 × 66.2 cm). Yale Collection of American Literature, The Beinecke Rare Book and Manuscript Library, Yale University, New Haven, Connecticut

veils, and a fur with a flower pinned to it.[26] A masterly introducer, Van Vechten incorporated Dodge into his teeming social life. Through his "Monday Interviews" in the *New York Times,* he gained entrée to the most glittering scenes in the world of dance, music, and theater. He introduced Dodge to the popular playwright Avery Hopwood and the music critic Pitts Sanborn, as well as the actresses Helen Westley and Fania Marinoff (the young Russian who would become Van Vechten's second wife). He injected a note of frivolity into the Evenings, bringing Broadway soubrettes and Harlem dancers, purveying gossip about Mary Garden and Léon Bakst. He also brought along the poets Donald Evans and Allen Norton (his associates at the *Times*) and Louise Norton, who formed the Patagonians, a now-forgotten coterie of poets who were the Village's chief exemplars of a fin-de-siècle manner.

"It was *you* who really started it there," Dodge wrote to Hutchins Hapgood years later. "You were the initiation."[27] From his first appearance at 23 Fifth Avenue—when he announced, "I am in revolt, I consider it my first duty to undermine subtly the foundations of the

Let me make the simple statement . . . that I merely defend and exalt what is generally condemned; that I do this irrespective of the merits of the case, and simply in order to defend the extremely small minority, just because it is the minority, irrespective of whether the minority is right or wrong; that I attack the powerful and prevailing thing, in art, industry, in all fields, just because it is prevailing, irrespective of the merits of the case; that my formula is a simple and false one which I apply and reapply with mechanical and monotonous precision.

Hutchins Hapgood

Dodge's life mask of Hapgood

community"—this columnist for the *New York Globe* was ideally suited to be Dodge's "general introducer" to New York.[28] The well-matched confidants were both incapable of dispassionate thought and spoke the same vocabulary of mystical ecstasy; to communicate the grandness of the cosmos one only had to say "It" to the other to be *understood*.

Always eager to share his friends, Hapgood introduced Dodge to worlds that ranged from the grittiness of Lower East Side saloons to the spirituality of 291. No Village figure embraced modern ideals more passionately than Hapgood. "[Henri] Bergson, Post-Impressionism, the I.W.W., anarchism, the radical woman movement, the thrill of the socially and politically new," Hapgood wrote during the Armory Show's run, "these things make up the sum and substance of my existence."[29] His position as a prolific journalist—he produced three signed columns a week—gave Hapgood enormous social mobility. The Harvard graduate (Class of 1892) was drawn to the denizens of Lower East Side bars, for he perceived "an instinctive feeling of sympathy between the aristocrat and the tough."[30] He listened to them intently and wrote sympathetic feuilletons about the proletarian life of thieves, prostitutes, and bums. He offered Dodge a glimpse of this seamy world, observed from the backseat of her chauffeur-driven limousine.

Hapgood called himself a "philosophical anarchist," a fashionable political stance that allowed him to espouse radical ideals while conducting a conventional life at the Harvard Club and at his home in suburban Dobbs Ferry. Max Eastman considered the "philosophical anarchist" label a symptom of "an irresponsible distaste for politics," but this equivocal position permitted alliances all along the political spectrum, and others who subscribed to it included Robert Henri, John Sloan, Lincoln Steffens, and even Eugene O'Neill. When Hapgood took Dodge to the *Masses* offices at 91 Greenwich Avenue, she met Eastman, the radical magazine's editor, and his colleagues.[31] Hapgood also introduced Dodge to the anarchist Emma Goldman, her colleague Alexander Berkman, and her associates at *Mother Earth*. He presented

Life in New York is one long-protracted thrill. You must spend next winter here and be in fashion.

Mabel Dodge to
Gertrude Stein, 1913

her to Bill Haywood, the hulking one-eyed labor organizer for the Industrial Workers of the World (known as the I.W.W. or the Wobblies), and to F. Sumner Boyd, whose advocacy of I.W.W. activity in Paterson, New Jersey, led to his arrest.

An indispensable stop in Hapgood's tour of modern New York was 291, where he saw people becoming "more and more alive, more and more sensitive to reality." [32] There Dodge met not only Alfred Stieglitz but also Andrew Dasburg, Marsden Hartley, and the Picabias. They came to her Evenings but "they also resented her," Agnes Ernst Meyer recalled. "She played with life as if it were a game in which the stakes were not very high." [33]

Dodge came to view herself as a collector. "It was not dogs or glass I collected now, it was people. Important people." [34] The throng of her visitors pushed through the dark double doors, then ascended two flights of red carpeting, past a table piled high with copies of "Portrait of Mabel Dodge at the Villa Curonia," and into the white rooms. The diversity of these guests was evident in their clothing, which ranged from Liberty silks and diamonds to batik shirtwaists, from formal black greatcoats to flannel shirts with rolled collars. Dodge, gazing demurely from beneath her dark bangs, offered her hand and murmured a faint hello. Vittorio, her Florentine manservant, poured Pinch Scotch and circulated trays of Gorgonzola sandwiches and Virginia ham on Catagalli plates. Gold-tipped Curtis cigarettes were heaped in white bowls and—to the shock of the press—women as well as men lit up. At midnight Vittorio opened the dining-room doors to reveal a refectory table spread with ham and olives, cold salads and beef; a side table held siphon bottles, rye, lemonade, and kümmel in bottles shaped like Russian bears.

Dodge's Evenings were a combination of town meeting, bohemian Chautauqua, and cocktail party. What made them important was the fact that they served the needs of a community that was just beginning to identify itself; before the avant-garde had organized institutions, it had Dodge's white rooms. Crowded into that space were people of all classes and political persuasions: "Socialists, Trade-Unionists, Anarchists, Suffragists, Poets, Lawyers, Murderers, Newspapermen, Artists, Clubwomen, Woman's-place-is-in-the-home Women, Clergymen, and just plain men." [35] In Van Vechten's words, it was "a strange salad." [36]

A guest might see Judge Learned Hand conversing in a corner with the birth-control advocate Margaret Sanger. Or goateed Lincoln Steffens talking with one of the recent Harvard graduates—such as Walter Lippmann or Lee Simonson—who described themselves with the new term "intellectual." Alfred Stieglitz might be sermonizing to the socialist Mary Heaton Vorse or to a Broadway ingenue who accompanied Carl Van Vechten. The new argot studded their conversations, and guests learned to speak of "released personality," "direct action," "paganism," "psyching," and "Freudism." Modern paintings by Arthur B. Davies, Marsden Hartley, Max Weber, and Andrew Dasburg began to appear on the white walls.[37] Attending Mabel Dodge's Evenings, one became modern by osmosis.

At the heart of the Evenings was General Conversation, a nineteenth-century social format adapted to the needs of the twentieth. The old rules were followed—the leader would orchestrate a single General Conversation within the room—but that conversation was no longer conducted with a coterie of tea-sipping ladies, but with several dozen modern artists, suffragettes, anarchists, and Ivy Leaguers who filled every available chair and patch of floor. Each Evening had a leader, and the leadership changed with each Evening. The conversation began with the leader's brief exposition on a set topic—often suggested and sometimes led by Hapgood, Lippmann, Steffens, or Van Vechten—followed by discussion among the guests for about two hours. To describe the relationship between the leaders and the others, Dodge invoked the Sermon on the Mount. "'And He spoke as one having authority, and not as the scribes.' That's just what I mean," she told a newspaper reporter, "the talker with authority, who seems to let forth a stream of creative psychic vitality when he speaks."[38] A more down-to-earth description of the leaders came from a reporter who observed: "They didn't read speeches, mind you. They hadn't 'got it up' beforehand; often they came not knowing what was to be talked of. . . . He (or she) spoke 'from the heart,' and the others—writers, thinkers, artists, travelers, philosophers, politicians, and mere ordinary people—spoke in discussion, laid before the rest their views and experience and hammered the matter out."[39]

The Evenings' topics provide an index to the concerns of the era. Margaret Sanger spoke on birth control, and John Reed recounted his adventures with Pancho Villa in Mexico. Frank Tannenbaum discussed the unemployed, and a slightly intoxicated Hutchins Hapgood led an Evening on Sex Antagonism.[40] Walter Lippmann moderated the Psychoanalysis Evening in early 1914, when the gnomelike Dr. A. A. Brill spoke on Freud's theory of the unconscious—often cited as the first group discussion of psychoanalysis in the Village.[41] The artists of the *Masses* challenged Will Bradley, art editor of *Metropolitan*, to print their drawings in his swanky magazine. At the Evening for New Poetry, the poets who read ranged from the eminent Edward Arlington Robinson to the experimenter George Sylvester Viereck—whose recitation was so raucous that Amy Lowell rose from the audience and moved out, Dodge recalled, "like a well-freighted frigate."[42]

The first Evening was unlike those that followed, for the dozen guests participated only as a passive audience for two black performers imported from Harlem by Carl Van Vechten. A woman in high-button boots and white stockings danced a jig while her male partner sang a

Beauty for the eye, satire for the mind, depravity for the senses! Of such is the new kingdom of art. Amen.

Dame Rogue
[Louise Norton], 1915

popular song and strummed a banjo. Van Vechten rocked and shrieked and clapped his hands, but Dodge considered it an embarrassing mixture of lewd lyrics, flashy leers, and suggestive skirt hiking. This paganism run riot was a far cry from her debut in Florence, but she consoled herself with the thought "One must just let life express itself in whatever form it will."[43]

The Evening led by Emma Goldman, Bill Haywood, and William English Walling—representing (respectively) anarchy, the I.W.W., and socialism—had a frisson of danger, for the trio risked imprisonment for inciting direct action against oppressors. Dodge hand picked the audience—what she called "the Live and Let Live kind of people"—and closed the front door against intruders.[44] Despite the inflammatory material and the charismatic speakers, there were no fireworks that evening. Bill Haywood reclined on a yellow chaise longue and looked, in Dodge's words, like "a large, soft, overripe Buddha with one eye, and the smile of an Eminent Man."[45] Despite Walter Lippmann's strenuous attempts to inject coherence into the proceedings, Haywood remained maddeningly inarticulate and Goldman sounded like a hectoring schoolteacher. Walling smiled complacently at socialism's apparent victory by default. In the middle of the discussion, the anarchist Hippolyte Havel shouted, "They talk like goddam bourgeois."[46]

The critic Malcolm Cowley and the historian Christopher Lasch have both summarized the Greenwich Village ethos in lists that neatly capture its confusion of political power and art, its attempt to create social and psychological revolution by political action, its embrace of life as a visceral experiment, and its identification with children, pagans, mystics, and outcasts. Mabel Dodge's Evenings became the first public expression of that diffuse doctrine, and she told one reporter that her gatherings would replace the press as the disseminator of a new gospel: "The time of the voice is at hand."[47]

Was the revolution discussed in Dodge's white rooms merely a metaphor for personal liberation? Could the interbreeding of artists, intellectuals, and anarchists survive outside the hothouse atmosphere of the Evenings? In the spring of 1913—when the Village cultural radicals joined the striking silk workers of Paterson, New Jersey—those questions were not simply academic. The two groups built an extraordinary alliance that one historian called "the fragile bridge."[48]

Late one evening in early May, Hutchins Hapgood, Mabel Dodge, and John Reed gathered in a Greenwich Village apartment to hear Bill Haywood tell the story of the Paterson strike. Local 502 had struck Paterson's silk companies in February 1913. Twenty-five thousand workers had closed down three hundred mills, demanding an eight-hour workday and an increase in their poverty-level wages.[49] The Industrial Workers of the World had dispatched their most charismatic leaders—Bill Haywood, Elizabeth Gurley Flynn, and her lover Carlo Tresca—and

Paterson silk strike, Paterson, New Jersey, 1913

TOP
Parade coming up Commercial Street

CENTER
Militia clearing the streets

BOTTOM
Funeral procession

*The I.W.W. is socialism
with its working
clothes on.*

Bill Haywood

their presence in Paterson attracted widespread interest. Just the year before, the I.W.W. had successfully organized the wool workers of Lawrence, Massachusetts; their militant demands had been met and local membership swelled from two hundred to fourteen thousand. Paterson was widely seen as a test of both the I.W.W.'s future and the possibility of nationwide revolution. By that evening in May, the strike had become deadlocked—funds were depleted, and hundreds of children had been temporarily resettled with foster "strike mothers" in New York. Newspapers helped the factory owners fight the I.W.W. by blacking out news about the strike, denying them the coverage that had been critical to their Lawrence success and essential for attracting wider labor support.

Exhausted, Haywood recounted in monotone the events the newspapers had ignored. He described the police brutality, the murder of a worker named Valentino Modestino, the arrests of strike leaders, and the restriction of free speech. "God! I wish I could show [the public] a picture of the funeral of Modestino, who was shot by a cop," Haywood said. "Every one of the silk mill hands followed his coffin to the grave and dropped a red flower on it. . . . The grave looked like a mound of blood."[50] Dodge, cloaked in crimson silk, shyly offered a suggestion. "Why don't you bring the strike to New York and *show* it to the workers? . . . Why don't you hire a great hall and re-enact the strike over here? Show the whole thing: the closed mills, the gunmen, the murder of the strikers, the funeral." Emboldened by her own vision, she proposed Madison Square Garden as the stage. Hutchins Hapgood caught Dodge's amorous glance at John Reed as Reed rose from his seat and exclaimed: "I'll *do* it! . . . We'll make a Pageant of the Strike! The first in the World!"[51]

Reed arrived in Paterson two days later at 6 A.M. Before the morning was over, he had been arrested on trumped-up charges and thrown into the Passaic County Jail. Among the forty men that shared his dank corridor, Reed witnessed a "cocaine-fiend," men with open syphilitic sores, faces bruised by billy clubs—as well as silk workers who sang I.W.W. songs and seemed unbowed by their inhuman treatment. "If you saw the strikers in here," he enthusiastically wrote to a Harvard classmate, "you would realize it is a *great strike.*"[52] His arrest proved to be a boon to the strikers, for it was widely covered in the New York papers—during four days in jail Reed garnered more attention than Haywood had during his several Paterson imprisonments. (After Reed's stint the Passaic County Court marshal tried to ban writers from the courtroom.) Reed's vermin-infested jail cell, shared with Carlo Tresca and Haywood, was the catalyst for his radicalism. His four days there inspired not only ideas for the Paterson Pageant but also "The War in Paterson," a *Masses* article that indicated Reed had found both his subject (radical politics) and his perspective (closeup).

Poster for the Paterson
Strike Pageant, 1913,
by Robert Edmond Jones

I. W. W.

THE PAGEANT OF THE PATERSON STRIKE

PERFORMED BY THE STRIKERS THEMSELVES.

MADISON SQUARE GARDEN

SATURDAY JUNE 7, 8:30 P.M.

BOXES $20 & $10: SEATS $2, 1.50, 1, 50¢, 25¢, & 10¢.

The Vocabulary of New Bohemia

THE ARTS

Cubism   A catch-all term for any form of avant-garde, nonacademic painting, used interchangeably with *modern art, futurism,* and even *Post-Impressionism. Cubist* and *futurist* were sometimes applied to literature and music, just as art was sometimes called *ragtime.*

Poets of revolt   A generic term for the new poets of the 1910s, also known as *free-versers* and *vers librists.* Their common tie was *free verse,* which replaced fixed stanzas, rhyme, and predetermined metrical patterns with *absolute rhythm.* In 1912 Pound wrote, "I believe in an 'absolute rhythm,' that is, in poetry which corresponds exactly to the emotion to be expressed." (In David Perkins, *A History of Modern Poetry,* p. 311.) Free verse had historical precedents dating back to *Beowulf* but not until the 1910s did the majority of important poets work in that mode.

The term *free verse* was associated with such disparate groups as the *tramp poets* or *hobohemians* (Vachel Lindsay, Harry Kemp), the *Patagonians* (Donald Evans, Allen and Louise Norton), the *Imagistes/Imagists* (H.D., Richard Aldington, Amy Lowell, Ezra Pound), and the *Otherists* (Mina Loy, William Carlos Williams, Alfred Kreymborg). Sinclair Lewis quipped that free verse was "so called because it doesn't pay." ("Hobohemia," *Saturday Evening Post,* April 7, 1917.)

POLITICS

Anarchism   Although anarchists composed only a small splinter group on the left, the belief that formal government should be abolished generated much passionate talk, both pro and con, during the early 1910s, especially at the uptown Ferrer Center. Alexander Berkman, Emma Goldman, Hippolyte Havel, and Polly Holladay called themselves anarchists. The term *philosophical anarchist* referred to those who believed in the tenets of anarchy but refused to engage in violent or illegal activities to bring them about. Clarence Darrow, Hutchins Hapgood, and Lincoln Steffens called themselves philosophical anarchists. Max Eastman castigated them as *sentimental rebels,* anarchists with "an irresponsible distaste for politics" (*The Enjoyment of Living,* p. 424), and others called them *souse anarchists* or *spit-in-the-fire growlers,* because they acknowledged the problems of society but did not take action to change them.

Direct action   Revolutionary rather than reform tactics—e.g., walking out or sabotaging a factory instead of negotiating to achieve labor demands—were labeled *direct action.* It was advocated by Wobblies, anarchists, and syndicalists, who cited the Boston Tea Party as an example of American direct action. A highly divisive issue among leftists, direct action was often presented as the opposite of *political action.*

Socialism   The Marxist doctrine eliminating private trusts and corporations had unusually broad support in the United States during the 1910s. The socialist candidate, Eugene V. Debs, won an unprecedented number of votes in the 1912 presidential election, and the party's Branch One in New York City attracted many prominent members. George Cram Cook, Floyd Dell, Max Eastman, John Reed, John Sloan, Margaret Sanger, and Art Young all called themselves socialists.

Syndicalists   An offshoot of the socialists, these militant trade unionists believed that socialism could be achieved only by engaging in industrial actions such as general strikes. A highly visible proponent of syndicalism was the *Industrial Workers of the World,* also called the *I.W.W.,* whose supporters were called *Wobblies.*

SOCIAL AND SEXUAL RELATIONS

Birth control   Coined in 1915 by Margaret Sanger, the term was a progressive alternative to *family limitation,* which had emphasized the reproductive function within a conventional marriage. Both terms were considered radical by the U.S. Post Office.

Bohemia   The term *bohemian* became popular after Henry Murger's newspaper sketches of life on the Left Bank were dramatized in 1849 as *La Vie bohème* and played to packed houses at the Variety Theater in Paris. As early as 1860 New York had its own Queen of Bohemia, Ada Clare, who observed, "The bohemian is not, like the creatures of society, a victim of rules and customs; he steps over them with an easy, graceful joyous unconsciousness, guided by the principles of good taste." (In Allen Churchill, *The Improper Bohemians,* p. 25.) The *New York Sun* of December 5, 1915, defined *bohemia* as "a place where everyone minds his own business. . . . free from lowbrows, barbers and scented soap." The *Burmingham Age Herald* of May 27, 1917, defined a bohemian as "one who wears his night shirt in the day time . . . who is listening to a Beethoven symphony when he should be paying his gasbill." By this time bohemia had become widely associated with Greenwich Village, and bohemians were sometimes called *Washington Square-ites.* The *new bohemia* was distinguished from the traditional one by its embrace of leftist politics, feminism, and modern aesthetics.

Feminism   Although the feminist movement encompassed supporters of women's right to vote, called *suffragists,* feminists attempted to improve women's position in all aspects of life, not just politics. They were sometimes called *Heterodites*—after the women who joined Heterodoxy, a women's club in the Village—or more popularly the *New Woman.* The prototypical New Woman supported everything from practical clothes and birth control to progressive education and sexual parity with men. H. L. Mencken used the term *flapper* to describe the New Woman in 1915, although the term didn't become popular until the 1920s. The New

Woman's opposite was dubbed the *parasite woman,* because she was dependent on men.

Free love   According to this doctrine, sexual relationships (or *free unions*) should not be restricted to married couples but enjoyed by any mutually consenting partners no matter what their marital state. Free love advocates distinguished their activity from promiscuity, describing the sexual impulse as a form of spiritual enhancement. Hutchins Hapgood lauded it as "the *higher sex companionship* that every conscious soul desires, and that is one of the few connecting links of the human with the divine." ("Cristine," p. 98.) Randolph Bourne called it *human sex,* "which is simply a generic name for those whose masculine brutalities and egotisms and feminine prettiness and stupidities have been purged away so that there is left stuff for a genuine comradeship and healthy frank regard and understanding." (Bourne to Prudence Winterrowd, April 28, 1913.) One version of free love popularized by the anarchists was *varietism,* in which couples engaged in sexual and emotional relationships with others as a way of overcoming jealousy and increasing mental hygiene. Lovers were called *soul mates,* and the word *mistress* was abandoned because it implied male ownership. By 1916 *affinity* had been overused to describe a couple's relationship and was replaced by *psychic harmony.*

Homosexuality   "Fairyland's not far from Washington Square," a line in a popular Village ballad, suggests that *fairy* was a popular term for homosexuals in the 1910s. They were also called the *intermediate sexes* or *Uranians.*

Intellectual   This was a new noun in America in the early twentieth century, imported by William James from Paris, where the Dreyfusards had been attacked as intellectuals by their enemies. "As it was used in the teens," observed the cultural historian Henry May, "the word *intellectual* associated one with Europe, and particularly with the young heroes of novels from Stendahl to Joyce: the young man from the provinces who had come to the capitals in search of experience and a role in the movement of their time." (*The End of American Innocence,* p. 281.) Walter Lippmann, Randolph Bourne, and Max Eastman were considered intellectuals.

Mysticism   The rejection of a materialist, rationalist approach to the world inspired a varied vocabulary. "*Vibrations* are the key to everything," the humorist Don Marquis wrote in 1916. "Atoms used to be, but atoms have quite gone out." (*Hermione and Her Little Group of Serious Thinkers,* p. 8.) Mabel Dodge and Hutchins

Hapgood invoked *It*, while others talked about *intuition, psychic vibrations*, Henri Bergson's term *élan vital*, and the *cosmic urge*.

Paganism   Denoting a rejection of Christian tradition and a revival of ancient Greek culture, *paganism* was used to describe everything from Isadora Duncan's dancing to the Villagers' pursuit of hedonism, as in their *Pagan Routs* (or variations such as the "Bal Primitif").

Psycho-analysis   This term and *Freudism* were widely, if imprecisely, used to describe all psychological exploration. Some of the avant-garde entered analysis, and many more casually practiced *associating* (spontaneously responding to words in psychoanalytic fashion) and *psyching* (analyzing one's associates) as a popular parlor game. Floyd Dell wrote in the December 1915 *Vanity Fair*, "Psycho-analysis is the greatest discovery made by intellectual conversationalists since Bergson and the I.W.W." There was talk of the *Ego*, the *Alter Ego*, and *Subliminal Consciousness*, along with an emphasis on *expression of self* and *released personality*.

BUZZWORDS

Free   An indication of the avant-garde's rejection of past rules, it was applied to politics (*free speech*—the opposite of *Comstockery*, named after Anthony Comstock, the nation's censor), to sex (*free unions*), and to aesthetics (*free verse*).

Little   A declaration of intimacy and exclusivity, it appeared in the *Little Room* in Chicago, Alfred Stieglitz's *little rooms* (or 291) in New York, the little theater (applied both to Maurice Browne's company in Chicago and to the movement throughout the United States), *little magazines*, and Margaret Anderson's *Little Review*.

New   A declaration of modernity, it was especially popular with journalists, who wrote about the *New Art*, the *New Woman*, the *New Commonwealth*, the *New Drama*, the *New Poetry*, the *New Paganism*, even the *New Baby*. Magazines also used it in their titles (the *New Freewoman*, the *New Republic*).

Revolution   This was the most widely used metaphor for cultural and political upheaval. Both Stieglitz and Reed were called *revolutionists*, and the Village bohemians were sometimes called the *romantic revolutionaries*. The term was also applied to art and poetry: "The new poetry *is* revolutionary. It is the expression of a democracy of feeling rebelling against an aristocracy of form." (J. B. Kerfoot, *Others*, November 1915.)

On his return to New York, Reed convened a meeting at Margaret Sanger's uptown apartment and formed an executive committee, composed of himself, Dodge, Haywood, Sanger, the feminist lawyer Jessie Ashley, and the radical socialist F. Sumner Boyd. They would force the newspapers to disseminate the truth about the strike by reenacting it at the old Madison Square Garden (between Twenty-sixth and Twenty-seventh streets on Madison Avenue) on Saturday night, June 7. Reed would write the scenario and direct the pageant. His apolitical Harvard classmate, Robert Edmond Jones, would design the sets, and John Sloan would supervise the artists painting them.[53] Dodge assumed the role of revolutionary muse. She wrote that she aided Reed by "pouring all the power in the universe through myself to him."[54] During this period Hapgood witnessed another of Dodge's glances at Reed, "a look of concentrated passion that I had never seen equaled."[55] Thus began the grand affair of Greenwich Village—John Reed and Mabel Dodge—a romance both inevitable and impossible.

On May 19 Bill Haywood introduced the strikers to Reed, who asked for one thousand workers to enact the pageant. Only three hundred volunteered. Unfazed, Reed took off his coat, rolled up his sleeves, and launched into his first rehearsal—just as if he were cheerleading back at Harvard. His rudimentary scenario dramatized six significant moments in the strike, enlivened with songs from the I.W.W.'s little red songbook and "Harvard, Old Harvard" sung with seditious I.W.W. lyrics. Reed traveled to Paterson each day with his megaphone, rehearsing first in a union hall and later in a vacant lot. By June 2, five days before the performance, the cast of men, women, and children had swelled to five hundred, and gradually the Polish, Italian, and German accents melded into one voice.[56]

Meanwhile, at emergency midnight meetings in New York, the planning committee worried over how to raise the eight thousand dollars needed to stage the event. But there was no turning back; Madison Square Garden had already been rented. Dodge added a thousand dollars to contributions made by Jessie Ashley, Reed, Margaret Sanger, and Upton Sinclair, but it was sympathetic New York unionists who finally assured that the money could be raised.

On the morning of June 7, 1913, 1,147 Paterson strikers bought nineteen-cent tickets on a chartered train to the Lackawanna Ferry and sailed to Manhattan. Led by Sanger and an eighteen-year-old striker named Hannah Silverman, who had been dubbed "Joan of the Mills," they marched from the Christopher Street pier up Fifth Avenue, waving red I.W.W. banners. Hundreds of unionists from Brooklyn, Astoria, and the Bronx simultaneously began the trek to Manhattan. With his huge cast finally convened at 2 P.M., Reed led a last rehearsal and then collapsed in nervous exhaustion.

By the time Reed had revived, the Garden was filling up with both Villagers and workers, the former paying two dollars for expensive tickets and the latter paying a quarter, a dime, or nothing at all. At 9 P.M. the doors were closed, with fifteen thousand people crowded inside, the majority of them workers. Everywhere were touches of red—I.W.W. banners, red bow ties, red carnations, and the red cover of the fifteen thousand programs that F. Sumner Boyd had written and Robert Edmond Jones had designed. (The cover design served as the I.W.W. logo for many years.) Outside, lines stretched for blocks—and although those queued up were unable to see the pageant, their spirits were lifted by hundreds of red light bulbs spelling I.W.W. ten feet high on the tower of Madison Square Garden. This electric sign beneath Augustus Saint-Gaudens's sculpture of Diana was a beacon visible for blocks. Inside, the houselights dimmed and the pageant began.

Robert Edmond Jones's two-hundred-foot-long silk mill set, backlit so that it glowed, dominated the huge stage. The audience heard piercing factory whistles and the clang and grind of machinery. When the noise subsided, the workers onstage began their strike, rushing from the mills, dancing, and embracing one another. Descending from the stage and singing *La Marseillaise,* they marched up a wide central aisle through the audience. The players trooped up this passage many times during the performance—as police leading strikers to jail, as union singers following a twenty-six-piece band, and as mourners.

Scene from the Paterson Strike Pageant, "Picketing the Mills"

United by that wide aisle, the players and the audience became one, the workers and the Villagers sensed momentary solidarity, and the gap between reality and its theatrical equivalent was blurred.

After the first scene the audience was on its feet throughout the evening, singing union songs, cheering the strikers and booing the police, and weeping—sometimes hysterically—at the funeral of Modestino, which was evoked by a silent cortege of workers a thousand strong, each dropping a red carnation on the coffin that slowly was buried beneath a vast blood-red mound. In the final scene Haywood stood before the now-shuttered silk mills and detailed the I.W.W. demands for an eight-hour workday. As the thousand players turned to face him, Madison Square Garden was transformed into a vast I.W.W. union meeting that ended with a rendition of the *Internationale.* As the assembly sang the refrain—"'Tis the final conflict / Let each stand in his place / The Industrial Union / Shall be the human race"—the editor from the *Paterson Evening News* listened with the uneasy sensation that "the era of social revolution is approaching."[57] The applause, as one reporter put it, "was one chronic roar," and Dodge declared years later, "I have never felt such a high pulsing vibration in any gathering before or since."[58]

All of New York's newspapers reported the event, and since many of the writers were drama critics evaluating the heartfelt performance, the coverage was surprisingly sympathetic. Hutchins Hapgood declared, "This kind of thing makes us hope for a real democracy, where self-expression in industry and art among the masses may become a rich reality, spreading a human glow over the whole of humanity. . . ."[59] Even newspapers hostile to the I.W.W. printed accurate articles that resoundingly satisfied the organizers' intentions to make the Paterson strike known to New York.

The pageant was a lively offspring of the marriage between political radicalism and cultural radicalism. Although working-class solidarity inspired the pageant, it depended on avant-garde theatricality for its effect. The event resembled neither labor propaganda nor the civic-minded pageants that were popular in that era—but it incorporated elements from each, rescuing the pageant form from musty historicism and propaganda from one-note stridency. Robert Edmond Jones's looming mills reflected Edward Gordon Craig's revolutionary stage designs, and the mechanical cacophony that opened the evening sounded like Futurism's "art of noise."[60] The evening prompted Randolph Bourne to observe, "Crude and rather terrifying, it stamped into one's mind the idea that new social art was in the American world, something genuinely and excitingly new."[61]

Members of the Village community made pilgrimages to Paterson, including Max Eastman, Mabel Dodge (who witnessed such police brutality that she declared, "I felt like shooting the policeman"[62]), Hutchins

Hapgood, the tramp-poet Harry Kemp, Walter Lippmann, Upton Sinclair, Lincoln Steffens, William English Walling, and the feminists Inez Haynes Gillmore and Henrietta Rodman. They wrote numerous articles that dispatched news of the strike to an audience beyond the strikers and union sympathizers. The pageant inspired other Villagers to pursue their own vocations. George Cram Cook and Susan Glaspell, for example, were so deeply moved by the event that they stayed up late into the night imagining what America's new theater could become. As if predicting his own future with the Provincetown Players, Cook had written a few days earlier, "It is possible that this pageant with a purpose may fail suggestively—that the impulse it generates may later be refined by greater artistic skill." [63]

The "terrible unity between all these people" felt by Mabel Dodge on the night of June 7 demonstrated the possibility of collaboration between workers, artists, and intellectuals.[64] That possibility did not survive. One note of strain was clearly voiced a few days after the pageant, when Harry Kemp exhorted Bill Haywood to speak more stirringly. "Hell, Harry," Haywood responded, "I'm not running this strike as a show for Greenwich Village." [65] What Christopher Lasch later called the cultural radicals' "'confusion' of power and art" proved disastrous to the I.W.W. Because so many workers had been admitted free, the pageant's expenses exceeded its intake by two thousand dollars, and the deficit prompted a breakdown in the fragile coalition. Soon newspapers followed their positive reports of the event with false reports of financial impropriety that discredited its organizers. A barrage of criticism came from within the labor ranks as former allies of the I.W.W. attacked from both left and right. The criticism of the conservative American Federation of Labor (A.F.L.) had been expected, but when the socialist newspaper the *Call* declared that the strike was not a revolution, and when Emma Goldman accused the strikers of lacking the "revolutionary spirit of active resistance to tyranny," the I.W.W. considered the remarks a bullet in the back.[66]

As the deadlocked strike dragged on throughout the hot summer of 1913, the workers grew demoralized and the radical political community splintered. At the end of July, Local 502 ended the five-month strike. The outcome was grim: two thousand workers were blacklisted and twenty-five hundred others left the city, fifteen hundred were arrested and five were killed, lost wages were estimated at $5.5 million, and worst of all, not one of the workers' demands had been won. Paterson would never again prosper as a textile center, and the I.W.W. would never again be a powerful force in American labor organizing.

The pageant's architects—Reed, Dodge, and Jones—knew nothing of this. In mid-June, Reed went to Paterson for the last time, where one of the strikers said to him, "We been lonesome for to sing—you come tomorrow?" [67] But when tomorrow arrived, Reed was writing to his mother, "I am not a Socialist any more than I am an Episcopalian. I now know that my business is to interpret and live life wherever it may be found. . . ." [68] Within a few days he was sailing with Dodge and Jones on the luxury liner *Amerika,* headed for Europe and the Villa Curonia.

Looking around him at the *Amerika's* glassed-in decks and the "many nasty, rich people with jewels softer than their faces and dogs scarcely less intelligent than they," Reed felt twinges of guilt but concluded that these days at sea with Dodge offered "a new, glamorous sensation." [69] During the feverish weeks before the pageant, their passion had been sublimated into politics, and while crossing the Atlantic, Dodge continued to resist Reed's advances. At midnight on the third night at sea, he delivered a poem to her entitled "The New Age Begins." Proclaiming that in the new age their love would replace God, Reed closed, "But the speech of your body to my body will not be denied!" Still Dodge resisted. "Oh, Reed, darling," she admonished, "we are just at the Threshold and nothing is ever as wonderful as the Threshold of things, don't you *know* that?" [70] By the time they had crossed it, they were ensconced in the Villa Curonia. Carl Van Vechten joined them there, and in the middle of one night Muriel Draper, dressed in ivory and gold, arrived at the villa with her husband and her new lover, the pianist Artur Rubinstein. Soon Mina Loy was there too, and Reed reported to his mother that he was witnessing "a real picture of ultra-modern ultra-civilized society." [71]

Life at the Villa Curonia—dominated by outrageous couture, high cuisine, classical music, and complicated couplings—was far removed from life in Paterson. Robert Edmond Jones spent hours dressing Muriel Draper in increasingly outré fashions, murmuring to his bizarrely beautiful mannequin, "Everything about you is *more* so." [72] Twenty-seven-year-old Artur Rubinstein spent his days practicing music with Muriel's husband, Paul, and his free time strategizing ways of being alone with Muriel. Left out of these couplings, Van Vechten sulked until he established a tie with Loy, encouraging her to write and offering to act as her New York agent. Reed fled the villa to swim in ancient Roman cisterns, continually rhapsodizing about Italy, "It's so *old!*" Feeling abandoned, Dodge descended into daily depression. But every night on the bed with golden lions at each corner, Dodge "recovered him, reconquered him, triumphing over the day's loss." [73]

This Florentine interlude soon ended. The Drapers returned to London to conduct their fashionable music salon at Edith Grove, Robert Edmond Jones traveled to Germany to study with Max Rheinhardt, Carl Van Vechten returned to Fania Marinoff. Mabel Dodge and John Reed sailed back to New York that fall and set up conjugal lodgings at 23 Fifth Avenue—providing grist for the Village gossip mill.

On Chicago's Fifty-seventh Street that summer, the spartan gin-in-a-sherbet-glass style of living furnished a stark contrast to the high

Please come down here soon. The house is full of pianists, painters, pederasts, prostitutes, and peasants. . . . Great material.

Mabel Dodge
to Gertrude Stein,
summer 1913

Muriel Draper with Paul
Draper and Artur Rubenstein
(at right), c. 1913

bohemia of the Villa Curonia. But it offered an equally complicated
roundelay of romantic attachments. After leaving Mollie Cook and
before marrying Susan Glaspell during the spring of 1913, George
Cram Cook had had affairs with the poet Eunice Tietjens and the photographer Marjorie Jones. Sherwood Anderson developed romantic
feelings for Floyd Dell's wife, Margery Currey, while twenty-five-year-
old Dell—who was beginning to feel like an elder in the modern community—pursued several affairs. He had liaisons both with Mollie Cook
(a Davenport vacation so exciting that it made him confront the sexual
disappointment in his marriage) and with Marjorie Jones (who later
lived with him for two years). "My lost youth," Dell wrote, "shone to
me never so appealingly as out of the eyes of girl poets." [74]

Dell's views about free love and marriage were widely known from
the pages of the *Friday Literary Review;* libertarianism, *élan vital,* leftist
politics, feminism, psychology, and modernity were all invoked in his
promotion of new relations between the sexes. (Members of the Fifty-
seventh Street community read between the lines to find in Dell's sexual politics a perfect rationale for his own open marriage.) But none of
Dell's newspaper columns provided any answers to his current dilemma;
he was obsessed with the Little Theater actress Kirah Markham but
seemed to be losing her to Theodore Dreiser, who was middle-aged,
unattractive, and charmless. Although Dell had indulged in many affairs, it was his infatuation with Markham that ended his marriage. He
and Currey parted in April 1913, and their separation followed what
had become almost a blueprint for modern relations between the
sexes. They rented separate residences at Fifty-seventh Street, with that
of the painter B.J.O. Nordfeldt between them. The back doors of their
houses abutted, they ate breakfast together, and they attended the
Little Theater and the Chicago Symphony together. Despite this façade
of amity, their relationship was crumbling; Currey soon accused Dell of

using their marriage as an "air cushion" for his affairs and suggested divorce. "There seems no other way but to drag it up by the roots," she wrote to him. "I'd rather do that than let it do the poetic *trash* flowers are accustomed to, such as withering slowly, becoming distorted, breaking, being choked by weeds, etc., etc."[75]

Floyd Dell left Chicago that October of 1913. He later claimed that his departure resulted from political disagreements at the *Friday Literary Review,* but he was also motivated by the end of his marriage and by Kirah Markham's presence in New York with Theodore Dreiser. As he made his way toward New York in the upper berth of the Empire State Express, he carried with him the manuscript of Sherwood Anderson's first novel and made plans to write his own bildungsroman. He composed a long, reflective letter to the rabbi who had married him and Currey. Calling himself "a rather different person than came to Chicago five years ago," Dell pledged that he would no longer "hurt anybody's feelings to prove the most beautiful theory ever invented."[76]

Currey continued to organize social gatherings on Fifty-seventh Street and pulled new figures such as Ben Hecht and Maxwell Bodenheim into the orbit of the Chicago Renaissance. But Dell's departure marked the beginning of the exodus to New York and the end of the period Sherwood Anderson called "a Robin's Egg Renaissance." Looking back on this era many years later, Anderson wrote, "It had perhaps a pale blue tinge. It fell out of the nest. It may be that we should all have stayed in Chicago."[77]

"We are revolutionaries without a revolution," Dell wrote to a Davenport friend in early 1914.[78] His comment neatly described the new bohemians of Greenwich Village, who revolutionized modern life without affecting the balance of political power. The ideas they popularized—free love, Freudian psychology, kindergarten, woman suffrage, expressive yet functional clothing, and liberated personal style—subsequently entered the mainstream of twentieth-century civilization.

Hutchins Hapgood dubbed Floyd Dell "the spokesman of the Village," and he enacted the role perfectly—not because he was its most formidable intellect or theoretician, but because he was sensitive to its slightest tremors.[79] As Hapgood observed, Dell's "mainspring seems always to be the instinct to conform," and Dell's close friend Max Eastman detected in his support of new ideas no "stability of opinion."[80] Poised between the village and the Village, between the nineteenth-century farm and the machine-age city, between poetry and politics, Dell espoused everything modern but freely confessed that "about nine-tenths of the new art, in painting, sculpture and poetry, seems to me to have no aesthetic value at all."[81] He was an outspoken feminist, but often called women "girls" and sank into the most Victorian sentimentality in his own romances. He wore flannel shirts but silk underwear. He considered himself a poet, but he is remembered as a social crusader. He organized and named the first of the Village balls, "The Pagan Rout," but was himself too shy to dance. Always he was in the thick of the action.

On his very first night in the Village, a beautiful bohemian dancer took Dell home and introduced him to her pet alligator. A few days later, an "incredibly naïve, preposterously reckless" schoolteacher named Henrietta Rodman asked Dell to write a housewarming play for the new Liberal Club, which called itself "A Meeting Place for Those Interested in New Ideas." "Why," she asked, "shouldn't intelligent people to-day have the same chance to know each other that the church and the tavern gave their grandparents?"[82] This chance encounter began a chain of events that linked Dell to the Liberal Club and later to the Provincetown Players.

Dell's *St. George in Greenwich Village,* which opened in November 1913, set the tone for the new Liberal Club. Presenting the Village through the eyes of a newcomer, Dell's play satirized modern ideas and was sprinkled with topical references to anarchism, Futurism, suf-

John Sloan (1871–1951). *Floyd Dell,* 1914. Oil and tempera on canvas, 24 × 20 in. (61 × 50.8 cm). Hood Museum of Art, Dartmouth College, Hanover, New Hampshire; Gift of John Sloan Dickey, Class of 1929

fragism, and Montessori schools. It was produced on a shoestring, with no costumes, no curtain, no stage, no lights. Sherwood Anderson, Helen Westley, and other cast members improvised new lines when they forgot the ones Dell had written. This was the first of Dell's plays, and Hapgood observed that they all dramatized the same idea: since marriage is doomed to failure and love inevitably wanes, only a succession of affairs could sustain the spirit. "Where these productions fell short of dramatic art," Dell observed, "they did succeed in being gay communal ritual."[83] The Liberal Club company, informally known as Dell's Players, boasted a few talented actresses—notably Kirah Markham, Ida Rauh (Eastman's wife), and Helen Westley. The plays, performed in the spirit of strictest amateurism, sowed the seeds of the Provincetown Players, the Washington Square Players, and later the Theatre Guild.

Often called the Village's first organized social center, the Liberal Club occupied the ground floor of a redbrick house at 137 MacDougal Street. Whereas 23 Fifth Avenue linked the Village to fashionable society, this building on the southwest corner diagonally across Washington Square was the cornerstone of bohemia. In the basement, Polly's restaurant became the favorite eating establishment for Village residents, and its yellow calcimined walls were sometimes appropriated for the Liberal Club's rotating art exhibitions. The Washington Square Bookshop next door, at 135 MacDougal, became the local literary center. Since customers were more likely to stand and read books than to

Polly's restaurant

WHEN LIFE IS VERY STRENUOUS AND SPIRITS ARE WAY DOWN
YOU'D BETTER GO TO POLLYS IN LITTLE GREENWICH TOWN
FOR THERE THE CLANS ARE GATHERED - ITS THERE YOU'LL FIND 'EM ALL
THE ARTISTS AND THE WRITERS RANGED ALONG THE WALL
MISS POLLY TAKES THE MONEY AND MIKE SAYS HE JUST CAN'T
WAIT ANY FASTER ON THE FOLKS IN POLLY'S RES TAU-RANT
J.T.B.
GREENWICH VILLAGE _ NEW YORK
JESSIE TARBOX BEALS
24

buy them, the owners, Albert and Charles Boni, began to feel that they were unintentionally operating the Village library.

The Liberal Club's two high-ceilinged parlor rooms were sparsely furnished with scattered wooden chairs and a few tables; the rooms' chief attractions were an upright electric pianola and a deep fireplace. These inviting rooms began to fill with Villagers each afternoon and did not empty out until early morning.[84] Members and their friends organized marches on Wall Street, practiced what Henrietta Rodman called "creative gossip" (as well as the old-fashioned kind), looked at exhibitions of "futurist" paintings on the club's walls, met with the feminist Heterodoxy Club, or joined the long-running poker game in the front room. When plays were produced, the mahogany doors to the Bonis' bookstore were opened to form a fourteen-foot-high proscenium. On Friday nights people paid a quarter for wine and danced such daringly modern dances as the turkey trot and the tango to the player piano. Intellectual ideas and trendy fashions received equal attention in the weekly lectures and symposia. One could hear about Freud, the tango, eugenics, Richard Strauss, "the intermediate sex" (homosexuals), white slavery, nudism, Technocracy, the slit skirt, sex hygiene, and the single tax.[85]

H. L. Mencken wrote to Dreiser that the Liberal Club "consists of all the tin pot revolutionaries and sophomoric advanced thinkers in New York."[86] A more neutral survey of its roster reveals slightly more men than women, mostly in their late twenties or early thirties, white, Protestant, Anglo-Saxon, and midwestern in origin. Two-thirds of the members lived within a five-minute walk of the club. Among them were such writers as Sherwood Anderson, George Cram Cook, Theodore Dreiser, Hutchins Hapgood, Alfred Kreymborg, Sinclair Lewis, Edna St. Vincent Millay, Eugene O'Neill, and Upton Sinclair; such arists as Charles Demuth and Marsden Hartley; and such *Masses* associates as Max Eastman, Floyd Dell, John Reed, Art Young, and Albert Boni.

Around mealtimes the club members spilled into Polly's restaurant downstairs and sat at brightly colored trestle tables that encouraged intimacy through proximity. Villagers lingered over thirty-five-cent extravaganzas of Hungarian goulash, liver and onions, and vegetable soup; alcohol had to be brought in from the outside. Hapgood described the restaurant as "a magnet for the expressively 'maladjusted' or 'unadjusted.'"[87] Presiding over it were the manager, Paula Holladay—known as Polly—and her lover, chef, and waiter, Hippolyte Havel.

Big-boned, dark-eyed, midwestern Polly seemed shyly maternal; Dell called her "the madonna of these truants and orphans."[88] Beneath her staid exterior, however, she was an avowed anarchist who suspected that the goings-on upstairs were all too organized. Short and rotund, forty-five-year-old Havel sported a bristly goatee and mustache, "hair flying in a self-created wind," and thick spectacles that

Her shoulders are square, her legs are long, her hips as vertical as a boy's are, with eyes that look neither to the right hand nor to the left hand, up the temptacious avenue she walks, bearing the banner with the strange device, Votes for Women!

Dame Rogue
[Louise Norton], 1915

magnified his large eyes.[89] A former lover of Emma Goldman, he had conceived the café years earlier as a place for people to eat and relax in an atmosphere sympathetic to cultural revolution, and he had raised start-up money from supportive artists, intellectuals, and revolutionists. He was the only born-in-Bohemia bohemian in the Village. The others only talked revolution, but Havel's political agitation had landed him in half a dozen European jails; Hapgood described him as "a revolte by temper and profession."[90] Although Havel's volcanic eruptions terrified some of Polly's customers on first meeting, he soon came to be regarded as a lovable Village mascot, a caricature of a bomb-throwing anarchist who played his role with relish, muttering "Bourgeois pigs!" as he shoved the diners' plates in front of them. "Without Hippolyte, the Village might have existed," Floyd Dell observed, "but it would not have been what it was."[91]

The Liberal Club played host to a variety of modern couples, and new ones were formed on its dance floor. The prototypical New Woman at the club supported suffragism, progressive education, birth control, and economic and sexual parity with men. As Hutchins Hapgood observed, "They had nothing to lose but their chains."[92] The prototypical New Man championed the feminist demands and encouraged his brethren to reject the masculine failings of competition, materialism, and militarism. The New Man and the New Woman practiced Human Sex (so named because it served the needs of both partners) and joined in nonbinding "free unions," which allowed for separate names, separate identities, and relationships outside marriage. Although the American public regarded the new relations between the sexes as base animality, the Villagers considered themselves aspirants to a more spiritual love. The following four couples exemplified the attempts to balance jealousies and power struggles with utopian ideals.

After returning from Florence in fall 1913, Mabel Dodge and John Reed lived together openly at 23 Fifth Avenue. Reed was the only one of her serious lovers that Dodge did not marry, and their relationship made her feel powerless, especially since Reed preferred traipsing around the streets of New York or following Pancho Villa in Mexico to languishing in her boudoir. Dodge attempted to redress the balance of power by making her Evenings larger and her name more prominent (her stylish presence at the trial of Frank Tannenbaum, champion of the unemployed, assured her space in the newspapers). She imagined that her celebrity would be an aphrodisiac for Reed, but it simply stimulated him to greater exploits of his own. Though Dodge resorted to increasingly hysterical pleas for constancy, Reed could no more be faithful to her than he could be to a single political movement. "To him the sexual gesture has no importance, but infringing on his right to act freely has the first importance," Dodge wrote to Neith Boyce. "Are we to 'make' men do things? Are men to change? Is monogamy better than polygamy?"[93]

In the fall of 1913 Dodge retrieved Reed from one of his trips by overdosing on Veronal. Finally Reed wrote: "Goodby, my darling. I cannot live with you. You smother me. You crush me. You want to kill my spirit."[94] That was merely the first farewell, however. Their dance of seduction and rejection continued for almost two more years. Reed attempted to marry another woman, then proffered Dodge a gold band, which she rejected. Only after finding him emotionally devastated and powerless did she agree to wear it, but she declared, "He never reached the core of me again as he once had."[95] To the Village, Dodge and Reed were symbols of the modern age, but the dynamics of their relationship resembled nothing so much as Victorian melodrama.

Hutchins Hapgood and Neith Boyce preserved the ideal of free love within the outlines of conventional marriage, complete with four children and a suburban home. Hapgood encouraged varietism (the anarchist belief that multiple sexual relationships strengthened a marriage) but cautioned Boyce, "Only don't fall in love with another and don't enjoy him more than you do me!"[96] Boyce reluctantly followed her husband's dictum and once wrote to Dodge, "Both Hutch and I feel that we are free to love other people, but that nothing can break or even touch the deep vital passionate bond between *us* that exists now as it always has."[97] They were a complementary pair—he was agitated and impetuous, she was self-contained and "moved like a slow river."[98] Hapgood complained to Dodge that "I do not seem able to find her, the soul of her," but he never stopped trying, and Boyce became another of his "mad unbridled quests for the absolute."[99] Believing that

---

Way down South in Greenwich Village,
*   Where the spinsters come for thrillage,*
Where they speak of "soul relations,"
*   With the sordid Slavic nations,*
'Neath the guise of feminism
*   Dodging social ostracism,*
They get away with much
*   In Washington Square*

Way down South in Greenwich Village,
*   Where the brains amount to nillage,*
Where the girls are unconventional
*   And the men are unintentional,*
There the girls are self-supporting,
*   There the ladies do the courting*
The ladies buy the "eats,"
*   In Washington Square.*

Bobby Edwards and others,
The Village Epic (sung,
accompanied by ukulele), 1910s

All women tell on their lovers. It is the way of showing their devotion to their husbands.

Dame Rogue
[Louise Norton], 1915

When you have got a woman in a box, and you pay rent on the box, her relationship to you insensibly changes.

Floyd Dell, 1914

sexual relationships with other women were acts of comradeship and that true lovers "must pass on restlessly from one woman to another," Hapgood pursued many extramarital affairs.[100] But he was able to feel emotional intensity only with his wife—and thus he considered himself a failure in his efforts to keep up with the modern world.[101] It was Boyce, who would have preferred mutual fidelity, who did find emotional fulfillment in another man, and this prompted her husband's charges of "spiritual infidelity." In 1914 he described their marriage in detail, convinced that his ruminations had yielded universal conclusions about human relationships. Hapgood circulated a typescript of "The Story of a Lover" among his friends, and at the suggestion of Theodore Dreiser he published it anonymously in 1919 (its sales suffered when the New York vice squad seized it for obscenity). At the end of his life Hapgood looked back on this intimate description of the new relations as "the very best thing I have written." [102] In 1916 he and Boyce dramatized their relationship into the play *Enemies* and played themselves in a modest production in Provincetown. "I've never been able to be essentially unfaithful, more's the pity," said the Hapgood character. "I cannot comprehend this wild swooning desire to wallow in unbridled unity," said the Boyce character.[103] And so they continued to wage marital conflict, warring with the responsibilities of freedom, periodically reaching an armed truce. The death of their oldest son in the influenza epidemic of 1918 changed their relationship completely: Boyce began to experience mystical visions, Hapgood buried himself in the Bible, and for the rest of their lives they practiced conventional marital fidelity.

Floyd Dell spoke for the New Man when he wrote, "Feminism is going to make it possible for the first time for men to be free." [104] Dell's writing mixed feminist philosophy with Freudian injunctions against sexual repression and such masculine truisms as "sweethearts are more fun than wives." (Affairs were one of the revivifying activities offered by the Village's atmosphere of "a moral health resort." [105]) He shared an apartment with Marjorie Jones—his photographer-lover from Chicago's Fifty-seventh Street community—and boldly posted both their surnames on the mailbox. They "lived on the square like a true married pair," wrote Dell, yet they "were going to behave *better* than any husband and wife!" [106] The rules of their free union decreed that outside affairs were acceptable, that Jones supported herself, and that they couldn't afford to have children. Dell's liaisons were carried on so publicly that Villager Dorothy Day commented that his "love encounters should really take place on the stage of the Hippodrome before a packed house." [107] In late 1916 Dell decided that he and Jones had "become too good friends to be lovers anymore," but their separation was like a strange divorce that deeply bewildered him.[108] His affairs were not nearly so satisfying without the foundation of his domestic partnership.

Polly Holladay and Hippolyte Havel's modern relationship overlapped with psychopathology; both spent years in mental hospitals.[109] Although Holladay followed the anarchist line on free love, Havel insisted on monogamy, often becoming insanely jealous about even nonexistent affairs. Holladay provided ample provocation by regularly and openly falling in love with her customers (who no doubt offered welcome relief from the turmoil in her relationship with Havel). Her family had prepared her for a certain amount of sexual unorthodoxy: her college-professor father had been murdered in a Saint Louis bordello, her mother was supported by a variety of lovers, and the most abiding of Polly's relationships was with her younger brother Louis, whom she had seduced as an adolescent.

Polly, hostess to Bohemia. *New York Sun,* December 5, 1915

Havel's jealousy repeatedly overpowered his anarchist beliefs, and during his frequent drunken bouts he would choke Holladay, attack her with a chair, or threaten to commit suicide. She responded to his hysteria with the placid complaint, "He promised me over and over again [to kill himself], but he just won't keep his word."[110] When she was healthy, she banished Havel from her presence, but when she was ill or in need, he nursed her tirelessly. "Like a fierce but devoted dog," Hapgood observed, "[he] vibrated in and out of Polly's graces."[111]

Hippolyte Havel by Ben Benn

Floyd Dell was walking down Greenwich Avenue one day in late December 1913—just two months after he'd moved to the Village—when Max Eastman summoned him inside Gallup's restaurant and offered him the managing editorship of the *Masses.* Dell accepted on the spot, with the single proviso that his twenty-five-dollar weekly salary was never to be more than a week overdue. "Life seemed extraordinarily simple and happy in Greenwich Village," he reflected; "one even got a job without asking for it!"[112]

Working for the *Masses* was more than a job, it was a vocation that positioned Dell at the vortex of Village activity. Just as the Liberal Club was the social center of the Village, so the *Masses* served as its moral and political conscience—or, as one radical wrote, "It is the recording secretary of the Revolution in the making."[113] The magazine's first issue appeared in January 1911, and it started out as a fairly orthodox muckraking socialist journal, distinguished primarily by its innovative illustrations by artists such as Glenn Coleman, John Sloan, and Art Young. When funds ran out in August 1912, several staff members refused to let the magazine die. Using a paintbrush, Sloan scrawled on a scrap of drawing paper a note to Max Eastman: "You are elected editor of *The Masses.* No pay."[114]

Their choice of a new editor ensured that the *Masses* would no longer adhere to socialist orthodoxy. At that time the twenty-nine-year-old Eastman was completing a dissertation under John Dewey at Columbia University, organizing and lecturing for the Men's League for Women's Suffrage, and writing *The Enjoyment of Poetry.* His chief

Max Eastman, 1916.
Photograph by Marjorie
Jones.

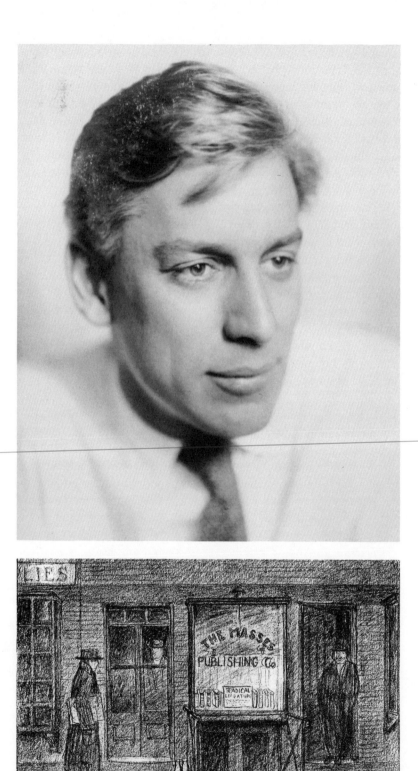

*Masses Office at 91
Greenwich Avenue* (detail).
Glenn Coleman, *Masses,*
June 1914

qualifications for heading the bankrupt cooperative magazine were charisma, intelligence, and the diplomacy needed to attract writers, artists, and backers and keep them working together. Entranced by the prospect of publishing a magazine—from first reading the manuscript to pasting it up—Eastman accepted the job, but with the thought that the magazine would soon be on its feet and could dispense with his services. ("One of the things I have learned from life," he later wrote, "is that magazines do not have feet."[115]) In his first issue of the *Masses*, which appeared in December 1912, Eastman declared,"Our appeal will be to the masses, both Socialist and non-Socialist, with entertainment, education, and the livelier kinds of propaganda."[116]

By the time he drafted Dell a year later, Eastman was exhausted from doing five jobs: editing the *Masses*, writing its editorials, directing the *Masses* company, raising money for the *Masses*, and earning his own living. He had enlisted the editorial help of John Reed and Harry Kemp. But he found that Reed's "too spirited help, somewhat like that of a wild colt eager to enjoy the harness, came near driving me out of the office for good."[117] And Kemp's tenure at the *Masses* ended after one day, terminated with a note that proclaimed, "I must live and die a poet."[118] Dell's arrival gave Eastman the relief he needed. These two constituted the only paid staff at the *Masses*, and their complementary talents kept it running for four years.

The laconic Eastman, Olympian and unruffled, avoided overt partisanship, and his reasonable manner provided a calm center for a tempestuous group of writers and artists. Equally important, he attracted patrons to fund the magazine. Dell described the money givers as "the skeleton in our proletarian revolutionary closet" and dubbed them the "Rebel Rich."[119] They included Mabel Dodge, Alva (Mrs. O.H.P.) Belmont (who was an ardent suffragist), Aline Barnsdall (a California heiress who was an admirer of the *Little Review* and a patron of Frank Lloyd Wright), Adolph Lewisohn (who also supported the Washington Square Players), and the publisher E. W. Scripps.

Dell brought to the magazine his years of experience on the *Friday Literary Review* and his ties to such Chicago writers as Sherwood Anderson, Vachel Lindsay, and Carl Sandburg. Dell's genial adaptability helped ground the highly charged atmosphere of the *Masses* editorial meetings, and his seasoned competence prompted Eastman to describe him as "the most perfect example of an associate editor that nature's evolution has produced."[120] That Eastman and Dell both valued poetry as much as politics encouraged the rich mix of literature, politics, and art that distinguished the *Masses*.

Around Eastman and Dell gathered writers that included such frequent contributors as John Reed, Margaret Sanger, Lincoln Steffens, Upton Sinclair, Louis Untermeyer, Mary Heaton Vorse, and William English Walling. The *Masses* artists were among the finest magazine illustrators in America. Many of them had been students of Robert

I believe that The Masses, *next to the masses of Organized Labor, the preamble of the I.W.W., the Panama Canal, Jess Willard and the Woolworth Tower is the biggest thing America has produced so far. It belongs to the realm of miracles as well as to the empire of portents.*

Arturo Giovannitti, 1916

*I am not so much inter-
ested in the man who
is paid to paint as I am
in the man who pays
to paint.*

John Sloan

Henri, including Maurice Becker, George Bellows, Glenn Coleman, Stuart Davis, Henry Glintenkamp, Robert Minor, Boardman Robinson, and Art Young. In his informal, unpaid role as the magazine's art editor, John Sloan skillfully led this cadre with confidence and an unwavering commitment to socialist principles. His technical expertise in magazine production enabled him to experiment with various ways to reproduce rough crayon drawings as well as line drawings, and the results made the magazine look as lively as any in America. The artists' loyalty to the magazine also reflected the fact that their "ashcan" realism had found no place in either the commercial or the academic branch of the art system. The *Masses*—with its two-color lithographed covers, its double-page spreads of illustrations, and its sophisticated reproduction techniques—served as an alternative exhibition space.

Working for little or no pay intensified the participants' commitment to the *Masses*. Dell and Eastman refused high-paying jobs in publishing, and the business manager, Berkeley Tobey, turned over much of his family inheritance to pay printing bills. "Strange thing was that if I got a good idea I gave it to *The Masses*," observed John Sloan. "If I got a second-rate one I might sell it to *Harper's*, but I could never have the same feeling when I was working for pay." [121] Without any motivation except belief in what the magazine stood for, the contributors gave it their best efforts; some, such as Reed, would never write more effectively than for the *Masses*.

Although the *Masses* was ostensibly a socialist magazine, the causes espoused on its pages were as catholic and freewheeling as those discussed at the Liberal Club or Mabel Dodge's Evenings. This unpredictable mixture was particularly evident in "the desultory and delightfully irresponsible *Masses* meetings." [122] About twenty men and women on the *Masses* editorial committee would meet each month in an artist's studio (most frequently Art Young's or John Sloan's) on Thursday nights, often joined by visitors such as Clarence Darrow, Theodore Dreiser, Bill Haywood, and Lincoln Steffens. Aspiring to socialist cooperative ideals, they conducted the meetings as a participatory democracy—everyone, including visitors, had an equal vote on the magazine's contents. Eastman and Dell read poems and articles aloud while the

EDITORIAL BOARD OF THE *MASSES*

WRITERS: F. Sumner Boyd, Robert Carlton Brown, Howard Brubaker, Arthur Bullard, Floyd Dell, Max Eastman, John Reed, Louis Untermeyer, Mary Heaton Vorse, William English Walling

ARTISTS: Cornelia Barns, Maurice Becker, George Bellows, K. R. Chamberlain, Glenn Coleman, Stuart Davis, Henry Glintenkamp, Alice Beach Winter, Charles A. Winter, John Sloan, Art Young

A FREE MAGAZINE

THIS MAGAZINE IS OWNED AND PUBLISHED CO-OPERATIVELY BY ITS EDITORS. IT HAS NO DIVIDENDS TO PAY, AND NOBODY IS TRYING TO MAKE MONEY OUT OF IT. A REVOLUTIONARY AND NOT A REFORM MAGAZINE; A MAGAZINE WITH A SENSE OF HUMOR AND NO RESPECT FOR THE RESPECTABLE; FRANK, ARROGANT, IMPERTINENT, SEARCHING FOR THE TRUE CAUSES; A MAGAZINE DIRECTED AGAINST RIGIDITY AND DOGMA WHEREVER IT IS FOUND; PRINTING WHAT IS TOO NAKED OR TRUE FOR A MONEY-MAKING PRESS; A MAGAZINE WHOSE FINAL POLICY IS TO DO AS IT PLEASES AND CONCILIATE NOBODY, NOT EVEN ITS READERS—THERE IS A FIELD FOR THIS PUBLICATION IN AMERICA.

HELP US TO FIND IT. SEND US YOUR NAME AND ADDRESS WITH ONE DOLLAR FOR AN ANNUAL SUBSCRIPTION. PASS US ALONG TO YOUR FRIENDS. TALK ABOUT US. PRAISE US. CRITICISE US. DAMN US PUBLICLY. WE MUST HAVE A LITTLE CONSIDERATION.

The AP and the Masses Editors. Art Young, *Masses,* April 1914

John Sloan (standing at table, wearing pince-nez), Art Young (seated, holding pen), Floyd Dell (seated, in profile), Max Eastman (standing, holding drawing), John Reed (seated at right end of table).

THE MASSES

Drawn by Arthur Young.

THE A. P. AND THE MASSES EDITORS.

Nature! Mountains! Scenery! What have they got to do with economic determinism!

Hippolyte Havel, after listening to a long poem at a *Masses* meeting

committee listened—although not necessarily all the way to the end. The unsparing critiques reflected Sloan's belief that "Since we have to speak well of the dead, let's knock them while they're alive." [123] (Not only alive, but often sitting in the same room.) Impatient listeners would call out "Chuck it!" or "Oh my God, Max, do we have to listen to this tripe?" [124] Some manuscripts set off hours of debate among the political factions in the room.

Once the articles were finally selected, unsigned cartoons were pinned to the wall and subjected to blunt critiques (John Sloan advised one artist, "There is only one thing left for you to do, pull off one of your socks and try with your feet." [125]) Finally, in the early hours of Friday morning, captions were submitted or composed on the spot, and everyone sat down to drink beer and smoke. Eastman felt like an "anxious parent" during these meetings, attempting to maintain amiable relations among the contributors while also ensuring that the magazine avoided the pitfalls of self-conscious Village bohemianism, art-for-art's-sake, and dogma of any sort. If the group's selections didn't add up to a full magazine, Eastman solicited articles on his own. He viewed the democratic editorial process with skepticism, balancing it with what Dell called the "practical dictatorship" of the two editors.[126]

Publishing a monthly magazine by consensus was quixotic. The potential for conflict was everywhere: members were vociferously partisan, and their politics were frequently at odds; debate among this highly verbal group could stretch on and on, conducted in the conflicting vocabularies of poetry, politics, and art. Uncompromising stances—John Sloan threatened to resign, for example, if a Stuart Davis drawing was voted down—made the process stormy. One of Hippolyte Havel's outbursts illuminates the inherent problems in the procedure. During one discussion he shouted: "Voting! Voting on poetry! Poetry is something from the soul. You can't vote on poetry!" When Dell replied that even *Mother Earth,* Emma Goldman's anarchist magazine, depended on such decision making, Havel replied: "Sure, sure. We anarchists make decisions. But we don't abide by them!"[127]

Yet the *Masses* appeared each month without fail, looking brighter and more audacious than any other magazine on the stands. The magazine epitomized the Village of the prewar years: it was a place where commitment to a group spirit could overcome internal dissension; where artists, poets, and political radicals could talk to one another; where culture and politics seemed to fuse; where inconsistency and contradiction were welcome. Floyd Dell's description of the *Masses* serves as a fitting epitaph for that first flowering of Village bohemia: "It stood for fun, truth, beauty, realism, freedom, peace, feminism, revolution."[128]

ART I:
EXPLOSION IN
THE ARMORY

On the evening of February 17, 1913, Lexington Avenue between Twenty-fifth and Twenty-sixth streets was lined with automobiles and horse-drawn carriages; a uniformed attendant summoned chauffeurs through a megaphone. Four thousand guests squeezed through the entrance into the Sixty-ninth Regiment Armory, an immense masonry pile customarily used to drill part-time soldiers in preparation for war. Tonight the fortress had been appropriated for a different sort of combat, for this was the opening of the *International Exhibition of Modern Art*—commonly known as the Armory Show.[1] Confronting some thirteen hundred works of art that ranged from Jean-Auguste-Dominique Ingres's mid-nineteenth-century drawings to Marcel Duchamp's 1912 *Nude Descending a Staircase,* this evening's stylish crowd was drilled in the revolutionary tactics of modernism.

The armory had been transformed into eighteen temporary rooms constructed of burlap-lined dividers and illuminated by jerry-rigged arc-lighting. Festive yellow streamers strung from the armory's glass ceiling created the effect of a circus tent pitched within a fortress. For the final touch Gertrude Vanderbilt Whitney had contributed a thousand dollars for white pine trees to flank the main entrance and for bunting of pine, laurel, and smilax to crown the burlap walls. Even the largess of a Whitney could barely touch the armory's vastness, but at least the air was filled with the fresh smell of the much-vaunted new spirit.

The guests had already heard a lot about the new spirit and modern art. In their eagerness to lure a large audience, the organizers of the Armory Show—the Association of American Painters and Sculptors—sought far more publicity than Stieglitz and his circle at 291 had ever tried to attract. At the urging of the lawyer and patron John Quinn—who informed the association that "New Yorkers are worse than rubes, and must be told"—the advance publicity included articles in news-

INTERNATIONAL EXHIBITION
OF MODERN ART
ASSOCIATION OF AMERICAN
PAINTERS AND SCULPTORS
69th INF'T'Y REGT ARMORY, NEW YORK CITY
FEBRUARY 15th TO MARCH 15th 1913
AMERICAN & FOREIGN ART.

AMONG THE GUESTS WILL BE — INGRES, DELACROIX, DEGAS,
CÉZANNE, REDON, RENOIR, MONET, SEURAT, VAN GOGH,
HODLER, SLEVOGT, JOHN, PRYDE, SICKERT, MAILLOL,
BRANCUSI, LEHMBRUCK, BERNARD, MATISSE, MANET, SIGNAC,
LAUTREC, CONDER, DENIS, RUSSELL, DUFY, BRAQUE, HERBIN,
GLEIZES, SOUZA-CARDOZO, ZAK, DU CHAMP-VILLON,
GAUGUIN, ARCHIPENKO, BOURDELLE, C. DE SEGONZAC.
LEXINGTON AVE.–25th ST.

ABOVE
69th Regiment Armory, 1913

LEFT
Poster for the Armory Show,
1913

Gallery A, American
Sculpture and Decorative Art,
Armory Show, 1913

THE ARMORY SHOW SCOREBOARD

Total Sales: $44,148 ($30,491 for work by European artists;
$13,675 for work by American artists)

Highest Price Paid: $6,700, by the Metropolitan Museum of
Art for Paul Cézanne's *Colline des Pauvres* (the first work by
Cézanne to enter a museum collection)

Most Popular American Artists (based on sales): Edward Kramer
($1,675), Robert Chanler ($1,500), Chester Beach ($500)

Most Popular European Artists (based on sales): Odilon Redon
($7,056), Cézanne ($6,700), Wilhelm Lehmbruck ($1,620, the
highest price paid for a sculpture), Marcel Duchamp (4 works
sold, for a total of $972)

papers as far away as Chicago, fifty thousand postcards mailed to the nation's tastemakers, free lapel buttons, and posters wheat-pasted up all over the city. The ubiquitous image in this campaign was an uprooted pine tree against a white background, a symbol borrowed from the Massachusetts flag carried into battle during the revolutionary war with its motto changed from "An Appeal to Heaven" to "The Modern Spirit." The association had appropriated for its crusade not only a military training ground but the American Revolution as well.

A fanfare of trumpets blasted from an upper gallery of the Armory. John Quinn mounted a platform, commanding attention with his ramrod demeanor and his urgent oratory. "The members of this association have shown you that American artists—young American artists, that is—do not dread, and have no need to dread, the ideas or the culture of Europe," he declared. "They believe that in the domain of art only the best should rule. This exhibition will be epoch making in the history of American art. Tonight will be the red-letter night in the history not only of American but of all modern art." [2]

But none of this—the newspaper articles, the revolutionary flag, Quinn's speech—prepared the audience for the jolt of the art itself. The exhibition began reassuringly with "old masters" such as Ingres and Eugène Delacroix and modern masters such as Jean-Baptiste-Camille Corot and Edouard Manet. They were flanked by nine galleries of American art; Americans outnumbered Europeans two to one. The American paintings depicted grittier subjects than the opening-night visitors were accustomed to, but they were tame in comparison with the art in the rooms beyond. As visitors worked their way toward the back of the armory, the images grew disconcertingly abstract and the crowds more vituperative. One room was devoted to the Impressionists—Edgar Degas, Claude Monet, Pierre-Auguste Renoir, Camille Pissarro. The Post-Impressionists Paul Gauguin, Vincent van Gogh, and Paul Cézanne were generously represented, and a side gallery was devoted to the Symbolist works of Odilon Redon. When the American press questioned the Gallic domination, the director of the show, Arthur B. Davies, replied simply, "All modern art speaks French." [3]

The most serious jolts were reserved for the final galleries, particularly the Cubist Room, in the southeast corner of the building. The most popular—and most notorious—gallery at the armory, it was the first to fill up and would be the last to empty out a month later. Promptly dubbed the "Chamber of Horrors," this small octagonal room embodied the shock of the new to the American public. Here was Constantin Brancusi's severely simplified sculpture *Mlle Pogany*. Seven Cubist paintings by "Paul" Picasso filled one wall, and four abstract works by Francis Picabia dominated another. The work that attracted the most attention was Duchamp's modest-size brown-toned painting *Nude Descending a Staircase*, which had been removed from the Salon des Indépendants in

Maybe you'll have more news of the great [Armory] Show. The "new spirit" gods how omnipotent they are. The Indians always said the "great spirit," but the New York Indians have to invent a "new" one.

Marsden Hartley to Gertrude Stein, January 1913

OPPOSITE, TOP
Suggestion to Futurists: Why Not Paint Four Pictures on One Canvas? George Carlson, *Life*, May 8, 1913

OPPOSITE, BOTTOM LEFT
Seeing New York with a Cubist: The Rude Descending a Staircase (Rush Hour at the Subway). J. Amswold, *New York Evening Sun*, March 20, 1913

OPPOSITE, BOTTOM RIGHT
Why Not Let the Cubists and Futurists Design the Spring Fashions? Peake, *World*, March 16, 1913

There is in my bathroom a really good Navajo rug which, on any proper interpretation of the cubist theory, is a satisfactory picture. Now if, for some inscrutable reason, it suited somebody to call this rug a picture of, say, "A well-dressed man going up a ladder," the name would fit the facts just about as well as in the case of the cubist picture of the "Naked man going downstairs."

Theodore Roosevelt, 1913

Paris the year before. As Henry McBride recalled, "the cumulative effects of so many cerebral shocks became unbearable at the far end of the Armory where Mr. Duchamp's painting hung."[4] Treated as a scandal and a joke, it became the public emblem for modern art and inspired more newspaper copy and more cartoons than any other work of the early modern era. The painting was seen as a deeply offensive mockery of the female form, which had been a staple of nineteenth-century art. Just as heretical was the fact that Duchamp looked to science for his inspiration, citing Eadweard Muybridge and Etienne-Jules Marey as inspirations for a work whose method was analytic and spirit ironic. To the audience at the Armory Show it seemed profoundly unnatural.

The American public typically countered threat with humor, and the *Nude* was the butt of most of the philistine jokes overheard in the Cubist Room. The painting was referred to as "an orderly heap of broken violins," as "a lot of disused golf clubs and bags," and, most lastingly, as "an explosion in a shingle factory." It became a national sport to ferret out Duchamp's nude as it descended the staircase, and everyone from ex-President Theodore Roosevelt to the art collector Arthur Jerome Eddy enthusiastically joined in. To those who asked where was the nude in Duchamp's painting, the painter Walter Pach replied, Where is the moon in the Moonlight Sonata?

ART—The portrayal in one perfectly stationary picture of about 5,000 feet of motion pictures: a "woosy" attempt to express the fourth dimension. FUTURIST ART—Same as the former, only more so, with primeval instincts thrown in; Cubism carried to the extreme or fifth dimension. POST-IMPRESSIONISM—The other two thrown together. HOW TO APPRECIATE IT—Eat three welsh rarebits, smoke two pipefuls of "hop" and sniff cocaine until every street car looks like a goldfish and the Masonic Temple resembles a tiny white mouse.

Chicago Record-Herald, March 20, 1913

There is an exhibition coming off . . . which is the most important public event that has ever come off since the signing of the Declaration of Independence, & it is of the same nature. . . . There will be a riot & a revolution & things will never be quite the same afterwards.

Mabel Dodge to
Gertrude Stein,
January 24, 1913

The Armory Show was not the avant-garde's first introduction to modern art—291 had supplied that—but it was the broad public's first encounter with it. They responded by repeatedly associating modern art with anarchy, immorality, epilepsy, and insanity. The *New York Times* cautioned, "It should be borne in mind that this movement is surely a part of the general movement, discernible to all of the world, to disrupt, degrade, if not destroy, not only art but literature and society too." [5] Looking back from this end of the century, it is easy to be smug about this public outcry, but in 1913 the American public had reason to feel profoundly threatened. The Armory Show was not simply another wave in the ebb and flow of fashion. It symbolized a seismic dislocation of everything that had ordered the nineteenth-century world, assaulting accepted modes of perception, paradigms of beauty, and standards of morality. To the uninitiated viewer the Armory Show looked like the apocalypse.

To the American avant-garde, the Armory Show meant just the opposite; it was a beginning, not an end. The idea that a revolution was underway was perceived as a source of hope, a portent not only of modernism but also of psychological, political, and sexual liberation. As such, it attracted artists, writers, and bohemians. A character in a Carl Van Vechten novel would later remark, "It was the first, and possibly the last, exhibition of paintings held in New York which everybody attended." [6] They welcomed the Armory Show as a heightening of art and of life, and no one expressed this optimism more clearly than Hutchins Hapgood. "It makes us live more abundantly," he wrote in the *New York Globe.* "And if this art has its logical effect it will help us all to understand more deeply what happens to us in life—to understand better our love and our work, our ambitions and our antipathies, and our ideals in politics and society." [7]

The Armory Show has been called a vortex, a crucible, a revolution, a circus, a touchstone; it was all of these and more. Invested with enormous symbolic power, the exhibition provided the climax of the avant-garde's first phase and inspiration for the next. That it was also a turning point in many lives—marking the start of friendships, art collections, and careers—is evident from the following "snapshots" of various characters in transition.

On March 8, 1913, the Association of American Painters and Sculptors held a dinner for the "Friends and Enemies of the Press." Of all the guests around the horseshoe table that evening, Arthur B. Davies aroused the most ambivalent feelings. Some association members felt that he had hoodwinked them, that he was not what he seemed to be—and of that he was certainly guilty. They had chosen the fifty-one-year-old painter as their president because he represented a middle course between the French-inflected avant-garde and the American independents. His refined manners and mild demeanor had suggested

Arthur B. Davies

Dinner for "Friends and Enemies of the Press" at Healy's, March 8, 1913

that he would be both effective and biddable. But, as Guy Pène du Bois later wrote, a "dragon evolved from the very gentle cocoon."[8] Davies's style was coolly aristocratic—his coworkers in the association called him Mr. Davies, or if they were feeling especially intimate, "the Chief." His curatorial choices were courageous and proved to be history making; they were also the work of a deeply secretive man who felt no allegiance to the group he represented and concealed his selections until they were a fait accompli. His enigmatic character was reflected in the double life he led. Davies not only had a wife and two sons in Congers, New York, but he also maintained a second household in New York City, where he called himself David A. Owen and lived with a former model named Edna Potter and their daughter. He kept the two families separate for nearly twenty years, and they did not discover each other until long after Davies's death in 1928.

Davies's conversion to modernism affected not only the Armory Show but also his own painting. Attempting to bring himself up to date, he imposed Cubist forms on his Symbolist canvases. The results were awkward concoctions that revealed how deeply his sensibility was rooted in the nineteenth century. Ironically, Davies became one of the Armory Show's victims. His subsequent contribution to art history would be limited to introducing wealthy women such as Lillie Bliss and Abby Rockefeller to the pleasures of collecting modern art. Bliss's purchases would later furnish the beginning of the Museum of Modern

John Butler Yeats (1839–1922). *John Quinn*, 1908. Oil on canvas, 27⅞ × 21⅞ in. (11 × 8.6 cm). National Portrait Gallery, Smithsonian Institution, Washington, D.C.; Gift of Dr. Thomas F. Conroy

Art's permanent collection, but by then Davies was dead and his reputation scarcely less so.

At that dinner for the "Friends and Enemies of the Press" John Quinn sat at the center of the head table, his arms folded, a cigar planted between his fingers. Quinn's unwavering gaze signaled the take-charge manner with which he handled both his law practice and the avant-garde community. Although he had no professional connection to art, Quinn had helped organize the Armory Show from the beginning. He drew up the association's constitution and papers of incorporation, helped secure the use of the armory, loaned more works to the exhibition than anyone else (seventy-seven paintings), and wrote an article for the special Armory Show issue of *Arts and Decoration* (March 1913).[9]

Born in Tiffin, Ohio, to Irish immigrants, Quinn had moved up quickly. He worked as the secretary (and nearly became the son-in-law) of Ohio's former governor Charles Foster, following him to Washington, D.C., where Quinn aspired to political power. He studied law at night school, opened his own law firm in 1906, and rapidly gained recognition as a brilliant financial lawyer. But Quinn did not respect the legal work that came to him so easily and brought him a small fortune; his devotion was reserved for art and literature.

Before the Armory Show, Quinn's nonprofessional pursuits had been so diffuse as to defy classification. He collected literary manuscripts and limited-edition books, worked for Irish home rule, sponsored American tours of Irish lecturers and Lady Gregory's Abbey Players (1911–12), served as a delegate to the Democratic convention of 1912, pleaded in court in defense of the salty language of J. M. Synge's *Playboy of the Western World,* and bought art by painters both living and dead. Quinn's collection at that time ranged from works of Oriental art to paintings by the English artist Augustus John and the French artist Pierre Puvis de Chavannes. His acquisition in 1912 of paintings by Cézanne, Gauguin, and van Gogh foreshadowed the interest in modern art that would come to dominate his collection.

The biggest lender to the Armory Show, Quinn now became its biggest buyer. He acquired "a whole heap of pictures," which cost $5,808.75 and made him "wildly happy."[10] His purchases ran the gamut from the Symbolist work of Odilon Redon to more experimental efforts by André Derain, Raymond Duchamp-Villon, Jules Pascin, André Dunoyer de Segonzac, and Jacques Villon. Although the Cubist Room aroused his blunt skepticism, he found that "after studying the work of the Cubists and Futurists, it makes it hard to stomach the sweetness and . . . sentiment of some of the other work."[11] The Armory Show also cemented Quinn's relationships with Davies, Walt Kuhn, Pach, and others who would guide his taste as a collector.

It wasn't only the thrill of purchase that drew Quinn to the Armory Show but also the pleasure of just looking. Whenever he could break away from his office on Nassau Street, he would call Lady Gregory or John Butler Yeats or even the mayor of New York to join him for the trip. "I enjoy a visit to the Armory with its pictures more than I would an old cathedral," Quinn wrote a friend. "This thing is living. The cathedrals, after all, seem mostly dead or remind one of the dead. When one leaves this exhibition one goes outside and sees the lights streaking up and down the tall buildings and watches their shadows, and feels that the pictures that one has seen inside after all have some relations to the life and color and rhythm and movement that one sees outside." [12]

After the Armory Show, Quinn committed himself to the international modernist community. As his closest friend and lover later observed, "He was, one might say, *mad to mix with genius.*" [13] Quinn was a welcome ally, for he had adventurous taste, money, and a savvy knowledge of the ways of the world. He loved combat and found no better battle than the one for modernism. Although he was politically conservative and hardheadedly practical, he contributed money and service to radical magazines such as the *Masses* and idealistic causes such as the 1917 Society of Independents. He has been called "a New World Puritan" and "a busy hodman of genius"; for the embattled American avant-garde this combination proved ideal. [14]

Although Robert Henri and Alfred Stieglitz had created the conditions that made the Armory Show possible, the two men played no role in planning the exhibition. The association did appoint Stieglitz honorary vice president, a title that accorded him respect without granting him power. (Henri was appointed head of the committee to select European art, an obvious irony for someone who stressed the importance of American art and an insult as well, since Davies and Kuhn had already made their European selections.) Several artists that 291 had introduced to America were prominently featured at the Armory, including Cézanne, Matisse, Hartley, Marin, Picasso, and others; Stieglitz's artists were second in number only to the bloc of Henri's protégés. [15] Stieglitz had also provided a wildly affirmative advertisement for the exhibition that ran below a six-column headline: "The dry bones of a dead art are rattling as they never rattled before. The hopeful birth of a new art that is intensely alive is doing it." [16] The Armory Show seemed to be a resounding confirmation of 291's long crusade, but for Stieglitz it was a bittersweet victory. He dourly pronounced it "a sensational success, possibly primarily a success of sensation." [17]

The hush of his little rooms had been drowned out by the cacophony of a three-ring circus, and he complained that "'Big Noise' is still too much of a feature." [18] To a public unfamiliar with 291, the Armory Show marked the American debut of modernism, and that became the verdict of history, too. Reacting against the public tumult, Stieglitz turned his back on the Armory Show, retreated into his little rooms, and filled them with his own photographs. At age forty-nine he was staging his first retrospective and, perversely, using the occasion to assess his photographs' power to compete with the riotous exhibition a few blocks away. "I am putting my work to a diabolical test," he wrote to a friend. "I wonder if it will stand it. If it does not, it contains nothing vital."[19] Some critics contrasted his straight photography with the subjective work at the armory, and others used it as the occasion to acknowledge his contribution to the avant-garde. Stieglitz's thirty prints stretched back twenty years, evoking a premodern age and a different era in Stieglitz's life as well. The circulation of *Camera Work* had dwindled to less than three hundred subscribers, and January 1913 marked its last appearance as a quarterly; henceforth the little magazine would be published at irregular intervals. The prominence that Stieglitz gave photography that month underscored the fact that it no longer commanded much of a place at 291, and the public attention to the art he had championed left Stieglitz upstaged by the very revolt he had fomented.

When Harriet Monroe first heard about plans for the Armory Show, she resolved to travel the thousand miles to see it in person. Chicago must be exposed to the newest advances in culture, she reasoned, and as the *Chicago Tribune*'s art critic since 1903, she was the one to make the introduction. Writing about the exhibition before leaving Chicago, she was an uneasy herald of modernity. In her disapproving words, Cézanne was reduced to "the shabby French vagabond," van Gogh became "the half-insane Flemish recluse and suicide," and Gauguin "the disreputable world wanderer."[20] On opening night the fifty-two-year-old critic trooped through each section of the Armory, earnestly gazing through her pince-nez. She reported that evening as a "grand time" and looked back on it as the high point of her journalistic career. But the final rooms in the Armory severely tested her aesthetic convictions. Matisse was an "unmitigated bore . . . talking blague in a loud voice," and the Cubist Room prompted her to sputter, "If these groups of theorists have any other significance than to increase the gayety of nations your correspondent confessed herself unaware of it."[21]

Monroe would not allow herself to remain complacently uncomprehending; she vowed to learn from modern artists. She returned to

---

Revolt is rarely sweetly reasonable; it goes usually to extremes, even absurdities. But when revolutionary feeling pervades a whole society or its expression in the arts, when the world seems moved by strange motives and disturbing ideals, then the wise statesman, the true philosopher, is in no haste to condemn his age. On the contrary, he watches in all humility the most extreme manifestations of the new spirit, eager to discover the deeper meaning in them.

Harriet Monroe on the Armory Show, April 6, 1913

---

the show repeatedly, and each report revealed that her nineteenth-century sensibility was giving way to acceptance of the modern. By the time she boarded the train back to Chicago, she had developed "an amused tolerance for the cubists," declared the event "a cosmopolitan modern exhibition," and carried with her a Symbolist lithograph by Redon, which she soon hung in the office of *Poetry*.[22]

Monroe saw the exhibition again in Chicago, where it was on view at the Art Institute from March 24 to April 16. In the provincial context of her native city she idealized the event into an embodiment of beauty, freedom, and aesthetic progress, and her earlier hesitancy was replaced by messianic fervor. Her final article on the exhibition summed up her wary new devotion to the modern crusade that would dominate the rest of her life: "We are in an anaemic condition which requires strong medicine, and it will do us good to take it without kicks and wry faces."

When William Carlos Williams stood in front of *Nude Descending a Staircase,* he laughed. But unlike the derisive chortles of the others crowded around him, the doctor's expression was one of profound relief, for the painters in the Armory Show presented what he later called "a break" for modern poetry. "Whether the Armory Show in painting did it or whether that was also no more than a facet—the poetic line, the way the image was to lie on the page was our immediate concern," he recalled.[23] His lifelong sensitivity to what poets could learn from painters dated from the show, where he encountered the works of the painters who would become his idols—among them Georges Braque, Cézanne, Duchamp, Hartley, Wassily Kandinsky, Picasso, and Charles Sheeler. The doctor understood that, in 1913, artists spoke in a more modern tongue than poets. (Even *Poetry,* the most progressive venue for poets in America, was devoted in February 1913 to *retardataire* rhyming verse by Arthur Davison Ficke and Witter Bynner.) The pursuits of painters and poets often overlapped during the early modern era. Williams had once considered becoming an artist, as did Marianne Moore, while the painters Charles Demuth and Hartley were, early in their careers, nearly as interested in writing poetry as in painting. Mina Loy practiced both expertly, and there were also painters, such as Max Weber and Florine Stettheimer, who wrote poetry as an avocation.

In the middle of the Armory Show's run, Williams received a rejection letter from Harriet Monroe. That the show had boosted his spirits can be deduced from his feisty response:

> Now life is above all things else at any moment subversive of life as it was the moment before—always new, irregular. Verse to be alive must have infused into it something of the same order, some tincture of disestablishment, something in the nature of an impalpable revolution, an ethereal reversal, let me say. I am speaking of modern verse. . . . It's the new seed, the one little new seed that counts in the end: that will ultimately cover fields with vigorous growth."[24]

William Carlos Williams, self-portrait from a letter to Harriet Monroe

This was the physician's first lecture to Harriet Monroe on behalf of modern poetry. It would not be his last.

The Armory Show gave Mabel Dodge her debut in America. She was at low tide when Frederick J. Gregg, the show's volunteer publicist, asked her to write about the links between Gertrude Stein's abstract writing and the work at the armory. Roused from her neurasthenia, she threw herself into the spirit of the exhibition. "It became, overnight, my own little Revolution," she declared. "*I* would upset America; I would, with fatal irrevocable disaster to the old order of things. . . . *I* was going to dynamite New York and nothing would stop me."[25]

The legends that grew up around Dodge turned her into a key participant in the Armory Show; years later she was even credited with having hired an ocean liner to transport modern art across the Atlantic. Her actual role was much less dramatic. She contributed two hundred dollars, rode around with her chauffeur to transport paintings from the drawing rooms of New York collectors to the armory, and was appointed an honorary vice president. She could often be seen at the armory, accompanied by her voguish friend Carl Van Vechten. Exhibition-goers got to know her name better than her face, for it appeared at the bottom of a small card that Davies distributed to some of the visitors. It called the Armory Show "the most important thing that ever happened in America, of its kind," and closed with a sweeping assessment, "What is needed is more, more and always more consciousness, both in art and in life."[26] When they read the signature on this provocative billet, many wondered, "Who is Mabel Dodge?"

Some hoped to find an answer in a small pamphlet that Dodge had bound in vivid Florentine wallpaper and circulated at the show. But Gertrude Stein's "Portrait of Mabel Dodge at the Villa Curonia" aroused the same frustration as looking for the nude in Duchamp's painting. "Portrait of Mabel Dodge at the Villa Curonia" attracted attention among the cognoscenti—Jo Davidson read it aloud at Mouquin's, Carl Van Vechten would recite it at the drop of a hat, and the association artists faked a Stein telegram at the dinner for the "Friends and Enemies of the Press." The "Portrait"'s renown increased with the corny jokes it provoked, and so did the publicity for Mabel Dodge.[27]

G is for Gertrude Stein's limpid lucidity
  (Eloquent scribe of the Futurist Soul),
Cubies devour each word with avidity:
  "Alone *words lack sense!*" they affirm with placidity.
  "But how *wise we'll be when we've swallowed the whole.*"
—G is for Gertrude Stein's lucid limpidity.

Mary Mills Lyall, *The Cubies' ABC*, 1913

Dodge, Stein, and the Armory Show proved mutually beneficial. The show garnered extra attention from Dodge's larger-than-life utterances, and Dodge in turn wrote an article on Stein for the Armory Show issue of *Arts and Decoration.* "In a large studio in Paris, hung with paintings by Renoir, Matisse and Picasso," wrote Dodge, "Gertrude Stein is doing with words what Picasso is doing with paint. She is impelling language to induce new states of consciousness, and in doing so language becomes with her a creative art rather than a mirror of history."[28] Stein thus received her first general recognition in her native land, a first taste of *la gloire* she desired. Perhaps Dodge benefited most of all, for the Armory Show elevated her to the status of what Van Vechten called "a new kind of woman."[29] After the Armory Show she was never "Mrs. Edwin Dodge" but always "Mrs. Mabel Dodge."

Francis Picabia docked in New York with his wife, Gabrielle Buffet-Picabia, on January 20, two days before his thirty-fifth birthday. As the sole on-site European representative of the Armory Show artists, he became a celebrity overnight; there were nearly a thousand references to Picabia in the press. His credentials as modern art's paladin were impressive: he had four paintings hanging in the Cubist Room, he lived in Paris and picnicked in Puteaux, his paintings had outraged officialdom at the Section d'Or and the Salon d'Automne, where he had reportedly "recubed" the Cubists and "refuturized" the Futurists.[30]

With his well-developed instinct for outrageousness, Picabia relished his public role, and to one reporter after another he trumpeted

Francis Picabia, Gabrielle Buffet-Picabia, and Guillaume Apollinaire, 1915

If you want to have clean ideas, change them as often as you change your shirts.

Our head is round so that our thinking can change directions.

Francis Picabia

his one-man manifesto: "Away with form! Out with perspective! Down with all effort toward materialization! Make way for the rhythm of impulse, the tonality of emotion, the equilibriumized expression of the inevitable." [31] When he wasn't acting as the local missionary of modernism—in the press or in person in the Cubist Room—he walked New York from the Battery to Central Park, listened to black singers on the Lower East Side, and absorbed inspiration for his art. "France is almost outplayed," Picabia proclaimed in a full-page interview in the *New York Times.* "It is in America that I believe that the theories of the NEW ART will hold most tenaciously. I have come here to appeal to the American people to accept the New Movement in Art." [32] For an impromptu exhibition at 291, which opened two days after the Armory Show closed, he created sixteen works that embodied his fascination with America. In the process of presenting his show at 291 he grew close to Stieglitz ("he is good; he is a God; I love him." [33]) and to his inner circle of Marius de Zayas and Paul Haviland. After Picabia sailed for France on April 10, Stieglitz wrote to a colleague: "All of 291 will miss him. He and his wife were about the cleanest propositions I ever met in my whole career. They were one hundred percent purity." [34]

When the thirty-five-year-old artist and collector Katherine Dreier arrived at the armory, she was well acquainted with modern art. She had been a visitor to the Steins' gatherings on the rue de Fleurus as early as 1907, and her burgeoning collection included a Rodin bronze, a Marin watercolor, and a van Gogh portrait of a young woman that she lent to the show. Dreier's family had emigrated from Germany in the middle of the nineteenth century, accumulated a small fortune exporting iron, and become upright Brooklyn citizens. Raised in a strict Teutonic household where only self-improving conversation was tolerated, Katherine was expected to espouse some cause that would better the human condition. She began painting at the age of twelve and pursued her training in France and England; her devotion to art was balanced by her social work on behalf of neighborhood settlement houses and female trade schools.[35] (Her love life was less successful: in 1911 she married Edward Trumbull, an American artist who already had a wife and children, and this day-long marriage was the only one she would ever have.)

Dreier was a woman whose opinions hardened into truth and whose missions were carried out with an iron will. Her determination was evident in the unswerving gaze of her piercing blue eyes and the pugnacious set of her jaw. "I am the reincarnation of Frederick Barbarossa," she casually remarked one day, without a hint of irony.[36]

Dreier's interest in modern art had been stimulated a few months before the Armory Show when she had attended the revolutionary Cologne Sonderbund (the exhibition that had shaped Davies's own vision of the show). She still lacked a daring imagination and a commitment to the advanced wing of modern art, as can be seen in her own timid

Katherine Dreier, c. 1910

still lifes that hung in the show and in her purchases from it: a twenty-five-dollar lithograph by Redon and a thirteen-dollar print by Gauguin.

The exhibition came as a shock. "Like a douche of cold water," Dreier wrote, "it left me gasping." [37] The Armory Show also convinced her that its artists needed her help. The newspapers' rabid attacks steeled this resolve, and she became indignant when modern artists were vilified as charlatans and degenerates. The best way to counter the vicious jibes, Dreier concluded, was by "getting to know the artists." [38] This cause, which would shape not only her own life but also the advancement of the American avant-garde, was inspired by the Armory Show. As she wrote, it "released an inner tension which was of tremendous importance, for at least the bonds had broken which bound the artist to the past." [39]

In the closing days of the exhibition thirty-four-year-old Walter Arensberg and his wife, Louise, made the trip from Shady Hill, his Cambridge home, to New York. According to a Harvard classmate, the Armory Show "hit him between wind and water." [40] Even to the intensely cerebral Arensberg the mind-bending jolt of the Armory Show was unprecedented, and he reputedly forgot to return home for three days. [41]

Given his moderate family fortune—and Louise's even larger inheritance—Walter Arensberg was in a position to buy. Although this was not the first time the Arensbergs had purchased art, their collection at the time of the Armory Show was neither modern nor distinguished. Their late arrival at the show frustrated Walter's collecting instincts, for many of his favorite works were no longer available. His inability to make rapid decisions cost him a Rodin drawing, bought by his Harvard classmate William Ivins for the Metropolitan Museum of Art, and Arensberg departed instead with an Edouard Vuillard lithograph, acquired for twelve dollars.[42] More important than this modest purchase was Arensberg's introduction to Walter Pach, the man who sold it. Pach would spur his new friend's most audacious purchases in art at a time when the common opinion of the Arensbergs' taste was mimicked by Henry McBride: "Walter Arensberg is quite mad. Mrs. Arensberg is mad, too."[43]

The Vuillard lithograph did not remain long at Shady Hill, however, for Arensberg compulsively worried over his faint-hearted purchase. When a selection of European work from the Armory Show traveled to Boston a few months later (April 28–May 13), Arensberg repeatedly returned to the exhibition at the distinguished Copley Hall; it was there that he took a pioneering step in collecting modern art. Arriving on the final day of the show with his Vuillard lithograph under his arm, Arensberg exchanged it for a small oil study of Puteaux by Jacques Villon. This purchase proved prophetic. Within a few years Arensberg's home would become the American outpost for the Puteaux group, and Villon's brother, Marcel Duchamp, would change Arensberg's life.

The circuslike atmosphere of the Armory Show reached a peak on March 15, the final day of the exhibition in New York. Over ten thousand viewers so crowded the cavernous armory that the doors had to be shut from 2 to 4 P.M. Celebrities and artists, collectors and millionaires packed together in the huge space, brushing against the sculpture and threatening the paintings. "It was the wildest, maddest, most intensely excited crowd that ever broke decorum in any scene I have witnessed," recalled one observer.[44] At 10 P.M. the guards began nudging the horde out onto Lexington Avenue, while the artists and the members of the Sixty-ninth Regiment continued to celebrate, with John Quinn supplying champagne and an Irish band furnishing the music. The din was punctuated by popping corks and exuberant toasts. The rite ended at 3:30 in the morning, with a fife-and-drum corps leading a spontaneous snake dance of artists, a dozen policemen, and as many guards. John Quinn directed the procession, while the giant D. Putnam Brinley, wearing a bearskin hat and twirling a baton, served as drum major. The line swept through each of the eighteen galleries, paying homage to artists past and present. They cheered the French, they cheered the Americans, and finally, they cheered the *Nude Descending a Staircase*. By ten the next morning the exhibition was completely dismantled, and the Sixty-ninth Regiment band marched across a strangely empty drill floor.

Long after the armory returned to its usual silence, the show's reverberations continued to be felt. "American art will never be the same again," the *New York Globe* had declared, and for once the hyperbole was justified.[45] From this point the American art world would develop a new orthodoxy, a new set of exemplary artists, and a new art market. "If its existence was transitory," Marius de Zayas observed of the Armory Show, "I am persuaded that the effect it caused was permanent."[46]

One of the biggest losers was the National Academy of Design. Although the institution survived, its imprimatur never again meant much. Its role as power broker and opinion maker was restricted to those painters who looked back to the nineteenth century, and henceforth it would be the headquarters only of the *derrière-garde*.

Certain members of the Association of American Painters and Sculptors perceived themselves as the Armory Show's victims. Although the exhibition had been initiated to showcase America's progressive artists, the French had attracted all the attention, and the inevitable comparisons between the two were unflattering to the Americans. "More than ever before, our great country had become an art colony," wrote Jerome Myers, one of the four founding members of the association, "more than ever before we had become provincials."[47] This group directed its anger toward Davies and even charged him with financial irregularities; despite the numerous sales, little money had come to the American artists or to the association. The most trenchant accusation was that Davies had "let the foreign lure rape him."[48] Max Weber, who had not shown in the exhibition, sourly observed about the association, "They invited their own drowning waves over their heads."[49] When Davies was reelected president, eight members of the Robert Henri faction walked out. The association never organized another exhibition and quietly ended in 1916.

In the wake of the Armory Show a new generation of artists were shown in New York's art galleries and noncommercial spaces.[50] Among them were Patrick Henry Bruce, Stuart Davis, Charles Demuth, Stanton Macdonald-Wright, Georgia O'Keeffe, Man Ray, Morton Schamberg, Charles Sheeler, and Joseph Stella. Modern art's new visibility was also encouraged by economic measures that John Quinn engineered at the

---

The public for "modern art" grows every day. . . . Something in the very name "modern art" seems to attract people. Besides, all over the world, a pathetic craze for honesty has broken out. . . . The wise ones are busily scanning the output and making their purchases with the identical acumen that the Havemeyers displayed years ago in purchasing their Manets, or Mr. Canfield used in his Whistler adventure.

Henry McBride, *New York Sun*, April 5, 1914

Matisse has reached the Montross Galleries—in other words become old-fashioned.

Carl Van Vechten to Gertrude Stein, January 21, 1915

time of the Armory Show. After October 1913 recent art from abroad was no longer subjected to the former fifteen-percent tariff. These new conditions—free international art trade, a broader audience, newly adventurous collectors, and innovative young artists—made it possible for European and American modern art to enter the mercantile precincts of the commercial art galleries. Henry McBride even slyly suggested a modern art bus tour, replete with refreshments and guides barking into megaphones. "The person who doesn't like the big general art movement of the day is an old fogy," he declared. "It occupies the centre of every art stage in civilization and affects all the arts."[51]

Among the new modern art dealers was N. E. Montross, a tall, pompous figure in the mold of the nineteenth-century dealer. Visiting 291, he was inspired to remark, "Surely, some time, Mr. Stieglitz, you are going into the art business."[52] For Montross, assimilating the new art seemed like a smart business move that capitalized on the economics of a changing art market. In his gallery at 550 Fifth Avenue he began to show modern American painting (his February 1914 exhibition attracted nine thousand people and yielded nineteen sales) and works by European modern masters such as Matisse (1915) and Cézanne (1916). Montross observed, "I consider it wiser to open the door from inside rather than to have it thrust in your face from outside."[53]

Charles Daniel, formerly a Forty-second Street saloon keeper commonly known as Pop, presented a contrast to Montross's blue-chip style. Introduced to modern art at 291 in 1910, he became so enamored of Marin's paintings that he immediately purchased two of them and soon bought work by Hartley, Abraham Walkowitz, and Max Weber. At the end of 1913 Daniels retired from his saloon to open a gallery at 2 West Forty-seventh Street. During his first two seasons he showed Stuart Davis, Charles Demuth, William Glackens, Man Ray, and William Zorach. Just as Stieglitz depended on the patronage of Agnes Ernst Meyer, so Daniels was supported from the beginning by the purchases of the collector Ferdinand Howald.[54]

An interior-decorating firm called the Carroll Galleries opened at 9 East Forty-fourth Street in March 1914. Financed by John Quinn and advised by Walter Pach and Walt Kuhn, the Carroll Galleries showed European and American modernist works to fashionable New York society. Stephan Bourgeois appealed to a similar audience. A French dealer in Post-Impressionism, he opened an American branch in February 1914 at 668 Fifth Avenue, and on its damask walls he hung paintings by van Gogh and Cézanne next to works by Anthony Van Dyck and Giovanni Battista Tiepolo. In June 1913 Bourgeois wrote to Walter Pach, "Unfortunately, Americans will begin to form interesting collections of modern art when the prices will have become exorbitant, a situation which in my opinion is not far off."[55]

Henry McBride was the ideal critic to introduce a broad audience to modern art. Although not the only American critic to support modernism, McBride was dubbed "the Chief of the Apostate of the Press," and he became modern art's most consistent and effective champion.[56] To the audience that read his Sunday pieces in the *New York Sun,* he was a mediator between them and the perplexing phenomenon of modern art; to the art world he was like a genial uncle whose support was unreserved and all-embracing. "*He is for the artist,*" observed one historian. "That is his only code."[57]

Henry McBride, 1903

The Armory Show was the first major event of McBride's long career at the *New York Sun.*[58] But this cub reporter was no fresh-faced youngster; he was forty-five years old and had risen to his new post from bleak circumstances in rural Pennsylvania.[59] McBride's late start as a critic proved to be an advantage. His enthusiasms belonged to the new era, and his incisive yet genial way of describing what he saw was unencumbered by the rhetorical strategies of earlier times; he was one of the few critics who could evoke the new art without resorting to either mysticism or moralism. Kuhn recalled that McBride "valiantly held high the torch of free speech in the plastic arts," but the critic would probably have cringed at this lofty encomium.[60] He was more comfortable with a characterization by his newest friend, Gertrude Stein, who simply stated, "You do make fun most charmingly."[61]

The prescience of McBride's judgment can be appreciated in retrospect; he was one of the first American critics to support the modern European masters (Brancusi, Duchamp, Matisse, and Picasso) and the most challenging American modernists (Demuth, Dove, Hartley, Marin, Nadelman, and Florine Stettheimer). His astute appraisals assure him a respected place in modern art criticism, but such a historical perspective ignores the qualities that most attracted his readers. In McBride's column, "What's Happening in Art," he made the *Sun* reader feel as if he were seated next to an entertaining dinner companion who could chat about the guests' couture ("What a Matisse dress!"), tell amusing art-world anecdotes, and deliver light but precise descriptions of artworks.[62] "The critic's business is not so much to be right as to inspire others to be right," he wrote,[63] and this humble credo was especially welcome in a period when so much modern art criticism was bombastic propaganda. In contrast, one recent critic noted, reading Henry McBride was "like getting the history of 20th-century art in a phone conversation."[64]

What was 291's function in this period when modern art was becoming fashionable? After the Armory Show, Stieglitz had considered closing the gallery—declaring its mission accomplished—and by the summer of 1914 the question assumed new urgency. The exhibition schedule of the season just ended had lacked the focus of earlier years, and fewer people had visited the gallery. "Curiosity seekers have fallen away," Stieglitz noted.[65] With de Zayas and Haviland traveling in Europe, Stieglitz spent his hours alone at 291, wrapped in his black cape and puffing on his pipe, brooding about an uncertain future.

In this country of rural pedagogues and long-faced parsons, to laugh at all is to be thought frivolous. I laugh a great deal (so do you). I laugh like an infant at what pleases me. Americans as a rule laugh bitterly, at what they hate, or at what they consider misplaced.

Henry McBride to Gertrude Stein, December 12, 1913

Edward Steichen (1879–1973). *Alfred Stieglitz at 291*, 1915. Platinum gum print, 11¼ × 9½ in. (28.6 × 24.1 cm). The Metropolitan Museum of Art, New York; The Alfred Stieglitz Collection, 1933

Teetering between inspiration and sardonic despair, he wrote to his mother in mid-June that he was recovering his sense of identity—he would find his way into the future by searching the past. Sharing his self-questioning with his circle, he asked them, "What is 291?" He proposed to print their responses in a special issue of *Camera Work*. (Stieglitz thought of this as a way to capture the spirit of 291; others saw it as a poll about the gallery's future and a clarion call to sycophancy.)

The sixty-eight respondents included not only the active members of the Stieglitz circle, but also such writers as Djuna Barnes, Alfred Kreymborg, and Henry McBride; the anarchist Hippolyte Havel; such cosmic appreciators of the new as Mabel Dodge and Hutchins Hapgood; and even 291's secretary and its West Indian elevator operator. Only four were photographers. They clearly understood that defining 291 was neither a documentary nor a historical task. Each writer groped to find the "common note" that Stieglitz hoped "would run through all the worded heart-beats." [66] These evocations of 291 resulted:

> "A modern 'Cour des Miracles' where kings can be found in beggar's clothes."
> "The Attic near the Roof."
> "An Idea . . . the expression of the soul of Alfred Stieglitz."
> "A room and a shrine, an adventure and a dream."
> "A cosmos-reflecting dew-drop."
> "A comradeship which is above prejudice."
> "An idea to the nth power."
> "An arena for disembodied souls."
> "A many-headed creature standing firm for every variety of truth."
> "The glory of the things beyond."
> "A spirit which fosters liberty." [67]

Interweaving strands of mythology, bohemianism, mathematics, Masonic spirituality, Platonism, and democratic American values, this tapestry of metaphors offers little insight into modern art but much into the spiritual values of the era.

The chief note of dissent within the community of 291 came from its cofounder, Edward Steichen, who considered "this inquiry into its meaning as being impertinent, egoistic, and previous." To Steichen, the issue of Camera Work resembled an obituary, and he wrote that "as far as 291 was concerned I was then ready to put an art movement such as futurism with anarchy and socialism into the same bag as Church and State to be labeled 'dogma' and relegated to the scrap heap—History." [68] Stieglitz was shaken not only by this negative response from his oldest colleague and valued partner but by the possibility that the analysis was accurate. As Henry McBride observed about the problem of consecrating a living enterprise, "The funeral sermon is preached in the presence of the corpse." [69]

POETRY I:
THE IMAGIST WARS

On a late summer day in 1912 Harriet Monroe walked into Chicago's Fine Arts Building, cradling in her arms a bulky bundle of manuscripts—the nascent *Poetry* magazine. She announced to her Little Room colleague Ralph Fletcher Seymour, "It is my child, and I have brought it to you to dress and help care for it." She leaned close, put her hand on his arm, and dropping her usual reticence, she exclaimed: "Oh, Ralph, you will do your best for our magazine. It does mean so much for all of us!" [1]

The first issue of the magazine appeared in late September 1912.[2] *Poetry*'s emblem, a black-and-red Pegasus, graced a gray cover of handmade stock with deckled edges. The cover satisfied Monroe as suitably uplifting, and she was pleased with the inspirational motto she had chosen from Walt Whitman: "To have great poets there must be great audiences too." Her editorial vowed to make the magazine "a place of refuge, a green isle in the sea, where Beauty may plant her gardens, and Truth, austere revealer of joy and sorrow, of hidden delights and despairs, may follow her brave quest unafraid."

Despite Monroe's aspirations, *Poetry*'s premiere issue was a microcosm of the poetry wars that would dominate the next few years. It was an era that one contemporary described as full "of cutthroat jealousies and vendettas, of gossip and wild parties, of murderous exclusions and, of course, of the all-too-eager joinings and belongings as well." [3] Ezra Pound's contribution to the first issue, "To Whistler, American," hinted at these tensions. Speaking in the curt twentieth-century idiom of a disillusioned expatriate, he accused his native land of provincial inhospitality to artists and called the American audience "that mass of dolts." These divisions—between America and Europe, the nineteenth century and the twentieth, democracy and elitism—would play crucial roles in the poetry wars to come.

The fiefdom over which the modern poets fought their battles was a small one—recalling George Russell's definition of a literary movement

It's the new seed, the one little new seed that counts in the end;—that will ultimately cover fields with vigorous growth. My idea of "Poetry" was that it must find this new seed, just as Burbank seeks and finds the new seed that is to grow his thornless cactus—pardon the moral.

William Carlos Williams to Harriet Monroe, March 5, 1913

as "Five or six men who live in the same town and hate each other."[4] Poets neither had nor hoped for a large audience; indeed, the coterie of poets largely formed their own audience. (Ordering one thousand copies of the first issue of *Poetry* was a strikingly optimistic act on Monroe's part.) In the eyes of the poets, however, their importance transcended popularity or material reward. Poets were, as Conrad Aiken put it, "the indispensable evolutionary fuglemen of mankind, the extenders of awareness and therefore of control, and therefore of wisdom."[5] In this light, *Poetry* was not just a modest office on Chicago's North Side but a civilizing outpost in America's cultural wilds.

There were no other magazines competing with *Poetry*—all of America's official organs of culture, from the *Dial* to *Atlantic Monthly*, published poetry only as column filler or as humorous jingles. For this reason Pound eagerly accepted Monroe's invitation to contribute his poems and welcomed the fledgling magazine as his only opportunity to establish a beachhead for modern literature. America, he thought, could be revolutionized by first revolutionizing its arts. He inundated Monroe with epistolary suggestions, contributions, and challenges. During the month before the first issue appeared, his letters arrived

---

No poet expects to earn money by his verse. If he does he is a fool and had better be disillusioned at the start. To compare him, the poet, to the painter is idle, for the painter produces a single piece incapable of reproduction, whereas the poet produces nothing more tangible than the paper which anyone can purchase for a cent and a few dabs of ink which cost still less.

William Carlos Williams to Harriet Monroe, July 17, 1917

My hair does stand on end. Habitually. I was born with it in that position.

Ezra Pound to
Harriet Monroe,
April 15, 1913

every few days, and a group of poets would crowd around Harriet Monroe's desk to read his large, loose scrawl punctuated by exclamation marks and heavy underlines. In his first letter he offered *Poetry* the right to exclusive American publication of his poetry and suggested that serious poets "boycott the rest of the press entirely." He also offered to keep "the magazine in touch with whatever is most dynamic in artistic thought. . . . I *do* see nearly everyone that matters." Enclosing his poem "To Whistler, American," he ended his letter with the hope that Monroe's magazine would be "an endeavor to carry into our American poetry the same sort of life & intensity which he [Whistler] infused into modern painting." [6]

Pound's letters were by turns bracing, condescending, encouraging, offensive, and funny, and he would occasionally beg Monroe to "Please forgive my constant imperative and didactic impulse." [7] His love-hate relationship with his native land animated the letters, and evident above all was his drive to create an authoritative position for himself in the modern literary establishment. Before the first issue even appeared he was presenting his views as "our policy," and by the second issue he was listed as *Poetry*'s foreign correspondent. [8]

Monroe did not enter into this alliance blindly, for Pound's first letter—all seven pages of it—sounded his key themes and made clear the intensity of his opinions. She must have understood that this volatile young modernist could never share the tastes of the civic-minded guarantors who financed *Poetry*. That she invited him anyway suggests her greatest contribution to the magazine: a readiness to endure vexation on behalf of poetry and to publish work that outdistanced her own understanding. "Still I give you your chance to be modern, to go blindfoldedly, to be modern," Pound wrote, "to produce as many green bilious attacks throughout the length and breadth of the U.S.A. as there are fungoid members of the american academy [*sic*]." [9] Harriet Monroe rose to his challenge.

Ezra Pound, letter to Harriet
Monroe, December 1912

Victor Plarr, Sturge Moore,
William Butler Yeats, Wilfred
Scawen Blunt, Ezra Pound,
Richard Aldington, F. S. Flint,
January 18, 1914

As the magazine's foreign correspondent, Pound immediately drew the lines of battle. *Poetry* would be a tale of two cities, London and Chicago. Both were ripe for a modernist takeover, Pound concluded, for diametrically opposed reasons. Britain's poets labored under the weight of their tradition; America's had no tradition. (Monroe still regarded London as a cultural center and wrote to Pound of her fervent hope that *Poetry* could reach England. Pound shot back in his next letter, "'England,' is dead as mutton." [10]) Alternately trumpeting the possibility of an American renaissance and chiding the nation for its provincial inadequacy, Pound warned Monroe, "Really you shouldn't stick yourself in between me and the 'country' while we are 'brunting' unless you can stand the inconvenience." [11]

"If I can help you make *Poetry the* center of the best activity, that will mean more to me than 'rates,'" he wrote Monroe. "And I do want a high standard kept." [12] This was not empty talk—Pound quickly mobilized his London connections and delivered a set of manuscripts that Monroe never could have mustered on her own. Following the model of Yeats's Monday Evenings, Pound began conducting Tuesday Evenings for poets in his cramped Church Walk flat. He solicited contributions from Ford Madox Ford and called in favors from William Butler Yeats. He introduced "THE *Scoop*"—the Bengali poet Rabindranath Tagore, who would win the Nobel Prize in 1913. Most important, he offered his just-formed school of Imagiste poets. All of them measured up to Pound's standards; he was less sure of the magazine itself.

Harriet Monroe's standards were as different from Pound's as Chicago was from Kensington. Her audience was not the literary cognoscenti of London but guarantors who had pledged their financial faith in her and local poets whose publication depended on her. She listened to Boston's and New York's jibes about "poetry in Porkopolis," and she

Harriet Monroe

read the local newspaper columnists who thought it witty to scramble cut-up pieces of the Congressional Record and print them as Imagiste poetry. Mixing civic pride, nationalism, aesthetic uplift and compassion, she pledged her allegiance to writers who were struggling to develop an American voice. (No one knew better than she the pain of being a poet neglected in her own country.) In the magazine's second issue Monroe declared that *Poetry* would not be the organ of any established group but would embrace as yet unknown masters scrivening in solitude across the land. "The Open Door will be the policy of this magazine," she announced, "may the great poet we are looking for never find it shut, or half-shut, against his ample genius!"[13]

Pound must have choked on her words. What would have offended him most? Monroe's awkward syntax? Her sentimentality? Or her hodgepodge policy? He shot back, "Of course if *I* don't keep up this harping on art *art* ART, nobody will."[14] His letter-sermons dropped off sharply after that, as if he had decided his brilliance was being wasted. Over the next four months he offered only his own poems and one by William Carlos Williams. Pound did not stop encouraging Monroe, but with fewer advisories from "the other side of the wet" (as Pound called it), *Poetry* was free to develop its own style and standards.

The *Poetry* office was set up in the former front parlor of a townhouse. It had a white marble mantel, which Monroe crowned with a French clock and a gilt-framed Victorian mirror; a Wilton rug was spread on the floor, books were piled precariously high on the two desks, and at the center was a wicker armchair called the "poet's chair." When Monroe returned from the Armory Show, she added a note of modernity to this elegant interior by hanging her newly purchased Odilon Redon lithograph and a photograph of his *Pegasus*.

The manuscripts that arrived in the mail circulated between the office's two desks. At the smaller of the two sat Alice Corbin Henderson, the friend from Lake Bluff, Illinois, whom Monroe had invited to be associate editor. A scrappy and articulate advocate of experimentation in verse, Henderson was the first reader of the submitted poems, and she passed them on to Monroe with her crisp editorial comments attached. From her position behind the supreme editorial desk, Monroe often would unintentionally intimidate young poets with her sharp gestures and methodical criticism. If Henderson informed her that she had deterred an aspiring poet, Monroe would chase after the devastated young writer and invite him for lunch. Henderson warned one of the new office girls (all of whom had to publish something in *Poetry* before working there): "Working with Harriet is like swimming in a sea which has warm and cold currents. One never knows where one is." [15]

The poets Monroe most avidly supported came to be called the Chicago School. Speaking in a distinctly American voice, these writers included Sherwood Anderson, Vachel Lindsay, Edgar Lee Masters, Carl

Vachel Lindsay, April 3, 1919

Sandburg, and such lesser talents as Maxwell Bodenheim, Floyd Dell, Arthur Davison Ficke, Ben Hecht, Eunice Tietjens, and Mark Turbyfill. Although she opened her pages to Pound's poets, Monroe's greatest devotion was reserved for purely American products; she hoped above all to provide the nurturing she had lacked. The poet that she was proudest to have introduced during that first year was Vachel Lindsay, though his eccentric conflation of religion, beauty, and the Midwest veered from her Little Room gentility.

Lindsay was a larger-than-life symbol for the Chicago Literary Renaissance. He preached a doctrine called "the New Localism," which valued the provinces above any city. His verse employed pure native inflections untainted by Old World sophistication, and his ragtime rhythms so vividly captured a new age that Pound called him a futurist. Tramping for months at a time through the plains of the Midwest, the rangy, sandy-haired poet resembled the medieval troubadours who interested Pound during this period. Lindsay mailed his poems to anyone he thought might be interested—a network that ranged from his former teacher Robert Henri to William James and fellow poet-painter Marsden Hartley. One of these epistles reached Floyd Dell, and through him Lindsay was introduced to Harriet Monroe, whom he found as "plain-spoken as the Old Testament, with an awful wallop." [16]

Modern poetry had so far defined itself in opposition to the overheated romanticism and sloppy abstractions of nineteenth-century verse, and its rallying cries were largely formulated in the negative: no more gentility, no more restrictions on syntax or subject, no more excess lyrical verbiage. Imagisme provided the first positive set of poetic principles, and offered the advantage of not limiting the writer to any particular subject or world view. The Imagistes' demand for verbal economy prompted Robert Frost to call them "a little group . . . who shortened one another's poetry." [17] Their basic doctrine could be reduced to three points: "1. Direct treatment of the 'thing,' whether subjective or objective. 2. To use absolutely no word that did not contribute to the presentation. 3. As regarding rhythm: to compose in sequence of the musical phrase, not in sequence of a metronome." [18]

Vachel Lindsay, letter to Harriet Monroe, November 22, 1912

Floyd Dell wrote in the *Friday Literary Review,* "We are for establishing Imagism by constitutional amendment and imprisoning without recourse to ink or paper all 'literary' ladies or gents who break any of these canons." [19] For an avant-garde movement in its first stage, Imagisme provided an ideal platform: it was broad enough to include many different poets, simple enough to be reduced to mottos, and flexible enough to be interpreted in various ways.

Imagisme's appeal is strikingly evident in Amy Lowell's reaction to it. She had been writing undistinguished Keatsian verse when, one January evening in 1913, she read "Hermes of the Ways"—H.D.'s poem that Pound had so admired at the tea-and-bun shop in the British Museum. Lowell paused at the signature, "H.D., Imagiste," then set down her *Poetry* magazine and declared, "Why, I, too, am an Imagiste!" [20] After a decade of writing verse alone at night in her library, she was thrilled to declare herself a member of a group. By the time her first poems (which were not identifiably Imagiste) appeared in the July 1913 issue of *Poetry,* she had sailed for London, armed with a letter of introduction to Ezra Pound from Harriet Monroe.

It was only a few days after Lowell descended on London that Amy Lowell stories began to circulate. The most often-repeated tale described her at the firm that had published her first book, *A Dome of Many-Coloured Glass.* She demanded to know where her books were and then refused to budge until the appropriate boxes were unpacked and the books distributed to bookstores. This event preceded her first meeting with Pound. The two took measure of one another over sumptuous dinners, and each reported back to Harriet Monroe. "Figure to yourself a young man arrayed as 'poet,'" wrote Lowell, "and yet making the costume agreeable by his personal charm; a sweep of conversation and youthful enthusiasm which keeps him talking delightfully as many hours as you please; the violence of his writings giving way to show a very thin-skinned and sensitive personality opening out like a flower in a sympathetic circle, and I should imagine shutting up like a clam in an alien atmosphere." [21] Pound in turn described Lowell as "pleasingly intelligent" and "ALL RIGHT"; he escorted her to Ford's South Lodge and Yeats's Monday Evening, and introduced her to John Gould Fletcher, an émigré American poet. [22] In Pound's eyes, Lowell was a prospective patron for himself and other poets. He saw the opportunity to blue pencil her verses into shape, and even considered one of her poems for inclusion in an Imagiste anthology he was planning. "When I get through with that girl," he wrote to his mother, "she'll think she was born in free verse." [23]

When Lowell sailed back to Boston in late summer, she was in high spirits. She had efficiently promoted her book, had glimpsed the abundant offerings of modern London, and—through Pound—had gained "a little wedge into the heart of English letters." [24] When Pound confided, "I agree with you that 'Harriet' is a bloody fool," she felt the

Modernity does not consist in rehashing labor disputes and rhetorizing about aeroplani.

Ezra Pound to
Alice Corbin Henderson,
October 14, 1913

frisson of conspiracy.[25] So buoyed was she by her new sense of power that on her voyage home she walked up to the ship's orchestra one evening, told them they were making a terrible racket, and suggested they just stop playing. They meekly complied.

That summer of 1913, in a cluster of ramshackle cabins perched on the sunset slope of the Palisades, a new little magazine was planned. Among the summer residents of Ridgefield, New Jersey, were the poet and mandolin player Alfred Kreymborg and the artist and jack-of-all-trades Man Ray (né Emmanuel Radnitzki).

At twenty-two, Man Ray had educated himself well. The son of an immigrant tailor, he quickly learned eclectic skills and took jobs engraving umbrella handles and designing layouts for a Fourteenth Street advertising firm. Through it all, he never abandoned the pursuit of art. During his lunches he went to 291 (Stieglitz even invited the young man to a few Round Tables), and at night he attended nude life-drawing classes at the Ferrer Modern School, taught by Robert Henri and costing twenty cents a session. There Man Ray met Hippolyte Havel, the sculptor Adolf Wolff, and the painter Samuel Halpert, and it was through these contacts that he came to Ridgefield's bohemian colony. Sharing a six-dollar-per-month cottage with Halpert and Kreymborg, Man Ray reported to his family that "it is the happy-go-lucky existence without any goal."[26]

With coffee and tobacco stains dotting his baggy pants, dark hair falling across his forehead, and a thick-lensed pince-nez dangling from a black cord, Alfred Kreymborg didn't look capable of organizing himself, much less a magazine. The twenty-nine-year-old was not without accomplishments: he had competed in national chess tournaments, had written a small volume grandly titled *Love and Life and Other Stories* (1909), and had been the editor of the *American Quarterly*. The novel disappeared immediately, and the magazine was stillborn—but in the process he was introduced not only to the harsh realities of literary life but also to Charles Demuth, Hutchins Hapgood, Marsden Hartley, and Joyce Kilmer. Through 291 he was acquainted with modern art, and he was one of the few journalists who recognized the Armory Show as "the business *coup d'etat* for which 291 was the artistic forerunner."[27]

In the wake of that exhibition Kreymborg hoped to catalyze similar experimentation in poetry, having concluded that Harriet Monroe was not up to the task. He had sent her his gnomic verses, which he called "mushrooms," and she had returned them with polite notes correcting their peculiarities. He had also received rejection slips from Mitchell Kennerley, New York's sole publisher of serious poetry. His only recourse, Kreymborg decided, was to start his own magazine; its pages would be the *salon des refusés* of American poetry. The magazine's spontaneous start-up could not have been more unlike *Poetry*'s carefully planned organization. Kreymborg peremptorily chose a title, the *Glebe* (an archaic synonym for "soil"), and divided the labor with Man Ray: Kreymborg solicited manuscripts and Man Ray printed the magazine. One Saturday afternoon in late summer the printing press made a circuitous journey via the Fulton Street Ferry and then horse and cart down the paths of the Palisades. Just as the two aged deliverymen reached the door of the shack, they dropped the press, and the *Glebe* seemed to have shattered with it.

Logo for the *Glebe*, 1914, by Man Ray

In fact, not one but three magazines were eventually published in Ridgefield: the *Glebe* (ten issues appeared sporadically from September 1913 to November 1914), the *Ridgefield Gazook* (one issue appeared March 31, 1915), and *Others* (twenty-six issues appeared from July 1915 to July 1919). Kreymborg published the first of these magazines with the financial support of Charles and Albert Boni of the Washington Square Bookshop. The *Glebe*'s policy of devoting each issue to a single author offered implicit criticism of *Poetry*'s hodgepodge, but unfortunately many of the *Glebe*'s contributors could not sustain a full issue. Charles Demuth's Greenwich Village comedy, *The Azure Adder*, was one exception, but the most important exception was the fifth issue, *Des Imagistes*.

At the end of summer 1913 Kreymborg received by special delivery a package from London, wrapped in butcher paper and addressed in Ezra Pound's commanding scrawl. Opening it, Kreymborg found a thick sheaf of manuscripts in different sizes, the editor's caustic notes in the margin, and an accompanying letter that concluded "unless you're another American ass, you'll set this up just as it stands!"[28] Pound promised more material if this issue was handled well and urged Kreymborg to meet William Carlos Williams ("my one remaining pal in America—get in touch with old Bull—he lives in a hole called Rutherford, New Jersey"[29]). Upon reading the poems by Richard Aldington, H.D., Lowell, Pound, Williams, and James Joyce, Kreymborg and Man Ray broke into a war dance.

Pound's reaching out to another little magazine was not without precedent.[30] But his generosity to a fledgling endeavor—known only through his recent acquaintance with the American émigré poet John Cournos—seems like a loony act of faith. He had rounded up the best younger poets and handed over their work to the unknown Kreymborg. Pound's contributions to the *Glebe* are most understandable in light of his deteriorating relationship with *Poetry*.

By the time of *Poetry*'s first anniversary, tensions between Pound and Monroe had reached a crisis, exacerbated by the selection of a poem to receive the $250 Guarantors' Prize. The award—to be determined by a six-person jury—raised questions that a nascent avantgarde was ill-equipped to answer. Could American standards be pitted against international standards? Should a little-known poet be favored over a widely recognized one? These questions nearly tore apart the Pound-Monroe alliance.

How are we to be two decades ahead of the country and cater to news stands at the same time?? . . . We can't afford to give the public what it wants.

Ezra Pound to
Harriet Monroe,
January 27, 1913

Complaining that "H. M. has gathered rosebuds in every field for a full year," Pound considered the prize a great opportunity to set the *weltliteratur* standard for modern poetry, something that no one had previously attempted.[31] "We must be severe if we are to count," he admonished Monroe, "and if our voice is going to be, as it should and must be, *the* authority."[32] He had no doubt about who should receive the Guarantors' Prize: William Butler Yeats, for his poem "The Grey Rock." Monroe, however, saw the prize as an opportunity to boost a native son and to vindicate the guarantors' faith in her local enterprise. She wanted to award the prize to Vachel Lindsay for "General William Booth Enters into Heaven."

Pound was enraged. To pass over Yeats's poem after Pound had ardently solicited it would be an embarrassment and a potential disruption of his close relations with Yeats. (His relationship with Yeats had already been threatened when Pound had the audacity to "correct" some of Yeats's poems, cutting out abstract language so that they became more Imagiste.) Pound feared that choosing Lindsay would destroy the magazine's credibility, whereas Yeats's acceptance would confer authority on both the magazine and the award.

The controversy over the first *Poetry* prize was one element that caused Pound to abruptly resign as foreign correspondent, turning the reins over to Ford Madox Ford. Only through complicated maneuvering could the break be mended. After just a few days in his new position, Ford implored Monroe to reinstate Pound, writing, "If I tried to help you that energetic poet would sit on my head and hammer me till I did exactly what he wanted. . . ."[33] Aldington, who had a stake in Pound's continued tenure at *Poetry,* urged Monroe to overlook Pound's bad manners: "Of course, he will insult you; he insults me; he insults Mr. Hueffer [Ford]; he insults everybody; most of us overlook it because he is American, and probably doesn't know any better."[34] Monroe not only urged Pound to return, but deferred to him in awarding Yeats the *Poetry* prize. She solicited one hundred dollars from the guarantors for a separate prize (which Pound dubbed "the prize for the village choir") to be awarded to Lindsay. Yeats, in turn, spent fifty dollars of his award on a ceremonial bookplate and gave the rest to Pound in recognition of his "vigorous imaginative mind."[35] (Yeats's munificence enabled Pound to buy a new typewriter and two small sculptures by his new friend Henri Gaudier-Brzeska.)

Encouraged by Alice Corbin Henderson, Monroe planned a *Poetry* banquet for March 1, 1914, and invited Yeats to speak at it and to stay in her modest apartment during his Chicago visit. When Yeats accepted, Monroe arranged for the banquet to be held in the Cliff Dwellers Room on the top floor of Orchestra Hall. Among the 150 guests invited were *Poetry*'s guarantors, members of Chicago society, the magazine's staff, and local writers and artists such as Carl Sandburg, Maurice Browne (of the Little Theater), and Margaret Anderson. Determined that Yeats acknowledge native talent, Monroe placed a copy of Lindsay's "General William Booth Enters into Heaven" by his bed. She volunteered to pay Lindsay's ten-dollar carfare from Springfield, and he offered to recite a new poem. "You must give me a license to rattle the Cliff Dwellers' windows," wrote Lindsay, "and pound the table *hard*." [36]

Yeats barely touched the banquet food set before him and presided at the head table in owlish distraction. He rose to speak, addressing his words to "a fellow craftsman," Vachel Lindsay, who was so overwhelmed that he later admitted, "I hardly saw him." [37] Yeats described his own earlier efforts to modernize poetry and then proffered advice to America's young poetry community: "I want you who are readers to encourage American poets to strive to become very simple, very humble. Your poet must put the fervor of his life into his work; he must give you his emotions before the world, the evil with the good. . . ." [38]

When Yeats sat down, Lindsay—as if carrying out Yeats's advice—rose to recite his poem, "The Congo." He faced a weary audience ready to go home. They were slightly unnerved by the poet's first line, "Fat black bucks in a wine-barrel room," and bolted upright when he came to his first chorus, "Boomlay Boomlay Boomlay BOOM." Lindsay hit the "BOOM" so loudly that it shook the room, and as he continued, the audience began to sway with the syncopated chant, while Lindsay rocked on the balls of his feet, his head thrown back, his arms pumping in time with the beat. The reading combined the passion of a gospel shouter with the rhythm of a vaudevillian. When Lindsay finished his seven-minute recitation, the black waiters applauded and the North Shore hostesses crowded around Lindsay, inviting him for dinners. [39] Many years later Lindsay confided to Yeats, "That instant remains, as it appeared then, the literary transformation scene of my life." [40] Harriet Monroe looked back on the *Poetry* banquet as "one of my great days, those days which come to most of us as atonement for long periods of drab disappointment or dark despair. I drew a long breath of renewed power, and felt that my little magazine was fulfilling some of our seemingly extravagant hopes." [41]

The next day Albert and Charles Boni published the *Glebe*'s *Des Imagistes* issue in hardcover format, selling it at their Washington Square Bookshop, and a month later it appeared in London's Poetry Bookshop, published by Harold Monro. *Des Imagistes* sold few copies and was widely ridiculed and parodied by critics, but it nonetheless proved an important publication within avant-garde circles. As the first published anthology of modern poets it determined who belonged in the clique—what Pound called "our little gang." [42] Its contents were exactly the same as the February issue of the *Glebe,* but the book did not mention the magazine, which had in turn neglected to acknowledge that thirty-one of its forty-seven poems had previously appeared in *Poetry.* Monroe threatened to sue until Kreymborg—who pleaded that he had just been following Pound's orders—offered to tuck an acknowledgment slip into each book. The space allotted to each contributor also proved divisive, for Pound had made no attempt at even-handedness. Some poets were heavily represented—Aldington led with ten poems, H.D. had seven, and Pound, six—but several others were restricted to a single poem. The most aggrieved of these was Amy Lowell, who characteristically turned her discontent into a practical plan.

In early July 1914 Lowell's claret-colored Pierce-Arrow eased out of the SS *Laconia* onto a Liverpool dock, and a chauffeur, dressed in matching claret livery, piloted Lowell and her companion Ada Russell to London's Berkeley Hotel, where Lowell had booked an entire floor. She plunged into the tumultuous cultural life of London, commanding boxes at the Diaghilev ballet, perusing volumes at Harold Monro's Poetry Bookshop, and selling her poems to English magazines. In these outward details Lowell's visit resembled that of the previous summer, but much had, in fact, altered.

London was in a state of frenzied gaiety, the crescendo at the end of an epoch. Champagne corks of the newly rich popped nightly in the Ritz ballroom; the Futurist Filippo Tommaso Marinetti howled and made machine-gun noises, only to be clangorously disrupted by the Vorticists; six-inch sans-serif type screamed *BLAST* across a shocking pink cover; Wyndham Lewis shrieked that he would kill T. E. Hulme for stealing his mistress. And charging the air was the threat of international explosion following Archduke Ferdinand's assassination, which had taken place during Lowell's transatlantic crossing.

Literary alliances were in flux, and the profound shifts that resulted can be glimpsed through a series of dinners held that summer. The first, at the Dieu-donné restaurant, celebrated the publication of *BLAST.* Pound invited Lowell to join his new confreres, the Vorticists, who had signed a manifesto that spring of 1914, designating what to Blast and what to Bless. Trumpeting their tenets with more noise than clarity, the Vorticists remained an even more amorphous group than the Imagistes. Pound variously described *BLAST* as a "revue cubiste" and as "a new Futurist, Cubist, Imagiste Quarterly."[43] What was clear about the new group were its kingpins—Ezra Pound, Wyndham Lewis, and Henri Gaudier-Brzeska—and its self-proclaimed position at the cutting edge of modern tendencies in poetry and art. It gave Pound the opportunity to act as the impresario of two movements simultaneously and to champion talents more major than Richard Aldington and H.D.

To the *BLAST* dinner Amy Lowell wore a formal floor-length black gown and matching cape, with white opera gloves, high heels, and

Henri Gaudier-Brzeska (1891–1915). *Portrait of Ezra Pound,* 1914. Brush and ink on paper, 20 × 15 in. (50.8 × 38.1 cm). Kettle's Yard, University of Cambridge, Cambridge, England

a large ornamental fan. In the company of the surly and revolutionary Vorticists, she appeared decidedly out of her element, as Pound
certainly had known she would when he issued the invitation. Lowell
dismissed Vorticism as "a most silly movement" that Pound was shame-
lessly using to keep his name before the public.[44] Unfazed by Pound's
opening salvo in what became the dinner wars, she announced an
Imagist Dinner to be held at the same establishment two days later.
Using an elegant restaurant as battlefield was decidedly to Lowell's advantage, for she could command a formal table with aplomb.

Lowell used this occasion to celebrate the British publication of *Des
Imagistes*. Because the selection of the anthology had been entirely
Pound's, Lowell's dinner ostensibly honored him. Among the thirteen
invitees were several couples—Pound and his bride of two months,
Dorothy Shakespear; H.D. and Aldington; Ford and his wife, Elsie;
Lowell and Ada Russell—and five single men: F. S. Flint, Allen Upward,
John Cournos, Henri Gaudier-Brzeska, and John Gould Fletcher. At
each place Lowell had put a copy of *Des Imagistes*. Pound's position
within this group was as embattled as his health (his hacking cough
prompted some to speculate that tuberculosis was attacking his brain),
for Pound's always-volatile alliances were especially conflict ridden
that summer. He was quarreling with Ford and Fletcher, and H.D. and
Aldington felt betrayed by the Vorticist alliance, which Aldington called
"a wearisome pose."[45] Lowell and Pound looked at each other from
one end of the table to the other, and one poet recalled that "the atmosphere from the start was one of embarrassed expectancy."[46]

After the guests had eaten their way through the ten-course dinner,
Lowell called on Ford as the Imagistes' éminence grise to make some remarks. He said that he had no idea what an Imagiste poet was: he

---

Menu for Amy Lowell's Imagist Dinner, July 17, 1914

Hors d'Oeuvres Norvégien

Consommé Sarah Bernhardt, Bisque de Homards

Filets de Sole Lucullus

Cailles en Gelée aux Muscats

Selle d'Agneau Richelieu

Canetons d'Aylesbury à l'Anglaise

Petit Pois aux Laitues, Jambon de York au Champagne

Haricots Verts Maître d'Hôtel

Bombe Moka

Dessert and Café

---

doubted whether Lowell was one, nor was he sure even about Pound. Looking around the table, he could identify only H.D. and Aldington as Imagistes, and then he sat down in abrupt and uncharacteristic silence. When Pound called on witty Allen Upward, the barrister-turned-writer made a joke about Lowell's girth by reading the concluding lines of "In a Garden," her sole contribution to *Des Imagistes.* Pound suggested that her closing line, "Night, and the water, and you in your whiteness, bathing!" referred to Lowell and her vast, pale body.[47]

During the next set of remarks by Aldington and Gaudier-Brzeska, Pound stole out to an adjoining room and returned with a large tin bathtub on his head. He deposited it before Amy Lowell, brushed his disheveled auburn hair from his forehead, and made a formal announcement: Les Imagistes would be succeeded by a new school of poetry, Les Nagistes, with this tub as its symbol. Perhaps Lowell, its inaugurating poet, should demonstrate her whiteness by bathing in it. During the laughter Lowell sat stiffly and observed that whether "imagiste" or "nagiste," the new movement in poetry would continue. Ford looked back on the evening as "a disagreeable occasion of evil passions, evil people, of bad, flashy cooking in an underground haunt of pre-war smartness."[48]

Over the next two weeks Lowell conducted smaller poetry dinners in her Berkeley Hotel suite. The newlyweds D. H. and Frieda Lawrence, Richard Aldington and H.D., and John Gould Fletcher dined in her drawing room, and over boxes of candied fruit they considered her seductive proposal for a new Imagiste anthology. As a democratic alternative to *Des Imagistes,* Lowell suggested that each poet be given equal space in which his or her own selection of poems would appear. To ensure publication by a reputable firm, Lowell would stake the venture. She secured their participation and then invited Pound. The anthology was in his own best interests, she told him, and added that she would never have suggested it had she thought he would disapprove. He roundly rejected her proposal, informing her that poetry was not "a democratic beerhall."[49]

Correctly perceiving that Lowell was on the verge of usurping his position among the Imagistes, Pound entreated his friends not to participate. Since H.D., Aldington, Ford, Fletcher, Flint, and Lawrence had all defected to Lowell, Pound was dispirited; his only major remaining ally was Yeats. For his last ploy, he asserted ownership of the term "Imagisme," and when Lowell simply stripped the word of its Gallic affectation to make it "Imagism," he riposted that the movement would henceforth be known as "Amygism." Lowell had maneuvered with such Yankee cunning that her raid made Pound appear the petulant dictator. *He* became the refuser, the impediment to the propaganda for modern poetry. Her last word on the matter was "Astigmatism," a poem dedicated "To Ezra Pound with Much Friendship and

Admiration and Some Differences of Opinion." The poem concluded: "Peace be with you, Brother, You have / chosen your part."

The dinner wars were interrupted by the Great War. The view from the French windows of Lowell's hotel room provided a fine perspective of London at the beginning of August 1914. The length of Piccadilly, with its bright electric globes lighting the parkway, stretched out below one window, with Green Park on the left. Another window overlooked Devonshire House, its doors opened wide and footmen in powdered wigs standing beneath its porte cochère. Within the month this view was transformed; sheds with corrugated roofs and canvas stretchers filled Green Park, Devonshire House had become the headquarters for the Red Cross, and marching down Piccadilly were crowds waving flags and chanting, "We want war!"

ENTR'ACTE

On the evening of August 3, H.D., Richard Aldington, and John Cournos stood before Buckingham Palace as the royal family walked onto the lighted balcony and the king declared war. It was H.D.'s second piece of unwanted news that day; earlier her doctor had told her she was pregnant. In everything from the outbreak of war and the fetus within her to Pound's marriage and his break with Imagism, she saw signs that her youth was over and an age was passing. Those feelings were intensified when she miscarried a few weeks later. She found comfort only in a new literary intimacy with D. H. Lawrence, who became her neighbor when the Aldingtons moved to Hampstead Heath in the fall of 1914.

Surveying war-torn London, Lawrence expressed the widespread sentiment that the city "in some way perished, perished from being a heart of the world, and became a vortex of broken passions."[1] Amy Lowell looked on the chanting, flag-waving London crowds calling for war and despaired that "the blood-lust was coming back. . . ."[2] After shipping her Pierce-Arrow back to Boston, she aided other stranded Americans by meeting them at Victoria Station, wearing a large sandwich board that directed them to an impromptu operation to return Americans safely home, set up at the Hotel Savoy by young Herbert Hoover. By early September, Lowell booked passage back to New York.

"I think the war is eating up all of everybody's subconscious energy," Pound wrote to Harriet Monroe in August 1915. "One does nothing but buy newspapers."[3] A year later he wrote her, "The war is still like a great cataclysm in nature."[4] *BLAST* turned out to be the apex of Vorticism; after a second issue in July 1915 the magazine and the movement died. Many of the Vorticists went to war. Wyndham Lewis volunteered as a gunner with the Royal Artillery. Henri Gaudier-Brzeska died in the trenches of Neuville Saint Vaast on June 5, 1915. Pound was devastated. "The arts will incur no worse loss from the war than this is," he wrote to a friend. "One is rather obsessed with it."[5] Ford Madox

Ford, old enough to escape military duty, was so disturbed by the sculptor's death that he enlisted, believing that old men rather than young should fight wars. The Imagist group scattered. T. E. Hulme enlisted with the Honourable Artillery Company, wrote articles from the trenches about "the heroic values" of war, and on September 28, 1917, while his fellow soldiers were eating lunch, was killed instantly by a burst of shellfire. Richard Aldington went to an army camp in Dorset and was quickly promoted up the ranks. John Gould Fletcher returned home to America in October.

Muriel Draper was determined that her musical salons at Edith Grove would continue, despite the fact that her husband had gambled away both his inheritance and hers and, at the war's outbreak, had sailed to America with the actress Jeanne Eagels. Muriel mortgaged her furniture and pawned her turbans, her bridal pearls, and her earrings, replacing an elegant wardrobe with hats fashioned from feather dusters and faded curtains. This was, she wrote, "an era of my life that must be lived out to its last moment. I knew with increasing conviction that it would not happen again."[6] That last moment occurred in 1915, and the London String Quartet continued to play as the sun rose on Draper's final morning in England. She breakfasted on champagne and pâté, then sailed to New York. She arrived penniless, with two sons, and for the next decade her poverty would consign her to living in drab railroad flats that made entertaining impossible.

Amidst the exodus there was one notable arrival: T. S. Eliot, who had been studying philosophy in Marburg, Germany. When war was declared, he moved to London and took a flat at 28 Bedford Place. On September 22, 1914, he met Pound, who became so excited by Eliot's poem "The Love Song of J. Alfred Prufrock" that he dashed off a letter to Monroe. "He is the only American I know of who has made what I can call adequate preparation for writing. He has actually trained himself *and* modernized himself *on his own.* . . . It is such a comfort to meet a man and not have to tell him to wash his face, wipe his feet, and remember the date (1914) on the calendar."[7]

Gertrude Stein and Alice B. Toklas were visiting Alfred North Whitehead in England when war was declared, and they were detained there for eleven weeks. Hearing the daily reports of the German troops' steady onslaught, Stein feared for her manuscripts, for the art collection at the rue de Fleurus, and most of all for Paris itself. By the time she learned that the Germans had been stopped at the Marne River, Stein could not bring herself to leave her room. The Paris that she and Toklas encountered when they returned late one October evening appeared unviolated and oddly quiet. As they strolled through the empty streets, the city seemed to belong to them alone.

By that time the summer visitors had gone home and the legion of art students had repatriated. Henry McBride noted in August that Paris had become "blue enough to get on one's nerves," and he hastened home at the end of the month.[8] Marius de Zayas and Francis Picabia (newly appointed as an "automobilist") were eager to accompany the French general staff to the battlefront so they could sketch it. They were refused permission, but de Zayas expressed wonder at hearing "the sound of German bombs and the French guns in Paris."[9] He escaped France with a trunk full of pictures by Picasso, Braque, and Picabia to be hung at 291, and fifteen of the best African sculptures "ever . . . brought to the civilized races (?)" [sic].[10] He wrote to Stieglitz, "I believe that this war will kill many modern artists and unquestionably modern art. . . . But what satisfies me is that at least we will be able to say the last word."[11]

The French art community was mobilized for war. Some, such as Georges Braque and Blaise Cendrars, sustained severe injuries that put them out of action. Others, such as Guillaume Apollinaire and Raymond Duchamp-Villon, were killed. Elie Nadelman sailed to New York that October on the *Lusitania*. The art dealer Daniel-Henry Kahnweiler, a German citizen, sat out the war in Switzerland and his gallery on rue Vignon was sequestered. The Salons were discontinued. The Bal Bullier became a clothing depot for soldiers, and even the noisy Latin Quarter cafés abided by a strict nine o'clock curfew. The pioneering era of Cubism was over, and the art world was suddenly moribund. One of the few young artists to remain in Paris was Marcel Duchamp, who was excused from military duty because of a heart condition. With his brothers and closest friends at the front, and all conversation dominated by the war, Duchamp led a monastic existence within the city he now called "a gloomy endroit. . . ." "Paris is like a deserted mansion," he told an American reporter. "Her lights are out."[12]

When Mabel Dodge, Carl Van Vechten, and Neith Boyce arrived in Florence at the beginning of August 1914, they found the city oblivious to the war that had been declared in France and England. The international colony was still pursuing its soignée life of tango teas and fancy balls, and after her first night back at the Villa Curonia, Dodge wanted to remain there forever. But Boyce lay awake all night, haunted by the specter that had reputedly visited other guests at the villa. Soon Dodge, too, was filled with foreboding. "We are doomed—our pleasant useless civilization effete and worn out," she declared when the reality of the war became clearer to her. "The Goths are upon us."[13]

Fearing that the Villa Curonia would be sacked, Dodge locked her most precious objects and books in one room and left in mid-August. She would never again set foot in the villa, and for many years it remained uninhabited. Retreating to the mountain village of Vallambrosa, Dodge and her guests soon learned that their money had been devalued and their return to America was blocked by the dangers of wartime travel. Mina Loy joined them, looking "like a Futurist poster."[14] Although she was as stranded as they, the war seemed to bring her to life as she recounted local gossip and chronicled the romances in her life. She read her latest letter from Marinetti, who declared his plan to attack Austria with his own Italian legion. She wanted to have his baby, she announced, for there was nothing else for women to do in wartime.

Worrying over the scarcity of money and the inflationary prices, Van Vechten became more and more hysterical about returning to America, while Dodge insisted on waiting for John Reed to arrive. By dispensing with luxuries, she believed that they could sit out the war in the tiny mountain village. As Dodge and Van Vechten grew increasingly at odds, she railed about his "great stupid eyes" and his "solemn greed," and he called her "the perfect tyrant." Nonetheless, in that topsy-turvy economy, Van Vechten and Boyce depended on Dodge to finance their trip back to America.[15] When Van Vechten finally found a rusty tanker, the *San Guglielmo,* that was leaving Naples with nine hundred Americans crowded into its steerage, Dodge paid their exorbitant fares. Van Vechten made his way kicking and swearing up the gangplank and sailed to New York; one month later he married the actress Fania Marinoff. He and Dodge didn't speak for many years.[16]

Dodge waited in Naples for Reed, and when he arrived at the end of August, she met him on the dock in a flowered hat and lace parasol. They boarded a train to Paris so that Reed could get closer to the front, and they found the city "like a great lady going to the Guillotine *en grande toilette. . . ."*[17] Dodge made a desultory attempt to join the Red Cross, but as Reed moved closer to the lines of battle her neurasthenia intensified. From her bed-ridden perspective, the war seemed like just one more competitor for Reed's attentions. She returned to 23 Fifth Avenue without him and wrote an article for the *Masses,* "The Secret of War: The Look on the Faces of Men Who Have Been Killing—And What Women Think about It."[18]

Mina Loy also noticed "these young men's eyes—going to the front," and she envied them.[19] She volunteered as a nurse in an Italian surgical hospital so she'd have a chance to hear the noise of battle. "But I'm so wildly happy among the blood and mess for a change," she wrote to Carl Van Vechten, "and I stink of iodoform—and all my nails are cut off for operations—and my hands have been washed in iodine, and isn't this a change."[20] Staying on in Florence until the fall of 1916, she became one of the international colony's last remaining members; most had fled to their respective homelands, where they could be closer to their money and their families. After the war was over, the international colony never returned in such glittering numbers, and Florence became a cultural backwater.[21]

Most of Greenwich Village summered at the tip of Cape Cod that summer of 1914, in the small Portuguese fishing village of Provincetown. Two streets wide and three miles long—the only directions needed were "up along" and "down along"—Provincetown provided an idyllic backdrop for the bohemians at play: weathered white cottages, dunes stretching to broad expanses of beach, and as Mabel Dodge recalled, "the cleanest smell of decaying fish and elm trees in the air."[22] Provincetown had been a popular vacation spot since 1911, when the socialist writer Mary Heaton Vorse began promoting the town, but this was the summer of the first full-fledged invasion by Greenwich Village.

Polly Holladay and Hippolyte Havel temporarily moved their restaurant from New York City to Commercial Street in Provincetown, and the local paper dubbed it "the headquarters of the nuts' convention."[23] Max Eastman and Ida Rauh rented a cottage, and together with Floyd Dell they edited the *Masses* from the beaches of Cape Cod. Hutchins Hapgood and Neith Boyce struggled through another marital crisis, and Hapgood tried to pin it down in *The Story of a Lover,* which he completed that July. Charles Demuth, arriving after two years in Paris, took a room in the same house as twenty-two-year-old Stuart Davis. Polly Holladay was falling in love with both of them—as well as with two vacationing Wobblies, Joe O'Carroll and F. Sumner Boyd—and she gave the artists an impromptu exhibition on her restaurant walls. Impeccably attired in a black shirt and white pants, with a plum scarf tied around his waist, Demuth surveyed the summer scene from the horse-drawn diligence as it made its way up and down the town's tiny thoroughfare, waving to friends as he passed by.

At night the vacationers gathered at the gaily painted cottage of George Cram Cook and Susan Glaspell.[24] Cook was prodigal with his jugs of red wine, dubbed Sappho and Bacchus, and by the end of the evening the guests were so intoxicated that they raised their voices to sing:

> *The song that we sing is the death of your day!*
> *The sledge that we swing is the smash of your sway—*
> *Blow after blow till your chains let go,*
> *And the hold of your gold gives way.*[25]

With everyone living in each other's backyard, swimming together in Cubist-patterned outfits or without any clothes at all, eating at Polly's and drinking Cook's flagons of wine, Glaspell observed, "We were as a new family."[26] That sunny moment of innocent bohemia ended abruptly with the declaration of war. The shocked community huddled around the town's stationery store, waiting for the papers to arrive. "Life goes on for us not visibly changed, as yet, but the European war cannot leave it unchanged," Cook wrote in his "New York Letter" that August. "After that we may find ourselves living in a world that has changed fundamentally—another epoch of human life."[27]

F. Sumner Boyd, just released from prison for advocating sabotage in the Paterson strike, proposed an immediate summit conference. "By a fortunate accident, we happen to have here assembled the brains of America," he said, and suggested that they issue a statement to the international working classes identifying the capitalist causes of the conflict and terminating the inhumane war at its outset.[28] The day after war was declared, the Village elders gathered at Hutchins Hapgood's— Eastman, Hapgood, Havel, Cook's mother, Vorse, and others. "No resolutions were drawn up," Hapgood recalled, "for the orthodox Socialist, the Anarchist, the I.W.W., the general poetry and the egotism combined, never reached an agreement. . . ."[29] Retiring to their respective cottages, they talked and drank tumblers of whiskey. "The War went to our heads," Hapgood wrote, "the whiskey helping merely to set free the emotions resulting from the War."[30]

In one cottage Havel raged against the war, against the bourgeois pigs, against Polly's infidelities, while I.W.W. poet Joe O'Carroll began lugubriously reciting his verses heralding the dawn of workers' freedom. Nearby, F. Sumner Boyd fell backward over the veranda of a beach house and disappeared. He went to the nearest telegraph office and tried to cable the committee's wisdom to the rulers of Russia, Germany, England, France, and Austria, and on his return to Provincetown he terrified residents by waving a revolver in the air. Meanwhile, Havel's rage was turning dangerously and quietly self-destructive, and soon he tumbled down a steep flight of stairs. O'Carroll tore off his clothes and ran screaming toward the beach, where his plan to drown himself was prevented only when Provincetowners beat him senseless on the sand. The noise aroused the neighborhood dogs, who engaged in such a vicious fight that Max Eastman had to stop them by throwing pepper in their eyes. Polly Holladay, too, was tempted to drown herself in romantic despair, but after racing into the water fully clothed, she quickly returned to land.[31] "I wanted to die, but the water was too cold," she declared so loudly that she could be overheard all along the beach.[32]

Hapgood captured the group anxiety that underlay those simultaneous explosions on a single summer night: "People felt the War as social upheaval rather than as war. . . . It was personal and impersonal, a turmoil from within as well as from without. Where was our Socialist propaganda now? What part had our ideas held with reality? Where were we? What were we?"[33]

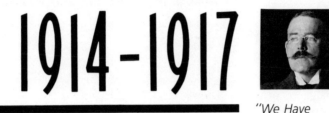

"We Have
Become the Capital
of the Arts!"
HENRY McBRIDE

VILLAGE II:
THE SELLING
OF BOHEMIA

A gainst a background of cloudless skies, dunes, and scrub grass, Provincetown in the summer of 1915 offered a haven from the European war. "Each seemed to hope that his or her particular enthusiasm was about to flower," Mabel Dodge recalled.[1] But the zeitgeist had darkened. The high-spirited drinking seemed boozier that summer of 1915, the romances more toxically jealous, the talk more aimless. "All existing theories had been shown to be impotent," recalled Hapgood. "Individuals had stopped their spiritual existence."[2] His sweeping statement—a mixture of projection and truth—set the tone for the Provincetown summer of 1915. The new bohemians confronted mid-life crises of stale marriages, blocked creativity, fragmented community, and dulled idealism.

In George Cram Cook and Susan Glaspell's bright cottage, Cook was facing middle age without the comfort of any solid achievement. His Village gossip columns for the *Friday Literary Review* were witty but ephemeral, and the grand books he planned to write were never set down on paper. Unable to support himself, he had to rely on the income from Glaspell's popular magazine writing, and her faith in her husband's greatness was increasingly an act of will unsupported by any evidence.

Mabel Dodge and her guests spent their time at Peaked Hill Bar, an abandoned coast guard station three miles from the village. They included her ever-faithful protégé Robert Edmond Jones—who was becoming recognized as a stage designer—and her new lover, the painter Maurice Sterne. Although Dodge relished her role as Sterne's muse and happily posed for his portraits, she feared that his physical advances would rob her of a personal identity. Beset by alternating waves of depression and jealousy, she hallucinated a liaison between Sterne and Neith Boyce and initiated a feud between the households. Exclaiming

I think there was a period in New York before the war when we were all keyed up to pretty high vibrations & we knew a good deal & then lost it.

Mabel Dodge to
Neith Boyce

"Houses have always been my antidote to love!"[3] she assuaged her feelings by redecorating the coast guard station with several coats of white paint. Leo Stein spent long hours with his old friends Sterne and Dodge, loudly discussing art and psychoanalysis (which had fascinated him since first reading Freud in 1909) and urgently counseling Sterne and Dodge not to pursue their relationship. ("Sterne doesn't want a mother except temporarily and unless you succeeded in dominating him more or less completely," Stein warned Dodge, "you'd find after a while that mother was out of a job, though there might be one for a house-keeper."[4])

In the aftermath of one of Hutchins Hapgood's most serious affairs (which Dodge had reported to his wife), relations were uneasy in that household. The strain was exacerbated by Hapgood's writer's block— following his prodigious output of books and columns for the *New York Globe,* he would not complete a piece of writing for the next two decades—and by his annoying habit of offering unsolicited psycho-analytic interpretation, which usually reflected only his own anxieties. Alarmed by the drying up of his flood of words, Hapgood blamed the war and longed for redemption. "Out of the outcast comes the new hope, out of the gutter the enkindling spirit of religious yearning, out of the moral death of the factories the energetic hope of labor organi-zations," Hapgood wrote years later. "And in the midst of the poison of Provincetown came the little movement which resulted in the Province-town Players."[5]

Drink and sex became a despairing ideal, instead of the constructive forms that we had dreamed about.

Hutchins Hapgood

The Provincetown Players was formed on a warm July evening. Several couples sitting around a driftwood fire complained about the New York theater. But instead of criticizing their usual target, Broad-way, they focused on the Washington Square Players: even though that Village organization offered New York's most up-to-date theatrical productions, it wasn't advanced enough for this fireside group.[6] By con-centrating on European playwrights, complained Cook, the Washing-ton Square Players neglected the promise of an American Renaissance. The theater he dreamed of would offer "a threshing floor on which a young and growing culture could find its voice."[7] Cook's bitterness was motivated by the Players' rejection of *Suppressed Desires,* a play he had written with Glaspell. It was witty and new, the Players acknowledged, but its satire of psychoanalysis was "too special" for their audience. Where was the theater that would portray the new Bohemia, that would fearlessly tackle any modern subject? Before the evening was over, the usually reserved Neith Boyce confessed that she, too, had written a play she would like to see produced. The group sponta-neously planned an evening of casual theater. They would stage the plays in the Hapgoods' living room, playing the roles themselves, and commandeer Robert Edmond Jones from Peaked Hill Bar to design the sets. As the group drunkenly drifted home to their white cottages, they

George Cram Cook, c. 1912

BUSINESSES

1. Art Mecca ("Home of the Soul Light Shrine"), 1 Sheridan Square (c. 1917–19). Run by Clivette, who called himself "an eternalist," a palmist, and an artist. Knickerbocker Window Gardens (from 1917). Specialized in the quaint window boxes that embellished the Village.

2. Bruno's Garret, 58 Washington Square South (1914–16). Run by Guido Bruno, this second-story garret appealed to uptown visitors willing to pay to ogle bohemians. In 1916–17 it became the site of the first of many bohemian restaurants run by the peripatetic Romany Marie (Mrs. Damon Marchand), a self-styled gypsy who often served artists free food and read fortunes in her customers' Turkish coffee. After she moved on, it became a spaghetti restaurant called Grace Godwin's Garret (opened 1917).

3. The Crumperie, 6½ Sheridan Square (1917–19). Tearoom run by Miss M. Aletta Crump.

4. *Dial*, 152 West 13th Street (1918–29). The editorial offices of the prestigious magazine, which reached its peak while edited by Scofield Thayer and Marianne Moore (1920–29).

5. Dutch Oven, 137 MacDougal Street (1916–c. 1919). Serving lunch, tea, and dinner, it took over the space occupied by Polly's and was run by Nora Van Loewen.

6. Greenwich Village Theater, 3 Sheridan Square (1917–30). The first plush theater in the Village, it attracted uptowners and staged Sinclair Lewis's *Hobohemia* and John Murray Anderson's *Greenwich Village Follies;* later O'Neill's *Desire under the Elms* and *The Great God Brown.*

7. *Liberator*, 138 West 13th Street (1918–24). A direct descendant of the *Masses*, run by Max Eastman, his sister Crystal Eastman, and Floyd Dell.

8. *Little Review*, 31 West 14th Street (1916–c. 1920).

9. Mad Hatter, 150 West 4th Street (1916–21). Called the Village's first tearoom and run by Edith Unger, its entrance sign read: NWOD EHT TIBBAR ELOH.

10. Modern Art School, 72 Washington Square South (from 1915). Founded by Myra Musselman and Frederick Burt, it moved to Provincetown for the summers.

11. My Tea Wagon, 118 Washington Place (from 1917). A tearoom decorated entirely in orange and black.

12. Open Door, 134 West 4th Street (from 1917). This restaurant advertised "Come Dance and Be Merry in Bohemia."

13. Polly's, 147 West 4th Street (1915–17). Polly's second restaurant, also known as the Greenwich Village Inn. Subsequently it became the Whitney Studio Club (1918–28). John Reed also rented a room for writing at this site (1918).

14. Polly's, 5 Sheridan Square (from 1917). Increasingly commercial, Polly Holladay expanded her new restaurant to two dining rooms and a basement grill.

15. Provincetown Players, 139 MacDougal Street (1916–17). The Players' first New York home. Christine's restaurant, run by Christine Ell, occupied the second floor; considered the spiritual descendant of Polly's, it was the favored hangout of the Players, who ate sixty-cent dinners cooked in the five-foot-square kitchen.

16. Provincetown Players, 133 MacDougal Street (1918–22). The Players' second New York home, with Christine's restaurant on the third floor.

17. Purple Pup, 38 Washington Square West (from 1917). Tearoom and restaurant popular with uptowners.

18. *Quill*, 133 Washington Place (1917–29). This monthly publication was a prime booster of the Village. Also the site of Romany Marie's (1918).

19. Samovar, 148 West 4th Street (from c. 1916). Run by Nanni Bailey, this tearoom was the site of many Provincetown Players' meetings. It inspired the Village verse: "Samovars twinkle, ukeleles tinkle, Villagers drinkel."

20. "Sixty," 60 Washington Square South (1915–16). This popular restaurant was run by Louis Holladay (Polly Holladay's brother), bankrolled by his lover Louise Norton, and cooked for by Christine Ell.

21. Strunsky restaurants, 19 West 8th Street (from 1917). The three family restaurants were the Washington Square Restaurant (first floor), Washington Square Cafeteria, and Greenwich Village Cafeteria (aka "Three Steps Down").

22. Ten Christopher Street. Starting in 1917 this four-story building became the first bohemian "mall." It housed Don Dickerman's Pirate's Den (1917–28), the first theme nightclub in the Village, featuring waiters dressed as buccaneers; the Aladdin Shop; Russian Tea Room; Black Parrot; Romany Marie's; and Vermillion Hound.

23. Thimble Theater, 10 5th Avenue (1915–16). Begun by Guido Bruno and Thomas Edison's son to promote phonograph concerts. Plays were also staged there, including the first regular American performances of August Strindberg's *Miss Julie;* a controversial pro-birth control play, *The State Forbids;* and religious plays by Harry Kemp.

24. Tiny Tim, 6th Avenue at Milligan Place (c. 1916–c. 1918). Candy store run by a Village character described by Village troubadour Bobby Edwards as: "Tiny Tim, all dressed up in white, / Makes those uptown suckers bite. / Makes nice candy, never stale, / Mixes it in a garbage pail."

25. Vincent Peppe & Brother, 40 Washington Square South (through 1910s). Headquarters of the Village's chief real estate brokers.

26. Washington Square Bookshop, 27 West 8th Street (from 1915). The shop's second site, operated by Egmont Arens and Frank Shay.

RESIDENCES

27. Margaret Anderson and Jane Heap, 24 West 16th Street (1917–c. 1922).

28. Maxwell Bodenheim, 228 West 11th Street (1916–17).

29. Randolph Bourne, 18 West 8th Street (1918).

30. Louise Bryant and John Reed, 43 Washington Square South (1916–19); George Cram Cook (1915).

31. Louise Bryant and John Reed, 1 Patchin Place (1919–20).

32. Clemenceau Cottage, 86 Greenwich Avenue. James and Susan Light rented a seventeen-room apartment in a tenement building and rented rooms to friends, including Berenice Abbott (1918), Djuna Barnes (1916), Kenneth Burke (c. 1919), Malcolm Cowley (c. 1919), Dorothy Day (1918), Matthew Josephson, and Ida Rauh.

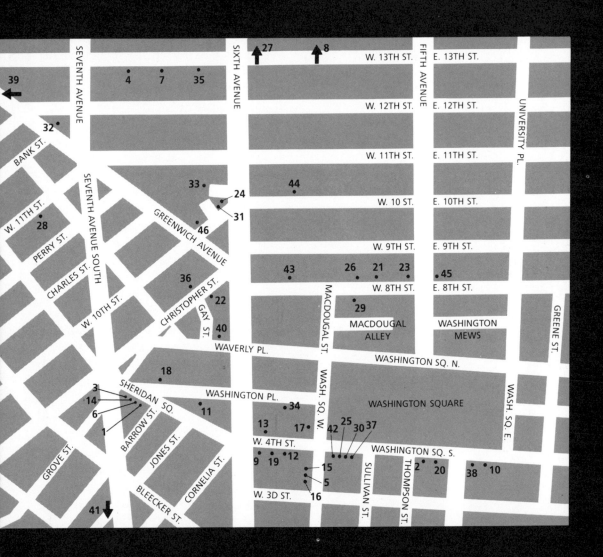

33. George Cram Cook and Susan Glaspell, 4 Milligan Place (1915–18).

34. Hart Crane, 78 Washington Place (1917).

35. Floyd Dell and Marjorie Jones, 106 West 13th Street (1916).

36. Floyd Dell, 11 Christopher Street (1918).

37. Charles Demuth, 45 Washington Square South (1915–16).

38. Max Eastman, 68 Washington Square South (1916–17).

39. Alfred Kreymborg, 32 Jane Street (1916–17).

40. Edna St. Vincent Millay, 139 Waverly Place (1917).

41. Marianne Moore, 14 St. Lukes Place (1918–29).

42. Eugene O'Neill, 38 Washington Square South (1915–17).

43. Man Ray, 47 West 8th Street (1918).

44. Maurice Sterne, 51 West 10th Street (1916–17).

45. Edgard Varèse, Hotel Brevoort (from 1915).

46. William and Marguerite Zorach, 123 West 10th Street (1917–20).

could not imagine that an eminent theater critic would later pronounce: "Among the sand dunes of Cape Cod—we must look for the real birthplace of the New American Drama." [8]

The first performance of the Provincetown Players began at 10 P.M. on July 15, on the veranda of the Hapgoods' bayside cottage. Neith Boyce and Joe O'Brien portrayed fictional versions of Mabel Dodge and John Reed in Boyce's *Constancy* while the audience watched from the adjoining sitting room. For the second play on the bill, Cook and Glaspell's *Suppressed Desires,* Robert Edmond Jones simply turned the audience around to face the living room, where a few carefully arranged sofa pillows and lamps implied a Greenwich Village apartment. The evening was such a lark that Cook promptly put together a second bill of two more one-act plays: *Contemporaries,* by Wilbur Daniel Steele, and Cook's own *Change Your Style.* No one took these lightweight bills seriously or even bothered to record the casts. Boyce closed a letter about the first performances with the casual remark "I wish I had more interesting things to tell you—but as I said, nothing happens here. . . ." [9]

With the exception of *Suppressed Desires*—which became a staple of community theaters throughout America—the plays expired after their extemporaneous productions in Provincetown. Like Floyd Dell's events at the Liberal Club, this quartet of "occasional" one-acts was created for a select audience that would catch all the personal references. *Constancy* satirized the new relations between the sexes by dramatizing the recently ended romance between Dodge and Reed. Just a few weeks before the production Reed, a war correspondent in Bucharest, had opened a letter and found the ring he had sent to Dodge, accompanied by an explanatory letter from Hapgood. "Mabel will never again be to you what she was," he wrote. "If I know her at all, I know she cannot repeat an experience, a feeling, that is gone." [10] Reed threw the ring into a nearby canal, but the romance was barely dead before the Provincetown Players exhumed it. [11]

The other three plays also reflected the moment. *Suppressed Desires* spoofed the effect of a Washington Square couple's being "psyched." Cook's *Change Your Style* satirized the avant-garde impulse in art, and prominent in the cast were Charles Demuth, B.J.O. Nordfeldt, Max Eastman, and his wife, Ida Rauh. Wilbur Daniel Steele's *Contemporaries* presented the story of a radical advocate of rights for the unemployed. Although the denouement revealed his identity as the Son of God, the audience knew that the protagonist was actually Frank Tannenbaum, whose crusade for the unemployed had dominated Dodge's Evenings during the winter of 1914. From that first informal season the Provincetown Players served as the mouthpiece of New Bohemia.

When the Provincetown vacationers resumed Village life in September, most of them looked back on their theatricals as nothing more than idle entertainment. Cook, however, saw greater significance in

A collective faith, collective energy, were good for the man who was lazy unless on fire with vision or purpose, and then had the strength of ten.

Susan Glaspell on
George Cram Cook

the productions. "True drama is born only of one feeling animating all the members of a clan," he wrote. "If there is nothing to take the place of the common religious purpose and passion of the primitive group . . . no new vital drama can arise in any people."[12] His dictum was that of a desperate man who saw a last opportunity for greatness. For Cook the Village community was the clan and the New Bohemianism stood in for the common religious purpose; the forty-two-year-old hoped to reincarnate ancient Greece in the modern era and to spark an American renaissance. Throughout the winter and spring Cook made plans for the next Provincetown season.

He optimistically announced four programs of plays for the next summer and offered $2.50 subscriptions for all of them. With the $217.50 raised, his crew set about refurbishing a weathered wooden fish house that stood at the end of Lewis Wharf, at 571 Commercial Street. Cook and the writer Mary Heaton Vorse were the first to recognize the theatrical possibilities in the rustic building (twenty-five feet by thirty-five feet) filled with barnacled anchors. A group that included Hutchins Hapgood, B.J.O. Nordfeldt, John Reed, and William Zorach created benches from planks resting on kegs and sawhorses, built a ten-foot-by-twelve-foot stage (ingeniously arranged in four sections so it could fit through the fish-house door), and wired rudimentary light-

Wharf Theater, Provincetown

Hutchins Hapgood and Neith Boyce in *Enemies*, 1916

ing. Cook was in his element leading this operation. Although he often pontificated in abstract language, his forte was physical labor, whether farming Iowa soil, refurbishing a cottage, or building a theater. "He was so intense that his esthetic creative excitement finally carried him into a nervous crisis," recalled Hapgood, "the crisis of the *exalté*."[13] When the new Wharf Theater caught fire two days before the opening and two walls were charred, Cook's crew simply painted the remaining walls black. The theater was primitive and production costs never exceeded thirteen dollars per bill, but the second Provincetown season signaled an enormous advance beyond the evenings on the Hapgoods' veranda. Now the group needed plays.

By recycling *Suppressed Desires* and adding Reed's *Freedom* and Boyce's *Winter's Night,* the Players mounted a strong first bill. But they needed a more substantial work to anchor the next one.[14] Sauntering along Commercial Street one June day, Susan Glaspell encountered Terry Carlin (an anarchist who played a key role in Hapgood's book, *An Anarchist Woman*) and asked if he had a play. "I don't write," replied Carlin, "I just think, and sometimes talk." He added, however, that he knew his housemate had a whole trunk filled with plays.

The trunk was actually a small wooden box bearing the legend MAGIC YEAST, and Carlin's housemate turned out to be Eugene O'Neill. By the summer of 1916 O'Neill had filled his box with eleven one-acts and three full-length plays. From them he selected *Bound East for Cardiff* and took it to the Cooks' house one evening. Too shy to read his play aloud or even to listen to it, he paced the dining room while the actor Fred Burt read O'Neill's lines to an audience that included Cook, Glaspell, Reed, Harry Kemp, and Kirah Markham. Their response was epiphanic. "Then we knew what we were for," Glaspell recalled. "We began in faith, and perhaps it is true that when you do that 'all these things shall be added unto you.'" [15]

O'Neill's chance encounter with the Provincetown Players was the felicitous meeting of a theater desperate for plays and a playwright without a theater. The son of the popular actor James O'Neill, Eugene knew the theater intimately, but none of his plays had ever been produced. The twenty-seven-year-old had been writing only a few years, inspired by a term in George Pierce Baker's playwriting class at Harvard in 1914–15. Though still a neophyte playwright, O'Neill had spent years working on cattle ships and tramp steamers, drinking heavily in waterfront dives in Europe and South America, prospecting for gold, recovering from tuberculosis in sanatoriums. He had been a husband and a father and had made one serious suicide attempt by overdosing on Veronal. A darkly handsome man, O'Neill was just coming out of a season-long drinking binge, and Max Eastman recalled that he was as "somber and sallow as a down-and-outer brought to Jesus by the Salvation Army." [16]

Despite his talent and his father's connections, O'Neill could find no niche in the American theater. Broadway was dominated by "well-made" plays and light comedies that bore no resemblance to O'Neill's works; even George Pierce Baker, on reading one of his student's early efforts, declared it not "a play at all." [17] Nor would O'Neill fight to establish a place for himself; morosely shy, he was too proud to push his own work, and he consorted with outcasts (alcoholics, prostitutes, the

John Sloan (1871–1951). *Hell Hole,* 1917. Aquatint and etching, 7⅞ × 9¾ in. (20.1 × 24.8 cm). Philadelphia Museum of Art; Purchased, Lessing J. Rosenwald Gift, and Farrell Fund Income

Eugene O'Neill is at upper right.

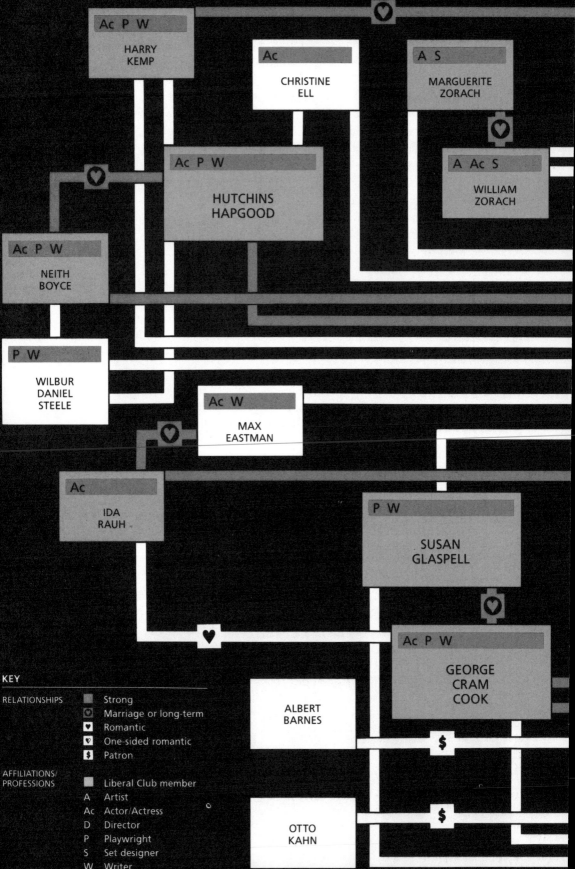

Ac P W HARRY KEMP

Ac CHRISTINE ELL

A S MARGUERITE ZORACH

A Ac S WILLIAM ZORACH

Ac P W HUTCHINS HAPGOOD

Ac P W NEITH BOYCE

P W WILBUR DANIEL STEELE

Ac W MAX EASTMAN

Ac IDA RAUH

P W SUSAN GLASPELL

Ac P W GEORGE CRAM COOK

ALBERT BARNES

OTTO KAHN

KEY

RELATIONSHIPS

Strong

Marriage or long-term

Romantic

One-sided romantic

Patron

AFFILIATIONS/
PROFESSIONS

Liberal Club member

A   Artist
Ac   Actor/Actress
D   Director
P   Playwright
S   Set designer
W   Writer

PROVINCETOWN PLAYERS

Ac
MARY
PYNE

A Ac P W
MINA
LOY

S
ROBERT
EDMOND
JONES

D P W
ALFRED
KREYMBORG

Ac W
WILLIAM
CARLOS
WILLIAMS

PROVINCETOWN PLAYERS

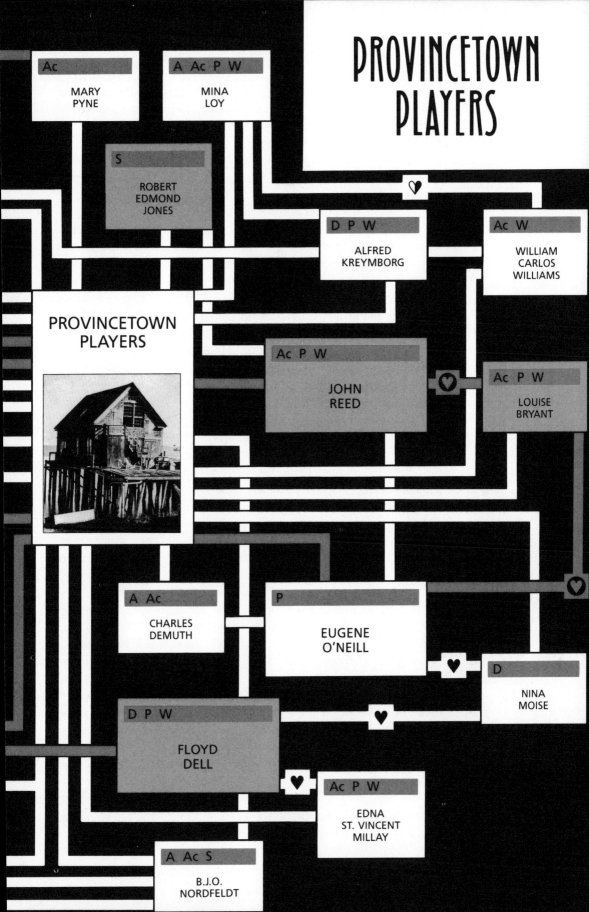

Ac P W
JOHN
REED

Ac P W
LOUISE
BRYANT

A Ac
CHARLES
DEMUTH

P
EUGENE
O'NEILL

D
NINA
MOISE

D P W
FLOYD
DELL

Ac P W
EDNA
ST. VINCENT
MILLAY

A Ac S
B.J.O.
NORDFELDT

unemployed) rather than with people who could pave the way for a theatrical production. O'Neill was most comfortable hanging out in sordid Village bars like the Hell Hole, and its crowd appears thinly disguised in *The Iceman Cometh*.

The Wharf Theater was filled to capacity on Friday evening, July 28, 1916, and the back door of the theater was rolled open. O'Neill's one-act drama of sailors, *Bound East for Cardiff,* was played with the ocean, the fog, and the lights of passing ships in the background, and the incoming tide spraying through holes in the theater's floor. The sound of waves lapping below was broken by the occasional toll of a fog bell. O'Neill stood behind the set, hoarsely prompting a cast that included Cook, Reed, and Harry Kemp, as well as himself. The play eschewed stock theatrical devices and conventional storytelling to create an atmospheric mood piece that had no model in the American theater. When the curtain fell, Glaspell recalled, "It was not merely figurative language to say the old wharf shook with applause."[18]

In the audience that night could be found the familiar Village crowd as well as several fresh faces. Floyd Dell had taken a cottage, and so had Kirah Markham, whose romance with Theodore Dreiser had just ended. Max Eastman and Ida Rauh were moving toward a separation; this holiday would be their last together. Polly Holladay had left Hippolyte Havel and was living with her brother Louis. Mabel Dodge kept her distance from Provincetown, her usual group activities having been supplanted by mysticism. "I feel fairly sick," she wrote to Alfred Stieglitz that summer, "when I am not somehow trying to add a mite more to the consciousness already in the world."[19]

John Reed's house was the center of Provincetown activity. Curtains and partitions had been added to accommodate his houseful of guests that included F. Sumner Boyd, Charles Demuth, Marsden Hartley, and the most attractive new face in town, Louise Bryant. Havel cooked for them all and railed incessantly: about the landlord (he "forgets about the Brotherhood when fresh Jews appear"), about Reed's radical talk ("You're just a parlor socialist," he said, and Reed replied, "And you're a kitchen anarchist").[20] About the romance between John Reed and Louise Bryant, however, Havel was uncharacteristically sentimental; it even inspired him to sing at work. When Provincetowners asked Havel about their relationship, he would reply, "There is nothing to tell—just that it is a dove cottage."[21] He said to Bryant that he had always thought quarreling was necessary to keep love stirred up. "But it's not so, why the wrong peoples get together is all—and dis is so lovely—you and Jackie."[22]

Twenty-four-year-old Bryant had left her dentist-husband and her hometown of Portland, Oregon, a few months earlier to live with Reed at 43 Washington Square South. He declared this vivid beauty with violet eyes "the first person I ever loved without reservation" and en-

Charles Demuth and Eugene O'Neill in Provincetown, c. 1916

LEFT
Louise Bryant sunbathing
nude in Provincetown, 1916

BELOW
O'Neill and Reed in Provincetown, 1916

thusiastically introduced her to everyone in the Provincetown colony.[23]
He lobbied for the production of her turgid allegorical drama *The
Game,* prompting one of the Players to complain, "Just because some-
one is sleeping with somebody is no reason we should do her play."[24]
Mabel Dodge had been introduced to Bryant, but whenever they passed
one another on Commercial Street, neither spoke a word.

O'Neill moved into a shack diagonally across from Reed and Bryant
but maintained his privacy by posting a sign that threatened, "May wild
jackasses desecrate the grave of your grandmother if you disturb me."[25]
The warm relationship between Reed and O'Neill was anchored in their
shared penchant for romantic adventure, but it was complicated by
O'Neill's growing attraction to Bryant. Uneasy in her presence, he communicated his desire only in covert glances, but most of the community
could see that Bryant was also attracted to him. She encouraged a romantic triangle by loaning O'Neill a volume of poetry that contained
between its leaves a note—"Dark eyes, what do you mean?"—and
then confided to O'Neill (falsely) that she and Reed could not enjoy sexual relations because of Reed's kidney ailment.[26] When O'Neill and
Bryant became lovers, the news raced through the Provincetown community, and Mabel Dodge came in from Peaked Hill Bar to offer Reed
unsolicited solace. In *Thirst,* on the season's last bill of plays, O'Neill and
Bryant played a bizarre love scene between a mulatto sailor (O'Neill
was sufficiently tanned that he didn't wear makeup) and a parched
dancer. O'Neill ended that summer in a state of unparalleled happi-
ness; after a long grim period he had found both vocation and love.

Louise Bryant, George Cram Cook, and Eugene O'Neill in *Thirst,* 1916

We Provincetowners were more successful in living our lives than in expressing them in our writings and pictures, though even in the art of living we were embry-onic as compared with some of our unconscious social instincts and intui-tions. We talked about art and revolution, but the talk was the main thing—and a delight-ful thing.

Hutchins Hapgood

"All the world will know Gene's plays some day," Cook declared. "Some day this little theatre will be famous."[27] Unable to bear the end of the theater season, he proposed to continue it in New York. Glaspell was appalled, convinced that neither Cook's summer-long Dionysian exaltation nor the summer vacationers' enthusiasm could be sustained back in the city. But Cook—buoyed by Reed's predictable enthusiasm, Dell's tempered support, and O'Neill's desire to have his plays pro-duced—called a meeting to establish an ongoing theater. Among the twenty-nine who signed the roster that evening were Louise Bryant, George Cram Cook, Floyd Dell, Charles Demuth, Max Eastman, Susan Glaspell, Hutchins Hapgood, Robert Edmond Jones, Eugene O'Neill, Ida Rauh, John Reed, Mary Heaton Vorse, and William Zorach. (Of the twenty-nine on the original roster, sixteen were members of the Liberal Club.) In just one day Cook, Eastman, Reed, and the actor Fred Burt wrote a constitution that set down the collective's first principles, de-spite Hapgood's warning that "Organization is death!"[28] The Province-town Players would encourage new American drama without bowing to Broadway's commercialism. The democratically selected plays would dramatize the moment and be produced in the playful spirit of ama-teurism. These principles would soon be violated, but the constitution nonetheless laid the foundation for Provincetown's summer high jinks to become an institution that would transform the American theater.

Could the pure and summery spirit of the Provincetown Players sur-vive year-round in Greenwich Village? Complicating that difficult tran-sition was the fact that the Village itself was in flux. By 1916 the bohemian Eden no longer seemed so innocent, and several Village "institutions" that had been created a few years earlier—Mabel Dodge's Evenings, the *Masses,* Polly's—reflected the significant changes in the neighborhood.

Dodge's career moved in impulsive surges—as she put it, "I just switched on one viewpoint and switched off another"—but its general trajectory resembled that of the Village at large.[29] Before her Evenings ended in the summer of 1914, the broad coalition of her guests had begun to dissolve.[30] Among the first to move on were the I.W.W. and the anarchists, who resented Dodge's return to the personal and aesthetic concerns of her years in Florence. Instead of the Villa Curonia, she now was preoccupied with her Finney Farm at Croton-on-Hudson. There she devoted her attention to the nearby school run by Isadora Duncan's sister, Elizabeth, where students lived their daily lives as a work of art.

The tendency among Villagers to drift from the political to the personal was evident, too, in the cult of psychoanalysis. After Dr. A. A. Brill introduced Freud's theory to the Village at the beginning of 1914, it became increasingly fashionable to enter psychoanalysis or at least to play the parlor game of "associating." Dodge led the way in 1916 when she began to see the psychoanalyst Smith Ely Jelliffe, having already sought mental balance through astrology, Christian Science healing, and theosophy. Other Village leaders soon followed: Floyd Dell, Max Eastman, and Hutchins Hapgood. "Psychoanalysis is going to do wonderful things," Cook wrote in his "New York Letter," "but for a while it is fated to be a fad."[31]

At the *Masses* the artist-writer coalition was strained to the breaking point, and in March 1916 a faction of the artists declared a strike. A sober business meeting of artists, writers, and editors was called at which parliamentary procedure was observed and minutes were kept, participants sat in straight-back chairs, drank no beer, and ate no cheese. "*The Masses* is no longer the resultant of the ideas and art of a number of personalities," said John Sloan on behalf of the artists' fac-

There was a real bohemia. Delightful. Why? Greenwich Village was filled with people doing absolutely nothing!

Marcel Duchamp

Way down south in Greenwich Village
 In the Freud and Jung and Brill age
People come with paralysis
 For the balm of psychoanalysis
Here the modernist complexes
 And the intermediate sexes—
Fairyland's not far from Washington Square.

Bobby Edwards and others,
The Village Epic (sung,
accompanied by ukulele), 1910s

tion. "*The Masses* seems to have developed a 'policy.'"[32] He suggested a return to utopian ideals in running the magazine: editors would be abolished, all decisions would be made by participatory democracy, and the costs of producing the magazine would be reduced so that it could be removed from "the Organized Charity class of drains on the purses of the rich."[33]

The artists (Maurice Becker, Glenn Coleman, Stuart Davis, Henry Glintenkamp, Sloan) objected to having the social content of their drawings spelled out in captions, which detracted from the drawings' artistic significance. Dell, in response, grumbled to Eastman, "We're running a magazine, not an art gallery."[34] Having grown increasingly skeptical of the cooperative process, Eastman answered Sloan's "blue-print for the millennium" by offering to resign. After Sloan's proposal failed (eleven to six), Dell swiftly moved to expel the rebels from the magazine. When his vindictive proposal also lost, the group tried to bind its wounds by electing members of the dissident faction to key positions on the executive board.[35] Eastman told a newspaper reporter that the meeting "was just our semiannual scrap. We live on scraps." But Sloan told the same reporter, "It just proves that real democracy doesn't work—yet."[36] The following day Sloan resigned, joined by Becker, Coleman, Davis, and the writer Robert Carlton Brown. This walkout did not end the *Masses,* but it did narrow the magazine's coalition; artists were now split off from "idea men."

A stroll around Washington Square revealed the changing bohemian landscape. One Villager complained in 1916 that the city had cut up the square with paths and would now "proceed to laboriously and without joy to stick tulips or some other straight official flower into these geometrical plots."[37] Bertolotti's was one of the few raffish Italian restaurants remaining on the south side of the square, and by the end of 1915 newspapers were nostalgically recalling the bohemian taste for spaghetti and garlic. "If Greenwich Village ever did gaze entranced upon the surrounding Italy, its eyes are turned away now," observed the *New York Tribune*. "For Greenwich Village is eating all to itself in little cubby holes off the main thoroughfare."[38]

Italian restaurants had been replaced by a new industry: tearooms. Inspired by the success of Polly's, they followed the same formula of cheap food in informal surroundings. The new tearooms boasted self-consciously bohemian names like the Purple Pup, the Samovar, the Black Cat, the Idée Chic, and the Mad Hatter. Tallow candles flickered on the tables and open fires burned in the grate; batik hangings or handicrafts covered brightly painted walls. Menus were invariably handwritten in ink on brown paper, offering teas and coffees, near-beer in egg cups, loganberry juice, and bran-nut muffins with Dundee marmalade. Comely young women wearing smocks and tan socks rolled below the knee served as waitresses. The new industry provided work

I flutter down the jocund aisles, the plaintively-garish corridors of New York, bumping into solemn-eyed, three-fourths happy poets, drained, humorous futurist-artists, wives of poets who have short strings to which their husbands are attached, enormous-bearded, bubbling sculptors, prostitutes who are not prostitutes, and Emma Goldman.

Maxwell Bodenheim to
Amy Lowell, c. 1916

LEFT
At the Mad Hatter

BELOW
The Samovar

for the surplus of single women in the Village, who not only served food in the tearooms but also offered ukulele instruction and sold batik blouses and negligées to order. By 1917 the *Quill* counted twenty-five tearooms in the Village.

Polly Holladay anticipated the Village emigration west by moving to larger quarters at 147 West Fourth Street in 1915 and to Sheridan Square in 1917. By that time Holladay ran two dining rooms and a basement grill, and Hippolyte Havel had been replaced by a less-ferocious waiter named Mike. "Polly's one touch of the spirit was with Hippo," Hutchins Hapgood observed, and he complained that her new cafés were used as "a bait for the uptowners and those who can not distinguish between the spirit and the vulgarly sensational." [39] A café opened by her beloved brother Louis at 60 Washington Square South carried on a more authentic tradition. Known as "the Sixty" and bankrolled by his lover Louise Norton (now separated from her husband, the poet Allen Norton), the basement café had walls of lavender, yellow, and blue, and a small red piano room, where customers sang popular songs such as "Frankie and Johnny," played cards, and nursed cups of coffee at bare pine tables. The waitress was "a golden haired Valkyrie" named Christine Ell, who had worked in the factories of Paterson, New Jersey. When interviewed by a reporter, Louis refused to give the café's address for fear of being stampeded by sightseers; his not unreasonable fear was in response to the ubiquity of a new element in the Village, popularly known as Uptown Swillage.

Some dated the uptown influx to the costume balls that Floyd Dell had started in 1914 to raise money for the *Masses* and the Liberal Club. Inspired by the popular Left Bank tradition of Quatre-Arts balls, Dell suggested costume dances and called them Pagan Routs. For the first one Art Young designed a poster—a naked golden girl astride a green faun streaking across a crimson sky—that awakened such aphrodisiacal fantasies that Webster Hall was mobbed. Other Village organizations capitalized on the financial success of these events; soon there was the

I don't know whether you know the pseudo-Bohemianism of Washington Square. It is nauseating to a decent man who doesn't need artificial sexual stimulation. It is a vulgar, disgusting conglomerate of second and third-rate artists and would-be artists, of I.W.W. agitators, of sluts kept or casual, clean and unclean, of Socialists and near Socialists, of poetasters and pimps, of fornicators and dancers and those who dance to enable them to fornicate—But hell, words fail me to express my contempt for the whole damned bunch.

John Quinn to Ezra Pound, January 12, 1917

Drawn by K. R. Chamberlain.

ANIMALS AT THE MASSES BALL

Animals at the Masses Ball.
Kenneth Russell Chamberlain,
Masses, June 1916

Liberal Club's "Arabian Nights," the *Masses'* "Futurist Ball," *Mother Earth'*s "Red Revel."[40] They became so familiar that by 1917 a Village magazine published the how-to formula for running a Village dance: pick an exotic theme and an unusual Oriental name like Taj Mahal, hire a band, rent Webster Hall, and sell cheap liquor.

In addition to becoming a popular solution to financial problems, the all-night balls gave Villagers the opportunity to celebrate the bohemian community they had created. As Dell recalled, "They were spontaneously joyous and deliberately beautiful, focusing in a mood of playfulness the passion for loveliness which was one of the things that had brought us to the Village. . . ."[41] Villagers didn't need to join the Provincetown Players to dress up and playact, to push the limits of accepted behavior by dancing such "immoral" steps as the bunny hug and the turkey trot, to stay out till dawn. George Bellows appeared at one ball as a matador, Stuart Davis as a dope fiend, Harry Kemp as an Assyrian king crowned by a tin washbasin. John Quinn dressed as a pirate, and many combined minimal (and strategically placed) costumes with

Way down South in Greenwich Village,
Where they eat Italian swillage,
Where the fashion illustrators
Flirt with interior decorators,
There the cheap Bohemian fakirs
And the boys from Wanamaker's
Gather "atmosphere"
In Washington Square.

Bobby Edwards and others,
The Village Epic (sung,
accompanied by ukulele), 1910s

bright body painting. Emma Goldman hosted the Red Revel (for those of "red revolutionary blood") dressed as a nun, and she demonstrated a waltzlike step she called the Anarchist's Slide.

Just a few years earlier George Cram Cook had suggested, "The transformation of a Villager would be a vital theme for a novel of 1914." [42] By 1917 this transformation had become a more complex subject, as Villagers began to metamorphose into marketable parodies of themselves. Even Mabel Dodge advertised her services as an interior decorator in the *New Republic,* and a few months later she dispensed tabloid wisdom to the masses in the *New York Evening Journal* under such headlines as "Supernormal, Normal, or Misfit: Which Are You?" "Choose Idol, Then Love Him Forever," and "Fear, Brutal Parasite, Feeds Our Soul Till It Dies." [43] Village poseurs began to flourish; Mr. Charles, the Village barber, announced that "his repertoire includes the artistic bobbing of women's hair"; and short-lived little magazines like the *Village Spectator,* the *Quill,* and the *Pagan* devoted separate advertising sections to "Greenwich Village Industries." [44] The Village increasingly depended upon uptown patrons: they were customers in its teashops, pagans-for-a-night at its dances, smokers of "Greenwich Village Cigarettes," buyers of "Fashions to be worn in the Village." Uptown newspapers published columns such as the *New York Tribune*'s "Who's Who in New York's Bohemia?" And when a reporter inquired, "Why doesn't somebody talk vorticistically so we could be sure this was the Latin Quarter?" someone in the crowd was likely to oblige. [45] By 1917 a mainstream, hardcover *Guide to Greenwich Village* had already appeared.

The most blatant commercializer of new bohemia was a middle-age immigrant who referred to himself as "I, Guido Bruno" and modeled himself on Hippolyte Havel. Ideally located across from the Fifth Avenue bus terminal on Washington Square South, Bruno's gen-u-wine Greenwich Village garret was lit by candles flickering in the gloom; he decorated it with half-finished modernistic canvases on easels and filled the small rooms with artists' model types chattering in Village argot and poets spouting free verse. Uptowners knew about the garret from the

Mrs. Mabel Dodge is prepared to assist in the furnishing and decorating of rooms, to supply ideas of her own, or to express those of her clients.

CONSULTATION BY
APPOINTMENT ——
23 FIFTH AVENUE

Advertisement in the *New Republic,* January 13, 1917

OPPOSITE, TOP
Webster Hall Ball

OPPOSITE, BOTTOM
Kit Cat Club

Way down south in Greenwich Village
   Came a bunch of uptown swillage
Folks from Lenox subway stations
   Come with lurid expectations
There the Village informalities
   Are construed as abnormalities
By the boobs that visit Sheridan Square.

Bobby Edwards and others, *The Village Epic* (sung, accompanied by ukulele), 1910s

various Village magazines that Bruno published and distributed, claiming a circulation as high as 32,000.[46] He charged visitors ten cents to enter and twenty-five cents for special events like the Monday Cabarets, where poets read by candlelight. Business was booming.

Most Villagers dismissed Bruno as a megalomaniacal charlatan who had divined as early as 1915 that Greenwich Village needed its P. T. Barnum.[47] He exploited the pool of single Village women—persuading them to play Village bohemians by feeding them and providing spartan sleeping quarters—and then advertised his premises as "First Aid for Struggling Artists." He bilked women who paid to have their poetry printed in his magazines, and when they threatened legal action he vowed to testify in court that he had slept with them ("I, Bruno, sleep with all girls"[48]). But as the supporter of the new generation of bohemians, as a staunch advocate of free speech, as a publisher of unknown writers, even this sleazy entrepreneur had his place in the burgeoning Village. He was the first to publish Hart Crane's poetry and a booklet by Djuna Barnes, he staged a controversial play in support of birth control called *The State Forbids,* and he successfully fought in court for the publication of Alfred Kreymborg's tale of a streetwalker, *Edna.*

The thriving Village real-estate market reflected bohemia's inadvertent role in colonizing marginal areas and paving the way for gentrification. As early as 1914 local merchants raised fifteen thousand dollars to advertise Greenwich Village and upgrade property values, and pale green window boxes were installed to enhance the effect of a quaint and neighborly village. By the following year, when the demand for artistic Village apartments outstripped the supply, a corporation was formed to renovate old Village homes and soon their rents were quadrupled. The *New York Times* described this sort of rehabilitator as one

---

Greenwich Village! A republic in the air! A gathering of constantly changing men and women that have a past or have a future and live in both. A gathering of people that worship the highest ideal, constantly building bridges from one illusion to another, not noticing the mud that covers their roads and that is thrown after them from all sides. Greenwich Village! Refuge of saints condemned to live in the crude, hard, realistic world. Greenwich Village! Where genius starved and gave the world the best it had, where fortunes are squandered and fortunes are made. . . . Where new ideas are developed into systems, into systems that will be overthrown to-morrow and substituted by others that will not live any longer.

Bruno Guido, "An Apostrophe to Greenwich Village,"
New York Tribune, November 14, 1915

---

who "seizes upon decayed tenements where free souls live in inexpensive dinginess and rebuilds them in studio apartments whose rentals are beyond the reach of any but the Philistine plutocrat."[49] In 1916 the Village's perpetual quaintness was ensured by new zoning laws that barred industry and by economic pressures that drove away the longtime Italian residents.

The chief rental agent, Vincent Peppe, benefited as every cranny in the Village became rentable, and large rooms were divided into three studio apartments. Rents for studio apartments more than tripled from six dollars a week to seventy-five dollars a month. A social worker from an earlier era observed, "It was certainly amusing and astounding to us who had fought against cellar lodgings as unhealthful, damp and unfit for human habitation as they were, to see them revived as 'one room studios' and let often at six times the price of former rentals."[50] By the end of 1917 the *Quill* was calling the Village "the Republic of Vincent Peppe."[51] The price increases around Washington Square pushed the community west to Christopher Street, Hudson Street, and Minetta Lane. "Our pseudo-Bohemia is always migrating," observed the *New York Times*, "as homeless as the Mormons before they found the Vale of Deseret."[52]

The old community was joined by a new generation arriving in the Village—among them Berenice Abbott, Malcolm Cowley, Hart Crane, Edna St. Vincent Millay, and Edmund Wilson. To some of the newcomers the Villagers' revolution seemed awkwardly earnest and their behavior tame. Bohemia is inevitably ephemeral, a brief moment poised between revolution and fad. As one Village magazine observed in June 1918: "Whatever else Bohemia may be it is almost always yesterday."[53]

The Village was just beginning its transition when the Provincetown Players rented an unheated brownstone at 139 MacDougal Street in the fall of 1916. Its location next door to the Liberal Club was ideal, and the rent was only a hundred dollars a month. Having already managed to create a theater from a fish house, the Players could certainly transform three and a half rooms on a parlor floor into something more elegant—even though the building was only fifteen feet wide and forty-four feet deep. They installed tiers of bare plank seating for 140 people, calcimined the walls a smoky gray, and painted the proscenium arch vermilion, gold, violet, and blue. The result looked as if someone had installed a circus grandstand in the front parlor. In the single dressing room a three-panel screen was installed and dubbed "The Paraphernalia for Modesty," and the Provincetown Players were ready for their first New York season.

The idealistic enterprise launched from the beaches of Provincetown almost foundered during its first New York season. On the premiere bill—O'Neill's *Bound East for Cardiff*, Bryant's *The Game*, and

Dell's *King Arthur's Socks*—the principle of amateurism was already being compromised when Dell ceded directorial responsibility to the professional actor Teddy Ballantine. The shift toward professionalization was probably inevitable, but the speed with which it occurred disquieted many. Barely a month after opening, the Provincetown Players moved further in that direction: they hired their first employee (stagehand Louis Ell) and appointed separate committees for revising plays, designing scenery, and mounting productions. Hapgood again railed against "the death which lurked in organization," and Reed and Bryant resigned from the executive committee.[54] A few months later Dell, Eastman, and Hapgood followed suit, and internal battles prompted the committee to request B.J.O. Nordfeldt's resignation as well.

Within that first month the Provincetown Players also demonstrated their aesthetic limits. They welcomed plays that were radical in subject but didn't know what to do with the formal radicalism of Alfred Kreymborg's *Lima Beans,* which he described as "a fantastic treatment of commonplace themes set to a stylized rhythm."[55] The play incorporated free verse, a musical rondo by Karl Maria von Weber, and a cast of four: the Wife, the Husband, the Huckster, and the Curtain. The re-

Provincetown Players arranging scenery for *Bound East for Cardiff,* November 1916

Left to right: Frances Burrell, Eugene O'Neill, Hippolyte Havel, William Stuart, B.J.O. Nordfeldt, Frank Jones, Henry M. Hall, George Cram Cook

Mina Loy and William Carlos Williams in *Lima Beans*, December 1916

sponse of the Provincetowners was initially cool—"They simply can't see beyond blood and thunder," reported William Zorach to Kreymborg—but John Reed threatened to quit unless the play was accepted.[56] The compromise they reached allowed Kreymborg to stage his play in their theater so long as he enlisted a cast outside the Provincetown Players, none of whom could imagine speaking his lines.

The best candidates for understanding his verse were poets, so Kreymborg enlisted his *Others* magazine cohorts William Carlos Williams and Mina Loy (who had just arrived in New York). Zorach created a set of black-and-white screens that cost $2.50. Kreymborg rehearsed his cast by beating time with a pencil, and the Players observed the rehearsals skeptically. The audience on opening night, however, so enjoyed the colloquy between Mina Loy in her décolleté creation and the stumbling, bizarrely clad William Carlos Williams that the canvas curtain went up and down sixteen times before the applause stopped. Nonetheless, the play's success did not inspire the Provincetown Players to challenge the conventions of naturalistic theater; modernist theater remained far more conventional than modernist art and poetry.

Before the first season ended, a professional director named Nina Moise began supervising the productions and many of the founding members departed. Some resignations resulted from overcommitment to other causes, some from the growing realization that the Provincetown Players were not in the vanguard of the class struggle or the modernist movement, and some from competition among the Players. "I saw new talent rebuffed," recalled Floyd Dell, "its fingers brutally stepped on by the members of the original group, who were anxious to do the acting whether they could or not—and usually they could not; but I wasted my sympathy, for the new talent, more robust than I supposed, clawed its way up on to the raft, and stepped on other new fingers, kicked other new faces as fast as they appeared."[57]

GEORGE CRAM COOK'S RECIPE FOR FISH-HOUSE PUNCH

4 quarts of three-star Hennessey brandy, 2 quarts of rum, 2 quarts of peach brandy, 2 quarts of lemon juice, and 10 pounds of sugar. Stir together over a block of ice. (More conventional recipes include 2 quarts of water.)

George Cram Cook provided the Players' chief support—one historian called him the "Atlas of the Provincetown Players"—not because he could organize the group but because he could inspire them.[58] His eyes, Hutchins Hapgood recalled, would "dance with the joy of ideas becoming poetic realities," as he staged opening-night parties like Hellenic rituals.[59] The collective spirit was restored as everyone gathered around the granite bowl that held Cook's potent fish-house punch. "It was important we drink together," recalled Susan Glaspell, "for thus were wounds healed, and we became one again. . . ."[60] As those parties continued into the night, ruffled feelings gave way to carousing, singing, and hugging. When the bottom of the punch bowl appeared, Cook would invariably raise the bowl high and proclaim, "Give it all to me and I guarantee to intoxicate all the rest of you."[61]

ART II:
NEW YORK HOSTS
TOUT LE MONDE

T he town is full of weird artists from all parts of the world," Henry McBride wrote to Gertrude Stein. "We have become the capital of the arts!"[1] Writing at the beginning of 1915, the art critic was the first to announce New York's new status. A note of hyperbole had crept into his customary jesting with Stein, but it was based on truth. After the outbreak of World War I, the pilgrimage to Europe was reversed, and New York became the modern Mecca.[2]

The signs of a great shift could be seen in New York's increasing numbers of modern-art exhibitions. According to the historian Judith Zilczer, the quantity steadily grew from 1907, when there were five shows, until 1917, when there were a dozen times that many.[3] Not until the 1930s would New York again host so many modern shows. Without leaving the city, one could see not only American artists but also the full range of European modernism: Fauves, Cubists, Vorticists, and Futurists. Dealers competed for exclusive rights to exhibit Picasso's paintings, and one gallery even mounted an exhibition that domesticated modern art for interior decoration. Paris and London combined could not offer so rich a menu.[4] Noting modern art's newly commercial status, Alfred Stieglitz remarked, "The game is being played fast and furious everywhere and to me it is disgusting."[5]

During New York's international years, throughout World War I, the Latin Quarter moved to the twisting streets around Washington Square. The Brevoort Café was dotted with the sky blue of French military uniforms, and carafes of Vichy Célestin sat on its bar. Paradoxically, New York's new sense of autonomy from Paris was inspired by these immigrants: they imported the prewar spirit of the avant-garde to the New World, and their fascination with American technology encouraged New Yorkers to value the city as the capital of modernity. The most influential expatriates were primarily French—Arthur Cravan,

Baron de Meyer, Marcel Duchamp, Albert Gleizes, Francis Picabia and Gabrielle Buffet-Picabia, Henri-Pierre Roché, Edgard Varèse—along with the Swiss Jean Crotti and the English Mina Loy. Nouveau New Yorkers also included recently repatriated citizens such as Leo Stein and the three Stettheimer sisters.

The French arrived in New York with preconceptions that dated back to the nineteenth century.[6] America, they contended, was such a young, materialistic country that it could not excel at the fine arts, but they admired the daring of its architects and engineers, the brashness of its advertisements, and the efficiency of its plumbing. In the geometric shapes of New York's skyline and its bright electric lights they discerned Cubist forms. They adopted the informality of American fashion, wearing flashy tweed suits, "Chicago ties more violent than American pickles," and bowler hats—or even no hat at all.[7]

The first wave, which began in the spring of 1915, was made up of artists: the Picabias, Crotti, Duchamp, and Gleizes. Frequently lumped

Jean Crotti (1878–1958).
Marcel Duchamp, 1915.
Pencil on paper, 21½ ×
13½ in. (54.6 × 34.3 cm).
The Museum of Modern Art,
New York; Purchase

together by the American press, they indeed formed a tight-knit group: Picabia, Duchamp, and Gleizes knew each other from their Puteaux days; Crotti would soon marry Duchamp's sister, Suzanne; and their paintings had hung in many of the same exhibitions. Above all, they shared a fascination with New York, which, one visitor observed, strives to be "as modern as possible, not to be merely New, but ever-new, York."[8] Duchamp's reaction was typical. Sailing into New York harbor on a sultry, windless day, he was dumbfounded by the soaring skyline. What had signified commercialism and lack of culture to Mabel Dodge, who had wept over its ugliness when she arrived three years earlier, Duchamp read as the jagged, dynamic contour of the future.

Some of the new arrivals, such as Gleizes, expected to find cowboys on Broadway. Others yearned to see the Brooklyn Bridge, ride the subway, inspect the latest in pistons and derricks, pulleys and beams.[9] Each sounded a note of admiration for these industrial creations. "The genius who built the Brooklyn Bridge is to be classed alongside the genius who built Notre Dame de Paris," Gleizes told a reporter.[10] Crotti flatly declared that New York had replaced Paris as the capital of modernity. Duchamp looked up the 792-foot-tall Woolworth Building and wrote a note to himself: "Find an inscription for the Woolworth Building as a ready-made."[11]

Not all the European expatriates were so enchanted. The Baron and Baroness Adolf de Meyer, for example, cared not a whit for subways or pistons. They had made the trip across the Atlantic on a private yacht chartered by rich friends, and they were accustomed to consorting with members of international society whose titles—unlike the de Meyers'—were both old and real. The de Meyers were a chic, parvenu pair, and their marriage was strictly à la mode. He was a forty-six-year-old half-Jewish homosexual ballet fan; she was a strikingly beautiful cocaine-addicted fencing champion who claimed Edward VII as her father. (One friend called them "Péderaste and Médisante [pederast and slanderer].") They arrived in New York with elegant clothes on their backs and nothing in their pockets. As *Vanity Fair* declared, "They are posters for fashions distinctly European and remote."[12] The baron and

---

The machine has become more than a mere adjunct of life. It is really part of human life . . . perhaps the very soul. In seeking forms through which to interpret ideas or by which to expose human characteristics I have come at length upon the form which appears most brilliantly plastic and fraught with symbolism. I have enlisted the machinery of the modern world, and introduced it into my studio.

Francis Picabia, *New York Tribune*, October 24, 1915

---

baroness found New York boringly prosaic, too young a society to have evolved the moneyed High Bohemia that had supported them in Europe. In New York the baron pragmatically decided to market his sense of the beau monde. He became a fashion photographer, quickly signing contracts with both *Vogue* and *Vanity Fair* and supplementing his income by giving finishing-school lectures to nouveau-riche women.

The composer and conductor Edgard Varèse arrived in New York during the last days of 1915, a representative of the latest thinking about musical composition. Hearing *Le Sacre du printemps* at its premiere, he had found Igor Stravinsky's music unshockingly natural, and he was a devotee of Erik Satie's and Claude Debussy's search for new sonorities. What distinguished Varèse from other composers was his exploration of sounds outside the traditional musical scale and beyond the capabilities of conventional orchestras. "My aim has always been the liberation of sound," he said near the end of his life, and one can trace that aim as far back as 1905, when the twenty-two-year-old Varèse was exploring the musical possibilities of sirens.[13] "*Let music sound!*" he exhorted in a manifesto. "Our alphabet is poverty-stricken and illogical."[14]

He shared with the Futurists a fascination with gongs, horns, sirens, and Klaxons, but he differed from them in his desire to make "not just noise but *noise being transmuted into sound,* noise becoming *beautiful,* noise becoming timbre, timbre revealing its spirit."[15] His music has been likened to Cubism, and he found support in the community of Paris artists as well as musicians. Before the war Varèse had helped plan an ambitious collaboration: he would conduct a musical production of *A Midsummer Night's Dream* at the Cirque Medrano, with a translation by Jean Cocteau, sets by Gleizes, and a potpourri of music composed by Varèse, Gabriel Astruc, Maurice Ravel, Satie, and Stravinsky.

When he set out for America, Varèse cherished hopes of finding a new universe of sound there. The supremely self-confident composer-conductor was convinced that the New York patron Otto Kahn would support him, for he had already won awards in France and conducted orchestras in Germany. Instead, he found himself fighting the battle of modern music alone in America. New York seemed to him "banal and dirty," its natives "sportsman types," and he was forced to support himself by copying scores and giving music lessons.[16] Although he did discover a brave new world of mechanical sounds in New York, he was also, ironically, the victim of its machinery. While standing on a sidewalk one day in the late summer of 1916, he was struck by an automobile and sent to the hospital for an eleven-week recuperation.

When Mina Loy arrived in New York from Florence in October 1916, she set her sights on making money. She had drawn fashion plates that delighted Florentine tailors and now hoped such American magazines as *Vogue* would publish her forward-looking couture on

The music that ought to be living and vibrating at this moment needs a new means of expression, and only science can infuse it with youthful sap.

Edgard Varèse,
manifesto in *391*

Joseph Stella (1880–1946). *Edgard Varèse*, c. 1920. Silverpoint drawing, 22 × 16 in. (55.9 × 40.6 cm). The Baltimore Museum of Art; Purchase Fund

their covers. Yet even at her most pragmatic, Loy had little sense of financial realities, and she found no niche in the business world. She was effusively welcomed by New York's avant-garde, however. Thanks to the informal press agentry of Carl Van Vechten and Mabel Dodge, her writings and her name had preceded her arrival. Besides her aphorisms and poems published in *Camera Work* and *Rogue,* she was best known for the controversial "Love Songs," which ignited the first issue of the poetry magazine *Others.* Shortly after she arrived she came into the orbit of the Provincetown Players when Alfred Kreymborg cast her opposite William Carlos Williams in *Lima Beans.*

No one who has not lived in New York has lived in the Modern World.

Mina Loy,
New York Evening Sun,
February 17, 1917

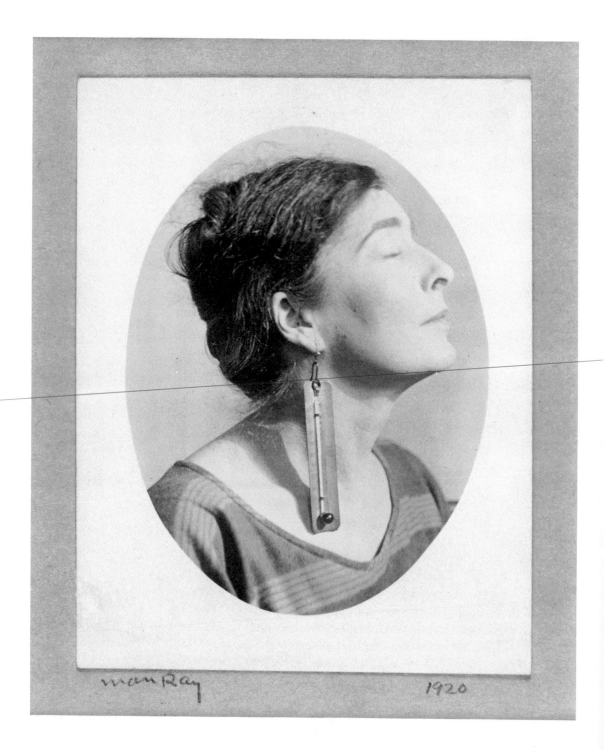

man Ray   1920

To the New York press Loy symbolized the New Woman. "This woman is half-way through the door into To-morrow," a reporter from the *New York Evening Sun* declared. (The reporter's list of candidates for the title of the Modern Woman also included Margaret Anderson, Louise Bryant, Jane Heap, the Baroness Elsa von Freytag-Loringhoven, Ida Rauh, and Margaret Sanger.) Loy, in turn, instructed the reporter about life. "The antique way to live and express life was to . . . say it according to the rules. But the modern flings herself at life and lets herself feel what she does feel then upon the very tick of the second she snatches the images of life that fly through the brain." [17]

Henri-Pierre Roché arrived in New York in November 1916, having been pressed into wartime service as a diplomat with the French High

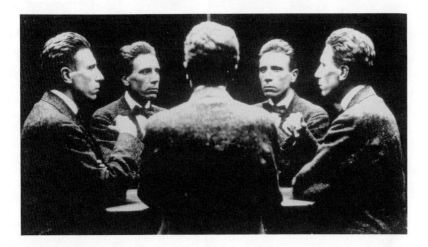

OPPOSITE
Man Ray (1890–1976).
Portrait (Mina Loy), 1920.
Silver print, 5 × 4 in. (12.7 × 10.2 cm). The Menil Collection, Houston

LEFT
Henri-Pierre Roché, 1917

Commission. In her portrait of Roché, Gertrude Stein wrote, "Certainly this one is liking very well to be knowing what any one doing anything is doing, in what way any one doing anything is doing that thing." [18] Her abstract sentence neatly captured Roché's métier; he made it his business to know everyone worth knowing. His address book was a rich source of artists and writers; he built a modest collection of modern art studded with works by friends such as Picasso and Braque, and he later acted as John Quinn's agent. But it was *la vie sentimentale* that held the most importance for Roché, and his sexual liaisons filled his diaries, which totaled seven thousand pages by his death in 1959. As Stein observed, "This one is certainly loving, doing a good deal of loving, certainly this one has been completely excited by such a thing, certainly this one had been completely dreaming about such a thing." [19]

The last of the significant expatriates to arrive was the Swiss-born Arthur Cravan. One wintry January day in 1917 he stepped off a dilapidated Spanish steamer. His fellow passenger Leon Trotsky recalled Cravan years later as a boxer "who openly pronounced that he preferred to slug Yankees in a noble sport than to get his chest driven in by

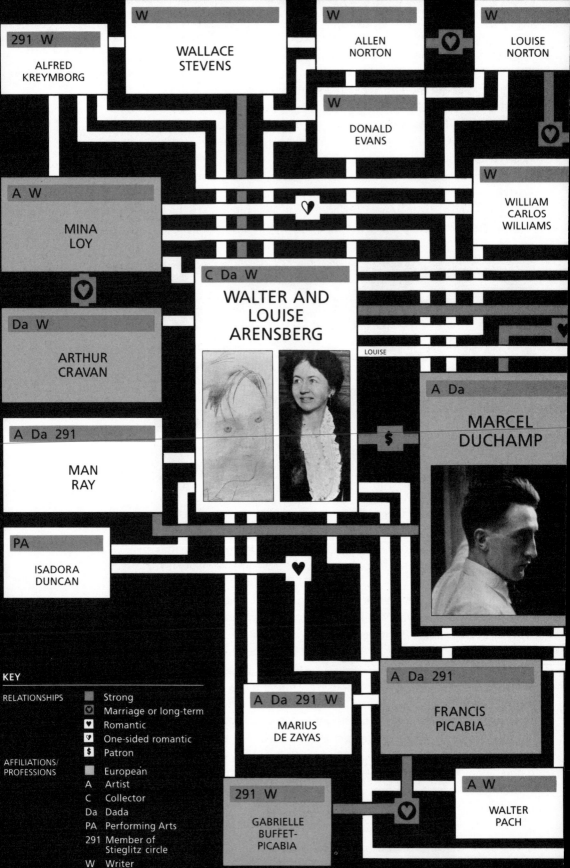

291 W
ALFRED KREYMBORG

W
WALLACE STEVENS

W
ALLEN NORTON

W
LOUISE NORTON

W
DONALD EVANS

W
WILLIAM CARLOS WILLIAMS

A W
MINA LOY

C Da W
WALTER AND LOUISE ARENSBERG

LOUISE

Da W
ARTHUR CRAVAN

A Da
MARCEL DUCHAMP

A Da 291
MAN RAY

PA
ISADORA DUNCAN

A Da 291 W
MARIUS DE ZAYAS

A Da 291
FRANCIS PICABIA

291 W
GABRIELLE BUFFET-PICABIA

A W
WALTER PACH

KEY

RELATIONSHIPS
- Strong
- Marriage or long-term
- Romantic
- One-sided romantic
- $ Patron

AFFILIATIONS/
PROFESSIONS
- European
- A Artist
- C Collector
- Da Dada
- PA Performing Arts
- 291 Member of Stieglitz circle
- W Writer

THE ARENSBERG & STETTHEIMER SALONS

A CHARLES SHEELER

A Da MORTON LIVINGSTON SCHAMBERG

PA EDGARD VARESE

A ALBERT GLEIZES

A Da JEAN CROTTI

A Da JOHN COVERT

A Da BEATRICE WOOD

A C Da KATHERINE DREIER

A Da W BARONESS ELSA VON FREYTAG-LORINGHOVEN

C W HENRI-PIERRE ROCHE

A W CARRIE, ETTIE, AND FLORINE STETTHEIMER

W HENRY MCBRIDE

A 291 CHARLES DEMUTH

ETTIE

A ELIE NADELMAN

A 291 W MARSDEN HARTLEY

C W LEO STEIN

W CARL VAN VECHTEN

W AVERY HOPWOOD

A 291 BARON ADOLF DE MEYER

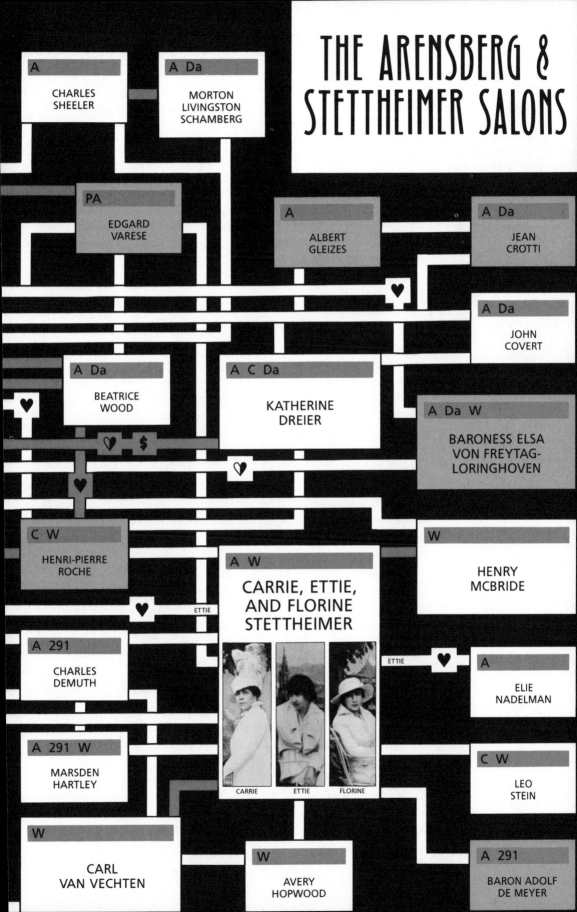

CARRIE ETTIE FLORINE

Arthur Cravan

some ignorant German."[20] It is not surprising that Trotsky would remember Cravan in such a combative stance, for he was a pugilist—in the ring and in print—of legendary proportions. He had won the Amateur Light–Heavyweight Championship of France without having previously fought a single bout, and he paid for his passage to America with his earnings from going six rounds with the former heavyweight champion Jack Johnson.[21]

For Cravan boxing was not simply a source of money; the boxing ring was the stage for his self-dramatization. When a referee announced him, Cravan would spring from his corner and boastfully call out his qualifications: "Hotel thief, muleteer, snake-charmer, chauffeur, ailurophile, grandson of the Queen's Chancellor, nephew of Oscar Wilde, sailor, gold prospector, poet with the shortest hair in the world."[22] His aggression was also played out on the pages of *Maintenant,* an avant-garde magazine that he started in 1912 as a platform for his abusive opinions and distributed from a wheelbarrow. Cravan's advice to artists always stressed the superiority of the physical: "Do a lot of fucking or go into rigorous training: when you have nineteen inches around the arm, you'll be gifted."[23] His sojourn among the American avant-garde lasted less than a year, during which he created nothing concrete. Yet the avant-garde regarded Cravan as a totemic figure. Raising sociopathy to an art form, he subverted everything that the nineteenth century had held dear and became the Antichrist for a new age.[24]

. . . a motley international band which turned night into day, conscientious objectors of all nationalities and walks of life living in an inconceivable orgy of sexuality, jazz, and alcohol.

Gabrielle Buffet-Picabia on the expatriates in New York

This expatriate cast of characters provided New York's avant-garde community with an on-site propagandist for Cubism (Gleizes), a pioneer in modern music (Varèse), an exemplar of international chic (de Meyer), the propagators of New York Dada (Picabia and Duchamp), a link between modern artists and collectors (Roché), a radical literary experimenter linked to the Futurists (Loy), and an all-purpose provocateur (Cravan). Their presence consolidated New York's position as the new capital of modernism. Where once there had been only Stieglitz's little rooms at 291, by 1915 the art world also encompassed the home of the Stettheimer sisters and the apartment of Walter and Louise Arensberg. The expatriates circulated through all three.

Francis Picabia arrived in New York in April 1915 in characteristically lawless fashion. When his navy ship stopped in New York en route to the Caribbean, Picabia debarked to visit his friends Marius de Zayas and Paul Haviland and never returned. This act did not express his antiwar sentiment so much as his devotion to the company of friends and his sense of independence. Just as Picabia's first trip to New York, for the Armory Show, had coincided with an upheaval in the avant-garde, so his second visit occurred at a significant moment in the Stieglitz circle: Picabia witnessed both the founding of the Modern Gallery and the most exciting months of the new magazine *291.* At the same time

Alfred Stieglitz (1864–1946).
Francis Picabia, 1915.
Platinum print, 9⅝ × 7⅝ in.
(24.5 × 19.5 cm). National
Gallery of Art, Washington,
D.C.; Alfred Stieglitz
Collection

Stieglitz was transformed from the avant-garde's loquacious knight to the "Old War Horse," the epithet with which he now closed his letters.

Picabia created a bittersweet valentine that wittily conveyed Stieglitz's becalmed state.[25] Entitled *Ici, c'est ici Stieglitz* (*Here, This Is Stieglitz*), it presents a slightly deflated camera that strains toward but never reaches the "IDEAL." "FOI ET AMOUR" ("faith and love") is printed in tribute to Stieglitz's enduring qualities, while behind the camera an automobile's shadowy stickshift remains in neutral, and a hand brake is in the engaged position. The portrait appeared at a time when Stieglitz's circle was dispersing and his finances were threadbare. He confided to

Francis Picabia (1878–1953).
Ici, c'est ici Stieglitz. From
291, July–August 1915

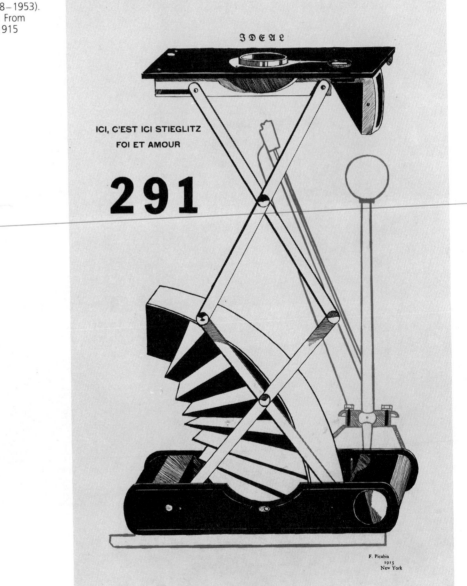

Gabrielle Buffet-Picabia that 291's patrons were no longer buying art at prewar prices, and he was forced to borrow money. Both John Marin and Arthur Dove were living outside the city, preoccupied with survival, and Paul Haviland had just been called home to manage the family business in France, never to return; the balance he had provided for the circle was sorely missed during this transition period. *Camera Work* had not appeared since the special issue "What Is 291?" In the meantime a new magazine appeared that carried on the spirit of 291 without retaining Stieglitz at its helm. It was on the cover of the July–August issue of this magazine, *291*, that Picabia's portrait of Stieglitz appeared.

The magazine's inaugural issue, in March 1915, represented an attempt to renew the waning spirit of the Stieglitz circle. His lieutenants—de Zayas, Haviland, and Agnes Ernst Meyer—had published it themselves only after unsuccessfully entreating Stieglitz to take action. "The attitude of *waiting for me to do something* was not fair to 291— to me—nor to the individuals themselves," Stieglitz wrote to de Zayas. "My own position had become disgusting to myself."[26] He contributed one-third of the money needed to publish the magazine (the rest was paid by Meyer and Haviland), advice, a back room at 291, and— symbolically most important—his benediction. De Zayas was the chief editor of *291*, but Haviland helped before his departure in July and Picabia's hand could be seen in the summer issues. Meetings were held to determine the magazine's contents—and these meetings sometimes included Agnes Ernst Meyer and Stieglitz—but since each individual was allowed to select whatever he or she wanted, the meetings rarely lasted more than ten minutes. Work by Stieglitz's favorite artists, Marin and Walkowitz, appeared on the cover as well as work by such French artists as Picasso and Picabia.

291 represented the international years more vividly than any other little magazine. Many articles appeared in French, without English translation, and the magazine reflected the up-to-date design of *Les Soirées de Paris,* a French journal edited by Guillaume Apollinaire. *291* published the Futurists' typographical experiments and Apollinaire's concrete poetry, and featured artworks (including many portraits of the avant-garde) designed specifically for its luxurious tabloid format of twelve by twenty inches. Just as other modernist forms explored the intrinsic nature of their media, so *291* experimented with the properties of type and image on the page.[27] Alone among America's little magazines, it looked truly modern.

Sensing *291*'s importance to the international avant-garde during wartime—when other little magazines had closed down—de Zayas sent sixty free copies of each issue to Paris "to people who have a real interest in modern art."[28] A set was sent to Ezra Pound in London in November 1915, and several copies went to the Zurich Dada group clustered around Tristan Tzara, who in turn mailed complimentary copies of the single issue of *Cabaret Voltaire* for de Zayas to distribute in New York. The readership of *291* was not large but it was influential.

At about the same time that *Ici, c'est ici Stieglitz* appeared on the cover of *291*, de Zayas was diplomatically arranging a summit conference with Stieglitz. When the founding of the Modern Gallery was first discussed in the summer of 1915—by de Zayas, Haviland, and Meyer— a sense of enormous possibility mingled with feelings of desperation. "At present it is in the power of Stieglitz to make of New York the world center of the best elements of modern art," de Zayas wrote to Meyer.[29] There was grave doubt, however, about Stieglitz's inclination and ability to seize that opportunity. The modern movement now urgently

Page of *291*, November 1915, by Marius de Zayas

needed not a chapel but a shop; with the European galleries shut down, artists were feeling the economic pinch. Unless they acted decisively, reasoned the cadre at 291, the war and Stieglitz's weariness would signal the end not only of the little rooms but of the modern movement itself.[30] Meyer voiced the group's concern when she wrote to Stieglitz, "It [a commercial version of 291] seems to me to be the only future left for us."[31]

It was in this charged atmosphere that de Zayas opened negotiations with Stieglitz. In fastidiously tactful letters de Zayas described the Modern Gallery as the next stage in the spirit of 291; just as artistic expression evolved, so must the commercial structure expand to support the needs of modern artists. By taking over the commercial responsibilities, the Modern Gallery could allow Stieglitz to maintain his vision of 291 as a pure laboratory for experimentation. The importance of these negotiations (in which Meyer and Picabia also participated) had little to do with financial requests and everything to do with the symbolism of Stieglitz's role. "We have you as our leader," de Zayas wrote him, "and I have to add, that as our leader you must have absolute confidence in every one of us . . . for otherwise we will not be able to carry our plans to success."[32] After darkly predicting the dangers of the endeavor, Stieglitz gave his wary blessing.

With Haviland, Picabia, and the Meyers sharing the six-thousand-dollar start-up cost, the Modern Gallery opened on October 7, 1915. Its inaugural exhibition would have been appropriate on the walls of 291; it included paintings by Braque, Picabia, and Picasso, and even photographs by Stieglitz. (291 opened the fall season with a little-known American artist, Oscar Bluemner.) In the three seasons of the Modern Gallery's existence it would continue to exhibit a mix of American and European moderns as well as African and Pre-Columbian sculpture—a particular fascination of de Zayas's.[33]

Marius de Zayas and Francis Picabia hand-tinting issues of *291*, 1915

Although both galleries showed many of the same artists, they had different aspirations. The Modern Gallery frankly attempted to sell modern art rather than to use it as a springboard for inner discovery. Gallery-goers were not subjected to a Socratic monologue nor interrogated if they wanted to buy a painting. The Modern Gallery fronted on the busy northeast corner of Forty-second Street and Fifth Avenue and displayed its wares behind an invitingly broad span of glass, so that passersby could glimpse the art from as far away as the steps of the New York Public Library. Unfortunately, de Zayas proved to be neither a persuasive salesman nor an orderly businessman, and the Modern Gallery failed to enlarge the number of modern art patrons beyond the usual core: Walter and Louise Arensberg, Arthur B. Davies, Eugene and Agnes Meyer, and John Quinn.

My advice to you is have nothing more to do with Stieglitz—Never see him, never think of him. That chapter should be closed for all of us. To have known S. is very beneficial, to let him hang on is sure destruction.

Agnes Ernst Meyer
to Marius de Zayas

Within a few months 291 and the Modern Gallery parted ways. The specific incidents that led to the separation are unknown and perhaps irrelevant; rupture was inevitable. Stieglitz could not accept mixing commerce and modern art, nor could he tolerate the idea of being replaced by a protégé. The break was gentlemanly but irreparable. De Zayas had his last word in the pages of *291*. He declared that Stieglitz, preoccupied with psychology and metaphysics, had failed to discover the essence of America and had been replaced by Picabia as the modern visionary. With this new rift and with Agnes Ernst Meyer's departure for Washington, D.C., Stieglitz concluded bitterly that "cooperation—really inner cooperation—is a mad dream." [34] He wrote to Haviland that his colleagues had outgrown the need for play. "I, for my part, seem never to outgrow the play period. Perhaps it is madness—perhaps it is cussedness. The fact remains, I play. Even with calamity and death. But I never play with friends. In fact with no human beings." [35]

New York's avant-garde swelled not only with the "strange artists . . . from all over" that Henry McBride reported to Gertrude Stein, but also with American expatriates forced home from Europe by the war. [36] Among New York's new residents were the three Stettheimer sisters—Carrie, Florine, and Ettie—who had been in Bern, Switzerland, in the summer of 1914. The war ended their decade-long European sojourn, and they sailed for New York. After their elegantly stylish residences in Europe, none of them was especially pleased with the house they rented at 102 West Seventy-sixth Street, which Ettie referred to as the "salle d'attente deuxième classe" (second-class waiting room). [37] But the sisters soon transformed it into a fantastic stage setting, where they would entertain their distinguished friends for the next decade. As McBride put it, the Stettheimers "enacted the roles of Julie de Lespinasse, Mme. du Deffand and Mme. de Stael in modern dress," creating a salon where "hardy ideas were put into words which echoed sooner or later in other parts of the city." [38]

European expatriates felt entirely at home in the salon, for an Old World atmosphere prevailed: the attire, manners, and multicourse meals were formal, with conversations frequently conducted in French. Not surprisingly, the guest list consisted largely of people like the Stettheimers, whose lives had been shaped by Europe. Here were Parisians—the dancer Adolf Bolm, Baron de Meyer, Marcel Duchamp, Albert and Juliet Gleizes, Elie Nadelman, and Francis Picabia. Here, too, were Americans recently repatriated—Jo Davidson, Marsden Hartley, Edward Steichen, Leo Stein—and Europhiles such as Charles Demuth, McBride, and Carl Van Vechten. "The personae gratae to the house," as McBride called them, gathered for intimate dinners at 7:30 P.M. and larger At Homes after 9:00 P.M.[39]

The Stettheimer sisters, on the brink of middle age when they returned to America, were Carrie (approximately forty-three), Florine (forty-one), and Ettie (thirty-nine). They were accompanied by a formidable mother, Rosetta Walter Stettheimer. A guest stepping from West Seventy-sixth Street into the Stettheimer salon entered the domain of aristocratic Continental taste. As Van Vechten noted, "It was like a room in a royal palace."[40] On the walls were gold moldings and red taffeta curtains that undulated to the floor in rich folds. Red velvet and fringe, Nottingham lace and heavy brocade were accompanied by cut-crystal bowls, glittering chandeliers, and Aubusson rugs. The grand dining table, laid with Italian antique lace altar cloths, was graced with

They have no salons. They entertain their friends, most of whom happen to be celebrated.

Virgil Thomson on the Stettheimers

The Stettheimer sisters on the verge of World War I. From left to right: Florine, Carrie, and Ettie

Florine's extravagant flower arrangements. The focal point of the dining room was a mural by Florine, depicting Spring scattering flowers.

Over the next few years Florine's portraits of the family began to dominate the walls throughout the house. These paintings depicted the three sisters in postures of exquisite lassitude, presided over by the ever-present Rosetta, august and aloof in black and lace, eternally laying out cards for a game of Patience. To some guests, like Van Vechten, Florine's witty paintings offered a clue that the decor was no straightforward re-creation of the European houses they had lived in but a camp joke about the German royal style.[41]

Champagne and rum cocktails were served until Prohibition, but these were such lightly alcoholic occasions that the tenor scarcely changed during the dry years, when the Stettheimers patriotically refrained from dealing with bootleggers. For the formal dinners Carrie devised menus that included such house specialties as feather soup, oyster salad, smelts stuffed with mushrooms, lobster in aspic and mayonnaise, chicken *chaud-froid,* and Brabanter Torte (a souvenir of Sacher's in Vienna). These meals, served on Worcester, Rockingham, and Crown Derby porcelain, tended toward the heavy end of haute bourgeois cuisine; some first-time guests mistook the hors d'oeuvres for the meal.

The Stettheimer salon was distant from downtown in both geography and sensibility. (When Ettie responded to a visit to the Village by getting "silly and prudish," Van Vechten complained, "I wish people like that would stick to their own environment."[42]) Intent on upholding their equivocal position among New York's leading banking families—they were on the fringe of the Jewish banking aristocracy, related to the Warburgs, the Seligmans, and the Lewisohns—the Stettheimers surveyed the modern age from a distinctly regal perspective, and their

---

Menu for a Gathering at the Stettheimers'

Mushroom Timbal

Soup

Halibut and Shrimps in Mayonnaise Aspic
with Mixed Green Salad

Poussins with Orange and Jelly Trimming

String Beans

Bermuda Potatoes

Meringue Filled with Fresh Strawberries
and Whipped Cream

Coffee

---

guests were the aristocracy of the avant-garde. "Occasionally a gifted refugee from Greenwich Village drifted in," recalled McBride, "but if there were too much of Eighth Street in his manner he was unlikely to re-appear."[43] One did not need to be European to attend the Stettheimers' salon, but a cosmopolitan outlook, cultural sophistication, and nuanced manners were essential. (Nor did being European guarantee approval; Ettie dismissed Varèse as rude and Picabia as a "womanish *enfant terrible*."[44]) Carl Van Vechten quoted George Santayana to illuminate the Stettheimers' sensibility: "The use of riches isn't to disperse riches, but to cultivate the art of living, to produce beautiful homes, beautiful manners, beautiful speech, beautiful charities. You individually can't raise the lowest level of human life, but you can raise the highest level."[45] The Stettheimers' salon was the American avant-garde's version of courtly society.

Whereas Mabel Dodge's Evenings had been keenly attuned to the moment, the Stettheimers' gatherings endured with little change for two decades. The salon's longevity depended on family bonds that had tightened considerably after Joseph Stettheimer left the family around the turn of the century. The two oldest children, Walter and Stella, escaped through marriage, but the three younger daughters accompanied their mother to Europe. As their mother became increasingly invalid, the daughters stayed home and entered a state of perpetual maidenhood.[46] When Rosetta Walter Stettheimer died in September 1935, the sisters dispersed and the salon ended.[47]

Family loyalty was exacted in complex rules, both spoken and tacit. One could not disgrace the family or upset its delicate balance. Most important of all, one sister must be available to their mother at all times. This had nothing to do with practical necessity (the house was always well staffed with able German servants) and everything to do with the psychological necessity that Mrs. Stettheimer never again feel deserted. Within this matrix of familial duty, it was essential for each of these intelligent and cultured women to pursue a vocation of her own. This was done, as Ettie wrote, in "strict singleness."[48]

Tall and stately Carrie acted as the official hostess of the salons, and she dressed for the part in white-and-gold dresses from Callot Soeurs and Bendel. The chicest of the sisters, she embellished her slight resemblance to Queen Mary with tiaras, dog collars studded with small pearls and rhinestones, and trains trimmed in miniver. When not on display, Carrie took care of the less royal tasks of devising menus, instructing a succession of German cooks, and periodically disappearing from the salon to ensure that dinner was progressing. She dictated orders with such dispatch that many who attended the salon assumed she derived satisfaction from her skill; it was only after her death that Ettie revealed that Carrie "had no liking whatever for this job."[49] She had been a martyr to domesticity, when her true calling was to be a

My attitude is one of love
is all adoration
for all the fringes
all the color
all tinsel creation
I like slippers gold
I like oysters cold
and my garden of mixed flowers
and the sky full of towers
and traffic in the streets
and Maillard's sweets
and Bendel's clothes
and Nat Lewis hose
and Tappe's window arrays
and crystal fixtures
and my pictures
and Walt Disney cartoons
and colored balloons.

Florine Stettheimer

stage designer. Perhaps her frustrated desires account somewhat for her melancholy demeanor and her frequent headaches.

Florine had found her vocation in early adolescence. She enrolled in the Art Students League at the age of fifteen, was elected to its governing body at eighteen, and painted throughout the family's years in Europe. Now back in New York, she retreated whenever possible to the seclusion of her gauzy, light-suffused studio in the Beaux Arts Studios at Fortieth Street and Fifth Avenue. Tailored to Florine's sensibility, the studio featured billowing cellophane curtains and glass tables with crystal flowers.[50] The least conspicuous of the sisters, Florine drifted through the salons in her trademark black velvet harem pants, her party behavior ranging narrowly from mousy silence to soft laughter. "She seemed often a furtive guest rather than one of the *genii loci* which she undoubtedly was," Henry McBride observed, "for her demure presence invariably counted."[51] What some interpreted as snobbery or coldness her friend Marsden Hartley ascribed to respectable reticence. Van Vechten noted, "She did not inspire love, or affection, or even warm friendship, but she did elicit interest, respect, admiration, and enthusiasm for her work in art."[52]

The Stettheimer salons proved especially meaningful to Florine as a painter. For many years her family and their guests constituted her sole audience. Even more important, the gatherings provided her key subject: about 1915 she began painting conversation pieces that depicted the lively interaction of the Stettheimers' circle. Her naive figures were limned in tendrillike lines and wispy strokes of Fauve colors brushed over a heavy impasto of china white paint that seemed to radiate light. Her canvases convey all the witty badinage that she repressed from her own conversation. Soon there were many such works, depicting soirées at home or festive outdoor gatherings, as well as individual portraits of her intimates. Florine described her vocation most succinctly in a short verse jotted on a paper scrap.

> Our Picnics
> Our Banquets
> Our Friends
> Have at last a raison-d'être
> Seen in color and design
> It amuses me
> To recreate them
> To paint them.[53]

Collectively, Florine's paintings provide a group portrait of America's first modern community: the Baron de Meyer, Muriel Draper, Marcel Duchamp, Albert Gleizes, Henry McBride, Elie Nadelman, Francis Picabia, Edward Steichen, Gertrude and Leo Stein, Alfred Stieglitz, and Carl Van Vechten. Florine Stettheimer was the avant-garde's court painter.

OPPOSITE
Florine Stettheimer's bedroom

BELOW
Marcel Duchamp (1887–1968). *Florine Stettheimer*, c. 1925. Pencil on paper, 19¾ × 13½ in. (50.2 × 34.3 cm). Estate of Virgil Thomson

Ettie's signature was a vivid note of red—a velvet cape, a puffy taffeta skirt, even a red wig. She was the intellectual of the three; her full title, Dr. Henrietta Stettheimer, acknowledged her doctoral degree in philosophy from the University of Freiburg, and her weighty dissertation on the metaphysics of William James reflected her interest in modern thought. James wrote to her, "There is no university extant that wouldn't give you its *summa cum laude*."[54] She encouraged serious conversation at the salons and acted as the family spokeswoman. When someone tried to shield the sisters from a racy piece of gossip, Ettie spoke up: "We may be virgins, but we know the facts of life."[55]

During the teens, Ettie's moral earnestness was balanced by coquetry. "I have developed a mania for being amused and amusing, perhaps a reaction to the horrible complexity of life," wrote Ettie soon after the soirées began, "and as I find that 1 follows 2, owing to the novelty of 2, I have become quite an amuser."[56] Nearing forty-one when she wrote this, Ettie still anticipated the possibility of an amorous liaison, and her flirtations introduced the frisson of romance into the repressed atmosphere of the Stettheimer household. She confided to her journal about her current "best," expressed her hopes of seeing an anonymous beau called "Don Juan," and asked a European friend to send her "an attractive Frenchman." The most characteristic expression of her mixed coquetry and intellectuality was her plan to write "The Emotion of Being Loved" for the *New Republic*.

Ettie's chief suitors were Elie Nadelman and Marcel Duchamp. With the handsome and self-possessed Nadelman she took long soulful walks and danced at the Coconut Grove. Although she was attracted by his charm, her ambivalence is suggested by her novel, *Love Days,* in which Ettie's fictional alter ego marries Nadelman and divorces him six months later: "He's become an egocentric—conceited—boring—egotist since he's the rage."[57] Duchamp conducted a friendly relationship with all three sisters—they helped support him by taking unnecessary French lessons each Wednesday afternoon—but with Ettie there were also private dinners and hints of engagement. She must have enjoyed having the attention of two desirable artist-suitors, but we will never know the seriousness of these flirtations because years later she took a razor and neatly excised everything personal from her journals.[58]

In the fall of 1916 Ettie wrote in her journal that these were "exciting days for the Stettheimer family."[59] Each of the sisters made a public debut—Carrie in the summer, Florine in the fall, Ettie in the winter.

Carrie's took place at Lower Saranac Lake, New York. For a raffle benefiting research for a cure of infantile paralysis, she improvised a dollhouse from a few wooden boxes. It was somehow inevitable that Carrie's mother won the raffle, but she returned the prize in order to generate more contributions, and in the process nearly a thousand dollars was raised. Encouraged by the small fortune that her ersatz

Elie Nadelman (1882–1946). *Bust of a Woman (Ettie Stettheimer),* c. 1926–28. Bronze painted with Prussian blue, height: 23⅝ in. (59.6 cm). Kathryn and Robert Steinberg

creation had brought, Carrie soon embarked on the more ambitious dollhouse that would remain her enthusiasm and her escape for two decades. She rented a studio at the Dorset Hotel and began her obsessive labor: needlepointing tiny rugs, carving settees from chalk, reupholstering furniture from F.A.O. Schwarz, hanging curtains of antique lace. Her friends created tiny paintings so that the ballroom became a modernist gallery, with works by Alexander Archipenko, Marcel Duchamp, Gaston Lachaise (who generously donated both paintings and sculpture), and William and Marguerite Zorach.

A retreat from the practical demands of the Stettheimer household and the sisters' exacting compromises, the dollhouse was dictated solely by Carrie's eclectic taste and symbolized her own personal ménage. Year after year she labored on it, adding pattern upon pattern—metallic foils, antique lace, chintz, velvet, and silk—until her mother died in 1935. Carrie never touched her creation again, and it remained unfinished at her death. Now on permanent display at the Museum of the City of New York, it is the apotheosis of the Stettheimers' gatherings.

In October 1916 Florine was offered an exhibition at Knoedler's. Although Knoedler's was a highly respected gallery, Florine hesitated to expose her paintings to the gaze of a public beyond her elite friends, and she was alarmed at the idea that one of her paintings might end up in the room of a stranger. "Suppose it were to hang in the bedroom of some man!" she once exclaimed in horror to Van Vechten.[60] Florine warily accepted Knoedler's offer, insisting that she would design not only the frames for her paintings but the frame for the entire exhibition: Knoedler's must be transformed to replicate her bedroom.[61] The gallery's walls were draped with white muslin, and a transparent gilt-fringed canopy was suspended from the ceiling. By minimizing the distance her paintings traveled out into the world, Florine tried to protect herself.[62] But her anxiety persisted. "I am very unhappy and I don't think I deserve to be," she wrote the evening her exhibition was installed. "I thought I might feel better after dinner but I have had dinner."[63]

Although Florine derided commercialism and publicity, she devoted more diary pages to the exhibition than to any other event of her life, and after she died, her ashes were scattered over the Hudson River on the anniversary of her Knoedler's opening. Referring to it with false bravado as "my X," she reported the response only in terms of sales. Although her exhibition was lauded by her friends and by some critics, her journal entry said, "Only one person asked to see the price list." On the night of the exhibition's close she penciled two ruthless words: "Nothing sold."[64] (Her first sale—fictional, alas—would come in 1923 to Ronald, Duke of Middlebottom, in Van Vechten's novel *Blind Bow Boy*.) The lack of sales seemed to underline the family dictum: venturing beyond the small circle of family and friends was dangerous.[65]

That fall of 1916 Ettie was anxiously awaiting the publication of

Carrie Stettheimer (c. 1870–1944). *Dollhouse*, 1916–35. Museum of the City of New York

ABOVE, TOP
The salon, with Gaston Lachaise, Marcel Duchamp, Rosetta Walter Stettheimer, and her married daughter, Stella Wanger

ABOVE, CENTER
The ballroom, with Henry McBride and Marcel Duchamp

ABOVE, BOTTOM
The nursery, with Walter Wanger (Stella's son) and an unidentified friend

Letting other people have your paintings is like letting them wear your clothes.

Florine Stettheimer

her first novel, a tale of romantic love with the characteristically cerebral title *Philosophy.* To ensure that the family name not be exposed to the vulgar light of publicity, Ettie employed the pseudonym Henrie Waste (derived from *Henrie*tta *Wa*lter *Ste*ttheimer). She was rewarded with a positive reception from her friends, a good review in the *New York Times,* and an especially admiring review "by one Randolph Bourne" in the *New Republic.* Had Ettie known that he was a leading young intellectual, she might have been more heartened by his praise: "Your first impression of Henrie Waste is that nobody could achieve such a fusion of vivid thought and exhilaration of a personal feeling," Bourne wrote. "She has the rarest gift of a lyric intellectuality which simply unhinges one's critical sense." [66] This acclaim did not long comfort her, however; she sourly wrote, "but I'm no nation-wide celebrity." [67]

Years later Ettie would write about the recognition from the intimates at their salon, which had sustained Florine: "It did not come like a refreshing stream, or even a grateful rain, but more like the morning dewdrop on flowers, that vanishes during the heat of the day, but comes again and again and again." [68] She could easily have been writing about Carrie and herself as well: throughout the years the Stettheimers' salon sustained the three sisters as their inspiration, their subject, and their audience.

Attributed to Joseph Stella (1887–1946). *Walter Conrad Arensberg,* c. 1915–20. Pencil on paper, 11 × 8½ in. (27.9 × 21.6 cm). Arensberg Archives, Francis Bacon Library, Claremont, California

The legend has grown up that reporters crowded around Marcel Duchamp as he stepped off the S.S. *Rochambeau* on June 15, 1915, eager to publish his first words in halting English. The actual events of that afternoon were less dramatic: Walter Pach met Duchamp at the pier and drove him to 33 West Sixty-seventh Street, the spacious two-floor apartment of the collectors Walter and Louise Arensberg, who had moved to New York from Cambridge less than a year before.

The alliance formed that June day between the artist and the patron-poet changed Walter Arensberg's life. One observer called the meeting "a kind of magical spell," and a friend who had known Arensberg since his Harvard days exclaimed, "Duchamp was the spark plug that ignited him." [69] Once ignited, Arensberg had generous reserves of money, taste, and hospitality to catalyze the modern movement. The artists and poets that gathered at his apartment from 1915 to 1918 included representatives of the Puteaux group and other European expatriates, the Patagonians and the *Others* poets, American painters, New York proto-Dadaists, and the Harvard old-boy network.

At first glance Walter Arensberg seems an unlikely figure to host this avant-garde community. In his well-worn suits, with a lock of hair straying across his forehead and his glasses perpetually sliding down his nose, Arensberg looked like a distracted academic. Indeed, he jumped effortlessly from Dante to dreams, Francis Bacon to the fourth dimension. He would speak sharply to guests if they didn't keep up,

*Arensberg always re-
minded me of the finest
vintage champagne:
heady, slightly biting, demanding, temperamen-
tal, and effervescent.*

Katharine Kuh

and even his close friend Duchamp observed that Arensberg had "a difficult character." [70] An intellectual high-wire act, he could not have performed so brilliantly without his solidly grounded wife, Louise. As a lifelong friend put it, "She was the rock on which the flower bloomed." [71]

Walter's domain was words, from classical literature to Symbolist poetry. Louise's was music, from bel canto opera to Arnold Schoenberg and Erik Satie. Walter was eternally in the ethers, while Louise remained planted in the everyday, enjoying nothing so much as peeling an apple and eating it. Abstemious in her habits, she completely shunned drink; her husband chain-smoked Murads and battled alcoholism. She loved sitting alone at a piano, and he loved a roomful of people. Walter was a political liberal, Louise a conservative. It was in their art collection that the Arensbergs collaborated most closely, and throughout their years of collecting, they differed over only two paintings.

The Arensbergs depended on family money to pursue their interests, and in this they were doubly blessed. Louise came into some of her inheritance before her marriage, and Walter inherited his money, derived from McCoullogh-Dalzell, the Pittsburgh crucible company, in the 1910s. With both these inheritances at his disposal, Walter bankrolled galleries and little magazines, paid artists' rent, bought art, and gave generous wedding presents.

The Arensberg circle encompassed the twin axes of poetry and art. His bonds to the poetry community extended back to his classmates from turn-of-the-century Harvard—Pitts Sanborn and Wallace Stevens. As music critic for the *New York Evening Globe*, Sanborn knew the world of music and performing arts well, and he was especially close to his fellow music critic and social arbiter Carl Van Vechten. Within a few months of arriving in New York, Walter Arensberg began informally participating in Sanborn's magazine, *Trend*. When that folded at the end of 1914, Arensberg financed *Rogue*, a short-lived little magazine, which in turn led to his financing *Others* (whose story belongs to the next chapter). Through the social networks of these magazines he met Donald Evans, Alfred Kreymborg, Mina Loy, Allen and Louise Norton, Carl Van Vechten, William Carlos Williams, and even Amy Lowell.

Gauging the effect of the Arensberg circle on any one of its members is tricky; focusing on Wallace Stevens to illustrate its impact seems especially perverse, for he was an obdurately unsocial character who spoke in "a voice on tiptoe at dawn" and received compliments with painfully embarrassed coughs. [72] But without the encouragement of the Arensberg circle at a crucial juncture in his life, he might never have achieved poetic maturity. Nearly half of Stevens's life was over before he embarked on the poetry career he brilliantly sustained through his remaining years. The circle provided precisely the atmosphere required for his timorous spirit to expand. [73]

Stevens's first visit to West Sixty-seventh Street occurred one Satur-

Louise Arensberg in the
Arensbergs' apartment,
c. 1915–20. Photograph
attributed to John Covert

day in late 1914. It began with a luncheon at the Brevoort, where
Stevens sheepishly extracted two poems, "Peter Quince at the Clavier"
and "Tea," and recited them in a nearly inaudible monotone. As Arensberg and Van Vechten both commended them and improvised prurient
variations, the poet became embarrassed, pleased, and boyishly clumsy.
He was, Van Vechten recalled, "so entirely unadept at acceptance of
anything pleasant, it became obvious shortly that he could have had
but little of this sort of thing in his life."[74] Eager to linger in this glow of
appreciation, Stevens announced that he would stay to dinner. He was
so anxious about his wife's disapproval, though, that he chose to telegraph his plans rather than risk her remonstrance by telephone.

When Stevens first entered the Arensbergs' apartment that evening, he felt uncomfortable in the vast studio room; its lighting was too
bright and its vivid paintings too overwhelming. Intuiting that Stevens
required enclosure within this arena of liberty, Van Vechten extinguished
the lights, lit the logs in the fireplace, and cozily arranged furniture
around it. Once ensconced in an armchair, Stevens indulged in all his
favorite but normally forbidden activities—he drank, he smoked, he
talked amusingly—and then he dozed until midnight. On waking he
confessed his dread of returning home. (Elsie did not smile until the
following Thursday.)

Stevens became a regular at West Sixty-seventh Street. In the course
of these evenings, his biographer has observed, "these literary friends
functioned as his mirror, his own great glass, as they replaced the Harvard circle and Elsie."[75] Stevens never blossomed into a bohemian, rarely
recited poetry, and always looked just like the lawyer-businessman he
was. Surveying the Duchamp paintings hanging on the walls, he confessed, "I made very little out of them."[76] Nevertheless, from his posi-

tion at the periphery of the group, Stevens silently absorbed the spirit of experimentation, and it was during these years that he produced *Harmonium,* his masterly first book.

The art axis of the Arensberg circle was dominated by the European expatriates—Crotti, Duchamp, the Gleizeses, the Picabias, Roché—though many of America's leading modern artists also attended: John Covert, Charles Demuth, Man Ray, Morton Schamberg, Charles Sheeler, Joseph Stella, and Marius de Zayas.[77] Works by many of these artists could be seen on the seventeen-foot-high walls of the Arensbergs' studio. Just as the first generation of modern American collectors had been dominated by the two sets of Steins, the Cone sisters, the Meyers, Stieglitz, and John Quinn, so the Arensbergs became the most adventurous of the next generation.

Walter Arensberg told William Carlos Williams, "Anything in paint that was truly new, truly a fresh creation, is good art." [78] This credo dictated not only Arensberg's art collecting but also the poetry he wrote, which moved rapidly from Symbolism to the most extreme experimentation with language. He pursued these activities with, in Duchamp's words, "the conviction of a man at play." [79] Seeking the "truly new," he bought not only work by modern masters such as Braque, Cézanne, Matisse, and Picasso, but also paintings with images of machines—a hydro cell, a chocolate grinder, a set of gears—that surpassed anything at the Steins' for sheer up-to-dateness.[80] These mechanical subjects represented one of the characteristic obsessions of the latest movement born of World War I: Dada.

Dada sprang to life nearly simultaneously in several expatriate colonies. The Zurich branch, centered in the legendary Café Voltaire, gave the movement its name and wrote its manifestos. New York Dada was less public—its arena was the Arensberg salon instead of a factory or a cabaret. Its little magazines published more jokes than manifestos and didn't formally take up the Dada label until 1921, when the first and last issue of *New York Dada* was published. What New York Dada shared with Zurich—and soon with Barcelona, Basel, Berlin, Cologne, and Paris as well—was an anarchic spirit that was at once playful and nihilistic. The Dadaists subverted not only bourgeois convention but art itself, experimenting with chance and erasing the lines between art and plumbing. As World War I so fatally demonstrated, the rational tradition of the nineteenth century was bankrupt; Dada shouted a raucous "NO!" to all that it represented.

At that time none of the New York avant-garde called themselves Dada; in fact, they didn't hear the word until November 1916, when Tristan Tzara sent Marius de Zayas copies of his Zurich-published periodical *Cabaret Voltaire.* By the time Dada officially came to New York, in the spring of 1921, it seemed distinctly after the fact. Picabia included New York in a diagram of the Dada movement that appeared on the cover of *391* in February 1919, but its first mention in America was in a newspaper on January 29, 1921, and its only official production was a four-page magazine called *New York Dada*. Edited by Duchamp and Man Ray, its cover featured Duchamp's new androgynous persona, Rrose Sélavy, and inside Tristan Tzara sanctioned the use of the word: "Dada belongs to everybody. . . . Like the idea of God or of the toothbrush." [81] Despite the magazine's extraordinary lineup—the Baroness Elsa von Freytag-Loringhoven, Rube Goldberg, Hartley, and Stieglitz—New York Dada fizzled. Its most fitting obituary is found in a note Man Ray sent to Tristan Tzara in 1921. It features a still from a film of the Baroness von Freytag-Loringhoven shaving her pubic hair, her leg forming the capital *A* in the word *America*.[82] "Cher Tzara," Man Ray wrote, "dada cannot live in New York." [83]

But unofficial Dada flourished in New York during the 1910s, and its roots can be traced to 1915. In that year Marcel Duchamp selected

ABOVE
Cover of *New York Dada*, April 1921. Photograph by Man Ray

LEFT
Still from a film of Baroness Elsa von Freytag-Loringhoven shaving her pubic hair, 1921. Photograph by Man Ray

a wood-and-galvanized-iron snow shovel from a New York hardware store, called it *In Advance of the Broken Arm,* and carried it to the Arensbergs' in the middle of a blizzard, at which point the guests laughed uncontrollably; it was his first American Readymade.[84] Also in 1915, *291* filled its pages with Picabia's machine portraits. Man Ray's one-shot magazine, the *Ridgefield Gazook* (March 31, 1915), was a proto-Dada publication blooming in the wilds of New Jersey. It was just a four-page hand-drawn sheet, with Man Ray's drawings of bugs copulating and sophomoric puns on Hippolyte Havel, Man Ray, and Pablo Picasso. But retrospectively the *Ridgefield Gazook* appears to be a progenitor of a string of ephemeral Dada publications: *The Blind Man* (1917), *Rongwrong* (1917), *391* (1917–24), *TNT* (1919), and *New York Dada* (1921).

For a group that aspired to anarchy, New York Dada had all the elements of an organization. Man Ray was its chief American artist; Francis Picabia its chief rule breaker; Baroness Elsa von Freytag-Loringhoven and Arthur Cravan its iconic figures; Walter Arensberg its patron; and Katherine Dreier its institutionalizer. Presiding over them, without seeming to preside at all, was Marcel Duchamp.

Francis Picabia and Marcel Duchamp had initiated their first antiart dialogue with one another in the backyards of Puteaux, and over the next few years their radical ideas took diverse visual forms. Picabia introduced mechanical imagery into his painting, beginning with spark-plugs and coil springs, and soon he adopted the anonymous visual vocabulary of machine catalogs. Having disdained to learn English, he spoke to American artists through the machine language of his paintings, which subsequently appeared in the work of Covert, Man Ray, Schamberg, and Sheeler. He told the New York press that machines had become "really a part of human life—perhaps the very soul," and his rejection of the easel tradition was characteristically breezy: "All my life I've smoked painting."[85] Picabia's and Duchamp's gestures tested

OPPOSITE
Man Ray (1890–1976). *Self-Portrait,* 1914. Ink on paper, 24 × 17¾ in. (61 × 45.1 cm). Robert Miller Gallery, New York

BELOW
Cover and inside spread from the *Ridgefield Gazook,* March 31, 1915, by Man Ray

Man Ray (1890–1976). *Rrose Sélavy,* c. 1920–21. Gelatin silver print, 8½ × 6¾ in. (21.6 × 17.3 cm). Philadelphia Museum of Art; Samuel S. White, 3rd, and Vera White Collection

Man Ray by Mina Loy

the boundaries of even the most advanced modern art; their only rule was the demolition of rules.

It was on the grassy hillocks of Ridgefield, New Jersey, in the fall of 1915, that Man Ray and Duchamp met. Duchamp had accompanied Walter Arensberg across the Hudson for a Sunday afternoon gathering of the *Others* magazine crowd. Surrounded by poets, Man Ray and Duchamp felt an immediate affinity, although their verbal communication was primitive. They began an impromptu game of tennis in front of Man Ray's white cottage; unhindered by the lack of a net, Man Ray simply called out the score—fifteen, thirty, forty, love—and to each of these utterances, Duchamp replied, "Yes." It was a perfect Dada introduction, and Duchamp became Man Ray's new mentor.

That fall Man Ray was preparing his first one-man exhibition, a series of Cubist-influenced paintings. His Dada instincts were already evident. As early as 1911 he had combined pages from a textile sample book and called it *Tapestry,* and before meeting Duchamp he had published the *Ridgefield Gazook*. But after meeting Duchamp his experimentation intensified. At the same time that Duchamp was turning his back on "retinal art," Man Ray pioneered one technique after another: within a few years he made oil paintings, collages, airbrush paintings, *cliché-verre* prints, assemblages, and photographs. In the process Man Ray became America's quintessential Dada artist.

Arthur Cravan epitomized Dada's iconoclasm long before the movement came into being. He valued physicality over rationality, athletes over artists, and defied whatever was deified. Cravan summed it up by saying, "Let me state once and for all: I do not wish to be civilized." [86] He was an ideal Dada icon; his powerful body, handsome face, and alabaster skin contributed to his larger-than-life presence. He enacted his defiance publicly and theatrically: he punctuated a lecture in Paris by firing a pistol into the air and walked through the streets of Berlin carrying four prostitutes on his shoulder. As Mina Loy observed, he was "a giant who carried the circus within him." [87]

As a Dada icon, Cravan was matched by the redoubtable Baroness Elsa von Freytag-Loringhoven. In true Dada spirit, the baroness eradicated the boundaries between life and art, and she carried the usual obsessions of the avant-garde to illogical extremes. Unlike other artists associated with New York Dada, the baroness did not keep herself at one remove from her art, and nothing she did was mediated by irony. In the words of a contemporary, she was "the Original Dada." [88]

When the war broke out, the Baron and Baroness von Freytag-Loringhoven were living at the New York Ritz. The baron decided that he must return to his German homeland, but having arrived there and directly experienced the war's organized fratricide, he felt compelled to protest and did so by taking his own life. Left behind in New York, the baroness declared his suicide the noblest deed of his life, but it left her

Arthur Cravan

penniless. She migrated downtown to Greenwich Village and began to model at the Ferrer Center for such painters as George Bellows, William Glackens, and Robert Henri. Although the baroness was not beautiful—her forty-year-old body was sinewy and worn, and her skin discolored—she was distinctive and would become even more so.

Every evening between five and six the baroness paraded through Washington Square with her legion of dogs on tangled leashes. No memoir of the period is complete without some report of her regalia. Her head was often shaved—or half-shaved—and then shellacked or painted vermilion. She alternately adorned her head with a coal scuttle, a French soldier's helmet, ice cream spoons, or even a lit birthday cake crowning a face smeared with yellow powder and black lipstick. Her wardrobe included a bolero jacket, a loud Scottish kilt, and a patchy fur coat, but these served merely as a base. An adept seamstress, she applied to her costume Kewpie dolls and stuffed birds, flattened tin cans, cigarette premiums, and chandelier pendants. On her bustle she installed an electric taillight. Friends of the baroness were often startled to find their own possessions turning up in her attire.[89]

The baroness pushed the limits of free love, too. One artist recalled her method of seduction like this: "Enveloping me slowly, as a snake would its prey, she glued her wet lips on mine." [90] She terrified some— William Zorach, for example, was unnerved to find her crawling out from beneath his bed one night, and Wallace Stevens was afraid to venture below Fourteenth Street for fear of running into her.

Her greatest passion, Marcel Duchamp, brought her into the orbit of the Arensbergs.[91] Her ardor for Duchamp—both sexual and aesthetic—was best dramatized in a vignette recounted by the painter Louis Bouché, who once gave her a newspaper reproduction of *Nude*

ABOVE
Baroness Elsa von Freytag-Loringhoven, 1921. Photographs by Charles Sheeler, *New York Dada*, April 1921.

RIGHT
Baroness Elsa von Freytag-Loringhoven (1874–1927). *Portrait of Marcel Duchamp*, c. 1919. Pastel and collage on paper, 12¼ × 18⅛ in. (31 × 46 cm). Arturo Schwarz Collection, Milan

Descending a Staircase. While posing nude, she rubbed it into every inch of her anatomy from top to bottom. She maintained her idée fixe that Duchamp was infatuated with her, despite all evidence to the contrary. "Although he loves me, he would never even touch the hem of my red oilskin slicker," she explained. "Something of his dynamic warmth—electrically—would be dissipated by the contact."[92] This psychotic interpretation of the relationship allowed her one-sided romance to continue unabated and inspired her to create both portraits and poems for Duchamp. At the Arensberg gatherings, for instance, she could be heard chanting one of her poems in a guttural German accent: "Marcel, Marcel, I love you like Hell, Marcel."[93]

In other times the baroness might have been dismissed as a schizophrenic street person. Within the avant-garde community, however, she embodied the most radical of personality experiments. In the world of Dada she was not just a baroness, she was queen.

Katherine Dreier seemed an unlikely supporter of Dada and virtually the opposite of the baroness. Dreier was earnest, didactic, unyieldingly proper. Both women, however, were German in background, both were infatuated with Duchamp, and both were equally militant. Between the time of the Armory Show and her introduction to the Arensberg salon by John Covert in 1916, Dreier had organized the Cooperative Mural Workshops (inspired by the ideas of John Ruskin and William Morris), which enlisted art in the improvement of the human condition. Unfazed by Dada, Dreier saw it not as nihilism but as the infusion of higher meaning in common objects.[94] "They are the tillers of the soil," she wrote of the Dadaists, "the men who are trying to prepare the ground for future development."[95]

Dreier always seemed out of place at the Arensbergs': the host made little attempt to hide his coolness toward her, and Henri-Pierre Roché likened her to an iceberg that would not melt. At those fleet and sardonic gatherings, she looked like a lumbering clubwoman whose autocratic seriousness seemed incapable of registering a note of irony. But she had qualities that made her useful to the Arensberg circle, for she added the anchor of organization to the brilliant airiness of the group. In her capable hands, ideas were transformed into a lecture or an item on a committee agenda. She also provided patronage to the modern artists and carried on the crusade with a Teutonic zeal that long outlasted this formative period.

That Duchamp was at the heart of New York Dada says as much about that avant-garde milieu as it does about his particular brand of leadership. He was the recipient of the community's philanthropy, the object of its romantic love, and the focus of its Francophile fixation.[96] Henri-Pierre Roché observed that "he was, along with Sarah Bernhardt, the most famous Frenchman in America."[97]

In a community that often split into factions, Duchamp was uni-

We are not limiting ourselves to the seven arts. No one has yet done much about the Art of Madness.

Jane Heap
on the baroness

Katherine Dreier

271

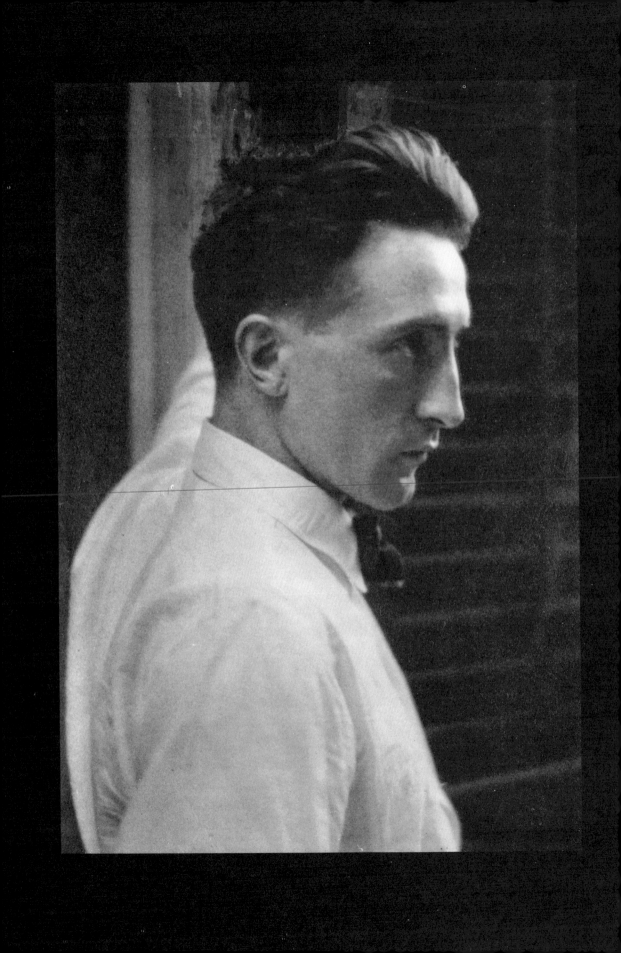

versally embraced. No other figure could provide the focus for both the Arensberg circle and the Stettheimer salon and elicit support from John Quinn and Alfred Stieglitz as well. His laconic elegance attracted the liberated women of Greenwich Village. The highbrow magazine *Current Opinion* published "The Iconoclastic Opinions of M. Marcel Duchamp Concerning Art and America," and even glossy *Vanity Fair* perceived him as sufficiently in vogue for its tony mainstream audience.[98] When the editors of *Rogue* needed a judge for their costume ball, they tapped Duchamp. And when a select group of six climbed the Washington Arch in January 1917 to declare the independence of Greenwich Village, Duchamp was among them. Although it was the scandalous *Nude Descending a Staircase* that had initially prompted his celebrity, Duchamp's persona was now as celebrated as his hermetic art, which was neither widely exhibited nor understood.[99] What was on display was the artist. McBride observed, "He is his own best creation," and a recent historian has aptly dubbed him "a self ready-made."[100]

Duchamp had spent his Paris years as a monastic librarian who would retreat to his studio for days, but as Gabrielle Buffet-Picabia observed, "Duchamp perfectly adapted to the violent rhythms of New York."[101] Walter Arensberg and John Quinn treated him to $1.25 dinners at the Brevoort, always preceded by a Bronx or a Manhattan. He became a gregarious figure who drank heavily, casually slept with many women, and went to bed at 5 A.M. Gleizes discerned in his friend "abysses of anxiety, of disenchantment, of protestation, of fatigue, of disgust," but none of this showed on the surface.[102] It was his beauty and his charm that his friends most often recalled. His chiseled Norman features and penetrating blue eyes aroused both men and women, and

OPPOSITE
Edward Steichen (1879-1973). *Marcel Duchamp*, 1917. Toned gelatin silver print, 9⅝ × 7½ in. (24.6 × 19 cm). Philadelphia Museum of Art; Louise and Walter Arensberg Collection

BELOW
John Sloan (1871–1951). *Arch Conspirators*, 1917. Etching, 4¼ × 5⅞ in. (10.8 × 15 cm). Delaware Art Museum, Wilmington; Gift of Helen Farr Sloan

On January 23, 1917, this group, later joined by Allen Norton, climbed the interior stairs to the top of the Washington Square Arch, strung Chinese lanterns and balloons, and signed a mostly illegible proclamation that Washington Square was a Free and Independent Republic. Marcel Duchamp is standing at left; John Sloan is crouching at right.

*Sometimes I think of you
as the Unknown Soldier
of the Cubist movement.
Once in a while you get
a wreath, but never a
definition. . . . If you are
the Unknown Soldier, let
me be the silent guard.*

Walter Arensberg
to Marcel Duchamp,
January 11, 1945

Duchamp's one-time paramour Beatrice Wood has speculated that even Walter Arensberg was sexually attracted to him. "Marcel at twenty-seven had the charm of an angel who spoke slang," she recalled. "But when his face was still it was as blank as a death mask."[103]

Duchamp attracted fame with what his friend André Breton called "a truly supreme ease."[104] He never smelled of oil paint or wore berets or fit any other stereotype of an artist. He didn't deliver earnest statements about the spiritual nature of art, and he seemed indifferent to conventional morality. His emotions were coolly reined in, ranging from amusement at one extreme to ironic disappointment at the other; his favorite phrase was "Cela n'a pas d'importance" (It doesn't matter).[105] Into the vacuum left by Stieglitz stepped Duchamp; as Roché observed, he became "the young prophet in spite of himself."[106]

A final catalyst within the Arensberg circle was the romance between French men and American women. In his first interview in the United States, Duchamp paid tribute to the American female as "the most intelligent woman in the world today," and added, "a wonderful beauty of line is hers, possessed by no other woman of any race at the present time."[107] Beatrice Wood exemplified this new brand of American woman that captivated the French émigrés. She had been brought up with hand-embroidered lace underwear, a governess, and a Pierce-Arrow. "But I was no doll beneath my childhood lace," she wrote, and by the time she was eighteen she lived in Paris, read Freud, and attended the first performance of *Le Sacre du printemps*.[108] The outbreak of war sent her back to America, where she acted in the French Repertory Company. To the visiting French, Wood and other liberated young

Beatrice Wood, 1915

women were nearly as captivating a feature of New York as its soaring skyline. Picabia would immortalize this American type in works like *Portrait d'une jeune fille américaine dans l'estate de nudité,* and Edgard Varèse would enjoy a lifelong marriage to one (Louise Norton), but the most idyllic of these Franco-American romances was the triangle composed of Beatrice Wood, Marcel Duchamp, and Henri-Pierre Roché.

Wood met Duchamp on one of her visits to Varèse, who was recuperating from his automobile accident in a bleak hospital room. (On an earlier visit the twenty-three-year-old actress was bravely conversing in her best Comédie Française French when—in mid-sentence—a fly buzzed into her mouth. Thinking it would be improper to spit it out, she bravely swallowed it, feeling every bat of its wings as it went down her gullet.) Wood was soon rewarded for her dutiful hospital visits when Duchamp came to call on his bedridden countryman, on September 27, 1916. Duchamp immediately addressed her in the familiar *tu*—signifying, as she knew from her French lessons, a daring intimacy.

Eighty years later Wood described herself during this period as "all romantic ectoplasm" eager to be molded.[109] Duchamp and Roché helped to educate her about love, but the difference between French and American sexual attitudes proved a barrier to consummating the relationships. Wood believed that sex should be a natural outcome of love, and since that condition was met she considered herself available to them both. Duchamp and Roché insisted that sex and love were entirely separate. Duchamp regarded Wood as a well-born virgin, and therefore sexually untouchable outside marriage. As Wood recalled, he "was well taken care of" by women he casually picked up on the sidewalk. Roché appalled Wood when he matter-of-factly informed her that he had slept with a hundred women; only after he "broke her heart" did she consummate her romance with Duchamp.

Wood called thirty-seven-year-old Roché her *vieux papa,* for he loved to correct her naive views of romance and teach her the nuances of lovemaking he had so frequently practiced. Duchamp became Wood's artistic mentor. He would invite her to spend afternoons in the disarray of his studio, amidst his unmade bed and his Readymades, the dust accumulating on the *Large Glass,* the walls hung with chessboards, and the windowsills piled with packages of his favored sustenance, crackers and chocolate. These afternoons were devoted as much to drawing as to romance, with Duchamp encouraging Wood to create abstract forms she considered unsightly scrawls. The threesome would often dine together, the two men instructing her in matters of taste, and then go on to spend the evening conversing at the Arensbergs'. Although she would sleep with Roché, it was Duchamp she dreamed about and would discuss the next morning over breakfast, at which point Roché would laugh and admit that he loved Duchamp too. "The three of us were something like *un amour à trois,*" Wood re-

Duchamp's studio, New York, 1917–18

Marcel Duchamp, Francis Picabia, and Beatrice Wood at Coney Island, 1917

called, and its reverberations could be felt years later in the classic triangle of Roché's novel *Jules and Jim*.[110]

The Arensberg salon was not as organized as Mabel Dodge's Evenings nor as sumptuous as the Stettheimers'. A dozen or more people would arrive after dinner or the theater and stay until the not-so-early hours of the morning. Although no one was formally invited, the gatherings were select occasions; in the words of Arensberg's biographer, the guests were "the avant-garde of the avant-garde."[111] Could any gathering be more exclusive?

The Arensbergs' apartment occupied the third and fourth floors of 33 West Sixty-seventh Street. Its chief room was a large duplex studio domesticated by an ensemble of Shaker furniture and worn Oriental rugs. The studio's main attraction was the art collection displayed on walls that soared seventeen feet up. Like the paintings at 27, rue de Fleurus, they were skied up to the ceiling, and like Leo Stein, Walter Arensberg never grew tired of speculating to his guests about the art's latent significance. Louise, who often arrived at the gatherings after an evening at the opera, was more reticent—especially if the work in question was as overtly erotic as Brancusi's *Princess X,* a bust in the form of a phallus. This ever-expanding exhibition provided a centerpiece to the gatherings. As one guest observed, it was here that "the super pictures on the walls / Had intercourse with the poems that were never written."[112]

The male guests wore jackets and ties and the women, conventional dresses; the Village dress code was not much in evidence here. The evenings were frequently alcoholic, the conversation encouraged

The Arensberg apartment,
c. 1918. Photographs by
Charles Sheeler

by glasses of whiskey and hors d'oeuvres, and at midnight Louise would wheel in a cart filled with chocolate eclairs and rice pudding as a sop for the liquor. Unlike Mabel Dodge's Evenings, conversation here was not General; it took place within small clumps of guests gathered around Louise's grand piano or seated on the Arensbergs' early American furniture, or standing before the paintings. One could overhear last night's dreams being analyzed, or artists' personalities being intuited from the forms on their canvases.[113] Walter discussed works as up-to-date as Duchamp's or as ancient as a Pre-Columbian figure. Although Louise usually lingered on the couch, she sometimes overcame her shyness and played the piano. Not all the activity was on a cerebral plane; there were also games of Twenty Questions and debates about fortune-tellers.

A chess game was always going in one corner or other, attracting players of consummate skill: Alfred Kreymborg had played professionally; Walter Arensberg's classmate Ernest Southard had been the president of Harvard's chess club; and Arensberg, Duchamp, and Allen Norton were devoted players. The game provided a form of discourse independent of language, which was especially useful since not all the

Beatrice Wood (b. 1893). *Soirée,* 1917. Ink and colored pencil on paper, 8¾ × 11 in. (22.2 × 27.9 cm). Francis M. Naumann, New York

French guests spoke fluent English and few of the Americans could converse in French.

The French visitors frequently banded together during these evenings, and the Americans sometimes interpreted this as condescension.[114] The American hypersensitivity is made vivid in a vignette recounted by William Carlos Williams. Standing before Duchamp's painting *Yvonne et Magdeleine déchiquetées,* the doctor was so intrigued by its Cubistic rendering of female heads that he wanted to compliment the artist. Although he knew his rusty French wasn't up to sophisticated conversation, Williams approached Duchamp, said simply, "I like your picture," and pointed at it. A slightly inebriated Duchamp gazed back at the doctor and said, "Do you?" From this plain and ambiguous response, Williams took such enormous offense that he fumed over it decades later:

> He had beat me all right, if that was the objective. I could have sunk through the floor, ground my teeth, turned my back on him and spat. I don't think I ever gave him that chance again. I realized then and there that there wasn't a possibility of my ever saying anything to anyone in that gang from that moment to eternity— but that one of them, by God, would come to me and give me the same chance one day and that I should not fail then to lay him cold—if I could.[115]

When guests later recalled the Arensberg gatherings, they emphasized the introductions—to new people and new ideas—that took place there and changed their lives. It was in the Arensberg studio that Dreier met Duchamp and began the relationship that lasted the rest of their lives. The poet Allen Norton remembered the Arensberg studio as the place "Where I first saw Time in the Nude / Where I first met Mme. Picabia."[116] Mina Loy first met Arthur Cravan at the Arensbergs' and "felt no premonition of the psychological infinity he would later offer my indiscreet curiosity as to the mechanism of man."[117]

Louise Norton (the ex-wife of Allen Norton and the future wife of Edgard Varèse) remembered Louise Arensberg playing Schoenberg's "Six Piano Pieces," which sounded to her "like an intricate shower of loud rain drops." Looking back on this moment, she wrote: "My ears had pricked up at the sound of my first modern music. They were quite ready for my musical future with Varèse."[118] Even the Francophobic William Carlos Williams prized his personal acquaintance with the French painters as a seminal influence that released his poetry from "stereotyped forms, trite subjects."[119] That these memories of the gatherings encompass poetry, music, art, and love suggests the broad impact of the Arensbergs' salon.

As 1916 drew to a close, the Arensberg circle began to organize more formally than they ever had before or ever would again: 33 West

Who's Who in Manhattan,
c. 1917, by Clara Tice.

Sixty-seventh Street became the headquarters of the Society of Independent Artists. How the "no jury, no prizes" concept was introduced to the Arensberg group is not known, but the idea itself was nothing new. Exhibitions staged without juries had begun in France with the Société des Artistes Indépendants in 1884, and the idea had been imported to New York in 1910 by Robert Henri. The artists who organized the Society of Independent Artists in 1917 descended from both sides of this transatlantic parentage.

One group, drawn from Henri's protégés, was resolutely American. Heading this cadre was William Glackens, who had previously presided over the domestic committee of the Armory Show and now served as president of the Independents. Among his cohorts were George Bellows, Robert Henri, Rockwell Kent, and Charles and Maurice Prendergast. For them, the Society of Independents was the vehicle to bring democracy to the art world. This group was outnumbered on the Independents' board of directors, however, by members of the Francophile Arensberg circle: Walter Arensberg was the managing director, Duchamp headed the hanging committee, John Covert acted as secretary, Walter Pach served as treasurer, and the board also included Katherine Dreier, Man Ray, Morton Schamberg, and Joseph Stella. These two blocs—who virtually repeated the Armory Show's split loyalties between America and Europe—made conflict inevitable.

In mid-January the fledgling organization mailed an announcement to artists throughout America that laid out the society's simple principles: a six-dollar membership fee guaranteed that each artist could exhibit two paintings at the Grand Central Palace.[120] On receiving the announcement, McBride declared it "great news, momentous news," and with characteristic enthusiasm he continued: "If the Liberty Bell were not so cracked already it should sound the glad tidings through-out the land. Young artists have been enfranchised. History is in the making. Breathe deeply of the air. Does not there seem to be already more ozone?"[121] Others clearly shared his feeling, for the society received over six hundred applications before the end of the month. They poured in from all over the country, and nearly one-third of them were from women. That the idea of a democratic exhibition elicited such a fervent response from artists throughout America came as a surprise.

Around the end of March 1917, Duchamp, Walter Arensberg, and Stella discussed submitting a piece that would test the limits of the Independents' democratic ideals. (Duchamp well remembered the timidity of the Salon des Indépendants when he submitted *Nude Descending a Staircase* to them in 1912.) After their conversation this trio went to J. L. Mott Iron Works at 118 Fifth Avenue. Looking at the plumbing appliances in their showroom, Duchamp selected and bought a porcelain, flat-back, Bedfordshire urinal. He signed his purchase R. Mutt (conflating the Mott company and the popular comic strip "Mutt and Jeff"), created a fictional Philadelphia address for himself, and submitted the piece to the Independents Show with his membership fee enclosed. Duchamp posed his challenge at the climactic moment of the most experimental phase of art making in American history. After the first shocks—delivered by Henri, Stieglitz, and the Armory Show—had been absorbed into the New York art world, Duchamp and the proto-Dada artists in New York subversively tested the most important issue: how far could the limits of art be pushed?

POETRY II:
NEW BATTLES

"There has undoubtedly been a great boom in vers libre rot, a huge production," Pound observed in the summer of 1916. "America will always grab any new mode or idea, or style, energetically and enthusiastically imitate and dilute it to death, WITH cheers, whoops and glorifications."[1] The popularizing of modern poetry had begun as early as the fall of 1913, when the estimable *North American Review* announced, "Poetry has now become a mentionable subject in decent society."[2] Over the next few years it became a virtual industry. In 1915 Houghton Mifflin, the chief publisher of mainstream poetry, replaced its pea green ribbed-cloth volumes with books sporting jazzy paper covers at half the price. The number of poetry books on the market soared: by 1916 the number of poetry and drama books published lagged only seventy-three volumes behind fiction. The *Little Review's* "New York Letter" reported in May 1916, "Poetry readings are now a well-intended form of afternoon time-killing."[3] By this time even magazines without avant-garde aspirations—*Poetry Review, Contemporary Verse,* and *Poetry Journal*—were publishing experimental verse, and the *New York Times Book Review's* annual poetry roundup lauded the ascendance of free verse.[4] The former agrarian troubadour Vachel Lindsay now toured under the auspices of the Pond's Lecture Bureau and chanted his Higher Vaudeville before women's clubs, President Wilson's cabinet, and Harvard classes. Modern poetry gave new life to a moribund poetry industry. In 1913 Harriet Monroe had mourned poetry as the neglected "Cinderella of the arts," but when she visited New York in 1916, she was astounded by the glut in the poetry market that had developed in just a few years.

The key little magazines of the period were *Poetry* (September 1912 to the present), the *Egoist* (January 1914—December 1919), the *Little Review* (March 1914—Spring 1929), *Rogue* (March 1915—September 1915), and *Others* (July 1915—July 1919). "A multitude of magazines is good in one way, but if it encourages diffuseness it is bad," warned

In the last six months practically every one of you has said that the tide of poetry is rising. . . . We need to have these verdicts restated in a way that will drown the automobile horns, the roar of the elevated railroads, the subways and the express trains and the guns of Europe.

Vachel Lindsay, speech at the annual dinner of the Poetry Society, January 26, 1915

Pound.[5] Each little magazine staked out its position within the suddenly crowded field. *Poetry*, the most established of the bunch, became a target among rebellious younger poets; as Pound observed in 1915, "*Poetry* is now an institution."[6] The *Egoist* offered the avant-garde an English headquarters; its mixture of American and English contributors gave it a transatlantic flavor.[7] The dandyish *Rogue* was called "the new little journal de fun," and it published not only poetry but also articles on amusing parties and trendy couture.[8] *Others* (like its predecessor, Alfred Kreymborg's *Glebe*) was always open to the newest experiments; William Carlos Williams called it "a free-running sewer."[9] The *Little Review* described itself as a "magazine of Art and Revolution" and ecstatically embraced both anarchism and Imagism—as well as free love and Margaret Anderson's various other passing enthusiasms.

The newly complicated poetry network required two rival impresarios, Ezra Pound and Amy Lowell. Harriet Monroe compared them to "two captains, each accustomed to command, who could not get together on the same boat."[10] Their changing alliances with the poets and with the little magazines proved as influential during this period as any of the publications themselves.

Certainly the jealousy of poets is quite equal to the proverbial one of opera singers.

Amy Lowell to
Margaret Anderson,
November 2, 1914

As the oldest of the little magazines, *Poetry* became a favorite scapegoat. Conservative critics chastised it for promoting free verse in America; experimental poets derided it as the ancien régime. Many of the attacks focused on Harriet Monroe. To some, this pinched woman with tightly waved hair represented a repressive parent; to Pound she em-

POETRY

"Chicago Poems" by Carl Sandburg . . . . March 1914
"Eros Turannos" by Edward Arlington Robinson . March 1914
"Song from the Player Queen"
    by William Butler Yeats . . . . May 1914
"On Heaven" by Ford Madox Ford . . . . June 1914
"Sketches" by Maxwell Bodenheim . . . . August 1914
"Blue Symphony" by John Gould Fletcher . . . September 1914
"Spoon River Anthology"
    by Edgar Lee Masters . . . . October 1914
"The Chinese Nightingale" by Vachel Lindsay . February 1915
"Exile's Letter" by Ezra Pound . . . . March 1915
"The Garden" by H. D. . . . . March 1915
"Root Buds" by William Carlos Williams . . . . May 1915
"To an Intramural Rat" by Marianne Moore . . . . May 1915
"The Love Song of J. Alfred Prufrock"
    by T. S. Eliot . . . . June 1915
"Phases I–VI" by Richard Aldington . . . . October 1915
"Sunday Morning" by Wallace Stevens . . . . November 1915
"Snow" by Robert Frost . . . . November 1916

Of course the plain
damn unvarnished fact
is that Harriet is a fool.
A noble, sincere, long-
struggling impeccable
fool. That is infinitely
better than being Amy-
just-selling-the-goods,
but it is damd [sic]
inconvenient.

Ezra Pound to
Alice Corbin Henderson,
May 5, 1916

bodied American provincialism. Her editorial limitations were significant: she overvalued negligible verse, pruned language to satisfy her
Victorian standards, recognized genius only dimly, and never really
grasped how to deal effectively with poets. However well-intentioned
her compulsive fretting over their manuscripts may have been, it was
rarely welcomed by the recipients. The writer Glenway Wescott, an
early office boy at *Poetry*, voiced a common sentiment when he informed her, "Your editorial habit of mutilation is unendurable; shows
also terrific lack of sympathy with the whole artistic process. . . ."[11]

Despite Monroe's shortcomings, *Poetry* reached its zenith in the
years 1914 and 1915. After introducing Pound's reforms in its first year,
Poetry accomplished the difficult task of publishing new literary tendencies without subscribing exclusively to any one school. Side by side
on its pages appeared Chicago poets such as Vachel Lindsay and Carl
Sandburg, modern masters such as Ford Madox Ford and William Butler
Yeats, sentimental romantics such as Arthur Davison Ficke and Monroe,
the Amy Lowell wing of Imagism that included Richard Aldington
and John Gould Fletcher, T. S. Eliot and other Pound protégés, and
such East Coast innovators as Marianne Moore, Wallace Stevens, and
William Carlos Williams.

This diversity attests to Monroe's strengths as an editor. Her role was
unenviable, for she had to please the guarantors who provided money,
the New York and Boston critics who took potshots at Porkopolis, Pound
and his English faction who demanded that modern international standards be met, local poets who considered it their geographical right to
be published in the Chicago magazine, and the Lowell faction who

*As I Imagine Miss Harriet
Monroe Editing "Poetry,"*
June 23, 1917, by William
Rose Benét

purveyed their own brand of Imagism. Monroe steered a wary course between these warring contingents. She kept the guarantors sufficiently content that they contributed emergency funds to keep the magazine afloat during its recurring episodes of near bankruptcy. She didn't succumb to Lowell's pressures, even when the poet became sufficiently ruffled to call Monroe "My Dear Girl," or to Pound's accusations that she was running an "ambulance corps for the incapable." [12] With young poets such as Maxwell Bodenheim, who attacked her as one of a breed of "editors who blow their careful challenge through a muffled trumpet," she maintained placid relations. [13] And she patiently nurtured poets who threatened suicide if their verse was not published (there were at least three during this period). Given the volatility of the poetry world, Monroe's uninspired evenhandedness was a relief. Alice Corbin Henderson observed that she was "a good deal of a brick. . . . I don't know anyone of her generation who would have proved so elastic." [14] Even Pound, reflecting on her at the end of his life, conceded that Monroe "was DUMB but honest, and honesty is a form of intelligence." [15] Monroe's relationships with three of *Poetry*'s most important contributors—William Carlos Williams, Wallace Stevens, and T. S. Eliot—demonstrate her editorial virtues and limitations.

In his first letter to Monroe, Williams demanded, "If *Poetry* does not open freely to me, in my absolute egotism, how am I to grow?" [16] His question echoed that of many poets who found their experimental verse clipped into conventional form by Monroe. She suggested new titles for Williams's poems, marked lines that fell a syllable short of the proper iambic, and offered to insert proper capitalization at the beginning of each line. Williams repeatedly accused her of being on the wrong side of the revolution. In an early letter she triggered Williams's rivalry with Pound by suggesting that, although she didn't like his poem, perhaps Pound could change her mind; Williams complained that she was afraid of experimentation "except when the divine Ezra bludgeons you into it." [17] Williams's emotionally extravagant letters were by turns hectoring, indignant, supplicating, and playfully shocking. He could write, "Whatever intellectual significance 'Poetry' ever had has long since departed," and then nine months later tell her, "You make me feel it worthwhile to be alive." [18] In their warmly combative exchanges Monroe entreated Williams, " 'Please punch my face in order to save my soul. . . .' " [19] She lifted the phrase from Pound, but the sentiment was her own; she gallantly tried to fight her drift toward conservatism. But this was not enough for Williams; when *Others* and the *Little Review* offered more adventurous outlets for his poetry, he took them. After 1915 his indignation at Monroe became chronic, and he submitted his poems elsewhere.

Wallace Stevens regarded Monroe as a source of unflagging support, but her appreciation of Stevens was, in fact, equivocal. After publishing the first group of poems he submitted in *Poetry*'s special war issue (November 1914)—bumping work by Lowell to squeeze his in—she rejected his next batch of poems. Stevens's early masterpiece, "Sunday Morning," prompted requests for substantive editorial changes. Unable to appreciate the poem's complexity and disturbed by its challenge to Christianity, she asked that he delete some sections and alter the sequence of others to fit the strictures of her own taste. Since "Sunday Morning" was Stevens's most complex poem to date, he might have felt disappointed by her response. Instead, he humbly thanked her for "clearly well-founded" criticism and allowed her to publish the poem as edited, but he restored it to its original state when he published his book *Harmonium*.

Stevens's self-effacement offered Monroe a welcome respite from the extravagant temperaments of Williams and Pound, and her meticulous attention to his poems offered a vivid contrast to the neglect he encountered at home.[20] "You are an encouraging person if there ever was one," he wrote to Monroe, "and I am grateful to you not only for that, but because, in addition, you give me more opportunity to do what you want, if I can. I shall try."[21] Stevens continued to submit poems to her for many years, and his warm correspondence with Monroe lasted until her death.

In October 1914 Ezra Pound sent T. S. Eliot's "Love Song of J. Alfred Prufrock" to Monroe, calling it "The most interesting contribution I've had from an American." He added a postscript: "Hope you'll get it *in* soon," but the poem made Monroe so uneasy that she hesitated.[22] The surface was too polished, the drawing-room sensibility too effete, and instead of feeling roused by an uplifting conclusion, she was disturbed by what she called "modern sophisticated dealing with the tag-ends of otherworldly cosmopolitanism."[23] Despite Pound's frequent epistolary bleats, Monroe stalled for nine months before publishing the poem, then buried it at the back of the issue.[24] And when Monroe published the next Eliot poem with a line cut from it, he never again submitted anything to her.

Eliot's poem became the focus of controversy in *Poetry*'s 1915 awards. After Pound cast his vote for Eliot, he listed the other potential candidates for the award (Skipwith Cannell, H.D., Orrick Johns, Carl Sandburg) as well as the must-avoids (Conrad Aiken, John Gould Fletcher, Amy Lowell, Constance Skinner, and Vachel Lindsay—"Oh gawd!!!"). Besides indicating his own preferences, this list demonstrates *Poetry*'s extraordinary accomplishments in 1915, certainly its most distinguished year. Pound concluded in a grand splutter: "No, if your committee don't make the award to Eliot, God only knows what slough of ignominy they will fall into—reaction, death, silliness!!!!!!"[25]

The committee's award selection shows how dimly *Poetry* understood its own achievement. It passed over unprecedented riches to give

T. S. Eliot. Photograph by E. O. Hoppe

the Levinson Prize to Illinois's perennial favorite son, Vachel Lindsay, and a second award to a series of Indian songs by the now-forgotten Constance Skinner. A special award for lyric poetry went to H.D. and at the bottom of the list, as third honorable mention, appeared Eliot's "Love Song of J. Alfred Prufrock." Pound reacted to the double insult of slighting Eliot in favor of two poets from his must-avoid list by simply noting that "the prizes were peculiarly filthy and disgusting" and letting the matter rest.[26] Although he would continue, on occasion, to fight the good fight with Monroe, he could now console himself with the fact that *Poetry* was no longer his sole American outlet.

The surfeit of new poetry heightened *Poetry*'s need to establish a new editorial course that would distinguish it from its competition. The recommendations that Monroe received—both solicited and un-solicited—were remarkably similar. At the end of 1915 Pound suggested that the magazine claim victory in having reformed poetry and "*go in for weight and mass attack. We must keep a monopoly of the* BEST *six or ten poets.*"[27] Echoing this idea six months later, Alice Corbin Henderson asserted: "The need for a perfectly fearless high standard was never greater than it is at this moment. What we need to do is to forget schools, forget Imagism, forget vers libre (now that that's back history) and talk poetry. . . ."[28] Aldington and even Williams prescribed a diet of only the best poets supplemented with critical prose, and John Gould Fletcher suggested closing *Poetry*'s pages to new poets and publishing only the best work of established writers.

These related strategies reflected the avant-garde's evolution: self-appointed gatekeepers now proposed to establish an elite, enforce standards, and close the door to newcomers. "If there is too great a flood of loose verse," Pound warned, "we shall kill the enthusiasm, the present enthusiasm, bore everyone and lose all we have gained."[29] But such an exclusive course contradicted Monroe's original desire to bring recognition to unpublished poets; she was constitutionally incapable of altering *Poetry*'s open-door policy. She protested to Fletcher in November 1916, "I should become merely a kind of register, and all the pleasure of gambling on the young and unknown would be gone."[30] However, what had been not only pleasurable but essential in 1912 was no longer a necessity by the end of 1916; by now there were so many places to publish that most of those poets who were still unknown deserved obscurity. By renewing her pledge to seek out the unknown, Monroe steered the magazine toward well-meaning oblivion, and by 1917 *Poetry* was no longer a standard-bearer in the modern movement.

After a day of unsettling depression Margaret Anderson was awakened in the middle of a Chicago summer night in 1913 by an epiphany. "First precise thought: I know why I'm depressed—nothing inspired is going on. Second: I demand that life be inspired every moment. Third: the only way to guarantee this is to have inspired conversation every moment. Fourth: most people never get so far as conversation; they haven't the stamina, and there is no time. Fifth: if I had a magazine I could spend my time filling it up with the best conversation the world has to offer. Sixth: marvelous idea—salvation. Seventh: decision to do it. Deep Sleep."[31]

Pursuing her inspiration a few weeks later, Anderson announced her venture at Margery Currey's storefront studio. Among the thirty friends Currey had invited for an informal dinner were Sherwood Anderson, Maurice Browne, Floyd Dell, Theodore Dreiser, and her Fifty-seventh Street neighbors. Anderson, in a severe black suit with her luxuriant strawberry blond hair spilling out from a small black hat, stood up after dinner and proposed the new magazine. The bohemian assembly greeted it with acclamation, and one of the guests—Dewitt Wing, a staff writer for the *Breeder's Gazette*—became so infatuated with the beautiful editor that he pledged his meager salary to finance the first issue.

This genesis of the *Little Review* well suited both the magazine and its editor: having emerged full-blown in a state bordering on dream consciousness, it was announced at the height of Chicago's Literary Renaissance; it depended on romantic chemistry between its editor and the bohemian community; and it was supported by the contributions of a class many rungs below *Poetry*'s guarantors.

Anderson promptly rented room 917 in her beloved Fine Arts Building and spent her first day staring at its sky blue walls, fantasizing

THE LITTLE REVIEW

Margaret Anderson

about the boundless future they promised for her magazine. The first issue appeared at the end of March 1914, bearing a simple white label on a plain brown cover. The contents of its sixty-four pages were a concise index of the interests of the Chicago avant-garde: Currey, Dell, and Cornelia Anderson (Sherwood's wife) each wrote about feminism. Essays appeared on Friedrich Nietzsche, Gertrude Stein, Rabindranath Tagore, and Ignace Paderewski. Describing "The New Note" in literature, Sherwood Anderson commended the subjectivity that became the magazine's guiding force: "It is the voice of the new man, come into a new world, proclaiming his right to speak out of the body and soul of youth, rather than through the bodies and soul of the master craftsmen who are gone."[32] Perhaps the most striking aspect of the first issue was the ecstatic tone of Margaret Anderson's editorial: "If you've ever read poetry with a feeling that it was your religion, if you've

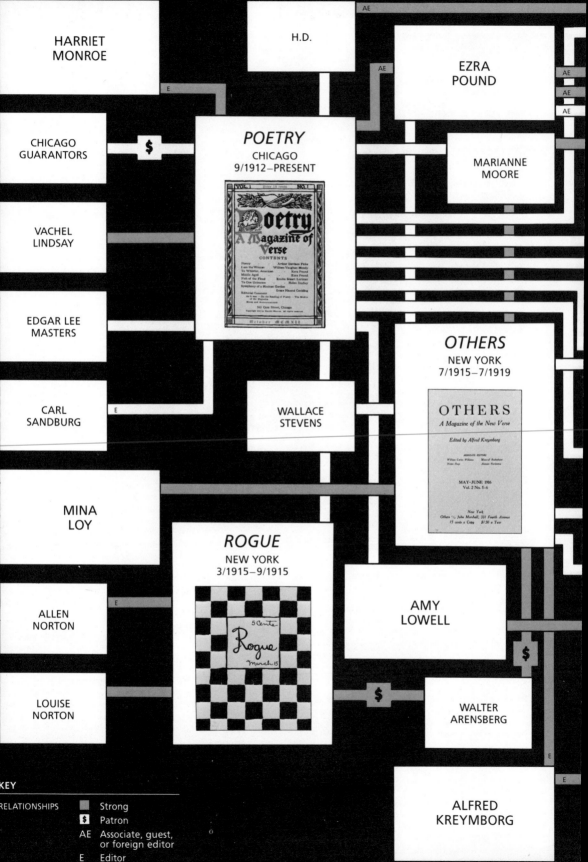

HARRIET MONROE

H.D.

EZRA POUND

AE

CHICAGO GUARANTORS

$

POETRY
CHICAGO
9/1912–PRESENT

Poetry A Magazine of Verse

MARIANNE MOORE

E

VACHEL LINDSAY

EDGAR LEE MASTERS

OTHERS
NEW YORK
7/1915–7/1919

OTHERS
A Magazine of the New Verse

Edited by Alfred Kreymborg

MAY–JUNE 1916
Vol. 2 No. 5–6

New York

CARL SANDBURG

E

WALLACE STEVENS

MINA LOY

ROGUE
NEW YORK
3/1915–9/1915

5 Cents
Rogue
march 15

AMY LOWELL

ALLEN NORTON

E

LOUISE NORTON

$

WALTER ARENSBERG

E

KEY

RELATIONSHIPS   ▮ Strong
                 $ Patron
                 AE Associate, guest, or foreign editor
                 E Editor

ALFRED KREYMBORG

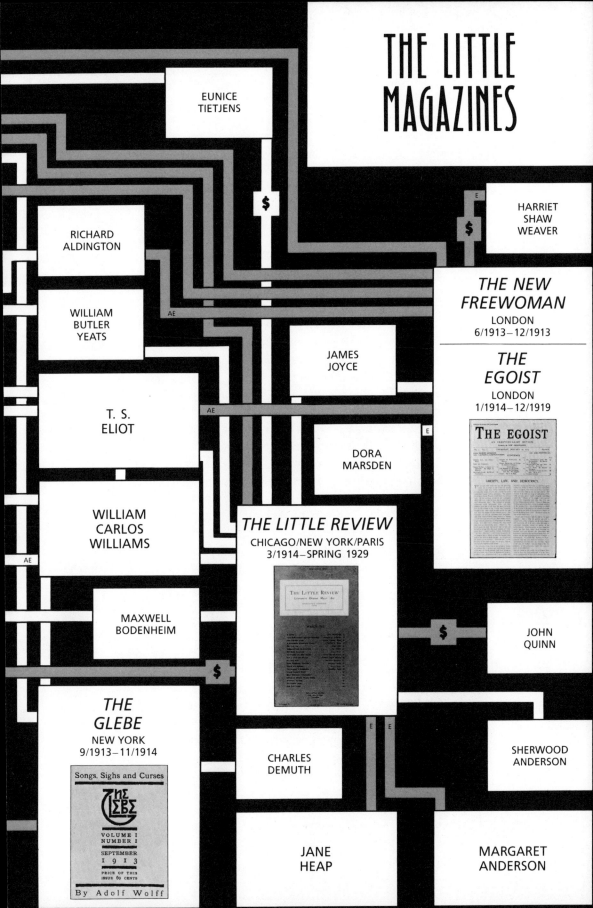

THE LITTLE MAGAZINES

EUNICE
TIETJENS

$

HARRIET
SHAW
WEAVER

RICHARD
ALDINGTON

THE NEW
FREEWOMAN
LONDON
6/1913–12/1913

WILLIAM
BUTLER
YEATS

AE

JAMES
JOYCE

THE
EGOIST
LONDON
1/1914–12/1919

T. S.
ELIOT

AE

DORA
MARSDEN

E

THE EGOIST
AN INDIVIDUALIST REVIEW

LIBERTY, LAW, AND DEMOCRACY.

WILLIAM
CARLOS
WILLIAMS

THE LITTLE REVIEW
CHICAGO/NEW YORK/PARIS
3/1914–SPRING 1929

AE

THE LITTLE REVIEW
Literature Drama Music Art

MAXWELL
BODENHEIM

$

JOHN
QUINN

$

THE
GLEBE
NEW YORK
9/1913–11/1914

E E

CHARLES
DEMUTH

SHERWOOD
ANDERSON

Songs, Sighs and Curses

THE
GLEBE

VOLUME I
NUMBER I
SEPTEMBER
1 9 1 3
PRICE OF THIS
ISSUE 50 CENTS

By Adolf Wolff

JANE
HEAP

MARGARET
ANDERSON

ever come suddenly upon the whiteness of a Venus in a dim, deep room, if, in the early morning, you've watched a bird with great white wings fly straight up into the rose-colored sun, if these things have happened to you and continue to happen until you're left quite speechless with the wonder of it all, then you will understand our hope to bring them nearer to the common experience of the people who read us." [33]

William Carlos Williams once wrote me: "As always, most of the stuff the Little Review prints is bad, I suppose, but the Little Review is good." How right he was.

Margaret Anderson

Readers were as often amused as impressed by the early issues of the *Little Review*. Dell lauded the magazine in the *Friday Literary Review* but ended by wondering, "Is this new magazine to be given exclusively to praise rather than to the art of criticism?" [34] Lowell considered it "amateurish and effervescent." [35] Pound didn't bother to get its name right when he wrote to Monroe that "the Small Review" was "A jolly place for people who aren't quite up to our level." [36] Even the praise had an inconsequential tone: "What an insouciant little pagan paper!" [37] Anderson freely confessed the magazine's glaring shortcomings; "We often printed rot," she later remarked. [38] But when she was asked if she had had any standards, Anderson bristled. "Standards? Mon dieu, did I have any *standards?* I had nothing *but*." [39]

Anderson considered herself both a "touchstone" and "a zig-zag idiot," and this combination determined the *Little Review*'s erratic course. [40] With each of the editor's enthusiasms, the magazine shifted. There were rhapsodic paeans to Hamlin and Garland pianos, Mary Garden, Henri Bergson, and little theater. Many pages were devoted to birth control, feminism, the new paganism, Futurism, and free love. Sometimes the magazine was dominated by articles on modern Europeans, at other times its pages were filled with the work of such Chicago literati as Sherwood Anderson, Maxwell Bodenheim, Ben Hecht, and Carl Sandburg. Through all the magazine's zigs and zags were two constants: the magazine always teetered at the edge of financial crisis, and its dilettante editor was always anchored by a formidable woman.

The financial crises were so frequent that they became a way of life. Anderson mastered the art of charming her way out of printers' bills and finding ways to delay the rent. Without the support of a moneyed class like *Poetry*'s guarantors, the *Little Review* relied on those who appeared on its pages. When Dewitt Wing backed away from the magazine's advocacy of anarchism in the third issue, others chipped in. Frank Lloyd Wright gave a hundred dollars, Vachel Lindsay contributed his *Poetry* prize money, and the poet Eunice Tietjens pawned her wedding ring. Amy Lowell (aka "Dear Fairy Godmother") sent $150, and occasionally anonymous donors contributed. The magazine scraped by on these contributions and the money raised from subscriptions (the circulation was approximately one thousand; subscriptions initially cost $2.50 a year but were cut to $1.50 six months later). Since the magazine survived on the slimmest means, it was taken for granted that contributors would not be paid. Many years later Gertrude Stein upbraided

Anderson for this policy. "Well, neither do I consider it a good principle for the artist to remain unpaid," Anderson replied, "—it's a little better than for him to remain unprinted, that's all." [41]

The magazine's resilience depended on its editor's adaptability to poverty. When Anderson invited guests for dinner, she served pickles and frankfurters. During low periods the magazine ran fewer pages or dispensed with a cover or was printed on cheaper stock ("We may have to come out on tissue paper pretty soon, but we shall *keep on coming out!*" Anderson wrote in 1916[42]). And when all the stamps and stationery ran out or the telephone was disconnected, the magazine simply appeared late.

The most theatrical of Anderson's adjustments to poverty came in the summer of 1915, when she lagged two months behind on the rent. Anderson, her sister and her two children, and *Little Review* associate Lois Dean carted their few belongings to the western shores of Lake Michigan, then nailed together nine dollars worth of boards, pitched tents, and cooked over a campfire. Embracing the summer rains and

Margaret Anderson's head-quarters, summer 1915

sleeping on a soldier's cot, Anderson looked back on those days as "lyrical." If she were not At Home, prospective contributors to the *Little Review* would simply pin their manuscripts to the tent flaps. "She was always exquisite," observed a friend, "as if emerging from a scented boudoir, not from a mildewed tent or a camp where frying bacon was scenting the atmosphere. . . . And she is valiant, always." [43]

The first of the three formidable women who affected the course of the *Little Review* was Emma Goldman. Hearing Goldman's lecture on anarchism just before putting the third issue to bed, Anderson became so inspired that she wrote an editorial proclaiming Goldman "the most challenging spirit in America." [44] At their first meeting Goldman was disoriented by the discovery that the editor of this radical magazine was a chic girl who lacked social consciousness. But when she heard Anderson's forceful piano playing, Goldman recognized a kindred desire for liberation and told Anderson she was an artist. Anderson later observed, "It was the first time in my magazine-cover existence that I had been taken at another valuation."[45] E.G., as Anderson began calling her, became her idol, and other sessions followed, with Anderson playing her Hamlin and Garland piano and Goldman singing Russian folk songs.[46]

During Anderson's anarchist phase she was bored by men in clean collars and grew fond of people that, she recalled, smelled of machine oil or herring. Sidestepping discussions of class and economics, she favored political analyses dominated by romantic non sequiturs like "You want free people just as you want the Venus that was modelled by the sea."[47] She reduced the complexities of sexual politics to a simple question: "When *will* people stop using that silly superfluous phrase 'free love'? We don't talk about 'cold ice' or 'black coal!'"[48] But when she wrote that "art and anarchism are in the world for exactly the same kind of reason," Anderson voiced the widespread sentiment of the American avant-garde that art and anarchy shared the common denominator of liberation.[49] Few felt this connection as viscerally as did Anderson. Opposition to authority was at the core of her character, and she believed that intellectuals, as well as conservatives of all stripes, constituted that authority. "I always thought of the *Little Review* as a crusade which could prove the superiority of the artist mind over the intellectual mind."[50] As her friend Eunice Tietjens recalled: "Margaret could never think, never distinguish one thing from another. She could only feel in a glorious haze."[51]

Anderson's support of anarchism aroused controversy within the *Little Review*'s community. The withdrawal of Wing's support forced Anderson to move to a smaller and cheaper room, number 814, in the Fine Arts Building. Lowell offered money only on the condition that an issue appear without a mention of anarchism. And the government even investigated Anderson when the *Little Review* suggested that the governor of Utah should be killed in retribution for the death of Joe Hill. But Anderson was unshaken in her radical beliefs; it was all part of what she later called her *Thirty Years' War*.

On January 4, 1915, Amy Lowell boarded the *Twentieth Century* for Chicago to convince Margaret Anderson that Lowell should edit the *Little Review*'s poetry section. Lowell had already approached other poetry magazines with similar propositions. The *Egoist* had offered her the position of poetry editor if she would contribute three hundred pounds a year, but Lowell could not imagine editing a magazine she couldn't even telephone. She had tried to insinuate herself into *Poetry* by cozying up to Harriet Monroe: "Please realize that I consider myself

Amy Lowell by Jane Heap

a kind of unofficial member of your staff, and glory to myself in the situation, and that anything I can write for you, and any labor which I can take off your hands, I consider to be a privilege." [52] Monroe maintained a cool, polite distance, while her associate editor, Alice Corbin Henderson, observed, "There is only one way to handle Amy, and that is with a pair of tongs." [53] In December, Lowell approached the *New Republic* to take her on as poetry editor, but again her offer was declined. Lowell knew that the *Little Review* might be her last opportunity to establish the base of power that only a magazine could supply.

Lowell strode into the *Little Review* office one afternoon accompanied by Monroe, who provided a formal introduction to Anderson. Listening silently to Lowell's account of her battles with Pound and her plans for promoting Imagism, Anderson concluded "that she wanted to subsidize modern poetry and push it ahead faster than it could go by its own impetus." [54] Lowell offered Anderson $150 per month in exchange for editing the magazine's poetry, adding that she would certainly never attempt to dictate policy. "No clairvoyance was needed to know that Amy Lowell would dictate, uniquely and majestically, any adventure in which she had a part," Anderson observed. "I should have preferred being in the clutches of a dozen groups." [55] She merely stated that she couldn't "function in association," and after Lowell's cajoling had no effect, she gave up and invited Anderson to lunch. Lowell never again attempted to take over a magazine, but she continued to court Anderson with contributions, flattery, and the occasional protest: "I do not think you would find me quite the fish you imagine." [56] Her patient persistence was rewarded with the informal position of poetry editor; just as *Poetry* had been the chief organ for Imagisme, the *Little Review* promoted Amygism from 1914 to 1917.

Poetry by Lowell (including her most famous poem, "Patterns"),

Unacademic, enthusiastic, appreciative and youthful. Free from propaganda and outworn tradition.

Advertisement for the *Little Review,* in the *Egoist,* 1915

Jane Heap, 1917. Photograph by E. O. Hoppe

Richard Aldington, H.D., and John Gould Fletcher appeared frequently in the pages of the *Little Review,* and its critical commentary about Imagist poetry consisted largely of promotion. *Some Imagist Poets* (1916) was glowingly reviewed in a collaborative piece by Lowell and Fletcher, pseudonymously signed George Lane; Aldington contributed articles about H.D.; and Lowell reviewed Aldington. Anderson was aware of the Imagists' group solidarity—and she shared it. One of the *Little Review* rules was that anyone who said that Lowell's poetry lacked feeling was to be promptly ejected from the office.

The third and most enduring of the formidable women who shaped the *Little Review* was Jane Heap.[57] Anderson recalled, "What I like to call my second life—a new, unexpected, extra life that to me was like a second birth—began when Jane joined the *Little Review.*"[58] The two women met one afternoon in February 1916, at an open house in the *Little Review* offices. Aline Barnsdall, a potential benefactor, was waxing passionate on the subject of Eleonora Duse and her sacrifice at the ignoble hands of Gabriele D'Annunzio. After listening carefully, Jane Heap chortled, "God love Duse, she has always given me a large pain."[59]

Heap defied categories. Her pronouncements didn't conform to the orthodoxies of either the bourgeois or the avant-garde, and her unique perspective owed something to the fact that she had grown up in the mental institutions where her father worked. She could discuss the most arcane subjects, but her style was that of a "breezy, travelling-salesman-of-the-world."[60] Most of all, she embodied authority. It was apparent in her heavy frame and the dark men's suits she wore, in the remark of a young admirer that "anything she starts, *Ends!*" and in the reaction of Emma Goldman on meeting her: "I felt as if she were pushing me against a wall."[61]

From Anderson's first encounter with Heap's odd, biting wit, she sensed the conversational genius and intellectual weight that could ground the *Little Review.* Where Anderson's friend Djuna Barnes detected "deep personal madness," Anderson saw "a supreme sanity" and "the most inspired mind that I knew."[62] By the summer of 1916 the two women had become lovers, and editing the *Little Review* together became an expression of Anderson's passion for Heap's original mind. Agreeing completely about the magazine's standards, Anderson wrote, "It was all expressed in the formula Jane found for the *Little Review:* TO EXPRESS THE EMOTIONS OF LIFE IS TO LIVE. TO EXPRESS THE LIFE OF EMOTIONS IS TO MAKE ART."[63] Although Heap's contribution is hard to pin down—it certainly extended beyond her monthly commentary as the "Reader-Critic"—she clearly added focus and organization to the *Little Review* and remained committed to it until the magazine's end, long after Anderson had left.

In both their ménage and their magazine, Anderson and Heap were opposites. Heap was earth to Anderson's fire, the butch to her femme, the depressive to her hysteric, the talker to her listener. Anderson made Heap the centerpiece of her life and decided it fell to her to bring this pungent critic to the world's attention. To translate Heap's conversation into magazine pieces, Anderson primed her with hours of "psychological gossip," locked her into a room, delivered food, and transcribed her talk. This arduous process resulted in a regular wide-ranging column bearing the tiny by-line "jh." In social situations, too, Anderson would incite quarrels so that Heap would be unable to resist getting into the fray. "It's an awkward role for me," Heap commented. "You're the buzz and I'm the sting." [64]

Now anchored in the relationship between Anderson and Heap, the *Little Review* no longer required an office in the Fine Arts Building. In the summer of 1916 the two women dramatized their absolute freedom by moving to the redwood forests of northern California and taking the magazine with them. In Muir Woods, across the Golden Gate from San Francisco, they set up a makeshift domicile lit by kerosene lamps. Days were filled with swimming and riding horses, eating fudge for breakfast and lounging about in pajamas—and through it all the two women *talked.* Anderson considered their talk so brilliant that the manuscripts submitted for the *Little Review* paled in comparison, so she published a number in which most of the pages were blank. This notorious issue—volume 12, number 2—was an avant-garde gesture and a plea: "*The Little Review* hopes to become a magazine of Art. The September issue is offered as a Want Ad." [65]

Upon returning to the Midwest that fall, Anderson decided that the magazine's Chicago phase was over. "It was just 'time to go,'" she concluded. "Chicago had had all it wanted from us, we had had all it could give." [66] Her intuition was accurate: the first flush of the Chicago Renaissance was over. [67]

As Christmas 1916 neared, Anderson and Heap made their goodbye rounds. They stopped by the *Poetry* office to bid adieu to Monroe, attended a concert in Orchestra Hall, and then strolled through the Fine Arts Building. "I went to walk through its corridors which always seemed to me filled with flowers," Anderson recalled, "[and] its shops, which gave me the emotion of a perpetual Christmas." Everyone from the elevator boys to the night watchman assured her that Chicago would not be the same without her. Last of all, Margaret Anderson saw the *Little Review* contributor Ben Hecht. "After you've gone," he told her, "I'm going to have an electric sign put across this building: WHERE IS ATHENS NOW?" [68]

In February 1915 Alfred Kreymborg sponged and pressed his Sunday suit for a party at the Washington Square apartment of Allen and Louise Norton. The party was being given in honor of *Rogue* magazine, which held an especially important place in Kreymborg's mind, because

I loathe compromising. . . . If there is only one really beautiful thing for the September issue, it shall go in and the other pages left blank. Come on all of you!

Margaret Anderson, *Little Review,* August 1916

Alfred Kreymborg. Marguerite Zorach, *Bruno's Bohemia,* April 1918

it was the first to ever request—and pay for!—one of his poems. The guest list consisted of the magazine's contributors—Donald Evans, the Nortons, Wallace Stevens, Carl Van Vechten and Fania Marinoff, and *Rogue*'s patron, Walter Arensberg. In contrast to Kreymborg's usual proletarian haunts—Lower East Side chess clubs and vaudeville back-stages—he was in the den of the Patagonians, the most dandified incarnation of the American avant-garde.

Trying to blend in with the stylish company, Kreymborg fingered his teacup nonchalantly and spoke languorously in imitation of a Harvard accent. But he soon realized the inadequacy of his impersonation compared with the others' "aesthetic fastidiousness in the matter of living as well of expressing art."[69] His next social gaffe was to tell Stevens that he liked his poem "Tea"—which made Stevens so uncomfortable that he waved his hand and muttered "something sounding like Jesus."[70] (Allen Norton took Kreymborg aside and politely informed him, "Cornering Stevens about his own work isn't done."[71])

Finally Kreymborg struck up a conversation with Arensberg about chess and Ezra Pound. Arensberg's formal reserve dropped (he knew about Kreymborg's professional chess career and his publishing *Des Imagistes*). They agreed on the need for a new poetry publishing venture—Arensberg found *Rogue* insufficiently experimental, and *Poetry* and the *Little Review* were a thousand miles away. They resumed the discussion a few days later at Arensberg's apartment and continued until 3 A.M., when Kreymborg fell asleep in a guest room. He awoke four hours later to Arensberg's insistent knock: they had a magazine to plan. According to Kreymborg, *Others* was born something like this:

> Arensberg: We'll have Wallace Stevens and Mina Loy to begin with.
> Kreymborg: They alone would create the paper we have in mind.
> Arensberg: So would you.
> Kreymborg: So would you.[72]

Would that we could rival Poetry. *Especially as rivalry is such a splendid stimulant to the boys.*

Alfred Kreymborg to Harriet Monroe, June 24, 1915

Others descended from two lines of little magazines: on one side, *Trend* and *Rogue;* on the other, the *Glebe* and the *Ridgefield Gazook*. It would be funded by Arensberg and edited by Kreymborg.[73]

Others may have been spawned in the elegant milieu of a Patagonian party and the Arensberg studio, but it was edited in bohemian fashion in rural Ridgefield, New Jersey. Beginning on June 4, 1915, a dozen poets gathered each Sunday to edit the magazine in a grassy clearing surrounding Kreymborg's two-room shack. For the local residents—the plutocrat poet Robert Carlton Brown, the poet Orrick Johns, Man Ray, and the painter Samuel Halpert—this required just a quick descent from the brow of the hill on the western slopes of the Palisades. William Carlos Williams escaped his medical practice to drive his

OTHERS

The *Others* group at William Carlos Williams's house, April 1916
Front row (left to right): Alanson Hartpence, Alfred Kreymborg, Williams, Skipwith Cannell. Back row (left to right): Jean Crotti, Marcel Duchamp, Walter Arensberg, Man Ray(?), Pitts Sanborn, Maxwell Bodenheim

Marianne Moore by Mina Loy

battered two-seater Ford five miles from Rutherford. Marianne Moore periodically made the twenty-mile journey from Chatham, New Jersey, accompanied by her friend Mary Carolyn Davies. Arensberg took the Fort Lee Ferry across the Hudson, along with Duchamp and Crotti.[74] (After the trek a baffled Duchamp inquired, "Why do you live so far? Is there something you do out here that can't be done nearer town?"[75])

The bundles that the poets carried contained not only sandwiches and bottles of cheap wine for a picnic but also the manuscripts that constituted the ostensible agenda for the afternoon. Kreymborg called them "Dutch Treats for the purpose of working together and of condemning the world at large."[76] Everyone played softball and tennis, then lolled on the grass that sloped down to the Hudson below, discussing Ty Cobb and Blanche Sweet. They carried on poetry shoptalk and chuckled over Kathleen Cannell's Ezra Pound imitations. Perhaps the finest talker was Marianne Moore, who arrived in boyish clothes, carrying her jug of carrot juice and a loaf of stone-ground whole wheat bread. "Marianne talked as she wrote and wrote as she talked," recalled Kreymborg, "and the consummate ease of the performance either way reminded one of the rapids of an intelligent stream." [77] Williams used a similar image when he recalled that "Marianne was our saint—if we had one—in whom we all instinctively felt our purpose come together to form a stream." [78] By the time the *Others* picnics ended late in the afternoon and the poets headed back to their scattered residences, the common emotion, as Kreymborg remembered, was "joyous bewilderment in the discovery that other men and women were working in a field they themselves felt they had chosen in solitude." [79]

At an early gathering Kreymborg suggested that each poet read his poetry, but these poets were invariably self-conscious about reciting. [80] Only Williams came forward, and his attempt to compensate for shyness by volume degenerated into unintelligible gasps. Kreymborg then assumed responsibility for reciting everyone's poems, and even though he had to devise his own rules for reading the irregular rhythms and eccentric spacing, hearing the new poetry excited the group. Williams recalled the shared feeling that "surely the present was the opening of a new era." [81]

Others first appeared in July 1915 and cost fifteen cents for its sixteen pages. The magazine's goldenrod covers and chaste layout offered no hint of the explosive poems inside. The first issue was dominated by Mina Loy's "Love Songs," which offered a clinical examination of a failed love affair, probably inspired by Loy's relationships with Marinetti and Papini. Its tone was ironic and cerebral, its lines oddly spaced, its meanings elliptical. New York's newspapers called it "swill poetry" and "hoggerel," complained that it was "erotic and erratic," and derided the magazine as "the little yellow dog." [82] Even the modern poetry community was shocked; Monroe called Loy "one of the long-to-be-hidden moderns," [83] and Lowell was so disturbed by the poem's treatment of eroticism that she and John Gould Fletcher made a pact not to publish their own work in the magazine. Lowell's conflation of free verse and free love was characteristic of the time. "Apparently all the questionable and pornographic poets are trying to sail under the name just now," she wrote to Aldington. [84] (Lowell even considered trying to copyright the term *free verse* so there could be no unseemly violations of the term.)

The magazine's laconic motto—"The old expressions are always with us, and there are always others"—positioned *Others* as the *salon des refusés* of the little magazines. The poet-critic Louis Untermeyer called the *Others* poets "crank insurgents." [85] Monroe staked out her position by writing to Kreymborg, "I assume that 'Others' stands exclusively for the radicals and for a rather more youthful effervescence than I am quite ready to endorse publicly. . . ." [86] Lowell dismissed the maga-

We always look for
Others, *no matter who
or what is waiting.
"There is an aviator spirit
in that magazine," says
Carl Sandburg—a gay
defiance of wind and
weather.*

Harriet Monroe, *Poetry,*
October 1916

zine as foolish, and at the *Egoist,* Aldington loftily concluded, "We have the talent, we have our public, and it is estimating that public and our success very low to think that Kreymborg . . . can do us a bit of harm." [87]

Others provided an arena for unfettered experiment that was unlike the other little magazines—its contents were not subjected to Monroe's stringent editing or to Anderson's mercurial enthusiasms. Kreymborg's libertarian and unassuming temperament was reflected in the magazine's editorial process (analogous to the participatory democracy of the *Masses* and the early Provincetown Players), and later the editorship rotated on an irregular schedule. [88] If Pound thought *Others* "a harum scarum *vers libre* American product chiefly useful because it keeps 'Arriet from relapsing into the Nineties," that was indeed a valuable function during this phase of modern poetry's development. [89]

Of *Others*'s impressive beginning, William Carlos Williams wrote in the *Egoist,* "This little magazine was said to be the sun of a new dawn—in its little yellow paper cover!" [90] The first few issues were its best. After the magazine's explosive debut with Loy's "Love Songs," the next issue published two poems by Stevens that had been rejected by *Poetry* ("Peter Quince at the Clavier" and "The Silver Plough-Boy"), as well as four poems by Williams. The next issue benefited from Pound's feud with Monroe over T. S. Eliot. In reaction to both her lukewarm treatment of "The Love Song of J. Alfred Prufrock" and Kreymborg's hands-off treatment of *Des Imagistes,* Pound submitted Eliot's masterful "Portrait of a Lady" to *Others* (at the same time writing to Monroe that he considered its publication there a waste).

The last prominent poet to appear in *Others* was Marianne Moore, who had five poems in the December 1915 issue. Having published once in the May 1915 issue of *Poetry,* Moore found her next manuscript heavily penciled by Monroe. She responded with stiff politeness ("Printed slips are enigmatic things and I thank you for your criticism. I shall try to profit by it." [91]) and refrained from submitting another poem until 1932. Nor did her astringent poems have any place in the *Little Review:* Anderson rejected her work with the firm conviction that "INTELLECTUAL POETRY IS NOT POETRY." [92]

Others offered an entry to little-known poets such as Djuna Barnes, Maxwell Bodenheim, and Lola Ridge, and it proved especially important to the development of Williams, who regarded *Others* as "the magazine which had saved my life as a writer." [93] But the qualities in *Others* that best served the dissemination of modern poetry—its openness to unknowns, its easy assimilation of the newest forms of modernism, its democratic editorship—also proved to be its undoing. Kreymborg was neither charismatic (like Anderson), nor a first-rate poet (like Pound), nor eternally devoted (like Monroe), nor a canny propagandizer (like Lowell). His egoless stewardship was praised for its enthusiasm and good intentions, but not for its brilliance. [94] Despite the shorthand terms "the Others group" and "the Otherists," the contributors embodied no independent school of poetry. By the end of its first year, *Others's* flexibility had degenerated into shapelessness, and its contents reflected all too vividly the glut of free verse on the market. The magazine became an inadvertent advertisement of the need for strict standards. "Kreymborg and his gang are going to pace-make for the last yell," Pound wrote to Alice Corbin Henderson at the beginning of 1916. "I suppose the double-Chestnuts are going to make some sort of a stand against the Kreymborg crowd and I hope and suppose that their slogan will be 'good English' and 'form.'"[95]

Others became a victim of its own openness when, in January 1917, the magazine devoted its entire issue to the Spectrist School, led by Anne Knish and Emanuel Morgan.[96] Some of their poems were reprinted in *Current Opinion,* and articles on the Spectrists appeared in the *New Republic* and the *Forum.* It was not until April 25, 1918, that the Spectrist School was revealed as a hoax concocted by two conservative poets, Arthur Davison Ficke and Witter Bynner, to expose the poetry renaissance to ridicule. Named at a performance of the Ballets Russes's *Spectre de la Rose,* the Spectrist canon was written in ten days over ten bottles of Scotch. Hoping to ensnare Amy Lowell and other editors in their joke, Bynner (aka Emanuel Morgan) and Ficke (aka Anne Knish) improvised "a sort of runaway poetry, the poet seated in the wagon but the reins flung aside."[97] The uncritical receptivity that was also its equivocal strength made *Others* the most vulnerable to the plot.

With Kreymborg (of no importance but as a symptom) and that gang, vers libre *as a principle has, and has for a long time become as fixed, stupid and academic as the* Century *or* Scribner *"laws of verse."*

Ezra Pound to Margaret Anderson, June 22, 1917

Smell me, a dead fish . . .
Taste me, a rotten tree . . .
Someday touch me, all you wish,
In the wide sea.

Emanuel Morgan, "Opus 79," *Others,* January 1917

The chief modern poetry impresarios, Amy Lowell and Ezra Pound, relied upon the little magazines to publish their poets. Operating at the behest of editors, Lowell and Pound aggressively and competitively colonized their respective territories, but each regretted the lack of a personal duchy from which to dictate.

With her aspiration to the editorship of a little magazine behind her, Lowell began a long, distinguished, and theatrical career lecturing about modern poetry. In Eliot's phrase, she became "a demon saleswoman."[98] It was commonplace to remark in Boston that if Lowell's figure had been less gross, she would have become an actress. By the time the forty-year-old poet took the stage, she had grown accus-

Amy Lowell, c. 1916

tomed to the fact that people would laugh both at her body and at modern poetry. Lowell's debut as modern poetry's propagandist occurred at a March 1915 meeting of the Poetry Society of America—known in Boston as "the New York Poetry Society" and known among modern poets as the ancien régime. Lowell had insisted on five minutes at the end of a long program, following Hamlin Garland's cordial introduction to Edgar Lee Masters's reading of *Spoon River Anthology.* In two weeks the first of Lowell's anthologies, *Some Imagist Poets,* would be published; she was determined that the official poetry establishment be prepared for it.

Lowell's selection of a poem to read carried curious echoes of the Imagist dinner in London; as if to prove that she was indeed a Nagiste, she opened with her poem "Bath." This provocative choice elicited repressed titters from an audience unable to dissociate the poem and the poet—especially when she recited the description of her body lying back, to "let the green-white water, the sun-flawed beryl water, flow over me." [99] It seemed to the audience that she was demanding, in the same breath, acceptance of poetic modernity and physical abnormality. As soon as she finished, the staid society erupted. Ignoring the strict rule against discussing the poems of guests, many even leapt from their seats to demand, "Do you consider that *poetry?*" Lowell would be answering that rude question for the rest of her life.

Lowell became a one-woman Chautauqua circuit, stumping for modern poetry in Chicago and Saint Louis; Springfield, Illinois; and New York. All doors opened to her. As a Lowell, she was welcomed into upper-class ladies' clubs, as a poet she went to writers' colonies and poetry academies, as a theatrical phenomenon she filled auditoriums across provincial America. Her fee escalated from fifty to two hundred dollars, her stage management became ever more finely tuned, and throngs had to be turned away from meeting halls even after extra chairs had been crowded into the aisles. "The life of a poet is by no means the dreamy aesthetic one people are led to suppose," Lowell said. "A mixture of that of a day-laborer, a travelling salesman, and an itinerant actress, is about what it amounts to." [100]

Lowell would seduce her audience, no matter what their poetic preferences, before a word about poetry had been uttered. Comically imperious, she stormed the stage and ordered it rearranged. The lectern had to be replaced with a table (which often had to be carried in over the heads of the audience), and her own blindingly bright reading light had to be plugged in. Lowell amused the audience by making sotto voce comments about the stagehands' progress and dramatized her strained eyesight by pulling out a small basket of spectacles and announcing, "These are my eyes!" She invariably ended the reading of her first poem by looking up at the audience to offer a mock challenge: "Well?—Clap or hiss, I don't care which; but for Christ's sake, do something!" [101] Her companion, the actress Ada Russell, had coached

*There was no still, small voice in Amy Lowell. Her bombs
exploded with a bang and came down in a shower of stars; and
she whizzed and she whirred, and she rustled and rumbled, and
she glistened and sparkled and blazed and blared. If at the end,
it seemed like the Fourth of July, it was a famous victory, none
the less, though the fields and the trees were littered with the
sticks and debris, with charred frames and burnt-out cases.*

Van Wyck Brooks

Lowell on tricks of the stage to incorporate into her declamation. Amy
whispered, chanted, shouted; she stamped out the poem's rhythm, she
swung her gold-mesh bag, she even cakewalked across the stage. But
reverberating through it all was her clear contralto voice, as effective an
instrument onstage as it was in conversation. Lowell turned the fusty
lecture format into a performance that invited audience participation
and undercut the temptation to laugh at her by doing so first.

As she had told Pound, it was all part of "American methods of
advertising." [102] And so Lowell concluded each of her lectures by grandly
descending from the stage to autograph books and stray slips of paper
and to pose for photographers before catching her train, leaving headlines in her wake. Lowell was a boon to the press, which relished reporting her eccentric habits. Traveling with Mrs. Russell and two maids
in a railway stateroom, she would book herself into the city's best hotel,
whose staff had orders to wrap all the mirrors and reflective objects, to
stop the clocks, to draw the shades, and (to replicate her Sky Parlor at
Sevenels) to set the double bed with sixteen plump down pillows and
Lowell's own handwoven bath towels and silk bed linens. "Publicity
first," the shrewd Lowell declared, "poetry will follow." [103]

Lowell's public tours were balanced by the serene constancy of
Sevenels. She called her private castle the Storm Center, and its thirty
acres of gardens and meadows were guarded by an imposing gate and
seven sheepdogs. There she conducted her private literary business
and her domestic life with Ada Russell.[104] Once Russell had settled at
Sevenels, around 1914, their relationship mirrored that of Gertrude
Stein and Alice B. Toklas. Russell fetched books, kept the household
quiet, and spent her evenings appreciatively criticizing Lowell's latest
poems. Lowell expressed their interdependence when she suggested
they put out a sign—"Lowell & Russell, Makers of Fine Poems." Russell
was not only a collaborator but a muse; Lowell called her "Peter" and
wrote love poems to her.[105]

Despite numerous medical complaints (hernias, gastritis, neuralgia,
high blood pressure, and pain that was eased only by double doses of
morphine), Lowell conducted her energetic course of literary diplomacy.

Amy Lowell in the garden at
Sevenels, 1922

I have the curious feeling that if a poet is any sort of a poet he ought to be able to do the other things of the world better than the people who can do nothing else. Therefore, being a soldier, I should wish to be a general; being a cook, nothing but a chef would satisfy me.

Amy Lowell to
Donald Evans,
June 7, 1918

Her favorite task was signing the royalty checks for the contributors to *Some Imagist Poets,* but she also sold editors poems by Aldington, Bodenheim, and Fletcher; she shipped her old typewriter to a destitute D. H. Lawrence; she wrote letters of introduction for the recent Harvard graduate E. E. Cummings and glowing reviews of work by Fletcher and Robert Frost. "Literary politicians have always abounded," observed Van Wyck Brooks, "but she was the prime minister of the republic of poetry." [106]

Lowell's intimate literary dinners followed a prescribed ritual. Guests arrived at seven o'clock and tarried in the yellow reception room for an hour, entertained only by themselves, the *Boston Transcript* handed to them by the maid, and the Monet painting of Battersea Bridge that hung over the dark oak mantel. Even after the guests were ushered into the dining room by Mrs. Russell, Lowell would not be present. Making her entrance during the meat course, she was heralded by the barking of her sheepdogs, who bounded down the stairs before her and obediently halted on the threshold. After dinner the company retired to the baronial library, where the maids lit a fire of four-foot logs, offered pale Manila cigars and cigarettes, liqueurs and coffee. Lowell's conversation commanded the guests' attention; in her mixture of gaiety and gusto she reminded Carl Sandburg of "a bright blue wave," and she inspired another guest to exclaim, "her conversation was a tonic for a year—a tonic not a stimulant." [107] At 12:05 the guests caught the last streetcar for Boston, and Lowell returned to the deep leather armchair before the fire, gathered her freshly sharpened pencils and "cameo sepia block" paper, lit a large colorado claro cigar, and through the uninterrupted night she wrote her poems and books.

Lowell's books about modern poetry—*Six French Poets: Studies in Contemporary Literature* (1915) and *Tendencies in Modern American Poetry* (1917)—provide a record of her lectures. She wrote as she talked, in a thoroughly engaging tone, and her books went through several printings. Lowell wasn't the pioneer of modern poetry anthologies, for Pound's *Des Imagistes* had appeared a year before hers. But Lowell's were the first anthologies to be published by a mainstream publisher (Houghton Mifflin) and to reach a wide audience. Beginning in 1915 a new edition of *Some Imagist Poets* appeared each spring, and by the time the third and last volume appeared in 1917 anthologies had become the fashion. Pound published his *Catholic Anthology* (November 1915); Monroe published *Modern Verse* (1917); and *Others* anthologies appeared in 1916, 1917, and 1919. [108]

To popularize poetry, Lowell used the language of advertising, which was more widely understood than the argot of the little magazines. Sidestepping discussion of modern poetry's hermetic subjects and styles, she appealed to her audience's belief in progress. In her crusade for modern poetry she sold America to itself:

We may not realize it, but slowly, before our eyes, the American race is being born. And one of the evidences of it is that we are beginning to hew new pathways for ourselves in this most intimate thing—Poetry, and to free ourselves from the tutelage of another nation. . . . Our artists are only just beginning to dare to be themselves. And the New Poetry is blazing a trail toward Nationality far more subtle and intense than any settlement houses and waving the American flag in schools can ever achieve. I might say with perfect truth that the most national things we have are skyscrapers, ice water, and the New Poetry, and each of these means more than appears on the surface.[109]

While Lowell triumphantly marched across America spreading the word of Imagism, the man who had founded the movement felt abandoned in a city across the Atlantic that no longer reigned as the capital of poetry. At the beginning of 1914 Pound had written to Alice Corbin Henderson: "Forgive this braggadocio. But I want you and H.M. to feel secure in the moderately certain knowledge that I can annihilate anyone who gets in front of us. Simply I've got the artillery . . . to take on the whole lot."[110] By the end of 1914 his boast seemed pathetically hollow. His artillery was gone, his ranks decimated. For Pound the period from late 1914 to early 1917 was marked by frustration and betrayal, by poverty and "cerebral gout."[111]

He had lost the Imagist war, and—adding insult to injury—the cover of Lowell's 1914 book, Sword Blades and Poppy Seed, proclaimed her "The foremost member of the Imagists."[112] Pound's angry plans to discredit the Imagists in print only alienated him even more from Aldington, Ford, and H.D. "I believe several of the contributors . . . consider that I have insulted them in their tenderest part, i.e., their nonextant critical faculty," Pound wrote to Henderson. "I trust that, relieved of my encumbering weight, their chariot will ascend Parnassus with the greater speed and convenience."[113] In May 1915 the Egoist began to expunge Pound from Imagism's history, when the "History of Imagism," written by F. S. Flint (an original member of T. E. Hulme's circle and a member of Lowell's camp), relegated Pound to the marginal position of an interloper. When Pound retorted "BULLSHIT," Flint responded, "You might have been generalissimo in a compact onslaught: and you spoiled everything by some native incapacity for walking square with your fellows."[114] Many of London's literary community harbored secret pleasure in the downfall of the upstart American; Flint merely seized the occasion to voice it. Aldington, during his tenure as the Egoist's deputy editor, banished Pound from its pages and privately called him "a small but persistent volcano in the dim levels of London literary society."[115] Meanwhile, one of Pound's other sources of income, the Quarterly Review, informed him that contributing to BLAST "stamps a man too disadvantageously"[116] to appear on the Quarterly's

Alvin Langdon Coburn (1882–1966). *Vortograph of Ezra Pound,* c. 1917. Gelatin silver print, 7⅞ × 6⅛ in. (20.2 × 15.4 cm). International Museum of Photography at George Eastman House, Rochester, New York

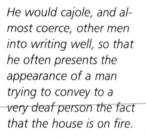

He would cajole, and almost coerce, other men into writing well, so that he often presents the appearance of a man trying to convey to a very deaf person the fact that the house is on fire.

T. S. Eliot on Ezra Pound

pages. Yet Vorticism provided no help, for *BLAST* died after a second issue, in July 1915. When Pound toted up his annual earnings in the fall of 1916, they amounted to a paltry forty-nine pounds.

Pound sometimes retreated from this grim reality into idealized fantasies of an artists' community. In the fall of 1914 he announced that "art is a matter of capitals" and set out his plans to create just such a capital in the form of a College of Arts.[117] "We aim at an intellectual status no lower than that attained by the courts of the Italian Renaissance," Pound proclaimed.[118] His fixation with a cultural rebirth filled three 1915 installments in *Poetry,* in which he described a society where visionary artists would create in harmony with an enlightened patron class. Pound's College of Arts came to nothing, and his idealistic vision of a renaissance bore little relation to the reality of wartime London, but both were symptoms of Pound's desperate grandiosity; his desire for a renaissance became even more urgent as the real thing crumbled around him. In the absence of former allies, who had sided with Lowell or gone to the trenches, Pound forged a new group, adding T. S. Eliot and James Joyce to his Vorticist colleague Wyndham Lewis. Although Lowell was modern poetry's most public figure, Pound was avatar to its most important poets.

Both in temperament and writing style Eliot and Pound were opposites, but their association proved critical to Eliot's development. Pound provided the younger poet with connections to Yeats's Evenings and to Ford Madox Ford. Pound introduced Eliot's poetry to the *Egoist* (which published it), began to push Eliot's poems in such American magazines as *Poetry* and *Others,* and assumed personal responsibility for anonymously financing Eliot's first book of poems, which was published under the auspices of the *Egoist.*

James Joyce, too, was a beneficiary of Pound's. "But for you I should have been a derelict," Joyce wrote him in an uncharacteristically generous note in 1917.[119] At Yeats's suggestion, Pound had first contacted the Irish author in December 1913, to enlist a contribution for *Des Imagistes,* and over the next few years he carefully shaped Joyce's career. He sold sections of *Dubliners* to *Smart Set,* he hammered at Harriet Shaw Weaver to serialize *A Portrait of the Artist as a Young Man* in the *Egoist,* he hectored Lady Emerald Cunard into sending Joyce money, he arranged for a good literary agent, he even offered his diagnosis of Joyce's astigmatism.

Pound's zealous sponsorship of Eliot, Joyce, and Lewis during this period seems remarkably selfless: many of his services were carried out in anonymity, he received no material rewards, and the three writers were not notably appreciative. But they did offer the poetry impresario a new clique who met *weltliteratur* standards. To Pound there was nothing like the joy of orchestrating the careers of geniuses, whom he treated, Eliot recalled, "almost impersonally, as art or literature machines. . . ."[120]

At the beginning of 1915 Pound began corresponding with John Quinn, perhaps the only patron who could make Pound's vision of an artistic renaissance come true. The exchange began in an atmosphere of challenge. In a January issue of the *New Age,* Pound had referred to "American collectors buying autograph MSS. of William Morris, faked Rembrandts and faked Vandykes"—a description that Quinn read as an inaccurate reference to himself as a collector of work by dead artists.[121] Quinn set the record straight by listing the modern paintings in his own collection, describing his practical legal services to modern art, and challenging Pound, "If there is a 'liver' collection of vital contemporary art in this country, for a man of moderate means, I should like to meet him."[122]

Pound's long reply to Quinn laid the foundation for their relationship: "A great age of painting, a renaissance in the arts, comes when there are a few patrons who back their own flair and who buy from unrecognized men. . . . If you can hammer this into a few more collectors you will bring on another Cinquecento."[123] Quinn and Pound were ideal partners—the self-made man of affairs who was "near the councils of power" met his match in the man who described himself as "a universal committee for the arts."[124] Through Pound, Quinn became not simply a collector and companion of artists but a full partner in fostering a great modern age of the arts.[125] And through Quinn, Pound found a way to establish a base of power in his native land. He proposed that America's only salvation was to elect Quinn president and Pound secretary of fine arts.

At first Pound barraged Quinn with a letter nearly every day; the garrulous Quinn, who kept three full-time secretaries busy with his dictation, replied in kind. Pound's letters set out plans to secure a pulpit

America has at least one great man in it and that man is John Quinn.

Ezra Pound to
Harriet Monroe,
May 3, 1916

from which he could preach his literary gospel. The two conspired to overtake a fusty weekly called the *Academy* or Mitchell Kennerley's *Forum*, to sponsor a new fortnightly magazine based on the *Mercure de France* (to be called the *Vortex* or the *Hammer*), and Quinn offered Pound a hundred pounds a year to assume editorial control of the *Egoist*. Although none of these plans came to fruition, the lively correspondence between two like-minded spirits was in itself tonic. Complaining about the "sugar teat optimism" of the women who ran the poetry establishment, Pound relished this opportunity for salty misogynism.[126] "I think America is getting fed up on gynocracy and that it is time for a male review," Pound wrote, seriously proposing a ban on women in its pages.[127] And both shared a sharp impatience with the public. "Je m'emmerde du public, they want shit and they get it, and they smack their dung smeared lips and holler for more," wrote Pound. "And when a good thing comes they hate it."[128]

Quinn furnished practical and financial support for Pound and his coterie of artists and writers. He arranged a New York exhibition for the Vorticists (at the Penguin Club), bought artwork by Wyndham Lewis, Jacob Epstein, and Gaudier-Brzeska; supported Eliot and Joyce by sending generous checks for their manuscripts; and arranged with the newly established publisher Alfred A. Knopf to publish Eliot's and Pound's first books in America.[129]

The most important product of their relationship was an alliance between Quinn, Pound, and the *Little Review*. When the magazine's blank issue appeared in September 1916 as a "Want Ad," Pound initiated a correspondence with Margaret Anderson that coincided with her move to New York. She had acknowledged the magazine's desperate need for higher standards and could even agree with Pound's judgment that the *Little Review* was "scrappy and unselective."[130] Quinn offered to give 750 dollars anonymously each year so that Pound could edit a section of the magazine without interference. After Anderson agreed to this arrangement, Pound wrote her a letter declaring his intentions to establish a base in America: "DEFINITELY then: I want an 'official organ' (vile phrase). I mean I want a place where I and T. S. Eliot can appear once a month (or once an 'issue') and where Joyce can appear when he likes, and where Wyndham Lewis can appear if he ever comes back from the war."[131]

For the first time the *Little Review* would be on firm financial footing, and the man who had initiated America's poetry revolution would return to power. Now, Pound wrote to Anderson, "We want all the available energy poured into our vortex."[132]

1917 & AFTER

"Sometimes it seems to be the end of the world's youth."

JOHN REED

APRIL 1917:
WAR BEGINS AND
AN ERA ENDS

A merica's avant-garde activity reached a peak in April 1917, just before the nation mobilized for war. The first days of the month were marked by Edgard Varèse's American debut on April 1 and by the opening of Georgia O'Keeffe's first one-person show two days later. But as the spring wore on, the sense of new beginnings was overridden by the feeling that an era was ending. It had begun with the Armory Show, and it closed in April 1917 with the Independents Exhibition. And just as Francis Picabia and Gabrielle Buffet-Picabia had sailed to New York for the Armory Show, they returned on April 4 to witness the avant-garde's final crescendo, "The Big Show."

The next day the artworks for the Independents Exhibition arrived at the Grand Central Palace in all their bewildering democratic diversity. The committee had four days to install 2,400 paintings and 350 sculptures by professional and amateur artists from thirty-eight states. As the conservative critic Royal Cortissoz observed, "Not art, but democracy, is in charge."[1] When John Quinn surveyed the assemblage, he called it "Democracy run riot!"[2] Included were academic landscapes, photographs, batik panels, family portraits, artificial flower arrangements, Cubist still lifes, wood carvings, a millinery dummy, and a bird bath.

The thousands of artworks without any common thread were assembled along two miles of ten-foot-tall beaverboard screens, which were divided into six boulevards and decorated with pine trees. Marcel Duchamp's solution to organizing the show proved both simple and controversial: works were hung alphabetically, and the letter leading off the installation was drawn at random (R, as it turned out).[3] This solution embodied ultimate democracy; its subversion of conventional aesthetics and order appeared quintessentially Dada. Robert Henri sourly responded to Duchamp's plan by observing, "We would not care for a

The principle of "No jury, no prizes" will not be vindicated by an uproarious excitement upon the part of the public over the affair, nor by impressive gate receipts and picture sales. It will be vindicated by only one thing, the future.

Henry McBride,
New York Sun,
April 15, 1917

musical program where Beethoven's Seventh Symphony would be followed by a fox trot, nor would it be possible to enjoy eating in sequence mustard, ice cream, pickles and pastry."[4] He withdrew his support before the exhibition opened.

One submission that arrived from Philadelphia tested the society's straightforward rules. Entitled *Fountain,* the sculpture was a urinal, placed on its back on a black pedestal, with the signature "R. Mutt" boldly scrawled in black paint. Now it is well known that R[ichard] Mutt was Marcel Duchamp, and *Fountain* has become the most notorious of his Readymades. But Mutt's identity was a mystery to most of the directors of the Independents show, and the controversy inspired by the sculpture demonstrated Duchamp's "veritable genius for perturbation and polemics."[5] In a heated argument with Walter Arensberg, George Bellows doubled his fist and punched the air while Arensberg caressed *Fountain*'s curved lip and offered a cerebral appreciation: "A lovely

Installation of the first exhibition of the Society of Independent Artists, Grand Central Palace, New York, 1917

form has been revealed, freed from its functional purpose, there a man clearly has made an aesthetic contribution."[6]

The disagreement within the Independents directors continued up to the final hours before the show opened. When an emergency meeting was called to decide Fountain's fate, the stormy emotional reactions split along predictable lines. Rockwell Kent divided the two camps into a "radical element" and "what I may without equivocation term the committee's saner members."[7] More neutral designations for these factions might be the Arensberg circle (Arensberg, John Covert, Duchamp, Man Ray, Morton Schamberg, and Joseph Stella) and Henri's protégés (Bellows, William Glackens, Kent, Charles and Maurice Prendergast, and John Sloan). The Henri branch considered Fountain a crude joke that insulted American art and the public, and they did not want it to usurp attention as Duchamp's Nude Descending a Staircase had done at the Armory Show. The Arensberg cadre saw Fountain as a gesture of absolute freedom and believed that any infringement of the society's basic principle—"No Jury, No Prizes"—constituted suppression. "Do you mean that if a man chose to exhibit horse manure we would have to accept it?" Kent demanded.[8] Fountain was rejected by a narrow margin, and William Glackens told the press, "It is, by no definition, a work of art."[9] Duchamp and Arensberg promptly resigned from the board of directors.

Perhaps the most torn among the committee members was Katherine Dreier. Her humorlessness kept her from appreciating Fountain, and she voted against its exhibition on the grounds that it lacked originality. But she could not bear to oppose Duchamp, being acutely aware, as she wrote, "of Duchamp's brilliancy and originality, as well as my own limitation which cannot immediately follow him. . . ."[10] Ruminating about the rejection, Dreier pleaded with Duchamp to remain a member of the Independents, reasoning that "a certain wholesome virility" found in American artists could not make up for the lack of Duchamp's European spirituality. She suggested as a compromise that Richard Mutt show his rejected artwork at a lecture given by Marcel Duchamp—although she still suspected that anyone who used a name evoking "Mutt and Jeff" was playing a joke.

The Independents exhibition opened for a private view on April 9, the day after Easter. Henry McBride described the evening as "very like the foyer of the Opera in Paris on a Ballet Russe night"; it reminded others of a vernissage at the Grand Palais.[11] The artists alone added up to a huge number, and they were joined by what seemed like half of Greenwich Village as well as an uptown crowd in smart evening dress. Heading the committee to greet such notables as the decorator Elsie de Wolfe, the Baron and Baroness Adolf de Meyer, Mrs. Condé Nast, Florine Stettheimer, Alfred Stieglitz, and Isadora Duncan's young troupe of Isadorables was Gertrude Vanderbilt Whitney. Dressed in opera gowns and swallowtail coats, flannel shirts and filmy negligées, the visitors strolled through the two miles of art, looking at the pictures and at each other. For relaxation they listened to a brass band and refreshed themselves at the mezzanine teashop organized by Katherine Dreier. A fleet of wheelchairs was available for the viewing marathon.

The alphabetical organization meant that innovative abstractions abutted the most conventional of flower paintings—and there was no climactic corner comparable to the Cubist Room at the Armory Show. "The proportion of inoffensive to offensive works is about ten to one," wrote McBride, "and offensive is meant in the complimentary sense of being challenging." [12] The democratic installation seemed to encourage the audience to act as critics. (Only Stieglitz found the system lacking in purity, and he suggested removing the artists' names as a way to focus attention on the art itself.) Louise Norton went so far as to turn the paintings she didn't like to the wall. [13] John Quinn reported to Ezra Pound that he had spent the opening arguing "that the whole damn thing went on the theory that art was democratic; that it never was; that art was aristocratic; that that meant choice, fastidiousness, taste, style." [14] Quinn's feisty opposition was, characteristically, balanced by generosity; he provided the Independents his legal services free of charge.

For the first time in an American modern art exhibition, women took center stage. Modern poetry had always been run by women, but modern art was still a male domain. At the Independents show women were newly visible because of their numbers (414 women and 821 men exhibited) and because of their work. One of the first pieces seen on entering the Grand Central Palace was Gertrude Vanderbilt Whitney's soaring granite memorial to those who sank on the *Titanic*. One of the show's hits was Dorothy Rice's huge painting *Claire Twins,* which caused de Zayas to exclaim: "I can't believe a woman did that. It's strong." [15] A more intimate work that attracted crowds was Beatrice Wood's *Un Peu d'eau dans du savon,* which depicted a woman arising from a bath, her modesty preserved only by a strategically placed bar of soap (into which several male onlookers inserted their calling cards). Wood became an instant celebrity, prompting a newspaper interviewer to ask, "Are you living for soul yearns?" Unfazed by the non sequitur, Wood replied in Dada fashion, "I want to return to the ecstasy and wild imaginings of childhood. To laugh is very serious. Of course, to be able not to laugh is more serious still." [16]

Mina Loy was a victim of the alphabetical order. Next to her modest painting *Making Lampshades* hung a reclining Venus with real jewels shining in her coal black hair. When it attracted such a crowd that Loy's work could scarcely be seen, a friend gazed at the gold pendant earrings that Loy was wearing and suggested she hook them onto her painting, since that seemed to be the only way to get attention. "Miss Loy's sad eyes flashed with opaline brilliancy for an instance," McBride

To point, as the Society has done, to the Paris Indépendants, is a misuse of the index finger . . . with art in abundance and our arteries young, why should we nibble on the dead end of Europe?

Robert Coady, *Soil,*
May 1917

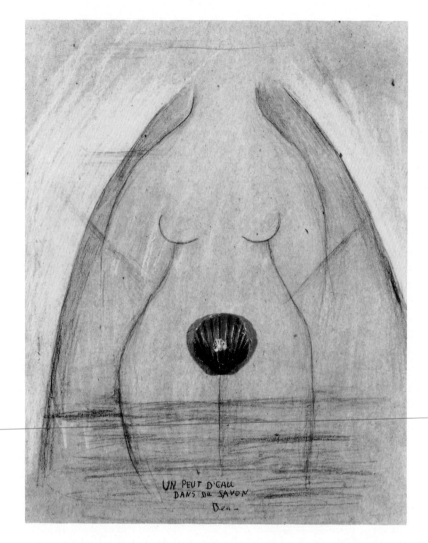

Beatrice Wood (b. 1893). *Un Peut* [sic] *d'eau dans du savon,* [A Little Water in Some Soap], 1977 replica of original from 1917–18. Colored pencil and soap on cardboard, 10¼ × 8¼ in. (26 × 21 cm). Francis M. Naumann, New York

observed, "and then as quickly dimmed. 'No, I could not do that. It would be plagiarism.'"[17]

It was easy to get lost in the endless beaverboard alleys, and McBride made several circuits looking for an exit. Each time he circled, McBride ran into Arthur Cravan, and on the third encounter the boxer exclaimed: "I am glad I do not owe you money. What an awful place this would be in which to escape a creditor."[18] On his fourth try McBride found his way out of this largest and most circuslike of all American exhibitions.

The foreword to the exhibition catalog closed with the statement "The purpose of the Society is to become a common ground for the free expression of all the arts." Though the paintings and sculptures provided the centerpiece of the show, there were other events that reflected the avant-garde's diverse interests. Robert Coady showed two movies, *A Daughter of the Gods* and *The Honor System,* on a fifty-foot screen hung at the Grand Central Palace and discussed the newest art-form. On April 18 fourteen poets read their work, including such familiar characters as Harry Kemp, Alfred Kreymborg, Mina Loy, Allen Norton, Pitts Sanborn, and William Carlos Williams. To demonstrate the absolute democracy of the event, members of the audience were then invited to read their own poems. On May 4 the psychologist Ernest Southard gave a lecture entitled "Are Cubists Insane?" Later, prisoners from Sing Sing talked about their lives and showed movies of prison life, after which the audience danced to a marimba band. Debutantes and society women wearing doily caps and yellow ribbons took over Dreier's teashop for two days, serving tea and cake on behalf of the suffragette movement. Dreier organized a Latin Quarter ball to benefit the Red Cross, stipulating that people dress in Cubist, Futurist, and Post-Impressionist costumes. (Only about two hundred showed up, but the costumes were amusing: Clara Tice wore the steam-radiator costume that was her staple for Village balls, and John Covert came as a Brancusi-esque hard-boiled egg.)

As a climax to the exhibition Arthur Cravan lectured. It was Duchamp and Picabia's idea that their friend Cravan give a lecture called "The Independent Artists in France and America." Cravan's critique of the last Salon des Indépendants in Paris before the war had triggered a duel, and his assessment of the current show promised to be similarly provocative. On the afternoon of April 19 (the same day, coincidentally, that Prohibition was proposed to President Wilson), they took Cravan out drinking, knowing full well that "alcohol liberated alarmingly terrifying properties in him." [19]

The trio arrived late at the Grand Central Palace, and Cravan made his way to the platform, his mammoth frame and uncertain gait arousing uneasiness in the smart audience. Cravan swayed slowly and then dramatically fell forward, as the *New York Sun* described it the next morning, "striking the hard surface of the speaker's table with an independence of expression plainly heard on Lexington Avenue." [20] Like a boxer loath to accept defeat, Cravan rose to his feet and hurled incoherent epithets. Then he slowly began to disrobe—proceeding from his coat and vest down to his suspenders—while the frightened audience fled the hall. House detectives encircled Cravan and quickly manacled him, as he challenged them to box. He would have ended up in jail had Walter Arensberg not interceded and taken him to 33 West Sixty-seventh Street. When the usual Arensberg circle gathered that night, Cravan was still recovering from the afternoon. Duchamp beamed, "What a wonderful lecture." [21]

Meanwhile, members of the Arensberg circle were waging a fight on behalf of Duchamp's *Fountain*. Shortly after the opening of the Independents show, Charles Demuth wrote to McBride suggesting an article on the sculpture for the *New York Sun*. He added a mysterious P.S.: "If you wish any more information please phone, Marcel Duchamp, 4225 Columbus, or, Richard Mutte [sic], 9255 Schuyler." [22]

This telephone number belonged to Louise Norton. Although it is unlikely that she was the "real" R. Mutt, Demuth's letter hints at the widening circle that perpetrated and then expertly milked the *Fountain* scandal: from inception to dissemination, it involved Arensberg, Demuth, Duchamp, Norton, Roché, Stella, and Wood. What became of *Fountain?* Some testify that William Glackens "accidentally" dropped it and broke it before the exhibition. Others claim that it was exhibited behind a partition so that no one, not even Duchamp, knew where it was. Still others believe that Arensberg bought it and lost it. None of these explanations is entirely convincing.

The original *Fountain* now exists only in a photograph by Alfred Stieglitz. Within the week of the Independents opening, the amorous trio of Duchamp, Roché, and Beatrice Wood took the urinal to 291 and asked Stieglitz to photograph it for their magazine *Blind Man,* which would be devoted to R. Mutt. Eager to participate, Stieglitz became engrossed in lighting the urinal. In his photograph the shadow from its lip falls in such a way that it looks, as Van Vechten wrote to Gertrude Stein, "like anything from a Madonna to a Buddha." [23] The photograph furnished the centerpiece of the second (and final) issue of *Blind Man,* and the list of contributors included many from the Franco-American crowd who assembled at 33 West Sixty-seventh Street: Walter Arensberg, Gabrielle Buffet-Picabia, Charles Demuth, Mina Loy, Allen and Louise Norton, Francis Picabia, Alfred Stieglitz, and Beatrice Wood. Over the title appeared the letters *PBT* (for Pierre, Beatrice, and Totor [Roché's nickname for Duchamp]), and inside appeared an editorial, "The Richard Mutt Case." Its closing line offered a parting shot at

OPPOSITE
Photograph by Alfred Stieglitz of Marcel Duchamp's *Fountain,* as reproduced in the *Blind Man,* May 1917

RIGHT
Cover of the *Blind Man,* May 1917, by Marcel Duchamp

P · B · T
THE BLIND MAN
33 WEST 67th STREET, NEW YORK

BROYEUSE DE CHOCOLAT   Marcel Duchamp

MAY, 1917   No. 2   Price 15 Cents

American provincialism: "The only works of art America has given are her plumbing and her bridges."[24]

At the last minute Duchamp and Roché worried that publishing the magazine might endanger their legal status as foreign residents in America. Could it be published under Wood's name? She agreed until her father strenuously objected, protesting that "there are words in there no young girl should ever know."[25] Frank Crowninshield, editor of *Vanity Fair*, suggested that the magazine be delivered by hand rather than through the mails. That Crowninshield would even envision such a solution—and that it was carried out by Wood, wearing sandwich boards—indicates the intimacy of the avant-garde community.

On May 25 the *Blind Man* threw a ball. Organized by a little magazine that had devoted itself to defending an artwork, it assumed the classic Village form of a costume ball at Webster Hall. "A new fashioned hop, skip and jump," declared the poster for it, "to be held at the Prehistoric, ultra-Bohemian Webster Hall. . . . The dance will not end till the dawn. The Blind Man must see the sun. Romantic rags are requested. There is a difference between a tuxedo and a Turk and guests not in costume must sit in bought-and-paid-for boxes." Mina Loy dressed for the ball in a smart costume she'd designed and sat at a table with Duchamp and the Arensbergs. Although Duchamp wouldn't dance, admirers approached him at the end of each number; Roché recalled, "It was like a great garland of fresh gowns renewing itself in some discreetly synchronized ballet."[26] Cravan arrived on the mezzanine floor dressed in only a bedsheet, his head wrapped in a towel. By the time he slouched into a chair next to Loy, he had shed the sheet and soon put his arm around her bare shoulders. "The putrefaction of unspoken obscenities issuing from this tomb of flesh, devoid of any magnetism," Loy recalled, "chilled my powdered skin."[27] She left while Cravan drunkenly lurched through the crowd ordering women to reveal their telephone numbers.

The "CONTINUOUS SYNCOPATION" promised by the poster included a performance by the Japanese dancer Michio Ito and a Russian peasant number by Beatrice Wood in an embroidered costume. (Joseph Stella challenged someone to a duel over Wood's honor, though she protested that it no longer existed.) Becoming increasingly drunk, Duchamp dropped a miniature American flag into his champagne, and in the early hours of the morning he made a grand theatrical gesture. Several people recalled it years later, but no one described the same event. Wood remembered Duchamp's ascending a chandelier while she and the Arensbergs applauded from a nearby box. Loy recalled Duchamp "with his robe afloat, the symmetry of his bronze hair rising from his beautiful profile, wavering as a flame, he was—actually—climbing a paper festoon hung from the top of the dome to the musician's gallery."[28] Roché remembered that Duchamp shinnied up a flagpole in-

THE
BLINDMAN'S
BALL

For the BLINDMAN
A Magazine of *Fine Art*

Friday May 25th

at Ultra Bohemian, Pre-
Historic, Post Alcoholic
WEBSTER HALL 119 East 11th Street

DANCING EIGHT-THIRTY

Tickets $1.50 each in advance—$2.00 at the gate. Boxes not
requiring Costume, but requiring Admission tickets $10.00

Everything sold by the BLINDMAN
7 East 19th Street   Telephone Vanderbilt 328.

Poster for the Blindman's Ball,
1917, by Beatrice Wood

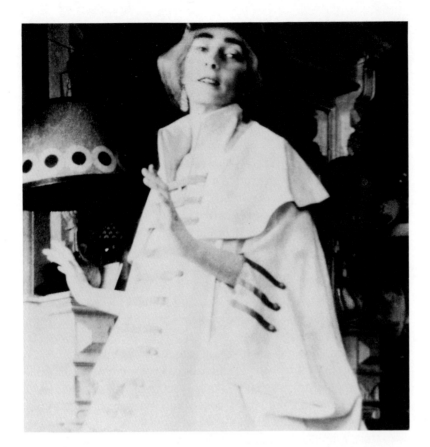

Mina Loy in New York
lampshade studio, dressed
for the Blindman's Ball,
May 25, 1917

clined at forty-five degrees and remained perilously suspended over the
audience, as if to say "Don't be afraid to be different and play it to the
hilt."[29] Duchamp's gesture, whatever it was, offered a fitting climax to
the twenty-third, and final, Village ball of 1917.

After the ball ended, a group headed uptown to the Arensbergs'
for a 3 A.M. meal of scrambled eggs and wine. Then Mina Loy led four
others upstairs and along a corridor to Duchamp's chamber, where
they pulled down his Murphy bed and laid themselves across it. Loy
took the bottom of the bed, along with an actress-painter named Aileen
Dresser. Charles Demuth positioned himself at right angles to the two
women, his leg dangling over the side of the bed and his trouser pulled
up to expose a garter. Next to the wall was Marcel Duchamp, and practically on top of him was Beatrice Wood. She was clothed, chaste, and
so excited that she could not close her eyes for the rest of the night.
Over sixty years later she remembered, "I could hear his beating heart,
and feel the coolness of his chest."[30]

This ménage offers a vivid image of an era when all the arts were
bedfellows—a period Floyd Dell recalled as "that glorious playtime in
which art and ideas, free self-expression and the passion of propaganda, were for one moment happily mated."[31]

"War means an ugly mob-madness," John Reed wrote in the April 1917 *Masses*, "crucifying the truth-tellers, choking the artists, side-tracking reforms, revolutions and the working of social forces." [32] As that spring turned into summer, patriotic songs such as "Liberty Bell, It's Time to Ring Again" were heard everywhere. Many in the avant-garde concluded that their personal liberties were being curtailed and their revolution derailed. The Selective Service Act was passed in May, and in June the passage of the Espionage Act made leftist speakers open to arrest and magazines vulnerable to suppression by the U.S. Post Office Department. By summer's end the postmaster general had stopped eighteen radical magazines, and Bill Haywood, Eugene Debs, Emma Goldman, and Alexander Berkman had been jailed in rapid succession, as had other I.W.W. leaders and picketers for woman suffrage. [33]

War fever began to infect even Greenwich Village, as recruiting stands sprang up near Washington Square. Isadora Duncan, a Village idol, danced at the Metropolitan Opera House in a filmy silk American flag, which she kissed and slowly unwound as the orchestra played the "Star Spangled Banner" and the audience stood on their chairs and cheered. "I tell you she drives 'em mad," Van Vechten reported to Gertrude Stein, "the recruiting stations are full of her converts." [34]

The war's invasion of the Village was dramatized most vividly that spring when the artists' stables along MacDougal Alley were tarted up with plaster and paint (at the cost of ten thousand dollars) to impersonate a quaint Italian street for a charity fête to raise money for the war effort. John Reed surveyed the incongruous situation and called it "New York's last real laugh." [35] When the real Italians from the south side of Washington Square tried to mingle with the Social Register set, they were pushed away and clubbed by policemen. "It was a bastard street," Jane Heap grimly observed, "a bastard hilarity, bastard plutocrats and bastard artists, with bastard soldiers guarding the scene." [36]

In a single season the New Bohemian atmosphere of freedom and hedonism was nearly wiped out. Only the commercial aspect of the Greenwich Village "revolution" thrived as uptowners visited the ever-increasing numbers of tearooms and nightclubs. By the time the IRT subway opened a stop at Sheridan Square in December 1917, visitors could ascend and step directly into the recently opened Greenwich Village Theater, a swanky establishment that presented slick comedies parodying bohemia and racy productions of the Greenwich Village Follies. When Seventh Avenue cut through Greenwich Avenue a year later, the Village became more accessible than ever. As commerce supplanted freedom, the *Masses* and the Liberal Club, two of the institutions essential to the Village bohemia, could no longer survive.

The postmaster general declared the August 1917 issue of the *Masses* "unmailable." He declined to identify the offending material, thereby preventing the magazine from removing or defending it. These tactics were already familiar to other radical magazines that had been suppressed, but the *Masses* was one of the few to fight back. Even though the distinguished judge Learned Hand established a landmark civil liberties precedent when he ruled in favor of the magazine's right to publish, the postmaster ignored the ruling. Using Kafkaesque reasoning, he closed down the magazine and had seven contributors to the *Masses* arrested for conspiring to obstruct enlistment.

Their two trials, which were widely covered in the press, gave the *Masses* one last public forum. Floyd Dell, who had recently been inducted into the army, delivered an impassioned defense of conscientious objection to his captive audience. Max Eastman spoke for three hours on the history of socialism and the necessity of free speech, and his extemporaneous speech was so lucid that it was later circulated as a pamphlet. The cartoonist Art Young provided the irreverent punch line to the nine-day trial. Having dozed through much of the proceedings, he awoke to the prosecution's final statement dramatically invoking an American soldier lying dead on a French battlefield: "He died for Max Eastman. He died for John Reed. . . . His voice is but one of a thousand silent voices that demand that these men be punished. . . ." "What!" Young demanded. "Didn't he die for me too?" "Cheer up, Art," stage-whispered John Reed. "Jesus died for you." [37]

The jury was deadlocked, and the defendants were freed in April 1918. By then the *Masses* was finished, but it had gone down in style. [38]

Another wartime casualty was the Liberal Club. By the summer of 1918 its remaining members were neglecting to pay their dues, and in the resulting economic crisis the club's maid, its second floor, and all its magazine subscriptions disappeared. The *New York Times* reported, "The members have been asked not to scatter cigar and cigarette ashes for their fellow members to clean up after them, and to place the piano rolls back in their boxes, owing to war-time economy in maid service." [39] It was a pathetic fate for the once raucous Liberal Club.

The Village balls that had previously filled the Liberal Club's coffers were canceled because of the war, but in the fall of 1918 Floyd Dell suggested one last Pagan Rout. This time, however, it was not only aimed at the pocketbooks of the Uptown Swillage but was conducted in their own territory, at the midtown Hotel Commodore. In addition to thousands of ticket holders many Villagers showed up and insisted on their right as Village residents to be let in free. After they threatened to riot, the entire crowd was admitted to the ballroom, which was already packed with costumed revelers. After midnight fighting broke out. It was the pretty Radcliffe graduate accompanying Malcolm Cowley (who would write the history of the avant-garde's next generation) who caused the most damage. Her behavior became increasingly bizarre: she bit her admirers' arms and shrieked loudly. After an especially vigorous chomp on the arm of an anonymous Pierrot, she knocked over a valuable Chinese vase. The ball's profits and any hope for the club's future were dashed along with the vase, and the club closed its doors in November 1918.

April 1917 marked the end of an era in poetry, as the campaign for Imagism concluded with the publication of the third and last of Amy Lowell's anthologies. *Some Imagist Poets, 1917,* published on April 24, was not as successful as its predecessors; whereas they had gone through multiple printings, the final installment sold only 406 copies. Although Lowell had originally planned five anthologies, she now concluded, "It has done its business with the American public. . . ."[40] H.D., who relied heavily on the income provided by the anthologies, agreed. "It was splendid for the 3 years—but its work, as you say, is finished— its *collective* work that is."[41]

God willing I shall make the L. R. a thorn in the face of the elder generation who have laboured all their lives to prevent American literature.

Ezra Pound
to Harriet Monroe,
July 2, 1917

In April's *Little Review,* Margaret Anderson announced that Ezra Pound had become the magazine's foreign editor. In his editorial that opened the magazine's next issue, Pound took potshots at America's cultural inadequacy and strategically sorted out his literary relations with the little magazines on both sides of the Atlantic. He made his peace with Harriet Monroe by praising her "spirited manner" in the face of Chicago's "peculiar milieu." He vowed to carry on the spirit of *BLAST* by publishing Wyndham Lewis, and he encouraged the *Little Review* "to aid and abet" the *Egoist.* (At the same time he was planning to install T. S. Eliot as the literary editor of the *Egoist.*[42]) Lowell was so offended by Pound's appointment that she vowed to never again publish in the *Little Review.* Monroe felt betrayed by his defection, and Alice Corbin Henderson consoled her that his alliance with the *Little Review* "is perhaps suicidal enough to be a sufficient punishment in itself."[43] But from his position in London, Pound felt that he had finally gotten everything he wanted: Quinn's financial support, the *Little Review's* editorial freedom, and a stable of fine writers–Wyndham Lewis, T. S. Eliot, James Joyce, and himself. He had momentarily regained control over modern poetry's complicated fiefdom.

Accustomed to internecine battles, the little poetry magazines seemed less shaken by the war. Amy Lowell faced it with her usual practicality, first stockpiling ten thousand Manila cigars and then supplying training-camp libraries throughout America with poetry. "Here was something I could do for my country," concluded Lowell, "without deserting the even more intimate preoccupation of poetry."[44] By the fall of 1917 she had edited her poetry lectures and published them under the title *Tendencies in Modern American Poetry.* The book put modern poetry in historical perspective and was her last word in the Imagist campaign.

Others limped through the war, publishing irregularly until July 1919, when William Carlos Williams unilaterally ended its four-year run with his bilious editorial, "Belly Music." In it he attacked a broad array of enemies—everyone from Lowell and her "ginger pop criticism" to Alice Corbin Henderson for "sullen backbiting" and Richard Aldington for supporting his wife's classicism at the expense of modernism. Williams's churlish tone shut down the magazine on a combative note that was entirely appropriate, given its pugnacious past.

When America declared war, Harriet Monroe was again making the rounds to Chicago patrons on behalf of *Poetry.* She was pleased to quickly enlist sixty percent of her former guarantors, but after war was declared the pledges dried up, and *Poetry*'s subsidy dropped over a thousand dollars between 1917 and 1918. During this shaky period the magazine was financially strapped and aesthetically diffuse. After Monroe's 1916 decision to keep the magazine open to new poets, it no longer set the course of modern poetry, and on *Poetry*'s tenth anniversary, in September 1922, Monroe expressed remorse that she might have wasted a "great opportunity." [45] Around this time *Poetry* assumed the hardy institutional character that has allowed it to survive to the present day; as Pound described it, it became "a very meritorious trade journal." [46] The magazine functioned as a clearinghouse for new poets, and it provided a respectable place to publish poems that had been rejected by magazines with more cachet.

Monroe, too, persevered, editing the magazine until 1936. A friend from the days of the Little Room, the novelist Hamlin Garland, suggested that she enjoy a quiet old age. "Not me!" Harriet replied. "I intend to go right on living till I drop. And what's more I intend to see every lovely far place there is left to see!" [47] Shortly after that she embarked on a final adventure, ascending the Andes to visit the ancient Inca ruins of Cuzco. The altitude induced a cerebral hemorrhage, and Monroe died a day later, on September 26, 1936. She was buried beneath the sacred city. Her letters continued to arrive in Chicago after her death; in one of the last she enclosed "a sprig of willow to prove that spring is coming." [48]

America's mobilization for war felt all too familiar to the European artists, for they had seen their own avant-garde disperse at the beginning of the war in Europe. During their last New York summer the international crowd carried on the Dada spirit, but by August, Duchamp reported that his crowd was going to bed at three instead of five. And then, one by one, they departed.

Francis Picabia set the manic pace for that last summer. He and Edgard Varèse shared one floor of Louise Norton's Upper East Side house; Albert and Juliet Gleizes rented the floor above. "Picabia could not live without being surrounded morning and night by a troop of uprooted, floating, bizarre people whom he supported more or less," recalled Madame Gleizes. "Noise at any time or knocks on the door, 'We are having a party. Come down.'"[49] One day Picabia presented himself as an art object; his current lover, Isadora Duncan, led Henri-Pierre Roché to a great armoire, opening it to reveal a nude Picabia seated before a tiny table sipping a cup of hot chocolate. His manic activity and steady diet of opium and sex alternated with delirium tremens, tachycardia, and preoccupation with death. Despite Picabia's emotional rollercoaster, he did publish three issues of *391* from New York. (One of his gossip columns snidely commented, "Isadora Duncan has certainly aged as much as the drawings [of her] of Rodin and Segonzac."[50] Nevertheless, Duncan told Picabia's next mistress, Germaine Everling, that she would gladly take him back whenever Everling was through with him.) By end of summer Picabia was under the psychiatric care of Dr. Collins, probably for manic-depression, and by mid-October he followed his wife back to Europe. He would never return to America.

By this time Arthur Cravan, alarmed at the growing number of military recruiting stations, had assumed the new identity of a soldier on furlough and hitchhiked along the New England coast to Newfoundland. Henri-Pierre Roché left New York in the spring of 1918 to resume his diplomatic work, and the Gleizeses moved away from New York that summer. The last to leave was Marcel Duchamp, who sailed for Buenos Aires with the artist Jean Crotti's first wife, Yvonne, on August 13, 1918. (Crotti had recently left to marry Duchamp's sister Suzanne in France.) A few days before Duchamp's departure he arrived at the Stettheimers' apartment bearing the smallest work of his oeuvre. Measuring a scant three by two inches, the miniature *Nude Descending a Staircase* was painted for Carrie's dollhouse, where it hangs today, between the ballroom's great Renaissance fireplace and its silver-and-ivory grand piano.

RIGHT
Cover for *391* (no. 8), 1919, by Francis Picabia

FAR RIGHT
Marcel Duchamp (1887–1968). *Adieu à Florine*, 1918. Watercolor, ink, and colored pencil on paper. Private collection

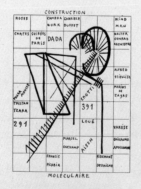

Louise Arensberg and
Henri-Pierre Roché

Duchamp was keenly missed in New York. For Ettie Stettheimer it meant the end of the most flirtatious phase of her life, which she fictionalized a few years later in her novel *Love Days* (1923). Disillusionment quickly set in, evident in Ettie's dour report to her journal: "It's a strange world and the more you know it, the less attractive it is. Others have found this out before."[51] Katherine Dreier felt Duchamp's departure so deeply that she followed him to Argentina five days later, ostensibly with the high-minded task of writing *Five Months in the Argentine from a Woman's Point of View*. Walter Arensberg later described Duchamp's absence as "the great lacuna" in his life and found some solace in the time he spent daily with Duchamp's artworks. "They are your conversation," he wrote to Duchamp.[52]

The decreasing frequency of the Arensbergs' evenings reflected not only the exodus of the international colony but also the disequilibrium of the Arensbergs' delicately balanced relationship. Walter was drinking heavily and becoming careless in his investments and loans, which cut into both his own fortune and his wife's. Finally, Beatrice Wood recalled, "Lou read him the riot act."[53] As unsettling as their shaky finances was Walter's discovery that Louise was having an affair with his friend Henri-Pierre Roché. Although Walter expected his own extramarital sexual activity to be tolerated, his wife's affair stunned him. In 1921 the Arensbergs moved to Los Angeles to escape such entanglements, and they remained there the rest of their lives. Having sold some of their art collection to John Quinn and Katherine Dreier, they put the rest in storage and moved into a Frank Lloyd Wright–designed house.[54] There they embarked upon a slow period of stabilization and recovery.

New York's international colony last assembled on July 28, 1917, at a party the Stettheimers gave for Duchamp's thirtieth birthday. A few days earlier Ettie had confided to her diary, "Duchamp's party won't amount to much I fear; no one knows for sure whether they're coming, so we can't ask the next."[55] But everyone came, the weather was cool and sunny, and the immaculate terraced lawns of André Brook (the Stettheimers' summer residence near Tarrytown, New York) provided the perfect setting. Ettie described the party in her diary as "a series of pretty pictures."[56] The fête began with Duchamp's tardy arrival in Picabia's red sports car and afternoon tea under the maples. The guests sat on the grass while Ettie read her story "Emotion" and Carrie, in virginal white, poured from the family teapot. Florine wandered among the guests, chatting with Carl Van Vechten (who wore a whimsical green suit) and the always serious Albert Gleizes. The sun's last light raking across the lawn gave way to a "windless and moony" evening illuminated by the glow of blue, green, and yellow Japanese lanterns over the three dinner tables that had been set around the terrace.[57] Standing at the head of her table, Ettie gazed the length of the terrace and raised her glass in a toast to Duchamp. Picabia and Roché were too busy chatting in French to hear, but Leo Stein, eager to catch every word, adjusted his cumbrous black hearing trumpet while Fania Marinoff clapped. Marcel Duchamp quietly rose to attention. Within a few days the party had become, in Florine's memory, "a classic."[58]

AFTERMATH: THE AVANT-GARDE MOVES ON

One of the theater's oldest conventions is a flurry of couplings just before the curtain falls. The first American avant-garde similarly culminated in a roundelay of romances that indicated a profound shift in its alliances, from the collective to the conjugal.

Floyd Dell dated his personal transformation to the spring of 1917. As the country was entering war with Germany, Dell was entering psychoanalysis with Dr. Samuel Tannenbaum. The patient free associated about the homosexuality latent in his affairs with his close friends' wives (Cook's among them), about his attachment to maternal figures, and about his inability to write his Davenport, Iowa, bildungsroman. Having turned thirty in the course of his year-long, irregularly scheduled therapy, he began to view his Village life as an adolescent playtime now over. This perception crystallized one night in a tearoom when an uptowner looked at Dell and inquired ingratiatingly, "Are you a merry Villager?"[1]

After a string of glamorous affairs—the last with Edna St. Vincent Millay, whose tremulous beauty affected him as intensely as it would Edmund Wilson a few years later—Dell met the woman he wanted to mother his children. B. Marie Gage was a golden-haired, blue-eyed midwesterner, as well as a socialist, a pacifist, a free-speech organizer—and a librarian. She embodied not only Dell's Iowa roots and his first love but also his Village radicalism; as he later wrote in a birthday verse, she was his "Goddess and girl-child, lover and guest and friend."[2] They married in February 1919 and moved to the Village outpost of Croton-on-Hudson, where Dell settled into the life of a writer-husband-father.

He called his marriage the beginning of maturity, and it ushered in an era of domestic harmony that lasted until his wife's death many years later. It also marked the end of Dell's influence as a cultural revolutionist. Many Villagers had felt betrayed by the marriage of their

Floyd Dell, c. 1921. Photograph by Marjorie Jones

spokesman for free love, and their fears about Dell's conservatism seemed to be confirmed by his paeans to matrimony and parenthood and his condemnation of experimental writers such as Pound, Eliot, and even Sherwood Anderson. Many of the younger generation of Villagers looked on him "as one of the pillars of a hated Village orthodoxy." [3] Dell did complete his coming-of-age-in-Davenport novel, *Moon-Calf.* When it became a best-seller in 1920 he followed up the next year with *The Briary Bush,* a roman à clef about his Chicago years, and in 1926 he wrote about his Village in *Love in Greenwich Village.* His books created an influential prototype for others writing about their own escapes from the village to the Village, but once Dell had used up the "imma-ture" years of his life, his novels became conventional. By the end of the 1920s Dell was considered a minor novelist who had failed to fulfill his early promise.

In April 1917, when Alfred Stieglitz presented Georgia O'Keeffe's first one-person exhibition at 291, he was in a despairing mood. He prophe-sied that the declaration of war would end America's great modernist leap forward, and the talk of prohibition meant that his wife's income from her family's brewery could no longer be counted on to finance his gallery and magazine. Stieglitz had already made some desperate ges-tures, the most poignant being his April 12 letter to the American Waste Company. He offered to sell nearly eight thousand copies of *291*—including special prints of *The Steerage* on Japanese Imperial paper—to be turned into pulp. When the lot was appraised at only $5.08, Stieglitz gave the money to his secretary, saying, "This may buy you a pair of gloves—or two." [4] He hawked back issues of *Camera Work* at sixty to eighty-five percent off and even sold his own photo-graphs at half price. For a man offended by commercial dealing, this shift into high-powered salesmanship signaled a state of crisis. The gal-lery and the magazine had come to an end. He began disbursing 291's artworks to the Modern, Daniel, and Montross galleries. He prepared a final June issue of *Camera Work,* devoted entirely to the work of his new protégé, Paul Strand, but the magazine's circulation had sunk to thirty-six subscribers.

Georgia O'Keeffe was teaching at West Texas Normal College in Canyon, Texas, when her show opened, and her first view of her water-colors, oil paintings, and charcoal drawings installed at 291 came in the photographs Stieglitz sent her. She spontaneously decided to travel the two thousand miles to New York, and she appeared at 291 late in May. The walls were now bare, but Stieglitz rehung O'Keeffe's show for the last, most private exhibition at 291. "So I closed the place in *Glory* in spite of all the treachery and cruelty," Stieglitz wrote to a colleague from the Photo-Secession days. "The little room was never more glo-rious than during its last exhibition. . . ." [5]

Alfred Stieglitz (1864–1946). *Georgia O'Keeffe: A Portrait at "291,"* June 1, 1917. Platinum photograph, 9⅝ × 7⅝ in. (24.7 × 19.5 cm). National Gallery of Art, Washington, D.C.; Alfred Stieglitz Collection

*I was born in Hoboken. I am an American. Photography is
my passion. The search for Truth my obsession.* PLEASE NOTE: *In
the above* STATEMENT *the following, fast becoming "obsolete"
terms do not appear:* ART, SCIENCE, BEAUTY, RELIGION, *every* ISM,
ABSTRACTION, FORM, PLASTICITY, OBJECTIVITY, SUBJECTIVITY, OLD MASTERS,
MODERN ART, PSYCHOANALYSIS, AESTHETICS, PICTORIAL PHOTOGRAPHY,
DEMOCRACY, CEZANNE, *"291,"* PROHIBITION. *The term* TRUTH *did creep
in but may be kicked out by anyone.*

Alfred Stieglitz, February 1921

Prior to the show O'Keeffe had represented to Stieglitz "A Woman
on Paper" whose drawings appeared in flimsy cardboard tubes. To her,
Stieglitz was a prodigious writer whose letters arrived up to five times a
week. O'Keeffe declared to a friend that she was glad she couldn't see
him—"I just like the inside of him."[6] After 291 closed in June 1917,
Stieglitz continued to write his letters, now from a tiny storage chamber he called "the Tomb," and he presented a morose figure seated
there in his black cloak. Though his first followers had dropped away,
he still held an occasional Round Table—at the Horn and Hardart instead of the Prince George Hotel—with a new set of protégés that
included Sherwood Anderson, Van Wyck Brooks, Waldo Frank, Lewis
Mumford, and Paul Rosenfeld. But this literary bunch could not take
the place of his lost circle; that role was assigned to O'Keeffe. By the
spring of 1918 he wrote, "She is the spirit of 291—Not I."[7]

O'Keeffe returned to New York in June 1918, depleted by lingering
influenza. Stieglitz ordered her to a sickbed and hovered over her, supervising her convalescence and talking endlessly. "Into one week," he
wrote his niece, "we have compressed years."[8] As O'Keeffe regained
her strength, art once again provided the bridge between her and
Stieglitz: she became his camera subject. He began photographing her
less than a month after her arrival, and when he finished twenty years
later he had created over three hundred images. On his glass-plate
negatives Stieglitz captured O'Keeffe's sharply modeled face, the fuzz
of her underarm, the contour of her breasts. The exposures would last
up to four minutes, but O'Keeffe complied, for Stieglitz was insatiable.
"When I make a photograph, I make love," he said, and O'Keeffe felt
his charged scrutiny as "a kind of heat and excitement."[9]

One month after O'Keeffe arrived in New York, Emmeline Stieglitz
discovered the couple in a photographic session that provoked the ul-
timatum that her husband leave either O'Keeffe or the marriage. It
took him exactly one hour and fifty minutes to clear out of the home
that had held him for twenty-four years. He and O'Keeffe moved into
his niece's house, at first separating their beds by a blanket hung over a
string. Six years were to pass before Mrs. Stieglitz would grant him the

divorce that would allow him to marry O'Keeffe, but long before that they had publicly announced their relationship to the world.

That announcement came on February 7, 1921, when Stieglitz exhibited 145 prints at the Anderson Art Galleries. Only twelve of them had been shown before, and most had been shot in the last two years; forty-five featured O'Keeffe, with her art prominent in the background. This was Stieglitz's first exhibition since the time of the Armory Show, and it revealed his late rebirth as an artist as well as his new intimacy with O'Keeffe. The exhibition caused one woman to burst into tears and murmur, "He loves her so." [10] The thousands of viewers who saw the exhibition were probably lured less by Stieglitz's aesthetic resurgence than by his explicitly erotic portrayal of O'Keeffe; these photographs became the vehicle for her early celebrity. Writing to Florine Stettheimer years later, Henry McBride instructed: "As for fame, you get it, as I often have told you, not by deserving it but by outraging public opinion. Georgia got hers by being so completely photographed." [11]

O'Keeffe married Stieglitz on December 11, 1924, and their relationship lasted until his death in 1946. They lived apart for much of the time—with O'Keeffe painting in her beloved New Mexico and Stieglitz holed up in his Manhattan galleries—and they each had other sexual partners. But their enduring relationship inspired each to produce greater work. By becoming her impresario, Stieglitz vitalized his own career and made some of his strongest photographs; O'Keeffe rapidly became a legend as the foremost female painter in America.

Shortly after America declared war, John Reed seemed to lose his bearings. Louise Bryant had left him that spring, supposedly to write in Provincetown but actually to resume her relationship with Eugene O'Neill. She returned home to Croton-on-Hudson when she received Reed's tender and desperate telegram—"PEACH TREES BLOOMING AND WRENS HAVE TAKEN THEIR HOUSE"—but she was greeted by Reed's confession that he had had an affair. [12] Bryant indignantly left again, this time to cover the war in France. Reed began to feel like an alien even in the Village, as former friends openly snubbed him for his antiwar beliefs. During the day he wrote indifferent articles for the *New York Mail,* and at night he fought insomnia and thoughts of suicide. "You thought you were getting a hero," he wrote to Bryant in July, "and you only got a vicious little person who is fast losing any spark he may have had." [13] Overwhelmed by his depression and the oppressive political climate, he called August 1917 "the blackest month for free men our generation has known." [14]

By this time Bryant had returned to New York, and the two planned to go to Russia together. [15] Reed and Bryant arrived in Petrograd in September and began the most exhilarating phase of their relationship. Interviewing Lenin, Trotsky, and Kerensky in the czar's billiard room, sitting through all-night meetings, joining the masses in singing the

John Reed. Photograph on his passport application to go to Russia, August 1917

Internationale, and hurrying back to their typewriters proved to be an aphrodisiac. Reed had found an event that "only the imagination of a revolutionary poet could have conceived," and that fall his disparate roles as adventurer, journalist, lover, and radical finally came together.[16] After Reed's best-selling chronicle of the Revolution, *Ten Days That Shook the World,* was published in March 1919, he was as much wedded to the Revolution as to Bryant. Speaking before crowds, testifying in Washington, enduring endless socialist meetings, and taking long trips to Russia left him little time for domestic life. Bryant also went on cross-country speaking tours after her book, *Six Months in Red Russia,* was published in 1918.[17]

The Revolution was only one element complicating their romance; O'Neill was another. Even the marriage of Reed and Bryant on November 9, 1916, hadn't ended the affair. When Reed had gone to Baltimore three days later for a serious kidney operation, O'Neill moved the five doors from his home at 38 Washington Square South into the Reeds' home, and Bryant may have become pregnant by O'Neill.[18] After Bryant left for Russia in 1917, O'Neill never saw her again, but the triangle continued. Agnes Boulton, the woman O'Neill married in 1918, bore such a striking resemblance to Bryant that many of his friends concluded that he had married on the rebound.[19] Nor could Bryant relinquish her ties to O'Neill. Upon returning from Russia in February 1918, two months earlier than Reed, she wrote to O'Neill that she had crossed three thousand miles of frozen steppes, fueled by her undying affection for him. When her letter arrived in Provincetown, O'Neill was writing *Beyond the Horizon*—a tragedy about two men in love with the same woman, which would win him his first Pulitzer Prize—and he declined her summons. Her letters continued to arrive in Provincetown, sometimes twice a day, even though O'Neill and Boulton were on the brink of marriage. Years after O'Neill had last seen Bryant, he wrote an epic nine-act play, *Strange Interlude,* whose central character was based on her.

In 1920, during the longest separation that Bryant and Reed endured, he spent thirteen weeks fighting fevers and delirium in a Finnish jail cell. Disguised as a sailor, Bryant made her way to Russia to meet her recently released husband. He bounded into her room, but she immediately saw that he was an utterly altered man. Dressed in rags, with dark circles around his eyes and sallow skin hanging loose on his bones, Reed seemed to her infinitely older and sadder, but beatific. He had a month to live. For the first week they walked through the Moscow streets and, as Bryant later wrote to Reed's mother, they "lived through a second honeymoon."[20] Then his body wasted away from spotted typhus, and a stroke paralyzed his right side. His thoughts became childlike, and he repeatedly remarked that the water he drank was filled with songs. With Bryant holding his hand through his last days, Reed died on October 17, 1920.

The official state funeral took place on a gray and snowy afternoon. Bryant marched alone behind the hearse to Red Square, then fainted during the endless rounds of official speeches. Reed was lowered into a grave next to the Kremlin wall, beneath a huge red banner whose gilt letters proclaimed: "The leaders die, but the cause lives on." [21]

However mercurial Reed's passions had been throughout his life, in death he was idealized into a Revolutionary hero, and in 1929 the Socialist party founded the John Reed Club. By that year Eugene O'Neill had won three Pulitzer Prizes and was regarded as the father of modern American theater. He was awarded the Nobel Prize in 1936—the year that Louise Bryant died at the age of forty-nine. After a short marriage to the socially prominent diplomat William Bullitt, she had begun a long alcoholic decline that ended in a Left Bank hotel. Shortly before Bryant's death, her friend Janet Flanner found her in a Montparnasse gutter; her face was so warped and her skin so colorless that Flanner could recognize Bryant only by the sapphire ring on her finger.

When the relationship between Arthur Cravan and Mina Loy began, each assumed an antagonistic stance. She was repelled by his coarse sexual advances, his heavy-lidded empty stare, his drunken soliloquies. Cravan "had sworn to 'break the face' of the modern movement" that Loy represented, and he was determined to destroy her ironic self-containment. [22] But during evenings at the Arensbergs' the two, the

Falling in love is the trick of magnifying one human being to such proportions that all comparisons vanish.

Mina Loy

Arthur Cravan

most introspective of the group, eventually found themselves drifting into a "spontaneous partnership," silently sharing a deep armchair and perusing the same book.[23]

At some point during the summer of 1917 their silence turned into unexpected passion. Loy discovered that her "emotions were primitive inversely to the sophistication of [her] brain. . . ."[24] She felt faint at the sight of Cravan's huge, superbly modeled body, which reminded her of a Greek statue in the British Museum. When he drew her onto his knees, she felt like "a face of silk—as it drifted from cheek to cheek of unshaven men the French so exactly describe as 'glabre.'"[25] After having slept with countless women, Cravan found Loy the first who was not attempting to "put something across" on him; he began to behave in so civilized a manner that the Arensberg crowd marveled that she had tamed him.[26] Before the summer was over, Loy and Cravan had grown into a couple with two fantasy children: a paper lion and tiger picked up in Chinatown for a nickel and christened Gaga and Mouche. This play family abruptly shattered at the summer's end, when Cravan fled America to escape the draft.

He bombarded Loy with letters, each from a different city, as he hitchhiked north to Newfoundland. Loy responded to the intensity of his feelings. "Tenderness in a strong man is always a deluge," she observed, "because it is a luxury which the weak can not afford."[27] By December, Cravan's letters were arriving from Mexico City: "I can't live without you," he entreated. "I want to marry you."[28] He had nothing to offer but the life of a vagabond and the companionship of a pugilist. Loy immediately departed for Mexico, where they were married in January. "Now I have caught you," said Cravan. "I am at ease."[29]

Cravan supported himself as professor of boxing at Mexico City's Escuela de Cultura Fisica, but in September 1918 he made the mistake of competing for the Mexican boxing championship against a local challenger known as the Black Diamond. Cravan lost not only the championship—he was knocked out in two rounds—but also his professorship. Cravan and Loy became itinerants, wandering the dusty roads of the provinces of Oaxaca and Veracruz, Cravan boxing in little towns for the meager purses that fed them. Loy felt displaced; her witty clothes and patrician beauty had no value here, and she had no time to draw the Mexican beggars who seemed like ideal subjects. In July 1918 Loy got pregnant, and as their money dwindled, the couple faced the bleak prospect of trying to feed a child when they themselves were barely subsisting on a diet of oatmeal and reboiled coffee grounds. Physically weak and fighting off disease, one evening Cravan suggested joint suicide. "You must get under your skull that *this* time the game is up," he told his wife. Loy replied, "How can we die when we haven't finished talking?"[30]

In November they formulated a plan to cope with their soon-to-be-born child. A Japanese hospital ship passed through Vera Cruz en route to Buenos Aires. One berth remained open. Loy sailed alone, and Cravan planned to join her as soon as possible so they could return to Europe and be reunited with her children. Loy never saw Cravan again.

His disappearance remains a mystery. Some identified a corpse found in a Mexican jungle as Cravan, his bloodied money belt nearby; others were convinced that he had drowned, or had been the victim of an FBI plot, or carried on an island existence incognito, or wrote novels under the name of B. Traven. "Looking for love with all its catastrophes is a less risky experience than finding it," Loy concluded. "The longer it lasts, so much the less can the habit of felicity when turned adrift withstand the onslaught of memory."[31] She continued her desperate search for him (again leaving her children in Florence), and in the remaining fifty years of her life she never again engaged in a romantic relationship. In 1929, when the *Little Review*'s "Confession-Questionnaire" asked, "What has been the happiest moment of your life?" Mina Loy replied, "Every moment I spent with Arthur Cravan." "Your unhappiest?" "The rest of the time."[32]

William Carlos Williams's interest in the Baroness Elsa von Freytag-Loringhoven began one evening in April 1918 when he noticed a curious sculpture of feathers and what looked like wax chicken guts in Heap and Anderson's apartment. They told him that he was looking at a portrait of Marcel Duchamp and encouraged him to meet its creator. The baroness was their current favorite in the *Little Review,* and Anderson considered her "the only figure of our generation who deserves the epithet extraordinary."[33] At the moment the baroness was residing in the Women's House of Detention for having stolen an umbrella, but on the day she was sprung, Williams treated her to breakfast. "She reminded me of my gypsy grandmother, old Emily," Williams recalled, "and I was foolish enough to say I loved her. That all but finished me!"[34]

Baroness Elsa von Freytag-Loringhoven. *Portrait of Marcel Duchamp,* c. 1922. Photograph by Charles Sheeler

Williams sent the voracious baroness a basket of peaches and told her that her lack of inhibition excited him. Visiting her cold-water flat, he found ashes piled high in the cold hearth and dogs mounting on a disheveled bed, but he was moved by her graciousness in this bleak environment. On another occasion he lightly kissed her in greeting, and she took his lips between her jagged teeth and bit hard. What Williams needed to free himself for art, she said, was to contract her syphilis.

Williams fled to the arms of his wife, Flossie, but not even Rutherford, New Jersey, was safe from the baroness. Her pursuit lasted several years. One evening the doctor received a call from a distraught father about his child, picked up his leather bag, and headed for his Ford. At this point someone grabbed his left wrist, and he heard the guttural voice of the baroness—"You must come with me"—followed by a solid blow to his neck.[35] When a policeman happened by, the baroness fled. Williams promptly installed a punching bag in his cellar, went into training, and when she next attacked him one evening on Park Avenue, the doctor flattened her and had her arrested. "What are you in this town?" asked the baroness. "Napoleon?"[36] As the police officer dragged her away, the irrepressible baroness amorously linked arms with him. "She revolted me, frightened me, beat me finally—out of a necessity I could not recognize," Williams confided to his journal after the baroness had died.[37] "I was really crazy about the woman."[38]

In 1923 the baroness's devoted friends (Berenice Abbott, Djuna Barnes, Margaret Anderson, Jane Heap) observed that "her spirit was withering in the sordid materialism of New York," and they collected a fund to send her back to Germany.[39] Williams sent her two hundred dollars, and when that was stolen by a go-between, he dispatched more. The baroness sailed to Germany and grimly survived by hawking newspapers on the street. In her last days she was supported by Djuna Barnes, who raised money by selling portions of Joyce's annotated manuscript of *Ulysses* so the baroness could live comfortably in a small Paris flat. There, on December 14, 1927, she and her small dog were asphyxiated by gas. Her friends debated whether it was a suicide (arguing that in life she had constantly courted death) or murder by one of her many lovers (she might have killed herself, but she would never kill her dog). Berenice Abbott turned away from her coffin, unable to "believe anyone as vibrant as Elsa could die."[40]

Death mask of Baroness Elsa von Freytag-Loringhoven

The romantic triangles that had dominated H.D.'s life did not end when she married Richard Aldington. The pregnancy announced at the outbreak of World War I ended in a stillbirth; and the Aldingtons' marriage was never the same. H.D. grew fearful of intercourse, and Aldington began several affairs, none of which he tried to hide, for they tried to maintain a modern marriage. Aldington could not only write "damn it, Dooley, I believe in women having all the lovers they want if they're in love with them," but he also accepted the fact that those lovers could be of either sex.[41]

Feeling deserted and betrayed when Aldington enlisted in the summer of 1916, H.D. developed new intimacies. The most important was with D. H. Lawrence, who lived with his wife, Frieda, one floor above H.D. during the winter of 1917. Whether their relationship went beyond criticizing one another's manuscripts and sharing frequent suppers cannot be determined, for they burned their letters to one another, but the relationship portrayed in their autobiographical writings was a passionate one.[42] In the spring of 1918 H.D. was the houseguest of a wealthy dilettante musician named Cecil Gray in Cornwall. Soon she became his lover and discovered that summer that she was pregnant; she never named the father, who was as likely to have been Lawrence as Gray.[43]

On July 17, 1918, in the wake of the news about her pregnancy, H.D. had a visitor named Winifred Ellerman. Realizing early on that a girl's name would never suit her, Ellerman adopted the name Bryher,

Richard Aldington, c. 1917

H.D., c. 1917

from one of the Scilly Islands off the coast of England. The daughter of one of England's wealthiest shipping magnates, Bryher was twenty-four, pampered, and suicidal. She had found an escape from her Victorian life in Imagism; when she discovered *Des Imagistes* in 1913, Bryher said, "[I] flung myself upon its contents with the lusty roaring appetite of an Elizabethan boy."[44] By the time she met H.D. she was desperately seeking salvation from her depression through poetry. Having read about H.D. in Amy Lowell's books and having memorized H.D.'s book *Sea Garden* (1916) in its entirety, she was emotionally primed to encounter her first goddess. As Bryher recalled, a tall figure with the sea in her eyes opened the door of the Cornwall cottage and in "a voice all wind and gull notes" said, "I have been waiting for you."[45]

At this vulnerable moment in H.D.'s life—husbandless, penniless, and pregnant, unwilling to name the father and fearing a second dead baby—Bryher's intense infatuation frightened her. "No man ever cared for me like that," she wrote.[46] Bryher's campaign for H.D. combined the promise of a trip to the Scilly Islands with the threat that if H.D. didn't give her the inspiration to go on living she would commit suicide. And so the pregnant poet and the blackmailing depressive rescued one another. Bryher's constancy and bottomless finances were new to H.D., and together the two women brought the baby to term. The day before the birth Ezra Pound showed up at the hospital carrying an ebony stick, which he used as both a baton and an instrument to pound against the wall. He looked at H.D. in a black lace cap, told her she looked like "old Mrs. Grumpy," and then admitted, "My only criticism is that this is not my child."[47] The baby was born May 31, 1919, named Perdita (lost one), and raised by the two women.

This marked the beginning of a relationship that was the most enduring of H.D.'s life. H.D. was the teacher to Bryher's student; the tremulous emotion to Bryher's Teutonic intellect; the feminine goddess to Bryher's pragmatic woman of the world. Bryher would marry twice—each time as a matter of convenience—and H.D. would repeatedly need to escape from her domination.[48] But for the rest of her long life H.D. would always return to Bryher.

In the middle of a night at the end of 1917 Mabel Dodge awoke to find herself in a state of superconsciousness. In the darkness over her bed hovered a vision of the large head of her husband, Maurice Sterne, and then the ghostly specter was slowly transformed into a new and unfamiliar face. Dark and calm, with wide-set eyes that stared intensely, the visage was unmistakably Indian. Mabel heaved a deep sigh and felt suddenly cleansed. Finding no hope among the shards of civilization left by the Great War, she turned her back on Europe. Armed with books about Aztec and Mayan deities given to her by Leo Stein, she left an oakwood fire glowing in the hearth at 23 Fifth Avenue and boarded a train for New Mexico. When she reached Taos, a mountain frontier community of two thousand, she concluded, "Now the world and I were met together in the happiest conjunction."[49] Dodge was especially drawn to the drumming and singing at the Indian pueblo, hearing in its rising and falling sonorities "the voice of the One coming from the Many."[50] In contrast, her own life seemed driven by a "singular raging lust for individuality and separateness."[51] While she was listening to one such singer sitting before a piñon fire in a bare white room, he raised his head and looked into Mabel's eyes; instantly she recognized this Tiwa Indian named Antonio Luhan as the face in her vision. When the pair explored the ancient New Mexican landscape together, Dodge recognized their mutual silence as the "It" that she and Hutchins Hapgood

Not with Genovese velvets and Renaissance chairs, nor with the repercussion of dangerous ideas fearlessly told, nor by any manner of means had I ever come so near before to the possibilities of abundant life, as in that empty place where firelight played upon bare walls.

Mabel Dodge Luhan

had so long discussed. By that summer Luhan had erected a tepee on her front lawn and was serenading her nightly with his drums. At summer's end Maurice Sterne returned to New York, and Dodge finally felt free to enter Luhan's tepee.

For Dodge, the consummation of their relationship surpassed sex; Luhan, she declared, "saw me into being." [52] She had felt similar ecstacy before, but this time her experience was lasting. Luhan satisfied her quest for spiritual integration, and she felt grounded in his tribal community. The hostess of the new age now looked back on New York as "a world that was on a decline so rapid one could see people one knew dropping to pieces day by day" and on her earlier self as "a zombie wandering empty upon the earth." [53]

In 1919 an occultist in New York informed Dodge that she would be chosen as a bridge between the Indians and the white race and that Taos would become a gathering place for "the great souls." She purchased twelve acres of high meadowland bordered on two sides by Indian fields, and there she began building Los Gallos, the grand hacienda that she considered her first real home. Its adobe walls and Indian relics reflected her new earthbound life, but in its grand proportions, its stark white walls, and its Italian divans there were echoes of former lives. Los Gallos would grow and grow, unfinished until the

LEFT
Mabel Dodge, c. 1918

ABOVE
Antonio Luhan

Life is like one long comic opera—with the most exaggerated costumes & colors, & impossible scenery and sunsets.

Mabel Dodge to Neith Boyce, April 21, 1918

1930s, and it would fill with new sets of people. People from earlier days would visit—Andrew Dasburg, Muriel Draper, Marsden Hartley, John Marin, Georgia O'Keeffe, John Sloan, Leo Stein, Carl Van Vechten— and she would make new friends, including Witter Bynner, Robinson Jeffers, and D. H. Lawrence. Taos became "the Garden of Allah in the New World," and as its hostess Dodge plied her cosmic vocation, proclaiming the "absolute static virtues" of truth, beauty, and the eternal.[54] Her life still went through manic-depressive swings, and sometimes she could not bear Luhan's endless mystical silences or his mistresses. But she no longer felt the urge to move on, and she remained in Taos with Luhan until she died, over four decades later.

By the time the first American avant-garde had dispersed at the end of the 1910s, with Paris replacing New York as the new beacon for writers and artists, the avant-garde had begun organizing the institutions that would perpetuate modernism in America. Those institutions survived even as the individuals moved on, providing the bridge between the avant-garde's brief revolutionary moment and its more enduring reign as the dominant culture of the twentieth century. Modern literature provided the new canon that became the basis for an academic industry, the little theater moved to Broadway, and contemporary art found shelter in new museums.

When William Carlos Williams attacked *Others* in 1919, he reserved a note of praise for the *Little Review*: "Margaret Anderson is the only one of them all who gets up a magazine that is not a ragbag," he wrote. "It is the NEW! not one more youthful singer, one more lovely poem. The *New*, the everlasting *New*, the everlasting defiance."[55]

Williams was right about the high quality of the *Little Review*— it was at its apex when *Others* ended—but he was wrong to credit only Margaret Anderson. The alliance responsible for the magazine— Anderson, Jane Heap, Ezra Pound, and John Quinn—constituted a formidable quartet. Each was accustomed to dictating, but their roles at

---

Gloria! Others *has come to an end. . . . Others* is not enough. It has grown inevitably to be a lie, like everything else that was a truth at one time. I object to its puling 4 x 6 dimensions. I object to its yellow cover, its stale legend. Everything we have ever done or can do under these conditions is being done now by any number of other MAGAZINES OF POETRY. Others *has been blasted out of existence.*

William Carlos Williams, editorial in final issue of *Others*, July 1919

---

the *Little Review* were clearly defined, and they all respected their limits. From the spring of 1917 to the spring of 1919 Pound served as the liaison between Quinn and the magazine's two editors, and he was granted editorial independence because of Quinn's annual contribution of $750, which guaranteed space for Pound to supply up to five thousand words in each issue. Anderson and Heap did not interfere with Pound's selection, editing only their own, largely American, section. Quinn also fought the magazine's legal battles and rounded up three other guarantors who ensured a period of financial regularity for the magazine, permitting the publication of sixty-four pages each month between February 1918 and May 1920.[56]

From the outset Quinn declared, "I cannot take the *Little Review* on my back," but within half an hour of meeting Anderson he had instructed her about her work and her life and then described the encounter to Pound as if he were writing a legal brief.[57] When she offered Quinn complimentary issues of the *Little Review,* he replied, "There is no more room for complimentary copies than there is for compliments on the deck of a battleship in action, or on the fields of the battle."[58]

Rigorous in his observance of the financial agreement with Quinn, Pound retained only $300 a year for himself and declined Quinn's offers to underwrite Pound's living expenses. As Pound explained to Anderson, "The point is that if I accept more than I *need* I at once become a sponger, and I at once lose my integrity."[59] What mattered most to Pound was editorial independence, or as he put it, "ABSOLOOTLY NO IN-TERFURRENCE." His first issue included work by T. S. Eliot and Wyndham Lewis and a translation of a poem by Jules Laforgue, followed in June by a rich selection of Yeats's poems and in July by more of Eliot's poems. Pound's domination appalled many of the magazine's readers; as one faithful reader complained, "An Ezraized *Little Review* is gargoylitic, monstrously so."[60] Jane Heap was characteristically unmoved by the complaint. "We have let Ezra Pound be our foreign editor in the only way we see it," she replied. "We have let him be as foreign as he likes: foreign to taste, foreign to courtesy, foreign to our standards of Art."[61] (Quinn roared with laughter when he read this passage.) The reaction didn't slow Pound, who gave the journal a motto: "A Magazine of the Arts Making No Compromise with the Public Taste." (To which Alice Corbin Henderson's husband appended *"And Having None of Our Own."*[62]) For a two-year period the best modern writers in France, England, and America appeared in the *Little Review.* The most important of them was James Joyce, and the serialized publication of his *Ulysses* in the *Little Review* assured the little magazine its place in history.

The first section of *Ulysses* arrived at the *Little Review* office in February 1918, and after reading it the two editors were on the verge of tears. "What Art," they murmured to one another, and Anderson cried, "We'll print this if it's the last thing we do!"[63] As a young man who was

John Quinn

*I told her [Margaret Anderson] she should stop admitting to any-
body that they had been hard up; that nothing succeeds like
success; that it was no damn body's business how they lived or
hard up they had been; that she should never again admit to
anybody that they got out one number by pawning a ring or
anything of that sort; that they should not talk about their
finances or personal affairs . . . that they ought to have a better
kind of cover; . . . that they must keep away from the
Washington Square bunch; that they mustn't be part of the
Washington Square bunch at all; that they must be austere and
exclusive in regard to their circulation, their finances and
secretive as a sphinx about any of their personal affairs. This is all
elementary common sense. I believe she will follow it.*

John Quinn to Ezra Pound, May 3, 1917

present at the moment later observed, "It almost was."[64] *Ulysses* ran for three years in the *Little Review*, beginning in March 1918. After twenty-three installments only half the book had appeared, the magazine had been confiscated four times for obscenity, and the Anderson-Heap-Pound-Quinn alliance had shattered.

For Pound, *Ulysses* was the prose masterpiece he had been seeking, and he wanted the text to be printed unexpurgated. For Anderson and Heap, *Ulysses* presented the opportunity for a spectacular battle on behalf of Freedom and Art; "lawless by nature," they wanted to challenge the legal process in the spirit of ecstatic defiance.[65] Quinn was in the most equivocal position. He wanted to serve a work that he considered a masterpiece—and by an Irish author to boot—but when he read Joycean words like "snotgreen" or "scrotumtightening," he was reminded of "toilet-room literature, pissoir art."[66] He considered causes like fighting censorship laws a foolish waste of time that could endanger publication of other works by Joyce in America. "I feel that I am on the ground," he wrote to Pound, "that I know the signs of the times *here;* the *'we'* are very young, very 'moral,' very crude, and now very virtuous, oh so virtuous—so WARY WIRCHEW-USS!"[67]

As the installments of *Ulysses* appeared each month, Quinn became increasingly perturbed. He no longer trusted the editors' judgment and followed each mention of their names with an inevitable "Damn!" or the wish that they would return to the stockyards from whence they had come. When he asked Pound to delete offending passages, the poet responded with an angry screed against censorship. In late September 1920 the inevitable occurred: Anderson and Heap were issued arrest warrants for having offended public morality by publishing the Gerty MacDowell episode of *Ulysses*. "And lo! The shadow of approaching martyrdom seems to loom!" Quinn wrote. "Mr. Sumner of the Vice Society seems to loom, and will probably be cast for the part of Judas or Herod. Ezra Pound will be the Apostle John. Jane Heap might get away in man's togs with St. Peter, and in a pinch Miss Anderson might be cast for the part of the blessed virgin."[68]

Ulysses had only a slim chance in the courtroom, and Quinn felt that the most he could do was minimize the damage. When he arrived for the first hearing, he encountered a courtroom crowded with uniformed policemen, petty thieves, and pimps. The *Little Review* section stood out immediately: "The two rows of them looking as though a fashionable whorehouse had been pinched and all its inmates hauled into court, with Heep [*sic*] in the part of the brazen madame," Quinn wrote to Pound.[69] Anderson yearned to play this courtroom scene to the hilt, using the spotlight to make speeches about freedom and beauty, and she was convinced that if Heap took the stand the case would be won. Quinn didn't call Heap and restrained Anderson from protesting that the judges wouldn't know the difference between

James Joyce and dirty postcards. "Quinn is merely legal," she concluded, "and it does no good."[70]

Quinn made no grand speeches on behalf of art. He simply tried to show that *Ulysses* would not incite a reader to desire. "I tried to pin his Lordship Corrigan [the judge] down on the syllogism that the average person reading the July–August number would either understand what it meant, or would not. If he understood what it meant, then it couldn't corrupt him, for it would either amuse him or bore him. If he didn't understand what it meant, then it couldn't have corrupted him."[71]

Moments of unintentional comedy leavened the hearings. The judge did not permit "libidinous" sections to be read, on the grounds that they would be offensive to the ladies present—meaning Anderson and Heap. Quinn got off some brilliant legal ripostes and convincingly argued that *Ulysses* was no more disgusting than Swift, Rabelais, Shakespeare, or the Bible. But the case was lost, *Ulysses* ended its serial run in the *Little Review,* and its editors were fined fifty dollars apiece. The dramatic scene that Anderson had been denied in the courtroom was played before the small audience of clerks who fingerprinted her. She haughtily declared that before she would "submit to such an obscenely repulsive performance," she would require that they produce a pristine cake of soap, a bottle of good eau de cologne, and an immaculate towel.[72] The bewildered clerks meekly complied.

After the trial Anderson wanted to end the *Little Review.* "I argued that it had logically begun with the inarticulateness of a divine afflatus," she wrote, "and should logically end with the epoch's supreme articulation—*Ulysses.*"[73] But Heap staunchly resisted. The magazine had always been as central to their relationship as a child; ending it would amount to desertion, of the magazine and of the relationship. According to Heap, Anderson couldn't end the magazine because she had founded it. "I certainly can give it up," Anderson responded. "I'll give it to you."[74] So Heap edited the *Little Review* beginning in 1922 and continued single-handedly during the magazine's Paris-based phase, from 1924 to 1929. Quarterly and then annually, the magazine continued to publish the newest movements in art—Dada, Constructivism, de Stijl, Surrealism, the machine aesthetic—until the end of the decade; Heap also exhibited works from these movements at the Little Review Gallery in New York (1925–27). The *Little Review* survived without Anderson, but Heap proved correct in predicting that the end of their editorship would also spell the end of their relationship.

In the wake of the *Ulysses* trial Anderson was tired of New York and of Heap's theatrical depressions. Her feelings crystallized one evening when William Butler Yeats, a guest of John Quinn's, regaled her with stories of Pound and Joyce; she intuitively decided that it was time to move on. Shortly after that evening Anderson attended a concert by Georgette Leblanc at a Washington Square salon and was enthralled by her performance of French art songs. Anderson recalled: "Ah, I said,

LEFT
Berenice Abbott (b. 1898).
Margaret Anderson, Paris,
c. 1925. Silver gelatin print,
14 × 11 in. (35.6 ×
27.9 cm). Berenice Abbott/
Commerce Graphics Ltd., Inc.

BELOW
Georgette Leblanc

when I first saw her marvelous mystic face: this is the land I have been seeking: I left home long ago to discover it—a new continent, an unearthly place, the great world of art. . . ."[75] Leblanc, a longtime companion of Maurice Maeterlinck, had aroused similar awe in others, which Jean Cocteau articulated most clearly: "Georgette was the model for a lyric saint—one of those strange great beings who move through the crowd, headless and armless, propelled only by the power of their souls, as immutable as the Victory of Samothrace."[76]

In May 1923 Anderson and Leblanc sailed for France and began a shared life that endured until Leblanc's death in 1941. For Anderson, who had struggled to live in beauty from her earliest midwestern days, life now assumed a fairy-tale quality. She played the piano for Leblanc's recitals and, though chronically poor, they managed to live in Norman chateaux, their days filled with music, books, and simple French food. "We realized that we were anachronisms—to live for art was no longer quite *apropos,*" Anderson observed. "In the world outside us the era of personal exaltation had waned."[77]

By 1929, as the final issue of the *Little Review* was going to press,

Anderson's life had come full circle. When she had entered Chicago in 1908 her eyes had been trained on the beacon of a lighthouse; now she lived in one, atop a white cliff overlooking the Seine. The beacon had long ago been removed from the glass-domed tower and replaced by a window seat; from this vantage point the two women surveyed the earth below, the morning mists, the forest filled with primroses and violets. In this celestial setting, Anderson recalled, "I always thought of myself as the happiest person in the world."[78]

For the final issue of the *Little Review*, in May 1929, Anderson joined Heap in sending out a "Confession-Questionnaire" to the magazine's chief contributors and friends. Looking back on the magazine's fifteen-year life, Heap contributed an editorial that, in dry-eyed remorse, she entitled "Lost: A Renaissance." "We have given space in the *Little Review* to 23 new systems of art (all now dead) representing 19 countries. In all of this we have not brought forward anything approaching a masterpiece except the *Ulysses* of Mr. Joyce. *Ulysses* will have to be the masterpiece of this time. . . . Self-expression is not enough; experiment is not enough; the recording of special moments or cases is not enough. All the arts have broken faith or lost connection with their origin and function. They have ceased to be concerned with the legitimate and permanent material of art."[79]

"The instigators of a little theater are no longer pioneers in a trackless and alluring forest," observed a commentator for the *Nation* in 1919. "It is not so much the work of exploration as of settling in the new land that confronts the promoters of the little theater today."[80] The most long-lived of those settlers was the Provincetown Players. In 1918 they moved three doors down MacDougal Street to a larger theater, and the seventeen hundred dollars needed for renovations came from such established patrons as Albert Barnes and Otto Kahn. The new theater had a deeper stage, a raked floor, and cushioned benches that seated two hundred.[81] Upstairs, Christine Ell opened a restaurant that became the Players' favorite hangout—and the spiritual successor of Polly's. From the Players emerged a constellation of downtown stars, with Ida Rauh, "the Duse of MacDougal Street," and Edna St. Vincent Millay prominent among them. Free tickets were given to critics, a clipping service was hired, and the Provincetown Players lost the atmosphere of an outpost on the bohemian frontier.

The Provincetown Players had outlasted other little theater groups despite a paucity of good scripts. They presented plenty of plays about romantic triangles and an abundance of works offering "a problem from [the playwright's] own little psychological laboratory," in Jane Heap's words. "But plays there were none."[82] Her negative verdict was only slightly overstated, for without the offerings of Susan Glaspell and especially Eugene O'Neill, the repertory would have been woefully thin.

Provincetown Playhouse, 133
MacDougal Street, New York

The Provincetown Players increasingly relied on their star playwright,
but now O'Neill was receiving offers from the Washington Square Players, the Greenwich Village Theater, *Smart Set* magazine, even vaudeville—and only the Provincetown Players paid no royalties. In early
1919 *Beyond the Horizon* opened on Broadway, winning O'Neill his
first Pulitzer Prize.

When O'Neill summoned George Cram Cook and Glaspell to hear
a new script in 1920, all three were living in Provincetown. O'Neill had
retreated to Peaked Hill Bar—Mabel Dodge's old house, given to him
by his father in a rare moment of generosity—hoping to write un-
distracted by his drinking partners at the Hell Hole. He settled into a
domestic life and wrote *Emperor Jones,* an expressionistic, hypnotic
one-act play about a black porter who imagines himself a king. Cook
and Glaspell were in Provincetown in self-imposed exile from the Players, for Cook was increasingly at odds with the new generation that
aspired to run the theater professionally. "He was a Great Man in dis-
habille," Floyd Dell recalled. "His life was, it seemed from the outside,
hardly within his own control; it was as if he were being driven on by a
daemon to some unknown goal." [83] Exhausted and dispirited, Cook
had turned the theater over to the young Turks for the Provincetown
Players' so-called "Season of Youth" (1919–20) and retreated to his
brightly painted cottage near the beach.

Susan Glaspell and George
Cram Cook in Provincetown

Cook and Glaspell trudged three miles through the dunes in the midst of a torrential late summer storm to hear O'Neill read from his pages of spidery handwriting. Even his halting voice and unconvincing rendition of black speech did not blunt the excitement they felt that night on first hearing *Emperor Jones.* "This marks the success of the Provincetown Players," Cook declared, and the next day he boarded the train for New York.[84] "Gene knew there was a place where such a play would be produced," Cook told his wife. "He wrote it to *compel* us to the untried, to do the 'impossible.'"[85]

The play gave Cook license to pursue his vision, sketched on stray napkins and menus, of building a dome over the Provincetown Players' tiny stage. The plaster cyclorama he envisioned would give the figures on stage "mystically deep significance from their background of infinity."[86] The Provincetown Players had opened the 1920–21 season with $530 in the bank, and much of that was earmarked for unpaid debts from the previous season. Undaunted, Cook declared that "Money or no money, the Emperor has got to play against that dome."[87]

The level-headed executive committee was bewildered by his insatiable drive; "Truly a madman" was the general verdict.[88]

Almost single-handedly Cook built the dome, laying plaster over interlaced iron rods, applying high-silica sand, and finally rubbing the curved surfaces with ice to remove all non-reflective particles. In constructing this dome—whose light gave an illusion of limitless depth to the shallow stage—Cook finally wed his visionary ideas to his earthbound artisan skills. Edna Kenton, a Provincetown Player, walked into the theater one morning to find him alone on stage amid a clutter of iron bars, steel netting, and bags of cement. "There's to be no argument about this," Cook asserted without introduction, and then he launched into a lyrical description of the set soaring from a dense jungle to the pure space of the dome. "Many, many times I was to see that play that made Gene O'Neill famous," Kenton recalled, "but I was never to see it so clearly as it played itself that morning in the dim little theater, with no voice but one, with no audience but one."[89]

The problems in mounting the play were daunting—from casting the black emperor to coping with O'Neill's heated complaints about the amateurish production. "The last five days," as Kenton recalled, "were nothing short of cyclonic."[90] When the curtain came down on opening night, however, it was clear that the production could not have been equaled in any professional theater of the time. The audience loudly cheered the leading man, Charles Gilpin—an unemployed actor who had been discovered running an elevator at Macy's—and after the curtain had been rung down repeatedly and the audiences still refused to leave, the curtain rose a final time. The dome stood alone, bathed in light, the pure theater of George Cram Cook's dream.

Emperor Jones, 1920,
New York

By the next morning a line of ticket buyers snaked down MacDougal Street, the meager list of subscribers jumped to fifteen hundred, uptown critics declared the play a masterpiece, and commercial Broadway producers campaigned for a move uptown. With the excited approval of Cook, O'Neill, and the executive committee, *Emperor Jones* went to Broadway and on to London. With this success, the Provincetown Players ended their phase as an amateur experimental collective and entered the realm of professional, institutionalized theater. Cook's response was to recite Plato to the Players and invoke the group's original principles: "to recreate in a group of modern individuals . . . a spiritual oneness underlying their differences—a oneness resembling the primitive oneness of a tribe. . . ."[91] His words demonstrated all too clearly his inability to recognize how much the tribe had changed.

After *Emperor Jones,* Cook and Glaspell finally accepted that they no longer had any place in the Provincetown Players. "We have not, as we hoped, created the beloved community of life-givers," Cook concluded. "We have valued creative energy less than its rewards—our sin against our Holy Ghost."[92] Cook drifted. He followed O'Neill to Broadway, throwing his family inheritance into a production of his own pretentious drama, *The Spring* (1921). He implored Floyd Dell to "gather the old Davenport crowd together, and go back there, and make it a new Athens!"[93] But the facts were brutally clear: Cook was an unsuccessful playwright, the deposed leader of a theater collective, and no longer exalted by any group. "If they had chosen to create the myth of me!" he later said to Glaspell. "I needed the power of that loving mythic lie."[94] One day during the spring of 1922 Glaspell came upon Cook seated beneath the dome in the Provincetown Players Theater, illuminated by blue stagelights. After a long silence he said, "It is time to go to Greece."[95]

Cook spent most of the four-week crossing on a Greek steamer absorbed in a dictionary, and on their arrival he made pilgrimages to the Parthenon and the Temple of Mysteries. He struck up friendships with shepherds, rhapsodized about the tinkling bells of grazing goats, the round loaves of peasant bread, and the flagons of retsina he drank so often. His hair and beard grew long and white, he wore a black spun-wool tunic, carried a carved staff, and wrote verse in a spruce-bough bower. As Cook drifted further from his life in New York, Glaspell observed that "more and more his eyes were the eyes of a seer."[96] She stood by Cook in his attempt to live out the vision that had obsessed him most of his life. Charitably understating the strain she had to endure, Glaspell later wrote, "An exasperating thing about him was that his enthusiasms often deprived you of your most righteous resentments."[97] It was the ironic fate of one of the era's most popular feminist writers to live her life in devout service to her husband's dream, even as he began to unravel. Cook wrote to his daughter, "I wish you were here to pick some golden fragments from the breakage of my life."[98]

George Cram Cook in Greece

The Delphi villagers and shepherds idealized him. "Now you are a hero," they told him, "now you are descendant of the Ancient Greeks."[99] Cook began to talk of his perennial dream for a theater, this time to be called the Delphi Players, where he could stage an epic pagan Passion play on the slopes of Mount Parnassus. But in January 1924 he contracted a rare disease called glanders (which usually attacks only horses), and he quickly died. Shepherds and villagers bore Cook's body on an open bier, washed in the wine of Parnassus, toward the Delphic temple. At the request of Greek poets, they placed on his grave a massive rock that had fallen from the temple of Apollo, bearing his name in its final, Greek incarnation: Kyrios Kouk.

As early as November 1916 there appeared an advertisement in the *Little Review* for *Modern Art Collector,* which called itself "an authoritative magazine published monthly in conjunction with the national movement instituted for the promotion and development of Modern Art in this country." It promised suitable-for-framing colored plates and cost a dollar per copy. Although this enterprise proved short-lived, the

And we will make the
cold world
Flame and music
The dance of flame
Obedient to dream.

George Cram Cook,
"Darkness," quoted on the
bronze memorial plaque
installed at the
Provincetown Theater

As I say to my friends, in buying art one does not go merely for numbers any more than in fishing one goes just for fish generally but one should look out for kingfish or brook trout or other game fish. Buying art indiscriminately or the work of an artist indiscriminately is very much like catching fish in a net, only it is more expensive.

John Quinn
to Walter Halvorsen,
November 17, 1920

mere idea that such a pricey, decidedly-not-little magazine could find an audience suggested a new stage in collecting: modern art could be a fashionable hobby and a good investment for the upper classes.[100]

At that time the largest modern art collection in America belonged to John Quinn, for whom it was neither a hobby nor an investment but an all-consuming passion. In 1918, while recovering from an intestinal operation, Quinn was confronted with his own mortality. "One looks at things out of hospital windows very differently from what one does out of other windows," he wrote to a friend.[101] In his remaining years he pursued modern art ever more urgently, selling off his huge manuscript library to subsidize his collecting. Quinn wanted to amass the best work of the modern era, and in his view that invariably meant French art.[102] His chief agent was Henri-Pierre Roché, whom Quinn charged in September 1919 with scouting "works of museum rank."[103] Roché was an ideal choice, for he had not only a practiced eye but also an unsurpassably keen ear; through his network of artist-friends Roché would hear about works before they came on the market.

Near the end of his life Quinn traveled to Europe, where Roché, "the general introducer," escorted him to the studios of artists Quinn had known only through their work. He drank with Braque, André Derain, and Picasso; he shot a round of golf with Brancusi (in a sombrero) and Erik Satie (in a bowler); he came face to face with the writers he had subsidized—Ford Madox Ford, James Joyce, and Ezra Pound. Their outpouring of gratitude was balm to the dying man. After this encounter with art and genius, Quinn found his grueling law practice "worse than the desert, like being sentenced to live in Gary, Indiana."[104] During his last trip to Paris, in 1923, Quinn was drawn and insomniac, but even as his body grew skeletal, his deathbed companion Jeanne Robert Foster observed that his eyes remained piercingly direct. "My girl," he said to her near the end, "when I get out of this I'm going to live. I've never lived."[105]

By the time of his death from cancer on July 28, 1924, Quinn had amassed over twenty-five hundred works (his final acquisition, Henri Rousseau's Sleeping Gypsy, was one of the collection's gems). The full scope of the adventurous collection—focused on Brancusi, Cézanne, Derain, Matisse, Picasso, Rousseau, and Georges Seurat—would remain forever unseen. Visitors to Quinn's eleven-room apartment found canvases stacked back to back against walls and under beds, sculptures

---

"Is Ezra a gentleman?" I asked.
"Of course not," Ford said. "He's an American."
"Can't an American be a gentleman?"
"Perhaps John Quinn," Ford explained.

Ernest Hemingway, A Moveable Feast

James Joyce, Ezra Pound, John Quinn, and Ford Madox Ford, November 1923

peeping out from dustcaps or still boxed in the basement, dim corridors choked with masterpieces that only Quinn's infallible memory could locate. The single exception to this warehouse jumble was his bedroom, which was hung solely with paintings by his sister and photographs of his family. "His room was Tiffin, Ohio," Foster observed, "the rest of the apartment was the world plus Olympus." [106]

Some of Quinn's intimates wanted the collection to be kept intact, and Henry McBride repeatedly called for a thunderingly dramatic auction to focus public attention on it. But it was soon sold off in small lots, bringing mostly disappointing sums from other American collectors (Katherine Dreier and the Arensbergs benefited significantly) and from art dealers who later sold the work at great profit. The haphazard dispersal of Quinn's collection underscored the necessity for a museum of modern art. As McBride observed, the sale left "the modern art situation in America precisely where it was and Mr. Quinn might just as well have dabbled in stocks or drygoods as in art." [107]

There was an institution that called itself a museum of modern art, but it had neither the space nor the money to take on Quinn's collection. It had begun in early 1920, when, over tea with Marcel Duchamp and Man Ray in her Central Park West apartment, Katherine Dreier proposed the first museum of modern art in America. Man Ray suggested

To go about Paris with Quinn was to see the doors of places, banks, offices, fly open as if propelled by gunpowder. . . . And before him even the notaries departed from the routines of their lifetimes. It was as if he carried about with him the power to make you see fairy tales.

Ford Madox Ford

Katherine Dreier, c. 1920

Traditions are beautiful—but to create—not to follow.

Adopted from Franz Marc
as a motto for
the Société Anonyme

ALREADY 1920 NEED FOR SHOWING MODERN ART STILL IN CHAOTIC STATE
OF DADA IN NON COMMERCIAL SETTING TO HELP PEOPLE GRASP INTRINSIC
SIGNIFICANCE STOP AIM OF S.A. TO SHOW INTERNATIONAL ASPECT BY
CHOOSING IMPORTANT MEN FROM EVERY COUNTRY UNKNOWN HERE
SCHWITTERS MONDRIAN KANDINSKY VILLON MIRO.

Marcel Duchamp, telegram to Katherine Dreier
recalling the founding of the Société Anonyme.

the name "Société Anonyme," which he had read in a French magazine and deciphered as "Anonymous Society." Duchamp explained that it was the French equivalent of "Incorporated" and declared Société Anonyme, Inc., to be the ideal name for a modern museum. Although the Société Anonyme's name seemed like a Dada Readymade, and the logo (a chess symbol that resembled a laughing ass) seemed antic, the organization's purpose reflected Dreier's entirely earnest, if somewhat mystical, faith, in art's capacity to advance human consciousness. By distinguishing important works of modern art from sensational charlatanism, the Société hoped to bolster the connoisseurship of modern art, and by offering the American public the chance "to study the serious expressions of serious men," it would elevate the nation's taste.[108]

Setting up headquarters at 19 East Forty-seventh Street, the three founders proved to be a complementary trio. Man Ray offered practical skills (he designed their logo, printed photographic postcards of the modern art shown by the Société, created a square wool flag for their office). Duchamp advised about exhibitions and provided the link to European artists, and his participation gave the Société international cachet. The Société's tireless engine was Katherine Dreier—the art world's counterpart of Amy Lowell, but without Lowell's charm or charisma. Dreier planned "a chain of Galleries which liberate the thoughts in the art world" and modern art exhibitions that would tour throughout the United States. She sponsored lectures (illustrated with real paintings rather than slides) for such New York organizations as the Woman's Trade Union and the People's Institute. She organized a reference library on modern art and wrote a book called *Western Art and the New Era.* She arranged for mainstream institutions such as the Cleveland Museum and the Detroit Institute of Arts to present the Société's exhibitions. She raised money for a permanent building for the Société (which was never built) and accumulated a vast collection. After the excitement of the Société's first years—what Dreier called "the sturm und drang period"—membership dwindled from a high of eighty-six members in 1921 to just a handful by 1924. But Dreier continued unabashed, assembling a collection (by 1925, she had acquired 190 pieces) and mounting a major modern exhibition at the Brooklyn Museum in 1926. Her crusade, as she wrote to Henry McBride, was to ensure that the public never forgot "that the modern movement is not dying out—is not a passing message—but is a *new vision in art*." [109]

Logo for the Société Anonyme, by Man Ray

Dreier considered her single-handed operation the first museum of modern art, but the institution formally bearing that name had no connection to her. The Museum of Modern Art was the sort of institution that would have benefited most from Quinn's collection. The museum opened on November 7, 1929, in three small twelfth-floor rooms in the Heckscher Building, whose entrance at Fifty-seventh Street and Fifth Avenue was crowded with "the socially elect" in cloche hats and black tie. The museum's founding mothers—Lillie P. Bliss, Abby Rockefeller, and Mary Sullivan—represented a different level of wealth than Dreier (the breed Bernard Berenson called "squillionaires"). The inaugural exhibition presented Post-Impressionist works by Cézanne, Gauguin, Seurat, and van Gogh; the works now seemed classical, and all but 14 of the 105 paintings had been borrowed from American collections. Alfred Barr, Jr., who had selected and fastidiously installed the work on beige monk's cloth, belonged to a new breed known as a museum professional. Like all the brightest of his generation's museum directors, Barr had been Harvard trained by Paul Sachs (Harvard, Class of 1900) at Shady Hill, the former home of the Arensbergs.

At the museum's opening there were few familiar faces from the era of the Armory Show, but that event still cast a long shadow and was repeatedly invoked by critics. Lloyd Goodrich's comment in the *Nation* suggests how far America had come since the first days of the avant-garde: "Just as the Armory Show of 1913 was the opening gun in the long and bitter struggle for modern art in this country, so the foundation of the new museum marks the final apotheosis of modernism and its acceptance by respectable society." [110]

These three chronicles suggest only a few ways in which the avant-garde arts of the 1910s were incorporated into American culture. "The bourgeois world," one observer noted, "absorbed their talent and expropriated their poses." [111] The luminaries of the little magazines now appeared in books by mainstream publishers—most frequently Alfred A. Knopf or Boni and Liveright—and in the fastidiously produced *Dial* (edited by Scofield Thayer and Marianne Moore, 1920–29). The look of modern art infused everything from Art Deco to the illustrations in *Vanity Fair*, and photographs by Edward Steichen and Baron de Meyer were used in chic advertisements. Mabel Dodge's Evenings were affectionately mocked in *Peter Whiffle*, Carl Van Vechten's best-selling novel of 1922. As the hectic gaiety of the Jazz Age took over, the Charleston replaced the turkey trot and the speakeasy replaced the Pagan Routs at Webster Hall. Many of bohemia's campaigns—for labor unions, Montessori schools, psychoanalysis, comfortable clothing, sexual freedom—spread far beyond Manhattan into America's suburbs.

The revolution had been won.

NOTES

Abbreviations of frequently cited collections

AAA — Archives of American Art, Smithsonian Institution

HRHRC — Harry Ransom Humanities Research Center, University of Texas, Austin

NL — Newberry Library, Chicago

NYPL — New York Public Library, Astor, Lenox, and Tilden Foundations

Poetry Papers — Papers of *Poetry* Magazine, 1912–36, Department of Special Collections, University of Chicago Library

YCAL — Yale Collection of American Literature, The Beinecke Rare Book and Manuscript Library, Yale University, New Haven, Connecticut

INTRODUCTION (pages 7–10)

1. Paul Rosenfeld, "When New York Became Central," *Modern Music,* Summer 1946, p. 84.

2. The motto of the Credo Club; in Albert Parry, *Garrets and Pretenders: A History of Bohemianism in America* (New York: Dover, 1960), p. 181.

3. Ezra Pound, "Patria Mia," *New Age* 11 (October 17, 1912): 588.

4. Hutchins Hapgood, *New York Globe,* January 27, 1913.

5. Hutchins Hapgood, "The Salon," *New York Globe,* c. 1913, Hutchins Hapgood Collection, YCAL.

6. Margaret Anderson, "A Real Magazine," *Little Review* 3 (August 1916): 1.

7. Mabel Dodge Luhan, *Movers and Shakers,* vol. 3 of *Intimate Memories* (New York: Harcourt, Brace, 1936), p. 39.

8. Quinn to Augustus John, February 7, 1915, John Quinn Memorial Collection, Rare Books and Manuscripts Division, NYPL.

9. Cook, in Susan Glaspell, *The Road to the Temple* (New York: Frederick A. Stokes, 1927), p. 245.

10. Louis Untermeyer to Harriet Monroe, September 24, 1915, *Poetry* Papers.

11. Heap, in Margaret Anderson, ed., *The Little Review Anthology* (New York: Hermitage House, 1953), p. 85.

CHICAGO (pages 12–27)

1. Francis Fisher Browne, *Dial* 13 (October 1, 1892): 206.

2. Membership in the Little Room was as exclusive as that of a gentlemen's club: after unanimous nomination by the executive committee, prospective members were evaluated by members of the nominee's profession and could be blackballed by any three members of the Little Room.

3. The Little Room had approximately one hundred members, although the gatherings themselves were much smaller.

4. On one such evening the distinguished writer Hobart Chatfield-Taylor played magician and extracted a three-hundred-page novel from the nose of Henry Fuller, Harriet Monroe read a poem, Fanny Bloomfield-Ziesler blindfolded herself and played both "If I Were a Bird" and Chopin's Etude in G-flat, and other members told stories in Irish and German dialect. (*Saturday Evening Herald,* March 30, 1901, pp. 2–3.)

5. Bernard Duffey, *The Chicago Renaissance in American Letters: A Critical History* (East Lansing: Michigan State College Press, 1953), p. 55.

6. Floyd Dell, "Daughters of Dreams and of Stories," Floyd Dell Papers, NL.

7. Floyd Dell, *Homecoming: An Autobiography* (New York: Farrar and Rinehart, 1933), p. 5.

8. Dell, "Daughters of Dreams."

9. Cook, in Susan Glaspell, *The Road to the Temple* (New York: Frederick A. Stokes, 1927), p. 191.

10. Ibid.

11. Ibid., p. 193.

12. Glaspell and Cook's brief first exchange signaled that they were cognoscenti in the cultural barrens of Davenport. Seeing Cook's open volume of Joseph Renan's *La Vie de Jésus* (1863), Glaspell remarked, "Oh, you read it in French." "Yes," Cook replied. (Glaspell, *Road to the Temple,* p. 148.)

13. Lawrence Langner, *The Magic Curtain* (New York: E. P. Dutton, 1951), p. 70.

14. Cook, in Glaspell, *Road to the Temple,* p. 111.

15. Dell, *Homecoming,* p. 151.

16. Cook appeared in Dell's novel *Moon-Calf* as Tom Alden; characteristically, Cook produced only a fragment.

17. Glaspell, *Road to the Temple,* p. 181.

18. Dell, "Daughters of Dreams."

19. Ibid.

20. Dell, *Homecoming,* p. 185.

21. Floyd Dell, *Moon-Calf* (New York: Alfred A. Knopf, 1920), p. 394.

22. Dell, *Homecoming,* p. 190.

23. Francis Hackett recalled: "He eagerly took over the *Review* when I said good bye to it, giving him the wheel and my charts and my blessing. He started off with gleaming eyes, as proud as any young pilot on the Mississippi." (Francis Hackett, *American Rainbow: Early Reminiscences* [New York: Liveright, 1970], p. 252.)

24. Dell was among the first Americans to call Ezra Pound "a true poet," and Pound returned the compliment by calling Dell America's only critic with "any worthy conception of poetry." (*The Letters of Ezra Pound,* ed. D. D. Paige [New York: Harcourt, Brace, 1950], p. 9.) Although Dell and Pound never met, the bond between them is suggested by Dell's unpublished story "The Portrait of Murray Swift," in which the Pound-based character (Swift) leads the Dell-based character through the Post-Impressionist Exhibition (the Armory Show in its Chicago venue) and explains to him the work of Marcel Duchamp and Francis Picabia.

25. Lindsay to Dell, December 1, 1912; in Duffey, *Chicago Renaissance,* p. 233.

26. Floyd Dell, *Looking at Life* (New York: Alfred A. Knopf, 1924), p. 119.

27. Margaret Anderson, *My Thirty Years' War* (New York: Covici-Friede, 1930), p. 8.

28. Ibid., p. 14.

29. Ibid., p. 30.

30. Ibid., p. 15.

31. Dell, *Homecoming,* p. 228. Anderson remembered his editorial injunction that she write subjectively: "Here is a book on China. Now don't send me an article about China but one about yourself." (Anderson, *Thirty Years' War,* pp. 36–37.)

32. These words, as Sherwood Anderson's secretary, Miss Chute, remembered them, are quoted in Dale Kramer, *The Chicago Renaissance* (New York: Appleton-Century, 1966), p. 172. Anderson remembered saying: "My feet are cold and wet and heavy from long wading in a river. Now I shall go walk on dry land." (Ibid.)

33. Anderson to Marietta Finley, December 8, 1916; in *Letters to Bab: Sherwood Anderson to Marietta D. Finley,* ed. William A. Sutton (Urbana and Chicago: University of Illinois Press, 1985), p. 28.

34. Other residents included Lou Wall Moore, a sculptor and dancer; Ralph Pearson, an etcher; Kathleen Wheeler, a portrait sculptor; Annette Covington and Blanche Menage, managers of a metalcraft studio; and Raymond Jonson, a painter.

35. Sherwood Anderson, *Sherwood Anderson's Memoirs* (New York: Harcourt, Brace, 1942), p. 236.

36. Dell, *Homecoming,* p. 211.

37. Floyd Dell, interview with Dale Kramer, May 1963, notebook 1, Dale Kramer Collection, NL.

38. Ficke, in Dell, *Homecoming,* p. 241.

39. Anderson, *Thirty Years' War,* p. 37.

40. Harriet Monroe, *A Poet's Life* (New York: Macmillan, 1938), p. 247.

41. Among the poets Monroe solicited were Floyd Dell, Arthur Davison Ficke, Vachel Lindsay, Amy Lowell, James Oppenheim, Ezra Pound, Edward Arlington Robinson, Edith Wharton, John Hall Wheelock, and William Butler Yeats.

42. Kramer, *Chicago Renaissance,* pp. 210–11.

HARVARD (pages 28–35)

1. *Letters of Wallace Stevens,* ed. Holly Stevens (New York: Alfred A. Knopf, 1966), p. 821.

2. William Ivins to Fiske Kimball, March 15, 1954, Arensberg Archive, Philadelphia Museum of Art.

3. *Letters of Wallace Stevens,* p. 44.

4. Katharine Kuh, "Walter Arensberg and Marcel Duchamp," *Saturday Review,* September 5, 1970, p. 37.

5. Holly Stevens, *Souvenirs and Prophecies: The Young Wallace Stevens* (New York: Alfred A. Knopf, 1966), p. 68.

6. *Letters of Wallace Stevens,* pp. 33–34.

7. H. Stevens, *Souvenirs and Prophecies,* p. 71.

8. *Letters of Wallace Stevens,* p. 822.

9. Jean Gould, *Amy: The World of Amy Lowell and the Imagist Movement* (New York: Dodd, Mead, 1975), p. 41; Lowell, in James Oppenheim, "The Story of the Seven Arts," *American Mercury* 20 (June 1930): 161.

10. Lowell described her social position as "one of the greatest handicaps that anyone could possibly have. I belonged to the class which is not supposed to be able to produce good creative work." (Gould, *Amy,* p. 73.)

11. Lowell to Eunice Tietjens, June 5, 1923; in S. Foster Damon, *Amy Lowell: A Chronicle with Extracts from Her Correspondence* (Boston: Houghton Mifflin, 1935), p. 148.

12. Ibid.

13. Lee Simonson, *Harvard Advocate,* January 1908.

14. John Reed, "The Harvard Renaissance," in Robert Rosenstone, *Romantic Revolutionary: A Biography of John Reed* (New York: Alfred A. Knopf, 1975), p. 45.

15. Ibid.

16. Walter Lippmann, "The Shaping of the Future in Our Hands," *Harvard Illustrated Magazine* 10 (November 1908): 56.

17. T. S. Eliot, "Henry James," *Little Review* 5 (August 1918): 49.

18. The Harvard organizations dominated by radicals included the Cosmopolitan Club, Dramatic Club, Equal Suffrage Club, *Harvard Illustrated Magazine, Harvard Monthly,* Pierian Sodality, Social Politics Club, and Socialist Club. In 1911, after hearing Max Eastman speak, students organized the Harvard Men's League for Women's Suffrage.

19. Reed, in Ronald Steel, *Walter Lippmann and the American Century* (Boston: Little, Brown, 1980), p. 12.

20. Reed, in Robert Hallowell, "John Reed," *New Republic* (November 17, 1920): 298–99.

21. George Martin to Granville Hicks, November 28, 1934; in Rosenstone, *Romantic Revolutionary,* p. 39.

22. John Reed, "Almost Thirty," ibid., p. 54.

23. Eliot, in *Harvard Advocate,* June 1910.

24. Reed to Eddy Hunt, October 21, 1910; in Rosenstone, *Romantic Revolutionary,* p. 70.

25. John Reed, "The Day in Bohemia, or Life among the Artists," in Mabel Dodge Luhan, *Movers and Shakers,* vol. 3 of *Intimate Memories* (New York: Harcourt, Brace, 1936), p. 174.

PARIS (pages 36–52)

1. Berenson, in Aline Saarinen, *The Proud Possessors* (New York: Random House, 1958), p. 180.

2. Mabel Dodge Luhan, *European Experiences,* vol. 2 of *Intimate Memories* (New York: Harcourt, Brace, 1935), p. 324.

3. Leo Stein to Fred Stein, July 1947; in *Journey into the Self: Being the Letters, Papers and Journals of Leo Stein,* ed. Edmund Fuller (New York: Crown, 1950), p. 298.

4. Maurice Sterne, *Shadow and Light: The Life, Friends and Opinions of Maurice Sterne,* ed. Charlotte Leon Mayerson (New York: Harcourt, Brace, 1965), p. 48.

5. Leo Stein, *Appreciation: Painting, Poetry and Prose* (New York: Crown, 1947), p. 151.

6. James to Stein, 1894; in James Mellow, *Charmed Circle: Gertrude Stein and Company* (New York: Holt, Rinehart and Winston, 1974), p. 47.

7. Robert Haas, ed., *A Primer for the Gradual Understanding of Gertrude Stein* (Los Angeles: Black Sparrow, 1971), p. 34.

8. *Selected Writings of Gertrude Stein,* ed. Carl Van Vechten (New York: Random House, 1946), p. 69.

9. *Fernhurst, Q.E.D., and Other Early Writings by Gertrude Stein,* ed. Leon Katz (New York: Liveright, 1971), pp. 29–30.

10. Billy Klüver and Julie Martin, *Kiki's Paris* (New York: Harry N. Abrams, 1989), vividly evokes the social life of Montparnasse.

11. L. Stein, *Appreciation,* p. 157.

12. Gertrude Stein, *Everybody's Autobiography* (New York: Random House, 1937), p. 75.

13. L. Stein, *Appreciation,* p. 58.

14. Barr, in Saarinen, *Proud Possessors,* p. 197.

15. L. Stein, *Appreciation,* p. 157.

16. Picasso's request was unusual, for the last time he had painted from a model had been eight years earlier, when he was a sixteen-year-old student.

17. *Gertrude Stein on Picasso,* ed. Edward Burns (New York: Liveright, 1970), p. 14.

18. Daniel Kahnweiler and Francis Crémieux, *My Galleries and Painters,* trans. Helen Weaver (New York: Viking, 1971), p. 81.

19. Cassatt, in Frederick A. Sweet, *Miss Mary Cassatt* (Norman: University of Oklahoma Press, 1966), p. 96.

20. Marsden Hartley, "Somehow a Past," Marsden Hartley Collection, YCAL.

21. W. James, in *Selected Writings of Gertrude Stein,* p. 67.

22. Daniel Kahnweiler, "Introduction," in *Painted Lace and Other Pieces* (New Haven, Conn.: Yale University Press, 1955), p. x.

23. Henry McBride, "Pictures for a Picture of Gertrude," *Artnews* 49 (February 1951): 18.

24. "I remember hearing Max sing 'Le Grand Frise' one whole long night, with different interpretations . . . waltzing with a chair." (Kahnweiler, in Kahnweiler and Crémieux, *Galleries and Painters,* p. 81.)

25. G. Stein, ibid.; Alice B. Toklas, *What Is Remembered* (New York: Holt, Rinehart and Winston, 1963), p. 28.

26. Matisse, in Fernande Olivier, *Picasso and Friends,* trans. Jane Miller (New York: Appleton-Century, 1965), p. 84.

27. Matisse, in Klüver and Martin, *Kiki's Paris,* p. 39.

28. Matisse's academy, which opened in January 1908, was an outgrowth of his critiques of the paintings of Sarah Stein and the German artist Hans Purrmann. Max Weber and Patrick Henry Bruce were also founding members. Financed by Michael Stein, Matisse's academy had eighty-three students during its four-year history; only three were French, seven were American, and the majority were Swedish and Norwegian.

29. Gertrude Stein, *The Autobiography of Alice B. Toklas* (New York: Harcourt, Brace, 1933), p. 54; L. Stein, *Appreciation,* p. 170.

30. *Selected Writings of Gertrude Stein,* p. 38.

31. Joseph Stella, "Discovery of America: Autobiographical Notes," *Artnews* 50 (November 1960): 42.

32. Mellow, *Charmed Circle,* pp. 25–26.

33. Georges Ribemont-Dessaignes, in Arturo Schwarz, *The Complete Works of Marcel Duchamp* (New York: Harry N. Abrams, 1969), p. 6.

34. Walter Pach, *Queer Thing, Painting* (New York: Harper and Row, 1938), p. 151.

35. Gleizes, in Maria Lluisa Borras, *Picabia* (New York: Rizzoli, 1985), p. 22.

36. Ribemont-Dessaignes, in Schwarz, *Complete Works of Marcel Duchamp*, p. 7.

37. Stein, *Autobiography of Alice B. Toklas*, p. 164; Ribemont-Dessaignes, in Schwarz, *Complete Works of Marcel Duchamp*, p. 7.

38. G. Stein, *Everybody's Autobiography*, p. 57.

39. Schwarz, *Complete Works of Marcel Duchamp*, p. 5.

40. Gabrielle Buffet-Picabia, "Some Memories of pre-Dada: Picabia and Duchamp," in Robert Motherwell, ed., *The Dada Painters and Poets: An Anthology*, 2d ed. (Cambridge: Harvard University Press, Belknap Press, 1989), p. 257.

41. Duchamp, in Borras, *Picabia*, p. 88.

42. Schwarz, *Complete Works of Marcel Duchamp*, p. 16.

43. Pierre Cabanne, *Dialogues with Marcel Duchamp* (London: Thames and Hudson, 1971), p. 31.

44. Guillaume Apollinaire, *The Cubist Painters: Aesthetic Meditations;* in Schwarz, *Complete Works of Marcel Duchamp*, p. 466.

45. Pach, in Saarinen, *Proud Possessors*, p. 192.

46. Although Gertrude Stein largely ignores Michael and Sarah Stein in her autobiographies, they were also pioneering collectors of modern art. Michael (who was seven years older than Leo and nine years older than Gertrude) managed the finances of his younger siblings. In 1903 Michael and Sarah Stein moved to Paris and settled near Leo and Gertrude at 58, rue Madame. They followed Leo's lead in collecting works by Cézanne, Picasso, and Renoir, but their huge collection soon focused almost exclusively on Matisse, who later described Sarah Stein as "the really intelligently sensitive member of the family." (Henri Matisse, "Testimony against Gertrude Stein," supplement to *Transition*, no. 23 [1934–35]: 3.) Their most active collecting years were 1905–8, but they continued to buy Matisse's works long after Gertrude and Leo had stopped. Sarah not only studied with Matisse but also helped him to organize his short-lived academy, and Michael and Sarah Stein conducted a Saturday night salon, with Matisse as its chief celebrity.

47. L. Stein, in John Malcolm Brinnin, *The Third Rose: Gertrude Stein and Her World* (Boston: Little, Brown, 1959), p. 82.

48. Leo Stein to Mabel Foote Weeks, February 4, 1913; in Irene Gordon, "A World beyond the World: The Discovery of Leo Stein," in *Four Americans in Paris: The Collections of Gertrude Stein and Her Family* (New York: Museum of Modern Art, 1970), p. 30.

49. Dodge to G. Stein, April 1911; in Gallup, *Flowers of Friendship*, p. 52.

50. Gertrude Stein, *Two: Gertrude Stein and Her Brother and Other Early Portraits* (New Haven, Conn.: Yale University Press, 1951).

51. "A Message from Gertrude Stein," in *Selected Writings of Gertrude Stein*, p. vii.

52. McBride to G. Stein, December 12, 1913, Gertrude Stein Collection, YCAL.

53. McBride, "Pictures for a Picture of Gertrude," p. 18.

54. Gertrude Stein, "One," in Gertrude Stein, *Geography and Plays* (Boston: Four Seas, 1922), p. 200. Although both Stein and Van Vechten maintained throughout their lives that they met at *Le Sacre du printemps*, Edward Burns has determined that they actually met three days earlier at rue de Fleurus. "But one must only be accurate about such details in a work of fiction," Van Vechten wrote to Stein. "The real point is that in my own consciousness I am not a bit muddled about the *facts*." (May 17, 1916; in Edward Burns, ed., *The Letters of Gertrude Stein and Carl Van Vechten, 1913–1946* [New York: Columbia University Press, 1986], p. 851.)

55. When Van Vechten arrived at 27, rue de Fleurus, he did not know that his ex-wife, Anna Snyder, had preceded him by a few weeks and told many tales; Gertrude used the information in the guise of a teasing clairvoyant. She also showed him a cache of Picasso drawings, "including men with erect Tom Toms bigger than mine." (Van Vechten to Fania Marinoff, June 2, 1913, Carl Van Vechten Papers, Rare Books and Manuscripts Division, NYPL.)

56. Dame Rogue [Louise Norton], "Philosophical Fashions," *Rogue* 1 (April 15, 1915): 16.

57. Van Vechten, in Bruce Kellner, *Carl Van Vechten and the Irreverent Decades* (Norman: University of Oklahoma Press, 1968), p. 47.

58. "Message from Gertrude Stein," in *Selected Writings of Gertrude Stein*, p. vii.

59. G. Stein, in Brinnin, *Third Rose*, p. 86.

60. Toklas, *What Is Remembered*, pp. 41–42.

61. L. Stein, *Journey into the Self*, p. 50.

62. L. Stein to Weeks, April 2, 1914; in Gordon, "World beyond the World," p. 29.

LONDON (pages 53–66)

1. E. Pound to Homer Pound, 1908; in Humphrey Carpenter, *A Serious Character: The Life of Ezra Pound* (Boston: Houghton Mifflin, 1988), p. 98. Pound, "White Stag," in *Personae;* this poem later provided the title for Lincoln Kirstein's distinguished Harvard-based magazine, *Hound and Horn*.

2. Ford Madox Ford, *Return to Yesterday* (London: Victor Gollancz, 1931), p. 389. Ford Madox Ford was then known as Ford Hermann Hueffer, which he changed to Ford Madox Hueffer in 1915, and to Ford Madox Ford in 1919. The name Ford Madox Ford will be used throughout this book.

3. Pound was dismissed when his landlady reported that a traveling performer, a male impersonator, had spent the night in Pound's room.

4. Van Wyck Brooks, *New England: Indian Summer, 1865–1915* (New York: E. P. Dutton, 1940), p. 523.

5. Pound, in Brita Lindberg-Seyersted, ed., *Pound/Ford: The Story of a Literary Friendship* (New York: New Directions, 1982), pp. 171–72.

6. Pound to Williams, February 3, 1909; in *The Letters of Ezra Pound*, ed. D. D. Paige (New York: Harcourt, Brace, 1950), p. 7.

7. Pound, *British-Italian Bulletin*, April 4, 1936; in Carpenter, *Serious Character*, p. 97.

8. Ford, in Carpenter, *Serious Character*, p. 130.

9. Iris Barry, "The Ezra Pound Period," *Bookman*, October 1931, p. 171.

10. *Letters of W. B. Yeats*, ed. Allan Wade (London: R. Hart-Davis, 1954), p. 543.

11. *Punch*, June 23, 1909; in Eric Homberger, ed., *Ezra Pound: The Critical Heritage* (London: Routledge and Kegan, 1972), p. 6.

12. Pound, in John Tytell, *Ezra Pound: The Solitary Volcano* (New York: Anchor, 1987), p. 51.

13. Pound to Harriet Monroe, August 13, 1913; in *Letters of Ezra Pound*, p. 21.

14. Olivia Shakespear was introduced to Yeats by her cousin, Lionel Johnson; she was married but began an affair with Yeats in 1895, after he had been rejected by Maud Gonne. Their active romantic relationship lasted just over a year, and by the time Pound entered the picture in 1909, Yeats and Shakespear were devoted friends but not lovers. In the meantime Shakespear had published five novels about strained marriages and Victorian conventions.

15. Pound to Isabel Pound, February 1, 1909; in Carpenter, *Serious Character*, p. 103.

16. Yeats, in Patricia Hutchins, *Pound's Kensington: An Exploration, 1885–1913* (London: Faber and Faber, 1965), p. 84.

17. George Moore, in Joseph Hone, *W. B. Yeats* (New York: Macmillan, 1942), p. 274.

18. Pound to John Quinn, July 10, 1916; in B. L. Reid, *"The Man from New York": John Quinn and His Friends* (New York: Oxford University Press, 1968), p. 292. Many years later Yeats described his protégé in this way: "Ezra Pound, whose art is the opposite of mine, whose criticism commends what I most condemn, a man with whom I should quarrel more than with anyone else if we were not united by affection." (William Butler Yeats, *A Packet for Ezra Pound* [Dublin: Cuala, 1929], p. 1.)

19. Douglas Goldring, *South Lodge* (London: Constable, 1943), pp. 48–49.

20. Ford, *Return to Yesterday*, p. 371.

21. The works that Ford published in the *English Review* included a play, essays, and stories by Arnold Bennett; one serialized book by Joseph Conrad; nine poems and three stories by John Galsworthy; four poems by Thomas Hardy; four stories by Henry James; thirteen poems and a story by D. H. Lawrence; three essays by Wyndham Lewis; nine poems by Ezra Pound; and two serialized books by H. G. Wells. (Information from Arthur Mizener, *The Saddest Story: A Biography of Ford Madox Ford* [New York: Harper and Row, 1971], pp. 169–70.)

22. Violet Hunt, ibid., p. 157.

23. Ford Madox Hueffer, "Literary Portraits: XXIII. The Year 1907," *Tribune* 2 (December 28, 1907).

24. For example, the *Times Literary Supplement, Quarterly Review*, and *Athenaeum*.

25. Ford, in Barbara Guest, *Herself Defined: The Poet H.D. and Her World* (Garden City, N.Y.: Doubleday, 1984), p. 57.

26. Violet Hunt (born September 28, 1862) descended from the bohemian aristocracy of the late nineteenth century: her father was an Oxford don who became a painter, and her mother was a popular novelist. She grew up knowing artists and writers, including Robert Browning, John Ruskin, Alfred Tennyson, and many Pre-Raphaelite painters. In her youth she was considered a Pre-Raphaelite beauty, and in her adult years she made a profession of sexual intrigue. As she put it, "I am a sensualist of the emotions." (Mizener, *Saddest Story*, p. 143.) She also published several novels. She was forty-six when she met Ford and had recently ended brief affairs with H. G. Wells and Somerset Maugham; she had even contemplated a romantic liaison with Henry James.

27. Goldring, *South Lodge*, p. 47.

28. Violet Hunt, in Charles Norman, *Ezra Pound* (New York: Macmillan, 1960), p. 53.

29. Ford, in Lindberg-Seyersted, ed., *Pound/Ford*, p. 87. Pound's energy proved more dangerous when he was inside South Lodge; he broke a favored gilt-and-cane chair and was thereafter remanded to the sturdy sensible kitchen chair that was always brought out for him.

30. R. A. Scott-James, "Ford Madox Ford When He Was Hueffer," *South Atlantic Quarterly* 57 (Spring 1958): 249.

31. Ford, *Return to Yesterday*, p. 388.

32. Epstein, in Glenn Coleman, *Imagism and Imagists* (Stanford, Calif.: Stanford University Press, 1931), p. 10.

33. Flint, in Hutchins, *Pound's Kensington*, p. 126.

34. Hulme, in Coleman, *Imagism and Imagists*, p. 17.

35. Ezra Pound, *Collected Shorter Poems* (London: Faber Paperbacks, 1984), p. 251.

36. F. S. Flint, *Review* 15 (Oxford) (April 1965): 40.

37. *The Autobiography of William Carlos Williams* (New York: Random House, 1951), p. 21.

38. Pound to Williams, May 21, 1909; in *Letters of Ezra Pound*, p. 41.

39. "Little Bill" was used to distinguish William Carlos Williams from William Butler Yeats.

40. E. Pound to Isabel Pound, March 6, 1910; in Carpenter, *Serious Character*, p. 142.

41. *Autobiography of William Carlos Williams*, p. 114.

42. Ibid., p. 117.

43. For example: "She hath some tree-born spirit of the wood / About her . . . / The moss-grown kindly trees, meseems she could / As kindred claim . . ." (Pound, in J. J. Wilhelm, *The American Roots of Ezra Pound* [New York: Garland, 1985], p. 104.)

44. Doolittle, in Carpenter, *Serious Character*, p. 61.

45. H[ilda] D[oolittle], *End to Torment*, ed. Norman Holmes Pearson and Michael King (New York: New Directions, 1979), p. 4.

46. Ibid., p. 12.

47. Williams, in Guest, *Herself Defined*, p. 3; *Autobiography of William Carlos Williams*, p. 67.

48. Doolittle to Williams; in Guest, *Herself Defined*, p. 5.

49. Williams to James Laughlin, June 25, 1938; in Paul Mariani, *William Carlos Williams: A New World Naked* (New York: McGraw-Hill, 1981), p. 49.

50. Norman, *Ezra Pound*, p. 5.

51. Doolittle, ibid., p. 5.

52. Doolittle, in Guest, *Herself Defined*, p. 27.

53. Doolittle to Isabel Pound, 1911; ibid., p. 28.

54. H.D., *End to Torment*, p. 12.

55. Pound, in Guest, *Herself Defined*, p. 28.

56. Williams to Babette Deutsch, January 19, 1943; in *The Selected Letters of William Carlos Williams*, ed. John C. Thirlwall (New York: McDowell, Oblensky, 1957), p. 210.

57. Olivia Shakespear to Pound, 1912; in Carpenter, *Serious Character*, p. 183.

58. Pound, *Ripostes*; ibid., p. 176.

59. Richard Aldington, *Life for Life's Sake* (New York: Viking, 1941), p. 135.

60. H.D., *End to Torment*, p. 18.

61. Pound to Monroe, August 18, 1912; in *Letters of Ezra Pound*, pp. 9–10.

NEW YORK (pages 67–84)

1. Roland Rood, "The 'Little Galleries' of the Photo-Secession," *American Amateur Photographer* 16 (December 1905): 567.

2. Anne Brigman, "What Is 291?" *Camera Work* 47 (July 1914): 17.

3. Marsden Hartley, "291—and the Brass Bowl," 1934, in *America and Alfred Stieglitz: A Collective Portrait*, ed. Waldo Frank, Lewis Mumford, Dorothy Norman, Paul Rosenfeld, and Harold Rugg (Millerton, N.Y.: Aperture, 1979), p. 119. Hartley was specifically referring to the spirit of James McNeill Whistler.

4. Arthur Dove observed, "His ears appear as though the roots of his feeling have grown out into the air in the form of hair for more room to breathe." (Dove, "A Different One," ibid., p. 122.)

5. Hartley, "291—and the Brass Bowl," ibid., p. 121.

6. Marius de Zayas to Stieglitz, January 25, 1911, Alfred Stieglitz Collection, YCAL.

7. For example, in 1899 F. Holland Day wanted to found a group called the American Association of Artistic Photographers, and a group in Philadelphia wanted to found the Organization of Friends of Pictorial Photography.

8. The Photo-Secession published a statement in December 1902: "The object of the Photo-Secession is: To advance photography as applied to pictorial expression; To draw together those Americans practicing or otherwise interested in the art; and To hold from time to time, at varying places, exhibitions not necessarily limited to the productions of the Photo-Secession or to American work." (William Innes Homer, *Alfred Stieglitz and the Photo-Secession* [Boston: Little, Brown, 1977], p. 56.)

9. The Photo-Secession council members were: John Bullock, Pennsylvania; William Dyer, Illinois; Frank Eugene, New York; Dallet Fuguet, New York; Gertrude Käsebier, New York; Joseph Keiley, New York; Edward Steichen, New York; Alfred Stieglitz, New York; Edmund Stirling, Pennsylvania; John Francis Strauss, New York; Eva Watson-Schutze, Pennsylvania; Clarence H. White, Ohio.

10. Steichen knew about Stieglitz through *Camera Notes*, the photography magazine that Stieglitz edited, and Clarence H. White encouraged Steichen to meet Stieglitz.

11. Alfred Stieglitz, "The Editor's Page," *Camera Work* 18 (April 1907): 37.

12. Alfred Stieglitz, "Photo-Secession Notes," *Camera Work* 30 (April 1910): 54.

13. The Camera Club expelled Stieglitz in February 1908 on the grounds of "conduct prejudicial to the welfare and interests of the Club." Stieglitz successfully sued, forcing the club to reinstate him as a life member, and then publicly resigned.

14. Stieglitz, in Dorothy Norman, "From the Writings and Conversations of Alfred Stieglitz," *Twice a Year* 1 (Fall–Winter 1938): 80–81.

15. John Marin, "Exhibition of Watercolors—New York, Berkshire, and Adirondack—and Oils by John Marin, of New York," *Camera Work* 42–43 (April–July 1913): 18.

16. Marsden Hartley, "Somehow a Past," c. 1933–39; in Barbara Haskell, *Marsden Hartley* (New York: Whit-

ney Museum of American Art and New York University Press, 1980), p. 10.

17. Dove, "A Different One," p. 122.

18. J. Nilsen Laurvik had suggested that Stieglitz meet de Zayas.

19. De Zayas to Stieglitz, October 28, 1910, Stieglitz Collection.

20. De Zayas to Stieglitz, December 22, 1910, Stieglitz Collection.

21. Paul Haviland financed the book and helped write it, but its Olympian perspective and content reflected de Zayas's thinking.

22. Haviland to Clarence H. White, June 10, 1912, Stieglitz Collection.

23. Jerome Mellquist, *The Emergence of an American Art* (New York: Charles Scribner's Sons, 1942), p. 192.

24. Agnes Ernst Meyer, *Out of These Roots: The Autobiography of an American Woman* (Boston: Little, Brown, 1953), p. 81.

25. Ernst to Stieglitz, January 5, 1909, Stieglitz Collection.

26. Stieglitz to Hartley, October 20, 1913, Stieglitz Collection.

27. His catalyzing zeal owed something to his mismated marriage to Emmeline Obermeyer in 1893. She received money from the family brewery (Obermeyer and Liebmann, Brewers, Maltsters and Bottlers, later known as Rheingold's) which, combined with Stieglitz's annual three-thousand-dollar stipend from his father, allowed the Stieglitzes to finance both a family and 291. Emmeline regarded Stieglitz's colleagues as boring, poorly dressed men likely to disrupt her dinner table, and she provided a luncheon allowance so that Stieglitz could entertain the 291 artists without bringing them home.

28. Lee Simonson, "What Is 291?" *Camera Work* 47 (July 1914): 48.

29. John Sloan recalled after a visit that Stieglitz "talked one ear off. It has grown back pretty well, but I never returned to 291." (Van Wyck Brooks, *John Sloan: A Painter's Life* [New York: E. P. Dutton, 1955], pp. 129–30.)

30. Marius de Zayas, "The New Art in Paris," *Forum* 45 (February 1911): 183.

31. Sadakichi Hartmann and Waldo Frank, in Edward Abrahams, *The Lyrical Left: Randolph Bourne, Alfred Stieglitz and the Origins of Cultural Radicalism in America* (Charlottesville: University Press of Virginia, 1986), p. 103; Edward Steichen, *A Life in Photography* (Garden City, N.Y.: Doubleday, 1963), n.p.

32. Stieglitz to Heinrich Kuehn, May 22, 1912; in Homer, *Stieglitz,* p. 78.

33. Stieglitz to Anne W. Brigman, June 24, 1914, Stieglitz Collection.

34. Brooks, *John Sloan,* p. 16.

35. This formulation comes from Milton Brown, *American Painting from the Armory Show to the Depression* (Princeton, N.J.: Princeton University Press, 1955), p. 12.

36. Their unidealized scenes of contemporary life inspired the group's designation as the Ashcan painters; this term was first used by Art Young in 1916 but did not come into popular usage until the 1930s.

37. It is probably Henri who is quoted in the *New York Sun,* May 15, 1907; in William Innes Homer, *Robert Henri and His Circle* (Ithaca, N.Y.: Cornell University Press, 1969), p. 131.

38. These evenings were not limited to the circle of painters who exhibited together; regulars included Alfred Kreymborg, Vachel Lindsay (a student of Henri), John Butler Yeats (the father of William Butler Yeats), and occasionally Isadora Duncan, in her trademark flowing garb. There were also the painters George Bellows, Rudolph Dirks, Walt Kuhn, Walter Pach; the art critics Charles Fitzgerald (married to Glackens's sister-in-law), Frederick James Gregg, and Byron Stephenson; the editors William Carman Roberts (editor of the *Literary Digest*) and Mary Fanton Roberts (editor of the *Craftsman*).

39. *The Eight* traveled to Philadelphia, Chicago, Detroit, Toledo, Indianapolis, and Pittsburgh. There were sales of two paintings by Davies, two by Henri, one by Lawson, one by Luks, and one by Shinn; Gertrude Vanderbilt Whitney bought four of the seven paintings sold.

40. Robert Henri, "The New York Exhibition of Independent Artists," *Craftsman* 18 (May 1910): 161.

41. John Sloan, *Joan Sloan's New York Scene, from the Diaries, Notes, and Correspondence, 1906–1913,* ed. Bruce St. John (New York: Harper and Row, 1965), p. 403.

42. Arthur Hoeber, *Camera Work* 36 (October 1911): 49.

43. Stieglitz to Heinrich Kuehn, May 22, 1912; in Weston Naef, *The Collection of Alfred Stieglitz* (New York: Metropolitan Museum of Art; Viking, 1978), p. 210.

FLORENCE (pages 85–96)

1. Mabel Dodge Luhan, *European Experiences,* vol. 2 of *Intimate Memories* (New York: Harcourt, Brace, 1935), p. 135.

2. Ibid., p. 139.

3. Mina Loy, "Mabel," p. 9, Mina Loy Collection, YCAL.

4. Luhan, *European Experiences,* p. 135.

5. Loy, "Mabel," p. 13.

6. Jo Davidson, *Between Sittings* (New York: Dial, 1951), p. 82.

7. Luhan, *European Experiences,* p. 184.

8. Ibid., p. 185.

9. Ibid., p. 389.

10. Ibid., p. 137.

11. Ibid., p. 184.

12. Virgil Thomson, interview with author, New York, June 27, 1985.

13. Luhan, *European Experiences*, p. 267.

14. Loy, "Mabel," p. 11.

15. Ibid.

16. Harold Acton, *Memoirs of an Aesthete* (London: Methuen, 1948), p. 9. Homosexuals were more accepted as guests here than in other metropolises; Mabel Dodge sweepingly declared that most of Florence's art critics, collectors, and club men were homosexual, and Acton noted that the social rule was "the queerer the dearer." (Ibid., p. 40.)

17. After Dodge proposed the idea of a Renaissance pageant, Craig petitioned her to devote herself to it exclusively—in time, money, and enthusiasm—for one year. Dodge declined.

18. M. Berenson, inscription in a copy of Mabel Dodge Luhan's *European Experiences* in the library at I Tatti, Fiesole, Italy. I am indebted to Naomi Sawelson-Gorse for bringing this to my attention.

19. Harold Acton, interview with author, Florence, May 23, 1987.

20. Although at this time she was Mrs. Stephen Haweis, she adopted the name Mina Loy. "The name is an assumed one, adopted in a spirit of mockery in place of that of one of the oldest and most distinguished families of England." (Roger L. Conover, "Introduction," in Mina Loy, *The Last Lunar Baedeker*, ed. Roger L. Conover [Highlands, N.C.: Jargon Society, 1982], p. lxiv.)

21. Luhan, *European Experiences*, p. 340.

22. Caroline Burke, "The New Woman and the New Poetry," in Diane Wood Middlebrook and Marilyn Yalom, eds., *Coming to Light: American Women Poets in the Twentieth Century* (Ann Arbor: University of Michigan Press, 1985), p. 41.

23. Loy to Carl Van Vechten, n.d., Loy Collection.

24. Ibid., in Conover, "Introduction," in Loy, *Last Lunar Baedeker*, p. lxvi.

25. Loy to Van Vechten, n.d., Loy Collection.

26. Loy, "Mabel," p. 3.

27. Luhan, *European Experiences*, p. 255.

28. Draper's aristocratic style can be accurately called "self-created," but there were also fertile conditions for it. Her deaf brother attracted much of the family attention, and a young man named Alexander Graham Bell served as his tutor, leaving Muriel alone to fashion her own verbal universe in contrast to the silence of her brother's world. Her own tutelage owed a great deal to her first visit to Italy at the age of fifteen. There she fell under the verbal spell of Norman Douglas, who instructed her to memorize a column of the dictionary each day and taught her to describe the taste of wine. He told Muriel that the first wine they sipped, for ex-

ample, could be described as a taste of "horse piss and violets." Many years later Muriel would repeat the story to her son, who observed, "I suspect an observation like that gives one an immediate sophistication." (Paul Draper, Jr., interview with author, Woodstock, New York, March 20, 1986.)

29. Luhan, *European Experiences*, p. 273.

30. Ibid., p. 257.

31. Acton, interview with author.

32. Loy, "Mabel," p. 10.

33. Her advice about the marriage even extended to the next generation: one day she told her son, John, to give a ring to Mina Loy's daughter, Joella, in the hopes that when they became adults they would marry. (Joella Bayer, interview with author, Montecito, California, August 16, 1986.) John eventually married the daughter of Alice Corbin Henderson.

34. Luhan, *European Experiences*, p. 258.

35. Mina Loy, "Feminist Manifesto," in Loy, *Last Lunar Baedeker*, p. 269.

36. Shortly before the Drapers left Florence, Muriel and Mabel discovered a feudal estate, dating back to the eleventh century, that housed three hundred peasants and had been put up for sale. The two women plotted to buy it and ply their social vocation on a large scale: an entire village to house their friends. The plan did not materialize, however, and the village was later purchased by the Sitwells, who found it too small to accommodate the whole family at the same time.

37. James Amster, interview with author, New York, April 10, 1986.

38. Gertrude Stein, *The Autobiography of Alice B. Toklas* (New York: Harcourt, Brace, 1933), p. 162.

39. Mina Loy's "Aphorisms on Futurism" appeared in *Camera Work*, January 1914.

40. After Dodge encouraged Haweis to leave, Loy wrote to her: "I wish I could shove all the responsibility of the consequences on your charming shoulders—I wish I had seen Edwin. I would have bewitched him off to Greenland or anywhere inconvenient." (Loy to Dodge, n.d., Loy Collection.)

41. In 1914 Loy wrote that Carlo Carrà, "a dear scrubby little person—about 3 years old . . . invited me to matrimony in his camera ammobiliata—where he paints his futurist pictures." (Loy to Dodge, February 1914, Loy Collection.) This did not lead to a serious relationship.

42. Loy to Van Vechten; in Conover, "Introduction," in Loy, *Last Lunar Baedeker*, p. lxviii.

43. Loy to Dodge, April 20, 1914, Loy Collection.

44. George Cram Cook, "New York Letter," *Chicago Evening Post*, September 25, 1914.

45. Loy, "Feminist Manifesto," in Loy, *Last Lunar Baedeker*, p. 269.

46. Loy, in Conover, "Introduction," in Loy, *Last Lunar Baedeker*, p. lxviii.

47. There is much in the allusive portrait that is suggestive of the goings-on in the adjoining room: heavy breathing, "adulteration," and an allusion to the tutor's entry: "A walk that is not stepped where the floor is covered is not in the place where the room is entered." The complexity of the situation is compounded if one accepts Dodge's perception that Stein was erotically interested in her at the time. Although Stein had been writing portraits since 1908, "Mabel Dodge at the Villa Curonia" marked a new step by Stein toward Cubism, in tandem with her friend Pablo Picasso. Leo thought that she was directly influenced by Picasso, and Gertrude corroborated this later when she remarked: "Well, Pablo is doing abstract portraits in painting. I am trying to do abstract portraits in *my* medium, *words*." (Stein, in Arnold Rönnebeck, "Gertrude Was Always Giggling," *Books Abroad,* Winter 1948.)

Gertrude Stein's excommunication of Dodge may also date from this episode. As Stein continued writing the portrait she grew closer to Dodge, who responded flirtatiously. One day when Edwin Dodge was away from the Villa Curonia, Stein sat in his chair across from Mabel, who recalled "such a strong look over the table that it seemed to cut across the air to me in a band of electrified steel—a smile traveling across on it— powerful—Heavens!" Toklas fled from the room, and thereafter she began to separate the two women. Leo Stein offered another motive for the split, which also hinged on the "Portrait of Mabel Dodge at the Villa Curonia." After Dodge was widely noticed for what she wrote about Stein's portrait, Gertrude began to feel "that there was some doubt as to which was the more important, the bear or the one leading the bear." (Luhan, *European Experiences,* pp. 332–33.)

48. Dodge's biographer, Lois Palken Rudnick, described the deep need that this work satisfied in Dodge. "Gertrude and Leo Stein were the first to teach Mabel a lesson which later became part of the aesthetic philosophy that shaped her memoirs: the individual could overcome the bonds of heredity and environment and make herself anew. All three of them worked, each in his or her own way, at the center of the American paradigm. And all three shared the hubris of its imperial selfhood: the artist took the place of God and could create out of his own will new ways of seeing and being." (Lois Palken Rudnick, *Mabel Dodge Luhan: New Woman, New Worlds* [Albuquerque: University of New Mexico Press, 1984], p. 46.)

49. Luhan, *European Experiences,* p. 452.

50. Ibid., p. 453.

VILLAGE I: NEW BOHEMIA ON WASHINGTON SQUARE (pages 122–65)

1. Allen Churchill, *The Improper Bohemians: The Re-Creation of Greenwich Village in Its Heyday* (New York: E. P. Dutton, 1959), p. 35.

2. Ibid., p. 20.

3. Albert Parry, *Garrets and Pretenders: A History of Bohemianism in America* (New York: Dover, 1960), p. 257.

4. Bohemians were named after the gypsies who first appeared in Bohemia during the fifteenth century, and the term came to be applied to all who consciously seceded from bourgeois life. As popularized by Henry Murger in *Scènes de la Vie de Bohème* (1847–49), the term referred to poor artists and writers who pursued their vocation in defiance of propriety. Sometimes known as European-style bohemians, they were signified by berets, garrets, colorful scarfs, garlic, and spaghetti, and they lived in America as well as Europe.

5. Caroline Ware uses this term in *Greenwich Village, 1920–1930: A Comment on American Civilization in the Post-War Years* (Boston: Houghton Mifflin, 1935).

6. Guido Bruno, "The Lost Village," 1916, in *Fragments from Greenwich Village* (New York: Privately printed, 1921), p. 91.

7. Floyd Dell, "Should a Young Writer Live in Greenwich Village?" Floyd Dell Papers, NL.

8. Dame Rogue [Louise Norton], "Philosophical Fashions: Trouser Talk," *Rogue* 1 (April 15, 1915): 18.

9. Orrick Johns, *Time of Our Lives: The Story of My Father and Myself* (New York: Stackpole Sons, 1937), p. 217.

10. Djuna Barnes, *Greenwich Village as It Is* (New York: Phoenix Bookshop, 1978), n.p.

11. Mary Heaton Vorse, *I've Come to Stay (A Love Comedy of Bohemia)* (New York: Century, 1918), p. 88.

12. Mabel Dodge Luhan, *Movers and Shakers,* vol. 3 of *Intimate Memories* (New York: Harcourt, Brace, 1936), p. 26.

13. Max Eastman, *Enjoyment of Living* (New York: Harper and Brothers, 1948), p. 523.

14. Luhan, *Movers and Shakers,* p. 6.

15. Ibid., p. 5.

16. Mabel Dodge Luhan, *European Experiences,* vol. 2 of *Intimate Memories* (New York: Harcourt, Brace, 1935), p. 100.

17. Steffens, in Luhan, *Movers and Shakers,* p. 81.

18. *The Autobiography of Lincoln Steffens* (New York: Harcourt, Brace, 1931), p. 655.

19. Hutchins Hapgood, *A Victorian in the Modern World* (New York: Harcourt, Brace, 1939), p. 347.

20. Ibid., p. 348; Eastman, *Enjoyment of Living,* p. 523.

21. Hartley to Alfred Stieglitz, February 1914, Alfred Stieglitz Collection, YCAL.

22. Luhan, *Movers and Shakers,* p. 15.

23. Ibid., p. 16; Carl Van Vechten, "Oral History," p. 149, Oral History Research Office, Butler Library, Columbia University.

24. Van Vechten, "Oral History," p. 149.

25. "Mike" was probably inspired by Oscar Hammerstein's practice of calling everyone he liked by that

name. Van Vechten customarily assigned affectionate monikers to members of his inner circle: Gertrude Stein was Baby Woojums; Van Vechten was Carlo or Papa Woojums.

26. Luhan, *Movers and Shakers*, p. 41.

27. Dodge to Hapgood, c. 1925, Hutchins Hapgood Collection, YCAL.

28. Churchill, *Improper Bohemians*, p. 43.

29. Hutchins Hapgood, *New York Globe*, February 21, 1913.

30. Hapgood, in Michael Marcaccio, *The Hapgoods: Three Earnest Brothers* (Charlottesville: University Press of Virginia, 1977), p. 63.

31. Eastman found "her witchlike fascination" resistible and attended only one Evening; nevertheless, he made Dodge a central figure (Mary Kittredge) in his novel *Venture* (1927), focusing on an Evening with Bill Haywood in a central chapter.

32. Hapgood, *Victorian in the Modern World*, p. 337.

33. Agnes Ernst Meyer, *Out of These Roots: The Autobiography of an American Woman* (Boston: Little, Brown, 1953), p. 102.

34. Luhan, *Movers and Shakers*, p. 84.

35. Ibid., p. 83.

36. Carl Van Vechten, *Peter Whiffle: His Life and Works* (New York: Alfred A. Knopf, 1922), p. 145.

37. When an uptown couple unfavorably compared the collection to Henry Clay Frick's, Carl Van Vechten responded by offering to introduce them to Alexander Berkman, the man who had shot Frick.

38. Mrs. Pearson, *New York Press*, June 1913, in "Many Inventions" (scrapbook), Mabel Dodge Luhan Collection, YCAL.

39. Luhan, *Movers and Shakers*, p. 82. The free-floating style of the Evenings was sometimes praised as their greatest strength, but others looked upon it as intellectual lassitude. Walter Lippmann, for example, saw them as missed opportunities to create something significant. "You've got enough endowment to run all of Greenwich Village half a century," he told Dodge, "and experience enough to supply a regiment, and all that's wrong with you is that your categories aren't any good. They remind me of a Fourth Avenue antique shop." (Lippmann to Dodge, July 20, 1915; in Ronald Steel, *Walter Lippmann and the American Century* [Boston: Little, Brown, 1980], pp. 52–53.) In response to the persistent prodding of the young Harvard phalanx that she called "these young cocksure boys," Dodge tried to impose on her gatherings a fitful order, however alien it was to her personality. "Walter is as much an instrument of It as Hutch or Steff," she concluded, and sat down to write an address that sternly sketched an orderly future for the Evenings. "They will have a more definite direction," she decreed, "there will be standards of ability, parliamentary rule, invitations!" (Luhan, *Movers and Shakers*, pp. 92, 93.) The Evenings soon returned to their original free-flowing format.

40. In the sole attempt made to formally record any of the Evenings, a reticent and blushing stenographer took notes that evening. Her vocabulary didn't include such words as *syndicalist* and *primordial*, however, and she finally quit rather than record a guest's opinion that Emma Goldman was better than the American government.

41. Several in the audience loudly took their leave in the middle, and Dodge's own doctor not only refused to come but warned his patient of the dangers of infecting her mind.

42. Luhan, *Movers and Shakers*, p. 91.

43. Ibid., p. 80.

44. Ibid., p. 88.

45. Ibid., p. 89.

46. Ibid., p. 90.

47. Dodge, in Mrs. Pearson, *New York Press*, June 1913.

48. The phrase is from Steve Golin, *The Fragile Bridge: The Paterson Silk Strike* (Philadelphia: Temple University Press, 1988), the most complete account of the Paterson Strike.

49. Average wages were as follows: Men earned $10.59 a week; women, $7.17; and girls under sixteen, $1.85. An additional source of worker discontent was management's demand that workers oversee four looms instead of two; known as the "speed-up," this practice resulted in a diminished labor force and increased output.

50. Haywood, in Luhan, *Movers and Shakers*, p. 188.

51. Reed, ibid., p. 189.

52. Reed to Edward Hunt, n.d.; in Robert Rosenstone, *Romantic Revolutionary: A Biography of John Reed* (New York: Alfred A. Knopf, 1975), p. 121.

53. Robert Edmond Jones was apolitical and entirely consumed by the theater; he agreed to design the pageant because Reed had been his hero during their Harvard undergraduate days.

54. Luhan, *Movers and Shakers*, p. 205.

55. Hapgood, *Victorian in the Modern World*, p. 351.

56. The ribbon weavers were usually English-speaking Americans, the dyers were Italian immigrants, and the unskilled laborers were Eastern European and Middle Eastern. Fifty-six percent of the workers were women and children.

57. *Paterson Evening News*, June 9, 1913, p. 4.

58. Luhan, *Movers and Shakers*, p. 206; ibid., p. 204.

59. Hapgood, in Granville Hicks, *John Reed: The Making of a Revolutionary* (New York: Macmillan, 1936), p. 103.

60. "There was a startling touch of ultra-modernity— or rather of Futurism—in the Paterson strike pageant." (*New York Tribune*, in Jesse Kornbluh, ed., *Rebel Voices: An I.W.W. Anthology* [Ann Arbor: University of Michigan Press, 1964], p. 212.)

61. Bourne, in Arthur Wertheim, *The Little New York*

Renaissance: Iconoclasm, Modernism, and Nationalism in American Culture, 1908–1917 (New York: New York University Press, 1976), p. 56.

62. Dodge, in Hapgood, "A Day at Paterson," *New York Globe,* Hapgood Collection.

63. George Cram Cook, "New York Letter," *Chicago Evening Post,* June 4, 1913. A year later he would call the Paterson Strike Pageant "the dramatic expression of social ideas which made this the most interesting winter New York has known. . . . Since then, they have been staging ideas in the streets and squares of Manhattan." (George Cram Cook, "New York Letter," *Chicago Evening Post,* May 8, 1914.)

64. Luhan, *Movers and Shakers,* p. 204.

65. Haywood, in George Cram Cook, "New York Letter," *Chicago Evening Post,* June 11, 1913.

66. Emma Goldman, *Mother Earth* 8 (June 1913): 102.

67. Rosenstone, *Romantic Revolutionary,* p. 131.

68. Reed to his mother, Margaret Reed, June 18, 1913; ibid.

69. Reed to Fred Bursch, June 27, 1913; ibid., p. 137.

70. Luhan, *Movers and Shakers,* p. 213.

71. Reed to Margaret Reed, August 1, 1913; in Rosenstone, *Romantic Revolutionary,* p. 139.

72. Muriel Draper, *Music at Midnight* (New York: Harper and Brothers, 1929), p. 122.

73. Luhan, *Movers and Shakers,* p. 219.

74. Dell, in Dale Kramer, *The Chicago Renaissance* (New York: Appleton-Century, 1966), p. 165.

75. Currey to Dell; ibid., p. 239.

76. Dell to William Fineshriber, fall 1913, Dell Papers.

77. Sherwood Anderson, *Sherwood Anderson's Memoirs* (New York: Harcourt, Brace, 1942), p. 199.

78. Dell to Arthur Davison Ficke, March 28, 1914, Dell Papers.

79. Hapgood, *Victorian in the Modern World,* p. 314.

80. Ibid., p. 316; Eastman, *Love and Revolution: My Journey through an Epoch* (New York: Random House, 1964), p. 223.

81. Dell to Arthur Davison Ficke, December 17, 1915, Dell Papers.

82. Floyd Dell, *Love in Greenwich Village* (New York: George H. Doran, 1926), p. 17. Henrietta Rodman led the secession from the mother Liberal Club, which had both a Gramercy Park address and a Gramercy Park sensibility. She was the ideal catalyst for such a change. A deeply earnest schoolteacher and a prominent feminist, she was, in Dell's words, "a *Candide* in petticoats and sandals." (Ibid.)

83. Ibid., p. 31.

84. The daily affairs of the Liberal Club were arranged by Ernest Holcombe, an engineer, and his wife, Grace Potter, a social worker and writer; they were sometimes called the mother and father of the club.

85. The lectures at the Liberal Club included Emma Goldman's "Is Man a Varietist or Monogamist?"; Alfred Kreymborg talking on music and poetry; Horace Traubel on Walt Whitman; Frank Tannenbaum on prison reform; Margaret Sanger on birth control; and Clarence Darrow on Voltaire.

86. Mencken to Dreiser, October 6, 1916; in W. A. Swanberg, *Dreiser* (New York: Charles Scribner's Sons, 1965), p. 209.

87. Hutchins Hapgood, "Cristine," c. 1918, p. 60, Hapgood Collection.

88. Dell, *Love in Greenwich Village,* p. 23.

89. Hapgood, *Victorian in the Modern World,* p. 358.

90. Hapgood, "Cristine," p. 58.

91. Dell, *Love in Greenwich Village,* p. 23.

92. Hutchins Hapgood, "The New Bohemia," Hapgood Collection.

93. Dodge to Boyce; in Lois Palken Rudnick, *Mabel Dodge Luhan: New Woman, New Worlds* (Albuquerque: University of New Mexico Press, 1984), pp. 96–97. To recapture Reed's attention, Dodge encouraged a new romance with the painter Andrew Dasburg, then enlisted Marsden Hartley to send Reed a poem about Dasburg's abstract portrait of Dodge.

94. Reed, in Luhan, *Movers and Shakers,* p. 242.

95. Ibid., p. 357.

96. Hapgood to Boyce, November 11, 1905, Hapgood Collection.

97. Boyce to Dodge; in Leslie Fishbein, *Rebels in Bohemia: The Radicals of the "Masses," 1911–1917* (Chapel Hill: University of North Carolina Press, 1982), p. 97.

98. Luhan, *Movers and Shakers,* p. 48.

99. Hapgood, in Churchill, *Improper Bohemians,* p. 44.

100. Hutchins Hapgood, "The Story of a Lover," 1914, Hapgood Collection.

101. Ben Reitman, Emma Goldman's lover, was sexually attracted to Hapgood, and Goldman encouraged Reitman to pursue the relationship; Reitman did not, concluding that Hapgood was enslaved to marriage.

102. Hapgood to Luhan, October 12, 1936, Luhan Collection.

103. Neith Boyce and Hutchins Hapgood, *Enemies,* in *The Provincetown Plays,* 2d series (New York: Frank Shay, 1916), pp. 103, 107.

104. Floyd Dell, "Feminism for Men," *Masses* 5 (July 1914): 19.

105. Floyd Dell, *Homecoming: An Autobiography* (New York: Farrar and Rinehart, 1933), p. 272.

106. Floyd Dell, "Daughters of Dreams and of Stories," Dell Papers; Dell, *Love in Greenwich Village,* p. 243.

107. Dorothy Day, *The Eleventh Virgin* (New York: A. and C. Boni, 1924), p. 169.

108. Dell to Arthur Davison Ficke, November 2, 1916, Dell Papers.

109. Hippolyte Havel spent time in mental hospitals in Europe and once was saved from the psychopathic ward of a prison by Kraft-Ebbing's diagnosis that Havel was sane; Polly Holladay spent the last fifteen years of her life in a mental institution on Wards Island, New York.

110. Holladay, in Hapgood, *Victorian in the Modern World*, p. 318.

111. Hapgood, "Cristine," p. 100.

112. Dell, *Homecoming*, p. 249.

113. Arthur Giovannitti, "What I Think of the *Masses*," *Masses* 8 (July 1916): 5.

114. Sloan, in Louis Untermeyer, *From Another World* (New York: Harcourt, Brace, 1939), p. 44. Eastman was not paid for his first two years; thereafter he was paid thirty-five dollars a week.

115. Eastman, *Enjoyment of Living*, p. 440.

116. Max Eastman, "Editorial Notice," *Masses* 4 (December 1912): 1.

117. Eastman, *Enjoyment of Living*, p. 443.

118. Ibid., p. 442.

119. Floyd Dell, "Memories of the Old *Masses*," *American Mercury* 68 (April 1949): 485.

120. Eastman, *Enjoyment of Living*, p. 443. Eastman's description of Dell at the *Masses* suggests his imperturbability: "He would sit down in the midst of all the ear-and-cortex-splitting roar and riot of a press room, where I could barely retain the faculty to measure a space, and write a shapely verse or paragraph, timely, witty, true, acute, and perfectly designed to fit." (Ibid.)

121. Sloan, ibid., p. 441.

122. Ibid., p. 550.

123. Sloan, in Churchill, *Improper Bohemians*, p. 107.

124. Karl K. Kitchen, "Artists for Art's Sake," unidentified newspaper clipping in the George Bellows Papers, Amherst College Library, Amherst, Massachusetts; in Rebecca Zurier, *Art for the Masses (1911–1917): A Radical Magazine and Its Graphics* (New Haven, Conn.: Yale University Art Gallery, 1985), p. 30. Mary Heaton Vorse, *A Footnote to Folly* (New York: Farrar and Rinehart, 1935), p. 42.

125. Sloan, in Churchill, *Improper Bohemians*, p. 107.

126. Dell, *Homecoming*, p. 251.

127. Untermeyer, *From Another World*, p. 49.

128. Dell, *Homecoming*, p. 251.

ART I: EXPLOSION IN THE ARMORY (pages 166–87)

1. The events leading up to the Armory Show are fully described in Milton Brown, *The Story of the Armory Show* (New York: Abbeville, 1988). The first recorded gathering of what became the Association of American Painters and Sculptors took place on December 14, 1911, with Walt Kuhn, Elmer MacRae, Jerome Myers, and Henry Fitch Taylor present. By January 9, 1912, the group had formally organized and elected Arthur B. Davies as president. Although the AAPS was formed to showcase progressive American artists who were slighted by the Academy, Davies broadened the organization's mission after seeing the catalog from the Cologne Sonderbund, which showed modern art from Europe. In September 1912 Kuhn was dispatched to see the Sonderbund and select works for the Armory Show. He subsequently traveled to the Hague, Amsterdam, Berlin, and Munich to see other artists' work, and Davies joined him in Paris in November. Guided by Walter Pach, they met the Steins (Gertrude and Leo, Sarah and Michael), many of the Puteaux artists (including Marcel Duchamp), and Paris's modern art dealers. After stopping in London to see exhibitions organized by Roger Fry at the Grafton Galleries, Davies and Kuhn returned to New York on November 30, 1912. Unknown to the membership of the AAPS, they had arranged an exhibition of revolutionary art.

2. Brown, *Armory Show*, pp. 26–27.

3. Davies, in "Art Radicalism on Exhibition," *Springfield Republican*, February 16, 1913; frame 397, Walt Kuhn Papers, AA.

4. Henry McBride, "Reappearance of Duchamp's *Nude Descending a Staircase*," *New York Herald*, March 9, 1924; in Henry McBride, *The Flow of Art: Essays and Criticism of Henry McBride*, ed. Daniel Catton Rich (New York: Atheneum, 1975), p. 189.

5. *New York Times*, March 16, 1913; in Brown, *Armory Show*, p. 167.

6. Carl Van Vechten, *Peter Whiffle: His Life and Works* (New York: Alfred A. Knopf, 1922), p. 123.

7. Hutchins Hapgood, "Life at the Armory," *New York Globe*, February 17, 1913.

8. Du Bois, in Brown, *Armory Show*, p. 58.

9. Quinn also suggested a portmanteau name for the Association: The Society for the Diffusion of Knowledge of Contemporary European and Particularly French Art in the United States. Although Quinn's suggestion was not used, it proved a prophetic description of the Armory Show.

10. Quinn, in John Butler Yeats, *Letters to His Son W. B. Yeats and Others, 1869–1922*, ed. Joseph Hone (London: Faber and Faber, 1944), p. 158.

11. Quinn to George Russell, March 2, 1913; in B. L. Reid, *"The Man from New York": John Quinn and His Friends* (New York: Oxford University Press, 1968), p. 151.

12. Ibid.

13. Jeanne Robert Foster to Aline Saarinen, May 20, 1957; in Judith Zilczer, *"The Noble Buyer": John Quinn, Patron of the Avant-Garde* (Washington, D.C.: Smithsonian Institution Press, 1978), p. 39.

14. J. B. Yeats, in Reid, *John Quinn*, p. 151; ibid., p. ix.

15. Other artists in the Armory Show who exhibited at 291 included Marion Beckett, Oscar Bluemner, Arthur B. Carles, Alfred Maurer, and Abraham Walkowitz. The two significant omissions were Arthur Dove and Max Weber. Weber felt slighted because the group did not ask him to be on its planning committee and invited him to exhibit only two works. His withdrawal was especially unfortunate since at that time Weber was probably the only modernist American painter whose work could stand comparison with his European counterparts.

16. Alfred Stieglitz, *New York American,* February 16, 1913.

17. Stieglitz, in Martin Green, *New York 1913: The Armory Show and the Paterson Strike Pageant* (New York: Charles Scribner's Sons, 1988), p. 174.

18. Stieglitz to Rockwell Kent, March 5, 1913, Alfred Stieglitz Collection, YCAL.

19. Stieglitz to Ward Muir, January 30, 1913, Stieglitz Collection.

20. Harriet Monroe, *Chicago Tribune,* February 16, 1913.

21. Ibid., February 23, 1913.

22. Ibid., February 27, 1913.

23. *The Autobiography of William Carlos Williams* (New York: Random House, 1951), p. 138.

24. Williams to Monroe, March 5, 1913; in *The Selected Letters of William Carlos Williams,* ed. John C. Thirlwall (New York: McDowell, Oblensky, 1957), pp. 23–24, 25.

25. Mabel Dodge Luhan, *Movers and Shakers,* vol. 3 of *Intimate Memories* (New York: Harcourt, Brace, 1936), p. 36.

26. Between the opening and closing lines she wrote: "Anything that will extend the unawakened consciousness here (or elsewhere) will have my support. The majority are content to browse upon past achievement." This card was originally a letter sent to Arthur B. Davies, who had it printed and autographed and distributed at the show. (Luhan, *Movers and Shakers,* p. 37.)

27. For example, the "Portrait" inspired the poet Donald Evans to embark upon the ambitious course of writing 1,001 portraits of Mabel Dodge in sonnet form. "Of course, I only hope to do ninety-nine, but that will be enough," he wrote to Dodge. "You yourself are quite ineffable; it is quite beyond belief that you exist." (Evans to Dodge, 1913; in Luhan, *Movers and Shakers,* p. 76.) In fact, Evans wrote only a few portraits of Dodge.

28. Mabel Dodge, "Speculations or Post-Impressionism in Prose," *Arts and Decoration* 3 (March 1913): 173.

29. Van Vechten, *Peter Whiffle,* p. 119.

30. Maria Lluisa Borras, *Picabia* (New York: Rizzoli, 1985), p. 98.

31. Picabia, in Henry Tyrrell, "Oh, You High Art! Advance Guard of the Post-Impressionists Has Reached N.Y.: One of Their Leaders, M. Picabia, Explains How He Puts His Soul on Canvas," *World Magazine,* February 9, 1913.

32. *New York Times,* February 16, 1913.

33. Francis Picabia, "What Doest Thou, 291?" *Camera Work* 47 (July 1914): 47.

34. Stieglitz to Arthur B. Carles, April 11, 1913; in William Camfield, *Francis Picabia: His Art, Life and Times* (Princeton, N.J.: Princeton University Press, 1979), p. 56.

35. Katherine Dreier was treasurer of the German Home for Recreation of Women and Children, president of the Little Italy Neighborhood House in South Brooklyn in 1903, and a director of the Manhattan Trade School Cooperative from 1903 to 1909.

36. Dreier, in Aline Saarinen, *The Proud Possessors: The Lives, Times, and Tastes of Some Adventurous American Art Collectors* (New York: Random House, 1958), p. 238.

37. Dreier, in Robert J. Levy, "Katherine Dreier: Patron of Modern Art," *Apollo,* May 1981, p. 314.

38. Dreier, in Saarinen, *Proud Possessors,* p. 241.

39. Dreier, in Levy, "Katherine Dreier," p. 314.

40. William Ivins to Fiske Kimball, March 15, 1954; in Francis Naumann, "Walter Conrad Arensberg: Poet, Patron, and Participant in the New York Avant-Garde," *Philadelphia Museum of Art Bulletin* 26 (Spring 1980): 6.

41. Known for his intellectual distraction, Walter Arensberg was frequently twitted by his wife for a remark he made on being asked if he would like some salad. Arensberg looked up quizzically and asked, "Salad? What's salad?" (Beatrice Wood, *I Shock Myself,* ed. Lindsay Smith [Ojai, Calif.: Dillingham Press, 1985], p. 68.)

42. Arensberg's concentration when looking at art is suggested by Wallace Stevens: "He told me once of having looked steadily at a piece of sculpture in one of the large museums for the three hours. He did a thing of that kind in the hope of some extraordinary disclosure coming to him." (Stevens to Fiske Kimball, February 23, 1954; in *Letters of Wallace Stevens,* ed. Holly Stevens [New York: Alfred A. Knopf, 1966], p. 823.)

43. Henry McBride, "The Walter Arensbergs," *Dial,* July 1920; in McBride, *Flow of Art,* p. 156.

44. Jerome Myers, *An Artist in Manhattan* (New York: American Artists Group, 1940), p. 37.

Present that last day was George Cram Cook. He skipped dinner and milled through the Armory for several hours until his "feet hurt something scandalous." A nude by Robert Henri inspired him to write a story about an artist who painted "a raw cold virgin" in photographic verisimilitude and then began to take liberties with her image, making her hair chrome and pale yellow against a background of infinity. (Cook to Susan Glaspell, March 15, 1913, George Cram Cook Collection, Henry W. Berg and Albert A. Berg Collection, NYPL.)

45. Brown, *Armory Show,* p. 109.

46. Marius de Zayas, "How, When, and Why Modern Art Came to New York," ed. Francis Naumann, *Arts Magazine* 54 (April 1980): 186.

47. Myers, *Artist in Manhattan,* p. 36.

48. Ibid., p. 41.

49. Max Weber, "Oral History," Oral History Research Office, Butler Library, Columbia University, p. 273.

50. For an accounting of early modern art exhibitions, see Judith Katy Zilczer, "The Aesthetic Struggle in America, 1913–1918: Abstract Art and Theory in the Stieglitz Circle" (Ph.D. diss., University of Delaware, 1975). Among the noncommercial spaces where modern art could be seen were the Cosmopolitan Club, the Gamut Club, the Liberal Club, the National Arts Club, and the Thumb Box Gallery.

51. Henry McBride, "The Growth of Cubism," *New York Sun,* February 8, 1914; in McBride, *Flow of Art,* p. 53.

 The new modern-art purveyors incensed many in the Stieglitz circle, who sniffed opportunism and aesthetic glibness. "The scavengers that always follow the pioneer are at work, and they ply their vulture craft," wrote one 291 regular. (Ernest Haskell, *Camera Work* 47 [July 1914]: 48.) Marius de Zayas railed against them as "Those lepers, those scullery maids of art, those Sudras of progress." He added, "They even believed themselves to be part of the evolution because, instead of copying trees, they copied a method." (Marius de Zayas, *291,* July–August 1915, n.p.)

52. Herbert J. Seligmann, *Alfred Stieglitz Talking: Notes on Some of His Conversations, 1925–1931* (New Haven, Conn.: Yale University Library, 1966), p. 40.

53. Montross, in "Modernist Exhibition at Montross Galleries," *New York Times,* January 30, 1914.

54. Ferdinand Howald was a bachelor who had made a fortune in West Virginia coal mines, retired in 1908, and then successfully invested in stocks. He quickly became a maverick collector of modern American art. From 1914 to the end of the 1920s he bought heavily from Daniel, and he left his collection of nearly three hundred works by Americans to the Columbus Gallery of Fine Arts. Among the other important collectors who bought from Daniel were Albert Barnes, Lillie P. Bliss, John O'Hara Cosgrave, Arthur Jerome Eddy (a lawyer-collector whose *Cubists and Post-Impressionists* was published in 1913), Morton R. Goldsmith, Philip Goodwin, Mrs. Meredith Hare, F. H. Hirschland, Charles B. Hoyt, Sturgis Ingersoll, Sam A. Lewisohn, Duncan Phillips, Mrs. John D. Rockefeller, Jr., Wolfgang S. Schwabacher, A. Mackay Smith, and John T. Spaulding.

55. Bourgeois to Pach, June 10, 1913; in Brown, *Armory Show,* p. 222. Walter Pach was a key advisor to these new galleries, for he provided the link to French modern art. A resident of Paris for much of the time from 1903 to 1913, he was a member of the Stein and the Puteaux circles. A central figure in organizing the Armory Show, he had guided Arthur B. Davies and Walt Kuhn through the Paris art world in 1912. After the Armory Show he became an advisor to John Quinn and Walter Arensberg, and he made exhibition arrangements in Paris on behalf of both the Montross and the Carroll galleries. Although Stieglitz's colleagues looked down on him as representing crass salesmanship, Pach achieved little personal gain from his agent activities, working for his expenses only. For further information on Pach, see Sandra Phillips, "The Art Criticism of Walter Pach," *Art Bulletin* 65 (March 1983): 106–21.

56. *American Art News,* 1916. Among the other critics who supported modern art during this period were Christian Brinton, Arthur Jerome Eddy, F. J. Gregg, Willard Huntington-Wright, J. Nilsen Laurvik, and Forbes Watson. At the conservative end of the critical continuum were Elizabeth Luther Carey, Royal Cortissoz, Kenyon Cox, and Frank Mather.

57. Jerome Mellquist, *The Emergence of an American Art* (New York: Charles Scribner's Sons, 1942), p. 314.

58. At the time of the Armory Show, McBride had no idea how important his position at the *New York Sun* would be. Within the year he would be promoted to senior art critic—obliged, as he later recalled, "to shift my brow into high"—and he carried on until his eighty-third year. (Henry McBride, "On McBride by McBride," in *Sun Rays,* 1931; quoted by Lincoln Kirstein in his introduction to McBride, *Flow of Art,* p. 5.) At that advanced age he began writing for *Artnews,* praising the newest modern generation, the Abstract Expressionists, and continued writing until he was ninety-one. McBride was modern art's most consistent critical champion until the generation of Clement Greenberg and Harold Rosenberg.

59. The youngest of a large family that disintegrated when McBride's mother died, the fifteen-year-old had been placed in a Quaker boardinghouse to find his own way in the world. He somehow developed the instinct and the judgment to pick his mentors well. The first of his teachers was an impoverished gentlewoman who had been at court in nineteenth-century Europe and conveyed to the adolescent McBride the manners essential to gracious living. By illustrating seed catalogs and working in the American Pavilion of the World's Columbian Exposition, he saved enough money to study at the Artist-Artisan Institute in New York under John Ward Stimson and then travel to Europe. "My experiences had been haphazard and unplanned," McBride recalled, "and if I had any conscious design in living, it had been then toward general culture rather than toward expertism in the arts." (Henry McBride, "Collecting from a Critical Viewpoint," *Artnews Annual,* 1939, p. 165.) His regular Continental journeys constituted his education—including exposure to new art in Paris and conversations with important critics such as Bernard Berenson and Roger Fry. From 1900 to 1905 McBride had taught drawing at the Educational Alliance to poor young men from the Lower East Side of New York and enjoyed treating them to chocolate and cookies. The work of several of his former students (among them Jo Davidson, Jacob Epstein, Samuel Halpert, and Abraham Walkowitz) hung in the Armory Show.

60. Walt Kuhn, *The Story of the Armory Show* (New York: Walt Kuhn, 1938), p. 17.

61. G. Stein to McBride, December 1913, Henry McBride Collection, YCAL.

62. Maximilian Miltzlaff, unpublished memoir of Henry McBride in Miltzlaff's collection.

63. Henry McBride, "The Palette Knife," *Creative Art* 8 (April 1931): 240.

64. Sanford Schwartz, "Henry McBride, an Era's Critic," in Schwartz, *The Art Presence: Painters, Writers, Photographers, Sculptors* (New York: Horizon, 1982), p. 210.

65. Alfred Stieglitz, *Camera Work* 47 (July 1914): 3.

66. Ibid., p. 4.

67. All citations are from *Camera Work* 47 (July 1914); the respondents, in the order quoted here, were: Paul Haviland, Djuna Barnes, Charles Caffin, Lee Simonson, John Wechsel, Arthur B. Carles, Arthur Dove, John Breyfogle, Marsden Hartley, Anne Brigman, and Hutchins Hapgood.

68. Edward Steichen, "What Is 291?" *Camera Work* 47 (July 1914): 65.

69. Henry McBride, "The Growth of Cubism," *New York Sun,* February 8, 1914; in McBride, *Flow of Art,* p. 53.

POETRY I: THE IMAGIST WARS (pages 188–204)

1. Ralph Fletcher Seymour, *Some Went This Way: A Forty-Year Pilgrimage among Artists, Bookmen and Printers* (Chicago: Ralph Fletcher Seymour, 1945), p. 139. Seymour was an etcher, fine-book designer, and publisher. *Poetry* was produced in his studio in the Fine Arts Building, where his models, sometimes nude, liked to dance, providing further incentive for those interested in poetry to frequently investigate the progress of the magazine's proofs.

2. Harriet Monroe published the first issue of *Poetry* a month ahead of schedule, after hearing reliable reports that Stanley Braithwaite from Boston might scoop her by publishing America's first magazine devoted to poetry. Rushing to print before she had enough poems to fill the magazine's thirty-two pages, she appealed to Harriet Moody, who dug into the trunk of her dead husband—William Vaughn Moody, the leading Chicago poet of the period—and met the crisis with a long poem entitled "I Am the Woman."

3. Conrad Aiken, *Ushant, an Essay* (New York: Duell, Sloan, and Pearce, 1952), p. 218.

4. William George Russell, in *A Book of Irish Quotations,* ed. Sean MacPherson (Dublin: O'Brien, 1984), p. 140.

5. Aiken, *Ushant,* p. 214.

6. Pound to Monroe, c. August 18, 1912; in *The Letters of Ezra Pound,* ed. D. D. Paige (New York: Harcourt, Brace, 1950), p. 10.

7. Pound to Monroe, October 12, 1912, *Poetry* Papers.

8. Pound's proposed policy: "My idea of our policy is this: We support American poets—preferably the young ones who have a serious determination to produce master-work. We import only such work as is better than that produced at home. The best foreign stuff, the stuff well above mediocrity or the experiments that seem serious, and seriously and sanely directed toward the broadening and development of The Art of Poetry. And 'TO HELL WITH HARPER'S AND THE MAGAZINE TOUCH!'" (Pound to Monroe, September 24, 1912; in *Letters of Ezra Pound,* pp. 10–11.)

9. Pound to Monroe, December 1912, *Poetry* Papers.

10. Pound to Monroe, 1913, *Poetry* Papers.

11. Pound to Monroe, December 3, 1912, *Poetry* Papers.

12. Pound to Monroe; in Ellen Williams, *Harriet Monroe and the Poetry Renaissance: The First Ten Years of "Poetry," 1912–1922* (Urbana: University of Illinois Press, 1977), p. 73. *Poetry*'s rate was ten dollars a page, slightly below that of popular magazines.

13. Harriet Monroe, "The Open Door," *Poetry* 1 (November 1912): 64.

14. Pound to Monroe; in Williams, *Harriet Monroe,* p. 37.

15. Henderson, in Eunice Tietjens, *The World at My Shoulder* (New York: Macmillan, 1938), p. 29.

16. Lindsay, in Eleanor Ruggles, *The West-Going Heart: A Life of Vachel Lindsay* (New York: W. W. Norton, 1959), p. 207.

17. Williams, *Harriet Monroe,* p. 64.

18. These principles were written by Ezra Pound, although when they appeared in the March 1913 issue of *Poetry,* they were signed by F. S. Flint, supposedly based on an interview with an Imagist. Pound actually wrote the whole piece and merely asked Flint to sign it.

19. Dell, in Glenn Coleman, *Imagism and Imagists* (Stanford, Calif.: Stanford University Press, 1931), p. 49.

20. Lowell, in S. Foster Damon, *Amy Lowell: A Chronicle with Extracts from Her Correspondence* (Boston: Houghton Mifflin, 1935), p. 196.

21. Lowell to Monroe; in Noel Stock, *The Life of Ezra Pound,* expanded ed. (San Francisco: North Point, 1982), p. 140.

22. Pound to Monroe, August 1913, *Poetry* Papers.

23. Pound to Robert Frost; in Charles Norman, *Ezra Pound* (New York: Macmillan, 1960), p. 106.

24. Lowell to Monroe, September 13, 1913, *Poetry* Papers.

25. Pound to Lowell; in Norman, *Ezra Pound,* p. 106.

26. Man Ray to Sam Ray; in Neil Baldwin, *Man Ray: American Artist* (New York: Clarkson N. Potter, 1988), p. 31.

27. Undated [1914] article by Alfred Kreymborg; in Mabel Dodge Luhan, "Many Inventions" (scrapbook), Mabel Dodge Luhan Collection, YCAL.

28. Pound, in Alfred Kreymborg, *Troubadour: An Autobiography* (New York: Boni and Liveright, 1925), p. 204.

29. Ibid., p. 205.

30. Pound submitted manuscripts by himself and others to the *Smart Set,* and that summer of 1913 he hoped to make the *New Freewoman* an outlet for Imagisme.

31. Pound to Henderson, October 14, 1913; Alice Corbin Henderson Collection, HRHRC.

32. Pound to Monroe, October 9, 1912, *Poetry* Papers.

33. Hueffer [Ford] to Monroe, November 12, 1913; in Williams, *Harriet Monroe,* p. 81.

34. Aldington to Monroe, c. November 28, 1913, *Poetry* Papers.

35. Yeats, in Harriet Monroe, *A Poet's Life* (New York: Macmillan, 1938), p. 330.

36. Lindsay to Monroe; ibid., p. 333.

37. Lindsay to Henderson, May 1, 1914, Henderson Collection.

38. From Carl Sandburg's transcription of Yeats's speech, *Poetry* Papers. Sandburg—a reporter who would follow Yeats as the winner of the Levinson Prize the following year—found it hard to keep up with his "delightful Irish burr that leaves a reporter with his pencil in the air wondering what in the divil [*sic*] the Celtic playboy has just been saying." (Sandburg to Monroe, March 5, 1914, *Poetry* Papers.)

39. Yeats commented about Lindsay's performance that the only remnants of the Greek lyric chanting and singing of poetry existed in American vaudeville. However apt was Yeats's comment, its effect was a mixed blessing for Lindsay, who thereafter built vaudeville's rhythms into his recitations, which he called "the Higher Vaudeville." Lindsay's performances increasingly resembled an act in Buffalo Bill's Wild West Show.

40. Lindsay to Yeats, 1928; in Joseph Hone, *W. B. Yeats* (New York: Macmillan, 1942), p. 298.

41. Monroe, *Poet's Life,* pp. 338–39.

42. Pound to William Carlos Williams, December 1913; in *Letters of Ezra Pound,* p. 27. *Des Imagistes* included ten poems by Richard Aldington, seven by H.D., five by F. S. Flint, six by Pound, one each by Skipwith Cannell, John Cournos, Ford Madox Ford, James Joyce, Amy Lowell, and Allen Upward.

43. Pound to James Joyce, c. April 1, 1914; in Forrest Read, ed., *Pound/Joyce: The Letters of Ezra Pound to James Joyce* (New York: New Directions, 1967), p. 26.

44. Lowell to Monroe, July 20, 1914, *Poetry* Papers.

45. Richard Aldington, *Egoist* 1 (July 15, 1914): 273.

46. John Gould Fletcher, *Life Is My Song* (New York: Farrar and Rinehart, 1937), p. 148.

47. Amy Lowell, *Sword Blades and Poppy Seed* (New York: Macmillan, 1914), p. 245.

48. Ford Madox Ford, "Henry Gaudier: The Story of a Low Tea Shop," *English Review* 29 (October 1919): 297.

49. Pound to Monroe, January 1915; in *Letters of Ezra Pound,* p. 48.

ENTR'ACTE (pages 205–10)

1. Lawrence, in Barbara Guest, *Herself Defined: The Poet H.D. and Her World* (Garden City, N.Y.: Doubleday, 1984), p. 73.

2. Amy Lowell, "A Letter from London," *Little Review* 1 (October 1914): 7.

3. Pound to Monroe, August 29, 1914, *Poetry* Papers.

4. Pound to Monroe, May 1915, *Poetry* Papers.

5. Pound to Dr. Felix Shelling, June 15, 1915; in *The Letters of Ezra Pound,* ed. D. D. Paige (New York: Harcourt, Brace, 1950), p. 61. Many years later Pound traced his first serious interest in politics and social programs to the untimely death of Gaudier-Brzeska.

6. Muriel Draper, *Music at Midnight* (New York: Harper and Brothers, 1929), p. 197.

7. Pound to Monroe, September 30, 1914; in *Letters of Ezra Pound,* p. 40.

8. McBride to Gertrude Stein, January 15, 1915, Henry McBride Collection, YCAL.

9. De Zayas to Stieglitz, August 13, 1914, Alfred Stieglitz Collection, YCAL.

10. De Zayas to Steiglitz, 1914, Stieglitz Collection.

11. Ibid.

12. Duchamp, in "French Artists Spur on an American Art," *New York Tribune,* October 24, 1915.

13. Dodge, in Neith Boyce, "August 1914" (unpublished manuscript), p. 8, Hutchins Hapgood Collection, YCAL.

14. Boyce, ibid., p. 4.

15. Boyce, ibid., p. 6.

16. There were several breaks in the Van Vechten–Dodge relationship, one lasting sixteen years.

17. Mabel Dodge, "The Secret of War: The Look on the Faces of Men Who Have Been Killing—And What Women Think about It," *Masses* 6 (November 1914): 8.

18. Ibid.

19. Loy to Van Vechten, Mina Loy Collection, YCAL.

20. Loy to Van Vechten, Loy Collection.

21. The great exception is Bernard Berenson, who reigned from I Tatti in Fiesole until his death in 1959.

22. Mabel Dodge Luhan, *Movers and Shakers,* vol. 3 of *Intimate Memories* (New York: Harcourt, Brace, 1936), p. 282.

23. "Cape Cod Town Is an Artistic Haven," unidentified newspaper, August 15, 1914; in Emily Farnham, "Charles Demuth: His Life, Psychology and Works" (Ph.D. diss., Ohio State University, 1959), p. 76.

24. The Cook-Glaspell home had recently been painted by communal decision: Demuth suggested yellow for one wall and black for the woodwork, Cook wanted an orange wall and green floor, and Cook's mother insisted on a purple door. Once repainted, it was called "the gay house." Cook and Glaspell had recently merged their libraries on new shelves, prompting Glaspell to observe, "Two people do not really live together until their books become one library." (Susan Glaspell, *The Road to the Temple* [New York: Frederick A. Stokes, 1927], p. 235.)

25. Ibid., p. 234.

26. Ibid., p. 236.

27. George Cram Cook, "New York Letter," *Chicago Evening Post*, August 7, 1914.

28. Hutchins Hapgood, *A Victorian in the Modern World* (New York: Harcourt, Brace, 1939), pp. 385–86.

29. Ibid., p. 386.

30. Hutchins Hapgood, "Cristine," c. 1918, p. 114, Hapgood Collection.

31. "With Fred [Boyd], [Joe] O'Carroll, Demuth and Hippolyte, the exigent lover and idealist," Hapgood observed, "her state of mind for a time was not unlike a War of Nations." (Hapgood, *Victorian in the Modern World*, p. 387.)

32. Ibid.

33. Ibid., p. 385.

VILLAGE II: THE SELLING OF BOHEMIA (pages 212–36)

1. Mabel Dodge, unidentified newspaper clipping, Mabel Dodge Luhan Collection, YCAL.

2. Hutchins Hapgood, *A Victorian in the Modern World* (New York: Harcourt, Brace, 1939), pp. 391, 393.

3. Mabel Dodge Luhan, *Movers and Shakers*, vol. 3 of *Intimate Memories* (New York: Harcourt, Brace, 1936), p. 408.

4. L. Stein to Dodge, late summer 1915; in Luhan, *Movers and Shakers*, p. 411.

5. Hapgood, *Victorian in the Modern World*, p. 392.

6. The Washington Square Players exemplified the Little Theater movement that mushroomed in America in the years 1910–16 (others included Chicago's Little Theater, the Vagabonds in Baltimore, and New York's Neighborhood Playhouse). Organized by Albert Boni, Lawrence Langner, Philip Moeller, and Ida Rauh, the Washington Square Players presented their first informal production (Lord Dunsany's *Glittering Gate*) in the Washington Square Bookshop, with mahogany door frames as the proscenium and columns created by Robert Edmond Jones from wrapping paper. Their first official season opened on February 19, 1915, with a bill of one-act plays by Edward Goodman, Lawrence Langner, and Maurice Maeterlinck. The other playwrights represented during that first season were Leonid Andreyev, Anton Chekhov, Octave Feuillet, Philip Moeller, and John Reed. The Provincetown Players and the Washington Square Players both grew out of the Liberal Club and involved many overlapping members, but they differed in the Washington Square Players' emphasis on European fare over American and in their relationship to the Broadway establishment. The Washington Square Players were reformist rather than revolutionary: they played in a conventional uptown theater and moved to Broadway as soon as success permitted; they paid royalties and courted the press by sending free tickets. By 1919 they had reorganized as the Theatre Guild, which became a prestigious and long-lived institution.

7. Cook, in Arthur and Barbara Gelb, *O'Neill* (New York: Harper and Brothers, 1962), p. 304.

8. William Archer, "Great Contribution of 'Little Theaters' to Our Drama's Future," *New York Post*, February 24, 1921.

9. Boyce to her father, July 17, 1915; in Louis Sheaffer, *O'Neill: Son and Playwright* (Boston: Little, Brown, 1968), p. 343.

10. Hapgood, in Luhan, *Movers and Shakers*, p. 383.

11. Some members of the audience undoubtedly also recognized parallels between Boyce's play, *Constancy*, and her own marriage. This topicality became the Provincetown Players' hallmark; as Hutchins Hapgood wrote, they were always looking for "a play that is felt to be in the moment of time." (Hutchins Hapgood, "The Provincetown Players," Hutchins Hapgood Collection, YCAL.) And the local Provincetown paper observed that the group was so modern "that they not only write about modern things, but satirize them." (Gelb and Gelb, *O'Neill*, p. 306.)

12. Cook, in Susan Glaspell, *The Road to the Temple* (New York: Frederick A. Stokes, 1927), pp. 252–53.

13. Hapgood, *Victorian in the Modern World*, p. 397.

14. The other plays on the second bill were of dubious quality: Louise Bryant's allegorical morality play, *The Game*, and Wilbur Daniel Steele's flimsy *Not Smart*.

15. Glaspell, *Road to the Temple*, pp. 253–54.

16. Max Eastman, *Enjoyment of Living* (New York: Harper and Brothers, 1948), p. 566.

17. Baker, in Barrett Clark, *Eugene O'Neill: The Man and His Plays* (New York: Dover, 1947), p. 28.

18. Glaspell, *Road to the Temple*, p. 254.

19. Dodge to Stieglitz, September 14, 1916; in Sheaffer, *O'Neill*, p. 355.

20. Bryant to Reed, June 8, 1916; in Robert Rosenstone, *Romantic Revolutionary: A Biography of John Reed* (New York: Alfred A. Knopf, 1975), p. 251. Anti-Semitism popped up elsewhere that summer; Provincetowners feared "the Jewish invasion," which formed "a sort of new Jerusalem at that end of town." (Bryant to Reed, June 12, 1916, John Reed Papers, Houghton Library, Harvard University, Cambridge.)

21. Bryant to Reed, June 12, 1916, Reed Papers.

22. Ibid.

23. Reed, in Granville Hicks, *John Reed: The Making of a Revolutionary* (New York: Macmillan, 1936), p. 205.

24. Sheaffer, *O'Neill*, p. 346.

25. Ibid., p. 356.

26. Agnes Boulton, *Part of a Long Story* (Garden City, N.Y.: Doubleday, 1958), p. 114.

27. Cook, in Gelb and Gelb, *O'Neill*, p. 315.

28. Hapgood, ibid.

29. Luhan, *Movers and Shakers*, p. 364.

30. By 1916 they furnished the subject of Don Marquis's satire *Hermione and Her Small Circle of Serious Thinkers*.

31. George Cram Cook, "New York Letter," *Chicago Evening Post*, May 27, 1914.

32. Sloan, in Eastman, *Enjoyment of Living*, p. 550.

33. Sloan, in Rebecca Zurier, *Art for the Masses (1911–1917): A Radical Magazine and Its Graphics* (New Haven, Conn.: Yale University Art Gallery, 1985), p. 35.

34. Dell, in Eastman, *Enjoyment of Living*, p. 549. This small revolt cannot be presented simply as a battle between an art-for-art's-sake faction and those favoring political engagement. Some of these same artists had objected to the modernists at the Armory Show—the magazine's only response to the exhibition was a cartoon by John Sloan—and their artwork for the magazine was almost always socially engaged. Although some art that had nothing to do with politics did appear in the *Masses*—works by Arthur B. Davies, Maurice Sterne, Abraham Walkowitz—those artists were only occasional contributors and played no part in the battle over captions.

35. John Sloan was elected vice president, Glenn Coleman treasurer, and Maurice Becker was promoted to the board of directors.

36. Sloan, in Eastman, *Enjoyment of Living*, p. 555.

37. Allan Ross MacDougall, "New York Letter," *Little Review*, April 1916, p. 29.

38. "Who's Who in New York's Bohemia," *New York Tribune*, November 14, 1915.

39. Hutchins Hapgood, "Cristine," c. 1918, pp. 98, 61, Hapgood Collection.

40. Other balls included the "Dance of the Feathered Flock," the "Bal Primitif," and the "Art Models' Frolic."

41. Floyd Dell, *Homecoming: An Autobiography* (New York: Farrar and Rinehart, 1933), p. 325.

42. George Cram Cook, "New York Letter," *Chicago Evening Post*, October 23, 1914.

43. Undated headlines from Mabel Dodge's scrapbooks, Luhan Collection.

44. *Quill*, June 1917. Examples of the new breed of self-conscious Village figures included Babs, who fought prostitution by offering her body free to any man who wanted it; Tiny Tim, who went from table to table in the tearooms, identifying the color of the customers' souls and selling them their appropriate shade of "soul candy" wrapped in paper on which his verse had been printed; and Doris the Dope, who bathed nude in the Washington Square fountain and made a living as a latter-day Camille, coughing and asking for money until she had enough to dine in the Brevoort basement that evening.

45. "Who's Who in New York's Bohemia," *New York Tribune*, November 14, 1915.

46. He changed the name of his magazine frequently and printed only a few issues of each—*Bruno's, Bruno's Review of Life, Bruno's Chap Book, Love and Literature, Bruno's Review of Two Worlds, Bruno's Bohemia, Bruno's Weekly,* and *Bruno's Scrapbook.*

47. One woman who had been swindled by Bruno described him this way: "He's not really human, he's a sinister shape of hell, without shame or pity or feeling for anything except money." (Andrew Field, *Djuna: The Life and Times of Djuna Barnes* [New York: Putnam, 1983], p. 73.)

48. Allen Churchill, *The Improper Bohemians: The Re-Creation of Greenwich Village in Its Heyday* (New York: E. P. Dutton, 1959), p. 152.

49. *New York Times*, March 5, 1918.

50. Mary K. Simkhovitch, in Edmund T. Delaney, *Greenwich Village* (Barre, Mass.: Barre, 1968), p. 104.

51. *Quill* 2 (December 1, 1917): 22.

52. *New York Times*, March 5, 1918.

53. Egmont Arens, *The Little Book of Greenwich Village* (New York: Washington Square Bookshop, 1918), p. 1.

54. Hapgood, "Provincetown Players," Hapgood Collection.

55. Alfred Kreymborg, *Troubadour: An Autobiography* (New York: Boni and Liveright, 1925), p. 308.

56. Zorach, ibid., p. 308.

57. Dell, *Homecoming*, p. 265.

58. Robert K. Sarlos, "Dionysus in 1915: A Pioneer Theater Collective," *Theatre Research International* 3 (October 1977): 41.

59. Hapgood, *Victorian in the Modern World*, p. 375.

60. Glaspell, *Road to the Temple*, p. 265.

61. Ibid., p. 266.

ART II: NEW YORK HOSTS *TOUT LE MONDE* (pages 237–81)

1. McBride to Stein, January 7, 1915, Gertrude Stein Collection, YCAL.

2. In George Cram Cook's unpublished essay "A Creditor Nation in Art?" c. 1915, he commented, "They [American modern artists] may be unconsciously spurred by the knowledge that if the significant move-

ment of which they were only a part in Paris is not now to die out of the world it must be in them that it finds life and in America." (George Cram Cook Collection, Henry W. Berg and Albert A. Berg Collection, NYPL.)

3. Art historian Judith Zilczer tabulated the number of modern and progressive art exhibitions in New York from 1907 to 1917 as follows: 1907: five; 1908: seven; 1909: ten; 1910: nine; 1911: thirteen; 1912: twenty-two; 1913: twenty-one; 1914: thirty-three; 1915: forty-five; 1916: fifty-three; 1917: sixty-three. (Zilczer, "The Aesthetic Struggle in America, 1913–1918: Abstract Art and Theory in the Stieglitz Circle" [Ph.D. diss., University of Delaware, 1975].)

4. Non-American art exhibited in New York during this period included work by Constantin Brancusi, Georges Braque, Paul Cézanne, Marcel Duchamp, Albert Gleizes, Henri Matisse, Amedeo Modigliani, Elie Nadelman, Francis Picabia, Pablo Picasso, Odilon Redon, Gino Severini, and Vincent van Gogh, plus African sculpture.

5. Stieglitz to Paul Haviland, April 19, 1916, Alfred Stieglitz Collection, YCAL. Daniel-Henry Kahnweiler appointed Robert Coady and Michael Brenner as Picasso's American agents. The Montross Gallery's show in April 1915 was Modern Art Applied to Decoration.

6. Direct encounters had also shaped the attitudes of the French avant-garde toward America. Arthur Cravan had lived there and returned to write about it in his scabrous publication Maintenant; the writer Blaise Cendrars came to the United States in 1911 and returned to Paris with a poem called "Easter in New York." Most influential was the Armory Show visit of Francis Picabia, who had carried his own impressions of America back to Paris.

7. Blaise Cendrars, "Two Portraits: Gustave Lerouge, Arthur Cravan," Paris Review 42 (Winter 1968): 164.

8. Richard Le Gallienne, "The Philosopher Walks Up-Town," Harper's Magazine 123 (July 1911): 228.

9. Duchamp introduced Albert and Juliet Gleizes to New York: he took them on a ferry in the East and Hudson rivers, up an elevator to the top of a skyscraper, to a drugstore soda fountain. For their second night in New York, Duchamp arranged a dinner at the Brevoort Hotel that, as Juliet Gleizes recalled, included the Arensbergs, Louise Norton, Man Ray, Joseph Stella, the Stettheimers, Alfred Stieglitz, and Max Weber. By the beginning of 1916, however, Albert Gleizes saw New York more darkly. His eye was drawn to shop windows filled with orthopedic devices and tin cans, and he imagined each fire escape a cage and behind each window a life going crazy. (Daniel Robbins, "The Formation and Maturity of Albert Gleizes: A Biographical and Critical Study, 1881 through 1920" [Ph.D. diss., Institute of Fine Arts, New York University, 1975].)

10. Gleizes, in "French Artists Spur on an American Art," New York Tribune, October 24, 1915.

11. Marcel Duchamp, Salt Seller: The Writings of Marcel Duchamp (Marchand du Sel), ed. Michel Sanouillet and Elmer Peterson (New York: Oxford University Press, 1973), p. 75.

12. Emily M. Burbank, in Philippe Jullian, De Meyer (New York: Alfred A. Knopf, 1976), p. 36.

13. Varèse, in Fernande Ouellette, Edgard Varèse (New York: Orion, 1968), p. 47.

14. Ibid., p. 39.

15. Ibid., p. 38.

16. Varèse to Mme Kauffmann, c. 1915; in Louise Varèse, Varèse: A Looking-Glass Diary (New York: W. W. Norton, 1972), p. 122.

17. "Do You Strive to Capture the Symbols of Your Reactions? If Not You Are Quite Old-Fashioned," New York Evening Sun, February 17, 1917.

18. Gertrude Stein, "Roché," in Gertrude Stein, Geography and Plays (Boston: Four Seas, 1922), p. 141.

19. Ibid., pp. 141–42.

20. Trotsky, in Roger L. Conover, "Introduction," in Mina Loy, The Last Lunar Baedeker, ed. Roger L. Conover (Highlands, N.C.: Jargon Society, 1982), p. xlvii.

21. Johnson and Cravan did go six rounds in this match (held April 23, 1916, in Barcelona's Plaza de Toros Monumental), but it appeared that Johnson was carrying him after the first round, for the benefit of a film that was being shot.

22. Cravan, in Conover, "Introduction," in Loy, Last Lunar Baedeker, p. xlix.

23. Ibid., p. lii.

24. Cravan's aggression was played out in the pages of Maintenant, a small Parisian avant-garde magazine that he started in April 1912 and, over the next three years, distributed from a wheelbarrow. He was, above all, a bellicose provocateur, and he systematically goaded people until their only possible response was to fight back. He so incensed Guillaume Apollinaire, for example, with his appraisal of the poet's lover the painter Marie Laurencin ("Now there's one who needs to have her skirt lifted") that Apollinaire assembled a tribunal of artists and had Cravan manacled and hauled off to jail for defamation of character.

25. I am indebted to William Camfield's interpretation of Picabia's portrait of Stieglitz in Camfield, Francis Picabia: His Art, Life and Times (Princeton, N.J.: Princeton University Press, 1979).

26. Stieglitz to de Zayas, September 2, 1915; in Peter Galassi, "Paul Burty Haviland, 1880–1950," in Photo-Secession (Washington, D.C.: Graphics International, 1977), p. 8.

27. Two editions were printed: 1,000 on heavy white paper, 100 of a special edition on heavy Japanese vellum. The regular edition sold for ten cents. One hundred people subscribed to the regular edition, and eight to the special edition. There were very few sales beyond those subscribers, and the magazine was considered a financial fiasco by the Meyers.

28. De Zayas to Stieglitz, August 16, 1915, Stieglitz Collection; in Douglas Hyland, Marius de Zayas: Conjurer of Souls (Lawrence, Kans.: Spencer Museum of Art, 1981), p. 44.

29. De Zayas to Meyer, July 15, 1915; in Eva Epp Runk, "Marius de Zayas: The New York Years" (M. A. thesis, University of Delaware, 1973).

30. "We had a firm conviction that something must be done to keep us all from getting into a deep gulf of inactivity and aimlessness, to keep 291 from dying an involuntary and nasty death. . . ." Meyer to Stieglitz, August 16, 1915; in William Innes Homer, *Alfred Stieglitz and the American Avant-Garde* (Boston: New York Graphic Society, 1977), p. 195.

31. Ibid.

32. De Zayas to Stieglitz, August 27, 1915, Stieglitz Collection.

33. Artists whose work had been exhibited at 291 and also at the Modern Gallery included Marion Beckett, Constantin Brancusi, Georges Braque, Frank Burty, Paul Cézanne, Arthur Dove, John Marin, Francis Picabia, Pablo Picasso, Paul Strand, Henri de Toulouse-Lautrec, and Abraham Walkowitz. In addition, the Modern Gallery exhibited work by Patrick Henry Bruce, André Derain, Juan Gris, Amedeo Modigliani, Diego Rivera, Morton Schamberg, Charles Sheeler, Vincent van Gogh, and Maurice de Vlaminck.

34. Stieglitz to Anne Brigman, May 17, 1916, Stieglitz Collection.

35. Stieglitz to Haviland, April 16, 1918, Stieglitz Collection. This was, in fact, the end of only this particular version of the Stieglitz circle. Younger men such as Waldo Frank, Lewis Mumford, Paul Rosenfeld, and Paul Strand would soon become key members of a new one.

36. McBride to G. Stein, January 7, 1915, Stein Collection.

37. E. Stettheimer to Henri Gans, October 22, 1918, Stettheimer Collection, YCAL.

38. Henry McBride, *Florine Stettheimer* (New York: Museum of Modern Art, 1946), p. 13.

39. Henry McBride, "Artists in the Drawing Room," *Town and Country,* December 1946, p. 76.

40. Carl Van Vechten, "The World of Florine Stettheimer," Carl Van Vechten Collection, YCAL.

41. Virgil Thomson, interview with author, New York, May 7, 1987. Maurice Grosser dubbed their furnishings "prickly Baroque." (Ibid.)

42. Van Vechten to Fania Marinoff, April 16, 1921, Van Vechten Papers, Rare Books and Manuscripts Division, NYPL.

43. McBride, "Artists in the Drawing Room," p. 77.

44. Ettie Stettheimer, journal entries, July 7 and July 25, 1917, Stettheimer Collection.

45. Santayana, *The Last Puritan,* 1935; in Carl Van Vechten, "The World of Florine Stettheimer," Van Vechten Collection, YCAL.

46. Parker Tyler, Florine Stettheimer's biographer, described "a virgin cult" developing within the family. (Tyler to Joseph Solomon, December 7, 1961, Parker Tyler Collection, HRHRC.) Marcel Duchamp observed that Florine "had no female body under her clothes." (Parker Tyler, *Florine Stettheimer: A Life in Art* [New York: Farrar, Straus, 1963], p. 86.) After the death of Rosetta Walter Stettheimer, Carrie stopped working on her dollhouse, and Ettie replaced her mother as the family invalid. Florine would continue to entertain in her studio, and Carrie and Ettie would entertain in their adjoining rooms in the Dorset Hotel.

47. The circumstances of Joseph Stettheimer's life after leaving his family were kept secret, as were the financial arrangements that supported the family after his departure. It has been speculated that either Walter, the only son, or members of Rosetta Walter Stettheimer's family supported them.

48. Ettie Stettheimer, "Introductory Foreword," *A Fabulous Dollhouse of the Twenties* (New York: Dover, 1976), p. 12. Virgil Thomson would later remark, "Three sisters are always three sisters." (Interview with author, New York, May 27, 1986.) The Stettheimers even corresponded neatly to the *Three Sisters* of Anton Chekhov: Carrie, the eldest, was practical like Olga; Florine, the middle sister, was creative like Masha; and Ettie, the youngest, was a hopeful coquette like Irina.

49. E. Stettheimer, "Introductory Foreword," *Fabulous Dollhouse,* p. 11.

50. Florine's drive to tailor her environment never let up; on seeing a waterfall in Connecticut, for example, she remarked that it would have been prettier falling up; she insisted on redecorating the Knoedler Gallery (1916) in preparation for her exhibition there; she wanted the black cast of *Four Saints in Three Acts* (1934) to wear white makeup so that it would better set off the costumes she designed for it.

51. McBride, *Florine Stettheimer,* p. 10.

52. Carl Van Vechten, "Prelude in the Form of a Cellophane Squirrel Cage," in Tyler, *Florine Stettheimer,* p. xiii.

53. Florine Stettheimer, *Crystal Flowers* (New York: Privately printed, 1949), p. 82.

54. W. James to E. Stettheimer, May 26, 1909; in Ettie Stettheimer, *Memorial Volume* (New York: Alfred A. Knopf, 1951), pp. 477–78.

55. Tyler, *Florine Stettheimer,* p. 93.

56. E. Stettheimer to Henri Gans, November 29–December 2, 1916, Stettheimer Collection.

57. Lincoln Kirstein, *Elie Nadelman* (New York: Eakins Press, 1973), p. 206.

58. The value that Ettie placed on private emotions can be seen in her reproach to a friend, the singer Marguerite d'Alvarez, for having "no calm depth of repressed emotion." (E. Stettheimer, journal entry, November 2, 1919, Stettheimer Collection.)

59. Ibid., October 17, 1916.

60. Tyler, *Florine Stettheimer*, p. 24. Florine revised her will upon returning to America, specifying that her paintings were no longer to be buried with her corpse in a mausoleum but given instead to her mother and sisters. (Stettheimer to her lawyer, Benjamin Tulka, September 22, 1914; ibid., p. 17.)

61. The otherworldly effect of Florine's ultrafeminine bedroom is suggested by two anecdotes. When the painter Max Weber first entered the bedroom, he fell on his knees, clasped his hands, and cried out, "Please God send me a man." (Marguerite Zorach, who recounted this tale in an undated letter to Parker Tyler [Tyler Collection], added that she didn't think the Stettheimers ever prayed to have a man in their lives.) And when a small fire broke out in Florine's bedroom, firemen were summoned. "When they first saw her fantasy world they were struck dumb and couldn't move; they thought they were visiting an alien." (Ruth Ford, interview with author, New York, February 13, 1990.)

62. "She was indulging herself in some first-class self-deception," her biographer observed, "she was pretending to be 'at home' while displaying her wares in order to sell them." (Tyler, *Florine Stettheimer*, p. 29.)

63. F. Stettheimer, journal entry, October 14, 1916; in Tyler, *Florine Stettheimer*, p. 28.

64. Ibid., p. 30.

65. During that same month of October 1916 Florine met one of the premier dancers of Diaghilev's Ballets Russes, the handsome Adolf Bolm. He was interested in her ballet *Pocahontas;* to show him how it might look, Florine transformed a large packing case into a cobalt-blue stage hung with two gold-fringed curtains and brightly lit with bare electrical bulbs. Florine reported to her sisters that Bolm had declared it "the real stuff—'grand theatre,'" and she allowed herself to hope that the ballet would come to pass. That production never went beyond this fanciful maquette, but it foreshadowed the next time that Florine would venture into the bright light of publicity, nearly two decades later, when she designed the sets for *Four Saints in Three Acts* (1934).

66. Randolph Bourne, *New Republic,* April 28, 1917; in E. Stettheimer, *Memorial Volume,* p. 359.

67. E. Stettheimer, journal entry, February 22, 1917, Stettheimer Collection. Near the end of her life, when she was editing her *Memorial Volume,* she described the same aim: "I want to be widely read." It seemed an odd statement for a writer who had not published for the last quarter century, and she sourly observed, "Memorial Volumes are not issued for authors who are likely to be remembered without them." (Stettheimer, *Memorial Volume,* p. x.)

68. E. Stettheimer, "Introduction," in F. Stettheimer, *Crystal Flowers,* p. iv.

69. Gabrielle Buffet-Picabia, interview with Malitte Matta, Paris, January 1974; published as "Un Peu d'histoire" in *Paris–New York* (Paris: Centre National d'Art et de Culture Georges Pompidou, 1977). The interview is translated by Francis Naumann in "Walter Conrad Arensberg: Poet Patron and Participant in the New York Avant-Garde, 1915–1920," *Philadelphia Museum of Art Bulletin,* Spring 1980, p. 11. Katharine Kuh, "Walter Arensberg and Marcel Duchamp," *Saturday Review,* September 5, 1970, p. 37.

70. Duchamp, in Pierre Cabanne, *Dialogues with Marcel Duchamp,* trans. Ron Padgett (New York: Da Capo, 1987), p. 51.

71. Beatrice Wood, interview with author, Ojai, California, August 15, 1986.

72. Arthur Davison Ficke, in Joan Richardson, *Wallace Stevens, a Biography: The Early Years, 1879–1923* (New York: William Morrow, 1986), p. 431.

73. Stevens's biographer has called this crucial contact "as important a single factor as ever played a part in Stevens's development." (Ibid., p. 401.)

74. Carl Van Vechten, "Rogue Elephant in Porcelain," *Yale University Library Gazette* 38 (October 1963): 43.

75. Richardson, *Wallace Stevens,* p. 430.

76. Stevens to Elsie Stevens, August 3, 1915; in *Letters of Wallace Stevens,* ed. Holly Stevens (New York: Alfred A. Knopf, 1966), p. 185.

77. Charles Demuth was introduced to the Arensberg evenings through the poetry community. Demuth had known William Carlos Williams since 1903, when they met over a boardinghouse breakfast, and more recently he had filled an entire issue of Alfred Kreymborg's *Glebe.* There were three points on Demuth's social compass: the provincial security of his residence in Lancaster, Pennsylvania; Village dives like the Hell Hole; and the Arensbergs' stylish apartment. He shared with Walter Arensberg a passion for novelty—one of Demuth's favorite expressions was "It's the last word in that kind of thing." (Emily Farnham, "Charles Demuth: His Life, Psychology and Works" [Ph.D. diss., Ohio State University, 1959], p. 141.)

Walter Arensberg shared with de Zayas an enduring interest in African and Pre-Columbian art. In de Zayas's galleries primitive art was exhibited alongside modern art, and visitors to the Arensbergs' soon found Aztec statuary and African tribal figures in the large studio room. Arensberg was a key buyer at the Modern Gallery, and in 1919 he helped finance the De Zayas Gallery. On the gallery's final financial statement (December 14, 1920), Walter Arensberg is owed $108,049.

Born in Italy, Joseph Stella emigrated to the United States at the age of eighteen. His continuing European contact—with the Futurists, with the Steins' salon—strongly influenced his painting, which depicted such Futurist motifs as movement and urban life, and in New York he found his ideal subject in the Brooklyn Bridge.

John Covert was Walter Arensberg's cousin, and his participation in the Arensberg circle crucially affected his painting, which became abstract and experimental in the materials he used. After the Arensberg circle dispersed and Covert could find no patrons, he donated his work to the Société Anonyme in 1923 and became a salesman in the family steel business.

Morton Schamberg had traveled to Europe in the early years of the twentieth century and was influenced by Cubism, Synchromism, and Orphism. He shared a house and photography business with Charles Sheeler. His contact with the Arensberg circle—notably Duchamp and Picabia—inspired the mechanomorphic work for which he is best known.

Charles Sheeler was not a newcomer to modern art when he became a part of the Arensberg circle; he had exhibited six works in the Armory Show, had met Stieglitz and de Zayas in 1915, had been a photographer of art for the Modern Gallery, and had exhibited at the Modern Gallery and the Daniel Gallery. Although he didn't move to New York until November 1919, he attended the Arensbergs' gatherings fairly regularly, and his relationship with the Arensbergs was lifelong. Sheeler shared an interest in Americana with the Arensbergs and was commissioned in about 1918 to photograph their apartment.

78. Arensberg, in William Carlos Williams, "Prologue to 'Kora in Hell,'" in William Carlos Williams, Selected Essays (New York: Random House, 1954), p. 5.

79. Duchamp, in Cabanne, Dialogues with Marcel Duchamp, p. 52.

80. For example, John Covert's Hydro Cell, Morton Schamberg's Mechanical Abstraction, Marcel Duchamp's Chocolate Grinder.

81. Tristan Tzara, in New York Dada, April 1921.

82. The still was one of few frames that survived from a film coproduced by Duchamp and Man Ray, Elsa, Baroness von Freytag-Loringhoven, Shaves Her Pubic Hair; most of the film was destroyed during a darkroom accident.

83. Man Ray to Tristan Tzara, [1921], Bibliothèque Littéraire Jacques Doucet, Paris.

84. This account of Duchamp's first American Readymade comes from Juliet Roché's memoirs, recounted in Robbins, "Formation and Maturity of Albert Gleizes."

85. Duchamp, in "French Artists Spur on an American Art," New York Tribune, October 24, 1915; and in William Rubin, Dada, Surrealism, and Their Heritage (New York: Museum of Modern Art, 1968), p. 23.

86. Cravan, in Conover, "Introduction," in Loy, Last Lunar Baedeker, p. liii.

87. Loy, ibid., p. 319.

88. Louis Bouché, "Oral History," 1963, AAA.

89. The baroness purloined stamps from the Little Review office and affixed them to her head; she also stole Hart Crane's typewriter.

90. George Biddle, An American Artist's Story (Boston: Little, Brown, 1939), p. 140.

91. The baroness met Duchamp through two sisters: Sarah MacPherson and Bessie Breuer. Breuer, editor-in-chief for the Sunday New York Tribune, had written the first article published on Duchamp; MacPherson was an artist who met the baroness in a life-drawing class.

92. Freytag-Loringhoven, in Biddle, American Artist's Story, p. 138.

93. Louis Bouché, "Oral History."

94. About Duchamp's Readymade In Advance of the Broken Arm, Dreier wrote, "The average eye was too untrained to notice a difference in snow shovels. . . . It ended in being just the right snow shovel." (Katherine Dreier, Western Art and the New Era [New York: Brentano's, 1923], pp. 70–71.)

95. Ibid., p. 118.

96. Walter Arensberg paid two to three hundred dollars for each of Duchamp's artworks and paid the rent on his West Sixty-seventh Street studio for two years in exchange for The Large Glass. John Quinn invited the artist for meals and paid $120 for a study of the Nude Descending a Staircase. When he noticed that Duchamp looked tired during his first summer in New York, Quinn paid for a week's vacation at Spring Lake, New York. Quinn also used his influence with his friend Belle Greene (librarian to J. P. Morgan) to secure Duchamp a position as librarian at the Institut Français. The Stettheimers, Katherine Dreier, and Louise Norton all paid for French lessons with Duchamp. When Norton repeated her new vocabulary to Albert Gleizes, he shuddered and warned her, "Madame Norton, if you speak like that all the doors of Paris will be closed to you." (Anne d'Harnoncourt and Kynaston McShine, eds., Marcel Duchamp [New York: Museum of Modern Art; Philadelphia: Philadelphia Museum of Art, 1973], p. 224.) Through the generosity of these figures, Duchamp's penurious existence was "slightly gilded." (Cabanne, Dialogues with Marcel Duchamp, p. 58.)

97. Henri-Pierre Roché, Victor, trans. Allan Jones.

98. "The Iconoclastic Opinions of M. Marcel Duchamp Concerning Art and America," Current Opinion 59 (November 1915): 346–47. For other contemporary accounts of Duchamp, see "The European Art-Invasion," Literary Digest, November 27, 1915; "A Complete Reversal of Art Opinions by Marcel Duchamp," Arts and Decoration 5 (September 1915): 427–28, 442.

99. Duchamp exhibited in only two group shows in 1916, one at the Montross Gallery and the other at the Bourgeois Gallery.

100. Henry McBride, The Flow of Art: Essays and Criticism of Henry McBride, ed. Daniel Catton Rich (New York: Atheneum, 1975). Moira Roth, "Marcel Duchamp in America: A Self Ready-Made," Arts Magazine 9 (May 1977): 92.

101. Gabrielle Buffet-Picabia, "Some Memories of Pre-Dada: Picabia and Duchamp," in Robert Motherwell, ed., The Dada Painters and Poets: An Anthology, 2d ed. (Cambridge: Harvard University Press, Belknap Press, 1989), p. 260.

102. Juliet Roché, "Souvenirs," in Robbins, "Formation and Maturity of Albert Gleizes."

103. Beatrice Wood, *I Shock Myself*, ed. Lindsay Smith (Ojai, Calif.: Dillingham Press, 1985), pp. 22–23.

104. André Breton, "Marcel Duchamp," in Motherwell, ed., *Dada Painters and Poets*, p. 209.

105. Duchamp's frequently used phrase comes from Beatrice Wood, "Marcel," in Rudolf Kuenzli and Francis M. Naumann, eds., *Marcel Duchamp: Artist of the Century* (Cambridge, Mass.: MIT Press, 1989), p. 16.

106. Roché, *Victor*.

107. Duchamp, in "The Nude-Descending-a-Staircase Man Surveys Us," *New York Tribune*, September 12, 1915.

108. Wood, *I Shock Myself*, p. 3.

109. Beatrice Wood, interview with author, Ojai, California, August 15, 1986.

110. Elements of the relationship seem to have been drawn from the triangle of Roché, Wood, and Duchamp; however, the chief model for Catherine was Helen Hessel, a girlfriend of Roché's and wife of the German writer Franz Hessel.

111. Naumann, "Walter Conrad Arensberg," p. 17.

112. Allen Norton, "Walter's Room," *Quill* 5 (June 1919): 20.

113. The psychiatrist Ernest Southard, a friend of Arensberg's from Harvard, would analyze the dreams of Beatrice Wood, who wrote them down in a notebook and recited them when she visited the Arensbergs.

114. Wallace Stevens to Weldon Kees, November 10, 1954: "One day one of his very oldest friends spoke with some soreness to the effect that Walter was giving a lot of time to these Frenchmen and neglecting others. I had not myself noticed this. But I thought I would do the man who had spoken to me a good turn and relieve his feelings by telling Walter what he had told me. . . . Walter froze up when I spoke to him and when he froze up, I froze up too." Carl Van Vechten attempted to arrange a reconciliation, inviting the Arensbergs and the Stevenses to a dinner in the Village; neither knew the other was to be invited. When they met, Stevens recalled, "Walter and I remained on our high horses. I never saw him again." (*Letters of Wallace Stevens*, p. 850.)

115. *The Autobiography of William Carlos Williams* (New York: Random House, 1951), p. 137.

116. Norton, "Walter's Room," p. 20.

117. Mina Loy, "Colossus," ed. Roger L. Conover, in Rudolf E. Kuenzli, ed., *New York Dada* (New York: Willis Locker and Owens, 1986), p. 104.

118. Varèse, *Looking-Glass Diary*, p. 203. Louis Holladay had just returned to New York from Washington state on January 22, 1918, when he heard that Louise Norton had fallen in love with Edgard Varèse. (Although Norton has said that she had written to Holladay about her new relationship, others have reported that he first heard the news from her during their reunion at the Hell Hole.) Holladay began drinking heavily, bought a large amount of heroin, and went off to Romany Marie's restaurant with a group that included Dorothy Day, Charles Demuth, and Eugene O'Neill. There Holladay overdosed on heroin and slumped over on Day's shoulder, dead. Everyone except Day fled Romany Marie's, and Hutchins Hapgood recalled Demuth's arrival at the Brevoort: "He literally seemed a being in hell. I never saw such a look of complete horror on any human being's face." (Hutchins Hapgood, *A Victorian in the Modern World* [New York: Harcourt, Brace, 1939], pp. 426–27.) The rest of the heroin was taken from Louis and secretly passed to Maxwell Bodenheim, and Polly Holladay testified to her brother's heart problems, so that the death certificate read "chronic endocarditis."

119. Williams, in Constance Rourke, *Charles Sheeler: Artist in the American Tradition* (New York: Harcourt, Brace, 1938), p. 137.

120. In addition, ten thousand dollars had to be raised for the exhibition. The guarantors included: Mrs. Walter Conrad Arensberg ($954.34), Katherine S. Dreier ($500), Archer M. Huntington ($500), Mrs. Rockwell Kent ($500), Mrs. Philip Lydig ($500), Eugene Meyer, Jr. ($500), Frederick B. Pratt ($1,000), Mrs. C. C. Rumsey ($1,000), Sydney Stevens ($1,000), Hans Stoehr ($1,000), Mrs. W. K. Vanderbilt ($1,000), and Mrs. Harry Payne Whitney ($1,000). About half of the guarantors' pledges did not come in until after the opening. A total of $4,302 resulted from sales of art, and artists' memberships and exhibition fees brought in $12,827, but expenses resulted in a net loss of $8,282 for the exhibition.

121. Henry McBride, *New York Sun*, January 21, 1917. The traditional Academy of Design mounted its own exhibition that winter, but it proved so tepid that McBride concluded, "not a ripple can be detected upon the intellectual life of the city." The Academy was always being declared dead by one progressive critic or another, but an alarming new symptom was evidenced by the failure of even its own members to attend. McBride jokingly suggested, "Academicians should be compelled by law to go to their own show or else resign and become 'Independents.'" The Academy, he noted, had been replaced by the burgeoning galleries that now constituted America's equivalent of the Salon d'Automne. (*New York Sun*, March 25, 1917.)

POETRY II: NEW BATTLES (pages 282–310)

1. Pound to Quinn, July 19, 1916, John Quinn Memorial Collection, Rare Books and Manuscripts Division, NYPL.

2. "The Muse in a Pet," *North American Review*, October 1, 1913, p. 246.

3. Allan Ross MacDougal, "New York Letter," *Little Review* 3 (May 1916): 16.

4. "A Year's Harvest in American Poetry," and "Poetry," *New York Times Review of Books*, November 18, 1915, pp. 464, 474.

5. Pound to Monroe, January 23, 1916, *Poetry* Papers.

6. Pound to Alice Corbin Henderson, March 29, 1915, Alice Corbin Henderson Collection, HRHRC.

7. The forerunners of the *Egoist* were two feminist magazines—the *Freewoman* (November 1911–August 1912) and the *New Freewoman* (January 1913–January 1914). Edited by Dora Marsden, they focused explicitly on issues of sexual politics: prostitution, sexual oppression, "Uranianism" (homosexuality), and free love. The change in title from the *New Freewoman* to the *Egoist* in January 1914 reflected the change from a feminist focus to humanist individualism that embraced literary experimentation. After Harriet Shaw Weaver assumed the positions of editor and publisher in June 1914, the magazine's emphasis on literature intensified. During her tenure the magazine was generously opened to modern literature, and it became England's primary propagandizer for Imagism. Pound rejected the chance to become the magazine's literary editor—that position was assumed by Richard Aldington (November 1913–June 1916), H.D. (June 1916–June 1917), and T. S. Eliot (June 1917–December 1919, when the magazine ended). Despite his lack of an official position on the magazine's staff, Pound shaped the magazine by pushing for the publication of his favorite writers.

 Although each issue of the *Egoist* ran only twenty pages, did not pay its writers, and had a circulation that hovered at about two hundred, it was critically important. This was due not only to its strategic position in the literary landscape—it was sufficiently influential that, at different points, Lowell, Pound, and John Quinn considered taking it over—but also to its distinguished and courageous record of publication. In addition to the Imagists, the *Egoist* published Marianne Moore and William Carlos Williams and serialized Joyce's *Portrait of the Artist as a Young Man,* Wyndham Lewis's *Tarr,* and sections of Joyce's *Ulysses.* The magazine also spawned the Egoist Press, which published Joyce's *Portrait of the Artist as a Young Man;* Eliot's first book, *Prufrock and Other Poems* (1917, subsidized by Pound); and Marianne Moore's first book, *Poems* (1921).

8. Louise Norton clearly voiced the *Rogue*'s sensibility: "It is in futile striving for new sensations and new gods that the modernite goes astray." Instead, she proposed that "the hope of the world lies in artificiality. . . ." (*Cleveland Leader,* June 21, 1914.) *Rogue*'s blend of chic bohemianism and fin-de-siècle elegance could be seen in the Aubrey Beardsley–influenced illustrations by Robert Locher and Clara Tice; in the magazine's arch fashion columns; and in its attention to the small coterie known as the Patagonians, led by Donald Evans, Carl Van Vechten, Walter Arensberg, Wallace Stevens, and the magazine's editors, Allen and Louise Norton. Calling itself "the cigarette of literature," *Rogue* had few pretensions to literary history; nevertheless it published such modernist heavyweights as Gertrude Stein, Mina Loy, and Wallace Stevens. Appearing semimonthly from March 15, 1915, to September 15, 1915, it maintained an airy tone best described by Henry McBride:

"*Rogue* is charmingly impertinent, and impertinence and sauciness are as necessary to youth and youthful countries like ours as the air we breathe and somehow all our tendencies to it have been ruinously choked out of us of late. Probably we were seeing too much of our English cousins." (*New York Sun,* March 25, 1915.)

9. Williams to Monroe, May 3, 1916; in Ellen Williams, *Harriet Monroe and the Poetry Renaissance: The First Ten Years of Poetry, 1912–1922* (Urbana: University of Illinois Press, 1977), p. 193.

10. Harriet Monroe, *A Poet's Life* (New York: Macmillan, 1938), p. 277.

11. Wescott to Monroe, *Poetry* Papers.

12. Pound to Monroe, March 28, 1914; in *The Letters of Ezra Pound,* ed. D. D. Paige (New York: Harcourt, Brace, 1950), p. 35.

13. Bodenheim to Monroe, December 4, 1916; in Williams, *Harriet Monroe,* pp. 195–96.

14. Henderson to Pound, February 17, 1917; ibid., p. 227.

15. Pound to Harry Meacham, March 22, 1959; in Harry Meacham, *The Caged Panther: Ezra Pound at Saint Elizabeth* (New York: Twayne, 1967), p. 172.

16. Williams to Monroe, March 5, 1913; in *The Selected Letters of William Carlos Williams,* ed. John C. Thirlwall (New York: McDowell, Oblensky, 1957), p. 210.

17. Williams to Monroe, October 10, 1913; ibid., p. 25.

18. Williams to Monroe, January 6, 1916; Williams to Monroe, October 6, 1916, both *Poetry* Papers.

19. Monroe to Williams, April 7, 1913; in Williams, *Harriet Monroe.*

20. The pains to which Monroe went in balancing her negative response can be seen in one of her early rejection letters to Wallace Stevens (probably concerning "Peter Quince at the Clavier," "The Silver Plough-Boy," and "Disillusionment at Ten O'Clock"):

> I don't know when any poems have "intrigued" me so much as these. They are recondite, erudite, provocatively obscure, with a kind of modern gargoyle grin in them— Aubrey Beardsleyish in the making. They are weirder than your war poems, and I don't like them, and I'll be blamed if I print them, but their author will surely catch me the next time, if he will only uncurl and uncoil a little—condescend to chase his mystically mirthful and mournful muse out of the nether darkness, in other words, please send more.

(Monroe to Stevens, January 27, 1915; in Joan Richardson, *Wallace Stevens, a Biography: The Early Years, 1879–1923* [New York: William Morrow, 1986], p. 439.)

21. Stevens to Monroe, May 19, 1916; in Williams, *Harriet Monroe,* p. 158.

22. Pound to Monroe, October, 1914; in *Letters of Ezra Pound,* p. 41.

23. Monroe, *Poet's Life,* p. 394.

24. Monroe's failure to recognize the poem that has become a modern classic should not be judged too harshly. At the time of its publication "The Love Song of J. Alfred Prufrock" was considered inaccessible by Eliot's colleagues. Even the *Little Review* parodied it, and the only positive American response came, oddly enough, from Vachel Lindsay. In London, Ford Madox Ford and Harold Monro were among the few who liked the poem.

Eliot was not the only poet whose manuscript *Poetry* stockpiled for months; even some of Yeats's manuscripts were held eight months, and one of Williams's poems remained with Monroe for a year before it was published.

25. Pound to Monroe, October 2, 1915; in *Letters of Ezra Pound,* p. 64.

26. Pound to Monroe, December 1, 1915; ibid., p. 66.

27. Pound to Monroe, December 15, 1915, *Poetry* Papers. Pound's selection of the best poets included H.D., T. S. Eliot, Robert Frost, Edgar Lee Masters, William Butler Yeats, and himself.

28. Henderson to Monroe, June 7, 1916, *Poetry* Papers.

29. Pound to Monroe, January 23, 1916, *Poetry* Papers.

30. Monroe to Fletcher, November 22, 1916; in Williams, *Harriet Monroe,* p. 200.

31. Margaret Anderson, *My Thirty Years' War* (New York: Covici-Friede, 1930), p. 35.

32. Sherwood Anderson, "The New Note," *Little Review* 1 (March 1914): 23.

33. Margaret Anderson, "Editorial," *Little Review* 1 (March 1914): 1.

34. Dell, in Anderson, *Thirty Years' War,* p. 47.

35. Lowell to Monroe, September 15, 1914, *Poetry* Papers.

36. Pound to Monroe, [summer 1914], *Poetry* Papers.

37. Sade Iverson, *Little Review,* April 1914. The *Little Review*'s first issue so excited a seventeen-year-old boy named Charles Zwaska that he telephoned to offer his services, arrived half an hour later, was dubbed Caesar, and began a career as the magazine's unpaid office boy that would continue for over a decade.

38. Anderson to Allen Tanner, c. 1970–71, Papers of Janet Flanner and Solita Solano, Library of Congress, Washington, D.C.

39. Anderson to Solita Solano, August 28, 1967, Papers of Janet Flanner and Solita Solano. Anderson continued: "Why would I have wanted to publish a magazine of Art if I hadn't had *standards*??? What were

they? What are they today? They are the standards of a 'touchstone'—which I considered myself to be. To me a touchstone is the kind of person who can prove that, in his case, the despised terms 'I like' or 'I don't like,' are important, authentic, 'right' (De gustibus non est disputandum.)"

40. Anderson, in Hugh Ford, *Four Lives in Paris* (San Francisco: North Point, 1987), p. 277.

41. Anderson, *Thirty Years' War,* p. 44.

42. Margaret Anderson, "To Our Readers," *Little Review* 3 (November 1916): 21.

43. Harry Hansen, *Midwestern Portraits* (New York: Harcourt, Brace, 1923), p. 105.

44. Margaret Anderson, "The Challenge of Emma Goldman," *Little Review* 2 (May 1914): 9.

45. Anderson, *Thirty Years' War,* pp. 73–74.

46. The difference between the two is clear in Goldman's weekend visits to Anderson's beach-side camp. "Looking like a disgruntled tragedy queen dispossessed from her rightful throne," as a friend recalled, Goldman sat on a low stool in heavy clothes and could concentrate only on the swarms of mosquitoes that attacked her, while Anderson's solution to the insect problem was to liberate herself by taking off her clothes and diving into the waters of Lake Michigan. "You see, she's a city Anarchist," Anderson explained, "and not used to real freedom. . . ." (Lawrence Langner, *The Magic Curtain* [New York: E. P. Dutton, 1951], pp. 84–85.)

47. Margaret Anderson, "A Real Magazine," *Little Review* 3 (August 1916): 1.

48. Margaret Anderson, "Knowledge or Prejudice," *Little Review* 1 (June 1914): 32.

49. Margaret Anderson, "Art and Anarchism," *Little Review* 3 (March 1916): 50.

50. Anderson to Solita Solano, January 22, 1964; in Jackson Bryer, "A Trial Track for Racers: Margaret Anderson and *The Little Review*" (Ph.D. diss., University of Wisconsin, 1965), p. 30.

51. Eunice Tietjens, *The World at My Shoulder* (New York: Macmillan, 1938), p. 66.

52. Lowell to Monroe, March 19, 1914, *Poetry* Papers.

53. Henderson to Monroe, January 23, 1918; in Williams, *Harriet Monroe,* p. 138.

54. Anderson, *Thirty Years' War,* p. 61.

55. Ibid.

56. Lowell to Anderson, March 19, 1915, Amy Lowell Collection, Houghton Library, Harvard University, Cambridge.

57. Jane Heap was born November 1, 1884, and died June 18, 1964, in London. She graduated from the Chicago Art Institute in 1905 and entered the Lewis Institute, where she designed costume jewelry. Around 1910 she spent a year studying in Germany and then returned to Chicago. She was a participant in the early years of the Little Theater, where she designed sets and also performed. Always masculine, she insisted on dressing with the men rather than the women.

58. Margaret Anderson, "Conversation," *Prose,* Spring 1971, p. 6.

59. Heap, in Anderson, *Thirty Years' War,* p. 107.

60. Robert McAlmon, *Being Geniuses Together: 1920–1930,* rev., with additional material by Kay Boyle (San Francisco: North Point, 1984), p. 37.

61. Max Ewing to Clara Ewing, letter no. 208, Max Ewing Collection, YCAL. Goldman, in Anderson, *Thirty Years' War,* p. 126.

62. Anderson, "Conversation," p. 11; Margaret Anderson to Solita Solano, Papers of Janet Flanner and Solita Solano.

63. Ibid.

64. Heap, in Anderson, *Thirty Years' War,* p. 108.

65. Margaret Anderson, *Little Review* 3 (September 1916): 1. Frank Lloyd Wright responded, "Your resolve is interesting—but it looks like the end." (Margaret Anderson, ed., *The Little Review Anthology* [New York: Hermitage House, 1953], p. 93.)

66. Anderson, *Thirty Years' War,* pp. 135–36.

67. Bernard Duffey, scholar of the Chicago Renaissance, concluded: "The renaissance was not stolen away from Chicago by New York but by two forces largely ideological. First, the intellectual heart of its being and growth, which had been formed by the militant ideas of personal liberation and personal fulfillment, seemed inadequate to younger writers and, in great part, proved finally unsatisfying to the older men. . . . As the idea of liberation grew less meaningful to the group, and finally even burdensome, its community grew less organic. . . . Second, the intellectual forces of the twenties, though much indebted to the Liberation for a ground-clearing operation, were developing new directions. In 1921, recorded the young Malcolm Cowley, the newer writers were 'not gathered in a solid phalanx behind H. L. Mencken to assault our American puritanism.'" (Bernard Duffey, *The Chicago Renaissance in American Letters: A Critical History* [East Lansing: Michigan State University Press, 1954], p. 159.)

68. Anderson, *Thirty Years' War,* p. 141.

69. Alfred Kreymborg, *Troubadour: An Autobiography* (New York: Boni and Liveright, 1925), p. 220.

70. Ibid., p. 219.

71. Ibid., p. 170.

72. Ibid., pp. 171–72.

73. Walter Arensberg withdrew from the magazine's leadership before the first issue was published, but he offered to pay the printing bills for a year. He got off lightly, for the printer, a Bronx anarchist who called himself Mr. Liberty, refused to make a profit from what he called "redicals." He produced 500 copies each month for $23.

74. Other participants at the *Others* gatherings included the poets Skipwith and Kathleen Cannell and Horace Holley, and the painters William and Marguerite Zorach.

75. Kreymborg, *Troubadour,* p. 187.

76. Ibid.

77. Ibid., pp. 238–39.

78. *The Autobiography of William Carlos Williams* (New York: Random House, 1951), p. 146.

79. Kreymborg, *Troubadour,* p. 241.

80. "Like most every other cultural activity of the new soil," Kreymborg observed, "the intercourse of these people was a novel experience. They had to approach it warily and grow up to the art of conversation with a painstaking, self-conscious *tempo* similar to their development as artists." (Kreymborg, *Troubadour,* p. 241.)

81. William Carlos Williams, letter to the *Egoist* 3 (November 1915): 137.

82. These comments are from Carolyn Burke, "The New Poetry and the New Woman," in Diane Middlebrook and Marilyn Yalom, eds., *Coming to Light: American Women Poets in the Twentieth Century* (Ann Arbor: University of Michigan Press, 1985); and Kreymborg, *Troubadour,* p. 235.

83. Monroe, in Roger L. Conover, "Introduction," in Mina Loy, *The Last Lunar Baedeker,* ed. Roger L. Conover (Highlands, N.C.: Jargon Society, 1982), pp. xxxiv–xxxv.

84. Lowell to Aldington, June 4, 1915; in S. Foster Damon, *Amy Lowell: A Chronicle with Extracts from Her Correspondence* (Boston: Houghton Mifflin, 1935), p. 311.

85. Louis Untermeyer, *American Poetry since 1900* (New York: Henry Holt, 1923), p. 183.

86. Monroe to Kreymborg, July 2, 1915; in Williams, *Harriet Monroe,* p. 150.

87. Aldington to Lowell, November 29, 1915, Lowell Collection. On first hearing about *Others,* Monroe wrote to Kreymborg, "Please make it very clear that we were the first in the field and the beginning of the present Renaissance." (Monroe to Kreymborg, July 2, 1915, *Poetry* Papers.) In sharp contrast to Monroe's growing sense of *Poetry*'s historical position, Kreymborg responded modestly: "It is good to be alive. That is all. We are not the big fishes." (Kreymborg to Monroe, July 6, 1915, *Poetry* Papers.)

88. William Carlos Williams edited a "Competitive Number" in July 1916 and July 1919; Maxwell Bodenheim edited a Chicago number in August 1916; Helen Hoyt edited a Women's number in September 1916; William Saphier edited numbers in December 1917 and February 1918; Lola Ridge edited an issue in December 1918.

89. Pound to Iris Barry, June 1916; in *Letters of Ezra Pound,* p. 82.

90. Williams, letter to the *Egoist* 3 (November 1915): 137.

91. Moore to Monroe, June 6, 1915; in Williams, *Harriet Monroe,* p. 155.

92. Anderson, ed., *Little Review Anthology,* p. 187.

93. *Autobiography of William Carlos Williams,* p. 135.

94. For example, Pound's appraisal: "She [Harriet Monroe] has more sense than any other American editor, save Kreymborg (who has no sense whatever, but excellent intentions)." (Pound to Alice Corbin Henderson, May 5, 1916, Henderson Collection.) Also: "Kreymborg (of no importance but as a symptom)." (Pound to Margaret Anderson, June 22, 1917; in *Pound / The Little Review: The Letters of Ezra Pound to Margaret Anderson: The Little Review Correspondence,* ed. Thomas L. Scott and Melvin J. Friedman (New York: New Directions, 1988), p. 80.

95. Pound to Henderson, January 29, 1916, Henderson Collection.

96. A third poet, a recent convert named Elijah Hay (Marjory Allen Seiffert), also published poems in this issue.

97. Witter Bynner, in William Jay Smith, *The Spectra Hoax* (Middletown, Conn.: Wesleyan University Press, 1961), p. 18.

98. Eliot, in C. David Heymann, *American Aristocracy: The Lives and Times of James Russell, Amy, and Robert Lowell* (New York: Dodd, Mead, 1980), p. 236.

99. Amy Lowell, *Men, Women and Ghosts* (Boston: Houghton Mifflin, 1916), p. 330.

100. Lowell to Carlotta Lowell, July 18, 1919; in Damon, *Amy Lowell,* p. 384.

101. Lowell, in Damon, ibid., p. 393.

102. Lowell to Pound, November 3, 1914; ibid., p. 274.

103. Lowell in Heymann, *American Aristocracy,* p. 236.

104. Eleven years older than Lowell, Ada Dwyer (Mrs. Harold Russell) was tall, brunette, and serene. She had conducted a distinguished career as a character actress and was particularly popular in the title role of *Mrs. Wiggs of the Cabbage Patch,* which she toured around the world. She and Lowell met on May 12, 1912, and immediately took to one another; Dwyer moved into Sevenels about 1914.

105. Although it is not conclusively known whether Lowell and Russell were lovers, their relationship had the domestic rhythms, emotions, and devotion of a marriage. This sort of domestic partnership between women was sufficiently common to have a name, the "Boston marriage."

106. Van Wyck Brooks, *New England: Indian Summer, 1865–1915* (New York: E. P. Dutton, 1940), p. 533.

107. Sandburg and unidentified guest, in Damon, *Amy Lowell,* pp. 265, 267.

108. Pound's *Catholic Anthology,* published by Elkin Mathews in November 1915 as a sort of reply to Lowell's Imagist anthologies, included T. S. Eliot's first poem to be published in a book, plus poems by Pound, Yeats, Williams, and (as if to prove its catholicity) Monroe.

109. Lowell, in Damon, *Amy Lowell,* pp. 339–40.

110. Pound to Henderson, January 20, 1914, Henderson Collection.

111. Charles Norman, *Ezra Pound* (New York: Macmillan, 1960), p. 155.

112. The advertising blurb for Lowell's book read: "Of the poets who to-day are doing the interesting and original work, there is no more striking and unique figure than Amy Lowell. The foremost member of the 'Imagists'—a group of poets that includes William Butler Yeats, Ezra Pound, Ford Madox Hueffer—she has won wide recognition for her writing in new and free forms of poetical expression."

113. Pound to Henderson, December 21, 1914, Henderson Collection.

114. Pound and Flint, in Noel Stock, *The Life of Ezra Pound,* expanded ed. (San Francisco: North Point, 1982), p. 179.

115. Richard Aldington, *Life for Life's Sake* (New York: Viking, 1941), p. 105.

116. Stock, *Ezra Pound,* p. 162.

117. Pound's faculty comprised a modern elite of all the arts: Henri Gaudier-Brzeska teaching sculpture, Wyndham Lewis teaching painting, Arnold Dolmetsch teaching music, Pound teaching poetry, and Alvin Langdon Coburn teaching photography.

118. The announcement first appeared in the *Egoist* 1 (November 2, 1914).

119. Joyce, in Stock, *Ezra Pound,* p. 210.

120. T. S. Eliot, "Ezra Pound," in Walter Sutton, ed., *Ezra Pound: A Collection of Essays* (Englewood Cliffs, N.J.: Prentice Hall, 1963), pp. 18–19.

121. Ezra Pound, "Affirmation," *New Age* 16 (January 21, 1915): 312.

122. Quinn to Pound, February 25, 1915; in B. L. Reid, *"The Man from New York": John Quinn and His Friends* (New York: Oxford University Press, 1968), p. 198.

123. Pound to Quinn, March 8, 1915; in *Letters of Ezra Pound,* p. 54.

124. Ibid., Pound to Quinn, March 18, 1916; in Reid, *John Quinn,* p. 248.

125. Although the self-made Quinn displayed confidence in all his practical and legal decisions, he depended on others in the area he valued most, the arts. His advisors included Arthur B. Davies, Marcel Duchamp, James Huneker, Augustus John, Walt Kuhn, Walter Pach (beginning in 1915), Ezra Pound (beginning in 1915), and Henri-Pierre Roché (beginning in 1917).

126. Pound to Quinn, October 13, 1915, Quinn Collection.

127. Pound to Quinn, August 26, 1915, Quinn Collection. On October 13, 1915, Pound suggested to Quinn "a bold plunge and hoisting the banner 'No woman shall be allowed to write for this magazine.' It would be a risk. It would cause outcry, boycott, etc. . . . BUT most of the ills of american magazines . . . are (or were) due to women. Young women, old women (male and female) both those who write and those who are catered for. Sugar teat optimism, etc." (Pound to Quinn, October 13, 1915, Quinn Collection.)

128. Ibid.

129. T. S. Eliot's *Poems* (1920), Ezra Pound's *Lustra* (1917).

130. Ezra Pound, "The Reader-Critic," *Little Review* 3 (April 1916): 36.

131. Pound to Anderson, c. January 1917; in *Letters of Ezra Pound*, pp. 106–7.

132. Pound to Anderson, September 13, 1917; in Scott and Friedman, eds., *Pound / The Little Review*, p. 124.

APRIL 1917: WAR BEGINS AND AN ERA ENDS
(pages 312–28)

1. Royal Cortissoz, *New York Tribune*, April 15, 1917.

2. Quinn, draft of a circular for the Society of Independents, Société Anonyme Archives, YCAL.

3. Henry McBride, while admiring the new society's attempts at complete even-handedness, concluded that "perfect justice, I fear, is not for this vale of tears." He suggested that some artists should change their names to achieve sympathetic groupings of paintings: Jules De Pascin, John De Marin, Charles Demuth, Abraham De Walkowitz, Arthur B. De Davies, Samuel De Halpert; Rockwell Von Kent, Walt Von Kuhn, Bryson Von Burroughs, Ben Von Benn, Man Von Ray, and William Von Zorach; Robert O'Henri, George O'Bellows, Randal O'Davies, Leon O'Kroll, Childe O'Hassam. (Henry McBride, *New York Sun*, April 8, 1917.)

4. Robert Henri, "The 'Big Exhibition,' the Artist and the Public," *Touchstone* 1 (June 1917): 175.

5. Gabriel Buffet-Picabia, "Arthur Cravan and American Dada," in Robert Motherwell, ed., *The Dada Painters and Poets: An Anthology*, 2d ed. (Cambridge: Harvard University Press, Belknap Press, 1989), p. 13.

6. Arensberg, in Beatrice Wood, *I Shock Myself*, ed. Lindsay Smith (Ojai, Calif.: Dillingham Press, 1985), p. 29.

7. Rockwell Kent, *It's Me, O Lord: The Autobiography of Rockwell Kent* (New York: Dodd, Mead, 1955), p. 316.

8. Ibid.

9. Glackens, in "His Art Too Crude for Independents," *New York Herald*, April 14, 1917, p. 6. In addition, a portrait of the crown prince of Germany painted by Madison Munsdorf of Boston was lost before the exhibition's opening and may have been the victim of de facto censorship.

10. Dreier to Glackens, April 26, 1917, Société Anonyme Archives.

11. Henry McBride, *New York Sun*, April 15, 1917; in Henry McBride, *The Flow of Art: Essays and Criticism of Henry McBride*, ed. Daniel Catton Rich (New York: Atheneum, 1975), p. 122.

12. Ibid.

13. Louise Varèse, interview with Francis Naumann, May 27, 1978; in Francis Naumann, "The Big Show: The First Exhibition of the Society of Independent Artists, Part II," *Artforum* 18 (April 1979): 50.

14. Quinn to Pound, May 3, 1917, John Quinn Memorial Collection, Rare Books and Manuscripts Division, NYPL.

15. De Zayas, in McBride, *Flow of Art*, p. 124.

16. Wood, in Francis Naumann, "The Big Show: The First Exhibition of the Society of Independents, Part I," *Artforum* 18 (February 1979): 36.

17. McBride, *Flow of Art*, pp. 123–24.

18. Ibid., p. 123.

19. Gabrielle Buffet-Picabia, "Arthur Cravan and American Dada," in Motherwell, ed., *Dada Painters and Poets*, p. 15.

20. *New York Sun*, April 20, 1917.

21. Duchamp, in Motherwell, ed., *Dada Painters and Poets*, p. 16.

22. Demuth to McBride, c. April 10–14, 1917; in William Camfield, *Marcel Duchamp/Fountain* (Houston: Houston Fine Art Press, 1989), p. 29.

23. Van Vechten to Stein, incorrectly dated April 5, 1917; in *Letters of Carl Van Vechten*, ed. Bruce Kellner (New Haven, Conn.: Yale University Press, 1987), p. 24.

24. It remains unclear who wrote this statement: although it is frequently attributed to Duchamp, he said it was a creation of the editorial board; Beatrice Wood has said that she wrote it.

25. Wood, *I Shock Myself*, p. 32.

26. Henri-Pierre Roché, *Victor*, trans. Allan Jones.

27. Mina Loy, "Colossus," ed. Roger L. Conover, in Rudolf E. Kuenzli, ed., *New York Dada* (New York: Willis Locker and Owens, 1986), p. 105.

28. Mina Loy, introduction to "O Marcel—Otherwise I Also Have Been to Louise's," *View* 5 (March 1945): 51.

29. Henri-Pierre Roché, "Souvenirs," in Robert Lebel, ed., *Marcel Duchamp*, trans. George Heard Hamilton (New York: Paragraphic Books, 1959), p. 87.

30. Wood, *I Shock Myself*, p. 33.

31. Floyd Dell, *Love in Greenwich Village* (New York: George H. Doran, 1926), p. 27.

32. John Reed, "Whose War?" *Masses* 9 (April 1917): 11.

33. The law meanwhile looked the other way when vigilantes attacked strikers, when race rioters killed thirty blacks in Saint Louis, when Boston's Socialist Party headquarters was wrecked by a mob of sailors and soldiers. "In America law is merely the instrument for good or evil of the most powerful interests," John Reed concluded. (John Reed, "One Solid Month of Liberty," *Masses* 9 [September 1917]: 6.)

34. Van Vechten to Stein, incorrectly dated April 5, 1917; in *Letters of Carl Van Vechten*, pp. 23–24.

35. John Reed, *New York Mail*, June 13, 1917; in Robert Rosenstone, *Romantic Revolutionary: A Biography of John Reed* (New York: Alfred A. Knopf, 1975), p. 267.

36. Jane Heap, "Push-Face," *Little Review* 4 (June 1917): 7.

37. Art Young, *Art Young: His Life and Times* (New York: Sheridan House, 1939), p. 351.

38. The *Masses* spawned two successors: the *Liberator* was founded in February 1918 and maintained the *Masses*'s combination of politics and art. Unlike its predecessor, it was conventionally edited by a small paid staff (Max and Crystal Eastman were editors, Floyd Dell was managing editor) and provided the chief source in America for news of Russia. It merged with the *Worker's Monthly* (the organ of the Communist Worker's Party) in 1924. In 1926 a new generation (Joseph Freeman, Hugo Gellert, and Mike Gold) founded the *New Masses*, which increasingly hewed to the doctrinal line of the Communist Party.

39. *New York Times*, July 25, 1918, p. 11.

40. Lowell to John Gould Fletcher, March 29, 1917; in S. Foster Damon, *Amy Lowell: A Chronicle with Extracts from Her Correspondence* (Boston: Houghton Mifflin, 1935), p. 404.

41. H.D. to Lowell, September 19, 1917; H.D. Collection, YCAL.

42. "If I can get Eliot in as an editor on *The Egoist* it will have several tactical advantages, and no drawbacks that I can see," Pound wrote to John Quinn. "He has not yet made enemies, and knows a number of people in the press here." (May 23, 1917, Quinn Collection.)

43. Henderson to Monroe, June 9, 1917, Alice Corbin Henderson Collection, HRHRC.

44. Lowell, in Damon, *Amy Lowell*, p. 436.

45. Harriet Monroe, "Mea Culpa," *Poetry* 20 (September 1922): 323.

46. Ezra Pound, "Small Magazines," *English Journal* 19 (November 1930).

47. Monroe, in Eunice Tietjens, *The World at My Shoulder* (New York: Macmillan, 1938), p. 36.

48. Monroe to unknown correspondent, September 4, 1936; in *Poetry* 36 (December 1936): 167.

49. Juliet Gleizes, in William Camfield, *Francis Picabia: His Art, Life and Times* (Princeton, N.J.: Princeton University Press, 1979), p. 102.

50. Picabia, *391* 5 (June 1917): 8.

51. Ettie Stettheimer, journal entry, February 3, 1919, Stettheimer Collection, YCAL. Ettie's disillusion was intensified by encountering Randolph Bourne, the critic most admiring of her first novel, and finding him a "hideous, hideous deformed dwarf."

52. Arensberg to Duchamp, May 23, 1930; in Anne d'Harnoncourt, "A. E. Gallatin and the Arensbergs: Pioneer Collectors of Twentieth-Century Art," *Apollo* 149 (July 1974): 54.

53. Beatrice Wood, interview with author, Ojai, California, August 15, 1986.

54. John Quinn bought a small Brancusi sculpture and a portrait by Henri Rousseau; Katherine Dreier paid two thousand dollars for the *Large Glass*. The Arensbergs sold the Duchamp glass largely out of fear that it would break in transit to California; it broke nevertheless, following its exhibition in the Société Anonyme's Brooklyn Exhibition (1926). When the major part of the Arensberg collection was given to the Philadelphia Museum of Art, it contained more than a thousand artworks, approximately one-third modern and two-thirds "primitive" art. The modern collection included works by Paul Cézanne (5), Salvador Dali (2), Duchamp (approximately 50), Max Ernst (3), Wassily Kandinsky (15), Paul Klee (19), Henri Matisse (5), Joan Miró (9), Henri Rousseau (4), Morton Schamberg (4), and Charles Sheeler (10). These numbers are from Naomi Sawelson-Gorse, who has written about the disposition of the Arensberg collection, "'For Want of a Nail': The Disposition of the Louise and Walter Arensberg Collection" (M.A. thesis, University of California, Riverside, 1987).

55. Ettie Stettheimer, journal entry, July 25, 1917, Stettheimer Collection.

56. Ibid.

57. Ibid.

58. Florine Stettheimer, in Parker Tyler, *Florine Stettheimer: A Life in Art* (New York: Farrar, Straus, 1963), p. 69. After *La Fête à Duchamp* was exhibited in the 1918 Independents exhibition, Henry McBride wrote, "The more I think of it, the more miffed I am that I wasn't asked to that party." (Henry McBride, *New York Sun*, April 28, 1918.)

AFTERMATH: THE AVANT-GARDE MOVES ON (pages 329–57)

1. Floyd Dell, *Homecoming: An Autobiography* (New York: Farrar and Rinehart, 1933), p. 325.

2. Ibid., p. 334.

3. Ibid., p. 281.

4. Stieglitz, in Dorothy Norman, "Introducing *291*," *291*, nos. 1–2 (1915–16) (reprint, New York: Arno, 1972), n.p.

5. Stieglitz to Anne Brigman, Alfred Stieglitz Collection, YCAL.

6. O'Keeffe to Anita Pollitzer, January 1916; in Roxana Robinson, *Georgia O'Keeffe* (New York: Harper and Row, 1989), p. 132.

7. Stieglitz to Paul Strand, May 17, 1918; ibid., p. 199.

8. Stieglitz to Elizabeth Stieglitz Davidson, June 16, 1918; ibid., pp. 203–4.

9. Stieglitz, ibid., p. 206; O'Keeffe, introduction to Alfred Stieglitz, *Georgia O'Keeffe, A Portrait* (New York: Metropolitan Museum of Art, 1978), n.p.

10. Hutchins Hapgood, *A Victorian in the Modern World* (New York: Harcourt, Brace, 1939), p. 339.

11. McBride to F. Stettheimer, August 20, 1932, Stettheimer Collection, YCAL.

12. Reed to Bryant, May 18, 1917; in Virginia Gardner, *"Friend and Lover": The Life of Louise Bryant* (New York: Horizon, 1982), p. 64.

13. Reed to Bryant, July 10, 1917; in Robert Rosenstone, *Romantic Revolutionary: A Biography of John Reed* (New York: Alfred A. Knopf, 1975), p. 270.

14. John Reed, "One Solid Month of Liberty," *Masses* 9 (September 1917): 6.

15. The Bell Syndicate sponsored Bryant, but Reed's reputation as a leftist made him untouchable, so Max Eastman solicited two thousand dollars from supporters of the *Masses* to send Reed to Russia as the magazine's correspondent.

16. John Reed, "News from France," *Masses,* October 1917; in Rosenstone, *Romantic Revolutionary,* p. 282.

17. Bryant had actually spent only four months in Russia; her book's title is only one example of her loose handling of time. As she grew older she shed years, admitting to only twenty-six of her thirty-one years on her marriage certificate and claiming only forty-one at the time of her death, when she was, in fact, forty-nine.

18. Two of O'Neill's biographers, Louis Sheaffer and Doris Alexander, believe that Bryant had an abortion after becoming pregnant by O'Neill during a period when Reed's kidney ailment prevented sexual intercourse.

19. Between Louise Bryant and Agnes Boulton, O'Neill had brief affairs with the Provincetown Players' director, Nina Moise, the restaurateur Christine Ell, and the writer Dorothy Day.

20. Bryant to Margaret Reed; in Barbara Gelb, *So Short a Time: A Biography of John Reed and Louise Bryant* (New York: W. W. Norton, 1973), p. 276.

21. Gardner, *Louise Bryant,* p. 207.

22. Mina Loy, "Colossus," p. 65 of original ms., collection of Mrs. Herbert Bayer.

23. Ibid., p. 6.

24. Loy, "Colossus," ed. Roger L. Conover, in Rudolf E. Kuenzli, ed., *New York Dada* (New York: Willis Locker and Owens, 1986), p. 107.

25. Ibid., p. 7.

26. Ibid., p. 57.

27. Mina Loy, "Arthur Cravan Is Alive!" in Mina Loy, *The Last Lunar Baedeker,* ed. Roger L. Conover (Highlands, N.C.: Jargon Society, 1982), p. 321.

28. Cravan to Loy, December 1918; in Roger L. Conover, "Introduction," in Loy, *Last Lunar Baedeker,* p. lviii.

29. Cravan, in Mina Loy, "Colossus," in Kuenzli, ed., *New York Dada,* p. 119.

30. Loy, ibid., p. 81.

31. Ibid., p. 58.

32. Loy, in *Little Review,* 1929; in Margaret Anderson, ed., *The Little Review Anthology* (New York: Hermitage House, 1953), p. 368.

33. Margaret Anderson, *My Thirty Years' War* (New York: Covici-Friede, 1930), p. 177.

34. *The Autobiography of William Carlos Williams* (New York: Random House, 1951), p. 166.

35. Ibid., p. 169.

36. Ibid.

37. Williams, in Paul Mariani, *William Carlos Williams: A New World Naked* (New York: McGraw-Hill, 1981), p. 163.

38. *Autobiography of William Carlos Williams,* p. 169.

39. George Biddle, *An American Artist's Story* (Boston: Little, Brown, 1939).

40. Abbott, in Robert Reiss, "'My Baroness': Elsa von Freytag-Loringhoven," in Kuenzli, ed., *New York Dada,* p. 96.

41. Aldington, in Barbara Guest, *Herself Defined: The Poet H.D. and Her World* (Garden City, N.Y.: Doubleday, 1984), p. 99.

42. This relationship is traced in Janice Robinson, *H.D.: The Life and Work of an American Poet* (Boston: Houghton Mifflin, 1982).

43. When H.D. informed Lawrence that she was pregnant, he never again wrote to her.

44. Bryher, *The Heart to Artemis: A Writer's Memoirs* (New York: Harcourt, Brace, 1962), pp. 152–53.

45. Bryher, *Two Selves* (Paris: Contact, 1923), p. 126.

46. H.D. to John Cournos, in Guest, *Herself Defined,* p. 106.

47. H.D. [Hilda Doolittle], *End to Torment,* ed. Norman Holmes Pearson and Michael King (New York: New Directions, 1979), p. 8.

48. Her husbands were the writer Robert McAlmon and the film aficionado Kenneth MacPherson; both were bisexual, both alcoholic.

49. Mabel Dodge Luhan, *The Edge of Taos Desert: An Escape to Reality,* vol. 4 of *Intimate Memories* (New York: Harcourt, Brace, 1937), p. 32.

50. Ibid., p. 62.

51. Ibid., p. 63.

52. Ibid., p. 219.

53. Ibid., pp. 221, 298.

54. Dodge, in Elida Sims, *New York Times Book Review*, December 25, 1921; Mabel Dodge Luhan, "A Bridge between Cultures," *Theater Arts Monthly* 9 (1925): 297.

55. William Carlos Williams, "Belly Music," *Others* 5 (July 1919): 28.

56. The guarantors were Quinn's friends James Byrne, Otto Kahn, and Max Pam. Each of them, and Quinn, contributed four hundred dollars at the beginning of 1918. Kahn, one of the key patrons of the era (he also supported the Metropolitan Opera, the American tour of Sergei Diaghilev's Ballets Russes, and the Provincetown Players), appended to his check a note that he would have contributed six hundred dollars but had deducted two hundred as a penalty for the badness of the magazine's American writers.

57. Quinn to Pound, May 3, 1917, John Quinn Memorial Collection, Rare Books and Manuscripts Division, NYPL.

58. Quinn to Anderson, June 4, 1917, Quinn Collection.

59. Pound to Anderson, May 17, 1917; in B. L. Reid, *"The Man from New York": John Quinn and His Friends* (New York: Oxford University Press, 1968), p. 446.

60. Letter from an "Old Reader," *Little Review* 4 (September 1917): 31.

61. Jane Heap, "The Reader-Critic," *Little Review*, September 1917; in Anderson, ed., *Little Review Anthology*, p. 272.

62. Alice Corbin Henderson to Harriet Monroe, December 12, 1917, Alice Corbin Henderson Collection, HRHRC. In August 1917 Pound wanted to change it to "The Magazine That is Read by 'Those Who Write the Others.'"

63. Anderson, *My Thirty Years' War*, p. 175.

64. Allen Tanner, in Hugh Ford, *Four Lives in Paris* (San Francisco: North Point, 1987), p. 247.

65. Janet Flanner, ibid., p. 275.

66. Quinn to Pound, March 14, 1918, Quinn Collection.

67. Quinn to Pound, December 2, 1917, Quinn Collection.

68. Quinn to Walt Kuhn, October 4, 1920; in Reid, *Man from New York*, p. 446.

69. Quinn to Pound, October 21, 1920, Quinn Collection.

70. Anderson to Pound, November 1920; in Jackson Bryer, "A Trial Track for Racers: Margaret Anderson and *The Little Review*" (Ph.D. diss., University of Wisconsin, 1965).

71. Quinn to Pound, October 21, 1920, Quinn Collection.

72. Anderson to Allen Tanner; in Ford, *Four Lives in Paris*, p. 249.

73. Anderson, *Thirty Years' War*, p. 230.

74. Ibid., p. 239.

75. Margaret Anderson, *The Fiery Fountains* (New York: Hermitage House, 1951), p. 6.

76. Cocteau, in Anderson, *Fiery Fountains*, p. 6. Leblanc had begun her relationship with Maeterlinck at the age of eighteen, when she gave up her position with the Opéra Comique to pursue Maeterlinck, having been inspired by one of his essays. "I had discerned a tendency of mind, a vision, ideas, and even a being whose secret inner existence corresponded to my own," she recalled. "I had staked my life on a purely spiritual intention." (Leblanc, in Ford, *Four Lives in Paris*, p. 251.)

77. Anderson, *Fiery Fountains*, p. 9.

78. Ibid., p. 10.

79. Jane Heap, "Lost: A Renaissance," *Little Review*, May 1929; in Anderson, ed., *Little Review Anthology*, p. 352.

80. *Nation*, May 3, 1919; in Louis Sheaffer, *O'Neill: Son and Playwright* (Boston: Little, Brown, 1968), p. 452.

81. The stage was twelve feet wide and twenty-six feet deep, about the same width as the previous stage and nearly twice as deep.

82. jh [Jane Heap], "Provincetown Theater," *Little Review* 6 (May 1919): 63.

83. Floyd Dell, *Homecoming: An Autobiography* (New York: Farrar and Rinehart, 1933), p. 267.

84. Cook, in Susan Glaspell, *The Road to the Temple* (New York: Frederick A. Stokes, 1927), p. 287.

85. Ibid.

86. Cook, in Robert Karoly Sarlos, *Jig Cook and the Provincetown Players: Theatre in Ferment* (Amherst: University of Massachusetts Press, 1982), p. 206.

87. Cook, in Glaspell, *Road to the Temple*, p. 287.

88. Kenton, in Arthur and Barbara Gelb, *O'Neill* (New York: Harper and Row, 1962), p. 444.

89. Kenton, in Sheaffer, *O'Neill*, p. 31.

90. Kenton, ibid., p. 33. Theaters at that point were still segregated, and black actors had been cast in leading roles only in black stock companies. One faction of the Players preferred a white actor in blackface, but it was overridden.

91. George Cram Cook, "The Emperor Jones," George Cram Cook Collection, Henry W. Berg and Albert A. Berg Collection, NYPL.

92. Cook, in Glaspell, *Road to the Temple*, p. 309.

93. Cook, in Floyd Dell, "A Seer in Iowa," in George Cram Cook, *Greek Coins* (New York: George H. Doran Company, 1925), p. 16.

94. Cook, in Glaspell, *Road to the Temple*, p. 366.

95. Cook, ibid., p. 311.

96. Glaspell, ibid., p. 388.

97. Ibid., p. 316.

98. Cook to Nilla Cook; ibid., p. 376.

99. Susan Glaspell, "Memorial," Susan Glaspell Collection, Henry W. Berg and Albert A. Berg Collection, NYPL.

100. Collecting modern art was accorded cultural respectability in May 1921, when the Metropolitan Museum of Art staged its first exhibition of Post-Impressionist art, with loans from the collections of the Arensbergs, Katherine Dreier, Agnes and Eugene Meyer, and John Quinn.

101. Quinn to Jessie Conrad, April 16, 1918; in Reid, *Man from New York*, p. 336.

102. Quinn's support of French art inspired his election to the French Legion of Honor (September 1919), and Quinn considered giving his collection to France, where he thought it would be understood more clearly than in America.

103. Quinn to Roché, September 17, 1919; in Judith Zilczer, *"The Noble Buyer": John Quinn, Patron of the Avant-Garde* (Washington, D.C.: Smithsonian Institution Press, 1978), p. 50. Roché played his most instrumental role in the American avant-garde as a collectors' art scout, serving as the European middleman for the Société Anonyme, the Arensbergs, and especially for Quinn. "I have the impression of acting like a dog trying to 'faire lever' [raise] some big birds in front of you," Roché wrote to Quinn, "and you shoot them or not, as pleases you." (Roché to Quinn, December 2, 1920; in Reid, *Man from New York*, p. 469.) Among the artists that Roché suggested and Quinn rejected were Marc Chagall, Giorgio de Chirico, Kees van Dongen, Paul Klee, Jacques Lipchitz, and Amedeo Modigliani. After Roché found works to recommend, Man Ray would photograph them, and from this evidence Quinn would make his decisions.

104. Quinn to Jeanne Robert Foster, August 29, 1921; in Judith Zilczer, *Noble Buyer*, p. 48.

105. Jeanne Robert Foster, diary entry, July 5, 1924; in Reid, *Man from New York*, p. 629. Pound wrote to Quinn that he would probably die with his checkbook in hand and would have a telephone installed in his coffin so his dictation to the office would not be interrupted.

106. Foster to Aline Saarinen, May 20, 1957; in Zilczer, *Noble Buyer*, p. 39.

107. Henry McBride, "The Quinn Collection," *Dial* 80 (March 1926); in Henry McBride, *The Flow of Art: Essays and Criticism of Henry McBride*, ed. Daniel Catton Rich (New York: Atheneum, 1975), p. 215.

108. Untitled Société Anonyme pamphlet, Société Anonyme Archives, YCAL.

109. Dreier to McBride, December 3, 1925, Société Anonyme Archives.

110. Goodrich, "A Museum of Modern Art," *Nation* 129 (December 4, 1929): 664.

111. Joseph Freeman, "Greenwich Village Types," *New Masses* 8 (May 1933): 9.

SOURCES FOR MARGINAL QUOTATIONS

The following sources are for quotations in the side columns and for those set off by rules in the text column. For abbreviations, see list of frequently cited collections, p. 358.

Page 13. Harriet Monroe, "Cantata," read at the dedication of Chicago's Auditorium Building, December 1889; in Harriet Monroe, *Valeria and Other Poems* (Chicago: McClurg, 1892), p. 213.

Page 14. Unidentified clipping, the Little Room Papers, NL.

Page 21. Dale Kramer, *The Chicago Renaissance* (New York: Appleton-Century, 1966), p. 220.

Page 23. Margaret Anderson, *My Thirty Years' War* (New York: Covici-Friede, 1930), p. 33.

Page 26. Harriet Monroe, *A Poet's Life* (New York: Macmillan, 1938), pp. 202–3.

Page 30. *Letters of Wallace Stevens*, ed. Holly Stevens (New York: Alfred A. Knopf, 1966), p. 44.

Page 31. Van Wyck Brooks, *New England: Indian Summer, 1865–1915* (New York: E. P. Dutton, 1940), p. 537.

Page 36. Calvin Tomkins, *Living Well Is the Best Revenge* (New York: Viking, 1971), p. 29.

Page 45. Judith Katy Zilczer, "The Aesthetic Struggle in America, 1913–1918: Abstract Art and Theory in the Stieglitz Circle" (Ph.D. diss., University of Delaware, 1975).

Page 49. Hutchins Hapgood, *A Victorian in the Modern World* (New York: Harcourt, Brace, 1939), p. 175.

Page 50. Gertrude Stein, *The Geographical History of America* (New York: Random House, 1936), p. 81.

Page 54. John Tytell, *Ezra Pound: The Solitary Volcano* (New York: Anchor, 1987), p. 72.

Page 55. Humphrey Carpenter, *A Serious Character: The Life of Ezra Pound* (Boston: Houghton Mifflin, 1988), p. 106.

Page 57. Tytell, *Ezra Pound,* p. 68.

Page 66. Ezra Pound, "Patria Mia," *New Age,* September 12, 1912.

Page 83. Van Wyck Brooks, *John Sloan: A Painter's Life* (New York: E. P. Dutton, 1955), p. 72.

Page 85. Jacques-Emile Blanche, *Portraits of a Lifetime,* trans. and ed. Walter Clement (London: J. M. Dent and Sons, 1937), p. 271.

Page 88. *Poetry* Papers.

Page 95. Mina Loy, *The Last Lunar Baedeker,* ed. Roger L. Conover (Highlands, N.C.: Jargon Society, 1982), p. 311.

Page 122, top. Jerrold Seigel, *Bohemian Paris: Culture, Politics, and the Boundaries of Bourgeois Life, 1830–1930* (New York: Viking Penguin, 1986), p. 3.

Page 122, bottom. Hutchins Hapgood, "The New Bohemia," c. 1913, Hutchins Hapgood Collection, YCAL.

Page 123. Adapted from Caroline Ware, *Greenwich Village, 1920–1930: A Comment on American Civilization in the Post-War Years* (Boston: Houghton Mifflin, 1935).

Page 127. C. Grand Pierre, ed., *Greenwich Village in Poetry* (New York: Greenwich Village News Weekly, 1932), n.p. Bobby Edwards is most frequently cited as the author of this song, but Clement Wood, Albert and Charles Boni, and others are also credited with having written some of the verses.

Page 128. Susan Glaspell, *The Road to the Temple* (New York: Frederick A. Stokes, 1927), p. 234.

Page 130. Mabel Dodge Luhan, *Movers and Shakers,* volume 3 of *Intimate Memories* (New York: Harcourt, Brace, 1936), p. 81.

Page 131, top. Mabel Dodge, "The Mirror," *Camera Work* 47 (July 1914): 9.

Page 131, bottom. Carl Van Vechten, *Peter Whiffle: His Life and Works* (New York: Alfred A. Knopf, 1922), p. 126.

Page 135. Allen Churchill, *The Improper Bohemians: The Re-Creation of Greenwich Village in Its Heyday* (New York: E. P. Dutton, 1959), p. 43.

Page 136. Robert E. Humphrey, *Children of Fantasy: The First Rebels of Greenwich Village* (New York: John Wiley and Sons, 1978), p. 31.

Page 137. Dame Rogue [Louise Norton], *Rogue,* April 1, 1915, p. 17.

Page 140. Max Eastman, *Enjoyment of Living* (New York: Harper and Brothers, 1948), p. 449.

Page 150. Lois Palken Rudnick, *Mabel Dodge Luhan: New Woman, New Worlds* (Albuquerque: University of New Mexico Press, 1984), pp. 94–95.

Page 156. Dame Rogue [Louise Norton], "Philosophical Fashions," *Rogue,* September 15, 1915, p. 13.

Page 157. Pierre, ed., *Greenwich Village in Poetry,* n.p.

Page 158, top. Dame Rogue [Louise Norton], *Rogue,* April 1, 1915, p. 17.

Page 158, bottom. Dell, "Feminism for Men," *Masses* 5 (July 1914): 19.

Page 160. Arturo Giovannitti, "What I Think of *The Masses,*" *Masses* 8 (July 1916): 5.

Page 162. Brooks, *John Sloan,* p. 83.

Page 164. Louis Untermeyer, *From Another World* (New York: Harcourt, Brace, 1939), pp. 48–49.

Page 168. Information based on Milton Brown, *The Story of the Armory Show* (New York: Abbeville, 1988), passim.

Page 169. Donald Gallup, ed., *The Flowers of Friendship: Letters Written to Gertrude Stein* (New York: Alfred A. Knopf, 1953), p. 70.

Page 170, top. Theodore Roosevelt, "A Layman's View of an Art Exhibition," *Outlook* 103 (March 29, 1913): 719.

Page 172. Gallup, ed., *Flowers of Friendship,* pp. 70–71.

Page 176. Harriet Monroe, *Chicago Sunday Tribune,* April 6, 1913.

Page 178. Mary Mills Lyall, *The Cubies' ABC* (New York: G. P. Putnam's Sons, 1913).

Page 180. William Camfield, *Francis Picabia: His Art, Life and Times* (Princeton, N.J.: Princeton University Press, 1979), p. xv.

Page 184. Edward Burns, ed., *The Letters of Gertrude Stein and Carl Van Vechten, 1913–1946* (New York: Columbia University Press, 1986), p. 35.

Page 185. Gertrude Stein Collection, YCAL.

Page 188. *The Selected Letters of William Carlos Williams,* ed. John C. Thirlwall (New York: McDowell, Oblensky, 1957), p. 41.

Page 190. *Poetry* Papers.

Page 195. Alice Corbin Henderson Collection, HRHRC.

Page 198. *Poetry* Papers.

Page 212. Rudnick, *Mabel Dodge Luhan,* p. 258.

Page 213. Hapgood, *Victorian in the Modern World,* p. 407.

Page 216. Glaspell, *Road to the Temple,* p. 188.

Page 224. Hapgood, "Cristine," p. 103, Hapgood Collection.

Page 225, top. Francis Steegmuller, "Duchamp: 50 Years Later," *Show,* February 1963, p. 28.

Page 225, bottom. Pierre, ed., *Greenwich Village in Poetry,* n.p.

Page 226. Amy Lowell Collection, Houghton Library, Harvard University, Cambridge.

Page 228. B. L. Reid, *"The Man from New York": John Quinn and His Friends* (New York: Oxford University Press, 1968), p. 285.

Page 229. Pierre, ed., *Greenwich Village in Poetry,* n.p.

Page 231. Ibid.

Page 240. Fernande Ouellette, *Edgard Varèse* (New York: Orion, 1968), p. 39.

Page 246. Gabrielle Buffet-Picabia, "Some Memories of Pre-Dada: Picabia and Duchamp," in Robert Motherwell, ed., *The Dada Painters and Poets: An Anthology,* 2d ed. (Cambridge and London: Harvard University Press, Belknap Press, 1989), p. 259.

Page 252. Eva Epp Runk, "Marius de Zayas: The New York Years (M.A. thesis, University of Delaware, 1973), p. 35.

Page 253. Carl Van Vechten, unpublished manuscript on the Stettheimers, Stettheimer Collection, YCAL.

Page 256. Florine Stettheimer, *Crystal Flowers* (New York: Privately printed, 1949), p. 23.

Page 260. Parker Tyler, *Florine Stettheimer: A Life in Art* (New York: Farrar, Straus, 1963), n.p.

Page 262. Katharine Kuh, "Walter Arensberg and Marcel Duchamp," *Saturday Review,* September 5, 1970, p. 37.

Page 271. Margaret Anderson, ed., *The Little Review Anthology* (New York: Hermitage House, 1953), p. 321.

Page 274. Arensberg Archives, Francis Bacon Library, Claremont, California.

Page 282. Alice Corbin Henderson Collection, HRHRC.

Page 283. Lowell Collection.

Page 284. Henderson Collection.

Page 292. Anderson, ed., *Little Review Anthology,* p. 11.

Page 298. *Poetry* Papers.

Page 303. Thomas L. Scott and Melvin J. Friedman, eds., *Pound/The Little Review: The Letters of Ezra Pound to Margaret Anderson: The Little Review Correspondence* (New York: New Directions, 1988), p. 80.

Page 306. Lowell Collection.

Page 305. Brooks, *New England,* p. 534.

Page 308. T. S. Eliot, "Introduction," in *Literary Essays of Ezra Pound,* ed. T. S. Eliot (New York: New Directions, 1968), p. xii.

Page 309. Ellen Williams, *Harriet Monroe and the Poetry Renaissance: The First Ten Years of "Poetry," 1912–1922* (Urbana: University of Illinois Press, 1977), p. 185.

Page 324. *Poetry* Papers.

Page 332. Sue Davidson Lowe, *Stieglitz: A Memoir/Biography* (New York: Farrar, Straus, and Giroux, 1983), p. 240.

Page 335. Mina Loy, "Colossus," p. 91 of original ms., collection of Mrs. Herbert Bayer.

Page 340. Mabel Dodge Luhan Collection, YCAL.

Page 341. Mabel Dodge Luhan, *The Edge of Taos Desert: An Escape to Reality,* volume 4 of *Intimate Memories* (New York: Harcourt, Brace, 1937), p. 95.

Page 344. John Quinn Memorial Collection, Rare Books and Manuscripts Division, NYPL.

Page 354, top. Reid, *Man from New York,* pp. 472–73.

Page 354, bottom. Ernest Hemingway, *A Moveable Feast* (New York: Scribners, 1964), p. 78.

Page 355. Ford Madox Ford, *It Was the Nightingale* (Philadelphia and London: J. B. Lippincott, 1933), p. 312.

Page 357. Duchamp to Dreier, January 16, 1948; in Robert L. Herbert, Eleanor S. Apter, Elise S. Kenney, eds., *The Société Anonyme and the Dreier Bequest at Yale University: A Catalogue Raisonné* (New Haven, Conn.: Yale University Press, 1984), p. 1.

CAST OF CHARACTERS

Key

A	Participant in Armory Show
Ar	Member of Arensberg circle
Ch	Resident of Chicago
D	Member of Mabel Dodge circle
Da	Participant in proto-Dada and Dada
E	Contributor to *Egoist*
Fl	Resident of Florence
GV	Resident of Greenwich Village
H	Member of Robert Henri circle
Ha	Attended Harvard
I	Proponent of Imagism
In	Participant in the Society of Independents exhibition
L	Resident of London
LC	Liberal Club member
LR	Contributor to *Little Review*
M	Contributor to *Masses*
O	Contributor to *Others*
P	Contributor to *Poetry*
Pa	Resident of Paris
PP	Participant in Provincetown Players
PS	Participant in Paterson Strike Pageant
R	Contributor to *Rogue*
S	Member of Gertrude and Leo Stein circle
SA	Participant in Société Anonyme
St	Member of Stettheimer circle
291	Member of Alfred Stieglitz circle

Boldface symbols indicate strong affiliation.

Richard Aldington (1892–1962). British poet, assistant editor of the *Egoist*. Married to Hilda Doolittle, 1913; separated, 1917. **E, I,** L, P.

Margaret Anderson (c. 1886–1973). Editor of the *Little Review*. Companion of Jane Heap, 1916–c. 1921. Ch, GV, **I, LR.**

Sherwood Anderson (1876–1941). Novelist. Ch, LC, LR, 291.

Louise Stevens Arensberg (1879–1953). Patron of modern art, salon hostess. Married to Walter Arensberg, 1907–53. **Ar.**

Walter Arensberg (1878–1954). Patron of modern art and poetry, salon host, poet, Francis Bacon scholar. Married to Louise Stevens Arensberg, 1907–53. **Ar, Da,** Ha, **O, R.**

George Bellows (1882–1925). Ashcan School painter. **H,** In, M.

Bernard Berenson (1865–1959). Aesthetician, collector. Fl, Ha, S.

Maxwell Bodenheim (1893–1954). Poet, avant-garde misanthrope. Ch, GV, LR, O, P.

Neith Boyce (1872–1951). Novelist, playwright. Married to Hutchins Hapgood, 1899–1944. D, LC, **PP,** S.

F. Sumner Boyd (n.d.). Anarchist. D, LC, PS.

Maurice Browne (1881–1955). Founding director of Chicago's Little Theater. Ch.

Guido Bruno (1883–1942). Bohemian entrepreneur, editor of many Village magazines. GV.

Louise Bryant (1890–1936). Playwright, advocate journalist for Russian Revolution. Married to John Reed, 1916–20. GV, LC, M, PP.

Witter Bynner (1881–1968). Poet, perpetrator of Spectrist hoax. Ha, O, P.

George Cram Cook (1873–1924). Founding director of the Provincetown Players. Married to Susan Glaspell, 1913–24. Ch, GV, Ha, LC, M, **PP.**

John Covert (1882–1960). Painter. **Ar,** Da, **In,** Pa, SA.

Arthur Cravan (1888–1918[?]). Swiss-born boxer, poet, avant-garde provocateur, editor of *Maintenant*. Born Fabian Lloyd. Married to Mina Loy, 1918. Ar, **Da,** In, Pa.

Jean Crotti (1878–1958). Swiss painter. Ar, Da, In, Pa.

Margery Currey (c. 1873–1959). Fifty-seventh Street colony hostess, teacher, journalist. Married to Floyd Dell, 1909; separated, 1913. Ch, LR.

Arthur B. Davies (1862–1928). Painter, organizer of the Armory Show. Married to Lucy Meriwether, 1892–1928. Simultaneously maintained a common-law marriage with Edna Potter, c. 1905–28. **A,** H, Pa.

Stuart Davis (1892–1964). Painter. A, In, M.

Floyd Dell (1887–1969). Novelist, essayist, editor of the *Friday Literary Review,* managing editor of the *Masses* and *Liberator.* Married to Margery Currey, 1909; separated, 1913. Married to B. Marie Gage, 1919–1969. Ch, GV, **M,** LC, PP.

Baron Adolf de Meyer (1868–1949). French-born photographer, bon vivant. Pa, St, 291.

Charles Demuth (1883–1935). Painter, poet. Ar, GV, In, Pa, PP, S, St, 291.

Marius de Zayas (1880–1961). Mexican-born caricaturist, aesthetician, director of the Modern Gallery, editor of *291.* Ar, Da, Pa, **291.**

Mabel Ganson Evans Dodge Sterne Luhan (1879–1962). Salon hostess, memoirist. Married to Karl Evans, 1900–1903. Married to Edwin Dodge, 1904; separated, 1913; divorced, 1916. Married to Maurice Sterne, 1917; separated, 1918; divorced, 1922. Married to Antonio Luhan, 1923–62. A, **D,** Fl, GV, LC, **PS,** S, 291.

Hilda Doolittle, also known as H.D. (1886–1961). Imagist poet. Married to Richard Aldington, 1913; separated, 1917; divorced, 1938. Companion of Bryher, 1918–61. **E, I,** L, LR, P.

Arthur Dove (1880–1946). Painter. In, Pa, **291.**

Muriel Saunders Draper (1886–1956). Salon hostess, writer, interior decorator. Married to Paul Draper, 1909–16. Fl, L, S, St.

Katherine Dreier (1877–1952). Painter, founder of the Société Anonyme. A, Ar, Da, **In,** Pa, **SA.**

Theodore Dreiser (1871–1945). Novelist. Ch, GV, LC.

Marcel Duchamp (1887–1968). Artist, chess player, editor of the *Blind Man, Rongwrong,* and *New York Dada.* **A, Ar, Da, In,** Pa, **SA, St.**

Isadora Duncan (1878–1927). Dancer. Ar, Pa.

Max Eastman (1883–1969). Editor of *Masses* and *Liberator,* essayist, poet. Married to Ida Rauh, 1911; separated, c. 1917. GV, **M,** PP.

T. S. Eliot (1888–1965). Poet, essayist, editor. **E,** Ha, L, LR, P, O.

Donald Evans (1885–1921). Poet, founder of Claire Marie Press. Ar, D, R.

Arthur Davison Ficke (1883–1945). Poet, lawyer, perpetrator of Spectrist hoax. Ha, LR, O, P.

John Gould Fletcher (1886–1950). Poet. Ha, **I,** L, LR, P.

F. S. Flint (1885–1960). British poet, translator. I, L, P.

Ford Madox Ford (1873–1939). British poet, novelist, editor of the *English Review.* Born Ford Hermann Hueffer; changed his name in 1918. E, I, L, P.

Baroness Elsa von Freytag-Loringhoven (1874–1927). German-born writer, artist, personality experimenter. Ar, **Da,** GV, **LR.**

William Glackens (1870–1938). Painter, president of the Society of Independents. **A,** GV, H, **In,** Pa.

Susan Glaspell (1882–1948). Playwright, novelist, journalist. Married to George Cram Cook, 1913–24. Ch, GV, LC, **PP.**

Albert Gleizes (1881–1953). French painter, aesthetician. A, Ar, In, Pa.

Emma Goldman (1869–1940). Anarchist leader, editor of *Mother Earth.* D, GV, LR.

Hutchins Hapgood (1869–1944). Muckraking journalist, bohemian mystic. Married to Neith Boyce, 1899–1944. **D,** Ha, LC, **PP,** S.

Marsden Hartley (1877–1943). Painter, poet. A, Ar, D, In, Pa, S, St, **291.**

Hippolyte Havel (c. 1870–c. 1940). Eastern European–born anarchist, writer, waiter. Companion of Polly Holladay, c. 1911–c. 1915. D, GV, LC, M.

Paul Haviland (1880–1950). French-born representative of Haviland porcelain firm in New York, photographer. Ha, Pa, **291.**

Bill Haywood (1869–1928). Leader of Industrial Workers of the World. D, M, **PS.**

Jane Heap (1884–1964). Writer, conversationalist, editor of the *Little Review.* Companion of Margaret Anderson, 1916–c. 1921. Ch, GV, **LR.**

Alice Corbin Henderson (1881–1949). Poet, associate editor of *Poetry.* Ch, **P.**

Robert Henri (1865–1929). Painter, teacher, leader of the anti-Academy faction. A, **H,** Pa.

Polly Holladay (c. 1885–c. 1940). Pioneering restaurateur in the Village and Provincetown. Companion of Hippolyte Havel, c. 1911–c. 1915. GV, LC.

T. E. Hulme (1883–1917). British philosopher, poetry aesthetician. **I,** L.

Robert Edmond Jones (1887–1954). Theater designer. **D,** Ha, LC, **PS,** GV, **PP.**

Harry Kemp (1883–1960). Playwright, poet, tramp. GV, LC, M, PP.

Alfred Kreymborg (1883–1966). Poet, editor of *Glebe, Others,* and *Broom.* Ar, GV, In, **O,** PP, 291.

Walt Kuhn (1880–1949). Painter, Armory Show organizer. **A,** GV, H, In.

D. H. Lawrence (1885–1930). British poet, novelist. I, L.

Wyndham Lewis (1884–1957). British novelist, essayist, editor of *BLAST,* artist. L, LR.

Vachel Lindsay (1879–1931). Poet, purveyor of Higher Vaudeville. Ch, H, **P.**

Walter Lippmann (1889–1974). Journalist, political commentator. **D,** Ha.

Amy Lowell (1874–1925). Poet, essayist, Imagist impresario, lecturer. Companion of Ada Dwyer Russell, c. 1914–25. D, **I, LR,** O, P.

Mina Loy (1882–1966). British-born poet, painter. Married to Stephen Haweis, 1903; separated, 1913; divorced, 1917. Married to Arthur Cravan, 1918. Ar, Fl, In, **O,** Pa, PP, R, S.

George Luks (1867–1933). Ashcan School painter. A, **H,** In, Pa.

John Marin (1870–1953). Painter. A, In, Pa, **291.**

Edgar Lee Masters (1869–1950). Poet, lawyer. Ch, P.

Henry McBride (1867–1962). Art critic for the *New York Sun.* A, Ar, In, S, SA, **St.**

Agnes Ernst Meyer (1887–1970). Journalist, art collector. Married to Eugene Meyer, Jr., 1910–59. Pa, S, **291.**

Edna St. Vincent Millay (1892–1950). Poet. GV, PP.

Harriet Monroe (1860–1936). Poet, editor of *Poetry.* A, Ch, I, **P.**

Marianne Moore (1887–1972). Poet, editor of *Dial.* **E, O,** P.

Elie Nadelman (1882–1946). Polish-born sculptor. A, Pa, S, **St.**

B.J.O. Nordfeldt (1878–1955). Painter, set designer. Ch, GV, In, PP.

Allen Norton (c. 1890–c. 1945). Editor, poet. Married to Louise Norton, 1911; separated, 1915; divorced, c. 1919. Ar, GV, Ha, **R.**

Louise McCutcheon Norton Varèse (1890–1990). Fashion columnist, poet, translator. Married to Allen Norton, 1911; separated, 1915; divorced, c. 1919. Married to Edgard Varèse, 1921–65. Ar, GV, **R.**

Georgia O'Keeffe (1887–1986). Painter. Married to Alfred Stieglitz, 1924–46. In, **291.**

Eugene O'Neill (1886–1953). Playwright. GV, Ha, **PP.**

Walter Pach (1883–1958). Painter, art critic. **A,** Ar, **In,** Pa, S.

Francis Picabia (1879–1953). French painter, editor of *391.* **A,** Ar, D, **Da,** In, LR, Pa, S, St, **291.**

Ezra Pound (1885–1972). Poet, essayist, founder of Imagiste movement, literary impresario, foreign correspondent for *Poetry, Little Review,* and *Dial.* **E, I,** L, **LR,** O, **P.**

John Quinn (1870–1924). Lawyer, modern-art collector, poetry patron. **A,** Ha, In, **LR.**

Man Ray (1890–1976). Photographer, painter, sculptor, editor of *Ridgefield Gazook* and *New York Dada.* Born Emmanuel Radnitzki; changed his name in 1911. **Ar, Da,** H, In, Pa, **SA,** 291.

John Reed (1887–1920). Journalist, historian of Russian Revolution. Married to Louise Bryant, 1916–20. **D,** GV, Ha, LC, **M,** P, **PP, PS.**

Henri-Pierre Roché (1879–1959). French writer, art agent, introducer. Ar, Pa, **S,** SA, St.

Pitts Sanborn (1879–1941). Music critic, editor of *Trend,* poet. Ar, Ha, R.

Carl Sandburg (1878–1967). Poet, journalist. Ch, LR, O, P.

Margaret Sanger (1883–1966). Leader of birth-control movement, editor of the *Woman Rebel.* D, GV, LC, **PS.**

Morton Livingston Schamberg (1881–1918). Painter. A, Ar, Da, In, Pa.

Charles Sheeler (1883–1965). Painter, photographer. A, Ar, In, Pa, 291.

John Sloan (1871–1951). Ashcan School painter. A, GV, **H, In,** LC, **M, PS.**

Edward Steichen (1879–1973). Photographer, painter. In, Pa, S, St, **291.**

Gertrude Stein (1874–1946). Writer, salon hostess. Companion of Alice B. Toklas, 1909–46. Pa, R, **S**.

Leo Stein (1872–1947). Collector, aesthetician, salon host. Fl, Ha, Pa, **S**, St.

Joseph Stella (1877–1946). Painter. A, Ar, Da, In, Pa, S.

Maurice Sterne (1878–1957). Painter. Married to Mabel Dodge, 1917; separated, 1918; divorced, 1922. D, In, Pa, S, St.

Carrie Stettheimer (c. 1870–1944). Dollhouse creator, salon hostess. **St**.

Ettie (née Henrietta) Stettheimer (1874–1955). Writer, salon hostess. **St**.

Florine Stettheimer (1871–1944). Painter, set designer, salon hostess. In, **St**.

Wallace Stevens (1879–1955). Poet, insurance lawyer. **Ar**, Ha, P, O, R.

Alfred Stieglitz (1864–1946). Photographer, editor of *Camera Work,* director of 291. Married to Emmeline Obermeyer, 1893; separated, 1918; divorced, 1924. Married to Georgia O'Keeffe, 1924–46. A, D, In, St, **291**.

Eunice Tietjens (1884–1944). Poet. Ch, LR, P.

Alice B. Toklas (1877–1967). Amanuensis, cookbook writer. Companion of Gertrude Stein, 1909–46. Pa, **S**.

Carl Van Vechten (1880–1964). Novelist, dance and music critic, photographer. Married to Fania Marinoff, 1914–64. Ar, **D**, Pa, **R, S, St**.

Edgard Varèse (1883–1965). French composer, conductor, founder of International Composers' Guild (1921). Married to Louise Norton, 1921–65. Ar, Pa, St.

Mary Heaton Vorse (1874–1966). Journalist, novelist. GV, PP.

Max Weber (1881–1961). Painter. In, Pa, S, 291.

William Carlos Williams (1883–1963). Poet, essayist, doctor, editor of *Contact.* Ar, E, In, LR, **O**, P, PP.

Beatrice Wood (b. 1893). Artist, actress, editor of the *Blind Man.* **Ar,** Da, In, Pa.

William Butler Yeats (1865–1939). British poet. L, LR, P.

Art Young (1866–1943). Cartoonist. A, In, **M**.

Marguerite Zorach (1888–1968). Painter. Married to William Zorach, 1912–66. GV, In, LC, Pa, PP.

William Zorach (1887–1966). Painter. Married to Marguerite Zorach, 1912–66. GV, In, LC, O, PP.

A MODERN CHRONOLOGY: 1900–20

1900

B.J.O. Nordfeldt appropriates as his studio one of the outbuildings of the World's Columbian Exposition; this marks the beginning of Chicago's bohemian Fifty-seventh Street colony.

SPRING
En route to Paris from Milwaukee, Edward Steichen meets Alfred Stieglitz in New York.

JUNE
Walter Arensberg and Wallace Stevens graduate from Harvard. Stevens goes to work as a reporter for the *New York Tribune* (until 1901). Arensberg takes his first trip to Europe.

FALL
Ezra Pound, age fifteen, enrolls at the University of Pennsylvania, Philadelphia, to study "Arts and Science" (remains until 1903).

OCTOBER
Leo Stein settles in Florence to write a book on Andrea Mantegna.

1901

Paul Haviland begins working in New York as a representative of his family's porcelain firm (remains until July 1915).

OCTOBER 31
Hilda Doolittle meets Pound at a Halloween party at the University of Pennsylvania.

1902

FEBRUARY 17
Stieglitz resigns from the journal *Camera Notes* and founds the Photo-Secession group, which makes its public debut in March at the exhibition Stieglitz organizes for the National Arts Club, New York.

FALL
After returning from Paris, Steichen re-establishes ties with Stieglitz.

SEPTEMBER 30
William Carlos Williams, in medical school at the University of Pennsylvania, meets Pound.

OCTOBER 21
After seeing Eleonora Duse perform in Boston, Amy Lowell is inspired to write her first poem.

1903

Mina Loy moves from London to Paris (remains until 1906).

Williams meets Charles Demuth over a bowl of prunes in Mrs. Chain's boardinghouse in Philadelphia.

Robert Henri begins teaching at the New York School of Art.

JANUARY
Stieglitz publishes and edits the first of fifty issues of *Camera Work* (published until 1917).

JUNE
Carl Van Vechten graduates from the University of Chicago and begins working as a newspaperman in Chicago.

SUMMER
Gertrude and Leo Stein vacation with Hutchins Hapgood and Neith Boyce in Florence.

FALL
The Steins set up house together at 27, rue de Fleurus, Paris.

Pound transfers to Hamilton College, in Clinton, New York.

OCTOBER 24
Gertrude Stein finishes *Q.E.D.*, her first completed full-length work.

DECEMBER 31
Mina Loy marries Stephen Haweis in Paris.

1904

Williams decides that he has a vocation as a poet.

John Sloan and George Bellows each move from Philadelphia to New York.

Demuth visits Paris for the first time, staying a few weeks.

Walter Pach moves to Paris (aside from visits to the U.S., remains until 1913).

SPRING
Leo Stein buys his first painting by Paul Cézanne, on the recommendation of Bernard Berenson.

APRIL
Pablo Picasso moves to Paris.

FALL
Leo Stein begins buying paintings at Ambroise Vollard's gallery; his first purchases include one painting by Cézanne, two by Paul Gauguin, and one by Pierre-Auguste Renoir.

1905
John Marin and Max Weber each move to Paris.

Chicago's Upward Movement begins to decline in importance.

Pound becomes Doolittle's boyfriend and mentor.

FEBRUARY
Gertrude Stein begins writing *Three Lives*.

APRIL
Williams meets Doolittle at a dinner hosted by Pound.

OCTOBER
Doolittle enters Bryn Mawr College near Philadelphia (remains until January 1907). There she meets Marianne Moore.

In Paris, Henri-Pierre Roché introduces Picasso to Leo and Gertrude Stein. (Some attribute the introduction to Picasso's dealer, Clovis Sagot.)

OCTOBER 18
The Salon d'Automne opens in Paris. Within a few days Leo Stein buys his first painting by Matisse, *Woman with a Hat*, and within a few weeks he buys his first by Picasso.

NOVEMBER 24
Stieglitz, with the help of Steichen, founds the Little Galleries of the Photo-Secession, 291 Fifth Avenue, which becomes known as 291. The inaugural exhibition features prints by thirty-nine photographers.

1906
Pound proposes to Doolittle. The engagement is a short one, since he has also proffered a ring to Mary Moore of Trenton, New Jersey.

Steichen settles in France and establishes ties with French artists (Matisse, Auguste Rodin, and others) that result in the first European exhibitions at 291.

SPRING
Van Vechten moves from Chicago to New York; in November he becomes assistant music critic for the *New York Times*, writing about music and opera (until 1907 and again from 1910 to spring 1913).

SUMMER
Gertrude Stein begins writing *The Making of Americans*.

FALL
Floyd Dell and George Cram Cook become friends and together found the Monist Society, a discussion club in Davenport, Iowa.

Loy exhibits her paintings at the Salon d'Automne and emigrates to Florence with her husband, Stephen Haweis.

1907
The MacDowell Colony is formed in Peterborough, New Hampshire.

Katherine Dreier becomes friends with Steichen, and he photographs her.

Demuth takes his first extended trip to Paris (remains until early 1908).

Gertrude Vanderbilt Whitney moves into a MacDougal Alley studio in New York; she organizes exhibitions for the Colony Club.

Georgia O'Keeffe studies at the Art Students League, New York.

The Liberal Club, a group of upper-class reformers, is founded; it sponsors lectures and discussions in its Gramercy Park meeting place.

JANUARY
Doolittle withdraws from Bryn Mawr because her grades are low and she fails English.

JANUARY 5
An exhibition of drawings and paintings by Pamela Colman Smith opens at 291, the gallery's first nonphotography show.

MARCH
In New York, Emma Goldman begins publishing the anarchist periodical *Mother Earth* (continues monthly until 1918).

SPRING
Dell becomes a hired hand on Cook's farm.

Forced out of Mexico by the Porfirio Díaz dictatorship, Marius de Zayas emigrates to New York. He immediately begins working as a caricaturist for the *New York Evening World*. During this year he meets Stieglitz.

MARCH 21
In London, Ford Madox Ford (then Ford Madox Hueffer) meets Violet Hunt, and they begin an affair.

JUNE
Stieglitz and Steichen visit an exhibition of work by Cézanne at the Galeries Bernheim-Jeune in Paris; Stieglitz laughs at the paintings.

JUNE 7
In Boston, Arensberg marries Louise Stevens.

AUGUST
Pound is hired to teach at Wabash College, a Presbyterian college in Crawfordsville, Indiana, but is dismissed a few months later on charges of sexual impropriety.

1908
Leo Stein buys his last Matisse painting.

Camera Work, heretofore devoted solely to photography, opens its pages to contemporary fine arts and criticism.

Sloan runs for the New York State Assembly on the Socialist Party ticket and loses.

At 291 Stieglitz presents the first American exhibitions of modern art: Rodin drawings (January) and Matisse works on paper (April); Steichen arranges both exhibitions from Paris.

JANUARY
Haviland visits 291 to see the Rodin drawings and becomes a member of the Stieglitz circle.

FEBRUARY 3
An exhibition of work by the Eight (Arthur B. Davies, William Glackens, Robert Henri, Ernest Lawson, George Luks, Maurice Prendergast, Everett Shinn, and John Sloan) opens at the Macbeth Gallery, New York.

FEBRUARY 25
Steichen founds the New Society of American Artists in Paris in his studio there; charter members include the sculptor Jo Davidson and the painter John Marin.

APRIL
Agnes Ernst, a reporter for the *New York Sun*, meets Stieglitz and Steichen and becomes a key figure in the 291 circle.

Stieglitz considers closing 291 when its rent doubles, but Haviland guarantees money for a three-year lease.

MAY
Van Vechten goes to Paris as the *New York Times* correspondent.

Arthur Dove abandons commercial art to paint in Paris (remains until July 1909).

AUGUST 14
Pound moves to London, taking up residence at 10 Church Walk, Kensington.

LATE SUMMER
In Davenport, Iowa, Dell meets Margery Currey.

FALL
Dell moves to Chicago.

Margaret Anderson moves from Columbus, Indiana, to Chicago and lives at the YWCA.

DECEMBER
In London, Ford starts the *English Review* (continues monthly until July 1937).

DECEMBER 1
The Little Galleries of the Photo-Secession moves to 293 Fifth Avenue; it is still known as 291.

1909
Muriel and Paul Draper move to Florence (remain until 1912).

Loy meets Mabel Dodge and Muriel Draper in Florence at the Villa Curonia.

Max Weber arrives in New York, meets Stieglitz, and lives with Abraham Walkowitz.

Marsden Hartley meets Stieglitz (through Seumas O'Sheel), who promptly offers him a one-man show in May at 291. Hartley also meets another gallery dealer, N. E. Montross, who gives him a four-dollar-per-week stipend for the next two years and introduces him to Albert Pinkham Ryder.

JANUARY
Henri opens the Robert Henri School of Art at the old Lincoln Arcade Building (continues until 1912). His students include George Bellows, Patrick Henry Bruce, Glenn Coleman, Guy Pène du Bois, William Gropper, Edward Hopper, Rockwell Kent, and Walter Pach.

JANUARY 4
De Zayas has his first exhibition at 291.

MARCH
In London, T. E. Hulme forms a group that secedes from the Poets' Club, to meet at the Tour Eiffel Restaurant on Percy Street. They include Joseph Campbell, Florence Farr, F. S. Flint, Pound, Edward Storer, and F. W. Tancred.

MARCH 5
Francis Hackett (age twenty-five) begins the *Friday Literary Review* (eight tabloid pages, part of the *Chicago Evening Post*); Dell soon becomes his assistant. This event is generally cited as the start of the Chicago Literary Renaissance.

MARCH 30
Marin has his American debut at 291.

ABOUT APRIL
Pound meets Ford.

APRIL
Van Vechten returns to New York from Paris.

APRIL 22
Pound reads at a meeting of Hulme's group.

MAY 8
Hartley has his New York debut at 291.

BY MID-YEAR
Pound is regularly attending William Butler Yeats's "Monday Evenings."

JUNE
Pound makes his English publishing debut with "Sestina: Altaforte" in the *English Review*.

Steichen introduces Stieglitz to Marin in Marin's Paris studio.

JULY
Dove returns to New York and meets Stieglitz a few months later.

JULY 30
Grafton Press (New York) publishes Gertrude Stein's *Three Lives*.

AUGUST
Dell and Currey marry and rent an apartment at 1307 Morse Avenue, Chicago.

1910
Against her parents' wishes, Doolittle wants to marry Pound; she also begins to write poetry.

Leo Stein buys his last Picasso painting.

T. S. Eliot begins writing "The Love Song of J. Alfred Prufrock" (finishes a year later).

Chicago's Little Room begins a long waning period.

Dove moves to Westport, Connecticut, and begins a series of landmark abstract paintings.

JANUARY 28
Dell becomes associate editor of the *Friday Literary Review*.

MARCH 3–11
Williams visits Pound in London.

APRIL 1
The Independent Artists Exhibition opens in a loft at 29 West Thirty-fifth Street; two thousand people attend the opening. It is organized by Davies, James Fraser, William Glackens, Henri, Walt Kuhn, Ernest Lawson, Everett Shinn, and John Sloan.

JUNE 15
Pound sails for the United States (remains until February 22, 1911).

SUMMER
Pound meets John Quinn in New York through John Butler Yeats (William Butler Yeats's father).

JUNE 24
Eliot, Robert Edmond Jones, Walter Lippmann, and John Reed graduate from Harvard.

OCTOBER
De Zayas takes his first trip to Paris (remains until fall 1911).

A group of artists and writers in France begins to meet on Sunday afternoons in the garden behind the detached studios of Raymond Duchamp-Villon, František Kupka, and Jacques Villon. Known as the Puteaux group, this loose confederation includes Guillaume Apollinaire, Marcel Duchamp, Albert Gleizes, Fernand Léger, Walter Pach, and Francis Picabia.

NOVEMBER
Stieglitz and the Photo-Secession arrange an international exhibition of Pictorial photography at the Albright Art Gallery in Buffalo; it is generally cited as the first exhibition of photography in a fine-art context.

NOVEMBER 22
Provença is Pound's first book of poetry to be published in the United States.

LATE FALL
Agnes Ernst marries the financier Eugene Meyer, Jr.

Duchamp meets Picabia (through Pierre Dumont), and they immediately become friends.

1911
Allen Norton, after dropping out of Harvard to become a journalist, marries Louise McCutcheon, who has dropped out of Smith to marry Norton.

Emmanuel Radnitzki changes his name to Man Ray.

Theodore Dreiser's *Jennie Gerhardt* is published; his *Sister Carrie* is reissued after being suppressed since 1900.

Eliot writes "Portrait of a Lady," sometimes cited as the beginning of modernism in American poetry.

JANUARY
Piet Vlag founds the *Masses* in New York. Vlag is a Dutch immigrant who worked as the chef for the socialist Rand School.

Max Weber ends relations with Stieglitz and his circle.

FEBRUARY
Soirées de Paris, edited by Apollinaire, begins publication in Paris (twenty-seven issues are published, until August 1914).

FEBRUARY 22
Pound goes back to London; he will not return to the United States for twenty-eight years.

MARCH
Cook moves from Davenport to Chicago, in part because of local disapproval of his affair with Susan Glaspell.

Man Ray begins frequenting 291, initially attracted by an exhibition of Cézanne drawings.

SPRING
Mabel Dodge visits 27, rue de Fleurus (with Mildred Aldrich) and meets Leo Stein, Gertrude Stein, and Alice B. Toklas. When the trio goes to Italy that summer, they take tea with Dodge at the Villa Curonia in Florence.

MARCH 28
At 291 Picasso receives his first one-man exhibition anywhere.

MAY 4
Max Eastman marries Ida Rauh in Paterson, New Jersey; no rings are exchanged.

JUNE
Dreier goes to Stockholm as a delegate at the Sixth Convention of the International Woman Suffrage Alliance.

SUMMER
John Reed moves to Greenwich Village, living with three Harvard friends at 42 Washington Square South.

Villagers explore Provincetown, Massachusetts; the pioneers include Neith Boyce, Hutchins Hapgood, Wilbur Daniel Steele, and Mary Heaton Vorse.

Stieglitz takes his last trip to Europe, spending the final three weeks in Paris. With Steichen and de Zayas serving as guides, he meets Matisse, Picasso, and Rodin.

JULY 22
Doolittle sails from New York for London, with Williams and her father seeing her off at the pier.

JULY 28
At age twenty-four Dell becomes editor of the *Friday Literary Review*.

AUGUST 8
Dreier marries Edward Trumbull, an American artist she met in London. On the same day she discovers that he already has a wife and children.

FALL
Pound meets A. R. Orage (through T. E. Hulme), editor of the *New Age*; the magazine becomes a primary publishing outlet for Pound and a source of income.

Henri joins the Ferrer Modern School and donates his teaching services for seven years.

De Zayas returns to New York from Paris.

NOVEMBER
Harriet Monroe meets with Hobart Chatfield-Taylor, an associate from the Little Room and Chicago's most active literary patron, to discuss plans for a poetry magazine.

DECEMBER 6
Cook becomes associate editor of the *Friday Literary Review*.

DECEMBER 14
The first recorded gathering of what will become the Association of American Painters and Sculptors (AAPS) takes place in New York; Walt Kuhn, Elmer MacRae, Jerome Myers, and Henry Fitch Taylor are present.

DECEMBER 19
The AAPS meets officially for the first time. J. Alden Weir is elected president but resigns when the association attacks the National Academy of Design.

1912
Muriel and Paul Draper leave Florence to live in London.

Du Cubisme by Jean Metzinger and Albert Gleizes is published in Paris.

Early in the year Pound meets the poet Richard Aldington.

JANUARY 9
Davies is elected president of the AAPS.

FEBRUARY 27
At 291 Arthur Dove has his first show anywhere.

MARCH 12
Amy Lowell meets the popular actress Ada Dwyer Russell in Boston; they become lifelong companions.

SPRING
Pound introduces Doolittle to Aldington; Doolittle and Aldington soon move into separate quarters at 6 Church Walk, across a courtyard from Pound. After much discussion the three decide on the principles of Imagisme.

SPRING AND EARLY SUMMER
Monroe sits in the Chicago Public Library, reading all verse published in English in books and periodicals from 1907 to 1912.

APRIL 11
Hartley arrives in Paris on his first trip abroad.

SUMMER
Van Vechten meets the actress Fania Marinoff in New York.

The Heterodoxy Club, a new feminist women-only luncheon group with twenty-five members, starts to meet in the Village for discussions every other Saturday.

Everett Shinn organizes what may be the first little theater performances in New York: burlesques in his Village studio, with such titles as "More Sinned against Than Usual" and "The Prune-Hater's Daughter."

AUGUST
Camera Work devotes its issue to modern art; it includes Gertrude Stein's word portraits of Matisse and Picasso, which are her first writings to appear in a periodical.

Monroe mails a circular to a selected group of poets, soliciting contributions to *Poetry: A Magazine of Verse*, a monthly journal.

AUGUST 18
Pound begins corresponding with Monroe, responding enthusiastically to her announcement of *Poetry*.

SEPTEMBER
Doolittle shows Pound her new poem, "Hermes of the Ways," in the tea-and-bun shop at the British Museum. He likes it and signs it "H.D. Imagiste," thus giving Doolittle her pen name.

Max Eastman, who is living in Connecticut and writing *The Enjoyment of Poetry*, receives a letter written by John Sloan and signed by the *Masses* staff: "You are elected editor of the *Masses*. No Pay."

Dreier sees the Sonderbund show, which sparks her lifelong interest in modern art.

SEPTEMBER 21
Pound agrees to be *Poetry*'s foreign correspondent. At about the same time he begins to host "Tuesday Evenings" in his cramped quarters.

SEPTEMBER 23
The first issue of *Poetry* appears. Edited by Monroe, with Alice Corbin Henderson as associate editor, the magazine operates from an office at 543 Cass Street, Chicago.

FALL
Man Ray enrolls at the Ferrer Modern School.

Muriel Draper begins a salon at Edith Grove, London, dominated by all-night musical performances.

SEPTEMBER 30
Walt Kuhn sees the Sonderbund exhibition in Cologne, Germany, and selects many works for the Armory Show.

OCTOBER
Aldington and H.D. move from Church Walk to Holland Place Chambers.

Gertrude Stein and Toklas arrive at the Villa Curonia, staying several weeks. On the third day of the visit Stein writes "Portrait of Mabel Dodge at the Villa Curonia."

OCTOBER 26
Samuel Swift invites Henry McBride to write art features and criticism for the *New York Sun*. He begins in November (remains until 1950).

NOVEMBER
Aldington debuts in *Poetry*.

Dodge departs Florence for New York. She settles at 23 Fifth Avenue, on the north side of Washington Square, and decorates her apartment entirely in white.

Monroe writes an editorial for *Poetry*, "The Open Door," which articulates her democratic editorial philosophy.

NOVEMBER 6
Davies arrives in Paris and spends ten days with Kuhn and Pach selecting work for the Armory Show.

NOVEMBER 28
Sherwood Anderson has a nervous breakdown in Elyria, Ohio; he is found December 1, amnesiac and bedraggled, in a Cleveland drugstore.

ABOUT DECEMBER
Van Vechten meets Dodge at Mrs. Jack Oakman's dinner party.

DECEMBER
The first issue of the *Masses* under the editorship of Eastman is published. Reed joins the *Masses*.

Demuth leaves Lancaster, Pennsylvania, for his third and most extended period of study in Paris (remains until spring 1914), where he meets Hartley and Gertrude Stein.

In Chicago, Maurice Browne begins the Little Theater, which rehearses in a storefront in the Fifty-seventh Street colony and performs in the Fine Arts Building.

Theodore Dreiser arrives in Chicago and stays for two months; he propagandizes for Edgar Lee Masters, attends the first production of the Little Theater, and falls in love with one of its actresses, Kirah Markham, whom Dell is also pursuing.

Poetry Journal begins publication in Boston, edited by Stanley Braithwaite (published monthly until March 1918).

DECEMBER 12
Williams marries Florence Herman in Rutherford, New Jersey.

1913
Smart Set, under the editorship of Willard Huntington Wright, begins publishing modern European writers (continues monthly until December 1923).

Cubists and Post-Impressionists by Arthur Jerome Eddy is published.

Marcel Duchamp buys a bottlerack at a Paris bazaar and inscribes it, creating his first Readymade, *Bottlerack*.

JANUARY
"H.D., Imagiste" debuts in *Poetry*. Upon reading H.D.'s poems, Lowell decides that she, too, is an Imagiste.

JANUARY 8
Harold Monro opens the Poetry Bookshop at 35 Devonshire Street, London.

JANUARY 20
Picabia and his wife, Gabrielle Buffet-Picabia, arrive in New York (remain until April 10); he is the only European artist to attend the Armory Show.

LATE JANUARY
Dodge begins her Evenings at 23 Fifth Avenue; they are variously held on Wednesday and Thursday evenings, sometimes more than once a week (until summer 1914).

JANUARY 27
Eight hundred employees quit the Doherty Silk Mill, marking the beginning of the Paterson (New Jersey) Strike; the strike gains momentum in February.

FEBRUARY
Van Vechten, Donald Evans, and Allen Norton become colleagues at the *New York Times*. Each has literary ambitions beyond journalism, and they share an interest in fin-de-siècle poetry.

Reed's *The Day in Bohemia* is published.

FEBRUARY 9
Sherwood Anderson leaves Elyria, Ohio, for Chicago to take a position with the Taylor-Critchfield Advertising Company.

FEBRUARY 17–MARCH 15
The International Exhibition of Modern Art—known as the Armory Show—is held at the Sixty-ninth Regiment in New York. Organized by the AAPS, it includes 1,046 catalogued items plus at least 600 uncatalogued works. A selection of about 500 items is later exhibited at the Art Institute in Chicago (March 25–April 16) and Boston (April 28–May 14).

Arts and Decoration dedicates a special issue to the show (although the issue is dated March, it is circulated at the show). Largely written by Guy Pène du Bois, it also includes Dodge's article on Gertrude Stein, "Post-Impressions in Prose."

FEBRUARY 24
Stieglitz gives himself his first, and last, one-man show at 291.

Van Vechten writes his first piece on Gertrude Stein, entitled "Cubist of Letters Writes a New Book."

MARCH
In London, Flint introduces Robert Frost to Pound. Pound writes about Frost to Alice Corbin Henderson at *Poetry*: "Have just discovered another Amur'kn. Vurry Amur'kn, with, I think the seeds of grace."

An "interview" with Pound by Flint appears in *Poetry* (actually written by Pound, with Flint's revisions). Entitled "Imagisme," it is the first description in print of the movement.

Pound also begins promoting D. H. Lawrence, at the suggestion of Ford.

MARCH 1
The Photo-Secession Gallery publishes *A Study of the Modern Evolution of Plastic Expression* by de Zayas and Haviland.

MARCH 8
The organizers of the Armory Show throw a dinner at Healy's (Sixty-sixth Street and Columbus) for their "Friends and Enemies" in the press.

MARCH 17
The first American one-man exhibition of Picabia opens at 291.

APRIL
The Woolworth Building opens in New York; at 792 feet, it is the world's tallest skyscraper.

Dodge meets Reed in the Village home of Bill Haywood's girlfriend, B. Shostac. After Haywood's description of the Paterson Strike, Dodge and Reed vow to stage a pageant that will dramatize the strike to New Yorkers.

APRIL 8
De Zayas exhibits abstract caricatures at 291.

APRIL 14
Cook and Glaspell are married by the mayor of Weehawken, New Jersey; they eat a wedding lunch at the Hotel Brevoort and honeymoon in Provincetown.

APRIL 28
Reed goes to Paterson to observe the silkworkers' strike; he is arrested and jailed.

END OF APRIL
Dell and Currey move to separate but adjoining quarters in the Fifty-seventh Street area of Chicago; for several months Currey's store-front flat is the gathering place for Chicago artists and writers.

MAY
Van Vechten resigns from the *New York Times* and sails for Europe. On May 31 he meets Gertrude Stein and Toklas.

MAY 17
Hartley arrives in Berlin (remains until December 1915, except for one trip to the United States, November 1913–April 1914).

MAY 19
Reed begins rehearsals for the Paterson Strike Pageant.

JUNE
Pound meets Wright of the *Smart Set* and tries to parlay this relationship into another publishing outlet. After Pound presumptuously sends the magazine Robert Frost's "Death of the Farm-Hand," Frost ends his brief alliance with Pound.

Williams debuts in *Poetry*.

Through a letter of introduction from Dodge, Van Vechten meets Muriel Draper at Edith Grove in London and soon sees her again at the Villa Curonia.

The Picabias meet Gertrude Stein in Paris.

Stieglitz devotes the June issue of *Camera Work* to modern art.

The *Masses* moves its office to 91 Greenwich Avenue.

JUNE 7
The Paterson Strike Pageant—conceived by Dodge, organized by Reed, with sets designed by Robert Edmond Jones and painted under the direction of John Sloan—is held in Madison Square Garden. 1,147 strikers from Paterson march up Fifth Avenue to participate in the event.

JUNE 13
Harriet Shaw Weaver and Dora Marsden publish the *New Freewoman: An Individualist Review* in London.

JUNE 19
Dodge, Reed, and Jones set sail on the *Amerika* for Europe and the Villa Curonia.

SUMMER
Henry McBride meets Gertrude Stein in Paris.

Donald Evans and Allen and Louise Norton live on Lake Congamond in Massachusetts and encourage one another to write poetry.

Haviland visits Picabia in Paris.

John Gould Fletcher begins regular financial support of Pound's literary section in the *New Freewoman*.

Summer residents at Dodge's Villa Curonia include Jones, Reed, and Van Vechten. Loy meets Van Vechten there; he becomes her agent and is responsible for appearances of her poetry in *Trend* and *Rogue*.

JULY
Lowell makes her debut in *Poetry*.

JULY 8

With a letter of introduction from Monroe, Lowell embarks for London to meet the Imagistes (remains until October). Through meetings with Pound and Fletcher, she is introduced to London's literary world.

AUGUST

In Chicago, Margaret Anderson, after hearing a lecture by John Cowper Powys, conceives the idea of the *Little Review* and announces it at one of Currey's studio gatherings.

AUGUST 7

Wallace Stevens writes to his vacationing wife that he has begun writing serious verse again for the first time since graduating from Harvard in 1900.

SEPTEMBER

The first issue of the *Glebe* is published in Ridgefield, New Jersey, consisting entirely of "Songs, Sighs and Curses," by the anarchist and sculptor Adolf Wolff. Alfred Kreymborg edits the magazine, with support from Albert and Charles Boni, Samuel Halpert, and Man Ray. With the exception of one issue (*Des Imagistes*), each issue is entirely devoted to one writer, mixing poetry, drama, and fiction. (Ten issues are published, until November 1914, with a circulation of about three hundred.)

FALL

Polly Holladay and Hippolyte Havel open a pioneering Village restaurant at 137 MacDougal Street.

SEPTEMBER 26

The last issue of the *Friday Literary Review* under Dell's editorship appears; Lucien Cary becomes editor.

OCTOBER

Poetry gives its first Guarantors' Prize, of $250, to William Butler Yeats for "The Grey Rock." Monroe had favored Vachel Lindsay but deferred to Pound. Monroe raises $100 for a second prize, which she awards to Lindsay for "General William Booth Enters into Heaven."

OCTOBER 3

A bill that strikes down tariffs on recently imported art is enacted by the United States Congress. (The bill is largely written by John Quinn.)

OCTOBER 14–27

Dreier exhibits paintings at the Macbeth Gallery, New York.

OCTOBER 18

H.D. and Aldington are married in Kensington, with H.D.'s parents and Pound as witnesses.

LATE OCTOBER

Dell arrives in New York with eighteen dollars in his pocket.

NOVEMBER

In London, Pound begins a period of working as William Butler Yeats's personal secretary. During the winter months of every year until 1915, the two men retire to Stone Cottage, Coleman's Hatch, Sussex.

On Pound's recommendation, Aldington becomes assistant editor of the *Egoist*.

NOVEMBER 1

Due to a schism catalyzed by the feminist Henrietta Rodman, New York's Liberal Club splits, with the more progressive faction moving to 137 MacDougal Street, just above Polly's restaurant and three doors south of Washington Square. It becomes a center for bohemian Villagers.

NOVEMBER 8

Pound resigns as *Poetry*'s foreign correspondent and suggests that Ford take his place. Ford promptly begins petitioning Monroe for Pound's reinstatement.

NOVEMBER 21

In the Village, Dodge takes an overdose of Veronal. Reed then leaves Dodge for the first time, writing a note that says: "I cannot live with you. You smother me. You crush me. You want to kill my spirit."

NOVEMBER 23

Hartley returns to New York from Germany, bringing work for an exhibition at 291.

ABOUT DECEMBER

A. A. Brill leads a Psychoanalysis Evening at Dodge's; this is often cited as the introduction of Freud to the Village.

DECEMBER

Charles Daniel, a saloon owner, opens the Daniel Gallery at 2 West Forty-seventh Street, with the poet Alanson Hartpence as its director.

Eastman invites Dell to be managing editor of the *Masses*.

Claire Marie Press, New York, publishes its first book, Donald Evans's *Sonnets from the Patagonian*; this book gives a group of writers (Evans, Allen and Louise Norton, Van Vechten) its name—the Patagonians. The press, located at 3 East

Fourteenth Street, is named after the actress Claire Burke and continues until September 1914.

William Butler Yeats begins talking with Pound about James Joyce; on December 15, Pound first writes to Joyce in Trieste, Italy.

EARLY DECEMBER
Reed goes to Mexico to write about Pancho Villa.

DECEMBER 8
Pound is reinstated as *Poetry*'s foreign correspondent.

1914
During 1914 and 1915 the *Little Review* is the vehicle for Lowell's Imagist campaign.

Monroe loses her job as an art critic for the *Chicago Tribune* and begins drawing a salary from *Poetry*.

Weber's *Cubist Poems* is published by Elkin Mathews, London.

At Dell's suggestion, the *Masses* sponsors a ball at Webster Hall to raise money. Other Village groups follow with other balls, which usually have an exotic theme and involve costumes, drinking, and dancing. The most famous are the Liberal Club's Pagan Routs (named by Dell); they attract both Villagers and an uptown crowd.

JANUARY
Activities at the Liberal Club include the lectures "Intellectual Illiteracy" and "Liberal Club Consciousness," dancing classes called "Why Hesitate?" and Clarence Darrow speaking on Voltaire.

JANUARY 1
The *New Freewoman* (which published thirteen issues, until December 1913) becomes the *Egoist* (published semimonthly until January 1915, when it begins monthly publication). In January, Pound sends the magazine Joyce's *Portrait of the Artist as a Young Man*, which begins publication in the January 15 issue.

JANUARY 29
Dodge holds an Evening devoted to magazine illustration; artists from the *Masses* confront Will Bradley about their exclusion from his uptown magazine, *Metropolitan*.

FEBRUARY
The month's issue of the *Glebe*, edited by Pound and entitled *Des Imagistes*, is devoted to Imagiste poets, including Aldington, Skipwith Cannell, John Cournos, H.D., Flint, Ford, Joyce, Lowell, Allen Upward, and Williams.

FEBRUARY 23
Pound begins a series of letters to Lowell, attempting to persuade her to invest in the *Egoist*. Lowell declines (on April 7) because the publication would require too much money before it could pay its own way.

LATE FEBRUARY
Pound moves to 5 Holland Place Chambers, London, on the same block as H.D., Aldington, and D. H. Lawrence.

MARCH
Carroll Galleries (supported by Quinn, advised by Pach and Kuhn) opens at 9 East Forty-fourth Street as an expansion of a decorating business and shows modern art.

The *Woman Rebel*, edited by Margaret Sanger and called "a paper for the advancement of woman's freedom," begins publication in the Village (published monthly until October 1914).

MARCH 1
Poetry gives a dinner in honor of William Butler Yeats at the Cliff Dwellers' Room in Chicago. The evening concludes with Lindsay's recitation of his new poem, "The Congo." (This marks the beginning of the oratory style Lindsay called the Higher Vaudeville.)

MARCH 2
Albert and Charles Boni publish *Des Imagistes* as a book; it is an exact reproduction of the February issue of the *Glebe*, but neither mentions the magazine nor acknowledges the original publication of many of the poems in *Poetry*.

MARCH 12
Constantin Brancusi has his first exhibition anywhere at 291.

SPRING
Demuth returns to the United States from Paris.

Cook and Glaspell buy a house in Provincetown.

Eliot leaves Harvard, where he has been a graduate assistant in philosophy, to pursue studies at the university in Marburg, Germany.

LATE MARCH
The *Little Review*, edited by Margaret Anderson in the Fine Arts Building, Chicago, begins publication (continues monthly until 1924 and less regularly until 1929).

APRIL
Des Imagistes is published in London by Harold Monro's Poetry Bookshop.

APRIL 20
Pound marries Dorothy Shakespear at Saint Mary Abbots before six guests.

APRIL 29
A meeting of the AAPS ends with the resignation of many of Henri's colleagues, marking the effective end of the association.

MAY
Van Vechten reviews *Granny Maumee*, by Ridgely Torrence, for *Trend*, the first of his many articles championing black contributions to the fine arts.

MAY 3
May Ray marries Adon Lacroix in Ridgefield, New Jersey.

MAY 13
De Zayas arrives in Paris, where he lives with Picabia and becomes acquainted with the Futurists and Apollinaire's friends at *Les Soirées de Paris* (which will be a model for *291*).

JUNE
The Claire Marie Press publishes *Tender Buttons* by Gertrude Stein in an edition of one hundred; Van Vechten is the liaison between Stein and the publisher, Donald Evans.

JUNE 20
BLAST, the organ of Vorticism, is published in London, edited by Wyndham Lewis. The leading Vorticists include Jacob Epstein, Henri Gaudier-Brzeska, Lewis, and Pound. (*BLAST*'s second and last issue is published in July 1915.)

SUMMER
Villagers invade Provincetown en masse for the first time. Among them are F. Sumner Boyd, Cook and Glaspell, Stuart Davis, Dell, Demuth, Eastman and Rauh, Joe O'Brien, and Mary Heaton Vorse. Polly Holladay and Hippolyte Havel set up a restaurant called the Greenwich Village Inn.

Margaret Anderson meets Emma Goldman in Chicago, and the *Little Review* begins its anarchist phase.

JUNE 28
The Archduke Francis Ferdinand of Austria and his wife are assassinated in Sarajevo, Yugoslavia.

JULY
Lowell arrives in London to get support for an Imagist anthology that is more inclusive and more widely distributed than *Des Imagistes*. Pound refuses to participate but invites Lowell to a dinner on July 15 at the Dieu-donné restaurant to celebrate the appearance of *BLAST*. On July 17 she responds with her own "Imagist Dinner," where the guests include Aldington, John Cournos, H.D., John Gould Fletcher, Flint, Ford, Pound, Dorothy Shakespear, and Allen Upward.

JULY 27
Eastman separates from Rauh in order to undergo self-analysis.

JULY 28
Austria-Hungary, with German support, declares war on Serbia. Russia mobilizes for war.

JULY 30
Aldington, H.D., and D. H. Lawrence dine at Lowell's suite in the Berkeley Hotel, and she secures their participation in her Imagist anthology. Lowell also enlists the participation of Fletcher and Flint.

BEFORE AUGUST 1
The Stettheimers return to New York from their extended travels in Europe and settle on West Seventy-sixth Street.

AUGUST 1
Germany declares war on Russia.

AUGUST 3
Germany declares war on France. The German army's drive through neutral Belgium gives Britain cause to enter the war.

AFTER AUGUST 3
With the outbreak of World War I the American and English expatriate colony in Florence disperses. Loy remains in Florence, working as a hospital nurse, and has an affair with the Futurist leader Filippo Tommaso Marinetti.

SEPTEMBER
Macmillan publishes *Sword Blades and Poppy Seed* by Lowell. This is her first book of Imagist poems.

Wallace Stevens publishes "Carnet de Voyage," his first poetry since college days, in *Trend*, a magazine edited by his Harvard classmate Pitts Sanborn.

ABOUT SEPTEMBER 22
On the recommendation of Conrad Aiken, Eliot calls on Pound.

FALL

H.D. and Aldington move to 7 Christchurch Place, Hampstead Heath, London; D. H. and Frieda Lawrence are neighbors.

Walter and Louise Arensberg move into a two-story apartment at 33 West Sixty-seventh Street, New York.

The idea of the Washington Square Players is first discussed by Albert Boni, Lawrence Langner, and Rauh.

OCTOBER

Poetry abolishes its $250 Guarantors' Prize and establishes the $200 Levinson Prize, which is limited, by donors' instruction, to an American poet. The prize goes to "Chicago Poems" by Carl Sandburg, despite Pound's objections.

Pound submits Eliot's "Love Song of J. Alfred Prufrock" to *Poetry*; Monroe waits nine months before publishing it.

Demuth has his first solo exhibition, at the Daniel Gallery, New York.

OCTOBER 21

Van Vechten marries Fania Marinoff in Connecticut.

NOVEMBER

The *Egoist* offers Lowell the editorship of its literary section in exchange for three hundred pounds a year; Lowell declines.

Herbert Croly begins the *New Republic*, "a journal of opinion which seeks to meet the challenge of a new time."

NOVEMBER 2

Pound announces (in the *Egoist*) his plan for a College of Arts to be taught by himself, Alvin Langdon Coburn, Arnold Dolmetsch, Gaudier-Brzeska, Wyndham Lewis, and others. The plan is never realized.

NOVEMBER 3

291's *African Savage Art* is America's first major exhibition of "primitive" art.

NOVEMBER 21

Walter Arensberg introduces Van Vechten to Stevens at a luncheon at the Brevoort.

LATE IN THE YEAR

Lowell begins a campaign to discredit Pound in the eyes of Monroe, continuing actively into early 1915.

DECEMBER

Stevens meets the Patagonians after seeing their writing in *Trend*, and for a while his work reflects their interest in fin-de-siècle poetry.

Lowell suggests to the *New Republic* that she become the magazine's poetry editor; her offer is declined.

Washington Square Gallery (directed by Robert Coady) opens at 47 Washington Square South (continues until late 1916, when Coady opens the Coady Gallery at 489 Fifth Avenue).

DECEMBER 1

Lowell gives her first public poetry reading, at a benefit for Belgium in Steinert Hall, Boston. Four hundred applaud.

1915

About this time Florine Stettheimer paints the first of her group pictures, *Studio Party* (also known as *Soirée*).

The Stettheimers meet Van Vechten and Marinoff (through Hopwood).

As the Village starts to be gentrified, the blocks west of Washington Square are reconstructed.

Holladay moves and expands her restaurant; Havel has been replaced by a more genial waiter named Mike. Other Greenwich Village tearooms proliferate.

Although *Poetry* has published the best new poets, it begins to lose them. Monroe offends some by delayed publication (Eliot, Williams), some by rejection (Marianne Moore), and some by emendation (Stevens).

Paul Strand shows Stieglitz his abstract photographs and becomes a member of the Stieglitz circle.

Freud becomes increasingly fashionable. Max Eastman and Floyd Dell write about his theories for the popular magazines; Dell, Dodge, Eastman, and Hapgood are among those who will enter psychoanalysis.

JANUARY

The July 1914 *Camera Work* is published, a special issue devoted to the question "What is 291?" Sixty-eight people respond, only four of them photographers. *Camera Work* then ends regular publication; two more issues appear before publication ceases entirely in June 1917.

JANUARY 5

Lowell meets Margaret Anderson in Chicago and proposes that she edit the poetry section of the *Little Review* in exchange for contributing $150 to the magazine. Anderson declines the offer.

ABOUT FEBRUARY
Walter Pach begins advising Quinn on his art collection.

FEBRUARY
In recognition of Quinn's work on legislation to permit the duty-free importation of art, the Metropolitan Museum of Art makes him an honorary fellow for life.

FEBRUARY 19
The Washington Square Players present their first bill, four one-act plays, at the Bandbox Theater (Fifty-seventh Street and Third Avenue).

FEBRUARY 25
Quinn begins a correspondence with Pound.

MARCH
291, edited by de Zayas and financed by Stieglitz, Haviland, and Agnes Ernst Meyer, begins publication (continues monthly until February 1916).

MARCH 15
Rogue, edited by Allen Norton and financed by Walter Arensberg, begins publication (continues semimonthly until September 15, 1915; publishes three additional issues in September–December 1916). Contributors include Arensberg, Evans, Loy, Louise Norton, Stevens, and Van Vechten.

At a dinner given by Allen and Louise Norton, Alfred Kreymborg meets Walter Arensberg and plans are first made for a little poetry magazine that will become *Others*.

MARCH 30
Lowell reads Imagist poems at the Poetry Society of America in New York. The event marks the beginning of her public-speaking campaign on behalf of new verse.

MARCH 31
Man Ray publishes the first and only issue of the *Ridgefield Gazook*, which is considered a proto-Dada periodical.

APRIL
Marianne Moore debuts in the *Egoist*.

APRIL 15
Houghton Mifflin publishes the first of Lowell's three anthologies, each called *Some Imagist Poets*. They all include six poets: Aldington, H.D., Fletcher, Flint, Lawrence, and Lowell.

MAY
Picabia sails for New York, on a mission for the French army. He promptly abandons his mission, instead spending his time with de Zayas, Haviland, and members of the Arensberg circle. During this seven-month visit Picabia is an active collaborator on *291*.

Moore makes her American debut in *Poetry*.

JUNE
E. E. Cummings delivers a commencement address at Harvard, "The New Art." He quotes one of Lowell's poems and notes its "clear development from the ordinary to the abnormal." The next day's *Boston Transcript* runs the headline "Harvard Orator Calls President Lowell's Sister Abnormal."

JUNE 4
Others holds its first meeting of poets (called a Dutch Treat) in Grantwood, New Jersey; twelve poets attend.

JUNE 5
Henri Gaudier-Brzeska is killed in battle at Neuville-Saint-Vaast, France. Pound compiles a memorial volume.

JUNE 15
Duchamp arrives in New York on the S.S. *Rochambeau*.

SUMMER
About this time the Village avant-garde becomes more widely known; articles such as "Who's Who in New York Bohemia" (in the *New York Tribune*) appear.

JULY
Others, edited by Kreymborg and initially financed by Arensberg, begins publication (continues monthly for fourteen issues then more sporadically until July 1919). Loy's "Love Songs" makes the first issue the subject of much controversy.

Dodge sends Reed's ring back to him, accompanied by a letter from Hapgood telling Reed the affair is over; Reed receives it in Bucharest and throws the ring in a canal.

Haviland is summoned to Limoges, France, to conduct the family business; a farewell party is held on July 4, a few days before his departure. His working association with Stieglitz ends.

JULY 15
The first production is staged by what will become the Provincetown Players: *Constancy* by Boyce begins the bill at 10 P.M., followed by *Suppressed Desires* by Glaspell and Cook. The plays

are presented in the front room of the Provincetown bungalow rented by Hapgood and Boyce. The second bill, including *Change Your Style* by Cook and *Contemporaries* by Wilbur Daniel Steele, begins September 5.

MID-AUGUST
De Zayas, Picabia, and Stieglitz gather in Oaklawn, New Jersey, to confer about the Modern Gallery.

SEPTEMBER
Albert and Juliet Gleizes arrive in New York on their honeymoon (aside from trips to Europe, they remain until 1919).

FALL
Demuth moves to the Village and lives on the south side of Washington Square (until spring 1916).

Poetry's Levinson Prize is given to Vachel Lindsay for "Chinese Nightingale." Monroe has raised an endowment for a $100 second prize, which is not limited to Americans only, and it goes to Constance Skinner. Pound's nominee for the Levinson Prize, Eliot's "Love Song of J. Alfred Prufrock," receives honorable mention.

Otto Kahn starts to provide financial support for the Washington Square Players (until September 1917).

OCTOBER
Gabrielle Buffet-Picabia arrives in New York to escort her husband to Cuba and Panama to finish his military mission.

Pound and Alvin Langdon Coburn invent the Vortoscope (a machine that uses mirrors and a camera to produce abstract photographs).

Man Ray has his first exhibition, at the Daniel Gallery; he photographs it, marking the beginning of his career as a photographer.

OCTOBER 7
The Modern Gallery opens at 500 Fifth Avenue (continues until April 1918). De Zayas conceives the gallery and serves as its director; Eugene Meyer finances it (with additional financing by Haviland and Picabia); and Picabia provides much of the initial stock of artworks by various artists. Its opening exhibition features Braque, Picabia, and Picasso.

Paul Sachs buys Shady Hill in Cambridge from his Harvard classmate Walter Arensberg.

NOVEMBER
Duchamp begins working for Belle Greene at the Morgan Library; the job was arranged by Quinn.

ABOUT DECEMBER
Francis Picabia and Gabrielle Buffet-Picabia return from Cuba and Panama to New York (remain until summer 1916). Possibly ill, Picabia reduces his public activity.

DECEMBER
Hartley returns from Berlin to New York and resumes relationships with the Dodge and Stieglitz circles.

Marianne Moore first visits New York from Pennsylvania; she dines with Kreymborg and visits 291 twice. Five of her poems are published in the December *Others*.

LATE WINTER
Stieglitz severs the connection between 291 and the Modern Gallery.

DECEMBER 29
Edgard Varèse arrives in New York after a twelve-day crossing from France, intending to stay only a few weeks (remains for the rest of his life).

1916
The Village is zoned as a residential area.

Jack Jones founds the Dill Pickle Club on Tooker Alley in Chicago and this restaurant becomes a bohemian gathering place. Although it lasts a decade, after the first few years it is largely a tourist attraction.

Florine Stettheimer holds her first unveiling party, in her studio in the Beaux Arts Building, on Fortieth Street between Fifth and Sixth avenues, for her portrait of Avery Hopwood. Among those present are Van Vechten and Duchamp.

JANUARY
Louise Bryant and Reed move in together at 43 Washington Square South.

JANUARY 1
Stieglitz, on his fifty-second birthday, sees a portfolio of charcoal drawings by O'Keeffe and exclaims, "Finally a woman on paper."

JANUARY 17
Diaghilev's Ballets Russes makes its American debut at the Century Theater in New York.

FEBRUARY
Witter Bynner and Arthur Davison Ficke conceive the Spectrist School of poetry (a hoax parodying Imagism) and, under the pseudonyms Emanuel Morgan and Anne Knish, they write the poems that form the Spectrist canon.

Margaret Anderson meets Jane Heap.

MARCH

Led by John Sloan, the artists at the *Masses* strike against Eastman and Dell. They want to replace the power of the editors with participatory democracy and to prevent the editors from adding captions to their drawings. When this resolution fails, Dell suggests that the rebels be expelled. In a conciliatory gesture they are elected to powerful positions, but instead resign.

Alfred A. Knopf publishes the first *Others* anthology.

MARCH 13

At 291 Paul Strand has his first exhibition anywhere.

MARCH 13–25

The Forum exhibition of work by nineteen American artists is held at the Anderson Galleries, New York, organized by Willard Huntington Wright and a committee that includes Stieglitz. Its purpose is to focus on Americans who had been overshadowed by the Europeans in the Armory Show.

MARCH 15

Quinn offers Pound a 100-pound-per-year subsidy to edit the *Egoist*; by April he increases this to 150 pounds.

SPRING

Heap joins the *Little Review* and immediately gives it a new sense of organization. She becomes Margaret Anderson's lover.

Alice Corbin Henderson moves to Santa Fe to recuperate from tuberculosis; her effect on *Poetry* diminishes.

Monroe visits New York and is fêted by Kreymborg and nearly sixty members of the poetry community.

APRIL

After receiving a copy of the *Little Review* from Anderson, Pound begins a correspondence with her.

APRIL 23

Arthur Cravan goes six rounds with the former world heavyweight champion Jack Johnson in Barcelona. He loses the fight but earns the 50,000 pesetas he needs to book passage to New York.

MAY

Stevens leaves New York for Hartford, Connecticut, where he will spend the rest of his life, working for the Hartford Accident and Indemnity Company.

Poetry publishes Alice Corbin Henderson's negative review of the *Others* anthology, which she derides as the "I-am-it" school of poetry.

The *Poetry Review of America*, founded by Stanley Braithwaite and financed by Lowell, begins publication (continues monthly until February 1917).

MAY 6

Lowell's second *Some Imagist Poets* anthology is published.

JUNE

Others loses both its publisher, John Marshall, and its editor, Kreymborg. From now on *Others* is run by a series of guest editors.

H.D. becomes assistant editor of the *Egoist*.

JUNE 8

Mabel Dodge receives her divorce from Edwin Dodge.

SUMMER

Carrie Stettheimer begins the dollhouse that she will work on until 1935.

Francis Picabia and Gabrielle Buffet-Picabia leave New York for neutral Barcelona, a popular haven for those who have fled France because of the war.

Among the Villagers vacationing in Provincetown are Cook and Glaspell; Dell; Dodge; Eastman and Rauh; Harry Kemp and his wife, Mary Pyne; and Kirah Markham. Guests at Reed's house include not only Bryant but also Hartley and Demuth; Havel cooks for this crew.

Heap and Anderson set up a makeshift home in the Muir Woods, in California.

JULY

Williams edits this month's *Others*.

JULY 28

The Provincetown Players stage the first production of a Eugene O'Neill play, *Bound East for Cardiff*, at the Wharf Theater in Provincetown.

SEPTEMBER

Williams publishes a premature obituary for *Others* in the *Egoist*: "At last the movement is dead. Now for the advance." The magazine continues, however, publishing irregularly.

The *Little Review* publishes an issue of blank pages, stating that there were no contributions of sufficient merit to fill them and calling the issue a "want ad" for better writing.

SEPTEMBER 1
John Lane publishes Sherwood Anderson's first novel, *Windy McPherson's Son*, which had been recommended to the publisher by Dell and Dreiser.

SEPTEMBER 4
Cook calls a meeting at the Wharf Theater to propose that the Provincetown Players continue their activities throughout the year. Twenty-nine people sign the roster (sixteen of them are members of the Liberal Club). Cook, Eastman, Reed, and the actor Fred Burt write a constitution, which is ratified at a meeting the following day. Also at this second meeting, an executive committee is set up (Bryant, Dell, Reed).

FALL
Marianne Moore, after four years spent teaching at the U.S. Indian School in Carlisle, Pennsylvania, moves to her brother's home in Chatham, New Jersey.

The first discussions of the Society of Independent Artists take place at the Arensbergs' apartment and at John Covert's apartment. One contingent of the society had helped organize Henri's Independents show of 1910 (William Glackens, president; Charles Prendergast, vice president; and directors Rockwell Kent and George Bellows). Most of the other founders are associated with the Arensberg circle (Walter Arensberg, managing director; Duchamp, director of installation; John Covert, secretary; Walter Pach, treasurer; and directors Katherine Dreier, John Marin, Man Ray, Morton Schamberg, and Joseph Stella). The society adopts a "no jury, no prizes" credo.

In New York, Mitchell Kennerley publishes *Spectra: A Book of Poetic Experiments* by Emanuel Morgan (Witter Bynner) and Anne Knish (Arthur Davison Ficke).

Poetry's Levinson Prize is awarded to Edgar Lee Masters's "All Life in a Life."

SEPTEMBER 27
While visiting Varèse, who is in the hospital after having been hit by a car, Beatrice Wood meets Duchamp.

SEPTEMBER 29
The Rogue Ball, a costume ball judged by Duchamp, celebrates *Rogue*'s second series. (After three monthly issues appear, the magazine ceases publication in December 1916.)

OCTOBER
Loy moves from Florence to New York, where she immediately enters the circles surrounding the Arensbergs, *Others*, and the Provincetown Players.

OCTOBER 14
Florine Stettheimer's exhibition of twelve paintings opens at Knoedler's gallery; it is her only one-person exhibition during her lifetime.

LATE FALL
Covert introduces Dreier into the Arensberg salon, where she meets Duchamp and Man Ray.

NOVEMBER
Henri-Pierre Roché arrives in New York as a diplomat with the French High Commission.

Seven Arts, edited by James Oppenheim with editorial assistance from Randolph Bourne, Van Wyck Brooks, and Waldo Frank, begins publication in New York (continues monthly until October 1917).

NOVEMBER 3
The first New York production of the Provincetown Players opens at 139 MacDougal Street. The bill includes O'Neill's *Bound East for Cardiff*, Bryant's *The Game*, and Dell's *King Arthur's Socks*.

NOVEMBER 9
Reed and Bryant are married at city hall in Peekskill, New York.

NOVEMBER 17
The Provincetown Players stage their second New York production: Reed's *Freedom*, Boyce and Hapgood's *Enemies*, and Cook and Glaspell's *Suppressed Desires*.

DECEMBER
Soil, published by Robert Coady, begins publication in New York (continues monthly until July 1917). The magazine espouses modernism, "primitive" art, and American popular art, but is highly irreverent toward the avant-garde.

The Provincetown Players hire their first salaried employee and form a revision committee, a production committee, and a scenic committee; Reed and Bryant resign from the executive committee.

DECEMBER 1
The Provincetown Players stage their third New York production: Boyce's *Two Sons*, Kreymborg's *Lima Beans* (starring Loy, Williams, and William Zorach), and O'Neill's *Before Breakfast*.

DECEMBER 5
The Society of Independent Artists is formally incorporated; Quinn donates the legal work.

LATE DECEMBER
Anderson and Heap move the *Little Review* to New York, helped by funds given by Lawrence Langer.

Monroe decides that *Poetry* will reaffirm its original purpose of seeking young and unknown poets.

1917
Knopf publishes the second *Others* anthology.

The New Poetry, an anthology coedited by Henderson and Monroe, is published.

Steichen commands the aerial photography division of the U.S. army.

At the Brevoort Café, Edgard Varèse meets Louise Norton.

Dreier, Louise Norton, and the Stettheimers take French lessons from Duchamp.

Dreier meets Roché; he later becomes an intermediary in her collecting.

JANUARY
Spectrist School poetry fills the entire issue of *Others*.

Quinn encourages Knopf to become the publisher of Pound and his protégés; by the end of the month Pound and Knopf meet and work out a publishing agreement.

Nina Moise, a professional director, begins working with the Provincetown Players.

Dodge advertises her services as an interior decorator in the *New Republic*.

Pound writes to Margaret Anderson, requesting to edit a section of the *Little Review*.

Longmans, Green and Company publishes *Philosophy* by Henri Waste (aka Ettie Stettheimer).

JANUARY 13
Arthur Cravan arrives in New York from Barcelona.

MID-JANUARY
The Society of Independent Artists sends out exhibition announcements to artists.

JANUARY 23
Duchamp, Sloan, and four others climb a secret stairway within Washington Arch and declare Greenwich Village "a Free Republic, Independent of Uptown."

JANUARY 25
Picabia publishes the first issue of *391*, in Barcelona (nineteen issues appear erratically, until 1924; the first four are published in Barcelona, the next three in New York, the remaining twelve in Zurich and Paris).

JANUARY 30
The first review of the Provincetown Players appears in the *New York Tribune* ("Down an Alley on Drama Trail" by Heywood Broun).

FEBRUARY 23
Maurice Browne's Little Theater in Chicago goes bankrupt.

MARCH
Pound sends the first three of his "Cantos" to Monroe.

In New York, Jules Pascin introduces Quinn to Roché.

MARCH 21
Several founding members of the Provincetown Players—Dell, Eastman, Hapgood—resign from the executive committee.

APRIL
The *Greenwich Village Spectator* begins publication (publishes monthly until June 1918).

APRIL 1
Varèse makes his American debut conducting Hector Berlioz's Requiem Mass before a huge crowd at the Hippodrome in New York.

APRIL 2
President Wilson asks Congress to declare war on Germany.

APRIL 3–MAY 15
O'Keeffe has her first one-person exhibition, at 291; it is the last show held there.

APRIL 4
Francis Picabia and Gabrielle Buffet-Picabia return to New York.

APRIL 6
America declares war.

APRIL 9
The Society of Independent Artists holds a large private viewing of their exhibition. The society rejects Duchamp's *Fountain*; Duchamp and Arensberg resign.

APRIL 10

The First Annual Exhibition of the Society of Independent Artists opens at the Grand Central Palace (closes May 6). The exhibition includes approximately twenty-five hundred works, hung in alphabetical order, by over twelve hundred artists from thirty-eight states.

Duchamp, Roché, and Beatrice Wood publish the *Blind Man* no. 1, a special Independents periodical; financing comes from Gertrude Whitney.

APRIL 11

Isadora Duncan and her pupils perform at the Metropolitan Opera in New York; Duncan's performance of the *Star-Spangled Banner*, draped in an American flag, is transformed into a patriotic recruiting event.

APRIL 12

A Latin Quarter ball, organized by Dreier, is held at the Grand Central Palace; profits benefit the Red Cross.

APRIL 18

Poets read at the Independents exhibition. They include Maxwell Bodenheim, Harry Kemp, Loy, Allen Norton, Pitts Sanborn, and Williams. Members of the audience are also invited to read their own poems.

APRIL 19

Scheduled to lecture at the Grand Central Palace, an inebriated Cravan instead swears, begins to disrobe, and is handcuffed and taken away by the house detectives. Walter Arensberg bails him out.

APRIL 20

The Independents Ball, a fancy costume ball with guests dressed as schools of art, is held at the Grand Central Palace.

APRIL 24

The last of Lowell's *Some Imagist Poets* anthologies is published. The first two anthologies had gone into multiple printings, but this final one sells only 406 copies.

MAY

Pound begins as foreign correspondent for the *Little Review*. In his editorial he clarifies his complicated relations with the little magazines: *Poetry*, the *Egoist*, and the *Little Review*.

MAY 3

After meeting with Margaret Anderson, Quinn confirms his plan to give Pound $750 per year to pay contributors selected by Pound for the *Little Review*.

MAY 5

The *Blind Man* no. 2 focuses on the case of R. Mutt and *Fountain*.

MAY 18

The U.S. draft is enacted.

MAY 25

The Blindman's Ball is held at Webster Hall, in the Village.

LATE MAY

The *New York Mail* hires Reed to write daily articles.

JUNE

The last issue of *Camera Work* is published, devoted entirely to the photographer Paul Strand.

When H.D. vacates the position, Eliot becomes assistant editor of the *Egoist*. In the same month the Egoist, Ltd., publishes Eliot's *Prufrock and Other Observations* in an edition of five hundred.

JUNE 15

Congress passes the Espionage Act, making words as well as deeds treasonable.

SUMMER

After Buffet-Picabia departs for Europe, Picabia shares his flat, sublet from Louise Norton, with Varèse; the Gleizeses live upstairs. Picabia has an affair with Isadora Duncan.

Dodd, Mead publishes Anna Alice Chapin's mainstream, hardbound guide, *Greenwich Village*.

JUNE 30

The *Quill*, a Village magazine, begins publication (publishes monthly until May 1929). Its first issue notes that there are twenty-five tearooms in the Village, four of them in Washington Square and six in Sheridan Square.

ABOUT JULY

Rongwrong is published, edited by Duchamp and Man Ray. Picabia (representing *391*) challenges Roché (representing *Rongwrong*) to a chess match to determine which proto-Dada magazine will continue; Roché loses and *Rongwrong* ceases publication.

JULY 5

The U.S. Post Office Department informs the *Masses* that it has found the magazine "unmailable under the [Espionage] Act of June 15, 1917."

JULY 23

Pound ends his role as the foreign correspondent for *Poetry*, although this is not formally announced for two years.

JULY 28
At their summer home near Tarrytown, New York, the Stettheimers throw a thirtieth-birthday party for Duchamp, recorded in Florine Stettheimer's painting *La Fête à Duchamp*.

AUGUST
The Post Office again declares an issue of the *Masses* unmailable.

AUGUST 15
Reed sails for Russia to report on the Bolshevik Revolution.

AUGUST 23
Dodge marries the artist Maurice Sterne in Peekskill, New York, with Andrew Dasburg and Ida Rauh as witnesses.

SEPTEMBER
Williams's *Al Que Quiere!* is published; its title contains a punning tribute to Alfred Kreymborg.

Reed arrives in Petrograd.

To avoid conscription, Cravan hitchhikes to Canada with his friend the artist A. B. Frost, Jr.

MID-SEPTEMBER
Buffet-Picabia leaves New York for Switzerland.

FALL
The first five years of *Poetry*'s guarantors' subscription are over; Monroe solicits new guarantors.

OCTOBER
Loy and Haweis are divorced.

The Postmaster General revokes the *Masses'* right to second-class mailing privileges on the grounds that the magazine has skipped mailing an issue (which resulted from the refusal of the Post Office to mail the magazine). This strategy is upheld in a three-man circuit court in November.

The Post Office suppresses this month's issue of the *Little Review* for publishing "Cantleman's Spring Mate," by Wyndham Lewis.

Seven Arts ceases publication when its benefactor, Aileen Rankine, withdraws financial support due to its pacifist views (she commits suicide a few weeks later).

Picabia leaves New York for Switzerland; he never returns to New York.

OCTOBER 10
Houghton Mifflin publishes *Tendencies in Modern American Poetry* by Lowell.

NOVEMBER
Poetry awards its Levinson Prize ($250) to "Grotesques," a verse play by Cloyd Head; Robert Frost receives second prize ($100) for "Snow."

NOVEMBER 15
The Greenwich Village Theatre (capacity 450) opens at Sheridan Square (the juncture of Fourth Street and Seventh Avenue), the new center of Greenwich Village.

ABOUT DECEMBER
The IRT subway line opens its Sheridan Square station, connecting the Village to the rest of New York.

DECEMBER
As a result of the Post Office's harassment, the *Masses* goes out of business.

Cravan writes to Loy from Mexico City, asking her to marry him there.

MID-DECEMBER
Dodge leaves New York for Taos, New Mexico.

DECEMBER 19
Pound receives the first chapters of Joyce's manuscript for *Ulysses*.

DECEMBER 22
Haviland marries Suzanne Lalique, of the Lalique glass family, in France.

1918
The Arensberg salon is limited to one or two nights per week.

After Boyce Hapgood, the eldest son of Hutchins Hapgood and Neith Boyce, dies of influenza in Colorado, Boyce begins to have mystical experiences, and Hapgood begins reading the Bible.

Poetry's Levinson prize is given to John Curtis Underwood for "Song of the Cheechas." Later it is determined that the poem drew heavily from an unacknowledged source.

JANUARY
Loy joins Cravan in Mexico.

Dodge meets Antonio Luhan, a Tiwa Indian.

FEBRUARY
The *Quill* reports forty-three tearooms in the Village.

Margaret Anderson receives the manuscript for the first section of Joyce's *Ulysses*.

Dreier commissions Duchamp to paint *Tu m'* for the space above her bookcase at 135 Central Park West.

MARCH

Max Eastman and Crystal Eastman (his sister) found the *Liberator*, a self-censoring successor to the *Masses*. Dell is the managing editor and Reed is a contributing editor. (It publishes monthly until October 1924.)

The *Little Review* begins serializing *Ulysses*.

APRIL

Anderson and Heap introduce William Carlos Williams to the Baroness Elsa von Freytag-Loringhoven.

The Modern Gallery closes.

The first *Masses* conspiracy trial is held, in which the United States charges Josephine Bell, Floyd Dell, Max Eastman, Henry Glintenkamp, John Reed, Merrill Rogers, and Art Young with conspiring to obstruct enlistment. Due to a split jury, the case is dismissed.

APRIL 25

It is revealed in the *Dial* that the Spectrist School of poetry was a hoax.

JUNE

The Whitney Studio Club opens at 147 West Fourth Street. Run by Juliana Force and Gertrude Vanderbilt Whitney, it is both a club for artists and an exhibition space.

In a small rebellion against Pound's endorsement of English writers in the *Little Review*, Heap organizes an all-American issue. Included are Sherwood Anderson, Djuna Barnes, Ben Hecht, Kreymborg, Lowell, Sandburg, Stevens, and Williams.

JUNE 9

O'Keeffe arrives in New York, having traveled with Paul Strand from Canyon, Texas; her romantic relationship with Stieglitz begins within the year.

JUNE 22

Dodge buys twelve acres of meadow, orchard, and high land in Taos.

SUMMER

Luhan serenades Dodge from her lawn, and they soon become lovers.

JULY 17

H.D. meets Winifred Ellerman, known as Bryher.

JULY 23

Duchamp gives Carrie Stettheimer a miniature version of his *Nude Descending a Staircase* for her dollhouse.

AUGUST 13

Duchamp leaves the country for Buenos Aires, largely in order to avoid American military service. He is accompanied by Yvonne Crotti and a *Sculpture for Travelling*.

AUGUST 18

Dreier follows Duchamp to Buenos Aires.

OCTOBER

The second *Masses* conspiracy trial is held, ending in a divided jury, and the defendants are dismissed.

OCTOBER 13

Morton Schamberg dies in the worldwide influenza epidemic.

NOVEMBER

The close alliance between Williams and Kreymborg ruptures. They are partly reconciled, and Williams dedicates his next book of poems to Kreymborg, but its title, *Sour Grapes*, suggests Williams's mixed feelings.

Loy sails on a Japanese hospital ship from Mexico to Buenos Aires. Though he had planned to follow, Cravan is never heard from again.

NOVEMBER 11

World War I ends.

NOVEMBER 22

The Provincetown Players begin a new season in a new, larger location, at 133 MacDougal Street, where they will remain until 1922.

DECEMBER

The Theatre Guild, an outgrowth of the Washington Square Players, is founded.

The *Little Review* publishes a second Americans-only issue (Djuna Barnes, Elsa von Freytag-Loringhoven, Hartley, Moore, Stevens, Williams).

1919

John Marshall publishes the third and last *Others* anthology.

Loy travels from Buenos Aires to Florence, where she is reunited with her two children.

FEBRUARY 8

Dell marries B. Marie Gage, a socialist and pacifist.

MARCH

Man Ray and Adolf Wolff publish *TNT*, a one-issue anarchist and avant-garde art magazine.

APRIL

Dreier returns from Buenos Aires to New York.

H.D. and Aldington permanently separate.

APRIL 11
Varèse forms the New Symphony Orchestra in New York. Its first concert (with music by Debussy, Casella, Bartók, Dupont, and Bach) is held at Carnegie Hall.

MAY
Pound resigns as foreign editor for the *Little Review*.

MAY 31
H.D.'s child, Perdita, is born (most likely fathered either by Cecil Gray or D. H. Lawrence).

JULY
Asked to edit both the July and August issues of *Others*, Williams takes it upon himself to end the magazine.

Duchamp sails from Argentina to Paris. Once there, he stays with Picabia and becomes acquainted with the Dada group that gathers at the Café Certá.

Prohibition begins.

AUGUST
In Europe, Dreier meets Alexander Archipenko, Constantin Brancusi, and Max Ernst and visits Herwarth Walden's Sturm Gallery in Berlin.

SEPTEMBER
Roché assumes his role as the most influential agent of Quinn's collection.

In recognition of his service to French art, Quinn is named to the French Legion of Honor.

FALL
The de Zayas Gallery—financed by Walter Arensberg, with Marius de Zayas as director—opens at 549 Fifth Avenue, New York (continues until 1921).

Aldington becomes the foreign editor of *Poetry* (continues until summer 1921).

OCTOBER 3
Cook and Glaspell relinquish control of the Provincetown Players in order to write in Provincetown; the Players' so-called Season of Youth begins, under the direction of Ida Rauh and James Light.

LATE WINTER–SPRING 1920
Walter Arensberg's drinking increases, and the Arensbergs' finances are depleted by his ill-considered loans.

LATE IN THE YEAR
Elie Nadelman marries a wealthy widow, Mrs. Joseph A. Flannery.

DECEMBER
The *Egoist* ends publication.

1920
JANUARY
Duchamp returns from Paris to New York.

FEBRUARY 3
Beyond the Horizon premieres, the first O'Neill play on Broadway; it will win a Pulitzer Prize.

EARLY IN THE YEAR
Quinn helps Pound become the foreign correspondent for the *Dial* (continues until May 1923).

APRIL 29
The Société Anonyme, Inc.—founded by Dreier, Marcel Duchamp, and Man Ray—is incorporated. Its headquarters are at 19 East Forty-seventh Street, New York.

AUGUST
Walter and Louise Arensberg travel to Los Angeles; they move to Los Angeles in 1921.

SEPTEMBER
H.D. and Bryher arrive in New York.

OCTOBER
The editors of the *Little Review* and the proprietor of the Washington Square Bookshop are arrested on obscenity charges for serializing *Ulysses*. Only half of the novel has been serialized; copies have been confiscated four times since serialization began.

OCTOBER 17
Reed dies of typhus in Russia and four days later is buried next to the Kremlin wall.

DECEMBER
Contact, edited by Williams and Robert McAlmon, and financed by Bryher, begins publication (continues irregularly until June 1923).

ACKNOWLEDGMENTS

This book is dedicated to my father and mother
and to Robert Atkins, for loving support.
And to Beatrice Wood,
the pulchritudinous saint of the era.

This book could never have been written without the generosity of numerous individuals. Several scholars have been especially important to me. Francis M. Naumann has zealously unearthed—and shared—gargantuan amounts of information about this period; his work on Marcel Duchamp, Man Ray, and other members of the Arensberg circle has greatly enriched my own. Roger L. Conover has been supportive throughout this project, providing information and images related to Mina Loy and Arthur Cravan and expressing confidence in this book's significance. Naomi Sawelson-Gorse's meticulous archival research on the Arensbergs proved invaluable. Carolyn Burke graciously shared her research about Mina Loy (for her forthcoming biography) and was especially helpful regarding Loy's relationships with the Futurists. Barbara Kramer shared information from her long and sometimes frustrating labors in tracking the Stettheimer sisters. Terry Miller provided additions and corrections to the maps of Greenwich Village. I am, additionally, indebted to Lois Palken Rudnick's work on Mabel Dodge Luhan and to Steve Golin's re-creation of the Paterson Strike Pageant.

I greatly enjoyed and appreciated my interviews with the long-lived avant-gardists and with those who knew them. Beatrice Wood was a crucial source—not only for her specific memories but because she embodies the adventurous spirit of that vanguard era. Joella Bayer, charming and worldly, provided information about her mother, Mina Loy. Paul Draper discussed his mother, Muriel Draper, one of the period's lesser-known yet intriguing figures. Berenice Abbott engagingly recalled her first years in Greenwich Village and her memories of the Baronness Elsa von Freytag-Loringhoven. Sir Harold Acton wittily recounted his childhood experiences in Florence and at the Villa Curonia. Joseph Solomon shared his memories of the Stettheimer sisters. Monroe Wheeler spoke vividly of his early memories of Chicago. James Amster recalled Muriel Draper. Virgil Thomson described Gertrude Stein and the Stettheimers, and dispensed his Continental brand of Missouri wisdom.

Patricia Willis, curator of the Yale Collection of American Literature at Yale's Beinecke Library, has been especially helpful. My trips to this treasure trove were a great pleasure; a result of the wonderful setting, the prescient collecting instincts of Donald Gallup, and its first-rate staff (in particular Steve Jones and Lori Misura). I am also indebted to the Newberry Library in Chicago for a research fellowship and for the assistance of its helpful curator, Diana Haskell. I also wish to thank staff members at the other libraries that have contributed to my research: the Harry Ransom Humanities Research Center at the University of Texas, Austin, the New York Public Library, the Columbia University Library, and the Library of Congress.

I am especially grateful to the people who read my manuscript: Marsha Amstel, Robert L. Caserio, Mason Cooley, Eric Himmel, Don Shewey, and Beatrice Wood. Their insights helped shape the book and renewed my flagging energies. Many others helped in diverse ways both great and small: Rebecca J. Bates, Linda Ben-Zvi, Avis Berman, Jay Bochner, Edward Burns, William Camfield, Ulla Dydo, Betsy Fahlman, Peter Galassi, Maria Hambourg, Stanley Mallach, Cindy Mann, Faith Middleton, Max Miltzlaff, Ann Lee Morgan, Jan Pciun, Jan Ramirez, Robert Reiss, and James Sturm.

The enthusiastic dedication of those responsible for all the various stages involved in publishing this book has gone beyond mere professional duty. I'd particularly like to thank: Laura Lindgren and Philip Reynolds, for their carefulness as copy editor and production editor, respectively; Lisa Rosen, for doggedly tracking down photos; Joel Avirom, for elegantly solving the devilishly complicated problems of design, and to Dana Cole, for making sure the final results looked just right.

Two people have shared in the ups and downs of this five-year project, from the optimism of the initial conception to the exhaustion of the final details. To them I am especially grateful. My editor, Nancy Grubb, managed to balance intelligent enthusiasm with an appropriately ruthless editing pencil; she never lost perspective during her long stewardship of the manuscript. Robert Atkins read the manuscript repeatedly, in all its bits and pieces, and punched it into shape; his critical yet loving support was invaluable.

SELECTED BIBLIOGRAPHY

ARCHIVAL SOURCES

Archives of American Art, Smithsonian Institution, Washington, D.C.
Louis Bouché Oral History. Walt Kuhn Papers. Beatrice Wood Papers.

Columbia University, New York
Butler Library, Oral History Research Office
Carl Van Vechten Oral History. Max Weber Oral History.

Rare Book and Manuscript Library
Marius de Zayas Papers. Florine Stettheimer Papers.

Francis Bacon Library, Claremont, California
Arensberg Archives.

Golda Meir Library, University of Wisconsin, Milwaukee
Little Review Papers.

Harry Ransom Humanities Research Center, University of Texas, Austin
Alice Corbin Henderson Collection. Parker Tyler Collection.

Houghton Library, Harvard University, Cambridge, Massachusetts
Amy Lowell Collection. John Reed Papers.

Library of Congress, Washington, D.C.
Papers of Janet Flanner and Solita Solano (includes Margaret Anderson Papers).

Museum of Modern Art, New York
Aline Farelly Scrapbook. Edward Steichen Chronology, by Grace Mayer.

Newberry Library, Chicago
Floyd Dell Papers. Sherwood Anderson Papers. Dale Kramer Collection. The Little Room Papers.

New York Public Library, Astor, Lenox, and Tilden Foundations
Rare Books and Manuscripts Division
John Quinn Memorial Collection. Carl Van Vechten Papers.

Henry W. Berg and Albert A. Berg Collection
George Cram Cook Collection. Susan Glaspell Collection.

Philadelphia Museum of Art
Arensberg Archive.

University of Chicago Library, Department of Special Collections
Harriet Monroe Papers. Papers of *Poetry* Magazine, 1912–36.

Yale Collection of American Literature, The Beinecke Rare Book and Manuscript Library, Yale University, New Haven, Connecticut
H.D. Collection. Muriel Draper Collection. Max Ewing Collection. Hutchins Hapgood Collection. Marsden Hartley Collection. Mina Loy Collection. Mabel Dodge Luhan Collection. Henry McBride Collection. Gertrude Stein Collection. Société Anonyme Archives. Stettheimer Collection. Alfred Stieglitz Collection. Carl Van Vechten Collection.

BOOKS AND DISSERTATIONS

Abrahams, Edward. *The Lyrical Left: Randolph Bourne, Alfred Stieglitz and the Origins of Cultural Radicalism in America.* Charlottesville: University Press of Virginia, 1986.

Ackroyd, Peter. *T. S. Eliot: A Life.* New York: Simon and Schuster, 1984.

Acton, Harold. *Memoirs of an Aesthete.* London: Methuen, 1948.

Aiken, Conrad. *Ushant, an Essay.* New York: Duell, Sloan, and Pearce, 1952.

Aldington, Richard. *Life for Life's Sake.* New York: Viking, 1941.

Anderson, Margaret. *My Thirty Years' War.* New York: Covici-Friede, 1930.

———. *The Fiery Fountains.* New York: Hermitage House, 1951.

———, ed. *The Little Review Anthology.* New York: Hermitage House, 1953.

Anderson, Sherwood. *Sherwood Anderson's Memoirs.* New York: Harcourt, Brace, 1942.

Baldwin, Neil. *Man Ray: American Artist.* New York: Clarkson N. Potter, 1988.

Barnes, Djuna. *Greenwich Village as It Is.* New York: Phoenix Bookshop, 1978.

Benstock, Shari. *Women of the Left Bank: Paris, 1900–1940.* Austin: University of Texas Press, 1986.

Biddle, George. *An American Artist's Story.* Boston: Little, Brown, 1939.

Borras, Maria Lluisa. *Picabia.* New York: Rizzoli, 1985.

Brinnin, John Malcolm. *The Third Rose: Gertrude Stein and Her World.* Boston: Little, Brown, 1959.

Brooks, Van Wyck. *New England: Indian Summer, 1865–1915.* New York: E. P. Dutton, 1940.

———. *John Sloan: A Painter's Life.* New York: E. P. Dutton, 1955.

Brown, Milton. *American Painting from the Armory to the Depression*. Princeton, N.J.: Princeton University Press, 1955.

———. *The Story of the Armory Show*. New York: Abbeville, 1988.

Bryer, Jackson. "'A Trial Track for Racers': Margaret Anderson and *The Little Review*." Ph.D. diss., University of Wisconsin, 1965.

Bryher [Winifred Ellerman]. *Two Selves*. Paris: Contact, 1923.

———. *The Heart to Artemis: A Writer's Memoirs*. New York: Harcourt, Brace, 1962.

Burns, Edward, ed. *The Letters of Gertrude Stein and Carl Van Vechten, 1913–1946*. New York: Columbia University Press, 1986.

Cabanne, Pierre. *Dialogues with Marcel Duchamp*. Translated by Ron Padgett. New York: Da Capo, 1987.

Camfield, William. *Francis Picabia: His Art, Life and Times*. Princeton, N.J.: Princeton University Press, 1979.

———. *Marcel Duchamp/Fountain*. Houston: Houston Fine Art Press, 1989.

Carpenter, Humphrey. *A Serious Character: The Life of Ezra Pound*. Boston: Houghton Mifflin, 1988.

Chapin, Anna Alice. *Greenwich Village*. New York: Dodd, Mead, 1917.

Churchill, Allen. *The Improper Bohemians: The Re-Creation of Greenwich Village in Its Heyday*. New York: E. P. Dutton, 1959.

Coleman, Glenn. *Imagism and Imagists*. Stanford, Calif.: Stanford University Press, 1931.

Damon, S. Foster. *Amy Lowell: A Chronicle with Extracts from Her Correspondence*. Boston: Houghton Mifflin, 1935.

Delaney, Edmund T. *Greenwich Village*. Barre, Mass.: Barre, 1968.

Dell, Floyd. *Moon-Calf*. New York: Alfred A. Knopf, 1920.

———. *Looking at Life*. New York: Alfred A. Knopf, 1924.

———. *Love in Greenwich Village*. New York: George H. Doran, 1926.

———. *Homecoming: An Autobiography*. New York: Farrar and Rinehart, 1933.

d'Harnoncourt, Anne, and Kynaston McShine, eds. *Marcel Duchamp*. New York: Museum of Modern Art; Philadelphia: Philadelphia Museum of Art, 1973.

H.D. [Hilda Doolittle]. *End to Torment*. Edited by Norman Holmes Pearson and Michael King. New York: New Directions, 1979.

Draper, Muriel. *Music at Midnight*. New York: Harper and Brothers, 1929.

Dreier, Katherine. *Western Art and the New Era*. New York: Brentano's, 1923.

Duffey, Bernard. *The Chicago Renaissance in American Letters: A Critical History*. East Lansing: Michigan State College Press, 1953.

Eastman, Max. *Enjoyment of Living*. New York: Harper and Brothers, 1948.

———. *Love and Revolution: My Journey through an Epoch*. New York: Random House, 1964.

A Fabulous Dollhouse of the Twenties. New York: Dover, 1976.

Farnham, Emily. "Charles Demuth: His Life, Psychology and Works." Ph.D. diss., Ohio State University, 1959.

Fishbein, Leslie. *Rebels in Bohemia: The Radicals of the Masses, 1911–1917*. Chapel Hill: University of North Carolina Press, 1982.

Fletcher, John Gould. *Life Is My Song*. New York: Farrar and Rinehart, 1937.

Ford, Ford Madox. *Return to Yesterday*. London: Victor Gollancz, 1931.

Ford, Hugh. *Four Lives in Paris*. San Francisco: North Point, 1987.

Four Americans in Paris: The Collections of Gertrude Stein and Her Family. New York: Museum of Modern Art, 1970.

Frank, Waldo, Lewis Mumford, Dorothy Norman, Paul Rosenfeld, and Harold Rugg, eds. *America and Alfred Stieglitz: A Collective Portrait*. Millerton, N.Y.: Aperture, 1979.

Gallup, Donald, ed. *The Flowers of Friendship: Letters Written to Gertrude Stein*. New York: Alfred A. Knopf, 1953.

Gardner, Virginia. *"Friend and Lover": The Life of Louise Bryant*. New York: Horizon, 1982.

Gelb, Arthur, and Barbara Gelb. *O'Neill*. New York: Harper and Brothers, 1962.

Gelb, Barbara. *So Short a Time: A Biography of John Reed and Louise Bryant*. New York: W. W. Norton, 1973.

Glaspell, Susan. *The Road to the Temple*. New York: Frederick A. Stokes, 1927.

Goldring, Douglas. *South Lodge*. London: Constable, 1943.

Golin, Steve. *The Fragile Bridge: The Paterson Silk Strike*. Philadelphia: Temple University Press, 1988.

Gordon, Lyndall. *Eliot's Early Years*. New York: Oxford University Press, 1977.

Gould, Jean. *Amy: The World of Amy Lowell and the Imagist Movement*. New York: Dodd, Mead, 1975.

Green, Martin. *New York 1913: The Armory Show and the Paterson Strike Pageant*. New York: Charles Scribner's Sons, 1988.

Guest, Barbara. *Herself Defined: The Poet H.D. and Her World*. Garden City, N.Y.: Doubleday, 1984.

Hackett, Francis. *American Rainbow: Early Reminiscences*. New York: Liveright, 1970.

Hansen, Harry. *Midwestern Portraits*. New York: Harcourt, Brace, 1923.

Hapgood, Hutchins. *A Victorian in the Modern World*. New York: Harcourt, Brace, 1939.

Haskell, Barbara. *Marsden Hartley*. New York: Whitney Museum of American Art, 1980.

————. *Charles Demuth*. New York: Whitney Museum of American Art; Harry N. Abrams, 1987.

Herbert, Robert L., Eleanor S. Apter, and Elise K. Kenney. *The Société Anonyme and the Dreier Bequest at Yale University: A Catalogue Raisonné*. New Haven, Conn.: Yale University, 1984.

Heymann, C. David. *American Aristocracy: The Lives and Times of James Russell, Amy, and Robert Lowell*. New York: Dodd, Mead, 1980.

Hicks, Granville. *John Reed: The Making of a Revolutionary*. New York: Macmillan, 1936.

Hoffman, Frederick J., Charles Allen, and Carolyn F. Ulrich. *The Little Magazine: A History and Bibliography*. Princeton, N.J.: Princeton University Press, 1946.

Homer, William Innes. *Robert Henri and His Circle*. Ithaca, N.Y.: Cornell University Press, 1969.

————. *Alfred Stieglitz and the American Avant-Garde*. Boston: New York Graphic Society, 1977.

————. *Alfred Stieglitz and the Photo-Secession*. Boston: Little, Brown, 1977.

Humphrey, Robert E. *Children of Fantasy: The First Rebels of Greenwich Village*. New York: John Wiley and Sons, 1978.

Hutchins, Patricia. *Pound's Kensington: An Exploration, 1885–1913*. London: Faber and Faber, 1965.

Hyland, Douglas. *Marius de Zayas: Conjurer of Souls*. Lawrence, Kans.: Spencer Museum of Art, 1981.

Johns, Orrick. *Time of Our Lives: The Story of My Father and Myself*. New York: Stackpole Sons, 1937.

Jullian, Philippe. *De Meyer*. New York: Alfred A. Knopf, 1976.

Kahnweiler, Daniel, and Francis Crémieux. *My Galleries and Painters*. Translated by Helen Weaver. New York: Viking, 1971.

Kellner, Bruce. *Carl Van Vechten and the Irreverent Decades*. Norman: University of Oklahoma Press, 1968.

Kirstein, Lincoln. *Elie Nadelman*. New York: Eakins, 1973.

Klüver, Billy, and Julie Martin. *Kiki's Paris*. New York: Harry N. Abrams, 1989.

Kornbluh, Jesse, ed. *Rebel Voices: An I.W.W. Anthology*. Ann Arbor: University of Michigan Press, 1964.

Kramer, Dale. *The Chicago Renaissance*. New York: Appleton-Century, 1966.

Kreymborg, Alfred. *Troubadour: An Autobiography*. New York: Boni and Liveright, 1925.

————. *Our Singing Strength: An Outline of American Poetry (1620–1930)*. New York: Coward-McCann, 1929.

Kuenzli, Rudolf E., ed. *New York Dada*. New York: Willis Locker and Owens, 1986.

———— and Francis Naumann, eds. *Marcel Duchamp: Artist of the Century*. Cambridge, Mass.: MIT Press, 1989.

Kuhn, Walt. *The Story of the Armory Show*. New York: Walt Kuhn, 1938.

Langner, Lawrence. *The Magic Curtain*. New York: E. P. Dutton, 1951.

Lebel, Robert. *Marcel Duchamp*. Translated by George Heard Hamilton. New York: Paragraphic Books, 1959.

Lindberg-Seyersted, Brita, ed. *Pound/Ford: The Story of a Literary Friendship*. New York: New Directions, 1982.

Lisle, Laurie. *Portrait of an Artist: A Biography of Georgia O'Keeffe*. New York: Seaview, 1980.

Lowe, Sue Davidson. *Stieglitz: A Memoir/Biography*. New York: Farrar, Straus, and Giroux, 1983.

Lowell, Amy. *Sword Blades and Poppy Seed*. New York: Macmillan, 1914.

————. *Tendencies in Modern American Poetry*. New York: Macmillan, 1917.

Loy, Mina. *The Last Lunar Baedeker*. Edited by Roger L. Conover. Highlands, N.C.: Jargon Society, 1982.

Luhan, Mabel Dodge. *European Experiences*. Volume 2 of *Intimate Memories*. New York: Harcourt, Brace, 1935.

————. *Movers and Shakers*. Volume 3 of *Intimate Memories*. New York: Harcourt, Brace, 1936.

————. *The Edge of Taos Desert: An Escape to Reality*. Volume 4 of *Intimate Memories*. New York: Harcourt, Brace, 1937.

McBride, Henry. *Florine Stettheimer*. New York: Museum of Modern Art, 1946.

————. *The Flow of Art: Essays and Criticism of Henry McBride*. Edited by Daniel Catton Rich. New York: Atheneum, 1975.

Macleod, Glen. *Wallace Stevens and Company: The Harmonium Years, 1913–1923*. Ann Arbor, Mich.: UMI Research Press, 1981.

Marcaccio, Michael. *The Hapgoods: Three Earnest Brothers*. Charlottesville: University Press of Virginia, 1977.

Mariani, Paul. *William Carlos Williams: A New World Naked*. New York: McGraw-Hill, 1981.

Marling, William. *William Carlos Williams and the Painters, 1909–1923*. Athens, Ohio: Ohio University Press, 1982.

Marquis, Alice Goldfarb. *Marcel Duchamp: Eros, C'est la Vie*. Troy, N.Y.: Whitson Publishing Company, 1981.

May, Henry. *The End of American Innocence: A Study of the First Years of Our Own Time, 1912–1917*. New York: Alfred A. Knopf, 1959.

Mellow, James. *Charmed Circle: Gertrude Stein and Company*. New York: Holt, Rinehart and Winston, 1974.

Mellquist, Jerome. *The Emergence of an American Art*. New York: Charles Scribner's Sons, 1942.

Meyer, Agnes Ernst. *Out of These Roots: The Autobiography of an American Woman*. Boston: Little, Brown, 1953.

Middlebrook, Diane Wood, and Marilyn Yalom, eds. *Coming to Light: American Women Poets in the Twentieth Century*. Ann Arbor: University of Michigan Press, 1985.

Miller, Terry. *Greenwich Village and How It Got That Way*. New York: Crown, 1990.

Mizener, Arthur. *The Saddest Story: A Biography of Ford Madox Ford*. New York: Harper and Row, 1971.

Monroe, Harriet. *A Poet's Life*. New York: Macmillan, 1938.

Morgan, Anna Lee. *Arthur Dove: Life and Work, with a Catalogue Raisonné*. Newark, Del.: University of Delaware Press, 1984.

Motherwell, Robert, ed. *The Dada Painters and Poets: An Anthology*. 2d ed. Cambridge and London: Harvard University Press, Belknap Press, 1989.

Myers, Jerome. *An Artist in Manhattan*. New York: American Artists Group, 1940.

Naef, Weston. *The Collection of Alfred Stieglitz*. New York: Metropolitan Museum of Art; Viking, 1978.

Norman, Charles. *Ezra Pound*. New York: Macmillan, 1960.

Olivier, Fernande. *Picasso and His Friends*. Translated by Jane Miller. New York: Appleton-Century, 1965.

O'Neill, William. *The Last Romantic: A Life of Max Eastman*. New York: Oxford University Press, 1978.

Ouellette, Fernande. *Edgard Varèse*. New York: Orion, 1968.

Pach, Walter. *Queer Thing, Painting*. New York: Harper and Row, 1938.

Parry, Albert. *Garrets and Pretenders: A History of Bohemianism in America*. New York: Dover, 1960.

Poggioli, Renato. *The Theory of the Avant-Garde*. Translated by Gerald Fitzgerald. Cambridge: Harvard University Press, Belknap Press, 1968.

Pound, Ezra. *The Letters of Ezra Pound*. Edited by D. D. Paige. New York: Harcourt, Brace, 1950.

Ray, Man. *Self-Portrait*. Boston: Little, Brown, 1963.

Read, Forrest, ed. *Pound/Joyce: The Letters of Ezra Pound to James Joyce*. New York: New Directions, 1967.

Reid, B. L. *"The Man from New York": John Quinn and His Friends*. New York: Oxford University Press, 1968.

Richardson, Joan. *Wallace Stevens, a Biography: The Early Years, 1879–1923*. New York: William Morrow, 1986.

Richwine, Keith Norton. "The Liberal Club: Bohemia and the Resurgence in Greenwich Village, 1912–1918." Ph.D. diss., University of Pennsylvania, 1968.

Robbins, Daniel. "The Formation and Maturity of Albert Gleizes: A Biographical and Critical Study , 1881 through 1920." Ph.D. diss., Institute of Fine Arts, New York University, 1975.

Robinson, Janice. *H.D.: The Life and Work of an American Poet*. Boston: Houghton Mifflin, 1982.

Robinson, Roxana. *Georgia O'Keeffe*. New York: Harper and Row, 1989.

Rosenstone, Robert. *Romantic Revolutionary: A Biography of John Reed*. New York: Alfred A. Knopf, 1975.

Rudnick, Lois Palken. *Mabel Dodge Luhan: New Woman, New Worlds*. Albuquerque: University of New Mexico Press, 1984.

Ruggles, Eleanor. *The West-Going Heart: A Life of Vachel Lindsay*. New York: W. W. Norton, 1959.

Runk, Eva Epp. "Marius de Zayas: The New York Years." M.A. thesis, University of Delaware, 1973.

Saarinen, Aline. *The Proud Possessors: The Lives, Times, and Tastes of Some Adventurous American Art Collectors*. New York: Random House, 1958.

Sarlos, Robert Karoly. *Jig Cook and the Provincetown Players*. Amherst: University of Massachusetts Press, 1982.

Sawelson-Gorse, Naomi. "'For Want of a Nail': The Disposition of the Louise and Walter Arensberg Collection." M.A. thesis, University of California, Riverside, 1987.

Schwarz, Arturo. *The Complete Works of Marcel Duchamp*. New York: Harry N. Abrams, 1969.

Scott, Thomas L., and Melvin J. Friedman, eds. *Pound/ The Little Review: The Letters of Ezra Pound to Margaret Anderson: The Little Review Correspondence*. New York: New Directions, 1988.

Seligmann, Herbert J. *Alfred Stieglitz Talking: Notes on Some of His Conversations, 1925–1931*. New Haven, Conn.: Yale University Library, 1966.

Seymour, Ralph Fletcher. *Some Went This Way: A Forty-Year Pilgrimage among Artists, Bookmen and Printers*. Chicago: Ralph Fletcher Seymour, 1945.

Sheaffer, Louis. *O'Neill: Son and Playwright*. Boston: Little, Brown, 1968.

———. *O'Neill: Son and Artist*. Boston: Little, Brown, 1973.

Sloan, John. *John Sloan's New York Scene, from the Diaries, Notes, and Correspondence, 1906–1913*. Edited by Bruce St. John. New York: Harper and Row, 1965.

Steel, Ronald. *Walter Lippmann and the American Century*. Boston: Little, Brown, 1980.

Steffens, Lincoln. *The Autobiography of Lincoln Steffens*. New York: Harcourt, Brace, 1931.

Steichen, Edward. *A Life in Photography*. Garden City, N.Y.: Doubleday, 1963.

Stein, Gertrude. *The Autobiography of Alice B. Toklas*. New York: Harcourt, Brace, 1933.

———. *Everybody's Autobiography*. New York: Random House, 1937.

———. *Selected Writings of Gertrude Stein*. Edited by Carl Van Vechten. New York: Random House, 1946.

Stein, Leo. *Appreciation: Painting, Poetry and Prose*. New York: Crown, 1947.

———. *Journey into the Self: Being the Letters, Papers and Journals of Leo Stein*. Edited by Edmund Fuller. New York: Crown, 1950.

Sterne, Maurice. *Shadow and Light: The Life, Friends and Opinions of Maurice Sterne*. Edited by Charlotte Leon Mayerson. New York: Harcourt, Brace, 1965.

Stettheimer, Ettie. *Memorial Volume*. New York: Alfred A. Knopf, 1951.

Stettheimer, Florine. *Crystal Flowers*. New York: Privately printed, 1949.

Stevens, Holly. *Souvenirs and Prophecies: The Young Wallace Stevens*. New York: Alfred A. Knopf, 1966.

Stevens, Wallace. *Letters of Wallace Stevens*. Edited by Holly Stevens. New York: Alfred A. Knopf, 1966.

Stieglitz, Alfred. *Georgia O'Keeffe, A Portrait*. New York: Metropolitan Museum of Art, 1978.

Stock, Noel. *The Life of Ezra Pound*. Expanded edition. San Francisco: North Point, 1982.

Tanselle, George. "A Faun at the Barricades: The Life and Work of Floyd Dell." Ph.D. diss., Northwestern University, 1959.

Tashjian, Dickran. *Skyscraper Primitives: Dada and the American Avant-Garde, 1910–1925*. Middletown, Conn.: Wesleyan University Press.

Tietjens, Eunice. *The World at My Shoulder*. New York: Macmillan, 1938.

Tyler, Parker. *Florine Stettheimer: A Life in Art*. New York: Farrar, Straus, 1963.

Tytell, John. *Ezra Pound: The Solitary Volcano*. New York: Anchor, 1987.

Untermeyer, Louis. *From Another World*. New York: Harcourt, Brace, 1939.

Van Vechten, Carl. *Peter Whiffle: His Life and Works*. New York: Alfred A. Knopf, 1922.

———. *The Letters of Carl Van Vechten*. Edited by Bruce Kellner. New Haven, Conn.: Yale University Press, 1987.

Varèse, Louise. *Varèse: A Looking-Glass Diary*. New York: W. W. Norton, 1972.

Ware, Caroline. *Greenwich Village, 1920–1930: A Comment on American Civilization in the Post-War Years*. Boston: Houghton Mifflin, 1935.

Wertheim, Arthur. *The Little New York Renaissance: Iconoclasm, Modernism, and Nationalism in American Culture, 1908–1917*. New York: New York University Press, 1976.

Williams, Ellen. *Harriet Monroe and the Poetry Renaissance: The First Ten Years of "Poetry," 1912–1922*. Urbana: University of Illinois Press, 1977.

Williams, William Carlos. *The Autobiography of William Carlos Williams*. New York: Random House, 1951.

———. *Selected Essays*. New York: Random House, 1954.

———. *The Selected Letters of William Carlos Williams*. Edited by John C. Thirlwall. New York: McDowell, Oblensky, 1957.

Wood, Beatrice. *I Shock Myself*. Edited by Lindsay Smith. Ojai, Calif.: Dillingham Press, 1985.

Young, Art. *Art Young: His Life and Times*. New York: Sheridan House, 1939.

Zilczer, Judith Katy. "The Aesthetic Struggle in America, 1913–1918: Abstract Art and Theory in the Stieglitz Circle." Ph.D. diss., University of Delaware, 1975.

———. "The Noble Buyer": *John Quinn, Patron of the Avant-Garde*. Washington, D.C.: Smithsonian Institution Press, 1978.

Zurier, Rebecca. *Art for the Masses (1911–1917): A Radical Magazine and Its Graphics*. New Haven, Conn.: Yale University Art Gallery, 1985.

INDEX

CREDITS

Grateful acknowledgment is made for permission to use quotations by the following authors. For specific sources of individual quotations and additional credits to both archival and published sources, see the Notes.

Walter Arensberg: Courtesy Arensberg Archives, © 1991 Francis Bacon Foundation, Claremont, Calif. George Cram Cook: Courtesy Daphne C. Cook, Estate of Susan Glaspell. Floyd Dell: Courtesy Newberry Library, Chicago. Hilda Doolittle: Previously unpublished material by Hilda Doolittle copyright © 1991 Mrs. John Schaffner; used by permission of New Directions Pub. Corp. Agents. Susan Glaspell: Courtesy Daphne C. Cook, Estate of Susan Glaspell. Hutchins Hapgood: Courtesy Beatrix Hapgood Faust. Marsden Hartley: Courtesy Yale Committee on Literary Property. Mina Loy: Permission to quote from Mina Loy's published and unpublished writings is granted courtesy of Roger L. Conover, her literary executor. Amy Lowell: Courtesy G. d'Andelot Belin and F. Davis Dassori, Jr., Trustees under the Will of Amy Lowell. Mabel Dodge Luhan: Courtesy Yale Committee on Literary Property. Henry McBride; Courtesy of Maximilian H. Miltzlaff. Agnes Ernst Meyer: Courtesy Katherine Graham. Harriet Monroe: Courtesy Special Collections, University of Chicago Library. Ezra Pound: Previously unpublished material by Ezra Pound, copyright © 1991 by the Trustees of the Ezra Pound Literary Property Trust; used by permission of New Directions Pub. Corp. Agents. Ettie Stettheimer: Courtesy Estate of Ettie Stettheimer; Joseph Solomon, Executor. Florine Stettheimer: Courtesy Estate of Florine Stettheimer; Joseph Solomon, Executor. Alfred Stieglitz: Courtesy Stieglitz/O'Keeffe Archive. Carl Van Vechten: Courtesy Estate of Carl Van Vechten; Joseph Solomon, Executor. William Carlos Williams: Previously unpublished material by William Carlos Williams copyright © 1991 by William Eric Williams and Paul H. Williams; used by permission of New Directions Pub. Corp. Agents.

PHOTOGRAPHY CREDITS

Every effort has been made to contact the current owners of the works reproduced in this volume. We would appreciate hearing about any changes in ownership or credit lines so that future editions can be updated. Please send this information to: Strange Bedfellows, c/o Abbeville Press, 488 Madison Avenue, New York, N.Y. 10022. The photographers and the sources of photographic material, by page number, other than those indicated in the captions are as follows:

The American Labor Museum, Haledon, N.J.: 139 bottom. Archives of American Art, Smithsonian Institution, Walt Kuhn Papers, Washington, D.C.: 167 top, 168, 173. Francis Bacon Library, Claremont, Calif.: 28 top (Charles C. Arensberg Collection), 244 left and center, 263 (Arensberg Archives). Bibliothèque Littéraire Jacques Doucet, Tzara Papers, Paris, courtesy Francis M. Naumann, New York: 265 bottom. Courtesy William Camfield, Rice University, Houston: 251. Chicago Historical Society: 12 bottom, 22 left and right. Geoffrey Clements: 115. Ken Cohen Photography, New York: 110. Columbia University Libraries, New York: 235 (Current Opinion, February 1918). Columbia University Rare Book and Manuscript Library, New York: 160 bottom, 164, 338 top (Transition, February 1928). Roger L. Conover: 90, 246, 268 bottom, 269, 321, 335. Trustees of Dartmouth College, Hanover, N.H., copyright © 1991: 153. William Dove, Mattituck, N.Y.: 76. Pierre DuPuy, Stamford, Conn.: 37. Collection of Yvette (Mrs. Max) Eastman, Gall Head, Mass.: 160 top. M. Lee Fatherree: 120. Galerie de Paris, Paris: 337. Courtesy Golda Meier Library, University of Wisconsin–Milwaukee, Little Review Papers, Archives: 289 (photograph by Hutchinson), 293, 296, 347 bottom. Harry Ransom Humanities Research Center, The University of Texas at Austin: 51 (photograph by Mishkin), 191, 193, 243 (Carlton Lake Collection), 256 (copyright © Peter A. Juley and Son, New York). Paul Hester, Houston: 242. Lizzie Himmel, New York: 259 top, center, and bottom. Courtesy Hirschl and Adler Galleries, Inc., New York: 258. Hirshhorn Museum and Sculpture Garden, Smithsonian Institution, Elmer MacRae Papers, Washington, D.C.: 167 bottom, 172. The Houghton Library, Harvard University, Cambridge, Mass.: 5 bottom, 31, 33, 34, 139 top and center, 222, 223 top, 286, 304, 305, 311, 333. The Huntington Library, San Marino, Calif.: 28 bottom. Courtesy The Institute of Contemporary Art, Boston: 118. The International Museum of Photography at George Eastman House, Rochester, N.Y.: 43, 60, 74, 104. Copyright © Estate of Mrs. G. A. Wyndham Lewis, courtesy the Art Collection, Harry Ransom Humanities Research Center, University of Texas, Austin: 112 top. All rights reserved, The Metropolitan Museum of Art, New York: 70, 73 left and right, 75, 78, 80, 82, 100, 109, 113, 186. Maximilian H. Miltzlaff: 5 top, 185, 211. Museum of the City of New York: 154 (photograph by Jesse Tarbox Beals), 234 (Theatre Collection). National Museum of American Art, Smithsonian Institution, Washington, D.C.: 267. Francis M. Naumann, New York: 320. The Newberry Library, Chicago, Floyd Dell Papers: 4 top, 11, 17 left, 18, 329, 353. The Newberry Library, Chicago, Little Room Archives: 14. The New York Public Library, Astor, Lenox and Tilden Foundations, Art and Architecture Collection, Miriam and Ira D. Wallach Division of Art, Prints, and Photographs: 179. The New York Public Library, Astor, Lenox and Tilden Foundations, Henry W. Berg and Albert A. Berg Collection: 19, 128, 350. The New York Public Library, Astor, Lenox and Tilden Foundations, General Research Division: 16 and 21 (Victor Georg), 223 bottom, 295. The New York Public Library, Astor, Lenox and Tilden Foundations, John Quinn Memorial Collection, Rare Books and Manuscripts Division: 344 (photograph by Hollinger), 355. The Philadelphia Museum of Art: 244 right, 277 top, center, and bottom (Archives), 280 and 318–19 (Arensberg Archives), 326 right (courtesy the museum). Private collection, courtesy The Philadelphia Museum of Art: 47, 275. The Rosenbach Museum and Library, Philadelphia, Papers of Marianne Moore: 300. Bob Rubic, Precision Chromes, Inc., New York: 79. Perdita Schaffner and New Directions Publishing Corp., New York: 62 (courtesy The New York Public Library), 64 (courtesy the Yale Collection of American Literature, The Beinecke Rare Book and Manuscript Library, Yale University, New Haven, Conn.). The Schlesinger Library, Radcliffe College, Cambridge, Mass., photographs by Jesse Tarbox Beals: 227 top and bottom, 230 top and bottom, back cover. Courtesy Sotheby's, New York: 116, 257. Stevens Memorial Library, North Andover, Mass., Ed Eich Photography, Andover, Mass.: 327. Tamiment Library, New York University: 141, 147. Thomas J. Watson Library, The Metropolitan Museum of Art, New York: 102–3, 248, 250. University Libraries, University at Buffalo, The Poetry/Rare Books Collection: 299. The University of Chicago Library, Department of Special Collections: 12 top, 17 right, 177, 189, 190, 192, 194, 197, 284. University Research Library, University of California at Los Angeles, Department of Special Collections: 217, 221, 349. William Eric Williams and New Directions Publishing Corp., New York: 59. Beatrice Wood Collection: 274, 276. Yale Collection of American Literature, The Beinecke Rare Book and Manuscript Library, Yale University, New Haven, Conn.: 4 bottom, 40, 44, 86 top to bottom, 87, 121, 129, 130, 133, 135, 151, 159 bottom, 163, 181, 213, 218, 224, 229, 231, 265 top, 270 top, 271, 290 top, center, and bottom, 291 top, center, and bottom, 297, 313, 326 left, 338 bottom, 339, 341 left and right, 351, 356, 357. Courtesy Yale University Library, New Haven, Conn., photograph by Elliott and Fry, published in Bookman: 53. Zindman/Fremont, New York: 266. Works by Marcel Duchamp and Man Ray, copyright © 1991 ARS N.Y./ADAGP. Works by Francis Picabia, copyright © 1991 ARS N.Y./ADAGP/SPADEM. Works by Pablo Picasso, copyright © 1991 ARS N.Y./SPADEM.

EDITOR: NANCY GRUBB
DESIGNER: JOEL AVIROM
PRODUCTION EDITOR: PHILIP REYNOLDS
PRODUCTION MANAGER: DANA COLE
PICTURE RESEARCHERS: LISA ROSEN AND KAREL BIRNBAUM

Front cover: Florine Stettheimer (1871–1944). *Soirée,* c. 1915.
Oil on canvas, 27¾ x 29⅜ in. (70.5 x 74.5 cm). Yale Collection of American Literature, The
Beinecke Rare Book and Manuscript Library, Yale University, New Haven, Connecticut

Back cover: Photograph by Jesse Tarbox Beals

Copyright ©1991 Cross River Press, Ltd. All rights reserved under international copyright
conventions. No part of this book may be reproduced or utilized in any form or by any
means, electronic or mechanical, including photocopying, recording, or by any information storage and retrieval system, without permission in writing from the publisher. Inquir-
ies should be addressed to Abbeville Press, 488 Madison Avenue, New York, N.Y. 10022.
Printed and bound in U.S.A.

First edition

Library of Congress Cataloging-in-Publication Data

Watson, Steven.
   Strange bedfellows : the first American avant-garde / Steven Watson.
      p.   cm.
   Includes bibliographical references and index.
ISBN 0-89659-934-5
   1. Avant-garde (Aesthetics)—United States—History—20th century. 2. Arts, Ameri-
can. 3. Arts and society—United States—History—20th century.   I. Title.
NX504.W38 1991
700'.973'09041—dc20   90-47476
                                                                              CIP